DISCOVERING ELEMENTARY SCIENCE

METHOD, CONTENT, AND PROBLEM-SOLVING ACTIVITIES

Marvin N. Tolman
Garry R. Hardy
Brigham Young University

Allyn and Bacon
Boston • London • Toronto • Sydney • Tokyo • Singapore

Vice President, Education: Nancy Forsyth
Editorial Assistant: Christine Nelson
Cover Administrator: Linda Dickinson
Composition and Prepress Buyer: Linda Cox
Manufacturing Buyer: Megan Cochran
Marketing Manager: Ellen Mann
Editorial-Production Service: Thomas E. Dorsaneo
Illustrators: Robert Allen, Russell McMullin, Gregory L. Tolman
Text Designer: Andrea Miles-Thoma/Menagerie Design & Publishing

Library of Congress Cataloging-in-Publication Data
Tolman, Marvin N.
Discovering elementary science: method, content, and problem-solving activities/Marvin N. Tolman, Garry R. Hardy.
p. cm.
Includes index.
ISBN 0-205-14030-0
1. Science—Study and teaching (Elementary)—United States
@. Science—Study and teaching—Activity programs—United States
I. Hardy, Garry R. II. Title.
LB1585.3.T65 1995
372.3—dc20 94—5363
CIP

Review Copy ISBN: 0-205-16900-7

 This book is printed on recycled, acid-free paper.

Printed in the United States of America

10 9 8 7 6 5 4 3 2 1 99 98 97 96 95 94

DEDICATION

This book is dedicated to children everywhere. May their teachers be infectiously excited about science, incurably curious about the world around them, and may the pestilence spread to epidemic proportions among all children exposed to them.

BRIEF CONTENTS

CONTENTS

CONTENTS OF ACTIVITIES

PREFACE

For elementary teachers, involving students in science the way science should be taught is like eating the proverbial peanut—you can't eat just one. But try one, then another and another, and you'll almost certainly be hooked by the enthusiastic response of your students. In our admittedly biased opinion, science is the elementary teacher's single best opportunity to turn kids on about school. Students deserve to have a reason to want to come to school, and when given a proper chance science excels in providing interest and enticement.

We hope that you will find this book to be helpful in elevating both enjoyment and learning in science, whether or not you have a strong science background. We have tried to approach elementary science in a practical way, providing many hands-on classroom activities for topics commonly studied, with emphasis on the development of problem-solving skills.

You do not need to be a scientist in order to teach elementary science effectively, but having a solid foundation of some basic science concepts can enhance the level of confidence with which you pursue the teaching task. Content background information is provided for teachers who have need to review, to help you feel more comfortable in teaching science, and we have tried to present the content in a way that is meaningful to the nonscientist. Your own curiosity and willingness to dive in and explore with children the wonders of nature will help to assure your success and fulfillment as a teacher of elementary science.

Textbook-based science has received a great deal of criticism in recent years because of the tendency of many teachers to short-change the hands-on, discovery aspect of science. Elementary students should be immersed in doing science, not just in reading and talking about it. The research aspect of science is also important, and will hopefully involve a rich supply of resources. Students need to use encyclopedias, trade books, and other library resources, along with many hands-on activities. Textbooks are appropriate resources if used in their proper role along with many other materials, but much of what science should be is lost if the textbook becomes the entire science program.

The famous Chinese proverb, "Give a man a fish and you feed him for a meal; teach him how to fish and you feed him for a lifetime," has meaning in science education. While we don't ignore the need for content, major emphasis must be placed on the skills of learning—the process skills. John Quincy Adams has been credited with saying, "To furnish the means of acquiring knowledge is . . . the greatest benefit that can be conferred upon mankind." We furnish the means of acquiring knowledge when we involve students in hands-on science, problem-solving activities, and other experiences in exploring, discovering, and otherwise developing the tools of independent learning. These are the priceless gems that students can take with them from their schooling experience and use throughout their lives. The process skills—the problem solving skills—are the skills of "fishing," the means of acquiring knowledge. Let's teach our young people to be problem solvers, solidly endowed with critical thinking skills.

Content has its place, too, as we learn to appreciate the world around us and as we try to comprehend its vastness and the incredibly consistent laws of nature which apply to everything and to which everything is bound. Science content often provides the vehicle with which to explore and develop the thinking skills. Just as we must not go overboard in teaching the facts and figures, we must also not diminish their importance out of existence.

Elementary science has the potential to be both entertaining and instructive. When we achieve such a wedding of qualities, students look forward to coming to school. So go ahead—try a peanut—and then dive into the bag all the way up to your elbows. Immerse your students in daily, active science.

For additional hands-on activities for elementary science, we suggest three activity books prepared in similar format that were written by the same first author, Dr. Marvin N. Tolman and Dr. James O. Morton. These are collectively called the *Science Curriculum Activities Library,* under the separate titles of *Life Science Activities for Grades 2–8, Physical Science Activities for Grades 2–8,* and *Earth Science Activities for Grades 2–8.* Although the titles indicate that the books begin at second-grade level, many of the activities included in the three books were designed for the earlier grades—some even for prekindergarten. These books are available from Parker Publishing Co., West Nyack, New York.

We appreciate the many professional classroom teachers and others who have so willingly given their time to critique and advise through the years of writing this book: Joel Bass, Sam Houston State University; Betty Crocker, University of North Texas; George Dawson, Florida State University; Steven Fairchild, James Madison University; Gerald W. Foster, DePaul University; Barbara Manner, Duquesne University; Preston Prather, University of Virginia; Ronald E. Rowe, Beaver College; Lawrence Scharmann, Kansas State University; and Leroy Schiller, Mankato State University. We acknowledge especially the work and assistance of Dr. Kent Harrison, of the Brigham Young University Physics Department, and thank him for his patience and insights, and for his sincere interest in elementary science education.

SECTION

THEORY AND METHODOLOGY

CHAPTER

HISTORY AND GOALS

CHAPTER OUTLINE:

INTRODUCTION
HISTORY
WHY TEACH SCIENCE ?
SOCIAL AND ETHICAL ISSUES
- Gender Differences
- Ethnic Differences
- Sex Education
- Creationism vs. Evolution

IN CLOSING
LIST OF RESOURCES

I WONDER . . .

How important is science at the elementary level?
Will I really have time to teach science?
How did the Soviet Union boost science education in the United States?
What can I do when science activities don't work out the way they're supposed to?
What can I do to help girls feel comfortable about pursuing careers in science fields?
How should the topic of reproduction be handled?
Is there really a conflict between science and religion? Is it necessary?

INTRODUCTION

Welcome to the world of elementary science. What a remarkable time it is to be alive! You are living in a time of a veritable knowledge explosion. For many years, it has been estimated that knowledge in the world is doubling every ten years. It seems impossible that such a trend could continue, for this suggests that in any given ten-year period, as much knowledge is acquired by the human race as was learned from the time of the first human creature until the beginning of that particular ten-year period. At that rate, by the time a child born today is fifty years old, 97 percent of everything known in the world will have been learned since the time that child was born!

Well, hang onto your hat. With the arrival of the computer age, more recent estimates suggest that knowledge is quantitatively doubling every three years or less! Paul Hurd, a respected science educator at Stanford University, stated that the amount of new knowledge generated in the world in thirty minutes, day and night and week after week, is enough to fill about twenty-seven volumes of the *Encyclopaedia Britannica* (Hurd, 1987). If we are to keep pace with world advances, we must be very serious about encouraging a high level of science literacy throughout our society. This must begin at a very early age, both at home and in the schools.

One of the major goals of elementary science education today is to enrich the lives of young people by expanding their perception and appreciation of the world around them, while stimulating their curiosity and sense of wonder. For those who have a particular interest or aptitude for science, the result could be an early mindset for a promising career. Others will live more fully with an enhanced awareness of the beauties of nature, and an inclination to be curious and to discover more and more about the wonders of the world. Along with gaining information about the world, elementary students begin developing skills of observation, classification, communication, measurement, prediction, inference, and other science processes.

Experiences that are appropriate for elementary science need not create high anxieties for the nonscientist teacher. As the teacher, it is important that you lead your class with a keen sense of curiosity and an interest in exploring and discovering new information. Indeed, science at the elementary level can provide, for both you and your students, excited anticipation for each new day. One of the greatest gifts you can give to your students is an insatiable curiosity and an interest in exploring and pursuing new information.

For the elementary teacher, science provides some of the greatest opportunities to turn students on about school. Your classroom should be a place of excitement. With animals in the classroom for your students to care for, with daily hands-on activities designed to help students learn about sound, magnets, and plants, with model car racing, rocket building, and bubble blowing, science concepts come alive! Teachers who are not getting students *involved* with science don't know what they're missing!

HISTORY

Swings of the pendulum are plentiful in education, as evidenced by the coming and going of philosophies, trends, and teaching techniques. The degree of emphasis placed on the teaching of phonics, our outlook toward the various notions of individualized instruction, and the use of curriculum specialists at the elementary school level are examples of the many trends that are subject to the pulsations of educational philosophy.

Nor has the teaching of science at the elementary level escaped the effect of the pendulum, swinging sometimes in its favor and at other times to its detriment. In the 1870s, science was a curricular fledgling, just beginning to be widely recognized for the first time as a discipline that should be taught in the early grades. Since that time it has been struggling for a solid foothold as a full-fledged member of the elementary school curriculum. An early emphasis was placed on nature study, helping children to become more aware of their environment by first-hand observation of things around them, rather than from books alone. Taught by master teachers who were also specialists in science, the topic was met with interest. Early in the twentieth century, however, it was entrusted to teachers with little or no training in science. Learning activities involving first-hand observation were replaced by reading about nature in books, and interest waned.

Interest in science education was rekindled in the 1930s by a new emphasis in the inquiry approach to teaching and by the efforts of the National Society for the Study of Education (NSSE). The pendulum began to swing again in favor of elementary science education. Three yearbooks devoted to science by the NSSE are thought to have had considerable positive effect. The *Thirty-first Yearbook* (1932) recommended a continuous K–12 science program; the *Forty-sixth Yearbook* (1947) reaffirmed that recommendation and emphasized the importance of science education because of the rapidly increasing impact of science on society. It stressed that learning outcomes in science should include functional understanding of facts, principles, and concepts, and the development of functional scientific skills, attitudes, and interests. The *Fifty-ninth Yearbook* (1960) assumed that a continuous K–12 science program was then in place, and stressed the need for developing problem-solving and critical-thinking skills, and the importance of teaching science as a process of inquiry.

Elementary school science in the United States received a significant boost in the early 1960s as the nation recognized its need for more and better-prepared scientists in order to maintain its cherished worldwide technological lead. Strange as it may seem, those of us who advocate more and better science education can thank the Soviets, in part, for a huge financial transfusion. The launching of *Sputnik* in 1957, the world's first manufactured satellite to orbit this great planet, set the United States' pride back on its heels and fueled our effort to get into and win the space race. Competition can be an excellent motivator for nations, as well as for individuals and teams.

A substantial portion of the money appropriated to improve science education was earmarked for the development of programs that later became known as the "alphabet soup curriculum," a term ascribed to the collective acronyms by which those programs soon came to be known. Some of the best-known elementary programs included SAPA (Science, A Process Approach), ESS (Elementary Science Study), and SCIS (Science Curriculum Improvement Study). (For descriptions of these programs see chapter 7, "Curriculum Materials and Technology.")

WHY TEACH SCIENCE?

Some teachers are better at finding reasons *not* to teach science than they are at finding reasons *to teach* science. For example, there are many demands on the time available in the school day, schools are typically not well funded for science equipment and supplies, and few elementary teachers have a strong science background. Others teach science despite such drawbacks, and many of them do it very effectively and with exciting results in terms of student motivation and learning.

You don't need to be a scientist to teach elementary science. Your background in science will grow with your continued involvement in it. Your greatest assets include your positive scientific attitude, your contagious curiosity, and your willingness to dig in and explore with your students. Don't be afraid to say, "I don't know, let's find out." You will discover that much can be done with very little expense, and that you can enrich other areas of the curriculum by integrating science, when appropriate, with art, music, math, social studies, language arts, and so on. Long-sought incentives to practice reading can be discovered in science trade books written to capture the interest of children.

Perhaps the most important purpose of science education at the elementary level is to increase the quality of life for people in general by upgrading the level of science literacy in society and enhancing public awareness of the beautiful but fragile world in which we live. This is compatible with current efforts to shift the focus of science education from "science for scientists" to "science for all" (Duschl, 1990). At least in part, we will accomplish this as we achieve the following major goals:

1. **Broaden interest in, and appreciation for, things around us.** *Increased interest and appreciation for the world is a natural result of learning more about our surroundings. Our awareness of birds and other animals increases as we learn more about them; the weather forecast is more interesting and more meaningful when we understand movement of air masses and other basic conditions that affect weather.*
2. **Guide students to understand basic science concepts and generalizations.** *Science content is important, but it becomes much more meaningful when the information is learned in relation to broad concepts rather than memorized sets of facts in isolation. To know that warm air rises is more meaningful if the information is coupled with an understanding of the generalizations that materials expand when heated and that materials will float in fluids that are heavier (more dense) than they are. These concepts not only explain why hot air rises above cold air, but also why a helium-filled balloon floats in the air, and why a log floats on a pond. It is interesting to know that the parachute seed of a milkweed floats through the air. The information is more useful, however, if we also understand that this is nature's way of scattering these particular seeds and preserving the species, and that different types of seeds are dispersed in many ways.*
3. **Teach the processes of inquiry.** *Inquiry is the process of seeking new information and understanding. In addition to learning science concepts and generalizations, it is important that our students also learn how to learn. Some of the process skills*

commonly taught in the elementary grades include observing, communicating, measuring, classifying, predicting, inferring, hypothesizing, and experimenting. More information relating to these skills is developed in chapter 3.

4. **Develop problem-solving skills.** *As students become involved in scientific investigations and learn to seek answers to questions in a logical fashion, problem-solving skills that are applicable to everyday situations are sharpened. As students systematically study the effect of varying amounts of light on plant growth, or discover how magnets respond to each other, their skills of acquiring information and solving problems are strengthened. They will be faced with problems and questions throughout their lives. Learning early in life how to pursue answers and solutions in a systematic way can help them discover that the scientific method is not just for scientists or for science classes, but that it is also a logical procedure for acquiring information and solving problems of everyday life.*

   For example, to remove a tight ring from a fruit jar, you run hot water over it—not just because it worked for Grandmother, but because of a scientific principle: The ring was hot when it was put on the jar. As it cooled, it became smaller and cinched very tightly around the mouth of the jar. Running hot water over it causes the ring to expand (metal expands at a faster rate, when heated, than does glass), loosening it and making removal much easier. Life is full of such applications of scientific principles: We sprinkle salt on ice to lower the freezing point, we wear rubber-soled shoes to increase friction as we walk, we spray the carpet with a substance to reduce problems caused by static electricity, and so on. Scientific problem-solving skills are not just for the white-clad person in the laboratory; they have the potential to make our day-to-day lives easier and more fulfilling.

5. **Raise the level of scientific literacy.** *Recent studies suggest that both children and adults have many misconceptions with regard to everyday science concepts, such as what causes the moon to change phases, why leaves change color in the fall, and what brings about the change of the seasons. Many of these misunderstandings can be corrected by a more thorough and effective experience with science in the early grades. The effort to deal with these and other common science-based misconceptions is currently getting a lot of attention in elementary science education.*

6. **Science/technology/society relationships.** *Another major goal of science education today is to help children understand how science, technology, and society (STS) interrelate and influence each other. Today's students are tomorrow's decision makers. They must appreciate the value of science and technology in society, and they must understand the associated problems and limitations as well. Technology is the bridge between science and society; it is the application of scientific knowledge. In some ways, society is blessed by science, as lives are made easier, more comfortable, and more enjoyable through technological advances in transportation, medicine, and so on. In other ways, the quality of life may be diminished or threatened as the production and use of certain energy sources and goods pollute our environment and deplete our natural resources. Solving these problems will be of increasingly greater concern for the world society throughout the foreseeable future, and one of the responsibilities of science education is to help our young people prepare to deal with these and other issues related to science, technology, and society (see chapter 9).*

7. **Develop scientific attitudes.** *One of the greatest gifts you can give a child through experiences with science is an endless curiosity and willingness to investigate, explore, and search to find answers to the*

questions of an inquiring mind. Scientists must also be open-minded, as science is not a finite set of facts, but an ongoing enterprise. What is considered fact at one point in time might be questioned or even ridiculed later on. There must always be room in the mind for new information that adds to, supports, or even disproves long-held beliefs.

Another important scientific attitude is the willingness to change one's mind when found to be in error. Teach your children to recognize mistakes as learning experiences—even necessary at times—from which growth and knowledge evolve, instead of equating mistakes with failure.

Scientists are well known for their persistence, as illustrated by this story that is told of Thomas Edison. At one point in his effort to find a source of rubber in plant material, a discouraged assistant said to him, "Mr. Edison, we have tried 50,000 things and have no results."

"Results!" exclaimed Mr. Edison, "We have wonderful results! We now know 50,000 things that won't work!"

Edison persevered, and found what he seemed to intuitively know was there. Efforts that others saw as failure were perceived by Edison as vital learning experiences, moving him steadily toward his goal; therefore they were not failures at all, but successes. To Edison's persistence we owe, at least in part, the huge latex industry of today. We all have need for the Edison attitude to help us keep seeking solutions in the face of discouragement.

You can model an important scientific attitude if you erase from your mind the notion that science activities sometimes fail to work the way they are "supposed to." Materials we use in science behave in certain ways under certain conditions. They are bound by natural laws, and they obey those laws precisely; therefore there is no such thing as a science activity that doesn't work. It might not work just as you anticipated, but it *works the way it's supposed to* every single time, meaning that results will be in keeping with laws and principles determined by variables in the activity. Isn't that exciting? When results seem unusual, repeat the activity. That's how new discoveries are made, and often unexpected learning takes place. Ask students to try the activity at home, if practical, then compare results the next day. If you want a different result, think of something that can be changed (variable), and try it still another time. With the right attitude, the activity that doesn't work as expected can become a most valuable learning experience, because it raises new questions and provides new incentives to investigate, manipulate variables, and explore. And what's still more exciting, the process of investigating will raise more questions, resulting in still more investigation! (See also the discussion of Disequilibrium in chapter 2.)

A successful science activity is a question followed by study that leads to an answer, whether or not the answer is the one that was expected or desired. The new information may, in turn, give birth to new questions, starting the cycle once again.

SOCIAL AND ETHICAL ISSUES

Today's world is a world of science; our lives are filled with the influence of technology. Science-related controversial issues abound—from air quality to the use of seatbelts in automobiles, from the development of natural resources to the protection of endangered species, from space exploration to nuclear arms, to overpopulation. These issues are explored in chapter 9. But there are other social and ethical issues to deal with that directly affect the classroom.

Gender Differences

Much effort is being expended in an attempt to overcome the barrier of tradition that has stereotyped science as a man's world. Girls today are encouraged to consider science careers, to feel at home in the world of science if that is the direction of their natural inclinations. Many studies have been done to determine whether males and females are equal in their abilities to succeed and excel in fields of mathematics and science (Klein, 1989; Rowe, 1981). So little difference has been found when both have equal encouragement and opportunity, and so many women have proven themselves capable of excellence in a broad spectrum of science fields, that further debate seems pointless.

Nonetheless, a gender barrier does exist. Because of the effect of the long-established stereotype, parents and teachers alike must be very careful, both in what they say and in the nonverbal (and often unintended) messages they convey to girls regarding science-related pursuits. The National Science Teachers Association reported a study in which it was found that "adult expectations, subliminal cues, and encouragement or modeling can greatly influence how girls approach math and science" (NSTA Reports, September 1991). As an elementary teacher, you can have a significant influence for good by offering equal encouragement to girls and boys. You can also highlight some of the notable achievements of women scientists. Indeed, women have made significant contributions in anthropology (Margaret Mead, Jane Goodall), astronomy and space (Maria Mitchell, Valentina Tereshkova), chemistry (Ellen Richards, Marie Curie), and many other science fields (Noyce, 1980). Our students, both boys and girls, need to know about the achievements of these and other women scientists.

This is not just an issue for older girls. It is never too early to begin efforts to erase stereotypes and encourage each individual according to his or her talents and interests. Related impressions begin to form in a child's mind long before the child enters kindergarten.

Ethnic Differences

Girls and boys of all ethnic groups deserve similar encouragement and equality of opportunity to pursue science careers. Great contributions have been made by scientists of broadly varying nationalities. George Washington Carver, for instance, was an African-American who became a great botanist. His contributions include hundreds of products, from peanuts to sweet potatoes. Galileo Galilei was an Italian scientist, best remembered for his contributions in astronomy. The first woman in space was a Soviet, Valentina Tereshkova. José Bonifacido de Andrada e Silva was a well-known Brazillian chemist and statesman. Francis Bacon, an Englishman, is credited with the scientific method and other ideas for better organization of science. Andreas Vesalius was a Belgian anatomist. Louis Pasteur, a French scientist, contributed ways to control microorganisms in food. The periodic table of the elements was outlined by Dmitri Mendeleev, a Russian chemist. Gregor Mendel, known for his discovery of laws of heredity, was Austrian. And German scientist Albert Einstein was one of the greatest physicists of all time.

This list could go on and on to include many other nationalities, but surely it is sufficient to make the point that no one social group has a corner on scientific talent. Our responsibility as teachers is to encourage each individual child to maximize his or her potential, without regard to gender or national origin. We must help each child to recognize strengths and to expand them to the extent of the individual's interest and ability. Again, this is not an issue only for the upper grades; we must begin very early to recognize student interests and talents and to help them to develop their strengths.

Sex Education

As an elementary teacher, you have a unique opportunity to teach preliminary information about reproduction. It is unnecessary either to skirt the issue, or to invite controversies by teaching intimate information about human sexual relations.

The uniqueness of the position of the elementary school as the forum for building early concepts and attitudes toward reproduction is at least twofold. First, nature is on our side. At the mere mention of sex at the junior high school level, bells ring, lights flash, whistles blow, and the hormone count can go out of sight, with all of this accompanied by giggles, embarrassment, and other emotional responses both overt and suppressed. To conduct meaningful dialogue about the subject under these circumstances is, to say the least, a challenge. Most elementary-age students are of such an age and level of maturation that sexual drives and misconceptions have not yet developed, allowing concepts of reproduction to be learned as a matter of information, without being influenced by sexual connotations.

Second, some information about reproduction of plants and animals is usually taught in the elementary grades. Parallels with human reproduction are logical and natural, adding to the child's understanding and insight without embarrassment or offense. We speak comfortably, for example, of the male and female organs of plants. The female plant has an ovary that produces eggs and, if fertilized by pollen from the male, it can grow into a new plant that looks a lot like its "mom and dad." Female mammals—cats, dogs, horses, and hamsters—also produce eggs in an organ called an ovary. The egg, if fertilized by sperm from the male, can grow into a new animal that looks a lot like its mom and dad. Humans are also mammals, and they reproduce in a similar way.

When students come to you and say, "Teacher, the gerbils are being naughty," what will you do? Turn red with embarrassment? Punish the children for watching? Quarantine the gerbils? In a matter-of-fact way, you can remind students of what they learned earlier about plant reproduction—how the egg from the female plant is fertilized by pollen from the male plant. Then you can explain that it's much the same for gerbils and many other animals. In order to have baby gerbils, the male must fertilize the egg that is produced by the female. What they observed is nature's way of fertilizing the egg. If that didn't happen, there would never be any more baby gerbils. Wouldn't that be sad?

When such information comes from a teacher who is able to handle it matter-of-factly, yet with an attitude of respect for the reproduction process, students will more likely begin to understand and respect the intimate relation between male and female. That approach is much more appropriate than the attitude that sexual relations are unclean and shameful. The first-grade teacher will handle these situations differently than will the teacher of upper elementary grades, as each recognizes the background and maturity level of the students involved. With all ages, however, the situation should be turned into an appropriate learning experience, not ignored.

When teachers deal with the related issues of sex and morality, regardless of the position they take, they risk offending parents and social groups. Seek advice from your principal and colleagues to be certain that you understand school and district policies, and to learn about any unique local cultural implications related to this issue. The kind of basic information suggested above, conveyed with an attitude of respect for the reproduction process in nature, carries little risk of offending people.

Creationism vs. Evolution

The topic of science and religion will always provide plenty of ammunition for those who wish to debate it. Certainly, the full philosophical spectrum exists—from some (not all) creationists who reject scientific evidence of the age of this planet and the evolutionary process; to religionists and scientists who see no conflict; to scientists who are annoyed with any reference to religion and pass it off as superstitious hocus-pocus.

This is another pointless debate. Certainly, students of religion who have an interest in information regarding the beginning of Earth and life on it must be interested in whatever factual information can be found, whether in religious writings or from scientific exploration.

Arthur C. Clark said, "Sometimes I think we're alone in the universe and sometimes I think we're not. In either case, the idea is quite staggering" (Clark, 1989). Some well-known scientists see no conflict between science and religion. For others, the discoveries of science strengthen their religious belief. Albert Einstein said that religion without science is blind, and science without religion is lame. Stephen Hawking, a highly respected British astronomer, clearly portrays an open-minded attitude on this issue (Hawking, 1988).

However, when some people, claiming a basis of religious belief, dispute that which is supported by overwhelming scientific evidence (for instance, that a few thousand years is but a moment in the time of the earth's existence), it's no wonder scientists dismiss their position. From the viewpoint of one author, "Religious persons who believe that God is the creator of the Universe and the author of the laws by which it operates should find no conflict between science and religion . . . . Religious persons have no reason to fear the results of scientific research" (Skehan, 1986). Again, *open-mindedness* is an essential attribute in the learning process, and needs to be applied to both sides of this issue.

IN CLOSING

We live in a rapidly changing world, abounding with the effects of science and technology. We do not know what tomorrow's world will be like. In science education, it is our responsibility to help children understand and appreciate the earth's beauties and fragility. We must teach children to be problem solvers and prepare them for change. This is the best assurance of a quality existence for the generations that follow. The many time demands *must not* relegate science to last place among curricular priorities; science must be given its full rights and a chance to live up to its potential to enrich other subject areas and breathe life into each school day.

In elementary science, children should learn science content, concepts, and generalizations, with an emphasis on process skills, problem-solving skills, and attitude. We must also provide experiences that will help students to acquire an interest in and appreciation for their world. They should be introduced to issues they will face as adults, as they begin developing their own opinions and philosophies about how controversies should be handled and how contemporary problems might be solved. Such preparation will help young people know how to survive in a changing world, constantly maintaining and improving the quality of life for current inhabitants of this planet, while assuring the same for future generations.

Many of the topics that have been mentioned in this introductory chapter will be examined in more detail in other chapters of this book. Several programs and curricular materials currently available will be introduced. Some of these are exciting new materials and ideas designed to help us accomplish the goals outlined above. Whether you choose to use these and other materials in lieu of a textbook, or to supplement your text, you will find ideas that will help you accomplish your goals.

The last section of this book provides content information to help you brush up on science concepts in preparation for teaching. The content chapters also provide many activities for use in the elementary classroom, which will get your students actively involved in *doing* science. Many problem-solving activities are provided. Together, these can be a valuable resource for day-to-day science exploration. Here's hoping your use of this book will result in more excited students and a more fulfilled teacher. Good luck with your journey.

LIST OF RESOURCES

Bennett, William J., "Science: An Excerpt from *First Lessons*," *Science and Children* 24, no. 4 (January 1987).

Clark, Arthur, "Quotable Quotes," *Readers' Digest* (May 1989): 95.

Committee on Science and Creationism, *Science and Creationism: A View from the National Academy of Sciences* (Washington, D.C.: National Academy Press, 1984).

Duschl, Richard A. *Restructuring Science Education* (New York: Teachers College Press, 1990).

Fort, Deborah C., and Heather L. Varney, "How Students See Scientists: Mostly Male, Mostly White, and Mostly Benevolent," *Science and Children* 26, no. 8 (May 1989): 8–13.

Hawking, Stephen W., *A Brief History of Time* (New York: Bantam Books, 1988).

Hurd, Paul DeHart, "Science/Technology/Society: Modernizing the Science Curriculum," address, Utah Science Teachers Association, Salt Lake City, Utah, January 31, 1987.

Klein, Carol A., "What Research Says About Girls and Science," *Science and Children* 27, no. 2 (October 1989): 28–31.

Noyce, Ruth M., "Women in Science: Biographies for Young Readers," *Science and Children* 18, no. 3 (November-December 1980), 24–26.

National Science Teacher's Association, "Girls Should Be Encouraged to Take Risks, Get 'Dirty.' New Report Examines Girls' Participation in Science, Math," *NSTA Reports* (September 1991): 10.

Rowe, Mary Budd, "What Research Says About Science Ability and Achievement—Helping Girls Make the Connection," *Science and Children* 18, no. 7 (April 1981): 28–31.

Rutherford, F. James, "The Character of Elementary School Science," *Science and Children* 24, no. 4 (January 1987) 8–11.

Skehan, James W., *Modern Science and the Book of Genesis* (Washington, D.C.: National Science Teachers Association, 1986).

Stronck, David R., *Discussing Sex in the Classroom: Readings for Teachers* (Washington, D.C.: National Science Teachers Association, 1982).

CHAPTER

PRINCIPLES OF LEARNING

CHAPTER OUTLINE:

I WONDER . . .

Do the well-known learning theorists agree with each other about how children learn?

What kinds of backgrounds did some of these psychologists have, and how did it influence their thinking?

Which of Piaget's developmental stages do we deal mostly with in the elementary grades, and what implications does this have for the way we teach science?

INTRODUCTION

The timeworn struggle of people trying to understand people has made much progress during this century. Probably no profession has a greater need for that understanding, or benefits more from it, than the teaching profession. In the effective teaching of science at the elementary level, it is essential that teachers understand human development and how children learn.

Each learning theorist has a personal, unique perception of the human mind and how it functions. Comparing these perceptions is like comparing a football team with a baseball team to judge which team is better (Shulman, 1968). In the first place, they would never be on the same field. In the second place, they do not play by the same rules. Trying to decide which team is better is a fruitless task because their criteria for success are different. Rather than wholly accepting or rejecting any particular learning theory, educators should consider the conditions under which each can be used most beneficially and appropriately, given the age and personality of the learner.

An army of people are currently involved in studies to further this cause, and new researchers will no doubt add much insight to current information. At this time, however, a few names are broadly recognized by educators for their long-standing contributions to the field of learning theory and human psychological development.

This chapter will introduce six representative learning theorists who have made their mark in the field of educational psychology, with implications for science education: Piaget, Bruner, Gagne, Bloom, Guilford, and Skinner. Each theorist has both proponents and adversaries, and each sheds light on the nature and behavior of the human creature.

It is important for the student to recognize that the experts don't agree with each other on all points. Jerome Bruner, for example, expresses great respect for Piaget, but discomfort with some of what Piaget stands for, and he gives us every reason to think these feelings were reciprocated (Lindzey, 1980). As with each one of us, these theorists' thinking patterns and perceptions, though based on research and other professional experience, are influenced by their own total experience. Thus those perceptions, insights, and theories never reach either a static condition or point of completion. Furthermore, their own theories and beliefs evolve as they continue their observation and research activities. Continued research and experience, including exposure to the notions and findings of others, perpetuate the dynamic nature of the open scientific mind.

Theories of learning, therefore, continue to be altered and refined as new light is shed by additional experience and research. After all, if changes in perceptions were not expected, there would be no reason to continue research activities. All of this should help you, as a teacher of elementary science, to: (1) feel safe in questioning certain theories and long-held beliefs that are inconsistent with your classroom observations; and (2) be more inclined to study and compare children, behaviors, and teaching methods, contributing to the perpetual effort of the profession to develop new insights and more effective techniques. Such efforts don't need to be even noticed by others in order to be of value. With the very process of classroom research, you will grow; and you will be, forever after, a better teacher and more likely to try other new ideas. Through these efforts, your professional growth will continue.

The chapter begins with brief biographies of each theorist. The majority of the chapter describes theories and concerns, outlining some of the information put forth by the learning theorists described biographically, and by other learning theorists who have made their mark in the field of educational psychology.

MEET THE MASTERS

Biographical information is given for Piaget, Bruner, Gagne, Bloom, Guilford, and Skinner in hopes of helping you to relate to the individual theorists and to recognize the broadly varied backgrounds of these scholars. This should lend insight into the diversity of their theoretical positions.

Jean Piaget

Jean Piaget is a prime example of a person whose perceptions changed over the years. He left a promising career as a biologist to pursue a compelling interest in developmental psychology, and his psychological studies were definitely flavored with biological connections. A study of his life reveals that his experiences led to progressive changes in his thinking. He was actually disturbed by the attention given his first five books because he considered them to be only preliminary and tentative, not a definitive expression of his views of the nature of intelligence. He recognized the embryonic nature of his theories, and preferred to let them mature further before they underwent serious scrutiny. Piaget considered the greatest value of those early books to be a clarification of his own thinking as he wrote them.

Jean Piaget was born at Neûchatel, Switzerland, on August 9, 1896. He developed an early interest in mechanics, birds, fossils, and seashells. He wrote and published his first paper at age ten, about a partly albino sparrow he had seen at a public park. As a result of this interest, and anxious to learn more, he asked the director of the natural history museum in Neûchatel if he could help after school hours. The director, a specialist in mollusks, put young Jean to work labeling an extensive collection of shells. Such a great interest resulted that Piaget began spending his free time collecting mollusks. In exchange for his help at the museum, the museum director gave Piaget a number of rare species and helped him classify those he had collected on his own. When the director died only four years later, Piaget had learned enough to begin publishing articles on mollusks without help.

Piaget's writing received more attention than he was ready for at this young age. In his autobiography, he wrote, "Certain foreign 'colleagues' wanted to meet me, but since I was only a schoolboy, I didn't dare to show myself and had to decline these flattering invitations" (Boring, 1952). A Mr. Bedot, director of the Natural History Museum of Geneva, published several of Piaget's articles in the *Revue suisse de Zoologie* and also offered him a position as curator of the mollusk collection at the museum. After another magazine editor refused an article because he had discovered the "embarrassing truth" about the age of the author, Piaget sent the article to Mr. Bedot, who responded with kindness and good humor: "It is the first time that I have ever heard of a magazine director who judges the value of articles by the age of their authors. Can it be that he has no other criteria at his disposal?"

With the interests that had been inspired by these early experiences, Piaget pursued studies in the natural sciences and graduated with a baccalaureate degree from the University of Neûchatel at the age of eighteen. Just three years later, in 1918, he obtained a doctorate, also in natural sciences, having done extensive research in the study of mollusks. By the time he was twenty-one years old, he was already considered to be one of the world's few experts on mollusks.

Along with his interest in the natural sciences, Piaget, early in his life, explored logic, philosophy, and psychology. Sensing a link between biology and human logic and actions, and driven to understand more, he went to Paris in 1919 to study at the Sorbonne for two years. There he worked with Dr. Theophile Simon (coauthor, with Alfred Binet, of the first successful intelligence test), in the Binet Laboratory, who suggested that Piaget standardize Cyril Burt's reasoning tests. These questions included part-whole relationships, which Piaget discovered were very difficult for children under eleven or twelve years of age.

Piaget became more and more interested in the reasoning processes underlying children's responses, especially the wrong answers, and he began engaging his subjects in conversations aimed at discovering patterns of logic and reasoning. He found that similar wrong answers occurred frequently in children of about the same age, and that there were different types of common wrong answers at different ages. Piaget abandoned the notion of a standardized testing procedure and followed the child's own line of thought, without imposing any direction on it, concluding that a standardized procedure might lead to a considerable loss of information if the child did not understand the questions (Ginsburg, 1969).

Piaget returned to Switzerland and accepted an invitation to join the staff of the Institute Jean Jacques Rousseau in Geneva in 1921. At age twenty-five, the young biologist/psychologist determined that he would study the processes of thought and logic for different ages beginning at birth, and thus he began the research that became his life's work. In 1925, he joined the faculty of the University of Neûchatel. In 1929, he returned to the University of Geneva as Professor of History of Scientific Thought and Assistant Director of the Institut J. J. Rousseau. In 1939, he became Professor of Sociology, still at the University of Geneva; and in 1940, he was appointed chair of Experimental Psychology and Director of the Psychology Laboratory.

During these years at Neûchatel and Geneva, in studies collaborated with his students, Piaget discovered that younger children did not believe in the constancy of material quantity (conservation), that is, that the volume of a ball of clay remains the same after the ball has been flattened out or stretched to change its shape.

Piaget used a longitudinal approach to his work (long-term study of the same children), and based his research on observation and on asking individual children selected questions and recording their responses. His own children (two daughters, born in 1925 and 1927, and a son, born in 1931) were an important part of his studies, and his wife (one of his former students) helped him greatly by observing, recording observations, and subjecting the children to various experiments. As he observed children of various ages and analyzed their responses to questions, he developed the theory that there are stages of cognitive development through which all people progress.

Jerome Bruner

Jerome Bruner was born on October 1, 1915, to a prosperous New York watch manufacturer. Bruner's father had arrived in America from Poland in his early adulthood, with neither friend nor fortune. He died when young

Jerome was twelve years old. In his autobiography, Bruner said of his father, "He had treated me flatteringly as an equal. He would report on what he was reading and would solicit and respect my views—indeed, restate them in a way that always made me prouder of my points than I had proper reason to be" (Lindzey, 1980).

Bruner enrolled at North Carolina's Duke University at age sixteen. Bruner was born blind, but developed his sight by age two. His later interest in the part of psychology that deals with perception seems very logical, given this, yet he claims to have become a psychologist quite by accident. Bruner entered Duke intending to "shop around," but with some expectation of getting into law. In his second year, he was enamored by courses in comparative psychology, neuropsychology, and animal behavior. He finished his undergraduate coursework "on the double" and began graduate school a year early. In retrospect, Bruner reckoned that his real induction into the world of psychology was a result of having gotten involved directly in research with a respected teacher. He published his first paper in the *Journal of Comparative Psychology* in 1939.

In 1938, Bruner enrolled in graduate school at Harvard. During World War II, he was assigned to work with the Foreign Broadcast Intelligence Service in Washington, D.C., examining foreign broadcasts and keeping appropriate government officials apprised of information that might be useful. Later, from a restless desire for a more direct part in the war, and unable to enlist because of poor vision, he joined the Anglo-American Psychological Warfare Division of Supreme Headquarters Allied Expeditionary Force Europe, in London. After the war, Bruner returned to the United States and was offered a position at Harvard, which allowed him to get back to what he had long considered the "guts of psychology": the study of perception. In the fertile academic soil of Harvard, this interest flourished.

In 1955, during the last stages of writing *A Study of Thinking*, Bruner was visited by Dr. Barbel Inhelder, and a continuing association between Bruner and both Inhelder and Piaget began. In 1955 and 1956, Bruner taught at the University of Cambridge in England, and while on that assignment made his first visit to Piaget in Geneva. Both seemed to enjoy the association and the opportunity to share and compare philosophies about life and about human development.

In the summer of 1959, Bruner became involved, as director, in a workshop held by the National Academy of Sciences, to assess the post-*Sputnik* ferment of the science curriculum. In the company of such curriculum makers as Lee Cronbach, John Carroll, Barbel Inhelder, Kenneth Spence, George Miller, Richard Alpert, Donald Taylor, and, for a day, B. F. Skinner, Bruner wrote *The Process of Education*, which was the director's report of the workshop. The book was published in 1960, generating an explosion of interest. Senator John F. Kennedy phoned to discuss advisable educational legislation, and, said Bruner, "I was catapulted into the midst of the raging educational debate—flattered, bemused, and skeptical" (Lindzey, 1980, 120).

In *The Process of Education* (which was translated into twenty-two languages and revised twenty years later), Bruner had argued for the importance of "models in the head," and the importance of firsthand experiences in developing those models. He reasoned that the young learner should not be *talking about* physics or *about* history or *about* mathematics, he or she should be *doing* physics or history or mathematics.

Bruner taught that concrete experiences should be heavily emphasized in childhood learning. He claimed that it is to teach the student to *participate* in the process that makes possible the establishment of knowledge. He will long be remembered for that, and for his hypothesis that any subject can be taught effectively in some intellectually honest form, to any child at any stage of development. For the latter statement, Bruner has had much praise and many critics, including Piaget, who expressed much displeasure over the statement, holding to his own conclusions that a child's readiness to learn depends on maturation and intellectual development. Perhaps some have interpreted this famous statement too precisely. If taken very literally, one could easily take issue with it; we'd have a tough time getting first-graders to learn the scientific names of the members of the animal kingdom, for instance. But if we interpret it to mean that there is something about that body of information that could be taught meaningfully to young children, the idea becomes much more plausible.

In the early 1960s, with mathematician Zoltan P. Dienes, Bruner set out to explore both of those conjectures with respect to the field of mathematics. Particularly in terms of the need for emphasis on hands-on experiences, this association seems to have been an especially desirable arrangement, for Bruner described Dienes as a genius at finding concrete embodiments for abstract ideas.

In spite of his respect for Piaget, Bruner became uncomfortable with Piaget's approach. There followed a lively period of exchange between Piaget and Bruner. "Piaget presided over his seminars and discussions with the somewhat slow and determined direction of a glacier," said Bruner.

> *His response is never "oppositional"; it is invariably to show, in ever more "logical" detail, how* his *argument handles all the phenomena necessary to it. It is a magnificent single-mindedness and, I think, lies at the root of his singular systematic thrust. But it is not easy to live with theoretically. He ingests everything offered, and it comes out more Geneva than ever. (Lindzey, 1980, 126)*

Bruner maintained close working contact with Inhelder and others at Geneva, but not with Piaget.

Another of Bruner's involvements in the 1960s was his writing of the controversial *Man: A Course of Study*. Although it was the victim of a vicious negative campaign from the John Birch Society, Bruner's perception was that the work was appreciated in every other country where it was used. In the 1960s, Bruner helped initiate Project Headstart.

Bruner is a proponent of discovery learning, and is often associated with this approach. Although he did not initiate discovery learning, he has been a major spokesperson for it. He proposes that what the child discovers is not outside the learner, but is an internal reorganization of previously known ideas. His book *The Process of Education* "captured the spirit of discovery" (Shulman, 1968).

Bruner was for many years a professor of psychology at Harvard University, and the director of the Center for Cognitive Studies. In spite of his reservations, Bruner is a proponent of Piaget's theories and follows his stages of intellectual development, with some deviation.

Robert M. Gagne

Robert M. Gagne is often associated with the University of California and the University of Florida, though he spent a major portion of his early career as an Air Force psychologist. He perceives learning as a process in which behavior can be modified in rather permanent ways, so the same modification does not need to occur over and over in each new situation.

While for Piaget and Bruner the child is a developing organism, passing through cognitive stages that are determined biologically, Gagne is less concerned with considerations of genetic development. He believes that growth results from learning alone, and not from some internal preset maturational clock. If the child cannot conserve volume, as he or she sees a liquid pass from a short, fat container to a tall, narrow container, it is not due to a developmental stage, but rather it is because the child has not had the necessary prior experiences.

Benjamin Bloom

Benjamin Bloom was born in 1915 and is, at the time of this writing, Professor Emeritus at the University of Chicago, with which he has been associated for many years. His publications include the *Taxonomy of Educational Objectives*, *Human Characteristics and School Learning*, and *Handbook on Formative and Summative Evaluation of Student Learning*. Bloom was a founding member of the International Association for the Evaluation of Educational Achievement.

Bloom believes there are three interdependent variables that must be attended to for an error-free system of education. The first variable is termed cognitive entry behaviors, and considers the extent to which prerequisites have been learned. The second variable, affective entry behaviors, refers to motivation of the student. The third variable is quality of instruction, which is concerned with the appropriateness of the instruction to the learner. Bloom believes that the nature of learning outcomes is determined by variations in these three interdependent variables.

Mastery Learning is a concept embraced by Bloom. He claims that most students can attain a high level of learning capability if mastery is clearly defined, if instruction is sensitive and systematic, if students receive appropriate help with learning difficulties when needed, and if students have sufficient time to achieve mastery.

Joy Paul Guilford

Born on March 7, 1897, to a farming family in Marquette, Nebraska, Joy Paul Guilford grew up familiar with hard work and long hours. He enjoyed academic pursuits, and often helped his older brother with his math lessons. As a youth, he read a lot, wrote short stories for an Omaha newspaper, and graduated from high school as valedictorian of the class of 1914 in Aurora, despite a heavy load of courses in such subjects as physical geography, botany, physics, chemistry, and Latin. Guilford was captivated by a psychology class. He attributes his unusually high interest to a teacher who presented the material "with great enthusiasm." He also was attracted to books written by William James, which he obtained from the town library (Boring, 1967).

Guilford was initially interested in becoming a chemist, but he was eventually attracted to the field of psychology and also became interested in teaching. Eventually, he did graduate work in psychology and continued teaching in the field. As a clinical psychologist, Guilford was asked to help develop some tests that would assist in the classification of students in two beginning chemistry courses. During this and other early experiences in clinical psychology, his conviction grew that there is not just one form of intelligence, but that "intelligence" comprises a multiplicity of abilities.

Interest in the many different factors of human intelligence and the variations in creative ability, both from one person to another and within any given individual, grew through Guilford's years as a professor of psychology and as a psychologist in the armed services. His research showed that highly intelligent children may lack specific mental aptitudes, while many who score poorly on general I.Q. tests perform very well at certain kinds of mental activities. This is supported by the experience of many teachers who have seen children who were seemingly unmotivated and even incapable in other areas become shining stars when they "discovered" science.

B. F. Skinner

B. F. Skinner was born in 1904 and grew up in Pennsylvania. Many of his boyhood days were spent in building such curiosities as water pistols, slingshots, slides, and merry-go-rounds. His curious and adventuresome mind led him to enjoy many memorable experiences, including a 300-mile canoe trip on the Susquehanna River at age fifteen—the oldest in a party of three (Boring, 1967).

Skinner credits his pursuit of English and writing to his father, who collected a large library of books, and to a respected and challenging English teacher at Hamilton College. A chance to meet Robert Frost, who encouraged him in his desire to become a writer, helped sway Skinner from choosing a career at the law firm his father had hoped to include him in. Achieving little success as a writer, however, Skinner went to Harvard to study psychology. In retrospect, he surmised that many events throughout his life had led up to his ultimate interest in psychology, without his realizing it was happening.

Skinner, a behaviorist, acknowledged his professional and philosophical indebtedness to Bertrand Russell, Ivan Pavlov, and others. Among his many philosophical tidbits, one which Skinner confesses to learning very slowly is that, "Nature to be commanded must be obeyed." Said Skinner:

> *I remember the rage I used to feel when a prediction went awry. I could have shouted at the subjects of my experiments, "Behave, damn you! Behave as you ought!" Eventually I realized that the subjects were always right. They always behaved as they should have behaved. It was I who was wrong. I had made a bad prediction . . . . But that coin has another face: once obeyed, nature can be commanded. (Boring, 1967, 411)*

While his notion about obeying and commanding nature is intriguing, Skinner is probably best known for his work with what he called operant and respondent behaviors. According to Skinner, nearly all identifiable human behavior can be separated into these two categories.

FITTING IT ALL TOGETHER

Our task is not to decide which of all the learning theorists is right, but to determine what we can learn from each one, as we attempt to maximize science education for the benefit of the child. Here are some of their collective contributions that have application to science education.

Developmental Psychology

As Piaget studied the findings of his research, he identified four stages of cognitive development. He was quick to point out that these stages are not abrupt divisions, but that associated cognitive behavior develops continuously. Piaget also cautioned that although all children pass through these stages, they do so at their own rate. Ages given, therefore, are only approximations.

Sensorimotor stage
(from birth to about age two or three)

During the first two weeks, the infant's behavior is reflexive in nature, as exemplified by the sucking reflex. Then behavior patterns begin to develop, and motor coordination allows the child to grasp objects within reach. As the child begins to crawl and walk, he or she seeks new things to find out about new situations. The child's sense of permanence of objects develops, even when they no longer are in sight. This is noted when the child looks for an object that has been hidden. Toward the end of the second year the child begins to form mental images of objects no longer in sight. This skill leads to symbolic thought, which is the beginning of genuine thinking, as the child enters the preoperational stage.

Preoperational stage
(from ages two or three to six or seven)

The preoperational child's world is egocentric, and thus children perceive things from their own point of view. It is difficult for the child to see another person's viewpoint, even when presented with evidence that is contradictory to the child's thought. Language development and rapid conceptual development are characteristic of this period. As language skill develops, the child moves from the sensorimotor mode to a conceptual-symbolic mode (words are now used as symbols). Language moves from egocentric (noncommunicative) to being intercommunicative, where the child is able to share ideas with others.

The preoperational child bases quantitative judgment on what is seen at the moment, and is not yet able to conserve quantity in the mind. Piaget poured beads from a short, fat jar into a tall, skinny jar and asked the child, "Are there more beads, or fewer beads, than there were before?" The preoperational child, despite having watched as the beads were transferred from one container to the other, usually responds to such a question indicating that there are more beads (the column is taller), or fewer beads (the column is skinnier). Judgment of quantity is based on what is in view at the moment; the fact that quantity was not altered during the change process is not a consideration of the child at the preoperational stage.

The reality of this type of reasoning in the preoperational child was effectively brought to the mind of one of the authors in an incident with his own five-year-old daughter, Valorie. After finishing her evening meal, she spread a full slice of bread with salad dressing. Realizing, then, her lack of appetite, she said, "Daddy, I can't eat all of this." Valorie was obviously considering the "if-you-take-it-you-eat-it" rule, so Dad said nothing, but watched with interest to see what she would do about her problem. Her eyes moved several times, in despair, from the bread to Dad and back to the bread. They suddenly brightened as she exclaimed, "I know!" With that, she folded the bread in half and ate it. No problem! Not only did there appear to be less bread when folded in half, Valorie determined beforehand that it would be less.

Concrete operational stage
(from ages six or seven to eleven or twelve)

In the concrete operational stage, the child begins to develop the use of logical thought, but as yet is unable to apply logic to hypothetical problems. He or she can solve tangible problems of the present.

According to Piaget, young children must develop the ability to perceive reality and use language before they can deal intelligently with their environment. An important and intriguing development early in this stage is the *conservation* skill, referring to conservation of quantity, mentioned above. Early in the concrete operational stage, the child acquires the ability to conserve quantity in the mind. Piaget used several activities, in addition to the jars of beads, to determine the presence or absence of this skill. A ball of clay, either flattened into the shape of a pancake or rolled into a sausage shape, is perceived by the preoperational child to change in quantity. The concrete operational child recognizes that, although the material looks very different, none was added and none was taken away; therefore, there must still be the same amount of clay.

Several years after the bread and salad dressing incident mentioned above, Valorie, now age ten, took one too many tacos. Teasingly, Dad said, "Just fold it in half." Valorie replied, "Oh, Daddy, there would still be just as much." You see, it doesn't look the same to the child in the concrete stage as to the child in the preoperational stage.

Another comparison between children functioning in the two different stages is often experienced with sandwiches. When the child is in the preoperational stage, if a sandwich is prepared and the child insists that it won't be enough, the sandwich can be cut in half, and that will likely satisfy the child. If not, cutting it into fourths will almost certainly do the job; four sandwiches should be enough for anyone! That trick doesn't work for the child in the concrete stage, because the child possesses the conservation skill. The child reasons correctly that the fact that there are more pieces doesn't change the amount. On another occasion, when Valorie's younger brother Aaron's sandwich was being cut into fourths so he could handle it easier, he actually cried, saying, "I don't want to eat that many." One sandwich was enough, and Aaron was sure he could not eat four of them.

Formal operational stage
(from ages eleven or twelve through adulthood)

A child at the formal operational stage is able to apply logical operations to solve all types of problems, including problems involving the future. Concrete as well as abstract problems can be solved because of the increased ability to use hypothetical-deductive reasoning. The child can collect and organize data, generate hypotheses, and reason logically. These skills give the child a broader range of application of logical operations.

This does not imply that children under age eleven or twelve completely lack the ability to respond to abstract experiences. Visit any first-grade classroom, and you will find students writing numerals and alphabetic characters—abstract symbols. Each level of cognitive development builds on the previous level. At the formal operation level, the mind is much more adept at abstract learning than in earlier stages of development.

Can the process of cognitive development be speeded up with formal instruction? Results of some experiments indicate this is not possible. Yet, educational experiences that offer the child opportunities to observe and describe—to perceive—do aid more rapid cognitive development.

Piaget's theory, which was developed primarily from clinical observations of young children, appears to be supported by recent findings of brain physiologists. "The more researchers learn about the physiology and chemistry of the brain, the more they verify the educational applications of Piaget's theory" (Esler, 1982).

In spite of some reservations, Bruner is a proponent of Piaget's theories and follows his stages of intellectual development with some deviation. He labels three levels of intellectual/cognitive development in children. At the *enactive level,* children manipulate materials directly. At the *iconic level,* they deal with mental images of objects but do not manipulate them directly. In the *symbolic level,* children manipulate symbols and no longer deal with mental images of objects. These levels are sometimes called the concrete, semiconcrete, and abstract levels, respectively, thus they parallel Piaget's levels of development.

The Importance of Concrete Experiences

The concrete operational stage pretty well spans the elementary grades, and calls for an abundance of concrete experiences in learning. Elementary science programs should provide children with many interactions with the physical and social environment to observe, manipulate, ask questions, and experience science concepts.

Hierarchical Steps of Learning

Gagne believes learning is a process of acquiring new capabilities, many of which depend upon previously learned, simpler competencies. His learning hierarchy is based on the notion that all learning must proceed from the simple to the more complex, in well-defined steps. Observable changes are the only criteria that indicate learning has occurred. These behaviors, in turn, form the basis for learning more complex behaviors in the next level of the hierarchy.

For Gagne, instruction begins with a task analysis of the instructional objectives. While Piaget and Bruner would ask, "What do you want the learner to understand or feel?" Gagne first asks the question, "What do you want the learner to be able to do?" Understanding and feeling are not easily observable. This *capability*, Gagne insists, must be stated *specifically* and *behaviorally*. The capabilities then become the objectives of instruction.

After analyzing the task, Gagne asks, "What would you need to know in order to do that?" A map of prerequisites would next be prepared, after which Gagne would pretest to determine which of the prerequisites have already been mastered. When the diagnostic evaluation (pretest) is finished, the resulting pattern shows what must be taught, and a very precise teaching program develops.

Gagne claims children pass through an eight-step hierarchy of learning, but without a rigid sequence. These are as follows:

1. **Signal learning, or conditioning**

   Example: *The child learns to make a conditioned response to a given signal, such as a loud noise (fright or startled movement) or the sight of a favorite food (pleasure).*

2. **Stimulus-response learning**

   Example: *The child learns to repeat a word when the word is stated by the teacher, or to define the word.*

3. **Chaining, or skill learning**

   Example: *A succession of two or more stimulus-response connections. These are limited to physical, nonverbal sequences, such as walking, writing, or picking up a ball.*

4. **Verbal associations (a form of chaining, but the links are verbal units)**

   Example: *Naming an object, such as a turtle, or memorizing a poem or the letters of the alphabet.*

5. **Multiple discriminations**

   Example: *The capacity to make different responses to many different stimuli, such as learning names of people—being able to associate each person with his or her distinctive appearance and the correct name.*

6. **Concept learning (classification)**

   Example: *The ability to make a response that serves to identify an entire class of objects or events, even though the objects or events differ in many ways.*

7. **Principle learning (rule-governed learning; a chain of two or more concepts)**

   Example: *Being able to chain the concepts of number of legs and number of body parts to identify a bumblebee as an insect.*

8. **Problem solving (the highest level; calls for two or more previously acquired principles to be combined to achieve a goal or produce a new capability. The lower levels are prerequisites to this one.)**

   Examples: *Interpreting a graph depicting the comparative number of cougars in North America over the past 100 years; or setting up an experiment to test the effect of three different types of fertilizers on plant growth.*

Gagne emphasizes that problem solving is the highest level of learning, and that the lower levels are prerequisite to it. Bruner would have teachers begin with problem solving, which leads to the development of necessary subskills; Gagne asks that the teacher emphasize the lower-level skills first, building up to the point where children have a firm foundation of the prerequisites, then teach problem solving.

Constructivism

Constructivists claim that learning involves the construction of knowledge as new experiences are given meaning by prior knowledge. Our current perceptions impact the formation of new perceptions. This notion builds on much of what was taught by Bruner, Piaget, and others. Many educators today agree that this position is basic and sound. We interpret new experiences and acquire new knowledge based on the "realities" that have already been constructed in our minds.

Occasionally, we acquire new information that we can't connect to previously acquired information, and a new seed of knowledge and experience germinates, neither clarified nor cluttered by previous knowledge. The cognitive foundation on which we can build in future learning experiences is then expanded.

Since we process new information through our experiential base, we don't always perceive things the same as someone else perceives them. Each person's mind is unique. Consider a child who is raised with a family of avid fishermen, for example. This child has had many experiences in catching fish, cleaning them, and preparing them for eating. The family has an aquarium at home, and the child spends hours observing fish and studying their movements. This child has a very different mental picture of "fish" than the child who has seen these animals only in pictures and on dinner plates. If the two children are learning together about types of fish and their varying streamlining and navigational characteristics, these two children will not have the same learning experience—even though they sit side by side in class, listening to the same lecture, seeing the same pictures, and doing the same assignment of forming a clay fish and explaining the roll of the fins in navigation. Each child processes the information through the base of his or her previous knowledge and experience.

We noted earlier in this chapter that some of the great learning theorists perceived the very processes of learning and developing differently, due in part to the influence of prior perceptions as they gained new experience step by step along the way. Two very knowledgeable educators can observe the same behavior in a child and interpret it differently because their prior perceptions are different. Similar differences result, to some extent, from every shared learning experience. The more different the prior perceptions are, the more varied will be the interpretations of new information. Although these differences sometimes interfere with learning in a group setting, they also often enrich the experience as members of the group share their perceptions and learn from each other different ways of looking at things.

Sometimes we learn false concepts, commonly called "misconceptions." This data can enter into the processing of new information and interfere with the correct interpretation of new information or experiences. If a child has learned in the past that the phases of the moon are caused by the earth's shadow being cast on the moon, for example, this "knowledge" can actually make it more difficult for the child to learn the true cause of the lunar phases than if the false information had never been learned. The "unlearning" of misconceptions can be very difficult, even with deliberate effort on the part of the learner. In such cases, the teacher must try to understand the student's point of view in order to be able to effectively help the child to clarify the concept. Correct explanations can be very confusing to the learner until the misconceptions are identified and replaced by correct information. Students must confront the inconsistencies that lie between their mental notions and the new information before they can deal productively with the new ideas.

Discovery Learning

Discovery learning is consistent with the ideas of constructivism. Bruner, a proponent of discovery learning, postulates that what the child discovers is not outside the learner, but is an internal reorganization of previously known ideas. Bruner suggests the following benefits of discovery learning: (1) It focuses on problem-solving and inquiry skills, helping students to learn how to learn; (2) motivation is shifted away from that of satisfying others and toward intrinsic rewards; (3) the child becomes a more independent learner as he or she gains self-confidence in being able to find out things by him- or herself; and (4) information discovered is fully synthesized in the mind of the individual and more easily recalled when needed.

Some proponents of discovery learning would advocate that virtually all learning be done through discovery (Brooks, 1990). However, even good ideas can be carried to excess. Discovery adds meaning to the learning experience, but time does not allow for each learner to "rediscover the wheel" and every other concept that is learned. Neither must we shortchange the learner by excusing ourselves from incorporating discovery because of time constraints. Applying this concern to career preparation, the training of a geologist would be greatly extended in time if the student was required to discover firsthand all of the major geologic formations and the historical implications of each; but to be personally involved in significant studies that add insights is meaningful and well worth the time required.

Educators must use wisdom in applying discovery learning efficiently. From a constructivist point of view, firsthand learning through discovery strengthens the mental constructs through which future learning is filtered and interpreted.

Transfer

Bruner believes that transfer of knowledge is possible—even massive transfer from one learning situation to another. He also believes in the transfer of the knowledge-getting process. As we increase our skill in acquiring knowledge in one area, our ability to learn in another cognitive area is also increased.

Taxonomy of Educational Objectives

The Taxonomy of Educational Objectives is well known among educators. It began at a meeting of the American Psychological Association Convention in Boston in 1948, and has become widely known as "Bloom's Taxonomy." It consists of six major classes of objectives, as follows (Bloom, 1971):

1. **Knowledge:** *The knowledge level includes the recall of specific bits of information that can be isolated, of ways and means of dealing with specifics, or of patterns, principles, and generalizations.*
2. **Comprehension:** *The comprehension category represents the lowest level of understanding. It includes the interpretation, translation, and extrapolation of a message, idea, theory, principle, or generalization.*
3. **Application:** *At the application level, students are expected to use previously acquired ideas, principles, or generalizations to solve problems in new or unique situations.*
4. **Analysis:** *Analysis emphasizes the breaking down of given information into its constituent elements or parts, clarifying the related hierarchy of ideas. It is an analysis of elements or parts and their relationships.*
5. **Synthesis:** *Synthesis is the combining of elements or parts to form a whole. It involves arranging the pieces in such a way*

as to form a pattern not clearly evident before.

6. **Evaluation:** *Evaluation involves judgments about the value of materials, ideas, and/or methods for given purposes or applications. The judgments may be based on criteria or standards that are provided for the student or that are determined by the student.*

Model of Mental Operations

One of the many products of Guilford's research was a model of mental operations, in which he identified five types:

1. **Memory** *is the ability to store information in the mind and recall it when needed.*
2. **Cognition** *is the ability to recognize and understand information.*
3. **Evaluation** *is the ability to form conclusions and make judgments.*
4. **Convergent production** *is the ability to use information to draw "correct" or generally accepted conclusions.*
5. **Divergent production** *is the ability to view information in new and creative ways and thereby draw unique and unexpected conclusions.*

Any serious study of science is filled with the need to function in the full range of mental operations. New discoveries would be scarce with a staff of scientists who lacked the ability of divergent production, whose vision was tunneled toward verification and acceptance of previously formed conclusions. On the other hand, progress would come slowly if the same minds were weak in the ability to recall, understand, and make judgments about preliminary information. For elementary students, acquisition of these skills is enhanced by immersion in a program rich in hands-on experiences.

Behaviorism

Skinner taught that behaviors can be classified as *respondent* or *operant*. Respondent behaviors are involuntary reflex actions caused by environmental stimuli: We blush in response to someone's comment or to a mistake we make. Our hands fly up to deflect a rapidly approaching object. We blink when an insect flies near our eyes or shudder at a gruesome or frightening anecdote of a story. In elementary science, students might enjoy identifying one or more of these responses and testing them with family members and friends to see if everyone responds in a similar way. What happens, for instance, when you walk up behind an unsuspecting person and say, "Boo!"? Do some people jump, while others do not? Do some laugh, and some become emotionally upset? Do still others seem to be completely unaffected by such an effort to startle them? Or do they all respond in the same way? What respondent behaviors are triggered by tickling bare feet? Students will enjoy adding other ideas for testing respondent behaviors of family and friends.

Respondent behaviors are many, but according to Skinner, most human behaviors are operant behaviors. These are behaviors that affect the environment or the behavior of others. If the results are satisfying to the individual, the behavior will likely be repeated. A teacher's compliment to a student for a well-formulated experiment will likely result in additional experiments done right (respondent behavior); in turn, as the commendation (operant behavior) succeeds in improving student performance, the teacher will repeat the use of the technique of complimenting.

Both respondent and operant behaviors can be taught. Pavlov's famous research, in which he was able to elicit a salivating response from a dog at the sound of a bell by pairing the sound of the bell with the presentation of food, is a classic example of teaching an involuntary response, or respondent behavior.

Operant conditioning can be used to promote operant learning by following a behavior with a stimulus. If a child is belittled in front of the class for not being able to name the main parts of a flower, when asked, the tendency of the child to respond to questions will likely be suppressed. But if the child feels successful for trying, or for parts of the answer that were correct, the experience of trying will be satisfying and the child will be more likely to attempt an answer to another question. Either way, the behavior is altered by conditioning.

The stimulus used in operant conditioning can be either positive or negative. Perhaps a child causes frequent disturbances when working on a science project with a committee, instead of contributing to the task at hand in a supportive way. In order to alter the behavior of the disrupting child, reinforcement of appropriate conduct, when it does occur, is needed. However, a compliment from the teacher for responsible behavior could be greatly overshadowed by peers who are reinforcing the ploys for attention. Perhaps a private talk with some of the more mature students in the group could cut off the pipeline that has been nourishing the child's improper conduct. The lack of reinforcement for the distractions becomes a negative, but effective, stimulus. On the positive side, the child might respond to the responsibility of being the group chairman and apply his or her leadership talents in a positive, productive way. As the project moves along, the efforts of all participants are encouraged and coordinated by the child with a newly found source of attention and satisfaction.

A FEW MORE IDEAS

Implications and ideas related to learning theory could go on and on, far beyond the scope of this book. In addition to the ideas introduced above, however, let us share some impressions related to four more notions that might be helpful in teaching science to children: self-image, Gestalt, curiosity, and disequalibrium.

Self-Image

What does self-image have to do with teaching science to children? It plays the same role in teaching science as it does in teaching social studies or language arts or any other area of the curriculum. Concern for the self-image is universal in education. It has been said that the most important psychological discovery of this century is the discovery of the self-image. The self-image might be the fundamental key to understanding all of human behavior.

Everything we do, ultimately including our success in life, is hinged on the self-image. Its effect on our behavior and thinking was expressed by a girl of elementary school age in this poem, entitled "My Robot"*:

I have a little robot that goes around with me.

I tell him what I'm thinking; I tell him what I see.

I tell my little robot all my hopes and fears.

He listens and remembers all my joys and tears.

At first my little robot followed my command,

But after years of training, he's gotten out of hand.

He doesn't care what's right or wrong, or what is false or true;

No matter what I try now, he tells me what to do.

*Used with permission from the audio program *The Psychology of Winning* by Denis Waitley. ©MCMLXXXVII Nightingale-Conant Corporation, 7300 N. Lehigh Avenue, Niles, IL 60714.

Dumbo, the cartoon character, provides an excellent example of the power of the self-image. Dumbo wanted to fly. He had noticed that all animals that fly had feathers. Dumbo wished so much that he had feathers, because he just knew that if he had them, he could fly, too. Dumbo's friend Timothy had also been observant; he had noticed that Dumbo's ears had far outgrown his body, and Timothy felt certain that, feathers or no feathers, if Dumbo would just flap his ears, he could fly. However, Dumbo was so sure that feathers were necessary for flying that he just couldn't do it without them.

So, Timothy found a feather, gave it to Dumbo, and said, "Here is a magic feather, Dumbo. If you'll just hold it and flap your ears, you can fly."

Dumbo was so excited about the feather, because he knew that feathers were necessary for flying. He tried it, and it worked; he flew. That was so much fun—it was just what Dumbo had been wanting to do.

One day, as Dumbo was flying, enjoying all the beautiful scenery, he accidentally dropped the magic feather, and he plummeted to the ground—ker-plop! The feather had nothing to do with Dumbo's being able to fly, except for one thing—Dumbo was convinced that with the feather he could fly, and that without it he could not.

As with Dumbo, our self-image sometimes impedes our progress until we obtain a magic feather. The magic feather usually works best if it comes from someone important in our lives—someone in whom we have confidence. Consider, for example, Gina first learning to ride a bicycle. Dad (or Mom, or big brother, or someone else the child trusts) runs alongside the bicycle, holding onto the seat and supporting the bike as Gina concentrates on pushing the pedals to make the two-wheeler go. Before long, Dad notices that Gina, without even knowing it, is beginning to balance the bicycle on her own. If Dad lets go and stops running, Gina will most likely fall, because she doesn't think she can ride the bicycle without help. So Dad will probably continue to run alongside the bike with his hand on the seat, though not really providing any further physical support. Dad will probably tell Gina, as he runs along, that she is balancing the bicycle herself, and Gina will probably say, "Don't stop." Dad soon stops holding onto the seat, but continues to run alongside the bicycle for moral support. By now, all Dad is providing is a "magic feather." Eventually (and by now, Dad's legs are feeling like a pair of wet noodles), Gina realizes that she really is riding the bike by herself, and Dad can stop running. Gina no longer needs the magic feather.

As teachers, one of our jobs is to provide the magic feathers when students need them. Another job, just as important, is to help students recognize their own strengths and become independent learners, so they don't need magic feathers any more. Science education provides many opportunities to build self-confidence, as students sense their increasing abilities to solve problems and to learn independently.

Sometimes insecurity masquerades as a powerful self-image. Don't be fooled. A strong self-image does not show itself as the ability to dominate, to overpower, or to intimidate others. A healthy self-image provides a feeling of confidence in one's own ability, which frees that person to be supportive of others. As the self-image grows, one realizes that we elevate ourselves by lifting others, not by stepping on them. Or, as someone said, "Blowing out another person's candle will not make yours shine more brightly."

As teachers, we also need to develop our own self-image. We owe that to our students. You cannot lift someone else higher than you stand. You will be better able to help others develop a positive self-image if yours is also healthy. Being a supportive teacher does not mean being a wishy-washy pushover. Sometimes showing a student you care will mean caring enough to insist that behavior is appropriate and that work gets done.

Gestalt

Gestalt theorists postulate that seeing the overall pattern gives meaning to the parts. Although a simple concept, this is a very important idea, as we view the science curriculum. The spiral curriculum implies that we give students quite a broad view of topics very early, then each year we review and expand the major concepts learned earlier, and then add more topics to the child's repertoire. As we provide a rather broad base of topics, we are helping the child to see a pattern, or Gestalt. Some examples might be helpful.

Do you enjoy putting picture puzzles together? The challenge of a 500-piece puzzle is very enticing to many people. But wait—what if the puzzle comes in a shoebox? Even with the assurance that there are no missing pieces, many people would lose interest very quickly. Why? Because puzzles usually come in a box with a picture of the completed puzzle—the ever-important Gestalt. Then, as you lay all the pieces out on a table, if you see a puzzle piece with a bit of red on it, and you notice from the picture that the only red is on a girl's clothing in the lower left corner, you'll probably put that particular piece in the lower left corner of the table. The picture—the overall pattern—clarifies the role of each small part. Seeing the overall pattern really does give meaning to the parts.

A story that is told about six blind men and an elephant, based on a famous Indian legend, seems to have meaning here. This story is listed as folklore (Aarne & Thompson, 1961, #1317), and many versions have been written in both prose and poetry. Here's ours.

Six Blind Men and an Elephant

Six fine men of Indostan
To learning much inclined,
Who went to see an elephant
Although they all were blind,
That each by observation might bring
Satisfaction to his mind.

The First to approach the elephant,
Clumsily did fall
Against the broad and sturdy side,
He at once began to call,
"What a monstrous beast! The elephant
Is almost like a wall!"

The Second, feeling of the tusk,
Cried: "My, What have we here,
So very round and smooth and sharp?
To me it's very clear
This over-rated elephant
Is nothing but a spear!"

The Third approached the animal,
Surprised as he did take
The squirming trunk within his hands,
Boldly he sat up and spake:
"To me this wondrous animal
Is much more like a snake!"

The Fourth reached toward the monster's leg,
And felt about eagerly
"What this huge beast is like to me
Is plain enough," said he;
"This wonder of an elephant
Is something like a tree."

The Fifth, who reached and touched the ear,
Said: "Why, even the blindest man
Can see what this beast resembles most;
I can't deny. Who can?
This marvel of an elephant
Is nearly like a fan!"

The Sixth man, anxious for his turn
About the beast to grope,
Quickly seized the animal's tail
As it swung within his scope,
"I think," said he, "The elephant
Is clearly like a rope!"

The perceptions of these six men regarding the elephant were very different simply because each man experienced a different part of the elephant. Their learning experiences did not include a Gestalt. They needed to experience the entire elephant. If only they could have stood back and taken off their blinders for a moment, just to get a glimpse of the entire animal, then each of the parts would have born meaning in its relationship to the elephant.

It seems that the question of what the earth—the whole earth—looked like was a dominating thought in the minds of many explorers for a long time. What they sought was a Gestalt. They were too close to the forest to see the trees, and they had no way to back off and get a broader perspective. The voyages of Columbus and other early explorers contributed greatly to this effort of exploring and mapping the planet, yet such explorers could see only a small part of it at any one time. The human race glimpsed its first real Gestalt of the earth with the *Apollo* space flights. That was the first time a person was able to back off far enough from the earth to see the whole thing. As we look at photographs taken by *Apollo*, we realize that even the early explorers, with their relatively crude techniques and instruments, mapped the earth with amazing accuracy. It took hundreds of years, but they were able to put the pieces together and form a rather accurate Gestalt.

Curiosity

While curiosity has taken the rap for killing a lot of cats, it has long been recognized as a mighty motivator for learning. Science offers many opportunities to arouse curiosity with objects or events that are novel, incongruous, or complex. Bringing a Jerusalem cricket into the classroom for an introduction to a unit on insects; pouring two clear liquids together to form a blue liquid, at the beginning of a lesson on matter; or being kissed on the nose by a charged balloon during a study of static electricity, will almost certainly stimulate curiosity. The probability that student attention will prevail during the discussion and activities that follow is greatly increased.

Koran and Longino (1982) suggest keeping a record of students' curiosity behavior, recording both the frequency with which they examine and manipulate objects and the time they spend (by choice) in the vicinity of a particular object or event. From their research on curiosity and science learning, they made the following suggestions for stimulating a high degree of curiosity in students:

1. *Use variety, novelty, change, and discrepant events to stimulate curiosity.*
2. *Provide students with books, magazines, newspapers, brainteasers, puzzles, and objects to manipulate.*
3. *Deal with topics of interest as they come up, rather than putting them off until they "fit" into the lesson plan.*
4. *Create, or have students create, science learning centers for developing independent learning, as well as fostering curiosity behaviors.*
5. *Recognize and reward students when they ask questions, exhibit curiosity behaviors, or spend time exploring a wide range of objects or events.*
6. *Don't rush students when they act curious about something.*
7. *Act as a model for students—ask questions aloud, spend time exploring and learning while using all of your senses, and verbalize what you are doing.*
8. *Encourage parents to provide novel and complex objects and events for their children to experience, and also to act as models for their children.*

Disequilibrium

In addition to identifying the cognitive stages described above, Piaget also emphasized the function of equilibrium in the learning process. Very simply, the mind, in a state of equilibrium, is satisfied. When unanswered questions stimulate the curiosity, or otherwise create a need to know, a state of disequilibrium occurs. A natural tendency in humans is to strive to reach a state of equilibrium, satisfying the mind with needed or desired information or experience.

Events that bring about disequilibrium occur frequently: We hear a sound, and we look up to determine its source; a car door slams, and we run to the window to see who is there; someone slips on the floor and is injured, and we investigate to determine the cause. In each of these cases, equilibrium is quickly reestablished as the needed information is acquired.

In the science classroom, teachers sometimes devise an event to deliberately create a state of disequilibrium in the minds of students, and the resulting need for information becomes a motivating force toward learning. This is sometimes effectively accomplished by using "discrepant events" (see chapter 3). Students listen and participate with greater interest in an effort to satisfy the curiosity and reestablish equilibrium. An example might be a "kissing balloon" used as an introduction to a unit on static electricity. Hang a balloon from string, then draw a face on it and rub the nose with a piece of wool cloth. The balloon will react to students who come near. (A child leaning toward the balloon might be rewarded by a kiss on the cheek!) This will usually raise questions, the answers for which students will likely be willing to work at as they become involved with various activities in the study of static electricity. Applying this technique to constructivism, disequilibrium is brought about as the discrepant event creates an imbalance between the child's "realities" and the event that is presented. Desire to learn is thus heightened by the disequilibrium.

Central to Piaget's theory is the theme that a continuing state of equilibrium is never reached, since the intellectual process through which the individual moves from disequilibrium to equilibrium triggers new questions and problems, resulting in imbalance (disequilibrium) at a somewhat higher level. This was verified when a second-grade student reported, after a group assignment was completed, "We answered our question, and now we have two more questions."

That is an exciting report, and it can be the beginning of an endless chain reaction of learning sequences. Children who are turned on by their experiences with static electricity, magnetism, or some other topic, might continue to expand on their classroom experience by inventing new experiments on their own, or by asking questions and discussing the topic with others.

Sometimes the search for answers is joined by others and continues on and on. In the year 600 B.C., a Greek philosopher, Thales of Miletus, discovered the effect of static electricity as he rubbed amber and produced a force that would pick up straw (Kettering, 1959). This source of disequilibrium has been pursued for centuries by Benjamin Franklin, Samuel Morse, Thomas Edison, Alexander Graham Bell, and others. Today, the benefits of that pursuit are vast and the resulting new information and technology move forward at an increasing rate. This continues to occur from efforts to establish a state of equilibrium in the minds of additional investigators. In fact, scientists today continue to learn more about the force that caused a piece of amber to pick up a straw hundreds of years ago.

IN CLOSING

The human mind is very complex, and the effort to understand how it develops and functions is an arduous task. Although the science of psychology is probably still in its infancy, as compared to the knowledge that will exist in the future, our knowledge exceeds our practice. We know, for instance, that children of the elementary grades need lots of direct, hands-on experiences in their learning. Probably no area of the curriculum has a greater need for application of this knowledge than does science, and no area of the curriculum is more naturally suited to concrete forms of learning than is science. Children need plenty of opportunities to explore, investigate, and manipulate materials. Although the experts disagree on some points of psychological development, there is very little argument about the need for concrete experiences in learning. Piaget taught that readiness depends on the child's maturation and intellectual development; Bruner teaches that the child is always ready to learn a concept in some manner; Gagne feels that learning is related to the successful development of prerequisite skills, rather than to the child's developmental level; but all agree that elementary science should be taught as a process of inquiry, rich in hands-on experiences.

Just as important as involving children in plenty of concrete experiences is the need to provide frequent occasions for them to talk about it and write about it, for children don't learn *just* by doing things; they learn by reflecting on what they do. Learning in the science classroom will be more complete and fulfilling for both teachers and students, as many experiences are shared in *doing* science, and in *talking* and *writing* about those experiences and related information. (See more information about these aspects in the discussion of Integrating in chapter 8.)

LIST OF RESOURCES

Aarne, Antti, and Stith Thompson, compilers, *The Types of the Folktale: A Classification and Bibliography* (FF Communications #184, Helsinki, Finland: Finnish Academy of Sciences, 1961).

Bloom, Benjamin S., et al., *Handbook on Formative and Summative Evaluation of Student Learning* (New York: McGraw-Hill, Inc., 1971).

Bloom, Benjamin S., personal telephone conversation, May 23, 1990.

Boring, Edwin G., et al., *A History of Psychology in Autobiography, Volume IV* (Worcester, MA: Clark University Press, 1952).

Boring, Edwin G., and Gardner Lindzey, *A History of Psychology in Autobiography, Volume V* (New York: Appleton-Century-Crofts, 1967).

Brooks, Jacqueline Grennon, "Teachers and Students: Constructivists Forging New Connections," *Educational Leadership* 47, no. 5 (February 1990): 68–71.

Bruner, Jerome S., *The Process of Education* (Cambridge, MA: Harvard University Press, 1960).

Bruner, Jerome S., *Toward a Theory of Instruction* (Cambridge, MA: Belknap Press, 1966).

Esler, William K., "Brain Physiology: Research and Theory," *Science and Children* 19, no. 6 (March 1982): 44–45.

Gagne, Robert M., *The Conditions of Learning* (New York: Holt, Rinehart & Winston, 1965).

Ginsburg, Herbert and Sylvia Opper, *Piaget's Theory of Intellectual Development* (Englewood Cliffs, NJ: Prentice-Hall, Inc., 1969).

Kantrowitz, Barbara, and Pat Wingert, "How Kids Learn," *Newsweek* (April 17, 1989).

Kettering, C. F., *Short Stories of Science and Invention* (Detroit: General Motors, 1959).

Koran, John J., Jr. and Sarah J. Longino, "Curiosity and Children's Science Learning," *Science and Children* 20, no. 2 (October 1982): 18–19.

Lindzey, Gardner, *A History of Psychology in Autobiography, Volume VII* (New York: Appleton-Century-Crofts, 1980).

Shulman, Lee S., "Psychological Controversies in the Teaching of Science and Mathematics," *The Science Teacher* 35, no. 6 (September 1968): 34–38, 89–90.

Silverstein, Shel, *Where the Sidewalk Ends* (New York: Harper & Row, 1974).

Waitley, Denis, *The Psychology of Winning,* (audio tapes) (Niles, IL: Nightingale Conant Corp., 1987).

CHAPTER

PROBLEM SOLVING AND RESEARCH

CHAPTER OUTLINE:

I WONDER . . .

What are discrepant events?
How do I use guided discovery in my classroom?
What are the process skills that apply to elementary science?
How can I make the scientific method meaningful at the elementary level?
Can elementary students do research?
Can I use research to improve my own teaching?

INTRODUCTION

The importance of helping children to develop problem-solving skills is one of the most talked-about issues in education today. No other area of the curriculum offers such a wealth of opportunity to develop these skills as does science. We begin this chapter by defining discrepant events and suggesting that you use them to stimulate curiosity and generate questions—or problems to solve—in the minds of students. We describe guided discovery as an intermediate step between expository teaching and true independent inquiry by the learner. The science process skills are presented in this chapter as tools of inquiry—methods for solving problems and answering questions. Finally, we emphasize the scientific method as a valuable, systematic approach to solving problems and acquiring information.

In this chapter, we also discuss the value of using classroom research to improve teaching and learning, emphasizing the connection between research and the scientific method of problem solving. In addition to discussing the uses of research, we suggest ways that students can become involved as researchers in science, and ways that you as the teacher can apply research to improve classroom instruction.

Our overall goal is to develop independent learners. Students who acquire problem-solving skills, and a sense of how they can apply these skills to everyday situations, will have less need to search outside themselves for answers to questions and solutions to problems that arise in their lives.

DISCREPANT EVENTS

Disequilibrium is the desire to know, the condition of the mind when a problem or question exists. A discrepancy between what a student expects to happen with a science activity and what actually happens can be very effective in capturing the student's curiosity and attention. The discrepancy creates a state of disequilibrium in the mind of the learner, increasing curiosity and providing the magic of *motivation to learn*

Science activities often have surprising outcomes, and each one is a potential discrepant event. Let's consider, for example, a simple activity that uses a funnel and a ping-pong ball to demonstrate Bernoulli's principle (that pressure within a fluid decreases as the speed of the fluid increases). Give a student the funnel and ball, and ask her to predict how far she can blow the ball across the room if she places the ball in the large open end of the funnel and then blows into the narrow end (see Figure 3-1). After she has predicted the distance, challenge her to try it. The student should hold the funnel at enough of an angle that the ball will not roll out, and then blow very hard through

Figure 3-1

Student trying to blow ping-pong ball from funnel.

the funnel. What happens? As the student blows into the funnel, the ball holds its ground. This surprising outcome is a discrepant event, and you can be sure the student's interest and curiosity will soar.

If such an event ends here, with a puff of curiosity, it has little value beyond entertainment. But as the teacher, you can capture the teachable moment created by the event and lead the class into a search for answers, related activities, and applications. For example, your students may be surprised when you tell them that some baseball pitchers use Bernoulli's principle by spinning the ball, causing air to rush over one side faster than the other as the ball speeds through the air, resulting in a curve ball. You might also point out that airplanes are held aloft, in part, by the effect of Bernoulli's principle, as air flows over airfoils (wings) that are curved on top and relatively flat on the bottom. Because the air flows faster over the top than across the bottom, pressure on the top of the wing is reduced, having the effect of increased pressure under the wing, providing lift. Your students can demonstrate the lifting effect that supports an airplane wing by blowing over a curved piece of paper (an airfoil).

Use the disequilibrium created by the discrepant event of the funnel and the ball to explore additional applications of Bernoulli's principle. When someone compresses the squeeze-bulb of a perfume atomizer, for example, a gust of air is forced through a horizontal tube. A separate, vertical tube extends from the horizontal tube into a jar of perfume. As air rushes through the horizontal tube and over the top of the vertical tube, air pressure in the vertical tube is reduced (remember Bernoulli). Atmospheric pressure inside the bottle forces perfume up the vertical tube because atmospheric pressure is greater than the reduced pressure in the vertical tube. The perfume is pushed up and mixes with the air that is rushing through the horizontal tube. The force of the air *atomizes* the liquid (breaks it up into tiny particles), and the result is on every cosmetic counter—a perfume sprayer. The type of weed sprayer that attaches to a garden hose operates on the same principle, as does a certain device that is available for emptying waterbeds with a sink faucet. This device wastes large amounts of water, but it does apply Bernoulli's principle.

The exploration of this topic is not complete until your students have made their own two-straw atomizers (see Figures 3-2 and 3-3). Have them cut a regular soda straw into two pieces, with one piece being about half as long as the other. Then have them stand the short piece of straw in a cup of water and use the longer piece to blow across the top of the short piece. Oops, what a mess! Sorry about that, but your stu-

Figure 3-2

Girl with two-straw atomizer, ready to blow.

dents will always remember Bernoulli. And, by the way, we could have used the 2-straw atomizer as the discrepant event that started the whole investigation. (For more information about Bernoulli's principle, see chapter 20.)

In addition to these activities, you might set up another exciting discrepant event using the topic of air by demonstrating how air pressure can crush a metal can. Put a small amount of water (1/2 cup or so) in an empty can (with the cap removed!) and heat the can on a hot plate. Use a can that has a small spout—not a coffee can. When a hefty head of steam is escaping through the spout, remove the can from the heat source, seal the spout immediately with the cap, and set the can aside to cool. Your students will watch in wide-eyed amazement as the can is crushed. Caution: be sure to remove the can from the heat before sealing it with the lid; if you leave the can on the hot plate with the lid on, you have created a bomb!

GUIDED DISCOVERY

One of the goals of elementary school science is to launch students in the direction of independent inquiry, or free discovery. We want our students to develop an endless curiosity, and

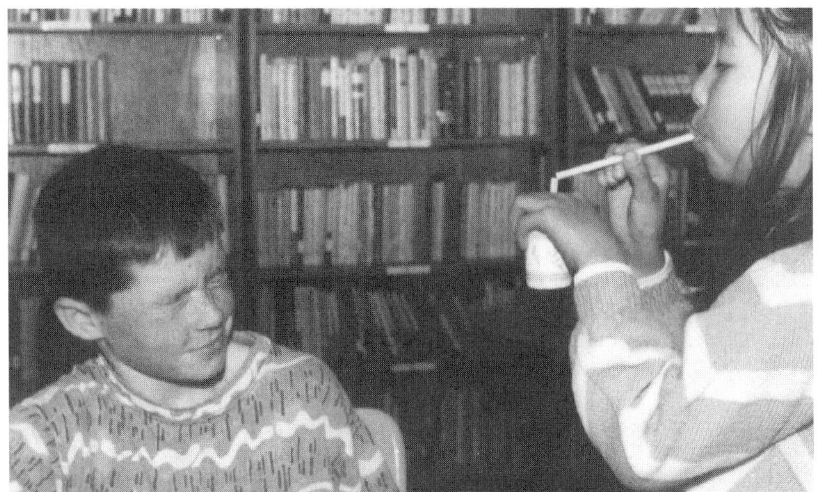

Figure 3-3

Student getting sprayed with two-straw atomizer.

with it such skill in the processes of learning that when they leave the classroom they embark on a lifelong quest for knowledge. We want them to explore the natural world spontaneously, enriching their lives and the lives of others with their constant zest for new knowledge and new insights.

The idea of discovery learning is consistent with constructivist theory (see chapter 2). New learning is influenced by prior perceptions as it is processed by the mind. As students acquire new information, perceptions are clarified and broadened and in turn become a part of the total cognitive base through which the next experience or idea will be processed. Information learned firsthand by discovery strengthens and clarifies perceptions.

How can we achieve this goal? Although expository teaching (direct instruction, lecture) is a time-efficient way to impart information, it lacks meaning. Students need frequent experiences that propel them toward independent inquiry. An important link in the transition between expository teaching and independent inquiry is a process of discovery under the direction of the teacher. This process is commonly called *guided discovery.*

When the formal years of schooling are finished, so possibly is the active pursuit of learning for the student who has experienced only expository teaching. For that student, all learning has come from teachers, and the teachers are no longer available. On the other hand, if children are effectively taught to be independent learners, the completion of formal schooling only marks a new dawn—the real beginning of a lifetime of inquiry, for which the student has prepared throughout the years of formal education. True education is not a process of teachers simply providing information; it must include honing the investigative skills of the learner. One measure of success for teachers is in how well we prepare students to get along without teachers. Is the graduate a self-guided learner who has discovered that learning offers its own reward, or is he or she still looking to an authority for direction, motivation, and reward in learning? Guided discovery is a way to help students discover and exercise their wings of independence in learning.

Guided discovery alters the role of the teacher. Instead of just dispensing information and rewards, you're a facilitator and guide—one who encourages the independent pursuit of knowledge. With discovery learning, the student discovers concepts. As the term "guided discovery" suggests, the teacher guides that process, asking questions to direct the child's thinking, and suggesting a new approach here and there, but encouraging independent investigation (see Figure 3-4).

Like other instructional techniques, guided discovery can take many forms. In general, it implies investigations on the part of the child. It also implies that the teacher has not first explained the concepts related to the topic at hand, which would likely get in the way of the discovery process. If you explain concepts first, and then instruct the child to do a related activity for which the outcome is known, the child is robbed of the discovery experience.

We know that time does not allow for all learning to be done by discovery. However, children need to learn how to investigate and

Figure 3-4

Teacher helping students as they study.

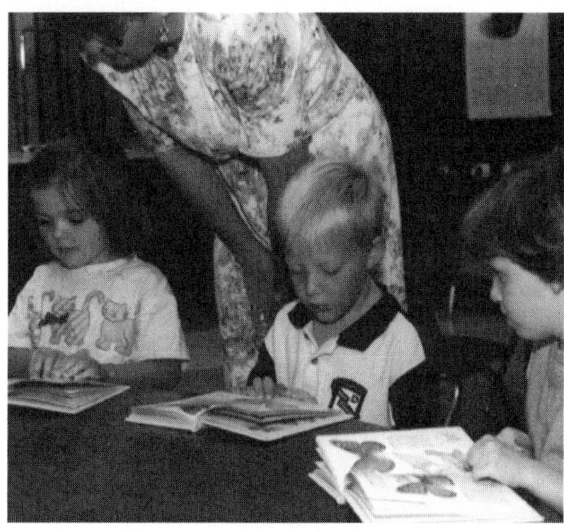

discover new information, and they acquire that skill only when they are given opportunities to investigate in a discovery setting. If the child knows what to expect before doing the activity, the process of doing the activity only verifies the expected outcome. In contrast, if the child does the activity without preestablished expectations of the outcome, he or she is free to investigate, to try to think of variables that will affect the outcome, to change one of those variables and try the activity again. With prior knowledge, the child is likely to be satisfied when the expected outcome occurs, whereas the condition of not knowing unleashes the curiosity to pursue additional investigations. Let's look at two examples.

Example 1: *Consider that your class is studying the topic of static electricity. You might explain that when a balloon is rubbed with cloth (wool works especially well), and brought near a sprinkling of salt and pepper, the salt and pepper is attracted to the balloon. This is due to a negative charge on the balloon, which results from being rubbed by the cloth, and a positive charge that is induced in the salt and pepper as the balloon comes near. If you give the materials to your students, they will try the activity and will likely watch the rapid movement of the salt and pepper particles with fascination. Having witnessed this phenomenon, they are ready to go on.*

Example 2: *Now let's change the approach slightly. Instead of explaining what will happen, you provide students with a balloon, cloth, salt, and pepper. You tell students to blow up the balloon, rub it with the cloth, sprinkle a small amount of salt and pepper on the table top, bring the rubbed side of the balloon near the salt and pepper, hold it steady, and observe. Then you ask them to describe what they see and hear. You invite them to explain what they think is causing the "rainstorm," and why they think the salt and pepper particles are behaving this way.*

What might you do next? Encourage students to think of some other things they could try that would be related to this. They will likely rub the balloon and make it stick on a wall, because they have seen that done before and they have probably done it themselves numerous times, and it's still fun to do. They might also try bringing the rubbed balloon near other small, light objects, such as small bits of paper, plastic foam, or the end of a string. If students don't try these things on their own, you could suggest one or more of them to kickstart the open investigation and discovery process. Encourage students to watch very patiently as they bring the balloon near the bits of paper; place it about 3 to 5 centimeters (1 to 2 inches) from the paper and hold the balloon steady—no matter what the papers do, just hold the balloon steady and watch. You might suggest that students run a stream of water over the balloon, let it dry (or dab it very carefully with a towel, don't rub, because that would charge the balloon all over again), and try it again with the bits of paper and other light objects.

The entire class can do the same activity, in small cooperative groups. Ask questions during the investigation process, encouraging students to try new ideas and see what new discoveries they can make. After they have had sufficient time for the investigation, invite students to share their findings—their discoveries—about what they did and what they observed. Following the discovery experience is a good time for you to add to the information and clarify concepts, perhaps with further demonstration of related activities, in which you still involve students wherever possible.

A successful variation of this technique is to select and prepare several related activities and to assign each discovery activity to a different table, with each of the cooperative groups working at one table. After five minutes (or whatever amount of time is appropriate), each group shifts to a new table (new activity) in a predetermined order. After all groups have experienced all activities, discussion can begin. Discuss one activity at a time, in an organized way. Here is one way to organize the discussion.

1. *Each group leads the discussion of the activity their group ended with.*
2. *The group captain assigns a speaker.*
3. *The discussion of each activity is done as follows:*
   a. *The speaker explains what the group did with that particular activity, what they observed, and whatever else the speaker would like to say about that activity.*
   b. *Others in the cooperative group add to the information if they care to.*
   c. *Others in the class may share additional information according to their investigations and observations with that particular activity.*
4. *When this process is finished, the speaker for the next group begins the discussion of the second activity.*
5. *The sharing of observations and discoveries progresses until all activities involved have been discussed.*
6. *In addition to guiding the discussion, the teacher now adds information that seems appropriate and needed in clarifying concepts and dealing with further questions.*

Research over a period of many years has shown that discovery learning is effective. One study showed that students who had experienced discovery learning with the use of SCIIS materials had a more positive general attitude toward science, greater feelings of success, and greater recognition of the usefulness of science in their daily lives (Kyle, 1985). Other studies have demonstrated that students of inquiry-oriented science have performed better in general science achievement, process skills, and related skills (Shymansky, 1982).

The most common objection to teaching by guided discovery is probably that doing it right is very time consuming. In discovery learning, there is no substitute for time and there are no real shortcuts. Students need time to think through a problem, to reason, to plan, to test alternatives, and to gain insights, in much the same manner as scientists approach a problem. But if students are genuinely interested in the problem, and are pursuing it creatively, the time is well invested. Although the expository approach is relatively time-efficient, as educators we would do well to consider this warning: "The fatal pedagogical error is to throw answers like stones at the heads of those who have not yet asked questions."

Guided discovery is consistent with the Learning Cycle model, as described in chapter 8. Knowledge acquired through problem solving is richer, with more embedded cues, than knowledge that comes through direct instruction. Retention is therefore likely to be more complete, and the knowledge is more readily transferred to related situations.

SCIENCE PROCESSES

Scientists are constantly searching for new information, new interpretations, new meanings. The processes by which scientists do their work are the processes that lead to problem solving and discovery. Although they are commonly referred to as *science processes,* these are skills that we all need. Everyone, not just the scientist, needs to have the skills necessary to take a scientific approach to learning and problem solving.

The science processes are the means used in acquiring and discovering science content. These are two distinct, yet inseparable, aspects of science education—the *how* and the *what.* Content information is the *what,* and the process skills collectively are the *how* of science. At the elementary level, a great deal of emphasis needs to be placed on learning how to learn—becoming competent in using the skills of inquiry. It is important to maintain a focus on developing the skills, not just on learning scientific facts. Students can memorize facts, but they must experience, practice, and internalize if they are to learn the skills. You don't learn how to swan dive by reading a book, and you don't learn science skills by memorizing definitions.

What Are the Process Skills?

Lists of process skills vary from one source to another, but the following skills are generally considered appropriate for the elementary grades:

1. **Observing:** *Perceiving events and the natural world through the five senses*
2. **Inferring:** *Interpreting or explaining one or more observations, often on the basis of prior experience or perceptions*
3. **Classifying:** *Grouping objects or events according to their characteristics*
4. **Measuring:** *Making quantitative observations*
5. **Predicting:** *Forecasting future events or conditions, based on patterns recognized in past observations*
6. **Communicating:** *Transmitting information to others through spoken language or written symbols, including charts, maps, or other visual demonstrations*
7. **Using space-time relationships:** *Identifying relative position and motion of objects, as well as changes over time*
8. **Formulating hypotheses:** *Making educated guesses on the basis of current information, prior to investigating or experimenting*
9. **Identifying and controlling variables:** *Identifying the variables that affect a system, and selecting those to manipulate and those to hold constant*
10. **Experimenting:** *Investigating through controlled manipulation of variables, using all applicable and appropriate process skills*

The first seven of these process skills are often considered *basic* processes, while the last three are referred to as *integrated* processes. Notice that the basic processes are used within the integrated processes. Primary grades (K–3) should concentrate on the basic processes. Intermediate grades should review and reinforce those skills, while developing the integrated processes. With the right approach, important groundwork can be laid for using the integrated processes even in the lower grades (see Kaplan, 1984).

Let's look at these skills one at a time. It would be helpful if we could identify activities for teaching each of the processes in isolation, with methods that involve one and only one process. That's not so easy. The great majority of the activities and investigations in science involve multiple processes. The difficulty is further complicated by the fact that processes are embedded within processes. Even the second skill on the list, *inference,* is based on the first, *observation.* Inversely, an understanding of the meaning of *inference* helps to clarify what is or is not a true observation. Still, we can introduce the basic processes one at a time, using relatively simple activities and concentrating our attention on the target skill. Here are a few ideas to consider when you introduce the process skills to elementary students.

Observing

Developing observation skills is compatible with the young child's need to practice verbal or written expression. Give primary grade students frequent occasions to express themselves—to talk about what they see, what they hear, and what they smell, taste, and feel. As they examine rocks, encourage them to talk about color, size, texture, and weight. As children develop their auditory observation skills through listening to music and learning to recognize and identify high pitch, low pitch, and loud and soft sounds, give them opportunities to describe what they learn. As they observe changes in nature—such as with new flowers and insects around the building in the springtime, or lack of them in the fall, or changes in temperature and weather patterns—encourage children to express their observations and feelings. Noting the changes in the taste, shape, and consistency of chewing gum as they chew it, or in candy as it dissolves away in their mouths, are observations that children will enjoy expressing.

Popping popcorn is an excellent activity for emphasizing observation. Ask children to see how many of the senses they use as they pop the popcorn and eat it. Children can also learn to use the word "observe," and begin to make connections between the term and the process of getting information through all of the senses—not just the eyes. (Caution: Before inviting children to taste or eat anything, check on possible problems such as allergies and school district policy. Similar precautions should be taken when using other senses.)

It is crucial that we provide students practice in recording observations. Before children can express their observations in written words, they can draw and sketch. Their vocabulary will be strengthened as they apply adjectives and verbs to verbal descriptions of their drawings. Sometimes students in the lower grades dictate their observations to the teacher, or to an older student, who records them on a chart. As students acquire writing skills, they can describe many of their observations on paper, as well as expressing them orally. Doing this will improve their writing skills through application. Make sure they continue drawing and sketching, continually sharpening their perceptions.

One good activity for encouraging observation is to challenge students to see how many observations they can record, as they closely observe a plant or other specific object. You might even set up this challenge in the form of a contest. Encourage both qualitative (such as color, shape) and quantitative (such as number, size) observations.

Inferring

An inference is an assumption that is based on observations. We frequently make inferences from our everyday observations. We hear a car door close and we say, "Mother is home." We see a robin on the grass and we say, "Spring is here." We feel a sore throat and we say, "I have the flu." All of these are inferences, based on our observations.

When pleasant aromas come from the kitchen, as lunchtime approaches and students mention hot dogs, pizza, or any other specific food, you have an excellent opportunity to talk about inferences. It's possible that frankfurters are being fried to be chopped up and put into a stew, or that pizza sauce is being used in the preparation of a dish other than pizza. On the other hand, maybe frankfurters are not on the menu at all, but something else on the stove smells a lot like them. If a student says, "Something smells like hot dogs," the student has expressed an observation. However, the statement "I smell hot dogs," would be an inference. Inferences are less certain and more susceptible to error than are observations.

Students learn to recognize the difference between observations and inferences by talking about and classifying them, by responding to the question, "Is that an observation or an inference?" As the teacher, you might ask, "Did you *see* a rock in your shoe, or did you *feel* a lump and you think it felt like a rock? When you said, 'There's a rock in my shoe,' were you making an observation, or an inference?"

Mystery boxes

Mystery boxes can add an exciting element to the classroom when you are working with inferences. Here are some examples:

1. *Place one or two small objects in a box, put the lid on, and seal the box with tape. Students can pick up the box and see how*

heavy it is, shake it, tip it back and forth and listen to the object(s) roll or slide, and so on, but they must not remove the lid. They infer *what is in the box by using senses other than sight (see Figure 3-5).*

2. *Cut an armhole in a relatively large box, and allow students to reach in and feel the object that is inside. The student whose hand is in the box describes the object to one or more others, but must not say what the item is or what it is used for; descriptions are limited to actual observations of size, weight, shape, texture, and so on. Those hearing the descriptions try to infer what the object is from the stated characteristics.*
3. *Fasten a cube, a ball, or other three-dimensional geometric shape to the bottom of a box—use more than one shape if desired. The box should then be sealed. Cut holes in the sides of the box and in the top, large enough for a pencil or dowel to be inserted. Students can then "feel" the contents of the box from different angles with the stick and infer the shape of the object(s) (see Figure 3-6).*

Figure 3-5

Student shaking mystery box.

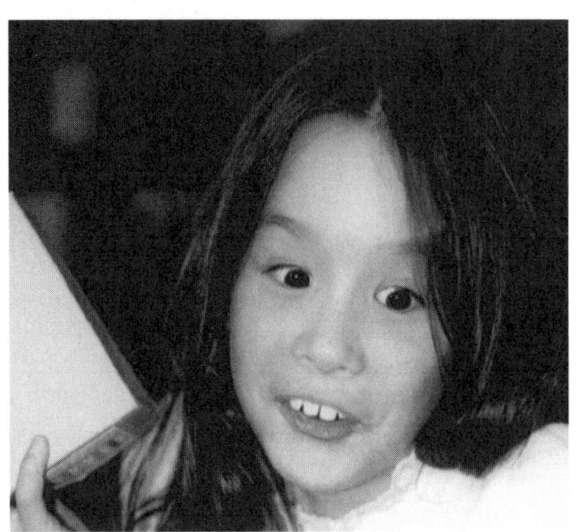

Figure 3-6

Student "feeling" shapes in a box with a stick inserted through holes.

4. *Place several paper clips (or washers or other magnetic objects) in some pattern between two layers of wood (or cardboard). Using a magnet, students infer where the objects are. They could even draw the pattern of paper clips on a sheet of paper.*

Children do a lot of observing and inferring as they have experiences with magnets, candles, growing plants, and myriads of other things. Your job as the teacher is to help them to recognize the difference and to connect them with the proper terms.

Classifying

Classifying, like inferring, relies heavily on observation. Children become skilled in recognizing characteristics of objects as they have more and more opportunities to express what they see and hear, for instance. Through these experiences they learn to recognize likenesses and differences between objects. If you give children an assortment of geometric shapes, and ask them to put all of those that are alike into one group, you'll get a variety of responses. One child might put all of the triangles together, another child might select only the red triangles, and a third might select only the small red triangles. Each of the three children completes the assignment correctly, though the second and third children may be more skilled at recognizing subtle differences than the first. You'd need to give them additional experiences before judging, since the first child might have noticed the other characteristics but simply decided to select the triangles because they have the same shape.

A collection of rocks provides excellent activities in classification for children. Ignoring the scientific classification of rocks (that can come later), you might ask young children simply to decide how the rocks are alike and how they are different, and group them accordingly. One child (or group) can begin by placing the rocks into two groups (or three or more, if they're ready). Another child (or group) then infers what characteristic the first had in mind in classifying the rocks. Continue the experience, encouraging students to consider color, texture, and other qualities—perhaps even hardness.

Other objects that you can use to provide excellent experiences in classifying include leaves, buttons, greeting cards, seeds, shoes, and the children themselves—or their fingerprints. A screen that is used to sort fine sand from coarse sand and rocks is a classifying machine.

Measuring

Science experiences provide many opportunities to experience numbers in action—to note application—to see where numbers fit in the children's lives. Even younger children do much describing and comparing in terms of quantity, even if only to suggest that one person is taller than another, one book is heavier than another, or one marble is larger than another.

Many properties of objects have to do with numbers. For example, children might classify buttons according to the number of holes they have for thread, or shoes by the number of holes they have for laces. When children have classified a set of objects into groups, they can count and compare subsets. Children may explore and discuss whether numbers have any implications as to which is best, or worst, or most preferred. They'll quickly notice that if the numbers represent scores on tests, such meaning is implied; or if they indicate time of day, and someone is running late. Even if the numbers do not suggest anything other than how many things there are in a group, students can see that the numbers mean something.

When children are ready, science experiences offer many opportunities to measure. Weight, height, and other numerical characteristics are constantly called for in science. Students are often intrigued by learning to use the width of their own fingernail, palm of their hand, handspan, and so on, as units of measure in determining sizes or distances (Roth, 1991). Doing so leads to many interesting experiences with numbers.

Children in the upper elementary grades can learn to apply their math skills by computing the maximum height of a model rocket in flight. Investigations of ramps involve measuring the height and length of the ramp, as well as the distance a ball, toy car, or other object travels when rolled down the ramp (see Figure 3-7). Working with a metric balance or with pendulums can provide additional activities dealing with numbers that will involve and interest children as they study science.

Predicting

There is much order in the natural world. The observation of conditions or events often

Figure 3-7

Child measuring the height of a ramp.

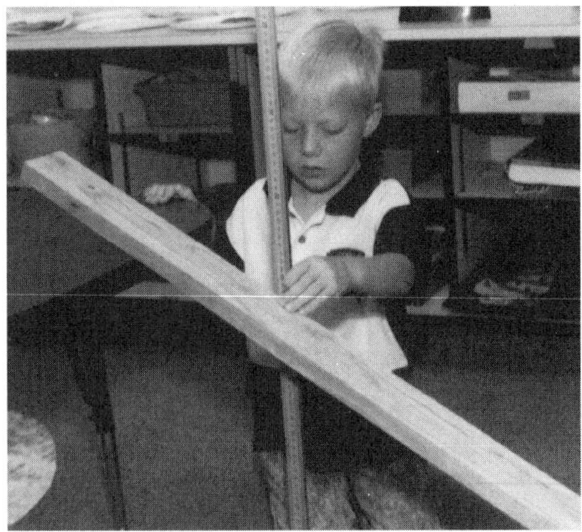

reveals patterns that make it possible to predict future conditions or events. The weather is notorious for being difficult to predict from day to day, and even meteorologists agonize over its complexity. General long-range weather patterns from season to season, however, are very predictable, even for the person untrained in the science of meteorology. In areas of the world that have cold winters, people can predict with great certainty that next winter will also be cold, even though in any given year the area might experience unusually warm weather, unusually cold weather, or more or less moisture than normal. Children in these areas learn at a very young age that in the winter they need a warm coat, and in the summer they expect to have warm days for swimming and for many other fair-weather activities. They soon come to expect the trees in the schoolyard to leaf out in the spring and to drop their leaves again each autumn. Other predictable patterns in the lives of most children include approximate bedtime, school vacations at certain times of the year, and their parent's or guardian's response to misbehaviors.

So children are not strangers to the notion of predictable events, and we can help them to make the connection between the term and its meaning by calling their attention to predictable patterns that are already familiar to them. For example, most children learn at a very young age to predict the behavior of a growling dog, and they keep their distance. In the elementary science classroom, pupils learn to predict events in nature that are difficult to believe even when observed, such as the emerging of a beautiful Monarch butterfly from a chrysalis spun by a caterpillar.

Prediction is based on observations, measurements, and resulting inferences about relationships between observed conditions or events. If children examine the weights of a few pumpkins and the numbers of their seeds, a pattern begins to emerge. Assuming the pattern will continue for other pumpkins, they can make inferences, and from those inferences they can predict the number of seeds in another pumpkin of a given weight. As students become familiar with pendulums, keeping track of data regarding pendulum length, distance of the first swing, and mass of the bob, they can learn to notice patterns and make inferences from the patterns about the effect of each variable on the number of swings per minute. From the inferences, they can eventually predict the number of swings per minute that will result from a given change in any of the variables—length of the pendulum, weight of the bob, or distance of the first swing.

Communicating

The ability to share information with others is an extremely important skill. As students learn to behave like scientists and to use the tools of learning that scientists use, they become aware that it is important to be clear and accurate in communicating their findings and thoughts. They learn to communicate ideas verbally by sharing their observations and ideas in discussions. They strengthen written communication skills as they read, discuss what they read, and write about their observations and ideas. As they receive feedback from teachers, peers, parents, and others who read what they write, they get valuable information about how well they are communicating, and as they adapt and practice they become better skilled at expressing themselves clearly and accurately. This feedback, amid other verbal communication, also helps to improve decoding skills related to both written and spoken language.

A curriculum rich with science experiences helps students to recognize that communication skills go beyond spoken and written words. Sometimes information and ideas are transmitted more clearly through the use of charts and graphs. The average height of students at each age group in the school can be expressed in a paragraph, but the information is communicated more quickly in the form of a chart. Better yet, a bar graph or line graph shows a picture of the information. In considering height, a vertical bar graph is appropriate, as it makes the upward trend of height with increasing age obvious at a glance (see Figure 3-8).

Sometimes charts, graphs, and paragraph descriptions are all needed to communicate information fully. While the graph clearly illustrates trends, it usually doesn't show exact numbers as precisely as they are shown in a chart, and a paragraph may be needed to explain and discuss trends and points of particular importance.

As we continue to emphasize the importance of many hands-on experiences in elementary science, remember that children also need to *reflect* on what they do. They need to talk about their observations, write about them, read information that is related, and communicate their quantitative observations by using charts and graphs as well as verbal and written descriptions. Children develop communication skills by having frequent occasion to transmit and receive information in different ways.

We must not overlook the importance of communicating with self. Often the information we record is intended only for later reference for ourselves. Charts, graphs, and pictures are still important. And the value in describing, charting, and drawing goes beyond providing information for later reference. The process of preparing information in these ways clarifies the information in the mind of the communicator.

Figure 3-8

Bar graph showing average height of each age group in school.

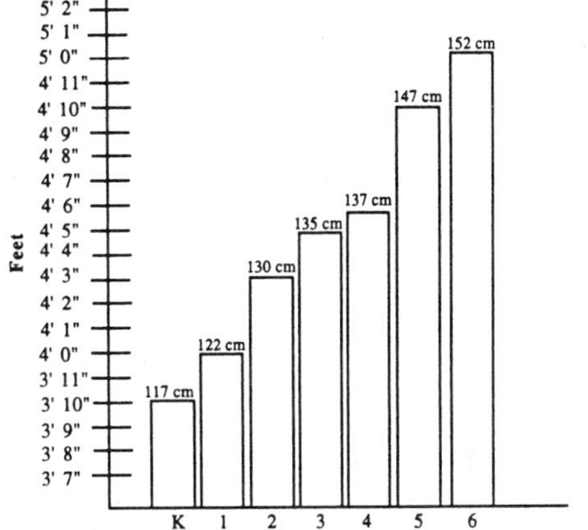

Using Space-Time Relationships

All events occur at certain times and in certain places. Location and timing are more significant with some events than with others. Consider the following examples.

Example 1: *If a child is studying the floatation of objects, using a bowl of water and objects to test, location and timing are unimportant. On the other hand, if the task is to check the outdoor temperature in the shade of the building each hour through the day, both timing and location are crucial in the comparisons that are to be made.*

Example 2: *If a rock is broken by a hammer to*

reveal the texture and coloring inside, exactly when and where it was broken might not matter. If the rock is split apart naturally, however, location and timing can be very important in terms of what can be learned from the event about the workings of nature. The investigator, in this instance, would want to know the conditions under which the rock broke.

Example 3: *In studying the metamorphosis of an insect, the timing of the different phases and where they occur are extremely important in teaching us about the habits and characteristics of that particular insect.*

We help children develop insights for the skill of using space-time relationships in a number of ways. They can relate stories or experiences, paying particular attention to sequence and location of events. They can keep a journal of the care and feeding of the classroom gerbil, of the movements and phases of the moon, or of other science experiences and events over a period of time. These projects are valuable in developing communication skills, and they strengthen children's perceptions of space and time.

Formulating Hypotheses

Before launching an experiment, or other effort to acquire new information about something, a scientist, teacher, or child should first examine the information already available. The next step is to clarify perceptions and thinking about that information, perhaps even making an educated guess about the cause of a problem or about what new information might be revealed through further study. Such an educated guess is called a *hypothesis.*

If your class is working with magnets and considering the question of what magnets do and do not attract, the children might make a list of items they remember seeing attracted to magnets. They might notice from their list that all objects they have seen attracted to magnets have been metals. (They will not correctly recall any nonmetal being attracted to a magnet.) Given this information, they might form a hypothesis that magnets attract all metals and do not attract any nonmetals. As they test this hypothesis, they will find that it is partially correct. If the experiment is structured carefully, students will find that some metals (brass and copper, for instance) are not attracted to magnets.

Knowing that fertilizers are commonly added to soil to promote plant growth, a group of students might hypothesize that the more fertilizer they use the faster their tomato plants will grow. By testing this hypothesis, they will discover that there is an optimum amount of fertilizer, and that when they apply more than the optimum, plant growth is actually effected negatively. Further investigation might reveal that certain types of fertilizer seem to affect the growth and health of the plant differently than others.

Identifying and Testing Variables

Variables are the inconstant factors or conditions that are involved in an experiment. Each variable may or may not affect a particular outcome. In fact, the outcome itself is one of the variables. The outcome is often referred to as the *responding variable,* as it changes in response to the varying conditions that affect it. Variables that might affect the outcome are called the *manipulated variables,* since they are the factors or conditions that the experimenter manipulates to test their effect on the outcome. In testing the effect of various amounts of fertilizer on tomato plants, the manipulated variable is the amount of fertilizer, and plant growth is the responding variable. The manipulated variable is sometimes called the *independent* variable, and the responding variable is sometimes called the *dependent* variable. We will use the terms manipulated and responding in discussing the two types of variables.

We could give many other examples of the use of variables in elementary science. If children are investigating to see how far a toy truck will roll across the floor after rolling down a ramp raised to varying heights, the height of the ramp is the manipulated variable, and the distance is the responding variable. If the question concerns the effect of different floor surfaces on how far the truck will roll, the surface becomes the manipulated variable.

Effective identification and testing of variables requires careful analysis of a situation to determine just what the possible variables are. Just as important is careful planning to increase the chances that when a change occurs in the outcome, or responding variable, it will be evident which variable(s) affected the observed change. We recommend using the following procedures to maintain careful control over the variables.

Testing the variables

Change or manipulate only one variable at a time. If the amount of fertilizer, type of fertilizer, amount of water, and amount of sunshine are altered, and different varieties of tomato seeds are used, the investigator has no way of knowing what effect each of these variables has on the final product, the mature plant. When your class is testing the effect of different amounts of fertilizer on the growth of tomato plants, several experimental plants can be used. All variables should be kept constant except the manipulated variable, the amount of fertilizer. Use the same variety of seed for each plant. The type of fertilizer and the amount of water should be the same for each plant, and each plant should be exposed to the same amount of sunlight. Each of the experimental plants (or each of several groups of plants) should receive a different amount of fertilizer, however, carefully measured and recorded.

Increasing the number of samples increases the validity of the results. Consider using clusters of two, three, or four plants, with plants being treated identically within clusters.

This procedure of testing variables has frequent real-life application. For example, a mechanic tests variables in the process of troubleshooting a problem with an automobile engine. If he is uncertain as to the cause of the problem, he will make only one change, try the engine, make another change, and try it again. He is testing the variables. If he replaces the spark plugs and distributor points, changes the timing, and replaces the computer module before checking the motor to see if it runs better, he has no way to know which of the changes ultimately affected how well the engine runs. For another example, if a recipe does not produce desired results and the reason is not immediately obvious, the cook might try the recipe again, altering one of the variables, such as an ingredient, cooking time, temperature, and so on.

As a final example, in experimenting with the toy truck and the ramp, the investigator should not change the height of the ramp, the type of floor surface, and the size of the truck at the same time. Determine which variable is to be tested and keep all other variables constant.

One teacher successfully impressed kindergarten students with the need to control variables in a "fair" way. In an effort to determine which ball bounces best, students quickly figured out the need to bounce the balls in the same way, on the same surface, and from the same height, as the balls are being compared (Kaplan, 1984).

Using controls

In the case of the tomato plants, a *control* should be used. The word "control" is a noun this time, and must not be confused with the process of controlling or manipulating variables discussed above. In the example given, the control is a plant, or cluster of plants, kept in normal conditions. In this case, the control should receive the recommended amount of fertilizer. The control becomes a standard with which all experimental plants can be compared, to determine the effect of the manipulated variable—in this case the amount of fertilizer.

If children keep all variables constant except the amount of fertilizer they give to the plant, they can compare mature experimental plants with the control. Differences between each experimental plant and the control should provide an indication of the effect of giving tomato plants more or less fertilizer than the recommended amount.

To use another example, if students are testing the effect of light on plant growth, they would keep the *control* in normal light conditions, while exposing experimental plants to varying amounts of light. Or if the question is whether hamsters prefer water of a particular color, the person doing the study needs to offer several pans of water, each with a different color of food coloring in it, in addition to a pan of water without any coloring. The uncolored water is the control. The amount of each color of water consumed by the hamsters in a given period of time would be compared with the amount of the control consumed, thus providing evidence of water color preference in hamsters.

Experimenting

Once students have acquired skill in using the processes we've just discussed, experimentation does not add anything new. It simply brings together much of what students have learned into a coordinated procedure. The term "experiment" is often used rather loosely in elementary science. Experiencing the effect of Bernoulli's principle by trying to blow a ping-pong ball from a funnel is not experimenting. Many of the experiences we call *science experiments* would more accurately be called *science activities*. An experiment involves a problem to which the experimenter does not know the solution. A true experiment includes testing a hypothesis and, where appropriate, using a control.

Because of the mature thought processes that are usually involved, true experiments are largely reserved for the intermediate grades and beyond. Primary grade children can use the same processes, however, with carefully selected projects that are designed for their level. For example, they can determine the effect of different types of surfaces on the distance a ball rolls, or how much moisture works best in a bucket of sand, when making sand castles.

Some purists would say that the experience really isn't an experiment if the outcome is already known to the field of science. For the student, we prefer to say that if the outcome isn't known to the investigator, the procedure is a bona fide experiment. Although the effect of light on plant growth has been demonstrated numerous times, the child who is eagerly living through the investigation, learning information that is new to him or her, is involved in true scientific experimentation. In the school setting, the process is usually more important than the data derived from the experiment.

An experiment involves testing variables, using the techniques described above. To be reasonably certain of the cause of any particular outcome, the same experiment would need to be repeated several times.

PROBLEM SOLVING

Problem solving is the application of the process skills we've just discussed. It involves testing an idea or pursuing new information. Such a pursuit often represents a struggle, but the end can be extremely rewarding, even if only in what is learned about the process of solving problems. In life, most people don't have to exert themselves looking for problems that need to be solved or questions that need to be answered—the challenge is to keep up with them. In the classroom, your challenge is to provide meaningful questions that students will pursue with interest in order to develop problem-solving skills. We hope the following ideas will help you do that.

Inoculating Ideas

To prevent disease, the body is sometimes inoculated with weakened or dead microorganisms; the body responds by building up antibodies that resist the disease. One teacher suggests that similar results can be obtained by "inoculating ideas," with the teacher taking an unpopular position on an issue (Shrigley, 1987). For instance, the teacher might ask the question, "Why should we spend so much money designing and building new cars that use less gas? We all know our geologists will find more oil so we won't we run out." As students respond (we hope) by building a case for the need to preserve the world's fossil fuel reserves, they will develop mental and attitudinal "antibodies" against careless attitudes that lead to exploiting precious natural resources.

Surveys

Class surveys are excellent problem-solving activities, and they frequently generate a great deal of interest. Students develop their skills of estimating, predicting, and inferring, as well as gathering data and charting and graphing results. Social skills, language arts skills, math skills, and more are strengthened as students interact in a cooperative way and perhaps persuade others to join in the effort.

The possibilities for questions that could be generated and then answered by a survey are endless. Weather patterns that change from season to season, or even from day to day, raise questions that can be surveyed, such as what percent of students wear coats, hats, boots, scarves, and so on. They can compare these numbers with outdoor temperatures. Children might gather data on color preferences in clothing, or clothing styles, either by asking people to state their preferences or by observing what colors and styles people actually wear. Better yet, how about doing both surveys, then comparing people's stated preferences with observations of clothing actually worn? Students can devise ways to display their data, perhaps with a variety of tables and charts.

Pairing Characteristics

Once students pair qualities or characteristics of objects, they can examine the results to analyze relationships. Examples of pairs of characteristics of elementary students might include: height and shoe size; eye color and hair color; and favorite school subjects and parents' occupation. For additional examples, gender can be paired with any number of questions, including height, running speed, occupational goals—the list could go on and on. With their active curiosity, students will generate plenty of questions to be surveyed once the idea has been "planted."

Problem-Solving Experiences

Try giving students a bowl of hard-boiled eggs mixed with raw eggs as a problem-solving experience (Wheatley and Walden, 1990). Ask your students to determine which eggs are raw and which ones are boiled—without breaking the eggs. As students reason that each of the hard-boiled eggs is a single, solid unit, and that the raw eggs are somewhat sloshy inside, you can lead them into comparing two cans of equal size. One can is filled with a solid material and the other with liquid—dog food and watery soup, for instance. Students then spin the cans and the eggs, and compare their spinning behavior. The soup can will wobble as the soup sloshes around, but the can of dog food will probably spin quite freely. As they spin the eggs, students will notice similar differences in the spinning action, depending on the nature of what is inside.

THE SCIENTIFIC METHOD

The scientific method of problem solving approaches the process of solving problems in a systematic way. Although it is often understood to pertain only to science, this is a mistaken perception. The scientific method is applicable to virtually all aspects of life and all individuals, in school and out. It is a systematic method of studying phenomena and solving all sorts of problems. It is a tool for all teachers and for all students, useful in dealing with everyday, nonscientific problems as well as with scientific questions.

Terms such as "hypothesis" and "theory" sometimes raise anxieties that interfere with learning. In teaching the use of the scientific method in the elementary classroom, it is a good idea to delay introducing these terms until the students feel at ease with the general process described in familiar terms. Connections to new vocabulary are then made more easily.

If you had a precise, detailed account of the development of the light bulb, the telephone, the radio, or thousands of other inventions, you would undoubtedly find that the scientific method was used many, many times by the inventors. They used it in the process of isolating various properties and effects to explain certain observations as they worked to get desired results. These inventors used the scientific method, not because they were dealing with science, but because the scientific method is a systematic way of finding information and solving problems. In this way, their needs were similar to ours—we all need new information at times, even if only to satisfy a curious mind. Sometimes the need can be satisfied simply by asking or reading. But when the needed or desired information is more difficult to acquire, a systematic method of obtaining it can be very useful. For this reason, everyone can benefit from some direct instruction and some guided activities that help them develop skill in using the scientific method of problem solving.

What exactly is the scientific method? The exact steps used in the scientific method vary from one source and time to another, but in general they include the following:

1. *Identify the problem*
2. *Consider current information*
3. *Form a hypothesis*
4. *Do experiments*
5. *Analyze the new information*
6. *Repeat steps 3 through 5, if necessary*
7. *State a theory or conclusion (can still be very tentative)*

As a teacher, you should attempt to capture the message of the scientific method. Specific terminology is far less important than the general idea. In solving a problem, the first logical step is to identify the problem, preferably in writing. The second is to determine what information is already known relative to the problem. Third, examine the known information for possible clues to a solution, and with that information make an educated guess about the solution. Fourth, find ways to test the idea. Fifth, examine your new information, and make a judgment as to the likely degree of accuracy of the hypothesis (best guess). And sixth, if needed, set up a new experiment to either support or contradict the previous outcome. If your earlier results are repeated, form a conclusion (explanation or theory) based on information you've acquired. If the earlier results are not repeated, alter the prediction and design additional experiments on the basis of new information.

It is important that we don't get log-jammed

by complex terminology and a long list of steps to memorize. If the formal sequence of seven steps makes heads spin, consider a simpler pattern of problem solving:

1. *Identify the problem.*
2. *Determine the most logical conclusion from the information already known.*
3. *Devise a way to check the accuracy of the tentative conclusion.*

It would be difficult to conclude that this three-step method belongs only in the laboratory, yet the general idea is still there. When mother comes home from shopping and finds milk spilled on the floor or toys scattered all over the house, step 1, the problem, is immediately apparent. Her mind quickly surveys current information by considering who has probably been in the house and, based on past behavior, age of children, and so on, who is most likely responsible for the mess—step 2. As she seeks out the culprit for clean-up patrol, she will consider alibis, witnesses, and additional information that contributes to a final conclusion—step 3.

This example does not involve clear-cut scientific experimentation, but it shows a logical sequence of steps for acquiring information or arriving at a solution to an everyday problem, which is just the point we're trying to make. The scientific method, in some form, is pervasive in daily living, even though it is not commonly recognized as such. If students are trained in the use of a logical, simple, systematic way to gather information and solve problems, they will be better equipped to meet life—whether dealing with science or anything else.

Your students may use this approach in a variety of subject areas. For example, in the science classroom they might apply the formal seven-step sequence as they experiment with the effect of light on plant growth, the effect of vinegar on baking soda and other powders, and do numerous other scientific explorations. In another setting, they might study diacritical markings and their uses in unlocking word pronunciations, making logical conclusions or predictions based on information at hand. Testing such predictions becomes a learning experience as students read and study further, compare known words, ask an expert (the teacher), and so on. Your students might also enjoy the challenge of identifying the steps of the scientific method as they read a mystery story. When students are introduced to a variety of experiences in applying this approach, they will recognize its universal application and down-to-earth logic.

Former Secretary of Education William J. Bennett (1987) put it this way:

> *The term "scientific method" has fallen into disfavor among educators, perhaps because it conjures up images of a white-coated man hunched over a petri dish. It ought to be restored. The scientific method is a method of thought, of reasoning, which applies not only to explorations of the physical universe but to all the realms of intellectual inquiry that require hypothesis, inference, and other tools of brainwork.*

CLASSROOM RESEARCH

One of the definitions given in *Webster's New Collegiate Dictionary* for the word *research* is "studious inquiry." Students who are learning and using the scientific method of problem solving are doing research.

The work of professional researchers usually involves an exhaustive study of what is already known about the target topic or problem, followed by a search for new information. Whether they are graduate students or professional researchers, they follow the scientific method. They use it because it is a logical sequence of steps for solving problems and acquiring information.

We've used several terms in this chapter to represent related concepts and practices as students develop into independent learners on a lifelong quest for new information. Such terms include *inquiry, process skills, experimentation, problem solving, scientific method,* and *research.* While these terms are often used together, they are also potentially confusing. Just how do they connect, to what extent do they overlap, or are they synonymous? Are all of them needed? We hope the following information will help to clarify the relationship of these terms.

Inquiry denotes seeking for information. It also means asking questions, and it is sometimes used synonymously with the term "research." In this chapter, the first meaning, "seeking for information," is most applicable. The **process skills** are the tools of inquiry. We observe, infer, classify, and so on, as **processes** of seeking information. **Experimentation** is last in the list of process skills, utilizing and applying all other process skills. Experimentation does not stand alone: It could be considered the pinnacle of a pyramid constructed of all the other process skills, which provide the foundation for experimentation. Having the ability to apply the skills of observing, inferring, and so on, all the way through controlling variables and hypothesizing, enables the student to experiment.

Problem solving denotes an effort to solve unanswered questions, or questions for which existing answers are inadequate, incomplete, or uncertain. The **scientific method of problem solving** is a systematic sequence of steps to use in the effort to solve problems. **Research** is the application of the scientific method.

Elementary Students as Researchers

Many people seem to think that there is something mysterious about research. They think that it requires a laboratory and expensive scientific apparatus. We perceive research more as a state of mind: It is organized thinking that we employ as we go about the process of acquiring information. Research can be done almost anywhere at almost any time. Elementary students are doing research when they apply the scientific method to acquire information that is new to them. The scientific method helps to guide our thinking as we do research activities.

In considering the role of the scientific method in research, remember that the terms are less important than the general notion. You can lead even young children through the logic of considering known information about a question and deciding on a possible answer, then determining a way to find additional information, without using the terms *hypothesis, theory,* or *experiment* at all. New terms are often easier to grasp if the concepts are taught first. Then the terms can simply be attached to known concepts. Introduce the vocabulary when students are ready for it. Use labels when labels will clarify, but don't allow them to interfere with learning.

In addition to the topics and questions already suggested, elementary students can research many other questions. A group of fifth graders in Manchester, Iowa, decided to find out how much food was being wasted in the hot lunch program at school (Pizzini, Abell, and VanderWilt, 1987). Another group of intermediate-level students in Iowa (McShane, 1987) compared brands of toilet tissue for absorbency and strength. In both of these cases, the students helped to determine the questions to be studied.

Usually, the best questions for investigation are raised by students themselves. These are questions born out of curiosity: "Which ball falls to the ground faster?" "Does music affect the way plants grow?" "What is the most common eye color in our school?" Many researchable questions come from the endless curiosity of children. As one person said, "Children have an innate sense of wonder . . . . Their sense of wonder makes an ordinary world extraordinary " (Lundgren, 1979).

Are first-graders too young to do research? One teacher involved her first-graders in a study of apples, as a part of a unit on the senses (Steiner, 1990). Three types of apples were purchased at the local grocery store. The children practiced making observations and describing apples in objective, not subjective, terms. They learned that it was okay in their study to say an apple is red, but not to say it is pretty, since "pretty" is a matter of personal opinion. Then each member of the class judged the apples on subjective observations (including taste) and voted on their personal favorites.

At the fall open house, students were there with bowls of sliced apples—all three kinds—to involve parents in their survey of preferences. Parents were asked to taste the three kinds of apples, mark their preference on a ballot, and drop the ballot in a box. For parents, the apple slices were identified only as Apple 1, Apple 2, and Apple 3.

Students tallied the results the next day in class, and each child prepared his or her own bar graph. They talked about possible reasons why people have different preferences in taste. One child said, "Because it's the only kind of apple my Mom buys." In their own terminology, others suggested genetic factors—"Our tastes are alike because we are in the same family."

These first-graders worked with several processes as they completed their inquiry with apples, including *observing, classifying, predicting, inferring,* and *measuring,* and they applied their emerging math skills as they counted and tallied ballots. They *communicated* their results both verbally and graphically.

Teachers as Researchers

In this chapter, we have emphasized the scientific method as a logical sequence of steps in gathering information and solving problems. We've pointed out that the general notion of the scientific method applies to everyday life and can be used almost anywhere at almost any time. The teacher who is convinced of the usefulness of the scientific method will lead students in many exciting and memorable journeys along the trail of learning. Surely the same teacher must recognize the potential of his or her own classroom research, for improving organizational styles and teaching techniques. Much research gets published, but your own research as a teacher doesn't need to be reported in magazines and textbooks in order to have value. With the very process of research in the classroom, you will grow, becoming a more insightful teacher because of the experience. As you test ideas and techniques and find one that offers new insights to you, consider writing it up and submitting it for publication as an article in *Science and Children* or other professional journal. Other teachers will benefit from your work and insights.

Many questions can be answered through classroom research: How effective is teacher praise as a reward for appropriate behavior? If it does work, how often is praise needed in order to have an effect? Is candy really a more effective motivator than praise? Do students perform better on tests of science concepts if the teacher has emphasized hands-on activities? Does student selection of science trade books from the library increase when an activity-based approach to science is being used in the classroom? Does seating arrangement make any difference in the productivity of individuals or of cooperative learning groups? To these and a thousand other questions, we are too often content to assume answers. A little effort to devise and implement a method to test such questions in your own classroom can be rewarding, and sometimes quite surprising. Classroom research can involve the entire class, or it can focus on a single student.

How do you go about doing classroom research? Kyle and Shymansky (1988, 30–31) suggest that a teacher has several options in initiating classroom research:

replicate *the findings of previous research. Each replication study provides further evidence to support or refute a researchable notion;*

adapt *the conditions of a prior study to determine the variables and environmental conditions that make the intervention more effective. Refining a previous investigation may enable a teacher or school to identify important researchable topics and implement research findings on a regular basis;*

extend *the boundaries of prior investigations. If an intervention enhances student performance in grades 4–6, will it also work on students in grades K–3 or 7–12, in science or in all subjects? and*

identify *a new research focus. New technologies and current scientific knowledge have created numerous areas to investigate. Existing knowledge must serve as a basis for practical improvements in science education as well as for needed innovations.*

Emphasizing the importance of a widespread research effort, the same authors suggest:

> *The process of schooling, especially as it relates to science education, must change if we are to prepare children for life in the twenty-first century. This cannot possibly occur without the collaboration of classroom teachers as active researchers.*

In the 1980s, the National Science Teachers Association launched a program called "Every Teacher a Researcher." This program is based on the argument that effective research on science teaching and learning begins with classroom teachers. Involvement of elementary teachers in this program has shown that they are most interested in research on the topics of hands-on experience, science content of the curriculum, cognitive development and learning styles, problem solving, and teaching strategies (Gabel, 1986).

IN CLOSING

Science answers a lot of important questions, but in the elementary classroom the questions science asks are probably more important than the answers it gives. It is important to develop curiosities, supported with both the ability and willingness to seek out answers. Curious minds with a yen to solve problems are responsible for the great scientific advances of today. The sewing machine, the printing press, the computer, the airplane, the automobile, the space shuttle, and countless other products of technology came about through problem solving and research. In turn, each of these has a long history of earlier problems that were solved, one by one, in the endless quest for improvement and new information.

Even more important than any of these monumental milestones are the problem solving and research that occur in the minds of each individual, as he or she deals with the daily challenges of life. These challenges represent the greatest reason for teaching all children the skills of inquiry. Major technological advances will continue to occur, and certainly we need a steady supply of people who are prepared to keep them coming; but the quality of life for each individual is affected by his or her ability to independently apply the skills of inquiry in the daily routine.

LIST OF RESOURCES

Bennett, William J., "Science: An Excerpt from *First Lessons*," *Science and Children* 24, no. 4 (January 1987): 15, 155.

Brooks, Jacqueline Grennon, "Teachers and Students: Constructivists Forging New Connections," *Educational Leadership* 47, no. 5 (February 1990): 68–71.

Carin, Arthur A., and Robert B. Sund, *Teaching Science Through Discovery*, 6th ed. (Columbus, OH: Merrill Pub. Co., 1989).

Funk, H. James, et al., *Learning Science Process Skills* (Dubuque, IA: Kendall/Hunt Pub. Co., 1990).

Gabel, Dorothy, "What Research Says: What's *Your* Choice?" *Science and Children* 23, no. 4 (January 1986): 129–31.

Kaplan, Nancy, "But That's Not Fair!" *Science and Children* 21, no. 7 (April 1984): 24–25.

Kyle, William C., Jr., et al., "What Research Says: Science Through Discovery; Students Love It," *Science and Children* 23, no. 2 (October 1985): 39–41.

Kyle, William C., Jr., and James A. Shymansky, "What Research Says: About Teachers as Researchers," *Science and Children* 26, no. 3 (November/December 1988): 29–31.

Leyden, Michael B., "Discrepant Events," *Teaching K-8* 20, no. 5 (February 1991): 25–26, 28.

Lundgren, Ruth H., "Look for Happenings," *Science and Children* 17, no. 2 (October 1979): 39.

McShane, Joan B., "The Royal Flush," *Science and Children* 25, no. 1 (September 1987): 29–32.

Pizzini, Edward L., Sandra K. Abell, and Jill A. VanderWilt, "Scrape, Scrape, Scrape: Problem Solving in the Lunchroom," *Science and Children* 24, no. 6 (March 1987): 14–15.

Roth, Wolff-Michael, "Coming to Terms with Metric," *Science and Children* 28, no. 8 (May 1991): 14–15.

Shrigley, Robert L., "Inoculating Ideas," *Science and Children* 25, no. 2 (October 1987): 13–14.

Shymansky, James A., William C. Kyle, Jr., and Jennifer M. Alport, "How Effective Were the Hands-on Science Programs of Yesterday?" *Science and Children* 20, no. 3 (November/December 1982): 14–15.

Steiner, Patricia, "A-Peelin' Apples," *Science and Children* 28, no. 1 (September 1990): 34–35.

Wheatley, Jack, and Melanie Walden, "The Case of the Hard-boiled Detective," *Science and Children* 28, no. 1 (September 1990): 32–33.

CHAPTER

QUESTIONING

CHAPTER OUTLINE:

I WONDER . . .

How far-reaching are the effects of questioning strategies?
How often do students typically ask meaningful questions in the classroom?
What is "wait time"?
What are the results of using adequate "wait time"?
Are teachers usually good listeners?
What are the implications of predirecting and redirecting questions?
What is "parroting"?
How are questions classified, and how is one type different from another?
Do students need to be taught how to ask meaningful questions?
Does gender bias show up in our questioning behaviors?
What can teachers do to improve their questioning skills?

INTRODUCTION

Questioning skills are universally accepted as vital teaching tools in every subject matter area. The importance of questioning in the arena of teaching and learning science becomes even more significant, because science is an endless quest. The very heart of effective science education depends on the questioning minds of students and teachers.

If you are to become skilled in the use of questions, you must understand several concepts: first, questions are a vital part of the instructional process; second, you can elicit different types of responses and levels of thought from students through the effective use of questions; third, your questioning techniques can have a profound impact on the number and quality of responses offered by your students, the percent of students who become involved in classroom discussions, and even classroom management; and fourth, the skills of effective questioning usually require considerable time and effort to acquire and implement.

Improving questioning skills requires thoughtful work and diligent practice. Your payoff for this effort will be realized in a more positive rapport with your students and a better grasp of science processes and concepts on the part of your students. These skills are more easily acquired early in the teaching career; altering teaching patterns established over a long period of time is more difficult.

IMPORTANCE OF QUESTIONS

Questioning is basic to societal and scientific progress. From the newborn baby's first investigation of his or her environment, to the young child driving a parent or teacher up the wall with an endless stream of questions, to the college student puzzling over the meaning of some abstract text or contemplating which new car to buy upon graduation, to the scientist in the laboratory attempting to understand the outcome of a complex experiment, our ability and willingness to ask and answer questions greatly influences the information we obtain, and therefore our success in life.

Education is, to a great extent, a process of developing the skills of asking questions and getting answers. The infant goes about this task in a seemingly crude but effective manner, testing the environment by tasting, feeling, looking, and smelling most everything that is accessible. As the child grows and develops, an accumulation of knowledge should result in greater skill in the art of asking questions.

The skilled researcher asks a question, then questions the question, seeks and hopefully finds an answer, and then questions the answer. Often the researcher will mistrust the accuracy of the findings until the question has been tested several times, preferably by different individuals or groups. This is questioning in its most refined state, and the continuous application of this process provides society with a constant flow of valuable information.

No matter what level of formal education we attain, the role of questions continues to be important in finding new information. Yet, in many schools the importance of question-asking skills (for instructor and student) has not received adequate attention.

After observing 721 students in twenty-seven classrooms, Dillon (1988) reported that students in his sample asked an average of only two questions per hour (all 721 students combined!), and that 99 percent of the students observed failed to ask a single question. Dillon raises the question, "What series of events could have led to the quashing of the inquiring minds of these young people?" Perhaps we are doing more in our society to eradicate the questioning mind than to encourage it. "When students do not ask questions," he says, "both teaching and learning suffer."

On the other hand, Dillon found that *teachers* ask many questions. Approximately 60 percent of teacher talk in his study was used in asking questions—an average of about eighty questions per hour per teacher. The teacher seems to recognize the importance of questions in the learning process, yet teachers often are not promoting student questioning skills.

QUESTIONING MECHANICS FOR TEACHERS

Techniques and rationale related to the role of questions in the classroom could fill volumes—far beyond the scope of this text. We have chosen to highlight just a few sound techniques and ideas that can be effectively applied in the elementary science classroom.

Wait Time

A brief wait time after asking a question and before accepting a response can increase both the quality and quantity of responses you get from students. This short period of time provides a stimulus for thinking, on the part of the student. If you use wait time effectively, you can actually prevent impatient students from blurting out answers. You do this, in part, by communicating your expectations for responses and being sure to not react to inappropriate answers. Ignoring the blurted answer and calling on another student will both reinforce the appropriate behavior and send an important message to the impatient student. You might need to review your expectations from time to time with individual students or the entire class.

In analyzing more than 800 tape recordings of science lessons taught by teachers in urban, suburban, and rural schools, one researcher found that the average teacher in her study asked questions at the rate of two or three per minute (Rowe, 1978). (This is even a more rapid rate of questioning than found in the Dillon study cited above.) In order to have an opportunity to respond, a student had to start an answer within one second after the question; otherwise the question would be repeated, rephrased, or someone else would respond. "When wait times are so short," Rowe discovered, "students' answers tend to be fragmentary, and their thoughts have a corresponding tendency to be incomplete."

It takes time to reflect on information learned and on experience, and it takes time to generate a thought. In Rowe's study, the quality of responses was found to increase dramatically if the teacher inserted a pause of just three to five seconds after asking a question, before calling on a student to respond. The researchers were surprised to find a second wait time to be even more important than the first. Student responses were found to come in bursts, separated by pauses of three to five seconds. Often the teacher thinks the student is finished, when actually the student is only pausing to formulate the next part of the response. Waiting three to five seconds after a student response greatly decreases the chance of cutting the student off in the middle of a thought, and increases the probability that the student will continue and improve the response or that another student will expand on an idea initiated by the first student. It is very important for the teacher to listen carefully to student responses. When both wait times were increased to at least three seconds, Rowe noted that certain elements were found to increase:

- *length of student responses*
- *number of unsolicited but appropriate responses by students*
- *student confidence, as reflected in fewer inflected responses—those with a questioning tone, indicating uncertainty*
- *incidence of speculative thinking*
- *students listening to, and responding to, each other*
- *use of evidence and inference statements*
- *number of questions asked by students*
- *number of experiments proposed by students*
- *contributions by "slow" students*

and certain elements were found to decrease:

- *failures to respond.*
- *number of disciplinary moves on the part of the teacher, such as calling for attention, indicating a corresponding decrease in student restlessness*

As the teacher, it is crucial that you attend to what the responding child says and, perhaps at least as important, what the student does not say. The child providing an answer should receive clear signals that the teacher is attending to what is being said.

Listening to Student Questions

It is essential that you, the teacher, listen attentively to questions asked by students. Your students will read both verbal and nonverbal cues (eye contact, nods, approving sounds, and so on) that indicate whether they have your full attention. Nonverbal cues can be as strong as verbal cues, or even stronger, in terms of student interpretation of teacher interest and attention. Because students are asking appropriate questions, you know that they are thinking about the subject at hand and the door of student learning is open.

Responding in a manner that will encourage further student questions is critical to effective classroom instruction. Focusing your total attention on the responding student sends important messages to other students: First, they discover that the responding student's answer is worth their attention; and second, they realize that the teacher gives full attention to those who participate by answering questions.

Predirecting Questions

Calling on a student before the question is asked presents two problems: It can serve as an invitation to the rest of the class to take a "mental vacation"; and the student who has been called on may feel overburdened and find it difficult to think. When the teacher asks the question, uses appropriate wait time, and then calls on someone to respond, all students are motivated to think about the question because each has an equal chance of being called on for the answer. While there may be a reason to predirect, and alert a particular student to an upcoming question, as a general rule the question that is not predirected results in more thinking on the part of the class and a more effective discussion.

Redirecting Questions

Often the most productive questions are those that encourage divergent responses—they either have no absolute correct answer, or they have several possible correct answers. By redirecting questions from one student to another you can effectively encourage students to form their own opinions or solutions to problems. The resulting student-to-student responses can also be very effective in improving the quality of the discussion and in upgrading rapport among members of the class.

Dealing with Student Input

The number and types of student questions and responses are directly correlated with the way the teacher handles student input. If student participation is received respectfully by the teacher, the amount of student interaction will be much greater than if the instructor ignores, parrots, or ridicules students for what they say. Saying or implying that a student's question or answer to a question is dumb is unthinkable—a serious tactical error on the part of the teacher, to say the least. It is also critical that the teacher not allow a student to belittle the other students. "Students experience verbal (and nonverbal) put-downs if their classmates mutter 'Dummy!' or 'What do you know?'" (Blosser, 1991). The probability that the student will voluntarily participate in a discussion again any time soon is greatly reduced.

Not only is the student who has been embarrassed unlikely to risk another comment, but other students will also be less prone to become involved in the discussion. Any question or response from a student in an effort to get information or add to the discussion should be received in a positive fashion, reinforcing and encouraging future participation. The classroom needs to be a safe and secure environment where risk-taking is encouraged. If students are not able to test their thoughts and ideas, they will have difficulty developing critical thinking and other important skills. This does not mean that children should never be told that their answers are incorrect or inadequate. It means that feedback should be given in a manner that will encourage them to rethink and modify their response.

Parroting

Repeating student answers is generally not recommended. The rationale often given for this practice is to make sure the rest of the class hears the response. While this may occasionally have some merit, asking the student to repeat the answer is usually more effective. If the teacher accepts the answer in a supportive way, then asks the student to repeat it loud enough for the rest of the class to hear, at least two worthwhile things happen: first, the student has communicated the answer in his or her own words, thereby strengthening self-confidence and communication skills; and second, the student's response is not changed, watered down, or embellished by the teacher. Often the teacher responds to student answers with, "Oh you mean . . . ," inserting the information the teacher wanted to hear, which can be quite different from what the student wanted to say. Changing student answers can suggest to the student that the answer was inadequate. If the teacher really did not understand a student response, it is appropriate to ask the student to repeat, or for the teacher to use a clarifying technique like: "I understood you to say . . . Am I right?" In this response, it is the teacher who is at risk of being wrong.

The wise teacher will recognize that there are exceptions to most every rule. At times, there may be good reason to restate a student's question or response. Perhaps clarification by the teacher really is needed. Or maybe an important point was made, in a very low voice, by a student who has never spoken up in class before and who might be negatively reinforced if asked to repeat even a very worthwhile statement. The importance of the information given can be acknowledged, then briefly restated for clarification, and the discussion can continue, providing just enough of a spotlight to make the student feel successful in making the contribution but not enough to raise anxieties. As a general rule, however, students can be asked to repeat what they say, if repetition is needed, and parroting can be avoided.

Repeating student responses encourages students to listen to you rather than to each other. The expectation that students listen to each other adds validity to student input.

Prompting

To the extent possible, every student response or question should result in the student feeling that he or she has made a contribution. When a response misses the point of the question, a skillful teacher can often assist the student and turn a potential embarrassment into a successful experience. A prompt, such as "Did you think of . . ." or "What about . . ." or "You're close, now what about . . ." can rescue a student who is making an effort but experiencing difficulty in formulating a thought. The least a child should get for braving an answer to a question is credit for being a good thinker, or for being on the right track. Maybe the answer missed the question, but still made an important point, or perhaps it leads into the next question. Credit can be given for that. Prompting should be kept brief, so as not to create an awkward situation for the child, resulting in the very embarrassment you were trying to avoid. Rarely is there a student question or response that can't be recognized somehow to have value.

Establishing a Supportive Classroom Atmosphere

Students sense the level of risk in a classroom. A feeling should be established that it is okay to be wrong and that we all make mistakes. The notion that the teacher is always right must not prevail, even if the teacher has to deliberately fumble occasionally to avoid it (for most of us it happens quite naturally). An atmosphere of supportiveness should be established—teacher for student, student for teacher, and student for student, wherein everyone is interested in the success of everyone else, and no one is afraid to try an idea. Put-downs and ridicule have no place in the classroom.

Teachers Answering Their Own Questions

Questions are usually intended to elicit a response from another person. Some teachers unwittingly fall into the habit of answering their own questions. This can be confusing to students (especially young children) because it leaves them unsure when a response is expected and when the teacher intends to serve the answer along with the question. When questions are asked by the teacher, responses should generally be expected from students.

The need for exceptions, again, must be recognized. There might be times when you will ask a question to focus attention on a particular point prior to discussing that point. For example: "We have learned that water and nutrients flow throughout the plant. Is there a tiny water pump at the bottom of the plant? Well, not really, but there are forces at work that are just as effective as a pump." While students could certainly have been invited to respond to that question, sometimes we ask a question with no intention of getting an answer, but simply to focus attention on a point of interest.

Playing the Guessing Game

Sometimes teachers are guilty of unnecessarily locking onto a particular word or concept as the only acceptable answer to a question when other answers are really just as correct. Doing this transforms an open question into a closed question, with the result that students who should be reinforced for thinking are instead wrong. Such a practice can turn a question/answer session into a guessing game. Student participation is often easily discouraged if students are expected to guess a specific word or idea the teacher has in mind when they could more productively attack the problem or question creatively, thus developing their own solution or their own way of expressing an idea. Perhaps the real question has to do with whether we should require students to tell us what we have in mind, when we really should be asking questions to find out what is in their minds and to promote mental processes.

CLASSIFYING QUESTIONS

Questions are sometimes thought of in two categories—those that require only direct recall of memorized facts and those that require the learner to think and analyze information. Some educators, however, prefer a multilevel classification scheme that associates question types with the various levels of thinking required to answer them, such as the levels of thinking identified in Bloom's taxonomy. Both approaches are described below, including samples for each type of question defined.

Open and Closed Questions

Some questions have only one correct answer. For example, the answer to the question, "What is the name of the planet we live on?" is "Earth." This planet has no other commonly recognized name. Questions like this, which have only one acceptable answer, or which have a very limited number of acceptable answers, are considered closed, or lower-order, questions.

The best questions for class discussion are those that encourage divergent thinking, inference, or evaluation. For example, "How might our lives be different if magnetic forces suddenly did not exist?" Such questions are open (or higher-order) questions, and have a wide range of acceptable responses. Open questions call for opinions, explanations, implications, analyses, judgments, and so on, requiring thinking beyond direct recall of facts.

One team of researchers claims that teachers who frequently ask divergent questions elicit more divergent thinking from students than teachers who use more cognitive memory questions. In fact, they say, "Higher scores on tests of critical thinking and on standardized achievement tests result when teachers use a range of convergent and divergent thinking questions" (Costa and Lowery, 1989).

Others describe effective questioning as an art, saying that "questions are most often used by teachers to see if the learner can remember information that was presented. This use of questioning is limiting, in that students are merely required to recall previously memorized information. Memory-level knowledge is considered to be the lowest level of cognition" (Cain and Evans, 1990). We need to ask more open questions and fewer closed questions.

Managerial Questions

In the course of a school day, students ask many questions that do not deal directly with the learning process but are still important in knowing what to do at the time. These are called managerial questions and might include, "Where shall I put my paper? How much time do we have left? Shall we fold our papers the long way or the short way?" These and many other questions are asked as students seek to know what is expected of them for an assignment, what to do next, and so on. Managerial questions usually do not result in new knowledge or clarification of concepts, but often they are necessary in the management of time, space, and materials.

Questions Based on Bloom's Taxonomy

Probably the most common system for classifying questions is based on Bloom's taxonomy (Bloom, 1971). Six levels of thinking are identified in this well-known hierarchy of mental operations, including knowledge, comprehension, application, analysis, synthesis, and evaluation (brief descriptions are found in chapter 2). This classification scheme provides the teacher with a framework that can be used in formulating questions that will encourage certain levels of thinking as students respond. Sample questions for each level follow:

1. **Memory:** *(recall of information)*
   - *What are four major parts of a flowering plant?*
   - *Which planet is closest to the sun?*

2. **Comprehension:** *(show understanding)*
   - *Describe the process of metamorphosis as it applies to a Monarch butterfly.*
   - *Explain the importance of photosynthesis to human life.*

3. **Application:** *(apply information learned to a specific situation)*
   - *Using what you know about magnets, how would you make a compass using a bar magnet?*
   - *How would you set up a sealed terrarium to make it self-sustaining for a long time?*

4. **Analysis:** *(examine information, separating it into its component parts)*
   - *What do you think are the reasons that renewable energy sources are getting increased attention?*
   - *Using a hand lens and a classroom collection of insects, identify all the similarities and differences of insects that you can.*

5. **Synthesis:** *(forming a whole using components)*
   - *Now that we have finished our study of static electricity, explain what you would do if you and several friends were playing ball in a park when a thunderstorm approached and you notice the hair on your arms beginning to stand erect? Explain your answer.*
   - *I agree that remote areas of our state should become repositories for nuclear waste because . . .*

   or

   - *I agree that remote areas of our state should not become repositories for nuclear waste because . . .*

6. **Evaluation:** *(make a judgment)*
   - *What do you think are the strengths and weaknesses of the arguments of environmentalists regarding the need to protect endangered animal species?*
   - *To what extent do you think we should become involved in recycling plastics, aluminum, and other materials at our school?*

Gender Bias

Teachers usually do not make a deliberate effort to convince female students that they should not pursue science careers. Yet it seems that educators (and parents) may be guilty of unwittingly discouraging girls from participating in science-related activities. Girls' interest in this field might be swayed by the way teachers ask questions and by the way they respond to student answers.

In one classroom, a teacher posed a science-related question to a group of elementary students and then called on a boy for an answer. The boy's incorrect answer evoked a response from the teacher encouraging him to rethink his response. A girl then offered an answer which was also incorrect. The teacher immediately told the girl that she was wrong and then stated the correct answer (Shepardson and Pizzini, 1991). The difference in teacher response could be interpreted to imply that the boy is able to rethink the question and come to a correct answer, while the girl is incapable of thinking the question through.

Other studies found that boys were given a longer "wait time" for answers to questions than were girls (Rowe, 1978). It is possible that subtle cues (along with some that are more blatant) convince some girls that science is a topic for which they are not well suited. There is some evidence to support this contention. Teachers in one sample rated boys in their classes much higher (60 percent) than girls (43 percent) in cognitive intellectual skills (Shepardson and Pizzini, 1991). Perhaps teacher expectation for girls in the domain of critical thinking causes some girls to sell themselves short.

Not only do teachers need to direct thought-provoking questions and tasks toward girls as well as boys, they should also consider carefully how they respond to both genders. Teachers need to instill in students of both sexes the skills and confidence needed to succeed in any vocation or field of study they may select.

STUDENT QUESTIONS

It seems as if children barely make it out of the delivery room before they begin asking questions. It is never too early for children to begin to investigate their environment.

"What is this for?"

"Why are the flowers red?"

"Why can't I fly?"

"What is this?"

"What is that?"

"Why?"

Questions are a most natural method of acquiring information. The ability of small children to produce questions seems limitless, and their persistence in asking is often annoying to adults. Within a few years, however, this marvelous attribute is usually dampened. Sometimes children stop asking so many questions because they have learned that children are only to ask certain questions, and these are permitted only at stipulated times. Some have found that many of the questions children asked their teachers had little to do with academics. They were, instead, procedural in nature, such as, "What will the test be like?" or "How many lines do we skip before we start writing?" (Dillon, 1988).

Social subordinates are typically reluctant to ask questions of social superiors. Even adults often hesitate to ask questions of bosses and other people they perceive to be their superiors. Children are assigned a subordinate role when they enter school. In that role, many children hesitate to ask questions when they do not understand a concept. Often, when students are asked if they understand a concept, they will nod or otherwise respond in the affirmative to "save face." This is a clue to the alert teacher that changes are needed in the classroom atmosphere or in the lines of communication between the teacher and that particular student.

Student questions provide a window into the mind, revealing interests, curiosities, and what has or has not been learned. If that window is closed, the teacher loses one of the best sources of information for continuous formative evaluation of learning.

WHAT THE TEACHER CAN DO TO IMPROVE

The effective teacher will display an open and questioning mind, making it clear that learning never ends. This is perhaps more important in science instruction than it is in any other area of the curriculum because the world of science is changing and growing at such a rapid pace.

Many times the process of finding the answer to a question is far more important than the answer itself. The processes of science that will serve the student for a lifetime are too often ignored, while their minds are filled with information that is forgotten or outdated in a short time. Students learn to absorb information, pass the test, and promptly discard the concepts, because they perceive the concepts to have little application outside the classroom.

As a teacher, you should become aware of the mechanics and levels of questions you use during instruction. The video camera provides an excellent opportunity to obtain authentic, unbiased reflections of your own teaching practices. Place the video camera in a strategic location and use it to record classroom action for private review at your own convenience. Through this medium, you can examine your questioning behaviors and other teaching practices and work toward making appropriate modifications for improvement. Several sessions might be needed for students to become accustomed to the camera's presence and for you to practice the changes you are attempting to make.

An evaluation form is provided at the end of this chapter to help you evaluate and improve questioning skills. Use this form yourself, along with videotaped sequences of instruction time, or ask observers who are assisting in the evaluation to fill it out. Audiotaped segments of instruction time can also be used to evaluate questioning and answering behaviors of teachers and students. Although it will miss much of the nonverbal communication, the audio recording can provide an effective review of verbal interactions in the classroom.

IN CLOSING

Questions and answers are at the very foundation of learning, and they are especially vital in the world of science education. Try to foster a classroom atmosphere that will promote healthy student interaction. Your students should understand at the outset that school is the place to ask questions, that you, as the teacher, value a questioning attitude, and that you and they are partners in the learning process.

LIST OF RESOURCES

Bloom, Benjamin S., et al., *Handbook on Formative and Summative Evaluation of Student Learning* (New York: McGraw-Hill, Inc., 1971).

Blosser, Patricia E., *How to Ask the Right Questions* (Washington, D.C. National Science Teachers Association, 1991).

Blough, Glenn O., and Julius Schuartz, *Elementary School Science and How to Teach It*, 8th ed. (Fort Worth, TX: Holt, Rinehart and Winston, Inc., 1990).

Cain, Sandra E., and Jack M. Evans, *Sciencing: An Involvement Approach to Elementary Science Methods*, 3rd ed. (Columbus, OH: Merrill Publishing Co., 1990), 208.

Carin, Arthur A., and Robert Sund, *Developing Questioning Techniques* (Columbus, Ohio: Charles E. Merrill Publishing Co., 1971).

Costa, Arthur L., and Lawrence F. Lowery, *Techniques for Teaching Thinking* (Pacific Grove, CA: Midwest Publications, 1989), 22.

Dillon, J. T., *Questioning and Teaching: A Manual of Practice* (New York: Teachers College Press, Colombia University, 1988), 11.

Far West Regional Laboratory, *Minicourse One: Effective Questioning in a Classroom Discussion* (Berkeley: Far West Laboratory for Educational Research and Development, January 1968).

Rowe, Mary Budd, *Teaching Science as Continuous Inquiry: A Basic*, 2nd ed. (New York: McGraw-Hill Book Co., 1978), 274, 281–83.

Shepardson, D. P., and E. L. Pizzini, "Gender Bias in the Classroom—A Self-Evaluation," *Science and Children* 29, no. 3 (November/December 1991), 38–39.

TEACHER SELF-EVALUATION OF QUESTIONING SKILLS FOR USE WITH VIDEOTAPED LESSONS

As you observe or watch yourself teaching, keep a tally for each of the questioning skills listed below. You may be surprised by what you find!

1. **Wait time** *following a teacher question five seconds or longer:* ________________
2. **Wait time** *following a student answer three seconds or longer:* ________________
3. **Open** *questions:* ________________
4. **Closed** *questions:* ________________
5. **Managerial** *questions:* ________________
6. *Unsolicited* **topic-related** *student questions:* ________________
7. **Parroted** *answers (verbatim or restated):* ________________
8. **Non-volunteer** *responses solicited:* ________________
9. **Predirected** *questions:* ________________
10. **Redirected** *questions:* ________________
11. **Prompts** *students toward correct answer:* ________________
12. **Reinforced** *student answers:* ________________
13. *Number of questions directed to:*

    Girls: ________________

    Boys: ________________

CHAPTER

EARLY CHILDHOOD

CHAPTER OUTLINE:

I WONDER . . .

How important are the questions of a young child?
What is the role of the scientific method in the science experience of these children?
How do we teach classification and problem-solving skills to students of this age?
What are some science activities that are appropriate during the early childhood years?
Why does the spontaneous curiosity of the young child seem to diminish in the upper grades?

INTRODUCTION

Young children have a natural curiosity about the world around them. They love to learn about puppies, horses, insects, and other animals. Many nonliving things are also irresistible to children, from magnets to mud puddles. Explorations with water, air, pendulums, light, sound, motion, and other science topics, strengthen the curiosity and breathe life into the learning process. The important tasks of teachers include: (1) keeping the spontaneous curiosity of the young child alive, (2) encouraging the free flow of student questions, and (3) providing many opportunities for children to explore. During these critical years, children learn to ask questions and to investigate freely, or they learn to keep their questions to themselves, depending on the way their queries are received. It is *crucial* that their natural instincts for inquiry be accepted and encouraged.

Plato said, "There is no other beginning of learning than wonder." The curiosity and desire to explore blossom through firsthand experiences: touching, smelling, examining things up close, taking things apart and putting them together, and creating. Concepts children learn in a science activity can be integrated into other activities throughout the day (Raines and Canady, 1990). These experiences should be coupled with frequent opportunities for children to discuss what they do, and to share their observations and perceptions. Newly acquired information, ideas, and insights can be shared by telling friends, preparing and displaying charts, drawing pictures, keeping journals, and creating books.

While it is important for them to express their ideas freely, it isn't necessary for young children to pursue all questions to the point of finding "correct" answers. The process of asking questions, exploring, and sharing ideas is often more important than the answers themselves. Children might reason together about whether air takes up space, and whether it even exists after being released from a balloon, for example. Consensus of opinion is not necessary, but free expression of ideas and reasoning enhances the development of creative and inquiring minds.

For young children, experiencing is more important than experimenting. Exposure to the scientific method is general and low key. Having lots of informal firsthand experiences using all of the senses nourishes the natural sense of inquiry. A more formal approach to problem solving can come later, perhaps beginning in the upper elementary grades, building naturally on a firm foundation of readiness experiences.

The stages of psychological development of the young child are described in chapter 2, in the discussion of Developmental Psychology. Developmental steps of the young child described in this section include the acquisition of the conservation skill as the child progresses from the preoperational stage into the concrete operational stage.

Thinking patterns of the young child who has not yet developed the conservation skill provide fascinating study for the student of child development. Other characteristics that portray the child at this stage of development are discussed in chapter 2, and will not be further developed in this chapter.

CONCRETE EXPERIENCES IN EARLY CHILDHOOD

Some past theories have held that a child's ability to learn is unalterably established by inherited factors. It is broadly accepted today that, although inborn characteristics strongly influence the ease with which we learn, our ability to acquire information and skills is also affected by experience. The child who is spoken to and read to frequently during the critical early months and years of life will learn language skills more readily than the child who hears relatively little language spoken. Just as the budding athlete benefits from playing catch with a caring mentor during the formative years, so are language skills enhanced by early experience and practice (Trelease, 1989). Similarly, the child who has many experiences with pendulums, buoyancy of objects, simple machines, magnets, and so on, will be better prepared to learn concepts and principles of physics than the child who is deprived of those experiences. The nursery school and the home should provide many experiences in doing and in interacting with the natural world. These experiences prepare the child to learn, step by step, along the way of life.

The importance of interactions with the physical and social environment during these early years cannot be overemphasized. Imitation and manipulation lay the foundation for mental symbolism, which enable the child to bridge the gap between sensorimotor thought patterns and later formal levels of thinking. Science programs should allow children to observe, manipulate, ask questions, and experience science concepts. The development of thinking skills is enhanced as children live through these experiences.

CONSIDER THE DEVELOPMENTAL LEVEL OF THE LEARNER

Classification and seriation skills begin to develop during preschool and early elementary grades. Young children should be exposed to activities that develop these skills. Early experiences with classification could involve such familiar objects as buttons, marbles, beads, or rocks. Young students should first identify a single, obvious characteristic, such as size or color, and separate the items according to that attribute. They can progress to two or more attributes as their classification skills mature. When classifying rocks, they will probably use some of the same characteristics a scientist would use, that is, color, hardness, and shiny or dull. Along with classifying objects (rocks, buttons, apples, and so on) by size, they enjoy lining them up from largest to smallest, learning and reinforcing skills of seriation (arranging things in a series). Continuing with seriation skills, they can arrange rocks in order from dark to light in color, and as their level of sophistication increases, they can arrange the rocks in order of hardness.

When planning science investigations, the teacher should ask: Can the children do it? Will it make sense to them? According to Piaget, the answers to these questions depend on the child's conceptual or cognitive developmental level, experience with the materials, and ability to act upon the materials.

As children enter school, peer interaction is important. Children are leaving the egocentric stage of preoperational thought, and can begin listening and responding to the views of others. Some will be ready for small group work and sharing times.

PROBLEM SOLVING AND THE YOUNG CHILD

Since children below the ages of nine or ten years usually exhibit few systematic investigative skills, science experiences should be planned that provide new information and allow manipulation of objects, but that do not require following a hypothetical problem-solving process. Problem-solving experiences for young children should be clearly tied to concrete examples. For instance, children can investigate the effect of water on sand, in making the sand stick together, and determine the ideal amount of water to add to a gallon bucket of their sand for building sand castles and other structures. The amount of water needed will change according to the type of sand, the amount of moisture already in the sand, and so on, but students can still learn as they experience the process of investigating the question with regard to this particular sand in its current condition.

INTEGRATING THE CURRICULUM

While ideas for integrating the curriculum are more fully developed in chapter 8, Planning, Assessing, and Integrating, it seems appropriate to make a few comments here regarding this effort. Like so many other good ideas in education, integrating the curriculum is much more popular in theory than in practice. As educators, we applaud its potential benefits, but we are less certain about how to do it effectively. Success in this effort will grow as educators try ideas, share them, and learn from each other. The following ideas have been tried successfully and shared by teachers of young children.

One teacher was successful in getting primary grade children to prepare their own book, based on experiences with Penny the guinea pig and her three tiny offspring. They considered the probable birth order of the babies, based on the premise that the firstborn is usually the strongest and healthiest, and the last one born is often the runt. The mass and length of the babies were measured and graphed. They discussed the likenesses and differences of the babies, compared them with characteristics of the parents, and extended these observations to some basic human genetics. These and other experiences with the guinea pigs became the basis of a book, *Penny's Three Little Wishes*. As they prepared the book, students had experiences with math, science, art, language arts, and social studies (King, 1990).

After giving young children many different experiences with animals, ranging from elephants at the zoo to smaller animals in the classroom, another teacher suggested several ways that curricular areas other than science can be enhanced by such experiences (Gianelloni, 1987). Projects for art and language arts are included in her suggestions. For example, after the teacher reads a book about a particular animal to the class, students might draw the animal and tell what they learned about it. They could also make a tail, a beak, or ears that represent a particular animal, then wear the item and pretend to be that animal for a time.

Opportunities are plentiful for teaching science while young students are involved in art, music, language arts, and other subject areas. Shapes of cross-sections of different fruits and vegetables can be noted as children use these for printing patterns on paper. Students can compare lengths, thicknesses, and shapes of blocks as they use blocks, and as they clean up and organize the block center. If they have opportunities to experience bins of rice, beans, flour, water, and so on, the experiences can include measuring these materials in different ways. A kitchen center, in which students work with eating utensils and with food packages, such as soup and vegetable cans and cereal boxes, provide excellent opportunities for children to develop classification skills. Children can learn how shadows change in size and shape as they dance in front of a bright light that casts shadows on a blank wall (Schiller and Townsend, 1985). They can shine colored lights on a blank wall, discovering new colors that are created as the lights are combined.

Science can even be integrated with transitions. Such times usually serve only to move students from place to place, but they often provide opportunities for teaching science to young children, asking students to pretend to be a particular animal as they move down the hall, or to observe the change of state as ice cubes melt in their drinking glass at snack time. Students can also discuss cloud shapes, other weather conditions, and even try to predict the weather, as they prepare to play outdoors. Science has application and becomes meaningful as children make connections between science and the everyday world.

THINGS TO DO

Many popular science-related activities for young children require little instruction and use materials that are usually easily acquired or are already on hand in the classroom (see Figure 5-1). Here are a few examples:

1. **Building structures with clay.** *Children discover principles of physics, even though they can't express them verbally, as their clay towers topple and they have to broaden the base to make them stand.*
2. **Sand play.** *A variety of buckets, spoons, strainers, funnels, and magnifiers provide opportunities for children to discover that grains of sand are not all the same size, and that wet sand is easier to mold than dry sand, but it doesn't pour as well.*
3. **Dinosaurs.** *Books and pictures of dinosaurs fascinate children. They can also draw a dinosaur footprint on butcher paper and compare the size with their own foot.*
4. **The five senses.** *Many, many activities can be built around the topic of the five senses, including rattle cans, feely bags, and containers of "mystery" foods to smell (use caution in encouraging children to taste*

Figure 5-1

A group of young children involved in science activities together.

foods, as unexpected problems may result from allergies, diabetes, and so on).

5. **Cloud watching.** *Children can find shapes in the clouds, and they can make clouds by gluing cottonballs on blue paper.*
6. **Water.** *Children love to explore with water. A teacher can help them notice that water drops stick together; they can be tugged around on waxed paper with a toothpick. Water clings to water and to the toothpick. If the child touches the end of the toothpick with soap and then touches the drop of water with the toothpick again, he or she will notice that the drop will flatten out, and the drop of water can no longer be tugged around with the toothpick.*
7. **Collections.** *Young children love to make collections—rocks, leaves, grasses, shells, and so on. Collections of such items can then be used to sort and categorize. They can also make a sound collection or a smell collection by listing sounds and smells encountered during a specified period of time or in a particular location, or on a ten-minute walk around the school grounds or nearby.*
8. **Shadows.** *One child can draw the shadow of another on butcher paper. If the child comes back in an hour (or even less than that), stands over the paper, and tries to make his or her shadow fit the outline on the paper, there is a surprise in store. The child can be challenged to notice the differences, then compare again the next day at the same time of day that the shadow was drawn. Dealing with the "whys" is probably too abstract for most children of this age, but making a simple comparison can be of interest and stimulate the curiosity. Remember, we don't need to provide all the answers or pursue questions to finality. The process of investigating and stimulating the curiosity have value independent of the "answers."*
9. **Colors.** *Most children enjoy drawing pictures with crayons. They can mix some of the colors and see what new colors can be made. The same activity can be done with colored chalk and with water colors. Children enjoy comparing the results. (Some types of clay also work well for mixing colors and making color wheels.)*
10. **Colored lights.** *Children can shine colored lights on a blank wall, discovering new colors that are created as the lights are combined.*
11. **Prism.** *Shine a light through a prism to project the color spectrum on the wall. Children can then paint rainbows in the true rainbow series of colors. (An easy way to produce the color spectrum is to fill an aquarium with water and place it in the sunlight coming through a window.)*
12. **Magnifiers.** *Children are fascinated with magnifiers, such as hand lenses and simple microscopes. They delight in examining leaves, rocks, insects, grains of sand, their own fingernails, and so on. If possible, leave the lenses and microscopes out for children to explore with freely and spontaneously.*
13. **Magnets.** *Magnets fascinate children of all ages. They can investigate freely, finding out how magnets respond to each other and to many other materials. Classification skills can be developed as children place items that are attracted by magnets in one group and items not attracted in another group.*
14. **Seeds.** *Children can examine and classify seeds by size, shape, and color. They can also predict, and even draw, the type of plants they think will grow from different types of seeds.*

IN CLOSING

Many resources offer ideas and activities for the early childhood years. One excellent source is a regular feature in *Science and Children*, called "Early Childhood." This monthly article describes science learning experiences and activities for preschool through primary age children. *Science and Children* is the official publication of the National Science Teachers Association (NSTA) for the elementary level, and can be obtained from NSTA, 1742 Connecticut Avenue, NW, Washington, D.C. 20009. Other resources for teaching science to young children are included in the List of Resources at the end of this chapter.

Close association with nature during the early years provides a foundation for later interest and inquiry at higher levels of thinking. Children grow in their independence as learners by asking questions and making observations. Thinking skills grow out of hands-on experiences, best aided by a teacher who is skilled in asking thought-provoking questions and who is wise enough to not always give answers. A good supply of books, stories, and pictures, along with a curriculum richly laden with firsthand experiences in a variety of science areas, can launch the child on a lifelong journey of curiosity, exploration, and satisfaction in learning.

LIST OF RESOURCES

Bloom, Benjamin S., et al., *Handbook on Formative and Summative Evaluation of Student Learning* (New York: McGraw-Hill, Inc., 1971).

Carratello, J., and P. Carratello, *Across the Curriculum with Favorite Authors* (Westminster, CA: Teacher Created Materials, Inc., 1992).

Fisher, B., *Joyful Learning* (Portsmouth, NH: Heinemann, 1991).

Geller, Linda Gibson, "Conversations in Kindergarten," *Science and Children* 22, no. 7 (April 1985): 30–32.

Gianelloni, Marcelle, "Close Encounters of the Wildest Kind," *Science and Children* 24, no. 6 (March 1987): 37–38.

Goldberg, Lazer, "Learning How to Learn," *Science and Children* 19, no. 7 (April 1982): 10–11.

King, Charlotte, "Making First-Class Books," *Science and Children* 28, no. 3 (November-December 1990): 40–41.

McIntyre, Margaret, "Science Is Basic," *Science and Children* 16 no. 4 (January 1979): 45.

Neuman, Donald B., *Experiences in Science for Young Children* (Prospect Heights, IL: Waveland Press, Inc., 1992).

Poppe, Carol A., and Nancy A. Van Matre, *Science Learning Centers for the Primary Grades* (West Nyack, NY: The Center for Applied Research in Education, Inc., 1985).

Raines, Shirley C., and Robert J. Canady, *The Whole Language Kindergarten* (New York: Teachers College Press, 1990).

Raines, Shirley C., and Robert J. Canady, *More Story S-T-R-E-T-C-H-E-R-S: Activities to Expand Children's Favorite Books* (Mt. Rainier, MD: Gryphon House, 1991).

Schiller, Pam, and Joan Townsend, "Science All Day Long: An Integrated Approach," *Science and Children* 23, no. 2 (October 1985): 34–36.

Trelease, Jim, *The New Read-Aloud Handbook* (New York: Penguin Books, 1989).

CHAPTER

INDIVIDUAL DIFFERENCES

CHAPTER OUTLINE:

I WONDER . . .

What can I do to encourage respect for cultural differences among students? What does the term "at-risk students" mean, and how can I help these students? How can I identify the gifted students? What can I do to meet their needs?

INTRODUCTION

Not all educators agree on a common definition of *individualizing*, or subscribe to its implications in the same way. Most, however, agree that we should do our best to involve each student in appropriate learning tasks that enhance motivation to learn and maximize progress. Such a commitment requires that we consider the physical, mental, social, and emotional differences in children, including the handicapped and the exceptionally capable, as well as the "normal" child.

The first topic of this chapter deals with cultural diversity. Much attention is currently focused toward the changing ethnic structure of our society. Certain social groups traditionally perceived as majority groups and minority groups are experiencing definite shifts and some will, in time, possibly even reverse roles. Emphasis on ethnic differences demands more awareness on the part of the teacher, and therefore more effective preservice training.

The second topic deals with students at risk of failure. Federal law (Public Law 94-142) currently requires that all handicapped children be taught in "the least restrictive environment," the environment most conducive to learning and growth for the child, given the existing individual limitations and needs. Former Secretary of Education Bennett (1978) called to task those who would by-pass science for the handicapped on the assumption that science is too difficult for these students. He claimed that such students must be given the opportunity for success in science problem solving, and that some science learning may actually aid the students in handling their limitations, whether they be mental, physical, or emotional. Bennett reported a study of 113 boys and girls classed as physically handicapped, emotionally disturbed, educable mentally retarded, and trainable, who were involved in an activity-based science program. Not only did students in the study show significant gains in learning, but they often wanted to continue beyond the time allotted. Both teachers and students enthusiastically expressed interest in continued studying of science topics.

As a final topic, children on the upper end of the spectrum of learning abilities have received less attention than the handicapped, but they, too, deserve to be involved in learning tasks that are appropriate for their ability and skill level—tasks that challenge them. One issue considered in this section is the question of who the gifted and talented students really are.

We assume that specialized courses will provide the beginning teacher with basic training in dealing with cultural differences, children at risk of failure, and those who are gifted learners. Still, a brief description of selected issues, along with suggestions about the role of science in dealing with those issues, seems appropriate in the effort to make science connections and to raise awareness in the minds of new teachers, which is the goal of this chapter.

CULTURAL DIVERSITY

The cultural diversity of students in the classroom is becoming more inevitable as immigrants continue to enter the country from abroad, established minority groups increase in population and become more widespread geographically, and as all families become more mobile.

Cultural diversity brings with it the challenge of multiple languages. In some settings, bilingual children have been reprimanded for speaking in their native tongue at school. Test results sometimes mark bright children as slow learners due to a language barrier between the child and the test or between the child and the person who administers the test (Smith and Luckasson, 1992).

Differences in socioeconomic status bring additional challenges. Children are sometimes criticized for their clothing, when their families cannot afford to dress them as nicely as other students in the school. Poverty can cause a variety of handicaps; but in the United States, inequity of schooling opportunities must not be one of them.

Behavioral issues arise out of cultural differences, as well. As a teacher, you need to become acquainted with the value structures of social groups represented by your students. Some cultures value competitiveness, for instance, and some do not. While schools in certain societies would interpret assertiveness as a behavioral disorder, another social group would be concerned about a student's reluctance to compete. Such problems can be minimized as teachers and administrators become more sensitive to cultural differences.

Gender issues are also an important element of cultural diversity. The related problems that arise usually result from differences that we create, rather than from any inherent variable. In the early grades, achievement in science is equal for girls and boys. As children progress through the grades, the achievement scores of girls begin to lag behind those of boys. There is evidence that these growing differences do not stem from any difference in basic ability to learn science, but from differences in the level of encouragement in their science experience. "Girls are less likely than boys to participate in class discussions and to be encouraged by teachers to participate" (Banks, 1993).

It is important that you model a positive attitude and focus on identifying strengths in each of your students. Help children see the opportunities to learn from each other. Cultural differences in the classroom can produce very real advantages; students broaden their horizons as cultural differences are spotlighted, if it is done wisely. Student respect for these differences, and their interest in learning about each other's backgrounds, often result from a teacher's attitude of interest and respect for each student. Accentuate the positive; spotlight the cultural backgrounds of students individually, and praise them for their unique skills, interests, and experiences. Establish pride in the mind of the child for his or her own uniqueness and avoid the feeling that to be different from the majority group is to be less. After all, we are all different; but as humans we are alike in more ways than we are different. No cultural group has two heads, three eyes, or six arms. Such differences as the color of our skin, the language we speak, or whether we can afford to wear the latest fashions in clothing, are minor. The practice of labeling, ridiculing, and perceiving individuals as being of less worth than others, based on these characteristics, should be replaced by a respect for diversity. Differences that might be ridiculed, such as cultural beliefs or practices that some would label superstition, can be deemphasized in favor of focusing on the positive aspects. Bring out that for which the child can be praised, respected, and admired.

Just as we all have strengths, we all have weaknesses. Each one of us likes to be recognized for characteristics that people around us respect. Turning the spotlight on someone else's qualities that their social group looks down upon is grossly unjust. Labeling a social group as being of less worth because it is different from our own is equally wrong. Every American can trace his or her roots to cultures that were very different from the one we call the American culture today. Diversity must be perceived as a strength, not as a weakness.

Things to Do

Here are a few ideas to consider when working with culturally diverse groups:

1. *Include science topics that can be related to children's background. Students from various cultures bring with them unique experiences and perspectives. A child whose family roots are in Africa or Australia could probably make unique contributions when the class is studying animals. A child of an Air Force family might be particularly interested in a unit on flight. This child could probably add to the unit by giving a report or sharing information and experiences informally. Children who have a positive experience in making such a contribution in class will grow in their respect for themselves and for their own uniqueness.*
2. *Become aware of community resources, especially people from various ethnic backgrounds who have science careers or hobbies. Invite such a person to come into the classroom as a resource person, thus providing a positive role model for children who have a similar cultural background.*
3. *Arrange for a child to be invited to visit the workplace of a person in a science career who has the same ethnic background as the child, providing a positive role model.*
4. *Make opportunities to become acquainted with parents. In regular contacts with the parents, try to involve them with their child in school activities and projects. Emphasize the positive, praising the parent and child on strengths and contributions.*
5. *Where language barriers exist, try to arrange for the child to have adequate interaction with someone who speaks his or her native tongue to enhance the level of clarity of science concepts being learned while the child acquires additional communication skills .*

AT-RISK STUDENTS

The term "at-risk" has become broadly used in reference to students who are deprived socially, emotionally, physically, or in some other way that places their academic success "at risk." Some children who are mentally capable and have no obvious handicaps may be at risk due to less obvious deficiencies, such as low self-concept, lack of motivation, or very limited experiential background. A child who feels incapable often performs as though he or she really were incapable unless and until the child is made aware of a greater ability to learn and do. "The most important element in teaching these students is a positive attitude. . . . Hold the conviction that every child can learn, that there are no losers" (McLaurin, 1991). One teacher concluded, after reviewing a very difficult and extended experience with a handicapped child, "I learned to think through problems with him. This was good for both of us" (Schulz, 1993).

Learning the basic concepts of magnetic attraction and repulsion, for example, comes relatively quickly for the child who has had many previous experiences with magnets. The child who has had very limited experience with magnets lags behind in grasping the concepts. In examining microscopic organisms, a child who has never used a microscope is at a disadvantage among children who have had many previous related experiences. Very possibly, the child with less experience will become highly motivated with the activity, however, and become the microscope expert of the class.

Such a discovery of the self—recognizing an area in which one is capable—can launch the child into a new world of self-realization and raise him or her to higher levels of performance and self-expectation in other areas as well. At-risk learners need a great deal of encouragement, understanding, and support in developing a more positive sense of self-worth. Science experiences can provide opportunities for a teacher to empower the child to access his or her innate capabilities.

Mainstreaming

Many children with special needs spend part of the school day in the tutelage of a teacher with special training and part of the day in a normal classroom, in a cooperative effort to broaden the experience and maximize learning for the special-needs child. Placing handicapped children in a regular classroom for selected educational experiences is called *mainstreaming*. Mainstreaming is done in an effort to place the child in an environment that is least restrictive to learning by integrating students having various disabilities with students who have no apparent handicaps. The ultimate goal is for each child to become a self-reliant adult. For most children, this is usually best achieved if the child learns to deal with a broad spectrum of personalities rather than being limited to a relatively homogeneous group of peers. Isolating handicapped students from other students for their entire school experience can convey to them that they are not able to relate with other groups of people. This does not prepare them for the "real world" they face outside of school.

Some educators object to mainstreaming, taking the position that handicapped students should spend most of their time with the teacher who is trained to understand and deal with their special needs. On the opposite end of the philosophical spectrum, others object to handicapped students being removed from the regular classroom at all. Wang leans toward the latter point of view, suggesting that instead of assuming that poor social adjustment and inferior performance are attributable entirely to characteristics of the student, teachers should prepare the regular classroom learning environment to accommodate the educational needs of all students (Wang, 1986).

The question of whether the child with special needs is to be mainstreamed into regular classrooms for all or most of the school day will continue to provide fuel for debate. However, since there is widespread agreement that each child should spend at least a portion of the school day in the regular classroom, this chapter offers a few suggestions for the classroom teacher to provide a positive science experience for all children. Some teachers report that many "resource" students *shine* in science—that it is the only time in the day when they are leaders.

Peer Tutoring

The practice of having students assist students in the classroom is commonly referred to as *peer tutoring*. Some experts think that we often build false barriers to the handicapped, consisting of myths that these students can't learn science, that science is not important to them, or that having a handicapped pupil in the class will hold the others back (Thompson, 1979). The need to help someone else can provide some of the best opportunities for learning; the more able students learn in greater depth as they offer assistance to the one in need.

Educable Mentally Handicapped (EMH)

Severely retarded children are usually placed in centers that are equipped with facilities and specially trained personnel. The mildly retarded, or educable mentally handicapped (EMH), are often mainstreamed into the regular classroom in varying degrees, according to the needs of the child and the philosophy of the school system.

EMH children are as varied in abilities as any other group. These children learn many skills and concepts at slower rates than most other children do; but with appropriate adjustments of the school setting to their needs, they are able to learn and participate in science. EMH children need structure rather than open-ended instructions; they need direct instruction, including frequent review and repetition, to help them make connections between activities and concepts; they need to focus on a single task at each session. Work sessions must be kept within the attention span of the child (at times this will be surprisingly long, depending on the level of motivation sparked within the individual by a given activity or topic).

Children with Impairments of Sight and Hearing

A general goal of science education is to provide experiences through which children learn about their environment. Ideally, encounters with science enrich the lives of learners through all of the senses. Children who must function with less than normal sight or hearing are at a disadvantage in the regular classroom, but the disadvantage can be minimized if adjustments are made to accommodate their needs.

Students who are hearing impaired or sight impaired are not necessarily deaf or blind. These impairments occur in a variety of types and degrees, just as mental handicaps do. For example, hearing may be clear in a certain frequency range but limited above or below that range; and sight may be inadequate in distinguishing between objects or restricted to a narrow field of view, but functional within those limits. In any case, students who are limited in one sense must rely more heavily on other senses in their efforts to learn. The effectiveness of their learning in science can be greatly enhanced by modifying experiences to optimize the use of the impaired sense and maximize learning through the senses that are functionally whole.

Instructions can be given in both verbal and printed form to assure maximum assimilation of information. Students whose sight or hearing is impaired should be invited to sit in the location that is best for them. Given close proximity to the teacher, hearing-impaired students will be more able to read lips and facial expressions. Similarly, the sight-impaired need close proximity to assure that they hear information and instructions clearly, compensating for the reduction or absence of visual cues. As the teacher, you need to be sensitive to opportunities to involve these students in ways that will capitalize on their strengths and capabilities and build their self-confidence. We must be careful to avoid embarrassing handicapped students, or placing them in situations where they are expected to perform tasks they are incapable of or where their safety is compromised. Demonstrations and activities should be explained in careful detail, especially in the presence of a blind or partially blind student. For the hearing impaired, verbal descriptions and instructions can be heavily supplemented with demonstrations, written instructions, and additional hands-on experiences, wherever feasible. Some children with impaired senses develop exceptional keenness in other senses, the others being strengthened through greater use in the effort to compensate for the impaired sense(s).

Students can be paired in a peer-tutoring setting—a sighted student with a visually impaired student, a student with fully functional hearing with a student whose hearing is limited—and trained to work together for mutual benefit and growth. Students with full use of the senses can read assigned material to the sight-impaired student or record such material for use as homework. If a classmate is blind, other students can learn certain Braille symbols and in various ways gain insight into the world of the blind through cooperative interaction. If a student is deaf, classmates can

Figure 6-1

A group of students working together.

learn sign language and in many ways assist the student in the learning task.

In addition to those students specifically assigned as peer tutors, all classmates of the impaired should be instructed and encouraged to use methods that help the impaired students succeed, as they have opportunities for positive interaction with these students. Students whose senses are whole need to encourage sense-impaired students to use what remains of the impaired sense to the fullest extent possible, being careful to offer only needed assistance (see Figure 6.1). The goal is not to make handicapped students dependent on student partners, but rather to offer help as needed and assist them in becoming as independent as possible. Where feasible, reverse roles and capitalize on the strengths of the sense-impaired students, letting them be the leaders in other partnerships in areas where they excel, such as teaching signing, basic braille, math, physical education skills, and so on. Emphasize that everyone teaches and everyone learns.

Students with Special Social Needs

Students who have difficulty being attentive in class or who are awkward with social interactions often have a hard time working cooperatively with others. Negative behaviors may reflect negative attitudes and lack of interest in school. High-interest, hands-on experiences in science can provide the key for social change for some students. "Phantom Johnny," whose experience is shared in two separate articles, is representative of many students whose potential can be awakened through involvement with science (Hare, 1987; Crow, 1987). Johnny had stopped participating in much of anything at school. Although he was a discipline problem at times, he had mostly become socially invisible, withdrawn and unsuccessful. Many teachers had tried to reach him without success. He preferred to "float on the edges of the academic system rather than to swim in the mainstream." Johnny accidentally stumbled into a science lab, where a wise and perceptive teacher helped him to develop interests. A former teacher was later amazed at Johnny's excitement and depth of involvement with a study of crayfish, the seriousness with which he worked, and the sparkle in his voice as he explained what he had learned. Teachers reported that Johnny's transformation from phantom to student was not limited to his work in science, but that his success in science led to overall academic and social improvements.

Such successes in science, with students considered to have learning handicaps, have been experienced by many teachers. Behavior problems often result from students being academically withdrawn, with little interest or purpose in school. Science involvement can capture the interest of many such students, focusing energies in productive directions. As with Johnny, the desire to seek out information comes from within the student when the interest and perceived purpose are present. The positive impact on reading, writing, and other academic areas can be great.

A colleague shared with the authors an experience with a middle-school student who was perpetually a low achiever and a troublemaker, and was constantly turning productivity into chaos for both himself and others. We'll call this child Bill. In preparing for an Invention Convention in the school, Bill's teacher signed up participants by personal invitation rather than by open announcement, to avoid having Bill sign up and destroy the event for everyone. It didn't work—the word got out, and Bill requested permission to sign up for the Invention Convention. Surprisingly, Bill won not only the school-level competition, but each higher level necessary to progress to national competition. The teacher who had tried to avoid including Bill at the school level proudly escorted him to Washington, D.C., reporting later what a change had come over Bill in his overall behavior and achievement. All of this resulted from a child discovering in himself the ability to succeed with science, and finding fulfillment in productive behavior.

Sometimes the Johnnys and the Bills are the more capable learners, drifting along without purpose through boredom and lack of a perceived objective. Such students can be transformed, almost overnight, from unmotivated low achievers to highly motivated stars with exemplary behavior and performance. For many of these students, potential keys for change lie dormant in the science curriculum, waiting to be used by the teacher who recognizes their potential.

Other Special Needs

Many situations call for special treatment or modification of school programs. In addition to limitations of hearing, sight, motivation, or learning ability, other conditions can interfere with learning. Students with speech disorders may find it difficult to communicate verbally. The teacher might require special training to deal with a child who has limited control of physical movement, or with a child in a wheelchair. Even allergies may require special consideration to ensure a student's health and safety at school. Materials and procedures should be modified to the extent that is feasible to assure maximum participation and involvement of each child in science experiences.

Behavioral and emotional disorders can be very disruptive in a classroom. The assistance of trained personnel may be necessary to effectively encourage on-task behavior and acceptable interaction of the child with others.

The Physical Setting

In addition to providing instructional assistance to students who have special needs, a teacher must consider these needs when arranging the physical setting of the classroom. Students in wheelchairs should have enough space to work and move about comfortably. Doorways should be wide enough to allow them clear passage, and work tables must be at an appropriate height to accommodate the wheelchair (see Figure 6-2). Children on crutches may need special consideration concerning location and arrangement of equipment. Proper lighting should be provided for students whose vision is limited. Location of storage spaces, furniture, and work areas should be predictable for the student with limited vision; when changes are necessary, that student should be carefully oriented to the new conditions.

Problems and Profits of Peer Tutoring

The presence of the handicapped student in the regular classroom, coupled with the practice of having the more capable students assist those in need, can have both positive and negative effects. Care must be taken to avoid making the more able and willing students feel that they have become permanent tutors. The danger of making the at-risk student feel dependent and incapable should be met with similar caution; the objective of helping less capable students become as independent as possible must remain a priority. Used wisely, the responsibilities of peer tutoring can be rotated and limited, leaving both tutor and tutee looking forward to the next session.

Figure 6-2

A handicapped student in a science classroom.

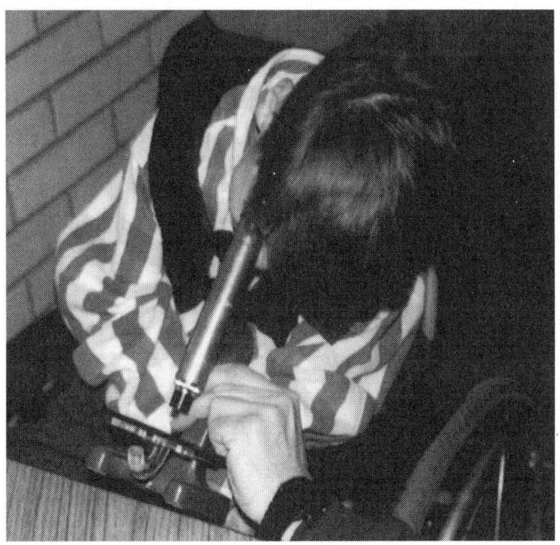

In considering the use of peer tutoring, the teacher must not overlook the excellent opportunities for service, for learning, and for developing empathy. These experiences can result in the "normal" child overcoming a much more common, though subtle, handicap—that of being insensitive to the needs of others. An additional benefit of this interaction is that misunderstandings and fears that "normal" students sometimes have, relating to the handicapped, are often dispelled.

Things to Do

Consider using these ideas with at-risk students:

1. *Be sure activities are well structured and within the child's capabilities, minimizing the chance for injury or damage to property and maximizing the likelihood of success.*
2. *Involve the at-risk student to the fullest extent possible in the same activities that other students do. If a child has a physical handicap that precludes full participation in a particular activity, the child can assist by helping with the planning, or perhaps by gathering some of the materials needed, and still benefit by sharing in the experience. Accentuate what the child* can *do, not what he or she cannot do, and capitalize on every opportunity for growth.*
3. *Provide cooperative learning activities in heterogeneous groups.*
4. *Give frequent* sincere *praise.*
5. *Communicate with parents on a regular basis, focusing on the positive as much as possible.*
6. *Provide opportunities for these students to share experiences that are unique to them with other students, whenever such sharing has a high likelihood of a positive experience.*
7. *Spotlight scientists that have succeeded in the face of obvious handicaps. Stephen*

Hawking, for instance, is a British astronomer who has persisted against great odds with physical handicaps, to become one of the most highly recognized and respected scientists of all time (Hawking, 1988).

GIFTED, TALENTED, AND HIGHLY MOTIVATED STUDENTS

Although children who are gifted have historically been included in discussions of special education, programs for gifted children are not universal, as programs for handicapped children are in the schools of the United States (Smith and Luckasson, 1992). It could easily be argued that the need is less for those who are exceptionally capable learners, because they are more able to progress on their own than are children with learning handicaps. Still, many gifted students can fall short of meeting their potential from lack of challenge and direction. With this issue, we must deal with the question of who the "gifted" really are.

Some educators recognize the "gifted and talented" as being those students who have outstanding academic abilities and are capable of unusually high levels of school performance. Many feel that in order to realize their full potential, such children should have educational experiences, programs, and services beyond those normally provided by the school system.

From an extended perspective, some define giftedness as an interaction of three traits: above-average ability, task commitment, and creativity. "Gifted and talented children are those who possess or are capable of developing this composite set of traits" (Esler, 1989). According to this view, the elementary teacher needs to go beyond merely giving more information to help gifted students focus their creative energies in appropriate directions. For example, educational experiences of students who are gifted can be enriched by extended challenges in experimentation and problem solving, or they may be encouraged to do research in STS topics (see chapter 9), including opinion surveys of students or the community.

Many would agree that students should not be identified as "gifted" and placed in special programs based solely on the results of an intelligence test. Such an approach presumes that all students who have demonstrated high scores on an intelligence test possess high task commitment and creativity as well. Often the performance of students who have less raw intelligence, but who have a high level of motivation and who are willing to stretch their creative talents, exceeds that of some students whose intelligence is measured to be exceptionally high. Thus the school should avoid using too narrow a definition of "giftedness" when inviting students to become involved in enrichment activities. Students who are *highly interested* in such extended study will learn and grow—and will probably do very well—whether or not their I.Q. scores predict that type of success. The Intelligence Quotient is not the only I.Q. to consider; a high "Interest Quotient" can often overcome a moderate Intelligence Quotient as a predictor of achievement and success.

Indeed, many children who are perceived as average students in school—or even below average—are found to be "gifted" in other settings. The traits necessary for advanced achievement can blossom when the right seed of interest is planted. Fortunate is the child in whose mind that seed germinates. Going one step further, every student is talented in some way; one of your challenges as a teacher is to help each child to recognize and build upon his or her individual talents.

Highly motivated and capable students will blossom and, at their own time, can enrich the educational experience for other students in the class by sharing insights, findings, and enthusiasm, and by encouraging others to explore. Realizing that different students have different talents, you should watch for opportunities to spotlight the science achievement of the child who shows some special talent for science but who struggles with reading or certain other curricular areas.

Talents Unlimited, a program that has evolved from the work of such learning theorists as Spearman, Thurstone, and Guilford, and more directly from the efforts of Calvin Taylor and Carol Schlichter (Barbieri, 1988), is based on the premise that when students' abilities are nurtured in five talent areas, their academic proficiencies and chances for success improve. The talents referred to are (1) productive thinking, (2) communication, (3) forecasting, (4) decision making, and (5) effective planning. Proponents of this project emphasize the importance of developing thinking skills, not just in the academically gifted, but in all children (Schlichter, 1988).

Bright students present a special challenge. Elementary teachers typically do not have a strong science background; their training must include all curricular areas, often without a specialty in any particular discipline. In addition to a background in curriculum, elementary teachers must receive training in child development, classroom management, and other areas related to the life and responsibility of a classroom teacher. Some teachers might be reluctant to become involved in science with students who are especially bright for fear of being overwhelmed by content and thus unable to give needed information and guidance. Such a situation need not be intimidating. Instead it can offer exciting opportunities for all to learn, including the teacher. As a teacher you can become the cheering section for advanced science students. Rather than presenting a facade of expertise that does not exist, or fearing embarrassment for what you do not know, you can encourage students to explore and research answers to their questions. A teacher who is willing to learn with the students will most assuredly learn from them as children explore and investigate new knowledge and skills. That's not intimidating—it's exciting!

Things to Do

Here are some ideas the teacher might consider when dealing with students who are gifted, talented, and highly motivated, in addition to regular classroom science activities.

1. *These children are generally self-starters. Although some guidelines and restrictions are still necessary, more freedom can be allowed for students to select and pursue their topics of study.*
2. *As the ability to take on more responsibility is recognized, and as they select their own topics of study, have these students prepare a contract for themselves. This approach recognizes the need for independence and at the same time the continuing need for some degree of structure. It provides structure within unstructure; students set their own guidelines as they outline the steps they will take and describe what they will produce.*
3. *Emphasize the process skills. These students are able to develop expertise in the use of experimentation and the skills of inquiry.*
4. *Local problems that involve issues of science and technology can provide stimuli for student involvement in the community: water and air quality problems, a bridge that is in poor repair, a flagrant animal rights violation, a park that has potential as a science learning center for the community. These and other issues can be influenced in a very real way as students study the needs, conduct interviews and surveys, attend town meetings to learn and express their findings, and write letters to appropriate local, state, and federal agencies, and so on.*
5. *Study the life of a great scientist, such as Thomas Edison or Marie Curie and prepare or present reports, skits, and so on about the lives and inventions of these people. Student creativity in the production can add a touch of humor, increasing the enjoyment of the end product by both producer and audience.*
6. *Involve students in science fairs, Invention*

Conventions, and any such activity that will stimulate their interest and creativity.

7. *Students enjoy constructing models. During a study of electricity, they can make such things as functional telegraph sets and electric motors. They can construct similarly appropriate models for other topics studied.*
8. *After-school science clubs can help to supplement the limited time allowed for science during the regular school day for highly motivated students. It might be a rocket club in which students design and build a variety of model rockets, learning about the principles of design and flight. The club could select some other specific topic of study that is of interest to those involved, or it might just become a general science club that studies a variety of high-interest topics.*

EXAMPLES OF MATERIALS DESIGNED FOR THOSE WITH SPECIAL NEEDS

Many science materials have been developed for the gifted, the handicapped, and the very young. The products described below are only a representative sample of such materials.

1. ESS Special Education Teacher's Guide *(Ball, 1978) is designed to help special education teachers use the regular ESS materials with children who have special needs. Many suggestions and ideas given can also be used effectively by regular classroom teachers.*
2. *Taped lessons and Braille or large-print copies of science textbooks are available from the State Library for the Blind or the American Printing House for the Blind (1839 Frankfurt Ave., Louisville, Kentucky 40206). "Talking Books" are available through the National Library Service for the Blind and Physically Handicapped (1291 Taylor Street NW, Washington, D.C. 20542). For the SCIS materials, Braille versions of student manuals are available, as well as teacher aids for those working with visually impaired students.*
3. Science for Children with Learning Difficulties *(Kincaid,* et al., *1988) was published in England and written for teachers of children who are unable to manage learning tasks with which the majority of their peers succeed. No attempt is made to focus on specific handicaps. Activities include experience observing firsthand, examining, comparing, measuring, sorting and classifying real things, finding similarities and differences, discovering patterns and relationships, asking questions about observations and devising tests to find answers to questions, predicting, looking for patterns and relationships, and communicating with others.*
4. Curriculum Activities for Gifted and Motivated Elementary Students *(Kamiya and Reiman, 1987) comes from the efforts of a group of teachers committed to nurturing students who have high academic potential, providing interesting and challenging learning experiences for the gifted and motivated.*

IN CLOSING

Attitudes of teachers and other adults permeate the lives of children, deliberately or inadvertently. Orchestrated by a master teacher, cultural diversity can enliven a classroom with interest, turning potential prejudice into understanding and acceptance. To a great extent you, the teacher, control whether prejudices are perpetuated or overcome in your classroom. Science provides an opportune setting for a positive impact. A science program properly implemented involves students in many activities in which students interact, working together in cooperative groups. They help each other in problem-solving situations, sharing observations and exploring new ideas. As students work together in an atmosphere of acceptance, they become more and more inclined to respect each person as a unique individual. The tendency to associate individuals with some stereotyped group and mentally assign them to a higher or lower status diminishes as we recognize strength in diversity.

Children, like adults, thrive on success. At-risk students frequently come to perceive themselves as incapable. To progress they must succeed, they must expect to succeed, and they must be expected to succeed. For the handicapped, manipulative science programs can play an important role in providing success through meaningful learning experiences. Programs can be adapted to meet the needs of those who can be mainstreamed, and special activities can be developed to serve those whose handicaps are so severe that they must remain in special classrooms.

Over the years, much has been said about individualizing. In providing for the needs of the handicapped, you need to be sure that those who have limited hearing or vision are located where their acquisition of information will be maximized. Be certain that the physically handicapped are involved to the extent of their capabilities, and assign students who are able and caring to assist those with special needs. To the extent that these and other needs are cared for, individualization is taking place. Each child should be provided with challenges and opportunities to learn within his or her realm of capability. All children should be encouraged to participate as fully as they are able.

Often students can assist other students and help to accomplish what you the teacher cannot do alone. The child who assists another, in an effort to enhance and maximize learning for a classmate, is often the one who benefits most. Also, careful placement of handicapped students in cooperative learning groups, wherein students work together toward a common goal, can result in positive learning and social experiences for the handicapped. Self-concept is enhanced for those who obviously need help. Others in the group experience growth, both in learning while teaching and in giving service to others. "By helping children interact positively with their peers who are visibly different, we remove a handicap from the 'normal' child—that of an additional lifelong prejudice" (Abruscato, 1988).

While making every effort to enrich the lives of gifted students with meaningful challenge in their learning experiences, you should maintain constant awareness of the talents in every child. A life can be forever elevated by a caring teacher who recognizes a spark of interest and talent, and who encourages the child to develop strengths that have been dormant or previously unrecognized.

LIST OF RESOURCES

Abruscato, Joseph, *Teaching Children Science,* 2nd ed. (Englewood Cliffs, NJ: Prentice-Hall, Inc., 1988): 89.

Ball, Daniel W., *ESS/Special Education Teacher's Guide* (St. Louis, MO: Webster/McGraw-Hill, 1978).

Banks, James A., "Multicultural Education: Characteristics and Goals." In James A. Banks and Cherry A. McGee Banks, eds., *Multicultural Education: Issues and Perspectives* (Needham Heights, MA: Allyn & Bacon, 1993): 3–28.

Barbieri, Edmund L., "An Overview of Talents Unlimited," *Educational Leadership* 45, no. 7 (April 1988): 40.

Bennett, Lloyd M., "Science and Special Students," *Science and Children* 15, no. 4 (January 1978): 12–14.

Cain, Sandra E., and Jack M. Evans, *Sciencing: An Involvement Approach to Elementary Science Methods,* 3rd ed. (Columbus, OH: Merrill Publishing Co., 1990).

Carin, Arthur A., and Robert B. Sund, *Teaching Science Through Discovery,* 6th ed. (Columbus, OH: Merrill Publishing Co., 1989).

Crow, Linda W., "Science Saves Johnny," *Science and Children* 25, no. 2 (October 1987): 37–39.

Esler, William K., and Mary K. Esler, *Teaching Elementary Science*, 5th ed. (Belmont, CA: Wadsworth, 1989), 143.

Hare, Donna, "Phantom Johnny, Real Science," *Science and Children* 25, no. 2 (October 1987): 34–36.

Hawking, Stephen W., *A Brief History of Time* (New York: Bantam Books, 1988).

Kamiya, Artie, and Alan Reiman, *Curriculum Activities for Gifted and Motivated Elementary Students* (West Nyack, NY: Parker Publishing Co., 1987).

Kincaid, Doug, *et al., Science for Children with Learning Difficulties* (London: Macdonald & Co., 1988).

McLaurin, William D., "Exploring Science with At-Risk Students." In *Science Horizons: Professional Handbook* (Morristown, NJ: Silver Burdett & Ginn, 1991), 8.

Schlichter, Carol L., "Thinking Skills Instruction for All Classrooms," *Gifted Child Today* 11, no. 2 (March-April 1988): 24–28.

Shulz, Jane B., "Teaching Students with Disabilities in the Regular Classroom." In James A. Banks and Cherry A. McGee Banks, eds., *Multicultural Education: Issues and Perspectives* (Needham Heights, MA: Allyn & Bacon, 1993), 262–78.

Smith, Deborah Deutsch, and Ruth Luckasson, *Introduction to Special Education: Teaching in an Age of Challenge* (Boston, MA: Allyn & Bacon, 1992).

Thompson, Ben, "Myth and Science for the Handicapped," *Science and Children* 17, no. 3 (November-December 1979): 16–17.

Wang, Margaret C., Maynard C. Reynolds, and Herbert J. Walberg, "Rethinking Special Education," *Educational Leadership* 44, no. 1 (September 1986): 26.

Zeitler, William R., and James P. Barufaldi, *Elementary School Science: A Perspective for Teachers* (White Plains, NY: Longman Inc., 1988).

CHAPTER

CURRICULUM MATERIALS AND TECHNOLOGY

CHAPTER OUTLINE:

I WONDER . . .

What is the "alphabet soup curriculum," where did it come from, and what effect has it had on elementary science?

Why should I or shouldn't I use a science textbook?

How do trade books fit in with the elementary science curriculum?

What supplementary programs are available that have been proven effective and useful?

In what ways can today's technology be used to enhance science in the elementary classroom?

What can I do to acquire needed science materials on a very limited budget?

What is the role of elementary science curriculum guides?

INTRODUCTION

The post-*Sputnik* era brought a landslide of materials designed for teaching science in the elementary school. This movement was launched with funds appropriated by the United States Congress to equip the schools for science, to raise the general level of science literacy of American citizens, and to provide specific preparation for scientists and mathematicians to better compete in a world of rapidly advancing technology and space exploration. The term "alphabet soup curriculum" was applied to an aggregation of curriculum projects because of the acronyms by which they were individually known: for example, SAPA (Science, A Process Approach), ESS (Elementary Science Study), and SCIS (Science Curriculum Improvement Study).

This chapter describes these materials along with several of the more recent programs that are widely used in the nation's elementary schools. It would not be possible in one short chapter to mention all of the materials currently available, so we'll concentrate on a few well-known examples of programs that have been produced in recent decades. In addition, we'll discuss the current attitude toward the use of textbooks, with comments added, and the recent impact of technology in the science classroom will be considered. The role of the curriculum guides produced by states and local school districts is also discussed.

ALPHABET SOUP

Of the federally funded post-*Sputnik* elementary science curriculum programs, those that are best known and have survived the test of time are SCIS, SAPA, and ESS. It is important to recognize that the impact of these programs on science instruction has been greater than their level of use would suggest. Born from research on new directions for science education, these programs stress providing hands-on activities and developing problem-solving skills. Commitment to this methodology and perspective spread beyond the programs themselves and altered the content of textbooks and other materials that were subsequently produced.

Although these programs consistently emphasize the need for active learner involvement and the development of process skills, they vary in other ways, especially in levels of structure and flexibility. In fact, on a continuum of structure versus flexibility, SAPA and ESS would be at opposite ends of the continuum, as indicated in the following descriptions of individual projects.

Science, A Process Approach (SAPA)

SAPA emerged as one of the most highly structured of the post-*Sputnik* curriculum projects. Both teachers and students are given rather explicit instructions for completing each activity, including objectives, materials, procedure, and evaluation. This program included 105 modules, based on process skills and written at varying levels of difficulty, each with a sequence of learning activities. Rather rigid adherence to the sequence and structure of the modules and learning activities is required. As the name implies, this project is process oriented.

The original SAPA materials were revised in 1975 to provide more flexibility, allowing teachers to choose from a selection of modules, and in some cases to choose from a selection of activities within modules. The 105 modules, which include manipulatives and printed materials, were also improved for efficiency in storage and use. The revision included some content changes, including a greater emphasis on ecology. The revised version of SAPA, called SAPA II, has fifteen modules per grade level, K–6, with each module focusing on one process. A total of eight basic processes are taught in grades K–3, with five integrated processes being added in grades 4–6. Although science content is used to teach the process skills, competence in using the processes themselves is the primary objective.

SAPA and SAPA II were developed by the American Association for the Advancement of Science (AAAS) and originally marketed by Ginn and Company, a subsidiary of Xerox Educational Company. SAPA II is currently marketed by Delta Education, in Hudson, New Hampshire.

Science Curriculum Improvement Study (SCIS)

SCIS differs from SAPA in that it emphasizes both science content and process skills, and it allows more freedom to select among the units and activities. With a main objective of developing functional understanding of science concepts, or *scientific literacy*, each lesson provides for student exploration with manipulative materials. These activities are followed by teacher explanations of the concept involved, and reinforced by further application of the concept through examples. At this point, the student is expected to recognize applications of the concept to more than one situation.

SCIS has undergone two near-simultaneous revisions, called SCIIS and SCIS II. In 1978, the copyright on the federally funded SCIS program expired and SCIS materials became public domain. SCIIS represents revisions made by the original developing team, responding to suggestions of users of the materials. Changes from SCIS to SCIIS are not extensive in terms of concepts and teaching methods, but some topics were expanded and others were added, including materials that emphasize the students' physical relationship to the earth and its ecological nature. "Extending Your Experience" (EYE) cards were added to facilitate individualization and to enrich basic concepts. Materials and packaging were redesigned to increase efficiency of storage and use.

American Science and Engineering (AS&E) designed and produced all of the materials used in SCIS during the copyright years, except for printed materials. When the copyright expired, AS&E published and marketed SCIS II. The original SCIS program was used as a foundation for SCIS II, with modifications to make it more manageable for the classroom teacher.

The most recent revision, SCIS 3, builds on the success of the earlier versions of this program to include:

1. *Increased emphasis on the concept of evidence, and how it is obtained, as the foundation for modern science;*
2. *Emphasis on the role of the teacher as a facilitator of learning rather than a source of knowledge;*
3. *New* Student Journals *that encourage students to become independent writers and provide them opportunities to report on their work;*
4. *Greater emphasis on the application of science to life.*

SCIS was originally developed by a team of scientists and educators at the University of California at Berkeley and published by Rand McNally. The revisions are currently marketed by Delta Education.

Elementary Science Study (ESS)

The ESS materials include a series of fifty-six child-tested units, presented in separate booklets along with manipulative materials in kits. Teacher guides and audiovisual materials are also available. Unlike SAPA and SCIS, ESS is very flexible, designed as nonsequential units to be used as desired any time during the elementary school years. Each unit is designed to be appropriate for a range of grade levels. These materials can be used as independent units or as supplements to an existing science program. Whereas SAPA and SCIS are dependent upon the materials provided in kits that come with those programs, most of the materials used with ESS are easily found around the house or the school, or are otherwise relatively easy to acquire. ESS units are therefore less dependent upon commercially produced kits, yet the kits are available and offer the obvious advantage of providing the materials conveniently packaged and easily accessible.

ESS materials are also currently marketed by Delta Education.

SCIENCE TEXTBOOKS

For years, many educators have discouraged using textbooks. Some feel that using textbooks removes from a program the flexibility to use a variety of resources. They also fear that many elementary teachers become overly dependent on the textbooks, that such use prevents them from implementing an activity-based approach; thus science becomes just another reading class. Lamenting such textbook dependence, one expert stated that "science textbooks should be removed from the elementary schools. They . . . actually get in the way of good science instruction" (Rutherford, 1987).

Favorable Aspects of the Textbook

Although overdependence on textbooks can severely limit the effectiveness of a science program, today's elementary science textbooks *can* be an important part of an exciting, active, and creative science program if used judiciously. Modern science texts do not stifle or discourage an active approach to science; it is teachers who sometimes do so by improper use of the book. The textbook is an excellent reference that provides a foundation or core program for the teacher to work from. Today's textbooks encourage frequent use of hands-on activities, and themselves provide many such activities. However, if used, they should be supplemented with a broad variety of other resources, including additional textbooks, activity books, encyclopedias, field manuals, and a rich supply of science trade books. Most of today's elementary science textbooks are well organized, interestingly written, and beautifully illustrated; if used properly, they can become an important part of an effective program.

Along with factual information, textbooks provide ideas for hands-on activities, demonstrations, and experiments. Science processes and content are taught through inquiry and discovery. The texts are also usually accompanied by teaching and learning aids, including activity sheets, additional pictures and illustrations, and transparency sets to accompany certain lessons. Kits of materials, which can usually be purchased separately, may save hours of gathering materials for hands-on activities. Another feature is the teacher edition, which provides organizational suggestions, background information for the teacher, evaluation techniques, and still more ideas for student activities.

Textbooks usually include a scope and sequence, to make it easy to see at a glance the scope of topics presented in the books and the sequence in which they are presented. If you prefer a different sequence, you do not need to feel bound by the sequence suggested by the publisher. Similarly, the scope of concepts and topics can be reduced by selecting only certain units, or certain parts of a particular unit; or the scope can be expanded by supplementing the text with other resources. Some would say that if a science textbook cannot be found that meets the requirements of the school, the school must modify its program to fit the text. More practically, however, schools and teachers can modify textbooks to meet their needs, recognizing that they are still in control of which parts of the book they use, and in what sequence they use those parts. Using a textbook does not require complete conformity to its contents. This is not an all-or-nothing proposition. The textbook is not the science program, but only one element of the program; thus it should be used to the extent that it benefits the program.

One reason behind the objections to textbooks is that they are frequently used as reading books, to the exclusion of other uses. Reading is, in fact, an important learning process; that students learn to read, understand what they read, and be able to discuss the material intelligently is crucial. The textbook can provide another avenue for teaching students the language skills of reading, comprehending, and discussing. It is the *overuse* of that application that has given the textbook a bad name in science. The teacher who adds lots of hands-on activities, trade books, and other supplementary material, should never be faulted for using a textbook. It is generally not the *use* of textbooks, but their *misuse,* which raises concern. The decision to use a textbook or not should be based on the value of the book's content, not on whether or not it is called a textbook.

Negative Aspects of the Textbook

On the negative side of the ledger, readability is often a problem with textbooks; the reading level of the books is often too high for many students in the class. Children whose reading skills are severely limited are especially penalized when they receive assignments that require them to acquire information by independent reading of the text. The problem can be reduced in several ways, including the following.

1. *The teacher can read the material aloud to slow readers. If appropriate for the particular needs and ability level, the student may be required to follow along in another copy of the book.*
2. *It may be advantageous to pair the slow reader with a strong reader and let the strong reader read aloud.*
3. *The teacher can read the material into a tape recorder, then let the student read along with the tape. Headsets can be provided at the listening station, so the use of the tape recorder by one or more students does not disturb the rest of the class.*
4. *The teacher may choose to give even slow readers (within reason, of course) opportunities to read specified selections to partners, to small groups, or to the entire class, with prior assignment and ample opportunity to prepare.*

Another potential drawback of textbooks is that, despite good intentions, some of them inhibit discovery. Instead of suggesting an activity with which students can explore and discover, they explain the outcome so students know what to expect. In such cases, students *verify* that the textbook was right, as they do the activity, but they are deprived of the opportunity to *discover* the outcome. With at least a large proportion of the activities they do, students need to discover outcomes. When they are told what to expect to happen, they are more inclined to be satisfied when the expected event occurs. If the expected outcome is not revealed before they perform the activity, students are more likely to try varying the procedure or to try the activity more than once and compare results. (See also the discussion of Guided Discovery in chapter 3.)

Worse yet, if the expected outcome is explained beforehand, and the activity does not work out the way it was "supposed to," children might feel that they failed. Students need to be taught that these activities never "fail." Science activities *always* work out the way they are supposed to. The materials that are involved in science activities are bound by laws of nature, which they obey *every single time*. They have no choice. However, sometimes conditions may vary: The investigator might have inadvertently changed something, or a variable might have been altered by a change in temperature, humidity, or some other factor that is difficult or impossible to control.

If students keep their minds open and are given a variety of experiences, opportunities to explore and discover, and encouragement to compare results, with multiple attempts if necessary, they will learn the real meaning of science and the satisfaction of having some control in the learning process. If students are allowed to repeat procedures, manipulate variables, and compare results, activities with unexpected outcomes can turn out to be some of the most valuable learning experiences.

Still another drawback of the textbook is that it eventually becomes outdated; however, that is true of virtually all printed material. It is important to replace textbooks every few years—especially in science because new information is being acquired so rapidly. You might want to keep a copy (or several) of each old text just to add to an existing collection of references. Much of the information and many of the activities remain valid and useful.

One way to use old textbooks is to remove selected sections and make individual science booklets by binding the pages of a section between two sheets of oaktag or cover stock. These booklets can be given to the students as supplementary text material for the study of certain topics, or they can simply be added to the library of materials freely accessible to all students. In addition, old texts can be compared with the new ones to illustrate how information changes over the years.

Using the Textbook

To preserve the process of discovery, involve your students first in hands-on activities. As a part of your preparation you might want to first read sections from the textbook and other available resources that are pertinent to the topic at hand, then prepare hands-on activities related to the topic or skill you are trying to develop. Following the hands-on activities, students should discuss the results, share experiences and observations, and compare outcomes with others who have done similar activities. This is a good time for students to read materials that you think are appropriate and helpful, some of which might be from textbooks. The reading will often generate more comparisons, more discussion, and perhaps repetition of the related hands-on activities for still further observation, comparison, and discussion. This cycle of doing, observing, discussing, reading, and comparing ideas and perceptions can expand to still more related hands-on activities and to additional research in encyclopedias, trade books, textbooks, and other resources.

Selecting Textbooks

Several good elementary science textbook series are currently on the market. They all differ, however, and the decision of which to choose can be difficult to make. Each series emphasizes different topics, arranges topics in a different order, includes them at different grade levels, and presents the topics in its own style and in varying degrees of detail. Each series is also unique in the information provided in the teacher edition. Numbers and quality of photographs and illustrations vary. Treatment of science processes differs. Other variables to consider include the size and attractiveness of the book, durability of the binding, and accessibility of material through index, table of contents, and glossary. Teachers should look for textbooks that encourage students to explore and discover, not always revealing the outcome of experiments and activities in the student edition. They should make sure that the teacher edition provides adequate instructions for teachers. The series should also provide hands-on activities that use simple, easily acquired materials.

Some textbook publishers have started offering their student books in booklet form. With this format, the student works with smaller manuals and doesn't need to keep the same book for an entire school year. Some of these are also in paper covers, which has a disadvantage in terms of durability, but the advantages of reduced cost and the fact that many young people prefer to use paperback books.

McLeod (1979) suggested an easy and practical approach to textbook selection as follows:

> *A good approach is to focus on two or three* most *important criteria. Let these criteria make your initial eliminations. Most likely you can quickly reduce the contending selections to three or four. Then decide again which two or three of the remaining (criteria) are most important. In this way, the committee will not be overwhelmed by too many criteria at a time.*

In selecting textbooks, the question of whether to use one text or multiple texts must also be considered. Probably the great majority of elementary science textbook orders are for classroom sets of one series. If funding policies allow, you might consider purchasing fewer copies of one text, then using remaining funds for one, two, or several copies of other series, to serve as additional classroom references. A multiple-text approach allows you to draw on the strengths of each, according to its contributions in meeting program objectives. Readability problems can also be reduced by providing texts designed for different grade levels.

SCIENCE TRADE BOOKS

Trade books play an important role in the elementary science program. Textbooks and trade books complement each other: Textbooks provide reference information over a broad spectrum of topics, while trade books usually focus on specific information on one narrow topic. For example, an elementary science textbook might have only one chapter on the broad topic of animals, while an entire trade book could be devoted to a specialized area such as birds, migratory waterfowl—or even just the topic of feathers, featuring illustrations, photographs, and vivid, colorful descriptions to capture the interest and imagination of the reader. A textbook must deal with many broad topics; it doesn't have the luxury of limitless space for a specialized topic. But use of trade books alone to cover all areas of science study might be impractical because of the large number of books that would be required, depending on the number of topics considered appropriate for your students. Trade books are very valuable for in-depth study of specific topics of interest, and a broad variety of them should be available for classroom use.

NSTA offers valuable assistance to the elementary teacher in evaluating recently published science trade books and identifying some that are especially well written. Each year, the March issue of *Science and Children* contains a feature article titled "Outstanding Science Trade Books for Children," which spotlights several excellent books published during the previous calendar year.

RECENT SUPPLEMENTARY CURRICULUM PROJECTS

In addition to the many textbooks and trade books on the market, a growing number of excellent supplementary projects are available to assist with the elementary science program, whether or not it is textbook-based. The following are representative of some of the better-known projects.

Project Wild

Project Wild is an interdisciplinary program focusing on wildlife, designed to provide environmental and conservation education for the schools. Its target audience is teachers, kindergarten through high school. However, the materials are used by parents, scouters, and other groups, both public and private. Project Wild offers books of activities for large or small groups of all ages (see Figure 7-1). These activities spotlight a variety of land animals and aquatic animals. They are designed to enhance awareness and appreciation of wildlife, and in doing so they represent a diversity of values and ecological principles. They introduce current issues and trends, considering a variety of responsible human actions and their potential consequences.

Figure 7-1

The Project Wild book offers wildlife-oriented activities for groups of all ages.

Project Wild workshops are conducted nationwide. The activity books are provided for those who attend a workshop and become trained in their use, and these materials are not available in any other way. Classroom teachers, parents, scouters, and all other interested groups are invited to participate in the workshops. Workshop participants spend several hours *doing* simulations and other activities that are in the books to assure that they are prepared to use the activities with children.

This project is sponsored by state wildlife agencies, state departments of education, and various other agencies. Its primary sponsors are the Western Association of Fish and Wildlife Agencies (WAFWA) and the Western Regional Environmental Education Council (WREEC). Information can be obtained by contacting Project Wild, Salina Star Route, Boulder, CO 80302.

Project Learning Tree

Similar in nature and purpose to Project Wild, Project Learning Tree (PLT) focuses on plant life. Activities provide opportunities for participants to explore the effects of natural resources on people, and the effects of people on the resources, historically and at present (see Figure 7-2). Materials provided by PLT represent a balance between the consumer perspectives of industries that rely on the products of the forest, and the views of environmentalists who seek to protect natural areas. This project represents the philosophy, expertise, and hard work of many people from widely diverse backgrounds, including classroom teachers, resource management personnel, foresters, consultants from state departments of education, environmentalists, college professors, and representatives of the wood products industry. Primary sponsors of PLT include the American Forest Institute and the Western Regional Environmental Education Council (WREEC).

As with Project Wild, materials providing numerous group activities are available to those who attend a training workshop. Such sessions are held nationwide. Information can be obtained by contacting the American Forest Institute, Inc., 1619 Massachusetts Ave., NW, Washington, D.C. 20036.

NatureScope

Ranger Rick's NatureScope is a series of paperbound books that provide a wealth of information and ideas for teachers (see Figure 7-3), including lesson plans, activity pages, transparency originals, and much more. Topics include mammals, birds, dinosaurs, astronomy, weather, trees, oceans, and so on. This program is dedicated to helping children appreciate the natural world, while developing the skills that they need to make responsible

Figure 7-2

Activities in the Project Learning Tree focus on plant life and natural resources.

Figure 7-3

Ranger Rick's NatureScope *books are dedicated to helping children appreciate the natural world.*

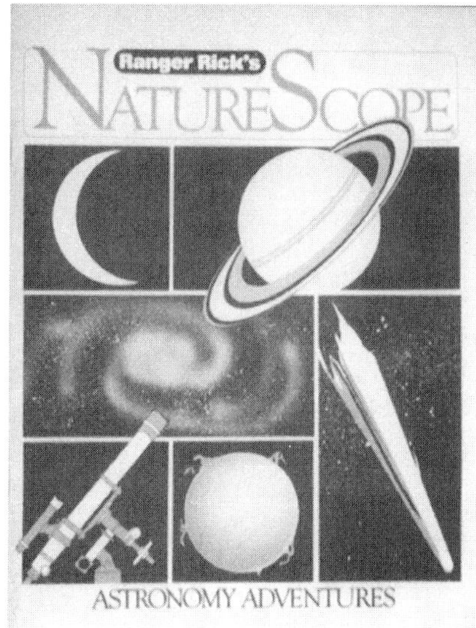

Figure 7-4

GEMS teacher guides use guided discovery and emphasize direct participation.

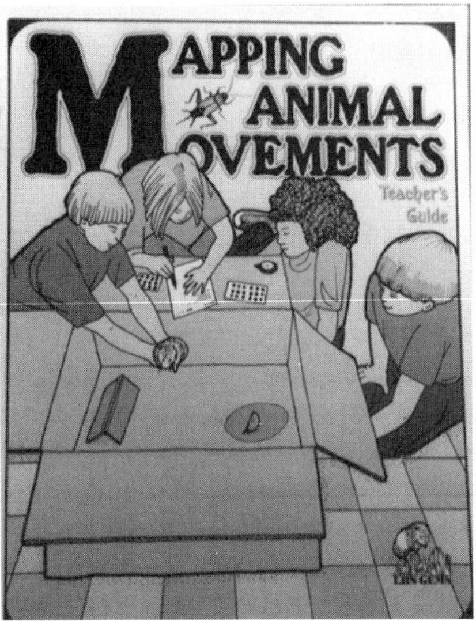

Figure 7-5

The AIMS materials integrate math and science with hands-on learning activities.

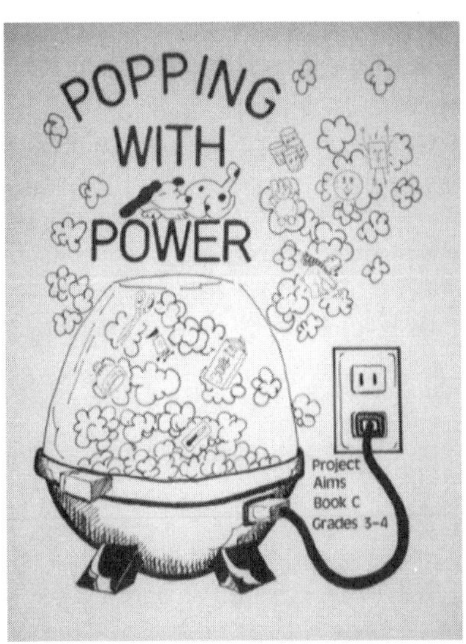

decisions about the environment. *NatureScope* is published by the National Wildlife Federation, 1412 Sixteenth St., NW, Washington D.C. 20036-2266.

Great Explorations in Math and Science (GEMS)

GEMS produces a series of teacher guides designed to bring effective science and math activities into classrooms, activities that will captivate young imaginations, while teaching concepts and processes of science. These materials use a guided discovery approach, emphasizing direct participation by students, cooperative learning, and development of inquiry skills needed in everyday life. Designed for a broad range of grade levels, they include such titles as *Animal Defenses, Mapping Animal Movements, Liquid Explorations, Crime Lab Chemistry, Paper Towel Testing, Acid Rain, Global Warming and the Greenhouse Effect, The "Magic" of Electricity,* and many more (see Figure 7-4).

GEMS materials are developed at the Lawrence Hall of Science and tested in hundreds of classrooms nationwide. Information can be obtained from LHS GEMS, Lawrence Hall of Science, University of California, Berkeley, CA 94720.

Activities That Integrate Math and Science (AIMS)

Originally funded by the National Science Foundation, this project was initially developed at Fresno Pacific College. Currently, development and dissemination is under the auspices of the nonprofit AIMS Education Foundation.

Some of the basic assumptions of this program are that math and science are integrated in the real world, so they should also be integrated in the classroom, that math skills and science processes should be interwoven in hands-on learning activities, and that students should be active participants in the learning process, not just observers.

A series of materials are available for grades K–8 (see Figure 7-5). Information about publications and staff development programs can be obtained from AIMS Education Foundation, P.O. Box 8120, Fresno, CA 93747.

Full Option Science System Project (FOSS)

FOSS was funded by the National Science Foundation, developed at the Lawrence Hall of Science, and is marketed by Encyclopaedia Britannica Educational Corporation. The program is organized into twenty-seven modules for grades K–6, each addressing one scientific topic in depth. Each module is recommended for use at one or two grade levels, based on the model for cognitive development that guided the development of the program (see Figure 7-6). Each module includes a kit of hands-on materials that students use as they engage in the learning activities. Materials available also include a comprehensive teacher guide, student sheets, assessment materials, and a teacher preparation video. The FOSS program places equal emphasis on science content and science processes, and provides assistance for incorporating its materials into existing curricula.

Information can be acquired from Encyclopaedia Britannica Educational Corp., 310 S. Michigan Ave., Chicago, IL 60604.

CEPUP in the Schools

CEPUP in the Schools is a project of the Chemical Education for Public Understanding Program (CEPUP) at the Lawrence Hall of Science. Developed through a grant from the National Science Foundation and by contributions from industry and private foundations, materials are designed for students from middle school through high school (see Figure 7-7). This program highlights chemicals, particularly as they are used in the context of societal

Figure 7-6

Each FOSS module addresses one scientific subject in depth.

FOSS K-6 PROGRAM

GRADE LEVEL	Life Science	Physical Science	Earth Science	Scientific Reasoning and Technology	THINKING PROCESSES (Sequential and Inclusive)
Grades 5 and 6	Food and Nutrition	Levers & Pulleys	Solar Energy	Models & Designs	**Relating** Organizing Comparing Communicating Observing
	Environments	Mixtures & Solutions	Landforms	Variables	
Grades 3 and 4	Human Body	Magnetism & Electricity	Water	Ideas and Inventions	**Advanced Organizing** Comparing Communicating Observing
	Structures of Life	Physics of Sound	Earth Materials	Measurement	

GRADE LEVEL	Life Science	Physical Science	Earth Science	THINKING PROCESSES
Grades 1 and 2	New Plants	Solids and Liquids	Air and Weather	**Beginning Organizing** Comparing Communicating Observing
	Insects	Balance and Motion	Pebbles, Sand, and Silt	

GRADE LEVEL	Life Science		Physical Science			THINKING PROCESSES
Kindergarten	Trees	Animals	Wood	Paper	Fabric	**Comparing** Communicating Observing

LHS 3/93

Figure 7-7

CEPUP materials are designed for students from middle school through high school.

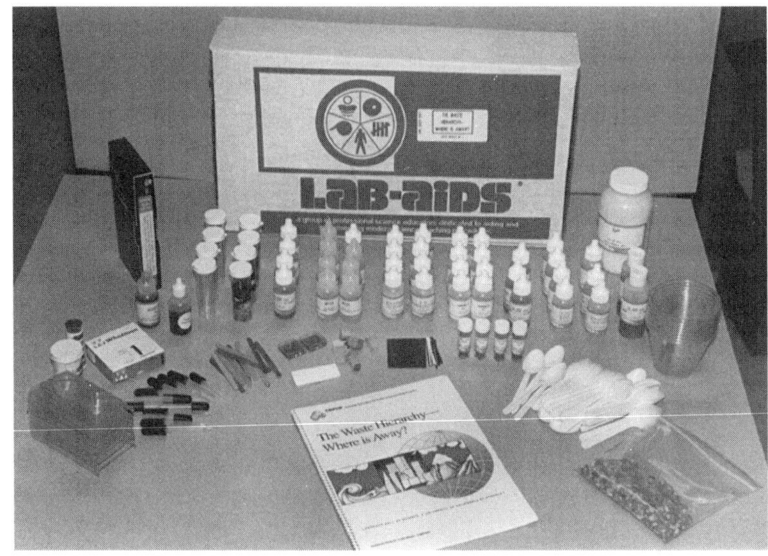

issues. Students collect and process scientific data, from which they reason and make practical decisions. Through these experiences they begin to appreciate both the power and the limitations of science.

CEPUP in the Schools seeks to enhance the role of science teachers as educational leaders and to improve the quality of science education in America. This project also promotes the use of scientific principles, processes, and evidence in public decision making. Information can be obtained from CEPUP, Lawrence Hall of Science, University of California, Berkeley, CA 94720.

Chemicals, Health, Environment, and Me (CHEM)

Like CEPUP in the Schools, CHEM is a project of the Chemical Education for Public Understanding Program at the Lawrence Hall of Science. This project involves a series of ten units designed for grades five and six (see Figure 7-8). With emphasis on science processes and learner involvement, the units provide lab experiences using household and classroom supplies that are easy to obtain. Students learn about the nature of chemicals, observing and studying how they interact with people and the environment. Students also learn that studying science and math can be productive and relevant in their lives.

Information can be obtained from CHEM/CEPUP, Lawrence Hall of Science, University of California, Berkeley, CA 94720.

IMPACTS OF TECHNOLOGY

Along with virtually all other phases of education, the elementary science classroom is feeling the impact of technology. Students are learning information and acquiring skills through the use of computers coupled with science-oriented software. Interactive video adds meaning to science lessons, as machines respond to instructional needs, providing still pictures or video clips, with either preprogrammed sequences or on-the-spot commands, enhancing the learning experience. Computers enable elementary students to link with other classrooms nationwide, and work together on projects that involve meaningful, cooperative research. For example, students witness live oceanic exploration, and have the

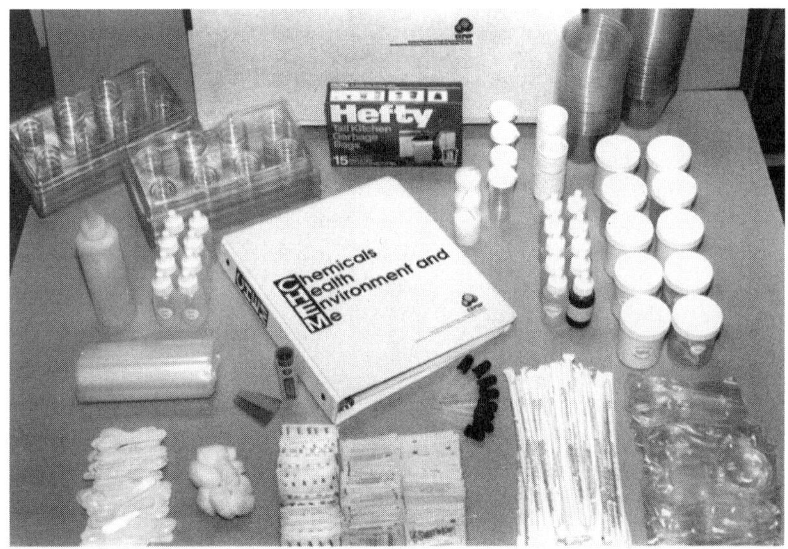

Figure 7-8

Fifth and sixth graders use CHEM materials to see how chemicals interact with people and the environment.

opportunity to ask questions of the divers and receive immediate responses as the exploration continues.

Computers

Today's computers have power, speed, memory, and interactive capability far beyond what most people would have imagined just a few short years ago. With their quickness and accuracy in gathering and analyzing data, computers are valuable in conducting laboratory experiments. Temperature, light, sound, and motion probes can be integrated into the gathering of data. Using a temperature probe connected to a computer, for example, students could collect outdoor temperatures periodically over several twenty-four-hour periods, then display their data using computerized graphics, and finally draw inferences and form hypotheses regarding temperature trends (see Figure 7-9). In a similar experiment, they might

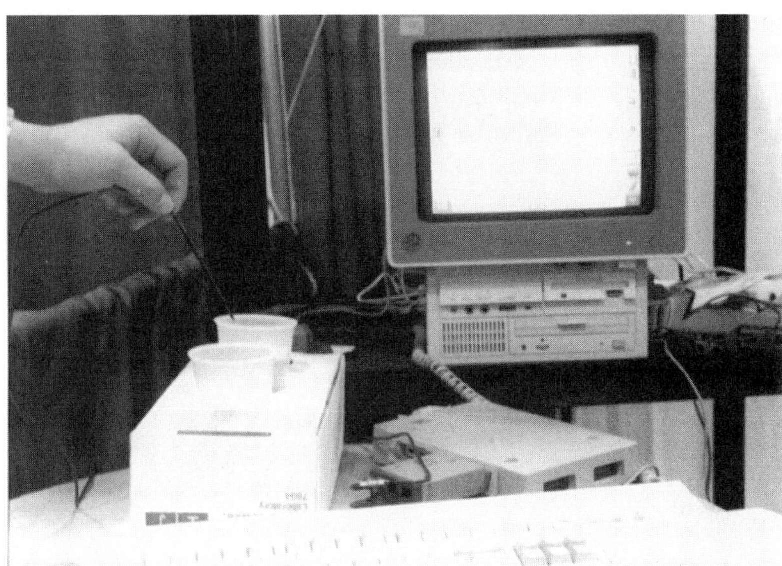

Figure 7-9

Using a temperature probe connected to a computer, students can use computer graphics to show temperature data.

test the effect of a ceiling fan by graphing temperatures of various parts of a room with and without the fan running. For inquiry with a sound probe, students could test the sound-insulating effects of various materials lining boxes, inserting the probe into boxes with several different liners and exposing the boxes to a given external sound. Many similar investigations could be made, giving students experience with the computer and at the same time building problem-solving skills.

Simulations

Experiences that are inconvenient, costly, dangerous, or otherwise impractical or even impossible can often be simulated to provide valuable learning experiences.

One popular computerized simulation, called *Fossil Hunter* (MECC) (see Figure 7-10), places students in the roles of scientists who set out on a fossil hunt for a museum. The goal is for the student to become proficient at locating fossils, to understand the relationship between certain geological periods and the types of fossils typically found in certain formations. Students apply their new-found skills to a set of problems using the tools provided. Clearly, school resources of time and money cannot provide thousands of elementary students with actual experiences in hunting for fossils in the various geological formations of the earth. The computer provides a meaningful educational experience with several advantages: It is possible to do, it is not very costly or time-consuming, everyone can do it, and the experience can be repeated over and over until the concepts are understood. And at the same time they are "discovering" fossils, students are developing the skills of observing, inferring, classifying, and others.

Operation Frog (Scholastic) (see Figure 7-11) provides students with the experience of dissecting a frog—without any mess or smell of formaldehyde! Again, the real thing may be a better learning experience, but the simulation has its advantages—especially for the frog. Students can have the experience over and over as they learn about the internal parts of the animal, without the cost of lab equipment. If students are to have the actual experience, they can practice beforehand with the computer simulation and increase their level of readiness for learning from the real dissecting

Figure 7-10

The* Fossil Hunter *program puts elementary school students in the role of paleontologists.

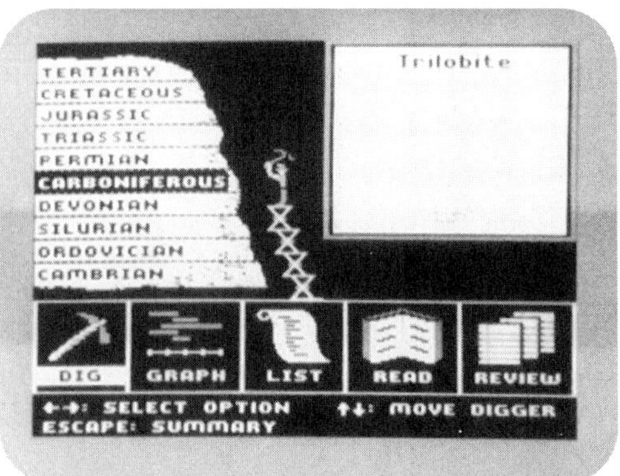

Figure 7-11

Operation Frog *allows students to dissect a frog without harming a live animal.*

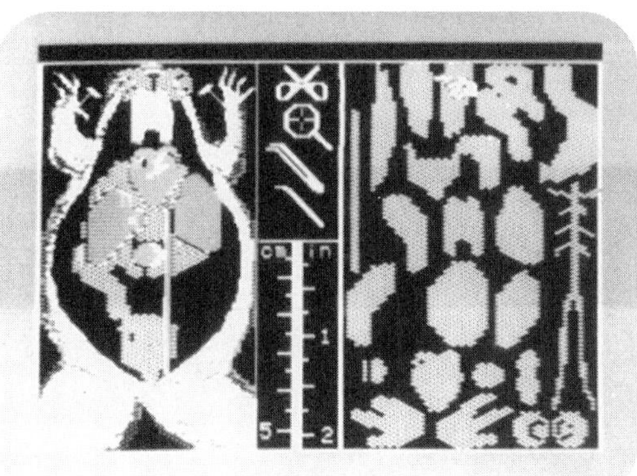

process, reducing significantly the number of animals necessary for the learning experience.

In the life sciences, simulations are expected to become more popular with experiments that otherwise involve live animals. The effects of various foods and chemicals on rats can be simulated by the computer, as can other experiments involving treatments of various animals; thus, student learning occurs without causing animals to suffer.

Interactive Video

The videodisc is very similar in appearance to a phonograph record (see Figure 7-12). Information is recorded in circular tracks of microscopic pits. Each side of the disc has up to 54,000 recorded tracks, with the information for one frame, or picture, recorded on each track. The microscopic pits are read by a laser beam, and the information is translated in the form of a picture on a TV screen or video monitor. The laser reads thirty frames per second, providing up to thirty minutes of movie on each side of a disc.

Figure 7-12

Videodisc technology opens up many opportunities in the science classroom.

Two sound tracks are used, which allows for stereophonic sound *or* for two separate languages. The user can select either sound track or both, allowing for a choice of languages for the bilingual student. In some applications, separate pictures are recorded on the disc as though they were slides, instead of movies, allowing for a collection of up to 54,000 slides on one side of the disc.

A code is recorded on each track, which enables the videodisc player to access any one of the 54,000 tracks, or frames. The user can select a given frame by entering the number of that frame into the control unit or by scanning a bar code with a light pen (see Figure 7-13). That frame can then be displayed as a still picture or as the beginning frame of a sequence showing movement, either in slow motion or at normal speed. If a still picture is called for, the laser beam reads the same track over and over again. Since the information is read by a light beam, nothing comes in contact with the disc physically; thus the still frame can be displayed as long as desired without causing any wear at all to the disc.

Figure 7-13

Using a remote-control unit with number pad and light pen, students can choose to see up to 54,000 graphics.

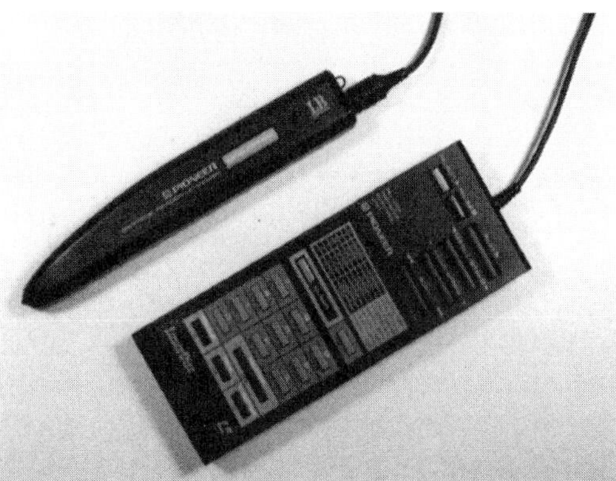

A very powerful instructional system can be created by attaching a videodisc player to a computer.

> *The computer can control the operation of the player and videodisc by sending commands that instruct the player to display a specific still frame, play a sequence of frames in normal or slow motion, or play a particular audio track with or without the corresponding video display. . . . The computer can be used to present questions to test the student's knowledge of concepts just presented and give immediate feedback. Depending on the student's response, the computer can set in motion the appropriate next sequence. . . . It is also possible to overlay computer-generated text and graphics on the videodisc images. For example, a lesson on anatomy may display a picture of a skeleton from a videodisc overlaid with arrows and labels generated by the computer. (Merrill,* et al., *1992)*

Although videodisc technology has been available for a number of years, schools have been slow in implementing it. Educators and software companies are developing quality software for elementary science and much more is expected in the very near future. *Windows on Science* (Optical Data Corporation, Warren, New Jersey), *Science Horizons* (Silver Burdett & Ginn), Videodiscovery (Videodiscovery, Inc., Seattle, Wash.), and *Mist* (Evergreen Laser Disc, Inc., St. Paul, Minn.) are examples of excellent materials that would be an asset in elementary science programs.

National Geographic Kids Network

Resulting from a cooperative effort of the National Geographic Society and Technical Education Research Centers (TERC), the Kids Network has been developed to involve students nationwide in cooperative scientific research. Students gather data and enter it into the computer, to be shared with other classrooms across the nation. In one of the units, "Acid Rain," students learn how to measure the acidity of rain water and other liquids. They build, test, and use their own collecting devices. Students study the causes and effects of acid rain and learn how wind patterns and factory emissions affect the problem. Through the network, their findings can be made available to students who might observe comparable conditions in other localities. Students learn to compare, contrast, and benefit from cooperative research.

With the Kids Network, students learn about computers, and they experience what it is like to be scientists gathering, sharing, and analyzing meaningful data. Information can be obtained from the National Geographic Society, Educational Services, Department 5389, Washington, D.C. 20036.

The JASON Project

The JASON Project was conceived and directed by Robert D. Ballard, a senior scientist at Woods Hole Oceanographic Institution. Dr. Ballard wished to spark new interest in science in the minds of the youth of this and other nations by involving them as observers of live explorations. Instead of just offering schools a video of completed explorations, Ballard wanted to give young people the opportunity to witness live expeditions and to interact, asking questions and making comments as the adventures progress, experiencing personally the excitement of exploration. With assistance from the National Geographic Society and other funding sources, the explorer's dream became a reality in May 1989, using "tele-present" technology and live satellite transmissions. For fourteen days, thousands of students in the United States and Canada watched the operations of Dr. Ballard and his crew as they explored geological and archaeological sites in the Mediterranean. This proved to be just the first of many such experiences.

The JASON Project will continue to offer young people the excitement of exploration through live broadcasts of investigations at museums and other educational locations, and of expeditions to underwater volcanoes, shipwrecks, pyramids, little-known islands, and other points of interest. For more information, contact the JASON Project, Woods Hole Oceanographic Institution, Woods Hole, MA 02543.

To enhance the educational value of the JASON experience, the NSTA, with funding from the National Science Foundation, developed a series of curriculum packages for grades 4–12. These materials can be acquired from NSTA Publications Dept., 1840 Wilson Blvd., Arlington, VA 22201-3000.

SCIENCE SUPPLIES

Most elementary schools that try to offer effective science programs struggle with the problem of budget for supplies. A great deal can be done in science at the elementary level with limited supplies, but some supplies are necessary. Here are some ideas for putting a little creative initiative to work.

The Science Resource Audit

It is not uncommon for teachers to find many science resources in a school where they had originally thought no science materials were available. Conducting a school "science resource audit" can be very productive. Each teacher explores his or her own classroom and makes a list of science books, hand lenses, microscopes, litmus paper, and all other science supplies. School supply rooms, supply closets, and media centers should also be included in the search. A master list of all materials should be prepared, and decisions can be made on the best places for these materials to be stored. Every teacher should get a copy of the list of materials and the location of each item; thus each teacher has access to all science materials in the building.

This exercise is usually very productive in revealing the existence and location of microscopes, filmstrips, magnets, and many other science materials that have been out of circulation for so long that they have been forgotten. Teachers sometimes mistakenly assume that the only science materials in the school are the two or three items in their own classroom—certainly inadequate to carry on an effective science program.

Acquiring Additional Supplies

The next step is to identify the most needed items that do not appear on the collective list and begin making plans to acquire them. Even a few dollars at a time from school funds can eventually make quite a difference. Parent-teacher organizations are frequently willing to help, as are local civic clubs, which sometimes solicit worthy projects. Students themselves can raise funds for science materials by selling popcorn, cookies, brownies, and so on. (Caution: Be sure to check on school and district policies regarding fund-raising before launching into such activities.)

Some teachers have been successful in acquiring science materials by preparing lists of needed items and sending the lists home with students, along with a note stating that if the family could help by providing one or more of the items on the list, it would be appreciated and would make a meaningful contribution to the science program of the class (or school). Parents are often more than willing to send a package of paper cups, balloons, aluminum foil, or any one of a number of other items that are needed for science activities; they only have to know what the needs are. Of course, this must be completely voluntary; students and parents should feel no pressure to contribute.

Free and Inexpensive Materials

Many industries and government agencies offer materials that are useful in elementary science, at little or no cost to schools. The references below provide comprehensive listings of such sources, updated annually. The listings themselves are not free, but they would be a valuable investment for purchase on a school or district level.

- *Educators Guide to Free Science Materials*
- *Educators Guide to Free Audio and Video Materials*
- *Educators Guide to Free Films*
- *Educators Guide to Free Filmstrips and Slides*

These are available from Educators Progress Service, Inc., 214 Center St., Randolph, WI 53956.

CURRICULUM GUIDES

District curriculum guides are provided for teachers in most of the larger school districts, and even many smaller districts. These are broadly varied in content, format, and in the extent to which they are intended to influence classroom instruction. Some district guides provide only very general guidelines and lists of suggested resources, in hopes of assisting the teacher and providing some degree of consistency in what is taught throughout the district at any particular grade level. Other districts prepare separate, detailed curriculum guides for each curricular area of each grade level. In addition to providing guidelines and suggested materials, some of these manuals include much of the content to be used for instruction, in an effort to assure quality and consistency of instruction throughout the school district. In these cases, the textbook and other resources become a supplement to the curriculum guide.

Most curriculum guides provided by school districts are somewhere between these extremes. They provide sufficient guidelines to offer some degree of consistency. They allow the teacher considerable freedom of choice, within certain limits, regarding specific content that is to be taught and instructional materials that are to be used, and they offer assistance in selecting appropriate activities, materials, and resources, again within certain limits established by district policy and dictated by the budget.

Most states also provide curriculum guides. These, too, vary in format and content. Some state guides establish only general guidelines and limits within which school districts are to operate, while others provide a certain amount of direction regarding instructional content at the classroom level. The degree to which states attempt to assure instructional quality and consistency varies greatly, just as it does at the district level.

IN CLOSING

This chapter has presented a few of the projects and programs that have been developed to enhance the teaching and learning of science in the elementary school. The curriculum projects and technological applications described represent current and earlier efforts to support classroom teachers in raising the level of science interest and science literacy in the schools and in society.

Programs stressing active learner inquiry

have been unpopular with many politicians and, unfortunately, some educators. As enrollment in secondary science courses declined throughout the 1970s, accusing fingers were pointed toward programs such as ESS, SCIS, and SAPA, claiming that emphasis on hands-on activities resulted in decreased learning efficiency. Shymansky (1989) and Shymansky, Kyle, and Alport (1982) analyzed many studies that were performed over a period of years on ESS, SCIS, and SAPA. They found the overall results of these programs to be positive, with no connection between these programs and the declining interest in secondary science. In fact, overall results favored the activity-based programs in nearly all cases. Attitude toward science, acquisition of process skills, and overall science achievement were actually found to be higher among students who had participated in an activity-based program. Although individual studies did not agree in all areas, these researchers found that in the overall results of the meta-analysis (study of studies), the programs encouraging active learner involvement were superior to those depending on the traditional approach of reading and discussing science concepts without active participation.

Finally, the contribution science textbooks can offer in supporting an activity-based science program should not be overlooked. Teachers who use textbooks must use them effectively, however, utilizing many hands-on activities. In addition, they should supplement the text with many activities from other sources and with science trade books, references, and other supplementary materials. The result will be richly rewarding for teachers and students, as science adds life and vitality to each school day.

LIST OF RESOURCES

Cain, Sandra E., and Jack M. Evans, *Sciencing: An Involvement Approach to Elementary Science Methods*, 3rd ed. (Columbus, OH: Merrill Publishing Co., 1990).

Carin, Arthur A., and Robert B. Sund, *Teaching Science Through Discovery*, 6th ed. (Columbus, OH: Merrill Publishing Co., 1989).

Fossil Hunter (computer program), (St. Paul, MN: Minnesota Educational Computing Consortium [MECC]).

Gega, Peter C., "Convert Your Text Series into a District Science Program," *Science and Children* 20, no. 3 (November-December 1982): 28–30.

McLeod, Richard J., "Selecting a Textbook for Good Science Teaching," *Science and Children* 17, no. 2 (October 1979): 14–15.

Merrill, Paul F., *et al.*, *Computers in Education*, 2nd ed. (Boston, MA.: Allyn & Bacon, 1992), 50.

Operation Frog (computer program) (New York: Scholastic).

Rutherford, F. James, "The Character of Elementary School Science," *Science and Children* 24, no. 4 (January 1987): 8–11.

Shymansky, James A., "What Research Says About ESS, SCIS, and SAPA," *Science and Children* 26, no. 7 (April 1989): 33–34.

Shymansky, James A., William C. Kyle, Jr., and Jennifer M. Alport, "How Effective Were the Hands-on Science Programs of Yesterday?" *Science and Children* 20, no. 3 (November-December 1982): 14–15.

CHAPTER

PLANNING, ASSESSING, AND INTEGRATING

CHAPTER OUTLINE:

- INTRODUCTION
- PLANNING
  - Organizing Materials
  - Organizing Students for Instruction
  - Lesson Planning
    - The learning cycle
    - A broader view
  - Unit Plan
    - Resource unit
    - Teaching unit
- ASSESSING STUDENT PROGRESS
  - Program Assessments
  - Classroom Assessments
    - Pencil-paper tests
    - Performance tests
    - Portfolios
- INTEGRATING
  - Integrating Science with Language Arts
    - Reading
    - Writing
  - Integrating Science with Music
  - Integrating Science with Mathematics
    - Life science
    - Earth science
    - Physical science
  - Integrating Science with Art
    - Life science
    - Earth science
    - Physical science
  - Integrating Science with Social Studies
    - Life science
    - Earth science
    - Physical science
  - Caution
- IN CLOSING
- LIST OF RESOURCES

I WONDER . . .

How important are lesson plans? Do teachers really use them?

What is the Learning Cycle?

What is one way that unit plans can be prepared? What information should they include?

What are some meaningful ways to assess science skills?

How can science be integrated with other areas of the curriculum?

How far should we carry the effort to integrate the curriculum?

INTRODUCTION

Instruction that occurs without adequate planning and assessment is usually both incomplete and diminished in its effectiveness. Without sufficient planning, objectives are unclear and classroom events often lack direction, purpose, and coordination. When classroom teaching is not accompanied by effective assessment, the extent to which objectives are achieved is not known. Assessment measures the effectiveness of past classroom events and offers direction in the planning of future events. These two elements of instruction—planning and assessment—are inseparable. As a final topic of this chapter, integrating means taking advantage of opportunities to apply the skills from all curricular areas, not just the subject of the moment.

PLANNING

Someone said, "To fail to prepare is to prepare to fail." This is certainly true of teaching; success literally hangs in the balance of planning. The successful teacher of elementary science has procedures and information well in mind, and has materials prepared and ready to use when needed. The teacher who is well prepared is able to be alert to on-the-spot needs as they arise. The teacher whose mind is constantly tied up with decisions about what to do next, and what to do if something doesn't work as expected, need not wonder why instructional activities lose their effectiveness and students are difficult to manage.

Organizing Materials

General order in the classroom benefits when materials are properly organized. One of the most obvious needs, in terms of organizing materials, is storage. In classrooms that have commercial science kits, this problem is minimized because the items are probably already conveniently stored in appropriate compartments and indexed for ease in locating the items. Another obvious advantage to commercial kits is that many of the materials needed for science activities are provided, saving the teacher the trouble of acquiring them from outside sources. The disadvantages of commercial kits include higher cost and having many materials in the kit which any given teacher will probably never use, resulting in waste of materials, money, and storage space. If commercial kits are available, the teacher should become thoroughly familiar with them in order to know what is there and maximize the use and benefit of the materials.

Teachers who do not have materials supplied in the form of commercial kits should consider preparing kits for favorite topics and activities. These can be stored in shoe boxes, apple boxes, magazine holders, or any box that is of appropriate size for needed items. Teacher-made kits have these advantages: (1) usually less costly materials; and (2) materials that are stored are those that are actually used—money and space are not used for unneeded materials.

Convenience is enhanced if science equipment and materials are kept in or near the classroom where they are to be used. If several teachers are sharing materials, every effort should be made to maximize convenience. For any items that might be needed by more than one teacher at a time, a check-out and accountability system can be worked out among the teachers involved, and perhaps multiple copies of some items can be obtained if needed. Also, someone must be in charge; one of the teachers in the group should be assigned as science specialist or materials coordinator and be responsible for coordinating the use of materials and equipment. Commercial science kits, and any other kits that are shared, should be inventoried periodically to be certain that expendables and broken or lost supplies are promptly replaced to assure that supplies are available and ready to use when needed. To increase the likelihood that materials will be there when needed, each user notifies the person in charge when such materials are used up, lost, or broken, rather than waiting until the materials are needed again, waiting for the next inventory time, or assuming that the materials coordinator is somehow intuitively aware of the need. Extra supplies of commonly used items, such as soda straws, paper cups, and balloons, should be kept on hand. Even when these procedures are in place, the embarrassment and frustration of missing or altered items can be avoided if each user will check kits prior to use.

Organizing Students for Instruction

One way to organize students for hands-on activities is to train them to work in **cooperative groups,** with assignments something like those suggested below. Within each group, one student is assigned to each role listed. Each person can be identified with his or her role for the day with a sign hanging around the neck, a label in front of the person on the table, or by some other method that is workable and acceptable to those involved. With the assignments described below, the teacher might assign only the leader, then request the leader to assign group members to the other roles. The role of leader could be passed around the group from day to day, or it could simply be assigned to a specific student, whatever works best for the class. These suggestions may be modified to meet the needs of each situation. Keep in mind, however, that students are given responsibilities not only because they are already responsible, but because through the experience they learn to handle responsibility. This might be the greatest benefit that comes from the activity.

1. Leader

- **a.** *Reads all instructions aloud to the group*
- **b.** *Assigns roles for the day*
- **c.** *Answers questions from the group*
- **d.** *If leader doesn't know the answer, he or she alone may ask the teacher*

2. Monitor

- **a.** *Picks up and returns all materials*
- **b.** *The only person who may leave his or her seat without permission during the activity*

3. Inspector

- **a.** *Takes inventory to be sure needed equipment and materials are there both before and after the activity*
- **b.** *Is responsible for the area being clean*

after the activity (everyone helps with cleanup, but this person is responsible to see that it happens)

4. **Secretary**
   a. *Records all data and findings for the group*
   b. *Reports data and findings to class or teacher as required*

Lesson Planning

There is widespread agreement regarding the importance of lesson planning, but there is no consensus of how it should be done or the format that should be followed. Still, certain elements of well-accepted strategy exist. The Learning Cycle provides a form of lesson planning that is effective in elementary science. This technique is briefly described below, then tied in with additional suggested parts of a lesson plan.

The learning cycle

The Learning Cycle is credited to the Science Curriculum Improvement Study (SCIS), one of the curriculum projects that resulted from the increased attention given to science education during the post-*Sputnik* era (see chapter 1). Over the years, the Learning Cycle has had broad acceptance, and research has shown it to be effective (Barman, 1989; Barman and Kotar, 1989; Saunders and Shepardson, 1987). In the Learning Cycle, SCIS suggested a three-phase approach: exploration, invention, and discovery. Others have suggested the second and third phases be renamed concept introduction and concept application (Barman and Kotar, 1989). We chose to use the terms suggested by Barman and Kotar. It is important to note that reading and researching activities are preceded by exploration.

1. **Exploration.** *In the exploration phase, students are free to manipulate materials and discover. Instruction on concepts has not yet been given (though guidance in the discovery process is often needed), so students are free to explore, pursuing questions and ideas. Students record observations and data, working either individually or in small groups. The teacher assumes the role of facilitator—observing, asking questions, and suggesting ideas to try. This is a time of guided discovery, with teacher-to-student interaction as well as student-to-student interaction (see the discussion of Guided Discovery in chapter 3).*
2. **Concept Introduction.** *Under the direction of the teacher, students organize data they have collected and look for patterns that may appear. They share their discoveries with the class and compare observations. An excellent time for the teacher to add information and introduce appropriate vocabulary is after students share their findings. Students might then do further research by reading about the concept from textbooks and other references, and share new information they learn.*
3. **Concept Application.** *Students are now given a new situation or problem to which they apply the information they have learned through discovery and research. This phase usually involves additional hands-on activities that reinforce earlier learning.*

As an example of the Learning Cycle approach, let's consider a situation in which your students explore the interactive behavior of magnets.

1. **Exploration.** *In the exploration phase, students are given two bar magnets (both have poles marked) and a thread. Instruct your students to tie the thread around the center of one magnet and hold the magnet up by the thread, with the magnet balanced horizontally. Next, ask them to bring one*

end of the second bar magnet near the one suspended from the thread, then turn the second bar magnet around and bring the other end near. Students should try this several times, observing carefully and recording their observations.

2. **Concept Introduction.** *Students share their observations with the class and compare their findings. They might report that the behavior pattern of the magnets is consistent. You could introduce the terms* attract *and* repel *at this point, making connections between the terms and what students have observed. Care should be taken to be sure students notice that like poles repel each other and unlike poles attract each other, not just that magnets sometimes attract and sometimes push apart. Students can do further research by reading about the concept from their textbooks, encyclopedia, and available trade books about magnets, then share the information they find. Be sure that in the process of research and discussion the students notice that the magnet suspended from a thread behaves as a compass—that if left alone and away from all magnetic materials, it will line up with the magnetic north and south poles of the earth. The end of the magnet that points north is called the* north pole *(north-seeking pole) and the end that points south is called the* south pole *(south-seeking pole).*
3. **Concept Application.** *Now give your students an unmarked bar magnet and a bar magnet that has the poles marked, and instruct them to use the marked magnet to identify the poles of the unmarked magnet. From what they have learned, students should be able to accomplish this task. The students will probably bring one end of the marked magnet near one end of the unmarked magnet and observe whether the two ends attract or repel each other. A second approach students might take is to suspend the unmarked bar magnet from a thread and identify the poles by letting the magnet line itself up with the magnetic poles of the earth; then test their results with the marked magnet. A third idea the students might try is to find a compass and identify the poles of the unmarked magnet by which end of the compass needle each end of the magnet attracts. (For additional information on the nature and behavior of magnets, see chapter 18.)*

The Learning Cycle model is appropriate for all grade levels, and with proper planning it can be used to teach most science concepts. Textbooks can be used as sources of activities and as material for study and research. Suggestions given on using textbooks in the previous chapter can easily be used with the Learning Cycle approach. Activity books can also be used as sources of activities, and reference materials should extend beyond the textbook to include encyclopedias, trade books, and other appropriate references that are available. The process skills of observation, inference, and communication, are clearly applied in the above sample lesson. These and many other process skills can be developed and reinforced through lessons on various science topics, using this technique.

A broader view

Through a seemingly endless flow of different styles and formats for lesson plans, certain elements of agreement seem to offer some degree of stability. For instance, a lesson plan for science should include a **list of materials and equipment** needed. There is also widespread agreement regarding the impact of an **activity that stimulates student interest** early in the study of a topic. Whether it is called a "grabber," "starter activity," "anticipatory set," or other, something is needed that captures student interest in the lesson. The lesson plan should include **procedural steps,** and those steps should frequently involve **hands-on**

activities and **problem-solving experiences.** The Learning Cycle fits well into the procedural steps of a lesson plan.

The effectiveness of a learning experience is often not known unless it is accompanied by some type of **assessment** to determine whether intended outcomes are achieved. Whether we call it "evaluation," "test," or "assessment," and whether we do it with every lesson or following a series of learning experiences, the degree of success in teaching and learning can usually be measured. Otherwise the extent to which the intended outcome is achieved is not known.

And speaking of intended outcomes, that brings us to a more controversial element of the lesson plan—the **objective.** The objective identifies the intended outcome. A variety of terms are used (learning objective, educational objective, performance objective, and so on), each suggesting a slightly different emphasis, but all identify an intended outcome of the learning experience. Controversies surrounding the use of objectives go beyond the question of whether we call them performance objectives or by some other term, however. Writing meaningful objectives often requires considerable time, and some teachers question whether the benefit justifies the cost of time and energy. Most educators agree that well-written objectives help to clarify the intended outcome of a lesson, especially if the person teaching the lesson writes the objective.

The format and scope of the following lesson plan is intended only to show an example of how the needed information can be organized, and is not intended to limit the creativity and personal touch of the individual. Hopefully these ideas will help you to develop a format that fits your teaching style.

The Learning Cycle can be incorporated into the lesson plan suggested above. The following lesson uses the Learning Cycle approach in the procedural steps. The parts of the Learning Cycle are labeled and underlined to make them clearly identifiable in this example. The topic of magnetism is used in order to apply the Learning Cycle example given above, showing that it can fit into a more standard lesson plan format.

SAMPLE LESSON PLAN: Magnetic Attraction and Repulsion

List of Materials *(for each group):*

- *Two bar magnets with poles marked*
- *One bar magnet with poles unmarked*
- *Thread*
- *Compass*

Objective: *Students will successfully discover the poles of an unmarked magnet.*

Procedure:

1. *Divide students into small groups.*
2. *Give each group two bar magnets (both have poles marked) and a thread.*
3. ***Exploration:*** *Instruct students to tie the thread around the center of one magnet and hold the magnet up by the thread with the magnet balanced horizontally. Next, have them bring one end of the second bar magnet near the one suspended from the thread, then turn the second bar magnet around and bring the other end near. Students should try this several times, observing carefully and recording their observations.*
4. ***Concept Introduction****: Have students share their observations with the class and compare their findings. Help them notice that the behavior pattern of the magnets is always consistent. Introduce the terms* attract *and* repel, *being sure that students are aware that like poles repel each other and unlike poles attract each other.*
5. ***Research****: Have students do further research by reading about the concept from their textbooks, encyclopedia, and available trade*

books about magnets, then share the information they find.

6. *Be sure that in the process of research and discussion, the students notice that the magnet suspended from a thread behaves as a compass—that if left alone and away from all magnetic materials, it will line up with the magnetic north and south poles of the earth. The end of the magnet that points north is called the* north pole *and the end that points south is called the* south pole.
7. ***Concept Application:*** *Give students an unmarked bar magnet and a bar magnet that has the poles marked. Instruct them to use the marked magnet to identify the poles of the unmarked magnet.*

   (The students will probably bring one end of the marked magnet near one end of the unmarked magnet and observe whether the two ends attract or repel each other. A second approach students might take is to suspend the unmarked bar magnet from a thread and identify the poles by letting the magnet line itself up with the magnetic poles of the earth; then compare their results with the marked magnet. A third idea the students might try is to use the compass and identify the poles of the unmarked magnet by which end of the compass needle each end of the magnet attracts.)

Evaluation: *Give students an unmarked magnet and instruct them to identify the north and south poles. Students may decide what method to use, but they should be asked to explain what they do and why.*

Unit Plan

Recognizing that the textbook is only one of the many important resources that should be used in teaching elementary science, the "unit" approach has been popular for many years. Using this approach, a topic of study is selected, then information and activities are gathered from a variety of resources, among which the textbook—or better yet a variety of textbooks—may be included. A unit is typically studied for two to four weeks or more, depending on the grade level, the topic, and the amount of time allowed in the schedule each day for science. The result is often called a "unit plan."

Resource unit

You can design the unit plan as a "Resource Unit," which is a collection of materials, ideas, and activities from which you can then draw as needed for use with any particular grade level or setting. The Resource Unit continually grows as you acquire materials and ideas pertaining to a given topic, and it usually contains more material than would be used with any given group of students.

Teaching unit

Another approach is to design the unit plan as a "Teaching Unit," which is a more specific plan, which you would prepare for a particular grade level, setting, and timeframe, to include materials that are specific to that situation. The Teaching Unit often includes specific lesson plans. The major difference between the Resource Unit and the Teaching Unit is in the degree of specificity—the Resource Unit does not target any particular grade level, time frame, or setting. Otherwise, the same general notions can be applied to the preparation of either a Resource Unit or a Teaching Unit, and the same parts can be used.

We should note also that even though you prepare Teaching Units for use with a particular group of students, it is still wise to collect materials in Resource Unit format. Teaching Units can be generated from Resource Units. If you have a well-developed file of science materials, the need for Resource Units is diminished, as Teaching Units can draw from the materials file.

The following sections are suggested as parts of a Unit Plan.

Conceptual Structure

The Conceptual Structure is an outline of major concepts and supporting concepts that are to be included in the unit. This becomes the framework of the unit. Here is an example of a conceptual structure for a unit on the moon.

Major Concept #1

The physical characteristics of the moon differ from those of the earth or other planets.

Supporting Concepts

A. *The moon is smaller than the earth in size and mass.*

B. *The moon has relatively little gravity and almost no atmosphere.*

C. *The moon's surface has rocks and soil but no water. The terrain includes plains, mountains, and craters.*

Major Concept #2

As the moon orbits the earth it appears in different phases.

Supporting Concepts

A. *The moon rotates counterclockwise on its axis as it orbits the earth counterclockwise. Its period of rotation and its period of revolution are equal, therefore the moon always faces the earth with the same side.*

B. *The moon appears in different phases, as we see varying portions of the moon's lighted surface.*

1. *The new moon has its shadowed side toward Earth and cannot be seen from the earth.*
2. *The first quarter is sometimes called a half moon. This is the first quarter after the new moon.*
3. *The second quarter is called a full moon.*
4. *The third quarter is sometimes called a half moon.*
5. *A crescent moon is between new moon and quarter moon.*
6. *When the moon is between a quarter and full, it is called a gibbous moon.*
7. *The moon passes through the entire cycle of phases in about twenty-nine and a half days.*

Major Concept #3

The earth and the moon sometimes pass into each other's shadow as they travel, creating eclipses.

Supporting Concepts

A. *A solar eclipse occurs when the moon passes between the earth and the sun in such a way that the moon casts a shadow on the earth, blocking the view of the sun from that area of the earth.*

B. *A lunar eclipse occurs when the earth passes between the sun and the moon in such a way that the earth casts a shadow on the full moon, "eclipsing" the moon from our view.*

Initiating Activities

Something needs to be done at the beginning of the unit to stimulate student interest in the topic. If students begin their study with curiosities high and with questions they would like to find answers to, they are ready to learn. Here is one suggestion:

> *Prior to beginning the unit, have students collect pictures and articles about the moon, including lunar explorations. Make a bulletin board or scrapbook with them. Discuss possible benefits and negative aspects of exploring the moon, such as cost and risking the lives of astronauts in the event of equipment failure.*

Learning Activities

The learning activities include all that students are to do in the process of learning information, skills, and attitudes. These might include such activities as experiments, demonstrations, audiotapes, videotapes, videodiscs, computer activities, learning center activities, direct instruction, and use of resource people, as well as research from textbooks, encyclopedias, trade books, newspapers, magazines, and other resources, and reports on this research. In the case of the moon unit, direct observation would also be appropriate.

As the Resource Unit is developed, it should be kept in mind that we are not just teaching subject matter, but we are developing skills and attitudes in the minds of children. Hopefully the plan will include plenty of hands-on activities and opportunities to develop skills of observing, measuring, predicting, inferring, and other process skills. Students should have opportunities to work in cooperative groups. A variety of activities will provide many opportunities to integrate experiences in other subject areas, applying skills related to math, language arts, social studies, art, music, and more.

Materials

Each activity in the Unit Plan should include a list of materials that are needed for that activity. A Teaching Unit should also include a master materials list to save time in determining the materials and equipment that are needed for teaching the unit. A master list for a Resource Unit would probably not be useful, since only part of the activities will be used with any given group of students; however, a list of needed materials should be included with each activity.

Culminating Activities

An experience that brings the unit to a memorable end will provide students with a referent that can be used to help recall the concepts, attitudes, and skills taught within the unit. Here is a possible culminating activity for a unit on the moon.

Have a moon-viewing party on an evening of a full moon. Invite students to bring their parents. Have binoculars and a telescope available. Students could also set up a display for their parents, demonstrating what they have learned about the moon.

Culminating activities for units of study on other topics might include a meal cooked by children at the end of a unit on nutrition; a visit to an airport after a unit on flight; a visit to the class by a local TV meteorologist, as a part of a unit on weather; or firing model rockets at the end of a unit on rockets and space exploration. Inviting parents to participate in these activities can be motivating to students and can do much to develop positive relationships between the school and the parents.

Assessment

The learning that results from involvement in a unit of study can be measured in a variety of ways. Assessment techniques should be consistent with knowledge and skills that were expected to be developed during the study of the unit. Acquisition of information can often be measured by pencil-paper tests, which might include multiple-choice and essay questions. Such tests are not usually adequate for assessing skills or attitudes, however. Students should have opportunities to demonstrate their competence by performing tasks that require measuring, classifying, or other process skills targeted for improvement. More is said about assessment as the next topic of this chapter.

ASSESSING STUDENT PROGRESS

Since the early 1960s, there has been a growing emphasis on the teaching of process skills in elementary science programs in the United States. National curriculum projects that strongly influenced this emphasis include: Science, A Process Approach (SAPA), Science

Curriculum Improvement Study (SCIS), and Elementary Science Study (ESS). Textbook-based programs and other curriculum materials have responded to the broadly recognized need to teach process skills, not just science content. However, evaluation measures have lagged behind the development and implementation of curricular objectives. Student progress continues to be measured in the cognitive areas, but effective measurement of skills presents a great challenge to teachers, curriculum developers, and experts in tests and measurement.

Program Assessments

Research is now being performed to determine the effectiveness of assessment practices in measuring student progress in light of current emphases in teaching and learning. Doran (1990) reviewed major broad-scale efforts in skills measurement that occurred over two decades, both in the United States and in other countries. The assessment projects reported were on a national and multinational scale. He concluded that continued effort is needed to provide assessment procedures that include situations in which the student directly interacts with materials and equipment. Hopefully, the attention these projects receive will result in more effective assessment of skills on both state and local levels.

With the growing recognition of the need for effective and efficient methods of assessing growth in the process skills, there have been some rather bold recent attempts to accomplish this task. The state of New York produced a syllabus in the mid-1980s that identified objectives for elementary science and contained ideas and information to help teachers meet those objectives (Isenberg, 1989). In 1989, they began evaluating the success of their efforts by administering the Elementary Science Progress Evaluation Test (ESPET) to all fourth-grade students in the state. The ESPET is a series of performance test items in which students manipulate materials in hands-on applications. This is a mammoth effort, involving all public and private schools in both rural and inner-city areas. The project is made possible, in part, by a mentor network of experienced teachers and administrators trained to administer and score the ESPET (Doran, Reynolds, Camplin, and Hejaily, 1992). Personnel in the science education department of New York have generously shared their information and findings, and have trained personnel in other states in the use of materials and techniques. California and Connecticut are also leading out with innovative programs of statewide performance assessment, and several other states have made similar efforts to improve effectiveness in measuring process skills.

Classroom Assessments

Let's now consider the assessment done in the classroom by the teacher, for the purpose of determining day-by-day effectiveness of instruction. With many educators, pencil-paper tests have acquired a bad name from misuse and overuse, but it is important that we don't overreact. Pencil-paper tests are usually not very effective in assessing the application of science skills, but such tests can provide information on the extent to which students have mastered certain kinds of content, such as terminology and facts. The relevance of such measures is limited to the importance of student acquisition of such information, and will vary from topic to topic and from teacher to teacher, according to the objectives. This is analogous to using the meter for all measurements—even for measurements of mass and volume. We are now becoming more fully aware of a need for grams and liters for some of our measurements, but we must not throw the meter stick away; neither grams nor liters measure linear distance between points, which is the specialty of the meter. So let's keep all of our pupil assessment instruments and become more skilled at using each one according to its strength.

Unfortunately, we must consider *efficiency* of testing, as well as *effectiveness;* the task must be doable in terms of available time, personnel, and financial resources. The school system has never been able to afford the hours of time necessary to assess each student individually on a one-on-one basis, and we still face that limitation. The computer is helping us to come much closer to individualized assessment, but even the computer has its limits and so do the budgets that provide the computers. The need for efficiency forces compromise in many walks of life, including measuring student progress.

Experience has shown that written tests can be used to assess content information, whereas both process skills and problem solving are more effectively assessed with performance tests or by interview (Meng and Doran, 1990). Performance tests and interviews, on the other hand, are limited by the seemingly unavoidable constraints of time, materials, and the number of students that can be assessed simultaneously. Getting back to our analogy, it may be that if we cannot afford liter measures, perhaps we can substitute cubic units, allowing us to use the meter stick that we do have and at least get by. Now, applying the analogy, although pencil-paper tests leave a lot to be desired in measuring process skills and problem-solving skills, perhaps limited information can be acquired by this method even with regard to these skills.

Pencil-paper tests

The most obvious advantages of *multiple-choice* tests are efficiency of time (often for the learner as well as the scorer) and consistency in scoring; everyone's paper is scored by the same criteria because of the objective nature of the test. *Fill-in-the-blank* tests are quite efficient in terms of scoring time, while having the advantage of requiring the student to produce information rather than just selecting from a list of choices. They are also fairly objective in nature, yet could potentially have answers that require subjective judgment on the part of the scorer. *Essay* questions usually require more time to take as well as more time to score. They have the potential advantage of requiring the student to *produce* information, *think* creatively, and *apply* concepts learned, and the disadvantage of requiring more subjective judgment on the part of the scorer. Overall, written tests also discriminate against poor readers, providing a score that is potentially a more accurate measure of reading ability than of science knowledge (Tolman, Sudweeks, Baird, and Tolman, 1991).

Performance tests

With a performance test, the student demonstrates a skill by performing a task. Such experiences are often called "authentic assessments," meaning that they use lifelike situations in which students apply their skills rather than just giving written responses to questions about the skills. For example, if the target skill is temperature measurement, a performance test will require the student to use a thermometer to measure the temperature of water or some other substance, whereas a traditional test item might ask the student to simply identify the temperature shown on a pictured thermometer.

The term "authentic assessment" is offensive to some, as it implies that modes of assessment previously used are not authentic. In the minds of many educators, this implication is neither valid nor intended. If used to imply an effort toward more worthwhile, significant, and meaningful assessment techniques, designed to more closely imitate lifelike conditions, the term communicates an important endeavor that could hardly be offensive to the teacher who is striving to improve.

The most obvious disadvantage of the performance test is the time-consuming nature of such tests. They not only take time to administer, but they also often require inordinate amounts of time to score. Other disadvantages include the need for materials, and subjectivity in scoring, which reduces scoring reliability from one student to another. The training of scorers in the use of precise scoring guidelines can greatly reduce subjectivity and improve reliability of scores, but again, this takes time. The more obvious advantages include (1) a more authentic (true-to-life) application of the skill; (2) less dependency on reading, listening, and writing skills; and (3) an opportunity for learners to demonstrate what they can *do*, not just what they can *say* or *write*, thus measuring science skills rather than reading skills, writing skills, or content information only. Students are also more likely, in this setting, to be allowed to ask for clarification of questions or instructions.

Performance tests don't necessarily need to be administered individually. Many different formats are used, including several students doing the same task at a given time, or even having two or more students working together as a team. Nor are written instructions and written responses necessarily ruled out; materials are sometimes provided along with written instructions *and* with written responses being required. The following is an example.

PERFORMANCE TEST: ROCK CLASSIFICATION

Skill: *Classifying*

Materials: *Assortment of rocks*
Two sorting trays, labeled A and B

Instructions to Students:

1. *Remove all of the rocks from the bag and place Trays A and B side by side in front of you.*
2. *Divide the rocks into two groups and place them in the trays, being sure that all rocks in each group are alike in some way and that each is different from the rocks in the other tray.*

   In what way are all of the rocks in Tray A alike?

   In what way are all of the rocks in Tray B alike?
3. *Divide the rocks again, this time using a different characteristic.*

   In what way are all of the rocks in Tray A alike?

   In what way are all of the rocks in Tray B alike?
4. *Can you think of a third way to sort the rocks? If so, try it.*

   In what way are all of the rocks in Tray A alike?

   In what way are all of the rocks in Tray B alike?
5. *Place all of the rocks back in the bag, stack the trays, and place the bag of rocks on top of the trays.*
6. *Raise your hand to show that you are finished.*

A response sheet to accompany this performance test item might look like this:

PERFORMANCE TEST: ROCK CLASSIFICATION

Skill: *Classifying*

Name: ____________________

Date: ____________________

2. A. ________________________________

____

B. ________________________________

____

3. A. ________________________________

____

B.____________________________________

____

4. A.____________________________________

____

B.____________________________________

____

Portfolios

In recent years, portfolios have become popular in assessing student progress. As for style and content, they are probably as varied as those who use them. Along with the variety, however, there are common elements that make a portfolio a portfolio. *Portfolio* has been defined as "a purposeful collection of student work that exhibits the student's efforts, progress, and achievements in one or more areas" (Paulson, Paulson, and Meyer, 1991). Vavrus (1990) described the portfolio as a "systematic and organized collection of evidence used by the teacher and student to monitor growth of the student's knowledge, skills, and attitudes . . ." Those most famous for using portfolios as evidence of one's talents and achievements are probably the artists, architects, and photographers. Even a collection of merit badges worn by a boy scout or girl scout, however, is a form of portfolio. Portfolios are also applied productively to the school setting, and can aid in developing independent learners—self-disciplined, self-regulating, and self-assessing.

For many elementary teachers, only the use of the term "portfolio" is new, because they have been keeping samples of student work all along for use in parent conferences and student conferences. Still, with emphasis on this form of record keeping, even these teachers can acquire new ideas and improve the effectiveness of the practice.

Objectives

If the portfolio is to be effective, objectives must be established. Is the portfolio kept for the purpose of showing the student's best work? Is it intended to communicate a progressive record of student achievement? Perhaps it has both of these purposes. Is it to be used for assessment, or just to display student work? The portfolio may not be adequate to stand alone as an assessment tool, but it can add significantly to the accumulation of evidence of student progress. The objectives can be modified as the portfolio is used and its actual contribution to the overall picture becomes clear.

What Does the Portfolio Contain?

If used as an assessment tool, it should include material that the teacher accepts as evidence of student performance in categories of work that are to be evaluated. From the standpoint of the student, the portfolio should include items the student judges to be representative of his or her best work. Those people designing the purpose and format of the portfolio might choose to select items that will provide a progressive record of student growth. (Many parents want to know how their child *compares* with others; this is not the role of the portfolio.)

Portfolios can be used even before children develop writing skills, with tape-recorded samples of oral expression: oral reading of simple, nonfiction science trade books; responses to stories; descriptions of observations; or conversation, perhaps while interacting with others during a science activity. To these could be added samples of art work, photos of projects, examples of student questions that indicate depth of thinking, and so on. As writing skills develop, appropriate samples, providing evidence of progress in written expression, can be added to the portfolio.

Conferences with students provide an excellent setting for deciding what is appropriate for the portfolio. The materials that should or should not be kept can be determined during review conferences held with students throughout the year. Care should be taken to see that the portfolio does not become cluttered, but that it contains items that meet the portfolio objectives. One benefit of using portfolios is that students develop the skill of self-critique, as they select pieces for their portfolio. They learn that having too few items in the portfolio makes it impossible to make a valid judgment of achievement, while too many items indicates lack of an ability to discern quality (Collins, 1990).

INTEGRATING

Attempting to teach any subject area in isolation is futile; the subjects are unavoidably interrelated and interdependent. We establish artificial, though sometimes necessary, boundaries between curricular areas for convenience of instruction. Planning in a way that maximizes the benefits of learning experiences in areas that are clearly linked makes a lot of sense. The study of science frequently requires children to read, for instance, and the benefit of that time can be maximized by recognizing and accommodating needed reading skills.

Similar connections can be made between science and other language arts areas, and with math, social studies, art, music, and other facets of the curriculum. The teacher should constantly consider opportunities to enhance other skills while teaching science, and to apply science skills meaningfully while involved in other curricular areas. When science is integrated with other subject areas, all of the areas benefit, as they are learned more effectively and often more quickly (Allen, 1981). Some specific suggestions for integrating science with other curricular areas follow.

Integrating Science with Language Arts

Communication skills are critical to productive daily life, and they can be frequently applied in science. We learn and we teach by reading, writing, listening, and talking; competence in language arts skills enables us to do it effectively. Science experiences in the classroom are rich with opportunities to apply and develop these skills.

Reading

In a study of books voluntarily checked out by elementary students for recreational reading, a disproportionate number of science books were selected (Graham, 1978). More science books were checked out than biographies, or books in the areas of social science, geography, or history. To accommodate this interest, a rich supply of science trade books, written on a broad variety of science topics and at all levels of reading difficulty, should be available to children.

Biographies of famous scientists can provide reading practice and at the same time motivate children to become more involved in science. Young girls and boys should become acquainted with the achievements of female scientists as well as the work of male scientists. They need to understand that major progress has resulted from the scientific contributions of both women and men. The work of scientists from various cultures and ethnic groups should also be included. Children from minority groups need role models they can relate to. As students follow printed instructions for highly motivating science activities, they improve their skills in reading and in following directions.

Science experiences also provide many opportunities for developing reading skills. Learning centers are often designed in such a way that students must read and follow simple directions in order to successfully complete the activities. Students should be encouraged to read weather reports in the newspaper and to share information about other science-related events that are reported in newspapers and magazines.

Writing

Writing skills are enhanced as students record observations from their scientific investigations. Students who keep a journal as they raise plants, care for gerbils, chicks, or other animals, or as they observe changes in seasons, get meaningful experience in developing sequences; and as they review their notes, they will experience the progression of events. Even children who have not yet learned to write can be introduced to the importance of recording their ideas by dictating their observations to their teacher, who records their words on a chart.

Science provides a natural launching pad for creative writing. Experiences with plants, animals, weather, and other science topics can open the floodgates of imagination and creativity for the child who is encouraged to record ideas that come to mind. Libraries of science fiction stories written by elementary students have been very successful in encouraging children to write and to read. Students enjoy reading small books written by fellow students. The reader is curious about what a friend or other student has written. The writer, in turn, has a new-found motivation to write clearly and meaningfully, as he or she senses the responsibility of communicating clearly to readers.

Poetry can be written with science topics as a central theme. Limericks, haiku, or some other type of poetry can be products of imaginations stimulated by experiences with science.

Integrating Science with Music

When studying the topic of sound, we study the ways sounds are produced by various musical instruments. This topic is not complete without considering ways to create music with soda straws, sandpaper blocks, soda bottles partially filled with water, and many other types and configurations of materials. So much can be done to enrich the study of the science of sound by expanding it to musical instruments, and one could not learn very much about musical instruments without studying the science of sound. Even the human voice is a musical instrument.

Integrating Science with Mathematics

Science provides real-world opportunities to apply math skills. Some instructional materials are specifically designed to assist in the meaningful integration of science with math (see the descriptions of GEMS and AIMS in chapter 7). As we estimate and measure, we use math skills. As we use or prepare graphs and as we read thermometers, we use math skills. Here are just a few examples of science experiences that apply some of these skills.

Life science

- *Measuring and graphing plant growth.*
- *Preparing fertilizer solutions in measured amounts for use with classroom plants.*
- *Keeping a record of the amount of water used by a plant.*
- *Using graphs to predict plant growth by a given date.*
- *Keeping personal record of weight, height, and food consumed.*

Earth science

- *Calculating the weight, volume, and density of different types and sizes of rocks.*

- *Measuring and graphing temperatures, precipitation, wind speed, and other weather-related information.*
- *Estimating the amount of garbage produced by the school and extending the estimates to the community and beyond.*
- *Estimating and computing the amount of water wasted by a dripping faucet.*

Physical science

- *Determining the strength of various magnets.*
- *Investigating the mechanical advantages of inclined planes and other simple machines.*
- *Determining the amount of liquid a vessel will hold.*
- *Computing the maximum height of a model rocket in flight.*

Integrating Science with Art

Virtually every science topic offers opportunities to enhance the science experience through artistic expression, and to develop artistic skills through such application. Children usually enjoy drawing, whether of their favorite animal or the setup of a first-class lever. Young children enjoy creating clouds when studying about weather. Topics of light and color could scarcely be taught effectively without applications of art, and art skills certainly could not be fully developed without learning something about the science of light and color. Here are a few specific suggestions for bringing science and art together.

Life science

- *Preparing accurate drawings of plants, leaves, flowers, and seeds develops skills of observing and illustrating.*
- *Using parts of plants (seeds, leaves, and so on) as components for a mosaic.*
- *Making paints and dyes from the extracts of certain plants, such as beets, berries, and leaves.*
- *Drawing what is seen as students dissect plants and simple animals, such as earthworms.*
- *Drawing a make-believe animal that can exist in a given environment.*

Earth science

- *Making an illustration of the solar system.*
- *Creating illustrations of space crafts and creatures from other worlds.*
- *Making accurate drawings of specific types of rocks and fossils.*
- *Cutting and polishing rocks to make jewelry or just to display in a collection.*
- *Drawing and labeling specific types of clouds.*

Physical science

- *Illustrating the setup for an experiment, and changes that occur as the experiment progresses.*
- *Creating images by sprinkling iron filings on a card that is placed over one or more magnets. Changing the positions or types of magnets will change the pattern of iron filings.*
- *Mixing colored lights on a white background, producing unique shadows when objects are placed between the light sources and the background.*

Integrating Science with Social Studies

The impact of science on society has often been the impetus of social change. The steam engine, the printing press, myriads of electrically operated equipment and appliances, the computer, and space travel, are all scientific developments that have heavily impacted how and where we live. Here are a few specific examples of activities that integrate science and social studies.

Life science

- *Investigate the social implications of chemical fertilizers and the demand for food.*
- *Study the social implications of pollution of the environment, ways that science has contributed to it, and what science is doing to control it.*
- *Start trees from seeds, then plant them on the school grounds or in the community.*

Earth science

- *Study the social differences in various climatic zones.*
- *Consider the possible implications of colonies of humans moving to other planets.*
- *Study the social impacts of natural phenomena such as earthquakes and volcanoes.*

Physical science

- *Discuss the impact of electricity or other broadly applied scientific developments on society.*
- *Consider how our lives would change if suddenly magnetism did not exist.*
- *Investigate how science has changed the way wars have been fought throughout history.*

Caution

Sometimes even good ideas can be practiced to excess. Some would have us integrate the curriculum to the point that there is no longer a specific time in the school day for studying science, or math, or language arts, or any other specific subject. While its advantages could be argued, and some teachers could no doubt implement that approach very well, we encourage a careful assessment of the personnel involved before moving that far in the effort to integrate. Do all teachers in the system have a sufficiently strong background and interest in all subject areas to effectively teach that way? Will this approach make it easy for certain areas of the curriculum to be ignored, perhaps even inadvertently?

There is little doubt, however, that constant effort to apply skills from one curricular area as we study another can enhance both. Science study offers some of the very best opportunities to apply math skills and language arts skills, for instance, and science applications abound in the area of social studies. Few could deny the advantages of integrating, but care must be taken to make sure all subject areas receive an appropriate amount of instruction.

IN CLOSING

The success of a science program depends on the teacher's preparation. Materials should be prepared beforehand, and decisions should be made as to how the class will be organized for planned activities. Careful preparation of Lesson Plans and Unit Plans helps to assure success and fulfillment in the school experience for all concerned—both teachers and students.

Planning should include ways of assessing

progress. Both portfolios and performance assessment techniques are gaining popularity in the broad effort to provide authentic assessment.

Deliberate efforts to enhance student growth in other subjects wherever they relate to science experiences can multiply positive learning outcomes. Removing the artificial boundaries between curricular disciplines increases opportunities to provide meaningful application of skills in all areas.

LIST OF RESOURCES

Allen, Dorothea, *Elementary Science Activities for Every Month of the Year* (West Nyack, NY: Parker Publishing Co., 1981).

Barman, Charles R., "The Learning Cycle: Making It Work," *Science Scope* 12, no. 5 (March 1989): 28–31.

Barman, Charles R., "A Procedure for Helping Prospective Elementary Teachers Integrate the Learning Cycle into Science Textbooks," *Journal of Science Teacher Education* 1, no. 2 (Summer 1989): 21–26.

Barman, Charles R., and Michael Kotar, "The Learning Cycle," *Science and Children* 26, no. 7 (April 1989): 30–32.

Cacha, Francis B., "Children Create Fiction Using Science," *Science and Children* 15, no. 3 (November-December 1977): 21–22.

Carin, Arthur A., and Robert B. Sund, *Teaching Science Through Discovery* (Columbus, OH: Charles E. Merrill Publishing Co., 1985).

Collins, Angelo, "Portfolios for Assessing Student Learning in Science: A New Name for a Familiar Idea." In A. B. Champagne, B. E. Lovitts, and B. J. Calinger, eds., *Assessment in the Service of Instruction* (Washington, D.C.: American Association for the Advancement of Science, 1990), 157–66.

Doran, R. L., "What Research Says . . . About Assessment," *Science and Children* 27, no. 8 (May 1990): 26–27.

Doran, R. L., D. Reynolds, J. Camplin, and N. Hejaily, "What Research Says . . . Evaluating Elementary Science," *Science and Children* 30, no. 3 (November-December 1992): 33–35, 63.

Graham, S. B., "Do Children Read Science Books?" *Science and Children* 15, no. 5 (February 1978): 29.

Isenberg, Susan, "New York—On the Cutting Edge," *Science and Children* 26, no. 7 (April 1989): 28–29.

Meng, E., and R. L. Doran, "What Research Says . . . About Appropriate Methods of Assessment," *Science and Children* 28, no. 1 (September 1990): 42–45.

Paulson, F. L., P. R. Paulson, and C. A. Meyer, "What Makes a Portfolio a Portfolio?" *Educational Leadership* 48, no. 5 (February 1991): 60–63.

Saunders, W., and D. Shepardson, "A Comparison of Concrete and Formal Science Instruction Upon Science Achievement and Reasoning Ability of Sixth Grade Students," *Journal of Research in Science Teaching* 24, no. 1 (January 1987): 39–51.

Tolman, M. N., R. Sudweeks, H. Baird, and R. Tolman, "Does Reading Ability Affect Science Test Scores?" *Science and Children* 29, no. 1 (September 1991): 44–47.

Vavrus, L, "Put Portfolios to the Test," *Instructor* 100, no. 1 (August 1990): 48–53.

Victor, Edward, *Science for the Elementary School*, 6th ed., (New York: Macmillan, 1989).

CHAPTER

SOCIAL CONTEXTS OF SCIENCE

CHAPTER OUTLINE:

- INTRODUCTION
- KEEP IT CURRENT
- HIGHLIGHT THE POSITIVE
- KEEP IT IN PERSPECTIVE
- NSTA GUIDELINES
- EXAMPLES OF SOCIAL CONSIDERATIONS FOR SCIENCE
  - Exploration of New Frontiers
    - Space
    - Oceans
  - Natural Resources and Environmental Concerns
    - Efforts for change
    - Another way of thinking
    - Developing energy sources
- TEACHER OPINIONS
- EXEMPLARY PROGRAMS
  - CAKE Project
  - JASON Project
  - Kid's Network
  - NSTA Spotlight
    - Energy audit
    - Earthscope
- MAKING CONNECTIONS
- IN CLOSING
- LIST OF RESOURCES

I WONDER . . .

In what ways do science and technology impact society?
What is STS and what are its goals?
What are some science programs in which we can see social objectives being met?

INTRODUCTION

Due to increased public concern about environmental problems, depleting natural resources, and the current technology explosion, the need to increase public awareness and sensitivity to these things has come into focus as one of the major emphases of science education today. Science literacy enables us to live intelligently in a society that is increasingly dependent on science and technology and improves our ability to contribute as informed citizens.

Science and technology are interrelated. Science explains principles and laws that govern the natural world. It is a study that seeks to understand and explain observed phenomena. Technology is the application of science—the link between science and society. It is the translation of science knowledge into new processes and products, and is reflected, in part, by the many conveniences in all phases of our lives. In the words of one author, "Science describes the world as it is and technology remakes the world to serve human desires . . . and our value concepts guide what we ought to do with both" (Hurd, 1975).

While distinctions in definition may seem clear enough, in reality "science and technology are no longer distinct enterprises—they operate as an integrated system," (Hurd, 1987). Though each has its unique role, differences between them are becoming cloudy as scientists depend more and more upon instruments made by technicians and engineers.

The rate of social change is greater than at any period of history, and it continues to increase. Our task as teachers of science is to help young people acquire a vision that will prepare them to keep pace with social change, supported by basic understandings of science principles.

KEEP IT CURRENT

Today's students need to know about new developments and events. Current issues of science deserve regular attention in the elementary classroom. You may find specific topics for day-by-day classroom consideration in sources such as journals, newspapers, television, radio, and personal observation, focusing on events and circumstances that are currently pertinent to society. This chapter provides several examples of topics that might be considered in an effort to heighten student awareness of the impact science and technology have on their lives. Some of these issues will be relevant for many years; others might diminish quickly in public attention and societal impact, as new concerns arise and demand the spotlight of attention.

Today's society faces numerous complex problems and issues, including food and fresh water shortages, environmental pollution, natural resource depletion, and other global issues. All of these require cooperative effort among nations if they are to be resolved. Science and technology are directly and unavoidably involved in efforts to find solutions to such problems. Science programs at the elementary level can contribute to solutions by helping children to be aware of the problems that face their world, and to recognize efforts that are being made or that might be made to deal with them. Some of today's young people will grow up to make significant contributions to environmental and social issues, partly because of interests that started with meaningful science experiences in the elementary school years.

HIGHLIGHT THE POSITIVE

We make a mistake if we expose only the gloomy side of science—to help clean up messes and try to save society from large-scale self-destruction. Science and its technological applications bring us computers, modern appliances, airplanes, automobiles, space travel, communication devices, miracle medicines, and artificial human organs. These are but a few of the numerous advances that raise the level of comfort and enjoyment in ways that earlier generations could not even imagine. What an exciting time it is to be alive!

KEEP IT IN PERSPECTIVE

Student involvement with activities and issues that highlight the impact of science and technology on society is very important, but even a good thing can be overdone. For many years, a major effort called Science, Technology, and Society, commonly known among science educators by its acronym, STS, has spotlighted the need to increase societal awareness of the importance of science in our lives. Some zealous supporters of STS would let it become the entire science experience of the child, and an education based entirely on current issues would likely leave many gaps in student knowledge. Issues become dated, while the processes of science do not. Basic structures, concepts, methods, and skills are still important, and students need to understand them in order to comprehend future developments and problems. The elementary science program must go beyond the emotional impact of social challenges and reap from them opportunities for meaningful application of science principles and attitudes.

NSTA GUIDELINES

In an official position statement issued in 1982, the National Science Teachers Association (NSTA) affirmed their support for an emphasis on STS (NSTA, 1982). They recommended that at the elementary level a *minimum* of 5 percent of science instruction be directed toward science-related social issues. The introduction to the NSTA position statement expresses the need:

> *Science and technology influence every aspect of our lives. They are central to our welfare as individuals and to the welfare of our society. All around us are examples of the importance of science and technology for production of food, shelter, clothing, medicines, transportation, and various sources of energy. There are an increasing number of science- and technology-related societal problems as well as increasing societal benefits.*

NSTA suggests that the following STS problems demand attention:

1. *Understanding of science and technology are central to our personal and national welfare, yet public appreciation of science education has declined.*
2. *An increasing number of individual and societal problems that have an impact on the quality of life are related to science-generated technology.*
3. *As the impact of science and technology on society has increased, the support for science education has decreased.*

4. *Compared to its recent past, the United States has fallen behind in the production of scientific and technological goods and services.*
5. *Women, minorities, and handicapped persons are under-represented in nearly all professional and technical roles in science and technology.*

To help clarify what science literacy means, the NSTA defines the scientifically and technologically literate person as one who thinks critically in the following ways:

1. *Uses science concepts, process skills, and values in making responsible everyday decisions.*
2. *Understands how society influences science and technology as well as how science and technology influence society.*
3. *Understands that society controls science and technology through the allocation of resources.*
4. *Recognizes the limitations as well as the usefulness of science and technology in advancing human welfare.*
5. *Knows the major concepts, hypotheses, and theories of science and is able to use them.*
6. *Appreciates science and technology for the intellectual stimulus they provide.*
7. *Understands that the generation of scientific knowledge depends on the inquiry process and on conceptual theories.*
8. *Distinguishes between scientific evidence and personal opinion.*
9. *Recognizes the origin of science and understands that scientific knowledge is tentative, and subject to change as evidence accumulates.*
10. *Understands the applications of technology and the decisions entailed in the use of technology.*
11. *Has sufficient knowledge and experience to appreciate the worthiness of research and technological development.*
12. *Has a richer and more exciting view of the world as the result of science education.*
13. *Knows reliable sources of scientific and technological information and uses these sources in the process of decision making.*

In the same position statement, NSTA makes the following recommendations for elementary school science:

> *Science should be an integral part of the elementary school program. It should be used to integrate, reinforce, and enhance the other basic curricular areas so as to make learning more meaningful for children.*
>
> *A carefully planned and articulated elementary science curriculum should provide daily opportunities for the sequential development of basic physical and life science concepts, along with the development of science process and inquiry skills.*
>
> *Elementary science should provide opportunities for nurturing children's natural curiosity. This helps them to develop confidence to question and seek answers based upon evidence and independent thinking. Children should be given an opportunity to explore and investigate their world using a hands-on approach, with instructional materials readily available.*
>
> *The focus of the elementary science program should be on fostering in children an understanding of, an interest in, and an appreciation of the world in which they live.*

EXAMPLES OF SOCIAL CONSIDERATIONS FOR SCIENCE

The following topics are not intended to dictate the curriculum for any classroom, but only to provide examples of some science and technology issues that currently impact society and, in varying degrees, raise controversies.

Exploration of New Frontiers

Few characteristics distinguish the human creature from the rest of the animal kingdom more dramatically than our curiosity and the insatiable desire to explore the unknown. Whether it be a medical cure yet to be developed, or uncharted territories on Earth or beyond, the urge to know is irresistible. The desire to know is not controversial, but it sometimes results in the human culture being imposed on the rest of Earth's creatures and on its resources. Therein lies the controversy.

Space

The exciting progress we have experienced in space exploration has been achieved through application of science principles. Because these efforts have come at great financial cost, some people bitterly criticize the continuous spending of public resources on the space program, while others note spin-off benefits, applauding the fruits of knowledge and products, even claiming that direct financial costs are more than offset by economic gains.

Techniques and products developed through space research have provided thousands of processes and consumer products now used in everyday living. Such societal benefits from space research include new and better ways to monitor hospital patients in intensive care; smaller, more powerful batteries with a much longer life of service; and improved wind generators. Sunglasses now can improve both day vision and night vision; other eyeglasses allow sounds to be translated into images by a microcomputer, so that the deaf may "hear."

In addition to products, opportunities are anticipated. One of the major goals for space research by the United States is to create contexts and settings for commerce in space (NASA, 1988). Indeed, some claim there is nothing in the national budget that promises American taxpayers more generous dividends than the money they are spending in space research.

Oceans

While some are probing deeper into outer space, others are exploring new depths on Earth. Among such efforts, one of the most significant is the JASON Project, directed by Robert D. Ballard, senior scientist at Woods Hole Oceanographic Institution, who located the *Titanic* in 1985. With the JASON Project, exploration of underwater volcanoes, shipwrecks, and other curiosities, are broadcast live by satellite transmission to a network of museums and other educational sites in the United States and Canada. Students at these sites are able to talk directly with those on board the experimental submarine as scientists probe beneath the sea. Such communication with students is not an afterthought of the JASON Project; it was a major objective from the outset. Director Ballard expresses this intent:

> *The JASON Project is really a voyage of discovery for educational motivation. We're losing kids from the sciences . . . [one reason] . . . is the images we've created for kids as role models in science and engineering. They see a scientist as an underdeveloped person who escapes reality*

by pursuing science . . . . We wanted, in our way, to begin to reshape that image by showing kids the excitement of exploration . . . . exploration and science in the sea are still in the Lewis and Clark phase. We now stand at the threshold of entering the deep sea; we have seen less than one-tenth of one percent of the planet beneath the ocean. We know more about the mountain ranges on Mars than we do about the mountain ranges beneath our own oceans. ("A Conversation with Robert D. Ballard," 1989)

Natural Resources and Environmental Concerns

Until the second half of the twentieth century, conserving natural resources was not a widely recognized priority, but the limited supply of fossil fuels, lumber, and other natural resources has, in recent years, captured worldwide attention and concern. In earlier times of fewer people demanding a share, the world's resources seemed endless. However, with increasing populations and greater technology, worldwide demand on these commodities is increasing at an alarming rate, and we are now acutely aware that the supplies are indeed vulnerable to the growing human appetite. Most thinking people now realize that we must change from exploiting the environment to conserving and using it wisely. In a related statement, one writer cautions that "technology demonstrates people's ability to create, but its unbridled application has demonstrated once again the world's inability to control its destiny and protect itself from its excesses" (McCormack, 1986).

Wise use will promise a continuous supply of wood, wildlife, clean air and water, and other renewable resources, and a long-lasting supply of resources that are not renewable within the brief time span of a human lifetime or two, such as oil, natural gas, and coal. Unwise exploitation will impose heavy penalties on future generations, in terms of both the quality and supply of these precious commodities.

Efforts for change

This goal requires a change in the level of awareness and concern of the general public. School science programs can provide backgrounds that are needed to help in promoting this change. It is very important that the future stewards of these resources grow up with an awareness of the critical decisions they face, and that they understand the possible consequences of their actions.

Broad-scale education in environmental awareness is necessary for significant changes to occur, especially in a democracy where public support is crucial. Uninformed people usually do not support the research or the policies that are essential to alter longstanding habits that harm the environment.

To be adequately motivated, the masses must understand that this planet is a closed system with limited resources and natural self-renewing cycles. These cycles cannot be rushed, and the resources cannot be exploited without harm to the inhabitants of the planet.

Far too many people wish for changes to preserve the environment only if such changes do not result in cost or inconvenience to them personally. Many people may insist that an oil company spend millions of dollars to clean up an oil spill, but are reluctant to pay the few dollars required to reduce the pollutants emitted from the exhaust of their own automobiles—one of the worst offenders of the environment. Some think that problems of nuclear waste can be solved by transporting the offending material to sparsely populated areas. In reality, passing the problem on to someone else does not represent a solution, but only another pretension that ignoring it will make it go away. At best, it is a way of passing the real problem on to future generations.

In 1970, an annual Earth Day was established to spotlight the need for citizens of the United States to clean up the environment and preserve our precious natural resources. Ironically, on the twentieth anniversary of this recognition, April 22, 1990, as reported by "Paul Harvey News," "America watched in disbelief while well-intentioned demonstrators carrying picket signs protesting pollution littered the landscape in many gathering places nationwide." Although the behavior was not universal, the seeming lack of direction is striking. Young people need to feel a genuine interest and concern for their environment, not merely vocalize a general discontent. Their actions will be productive only if they are founded in informed, sound scientific principles rather than simply in emotional behavior.

Another way of thinking

Young students might also benefit from discussing the perspective on the environment suggested by an expert who claims that the environment is not in any danger: the threat is that we'll spoil the conditions that support human life (Esterbrook, 1989). Whether there is room for humankind on planet Earth is up to us. While others warn of the fragility of the environment, this author broadens the perspective of the earth's existence and makes the point that only in terms of human needs and comforts is the environment of this planet fragile; the environment itself is, instead, almost indestructible. It got along quite nicely without us for a long time and it can do it again. The environment has survived ice ages, cosmic radiation, solar fluctuations, and collisions of comets and meteors. "Though mischievous, human assaults are pinpricks compared with forces of the magnitude nature is accustomed to resisting." Esterbrook points out that nature doesn't care if the globe is populated with trilobites, lizards, people, or slugs. If we spoil the environmental conditions that favor our species, other species will rise up that will thrive in the new environment. It is the survival and condition of our species, not the survival of the planet, that depends on our activity.

Developing energy sources

A growing concern about energy sources is deeply embedded in our efforts to conserve natural resources. Material progress increases energy use. The supply of easily accessible fossil fuels is limited and is being consumed at an alarming rate. As such fuels become less abundant, alternative energy sources such as solar energy, wind energy, tidal energy, geothermal energy, and nuclear energy become more attractive. Thus far, extracting energy from these sources has been more expensive than from fossil fuels. However, with increasing costs of fossil fuels, and the prospect of technology to develop other energy sources becoming more cost-effective, large-scale production and use of these sources becomes more feasible for future generations. Dealing with current issues in our science programs will generate student interest in this area of concern.

Many students will enjoy learning about the annual World Solar Challenge race, which has had a major impact on the development of solar energy. University research groups, automobile manufacturers, and other companies and agencies worldwide have developed vehicles powered solely by sunlight to participate in a 2,000-mile race across the continent of Australia. This event helps to spur development of practical uses of solar energy, not only for automobiles, but for numerous other future applications.

Among the efforts to develop alternative fuel sources, major attention is currently being given to the development of fuel cells, which transform the energy from any of a variety of fuels into electricity. One of the advantages of the fuel cell is that it can produce energy at the location of need, stationary or on the move, eliminating the need for costly and unsightly transmission lines. Its size is flexible enough to power a radio, an automobile, or a city (Skerrett, 1993).

TEACHER OPINIONS

In one survey, the majority of both elementary and secondary teachers expressed the opinion that STS considerations are an important part of the science education curriculum. This group ranked the following science-related social concerns as the five most significant: (1) air quality and atmosphere, (2) water resources, (3) population growth, (4) energy shortages, and (5) world hunger and food resources (Bybee & Bonnstetter, 1986).

EXEMPLARY PROGRAMS

Successful programs have demonstrated that when young people become involved with science-related social issues, they can make positive contributions as they learn. Let's look at several such exemplary programs.

CAKE Project

Students from the George C. Soule Elementary School in Freeport, Maine, formed CAKE (Concerns About Kids' Environment). The CAKE kids do not merely talk about how things should be, they go to work and do what they can, in hopes that the rest of us will follow their lead and together we will make an impact.

Each year, the students select a special project through which they can get involved in the effort to improve the environment. They study and learn about their topic; they find out what is happening—and why. For its first project, CAKE attacked polystyrene—the type of plastic used in most fast-food containers. When buried, polystyrene does not deteriorate into the soil, and when burned, it releases a poisonous substance into the air. Thus polystyrene and similar plastics are major concerns for environmental pollution and solid waste disposal. A core of nineteen CAKE members solicited community support and petitioned the town council to ban polystyrene packaging in Freeport. At a town meeting, representatives of a major fast-food chain argued against the ban, but CAKE students spoke in favor of it, and the council voted to outlaw the containers ("Styrofoam Forever? Never!" 1990).

In its second year, CAKE joined the worldwide concern about the rain forests of Central America. Joining other groups interested in rescuing this valuable area from destruction, these young environmentalists raised money and purchased several acres of rain forest land in Costa Rica. As owners of the land, the CAKE kids are now assured that the precious growth, at least on those few acres, will be allowed to stand. Yes, a few acres is only a small contribution, but these students are doing their part, and they know that a similar effort from enough such groups could save millions of acres of rain forest, and that *does* make a difference.

Projects selected by CAKE grow out of student interest and concerns. They are pursued with student leadership, under the direction of supportive parents and teachers who act as moderators and listeners, but who remain in a backseat, supportive role (Pennock, 1990). CAKE is truly an example of STS at its best.

Many concerned citizens applaud the efforts of CAKE. Plastic has many practical uses, but it is often hazardous to the environment. The problems caused by plastics provide a fruitful area for additional student research and involvement modeled by the CAKE project. In addition to using precious oil reserves as it is manufactured, plastic is clogging up landfills with nonbiodegradable material. If plastic does decay into the soil, it is estimated that the process will take hundreds of years, possibly producing dangerous material that will leach into the ground water. Further, plastic garbage discarded into the oceans is killing an estimated 2 million seabirds and 100,000 marine mammals each year. Some seagoing creatures get entangled in plastic garbage; others mistake certain items for food and ingest them (WREEC, 1987). Disposal of solid waste is one of the major challenges faced by present and future generations, and it is an issue with which young students can become involved in a well-structured STS program.

JASON Project

As discussed earlier, the JASON Project allows students at various educational sites throughout the United States and Canada to participate in oceanic explorations by communicating with scientists as they probe islands, underwater volcanoes, shipwrecks, and so on. See Exploration of New Frontiers, above, for more details.

Kids Network

The National Geographic Society's Kids Network is a program designed to promote genuine interest in protecting our environment. Students become involved in current events, as they gather data to share with other groups of students nationwide concerning the effects of acid rain, and other environmental issues. They are personally dealing with information they helped collect, rather than just reading in a textbook about the broadscale challenges of society. (See chapter 7 for a more complete description of the NGS Kids Network.)

NSTA Spotlight

The National Science Teachers Association encourages the development and use of programs that effectively heighten awareness of social considerations that relate to science at both the elementary and secondary levels by spotlighting model programs which increase student awareness. Science and technology issues that affect their lives encourage students to personally and collectively make a positive difference (Penick, 1984).

Energy audit

The NSTA gave special commendation to an energy conservation project implemented with high school students in Wallingford, Connecticut, which resulted in substantial savings to the school district in energy expenditures, as well as an exceptionally valuable experience for students. Students performed an extensive energy audit of the school, with the interest and cooperation of the administration, which implemented sound recommendations based on student findings (Wilson, 1984). Following the example of this successful project, groups of elementary students could also conduct an energy audit of their school, on a less complex level. The teacher, with the help of an interested principal and custodian, could share with students the costs of energy for the school, encourage students to brainstorm possible energy-conserving measures, then devise and implement a plan for monitoring and decreasing the costs by reducing energy waste.

Earthscope

In another program spotlighted by NSTA, an environmental center called Earthscope prepared students from the Monte Sano Elementary School in Huntsville, Alabama, to be more appreciative and responsive in their interactions with the environment (Black, 1984). Although the school had access to extensive state park facilities nearby, they spent the majority of their training time in the community at large, conducting classes in cemeteries, city parks, fields, and other local facilities, similar to those that could be accessed by most schools in other places. The program has received several awards. The Monte Sano project demonstrates that one of the factors of success with such efforts is to use local facilities as laboratories of learning.

MAKING CONNECTIONS

The real value of these experiences depends largely on the extent to which we make effective transitions from social issues to scientific principles and attitudes, and from there to decisions and actions. With the CAKE Project, for example, students are introduced to social challenges such as the buildup of plastics in landfills (issue) and the potential long-term impact on the environment (principle). Together they identified something that could be done to improve the situation, such as reducing the amount of plastic waste in their area (decision), and they set out to make it happen (action). The Energy Audit and Earthscope projects provide additional examples of students getting involved far beyond the point of acquiring information about the problem.

Each teacher can make a positive difference in the future by doing more than simply making students aware of science-related challenges that face society. Taking the next step of identifying *how* science and technology enter the picture heightens student awareness of the issue. If we then involve students in decisions and actions, the likelihood of lifelong commitments resulting from the experience is greatly enhanced.

IN CLOSING

Although producing responsible, informed citizens is a goal for the entire education community, science education clearly has a significant role. As with other aspects of the total science experience, learning about social issues is more effective if students are directly involved. Elementary science experiences lay the groundwork for positive change when they involve children in projects to improve the school, community, or world environment. Students can then internalize the satisfaction of knowing that what they do now can make a difference. These feelings will have a far-reaching impact on their responsible involvement as adult citizens.

Our challenge as citizens is to learn from the past and to serve the present with careful consideration for the future. Working harmoniously with nature does not mean that the quality of life must diminish. Failure to work harmoniously with nature *guarantees* that it will. Tomorrow's decisions lie with today's students. To be prepared to accept these responsibilities, young people must understand the societal problems and benefits associated with science and technology.

LIST OF RESOURCES

"A Conversation with Robert D. Ballard," *Instructor* (March 1990): 6.

Antonoff, Michael, "Living in a Virtual World," *Popular Science* 242, no. 6 (June 1993): 82–86, 124–25.

Black, Jim, and Dave Brotherton, "Earthscope." In *Focus on Excellence: Science/Technology/Society* vol. 1, no. 5, edited by John E. Penick and Richard Meinhard-Pellens (Washington, D.C.: National Science Teachers Association, 1984), 88–93.

Bybee, Rodger W., and Ronald J. Bonnstetter, "STS: What Do the Teachers Think?" In *NSTA 1985 Yearbook: Science Technology Society*, (Washington, D.C.: National Science Teachers Association, 1986), 117–27.

Esterbrook, Gregg, "Cleaning Up," *Newsweek* (July 24, 1989): 26–29, 32–42.

"Fighting Plastic," *National Geographic World* 177 (May 1990).

Hurd, Paul DeHart, "Science, Technology and Society: New Goals for Interdisciplinary Science Teaching," *The Science Teacher* 42, no. 2 (February 1975): 27–30.

Hurd, Paul DeHart, "A Rationale for a Science, Technology, and Society Theme in Science Education," In *NSTA 1985 Yearbook: Science Technology Society* (Washington, D.C.: National Science Teachers Association, 1986), 94-101.

Hurd, Paul DeHart, "Science/Technology/ Society: Modernizing the Science Curriculum," address, Utah Science Teachers Association, Salt Lake City, Utah, January 31, 1987.

McCormack, Alan J., "A Historical Evolution of Invention and Technology." In *NSTA 1985 Yearbook: Science Technology Society* (Washington, D.C.: National Science Teachers Association, 1986), 9–20.

NASA, *Spinoff 1988* (Washington, D.C.: U.S. Government Printing Office, 1988).

NSTA, *An NSTA Position Statement, Science-Technology-Society: Science Education for the 1980s* (Washington, D.C.: National Science Teachers Association, 1982).

Penick, John E., "Seeking Excellent S/T/S Programs." In *Focus on Excellence: Science/Technology/Society*, vol. 1, no. 5, edited by John E. Penick and Richard Meinhard-Pellens (Washington, D.C.: National Science Teachers Association, 1984), 1–3.

Pennock, Margaret, personal letter describing the CAKE project, July 10, 1990.

Skerrett, P. J., "Fuel Cells Update," *Popular Science* 242, no. 6 (June 1993), 88–91, 120–21.

"Styrofoam Forever? Never!" *Super Science Blue* 1, no. 4, (January 1990): 4.

Wilson, Carol A., "Wallingford Auditing Technical Team." In *Focus on Excellence: Science/Technology/Society*, vol. 1, no. 5, edited by John E. Penick and Richard Meinhard-Pellens (Washington, D.C.: National Science Teachers Association, 1984), 68–72.

WREEC, *Aquatic Project Wild, U.S.A.* (Western Regional Environmental Education Council, 1987), 159–61.

SECTION

CONTENT AND PROBLEM-SOLVING ACTIVITIES

INTRODUCTION TO SECTION 2

The purpose of Section 2 is to provide the elementary teacher with an interesting and useful reference of content information and a collection of hands-on problem-solving activities. The intent of the content portion of these chapters is not to offer an in-depth study of the topics, but to provide a meaningful reference for the teacher at a step beyond that which would be directly studied in the elementary classroom. An effort has been made to include points of interest to children in these content chapters.

Elementary science must not be a sterile textbook experience. We do not diminish the importance of learning to learn from the many excellent trade books, textbooks, and reference materials that we hope will be available to all classrooms. Hopefully students will have many opportunities to develop and apply their research skills, and with each experience they will learn and grow. By reading and researching, and comparing and discussing information and ideas with others, students will learn many things about the natural world, but even more importantly they learn how to learn. The interesting facts children acquire will fascinate them, and heighten their awareness and appreciation for the natural world, but as they perform the research activities they stretch their ability to learn more and more about the world around them. This is the point of the famous Chinese Proverb, "Give a man a fish and you feed him for a day. Teach him how to fish and you feed him for a lifetime."

Experiences with printed materials must be richly supplemented with experiences that provide interactions with the natural world. It is our hope that the elementary teacher will approach the topic of science with a clear priority on teaching the process skills with problem-solving applications, and with a heavy emphasis on direct involvement of students in hands-on activities that are appropriate for their level. The chapters that follow provide a number of activities that are appropriate for the elementary grades. We hope teachers will use the activities that are appropriate for their students according to established objectives, along with many other activities from additional sources, including the teacher's own creativity. We also hope that the content information in these chapters will provide a convenient reference and source of review for the teacher when needed.

CONNECTING ACTIVITIES WITH CONTENT

For each of the content chapters, the major headings are numbered with Roman Numerals. These numbered headings then appear again in the activities section at the end of the chapter. The hands-on activities are grouped according to the major headings, making it easy to know which activities tie in with each part of the content section. With the exception of the "Introduction" and "Closing," one or more activities are provided for all major topics. Most of the activities can be easily adapted for a broad range of grade levels. The step-by-step instructions, which are written to the student, are followed, in most cases, by extensions "For Problem Solvers" that provide higher levels of challenge for those who are motivated to do them. In some of these sections multiple activities are suggested. We hope that all students will be motivated to do the extensions for problem solvers on at least some of the activities.

FORMAT OF THE ACTIVITIES

The format of the activities is uniform throughout the book, and incorporates the following parts. For any given activity, the portion above the Teacher Information section can be copied and given to students, along with materials listed, and students should be able to complete the main activity with minimal direction and supervision.

The activities include the following parts:

1. ***Title:*** *The title of the activity is in the form of a question, which hopefully can be answered by students in the process of completing the activity.*
2. ***Materials:*** *A list of materials that are needed for the activity is provided.*
3. ***Procedure:*** *Step-by-step instructions are written for students. These instructions are designed to lead students in discovery and problem solving, and encourage frequent discussion and sharing of ideas. Conceptual information is deliberately not given here, as students are encouraged to explore and discover.*
4. ***For Problem Solvers:*** *For most of the activities, the numbered procedural steps are followed by a section "For Problem Solvers." Suggestions are given here to encourage students toward research and further problem-solving investigations related to the activity. These extensions often involve higher level skills, such as manipulating variables, formulating hypotheses, and experimentation, challenging students to expand their minds with additional discovery. Instructions in this section are more general and often materials are needed that are not listed at the beginning of the activity. This section is for students who are self-starters and motivated.*

   Note: Many of these activities could be developed into excellent science fair projects. They might also lead to ideas for Invention Convention projects.

   While some of the problem-solving activities could be assigned, and perhaps should be, there is something enticing about the challenge of an activity that is optional, and there is something magic about the motivation that can be added to the learning atmosphere by offering students choices.

   The terms "hypothesis" and "variable" are used sparingly in the step-by-step instructions for the activities to avoid encumbering the activities with terminology. However, these same terms are used freely in the extensions "For Problem Solvers," assuming that students who accept these challenges are willing to deal more directly with problem-solving thought processes and that by being immersed with these terms, students will come to feel comfortable with them. This involvement is likely to be more influenced by student interest and attitude toward science than by raw intelligence.
5. ***Teacher Information:*** *This section provides information that will be helpful to the teacher but is not needed by the student. Often conceptual information is provided which, if given to the student prior to beginning the activity, can inhibit the discovery process. Students need many experiences in finding out what is, not just verifying that what they read or hear is so.*
6. ***Integrating:*** *Many activities include experiences that integrate science with other areas of the curriculum. In cases where that connection is obvious, the subject areas are listed. You might include others by adding your own touch to the activities.*
7. ***Process Skills:*** *Process skills that are applied are listed here for most of the activities. Again, your embellishments to the activities will sometimes add others.*

THE SCIENCE CURRICULUM ACTIVITIES LIBRARY

Teachers who have used the series of three activity books written by Marvin N. Tolman and James O. Morton, called the *Science*

Curriculum Activities Library will recognize the format of the activities. The books referred to are titled, *Life Science Activities for Grades 2-8, Physical Science Activities for Grades 2-8,* and *Earth Science Activities for Grades 2-8.* Although the titles indicate that the books begin at second grade level, many of the activities included in the books were designed for the earlier grades — some even for pre-kindergarten. These books are available from Parker Pub. Co.

CHAPTER

ANIMALS

CHAPTER OUTLINE:

- INTRODUCTION
- LIVING ORGANISMS
- CLASSIFICATION OF ANIMALS
- VERTEBRATES AND INVERTEBRATES
- MAMMALS
  - Habitats
  - Value of Mammals to Humans
  - Commonalities and Differences
  - Reproduction of Mammals
- FISH
- AMPHIBIANS
- REPTILES
  - Snakes
  - Lizards
  - Turtles
  - Crocodilians
- BIRDS
  - Many Kinds and Many Places
  - Migration
  - Special Adaptations
    - Eyes
    - Feathers
    - Beaks and feet
- ARTHROPODS
  - Insects
    - Sensational survivors
    - Life cycles
  - Spiders
  - Crustaceans
- ANIMAL ADAPTATIONS
- IN CLOSING
- LIST OF RESOURCES
- ACTIVITIES

I WONDER . . .

What makes mammals different from all other animals?
Why are amphibians called amphibians?
The glass snake isn't a snake—so what is it?
How can you tell an alligator from a crocodile?
What one characteristic most clearly identifies a bird as a bird?
How hungry would you get if you really "ate like a bird?"
Which bird is the champion migrator?
Why doesn't the woodpecker beat its brains out?
Why do biologists like to study insects for hereditary factors?
Are spiders our enemies or our friends?

I. INTRODUCTION

With elementary students, the topic of animals is in a class by itself. Dinosaurs fascinate children, but they stand today only as lifeless forms, representing what once was. Magnets capture the attention of all age groups, but they have no eyes or cuddly fur. Only animals offer the magic of a live response to the voice and affections of a child. And beyond the cuddly qualities of puppies, kittens, and hamsters, the fascinating diversity of the animal kingdom can leave most any curious investigator in awe.

The first section of this chapter, Living Organisms, compares the unique characteristics of plants and animals, and introduces rationale used in classifying living things. The teacher should refer back to this section when reviewing the next chapter, Plants.

II. LIVING ORGANISMS

Compared with plants, animals have the disadvantage that they cannot make their own food, but they have the advantage of being able to move about quite freely in search of food. Despite their fundamental and conspicuous differences, though, plants and animals share some commonalities: both are living organisms, and both are made of combinations of cells that are specialized for certain functions.

Cells are the smallest functioning units of living things. In plants and animals, cells combine to make tissues, and tissues merge as organs, which in turn join together as systems, such as the circulatory system of a mammal or the vascular system of a flowering plant, enabling each plant and each animal to carry out the natural processes and activities of its species. Because of specialized cells, tissues, organs, and systems, a honeybee is able to function as a honeybee, a beaver as a beaver, and a delicate fern is uniquely able to carry out the functions that make a fern a fern.

The topic of *animals* is far too extensive to treat fully in a single chapter of a book that is committed to a broad treatment of elementary science. The information presented here is limited to a brief description of the animal kingdom, with some of the major classification rationale but only a scant introduction to scientific terms used in classifying animals. Information is given about a few major groups of animals, plus additional points of interest to the elementary grades. Most of our attention is given to mammals, birds, reptiles, and arthropods, which are among the animals commonly studied at the elementary level.

III. CLASSIFICATION OF ANIMALS

At first glance, one would not think that a black widow spider had anything in common with a crayfish, or that a mouse had any resemblance at all to a house cat or to an elephant. Looking closer, though, the cat, the mouse, and the elephant all have hair on their bodies, they all give live birth, and they suckle their young. Because of these and other characteristics the elephant, the cat, and the mouse are called *mammals.* As for the spider and the crayfish, both are called *arthropods* because they have certain common characteristics, including segmented bodies, jointed legs, and external skeletons. Other arthropods include sowbugs, pillbugs, and all forms of insects.

All of us know the names of many animals, such as the dog, cat, chicken, pig, horse, butterfly, and so on. These are called *common names,* and they are different for people in different countries. Even in the same language and in the same country, there can be many common names for a given animal. For example, mountain lion, cougar, and puma, are all names commonly used in reference to the same animal. To keep track of animals and to communicate clearly about them with others, scientists have found it useful to classify them according to certain characteristics. They assign a *scientific name,* in Latin, to each animal, and the scientific name is the same worldwide.

First, all animals are in a general category called *animalia.* By contrast, plants belong to a group called *plantae.* For a long time, all living things were considered to be either plant or animal. In the scientific classification scheme, these are called *kingdoms.* It is estimated that at least 5 million different kinds of living organisms exist, and some of them have caused considerable concern—even frustration—because they do not clearly fit as either plant or animal. For this reason, in recent years scientists have agreed on a five-kingdom system of classifying living things, adding the kingdoms *monera* (bacteria), *protista* (protozoa and algae), and *fungi* (yeasts, molds, and mushrooms). Indicative of the ever-changing nature of science, there is now considerable support among scientists for a sixth kingdom, to be divided from the monerans. This chapter will consider the animal kingdom.

In classifying living things, kingdoms are divided into *phyla,* which are further divided into *classes,* and so on, until a group of living things with very similar characteristics is identified. Such a homogeneous group is called a *species.* For example, the black widow spider is a species, and all female black widow spiders have shiny black bodies, long legs, and a certain type of red marking on the underside of the abdomen. Black widow spiders breed only with other black widow spiders, and their offspring are fertile black widow spiders. Small differences can be found even within species, however, forming a still finer category called a *subspecies.* In most parts of the United States, for instance, the red marking on the underside of the black widow's abdomen resembles the shape of an hourglass, but in the northern Mediterranean the black widow is usually marked with a series of red spots.

The hierarchy of groupings used in classifying animals is as follows:

- **kingdom**
- **phylum**
- **class**
- **order**
- **family**
- **genus**
- **species**
- **subspecies**

Humans are part of the animal kingdom; we have certain characteristics in common with other animals. Here is the scientific name of each level in the classification system for humans and for house mice. First, notice that the first three levels are identical. Like mice and other mammals, humans have hair on their bodies, they give live birth, and they have other characteristics by which mammals are identified. (Note: Names of species are commonly written in lowercase and italicized.)

	Human	**Mouse**
Kingdom	*Animalia*	*Animalia*
Phylum	*Chordata*	*Chordata*
Class	*Mammalia*	*Mammalia*
Order	*Primates*	*Rodentia*
Family	*Hominidae*	*Muridae*
Genus	*Homo*	*Mus*
Species	*sapiens (human)*	*musculus (house mouse)*

Scientists commonly refer to animals by their genus and species names. The scientific name for human beings, therefore, is *Homo sapiens*. Here are the family trees for the honeybee, the black widow spider, and the American crayfish.

	Honeybee	**Black Widow**	**Am. Crayfish**
Kingdom	*Animalia*	*Animalia*	*Animalia*
Phylum	*Arthropoda*	*Arthropoda*	*Arthropoda*
Class	*Insecta (insect)*	*Arachnida*	*Crustacea*
Order	*Hymen-optera*	*Araneae (spider)*	*Decapoda*
Family	*Apidae*	*Theridiidae*	*Astacidae*
Genus	*Apis*	*Latrodectus*	*Cambarus*
Species	*mellifera*	*mactans*	*virilis*

Many people consider spiders and insects to be closely related, in fact many people think spiders *are* insects, but they would not think of spiders as having anything in common with the crayfish. However, insects, spiders, and crayfish are all arthropods because of their external skeletons, segmented bodies, and jointed legs.

IV. VERTEBRATES AND INVERTEBRATES

Scientists have also found it helpful to classify all animals into two major groups, *vertebrates* (those with backbones) and *invertebrates* (those without backbones). Although they do not appear on the levels of classification listed above, these terms are commonly used in describing animals. Members of the subphylum vertebrata (phylum chordata) are the only vertebrates. The vertebrates include reptiles, amphibians, fish, birds, and mammals. The invertebrates are the animals in all other phyla, including spiders, insects, lobsters, jellyfish, and so on.

The remainder of this chapter will present information on a few major groups of animals that are of interest to the elementary grades: mammals, fish, amphibians, reptiles, birds, and arthropods.

MAMMALS

Kingdom	*Animalia*
Phylum	*Chordata*
Subphylum	*Vertebrata*
Class	*Mammalia*

There is little doubt that the class of animals children are best acquainted with are the mammals. If asked to make a list of living things, some children might include plants, people, insects, spiders, birds, snakes, fish, and animals. The word "animal," in the minds of many children, is synonymous with "mammal."

Habitats

Biologists and explorers have found mammals almost everywhere: in the Arctic, the Antarctic, the tropics, deserts, and forests. There are even mammals that fly (bats), and mammals that live in the sea (whales, porpoises). Most mammals are very mobile, they adapt relatively quickly to environmental changes, and they are able to move to new locations as food supplies and other environmental conditions change.

Some mammals migrate at different seasons of the year. Elk, for instance, live high in the mountains during the summer and in the winter they move to lower elevations. Seals of the Pacific Ocean prefer the cool waters north of the Aleutian Islands during the summer, but they move south toward California for the winter. Gray whales swim from their Arctic feeding grounds to warmer waters near the northwest coast of Mexico in the fall of the year. Food for them is scarce there, but they give birth at the end of the migration, and their young could not survive if they were born in the frigid northern waters.

Other mammals prefer to ignore the cold months of the year by hibernating, and still others just take a long winter's nap and pretend to hibernate. Ground squirrels and woodchucks are true hibernators. During this period of time, their heart rate slows down and their body temperature drops. Breathing rate decreases to as little as one breath in five minutes. Skunks and raccoons, on the other hand, are not true hibernators. They do go into a deep, extended sleep, their heart rate and breathing rate both slow down, and they live on food (fat) stored in the body. However, these animals can wake up on mild winter days, and maybe even go for a stroll, then go back to sleep again. Animals in true hibernation cannot be awakened. Bears seem to be somewhere between these two groups; they come closer to true hibernation than do skunks and raccoons, yet their body temperature does not drop and they sometimes wake up and go for a stroll, then return to their slumber.

Value of Mammals to Humans

Mammals have been hunted as an important source of food since prehistoric times. Animal skins were used for making clothing, and other body parts, such as bones, teeth, and horns, were used for making tools and ornaments. People began domesticating mammals thousands of years ago, especially dogs and such others as cows, horses, goats, and sheep. Many mammals are still raised as pets, and even with today's level of sophistication in ranching, wild animals are hunted for food and for skins. Also, in many parts of the world, horses, camels, dogs, and other mammals are still used for transportation of people and goods.

Commonalities and Differences

All mammals feed their young on milk produced by the mother. They have hair on their bodies, and they have a larger, more well-developed brain than do other animals. Mammals are warm-blooded, or *endothermic*, meaning that they maintain their own body temperature independent of environmental temperature. Endothermic animals have the advantage of being able to maintain vigorous activity within most normal atmospheric temperature ranges. If normal body temperature is not maintained, death occurs. Most mammals are protected from the cold by layers of fat or by protective coverings, such as fur, and most have cooling mechanisms for hot weather, such as perspiring, panting, or just lying quietly in the shade or wherever they can find refuge from the heat.

Mammals also have other common properties that are less obvious to the observer, such as a four-chambered heart. The only other endothermic animals are the birds, which also have a four-chambered heart. The internal temperature of other animals fluctuates with the environmental temperature. These are called *ectothermic,* or cold-blooded animals.

Mammals include some of the most familiar animals, such as dogs, cats, cows, horses, and humans. They also include some very unusual animals, such as anteaters, armadillos, flying squirrels, and the duck-billed platypus, and some of the most fascinating, including giraffes, bears, and kangaroos.

Mammals vary greatly in size. The tiny Kitti's hog-nosed bat of Thailand is a mammal about the size of a bumblebee and weighs about 2 grams (1/14 ounce)—about as much as a penny. On the other end of the size spectrum, the largest animal that has ever lived is a mammal! Larger than any dinosaur, the great blue whale can grow to more than 30 meters (100 feet) long, with a weight greater than 136,000 kilograms (150 tons).

The lifespan of mammals ranges from less than a year (such is the case with many mice and shrews) to approximately sixty years for elephants and sometimes over 100 years for humans.

Reproduction of Mammals

The duck-billed platypus and the spiny anteater, both of Australia, lay eggs. The hatched young are suckled by their mother, as is true of other mammals. All other known mammals are born alive. One or more tiny eggs inside the mother's body are fertilized by sperm cells from a male of the same species when the male and female mate. The fertilized egg attaches to the mother's uterus, where it receives oxygen and nutrients and develops as an embryo until it is ready for birth.

With *placental mammals* (including humans), the embryo grows in a protective sack, called the *embryonic sac,* which is attached to the uterus (an organ in the female's reproductive system). Nutrients flow to the developing baby from the placenta through an *umbilical cord,* and the baby's liquefied wastes are returned by the same cord, then disposed of by the mother's body. The umbilical cord is attached at the baby's abdomen; the navel, or "belly button," is a reminder of this early stage in the lives of humans.

Marsupial infants, such as kangaroos and opossums, are born at an immature stage. They crawl into a special protective pouch of the mother, attach themselves to a nipple, and continue their development.

The amount of time required for the embryo to develop varies from one mammal to another. The *gestation period* (from the time the egg is fertilized until the new baby is born) ranges from about sixteen days in golden hamsters to 650 days in elephants. It requires approximately twenty-one days for mice, sixty-three days for cats and dogs, and nine months for humans.

Mammals care for their young. Insects, spiders, turtles, and many other animals are able to find their own food and take care of themselves right from the start, never being dependent upon adults of their species. Baby mammals, however, are dependent on adults for food and protection. This period of dependency varies from species to species; for humans it extends for several years. However, the need of infants for parental care is not limited to mammals. Alligators and crocodiles, for instance, care for their young for up to a year or more.

VI. FISH

Kingdom	*Animalia*
Phylum	*Chordata*
Class	*Gnathostomata (jawed fish)*

Fish appear in a broad variety of shapes and sizes, and every color of the rainbow is represented in their diverse exterior designs. Some fish look like worms, others like rocks, some are flat, and still others can puff up like balloons.

What we might think is the largest fish—the great blue whale—is really not a fish at all, but a mammal. The largest fish is the whale shark, which can grow to be over 12 meters (40 feet) long and weigh more than twice as much as an African elephant. Although your heart might skip a beat if you met up with it in your bathing suit, this fish feeds on plants and small sea animals and is harmless to humans.

Some fish will attack people, however. These include hammerhead sharks, white sharks, sometimes barracudas, and certainly the bloodthirsty types of piranhas. Stonefish and sting rays will not attack humans in search of their next meal, but they have poisonous spines that can inflict injury and even death in humans.

Fish have lived on the earth for an estimated 500 million years, and more than half of all known species of vertebrates in the world are fish. A few species of fish, including sharks and rays, have skeletons composed of cartilage; a few have skeletons composed partly of bone and partly of cartilage; others have skeletons composed largely of bone. The latter group, called *modern bony fish*, comprises about 95 percent of all known species of fish.

VII. AMPHIBIANS

Kingdom	*Animalia*
Phylum	*Chordata*
Class	*Amphibia*

Amphibians are ectothermic (cold-blooded) vertebrates. They have thin, loose skin. Common amphibians include frogs, toads, and salamanders. The term *amphibia* means "two lives." The eggs of amphibians are laid in water and become larvae, which are strictly aquatic creatures. The larvae of frogs and toads are known as *tadpoles* or *polliwogs*. Tadpoles develop, through metamorphosis, into adults that look very different from the tadpoles. Frog and toad eggs are fertilized outside the female's body. They are laid in a pond, held together by a jellylike material, and the male immediately spreads sperm over them. Frogs lay eggs in masses, while the toad's eggs are laid in strings.

Many amphibians have glands that produce a thick, slimy mucus that covers the skin, providing moisture and protection. The adult toad lives on land, returning to the water only to lay eggs. Its skin is usually dry and covered with wart-like bumps.

Adult frogs, and some types of salamanders, are well adapted to both land and aquatic life. On land, they breathe with lungs; while in water, oxygen that is dissolved in the water is absorbed directly through the skin into the blood, and carbon dioxide leaves the blood and passes out through the skin. In the fall, in cold climates, frogs burrow into the mud at the bottom of a pond and hibernate until spring.

Most frogs and toads range from about 5 to 15 centimeters (2 to 6 inches) in length, but most tree frogs are no more than 2.5 centimeters (1 inch) long, while the African frog can grow as long as 30 centimeters (12 inches). Salamanders usually measure from about 5 to 65 centimeters, with the giant salamander of Japan being up to 1.5 meters (5 feet) in length.

VIII. REPTILES

Kingdom	*Animalia*
Phylum	*Chordata*
Class	*Reptilia*

Reptiles are ectothermic (cold-blooded) vertebrates with dry, scaly skin, and they breathe with lungs. Some reptiles lay eggs, which are then incubated by the heat of the sun and the heat of the soil. With other reptiles, the eggs mature inside the mother's body and the young are born alive. Their skin does not grow, so reptiles must shed their skin as they grow; most of them shed their skin several times each year. Those with feet have claws on their toes. Snakes are so well known as reptiles that the words "snake" and "reptile" are probably synonymous terms in the minds of many people; yet lizards, turtles, alligators, and crocodiles are also reptiles.

Most reptiles are harmless. They may not compete well with puppies for human affection, but many of them, especially snakes and turtles, do live as pets in human homes.

Figure 10-1

Snakes use the tongue and Jacobson's organ, as well as the nostrils, to smell.

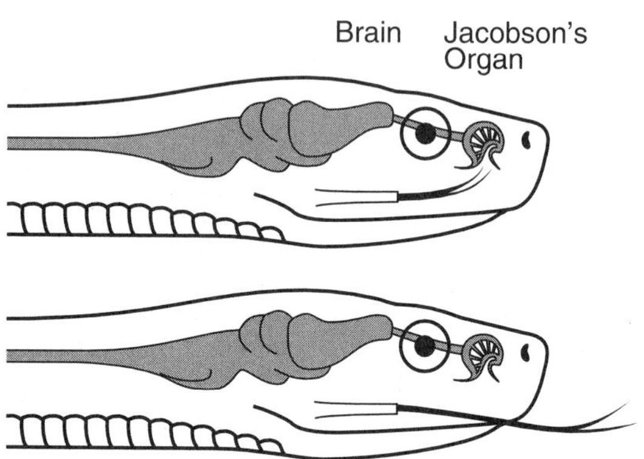

Snakes

Kingdom	*Animalia*
Phylum	*Chordata*
Class	*Reptilia*
Order	*Squamata*
Suborder	*Serpentes (snake)*

Snakes have no legs, ear openings, or eyelids. Their eyes are protected by transparent scales that do not move. Their senses of sight and hearing are not especially sharp, but their sense of smell is very keen. They smell with the Jacobson's organ as well as with the nostrils. The snake thrusts out its long, forked tongue and picks up scent particles from the air. When the tongue is drawn back into the mouth, these particles enter the Jacobson's organ (see Figure 10-1).

Snakes move by winding from side to side and by moving *scutes* (broad scales on the underside of their bodies) in a walking motion. Using the scutes, some can even move in a straight line, like a caterpillar, but they do so very slowly.

Small rodents make up a large part of the diet of these carnivores, and they always swallow their meal whole. Flexible jaws, with a detachable hinge, make it possible to swallow animals that are thicker than the snake's own body. They have two rows of teeth in the upper jaw and one row in the lower jaw. The teeth slant backward and are not used for chewing, but only to hold the food and assist in moving it down the throat.

Some snakes swallow their food alive. Others kill their prey by wrapping around it and squeezing until the animal suffocates. Still others poison the animal, then swallow it after it dies.

Venomous snakes have hollow fangs. When they strike their prey, poison is squeezed from venom glands, passes through the hollow fangs like a syringe, and into the body of the victim.

The only snakes in the United States that are a threat to humans are the rattlesnake, copperhead, water moccasin, and coral snake. People need to be very careful when they are in the territory of venomous snakes.

Lizards

Kingdom	*Animalia*
Phylum	*Chordata*
Class	*Reptilia*
Order	*Squamata*
Suborder	*Lacertilia (lizard)*

Lizards range in size from the very tiny swift to the Komodo dragon lizard of the Dutch East Indies, which grows to about 4.5 meters (15 feet) in length and can weigh close to 115 kilograms (250 pounds). One well-known lizard in the United States, the chameleon, has a total length of about 12 centimeters (5 inches). The chameleon is known for its ability to change its color and blend in with its surroundings. The poisonous Gila monster of Arizona and New Mexico grows to about 0.7 meters (2 feet) long. It is brown or black and covered with blotches of orange or pink.

Most lizards have four legs, and some can run very quickly. Some lizards can even run on the surface of water! A few legless lizards, including the glass snake, are often mistaken for snakes. The most obvious difference to the observer is the eyelids; lizards have eyelids that close, and snakes do not. Lizards also have external ear openings. The tails of some lizards break off easily, when seized by a predator, then the tail grows back again.

Turtles

Kingdom	*Animalia*
Phylum	*Chordata*
Class	*Reptilia*
Order	*Testudinata (turtle)*

The best-known distinguishing feature of the turtle is its shell. Turtles have an upper and lower shell with the body between, and the ability to withdraw head, tail, and legs into the shell. Some turtles can even close their shells tightly. Other distinguishing characteristics include the turtle's bony jaw that forms a sharp beak (no teeth), its short legs, and slow movement. Different species of turtles can be identified by markings and color patterns on their shells.

Some turtles live on land (these are often called tortoises), some live in fresh water (these are often called terrapins), and some live in the sea. Sea turtles are known to grow up to 2.5 meters (8 feet) long, weighing up to 450 kilograms (more than 1,000 pounds).

Crocodilians

Kingdom	*Animalia*
Phylum	*Chordata*
Class	*Reptilia*
Order	*Crocodilia*

Among the twenty or so species of crocodilians, all of which live in or near water, the best known are the alligators and crocodiles (see Figure 10-2). These animals live in tropical regions and have been hunted for their skins so broadly that hunting laws have been established to protect them. They have a long, low, lizard-shaped body, and a long snout with strong jaws and sharp teeth. These reptiles have short legs, webbed hind feet, and a long, powerful tail with which they swim. Bony scales cover their bodies and serve as an armor of protection from enemies. They are also equipped with built-in periscopes, as their eyes are positioned above their skull, enabling them to see above the water while their bodies are below the water.

Unlike most reptiles, alligators and crocodiles care for their young. The female lays eggs in a nest of grass, and generally remains near-

Figure 10-2

One way to distinguish crocodiles and alligators is by the shape of the snout.

by to protect the eggs from predators. When the eggs hatch, after about a nine-week incubation period, the young make high-pitched yelps. The mother responds to the call and helps the little ones out of the nest. She then looks after them until they are able to care for themselves, which can take up to a year or so.

Although alligators and crocodiles look much alike, there are a few characteristics by which they can be quite easily distinguished. The snout of an alligator is broadly rounded, whereas that of a crocodile is narrower and more pointed. The alligator typically has a heavier body than does a crocodile of the same length. The alligator also moves more slowly and is less aggressive than the crocodile. The fourth tooth in the lower jaw of the alligator fits into a cavity in the upper jaw and is concealed when the jaws are closed. The same tooth of the crocodile fits into a groove in the upper jaw and is visible when the jaws are closed.

Alligators and crocodiles eat many kinds of small animals that live in or near the water, including fish, turtles, small mammals, and birds. Occasionally, they will attack large animals.

Also of possible interest is a difference in their jaw muscles. Both have powerful jaws, but the crocodile can both open and close its mouth with force, whereas the alligator must lift its head and let the lower jaw drop. If you should see one of these beasts and you aren't sure whether it's an alligator or a crocodile, just sneak up behind it and throw your arms around its jaws. If it's an alligator, it won't be able to open its jaws. Before you try it, though, remember that crocodiles are quick and aggressive, and you could be on the menu for the next meal. And incidentally—if it's an alligator, don't ever let go!

IX. BIRDS

Kingdom	*Animalia*
Phylum	*Chordata*
Class	*Aves (bird)*

The attribute that best distinguishes birds from the rest of the animal world is the one that is probably the most obvious: birds have feathers. The fact that birds fly might run a close second place, but bats also fly, and so does the flying squirrel (okay, it doesn't really fly, but it glides), and both of these are mammals. To further complicate flight as a distinguishing feature, penguins and ostriches are birds, but they cannot fly at all. So for our purposes, let's stay with feathers as the trait that most clearly identifies a bird as a bird.

Also of interest are the scaly legs of birds, which are considered a sign of their relationship to reptiles. Feathers, in fact, are thought to be modified scales.

The bodies of most birds are well designed for flight, streamlined and relatively light. Hollow bones help to minimize body weight. With the wings and sleek body, birds have a lot of body surface compared to body volume. This is a disadvantage in cold weather, because heat is radiated from the body very rapidly and a great deal of energy is required to maintain body temperature. As we learned earlier, birds are endothermic vertebrates and maintenance of body temperature is literally a matter of life and death.

Because of high energy needs, birds eat a great deal for their size. Many birds eat their weight in food each day just to generate enough energy to stay alive. So if you know someone who "eats like a bird," you need to help your friend find some diet counseling fast!

Many Kinds and Many Places

Birds are found almost everywhere, and in many varieties. They come in large and small sizes, both colorful and dull. They can be found in the air, in trees, in water, and at times even under the water. The dipper, with its strong claws and sturdy legs, walks along the bottom of stream beds in search of insects and small fish. The common loon of North America has been seen at depths of 49 meters (160 feet), in pursuit of fish. And we mustn't forget that the penguin, a talented swimmer of the cold Antarctic waters, is a bird.

The smallest bird is the bee hummingbird, which grows to a grand size of 5 centimeters (2 inches) in length and weighs about 3 grams (1/10 ounce). The largest bird is the African ostrich, which may reach 2.4 meters (8 feet) tall and weigh up to 140 kilograms (more than 300 pounds).

Although the ostrich can't fly, it holds the record as the fastest bird on land, with running speeds up to 64 kilometers (40 miles) per hour. The peregrine falcon, holding the record as the fastest diver, can swoop down on its prey at speeds exceeding 320 kilometers (200 miles) per hour. The medal for the highest flyer goes to the bar-headed goose, which has been seen flying over the Himalayas at altitudes of over 7,625 meters (25,000 feet).

Migration

Certain insects and even some mammals migrate, but we're probably safe in suggesting that most people probably think of birds first when they think about migration. With changes in food supplies and weather patterns from one season to another, many birds spend their winters and summers in widely separated places. Reasons for selecting specific locations, or exactly what triggers the migration to begin, raises many questions that are only partially explained. Known factors include food supply, weather patterns, length of days, and glandular secretions within the bodies of the birds. The migration of birds stands today as one of the most fascinating and least understood events in nature.

Migration habits among birds vary from no migration at all to migrations of short distances to very lengthy journeys. Some grouse and many kinds of finches and sparrows are among those that are adapted to survive summer and winter in the same location. Blue grouse have a reverse migration; they inhabit lowlands in the summer and move to the tops of mountain evergreen trees in the winter. Some biologists think this strange migratory pattern may have developed through avoidance of predators that move in opposite directions.

Canada geese are well known for their **V**-shaped formation in flight as they travel between their summer nesting grounds (northern Canada) and their winter habitats (as far south as northern Florida and northern Mexico).

Some birds like living in the tropics year-round. Among these, certain species prefer the dry season and others are more fond of the rainy season, so they pass each other going in opposite directions to maintain their chosen climatic conditions.

Still other birds travel much longer distances. The British yellow wagtail nests in England and winters in Africa. The sharp-tailed sandpiper breeds in Siberia and spends its winters as far away as southeast Asia or even Australia. The blackpoll warbler, no bigger than a sparrow, flies nonstop for almost 90 hours, from North America to its South American winter home—a trip of approximately 4,000 kilometers (about 2,500 miles). The gold medal for distance goes to the Arctic tern, which spends its summers in the Arctic and its winters in the Antarctic, a yearly round trip of about 35,400 kilometers (22,000 miles).

Special Adaptations

Over the time of their existence (more than 200 million years), birds have adapted well to the requirements of many different habitats and conditions, resulting in some very unique characteristics. In considering special adaptations of birds, or of any other animals, we need to assume a restrained posture in implying cause and effect. Some would say, for instance, that the cedar waxwing and other seed-eating birds have short, stout beaks *so that they can* crack seeds, or that the great blue heron has long legs and a spear-like beak *so that it can* catch fish in shallow water. Perhaps, instead, these birds have developed eating habits within the limitations of, or which capitalize on the strengths of, their special body features and design. At the same time, we need to recognize that within any given species, those most able to cope with the demands and limitations of the current available habitat are the ones that survive and reproduce, thereby perpetuating the characteristics most suited to the conditions in which they live. Members of the species that are most able to cope with the environment will dominate the species. This process is called *natural selection*. Of course, it is not only true of birds but of all living things.

Evolutionists believe that many forces are at work in the evolutionary development of any species. Consider the following scenarios, for example:

Scenario 1. Characteristics that help a species to survive are strengthened and refined over time: *Assume that sparrows live mostly on seeds that have hard shells, that some sparrows have strong beaks, and that others with weaker beaks have a difficult time cracking the shells and getting enough to eat. The strong-beaked sparrows will have a higher survival rate and pass the characteristic of the strong beak on to their offspring. The frequency of weak-beaked sparrows will decrease, and sparrows, as a species, will evolve to have stronger beaks.*

Scenario 2. Changing conditions can redefine the success mechanisms and cause new features to be strengthened: *Suppose that seeds become scarce and some sparrows have beaks that are a bit longer and narrower than usual, and they are able to adjust to eating insects much more readily than are sparrows with the conventional short, stout beak. Sparrows with the nonconventional beak will flourish, while those whose food supply is dwindling will suffer a reduced survival rate, and in time the species will evolve toward having a longer, narrower beak.*

The woodpecker has acquired some interesting characteristics and habits. Did you ever observe one of these little hammerheads in the act of extracting insects from under the bark of a tree? For most animals, pounding on a tree with such force and rapidity would beat their brains out. The woodpecker, however, is equipped with special muscles that act as shock absorbers in the skull, protecting the brain from the impact, as the bird drills holes in trees. In addition, the woodpecker's tongue is of rather unusual design; it is attached to a structure of bone and elastic tissue called the hyoid, which loops around the skull and pushes the tongue out of the mouth, giving the tongue unusual length (see Figure 10-3). The tongue is also sticky and is equipped with a barbed tip, assisting significantly in the extraction of insects from their refuge beneath the bark. Most woodpeckers have feet designed with two toes in front and two in back, which helps them to climb without falling backward, and stiff tail feathers that press against the tree and support the body.

Today's woodpecker is probably a product of both forces suggested in the two scenarios above, and the same is probably true of most other species of animals. The bald eagle is a successful hunter of rodents, fish, and so on, because of its keen eyesight, its talons and beak that cling to animals and tear flesh, its power in flight, and other characteristics. If the pelican had only seeds and berries to eat, instead of fish, it would probably become extinct rather quickly. Each species has become skilled in certain feeding patterns made possible, at least in part, by its structural design.

Eyes

Birds are well known for their keen eyesight. Less well known are their built-in windshield wipers, which allow them to keep their eyes cleaned and lubricated without blinking. In addition to two eyelids similar to those of mammals, which can close the eye, birds have a third eyelid that sweeps back and forth, cleaning away dust and foreign matter.

Feathers

Not only do feathers help a bird to fly, but they are a great benefit in conserving body heat. Next to the skin are the small, fluffy *down* feathers that are famous for their insulating qualities. These have long been known as one of the best materials for lining sleeping bags, quilts, and winter coats. They also do a nice job of conserving body heat for the bird. *Contour* feathers lie close to the body, providing streamlining, and the larger contour feathers of the wings and tail, which might be called *flight* feathers, help to propel the bird through the air and provide maneuverability as it flies.

Figure 10-3

The hyoid loops around the woodpecker's head and pushes the tongue out of the mouth.

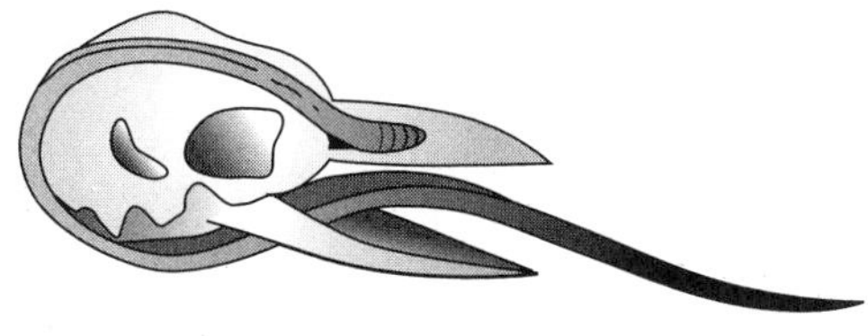

A contour feather usually has hundreds of parallel branches, called barbs, that branch out from a central shaft, forming a vein on each side of the shaft. Growing from the barbs are barbules. The barbules have tiny hooks that link the barbs together, providing both strength and flexibility to the vein. These parts, including the hooks, can be seen under a magnifying glass (see Figure 10-4).

Feathers provide color and variation in design. One could safely say they are largely responsible for the delightful way in which birds add variety to the wonders of wildlife. How drab it would be if there were only one style and color of feather. Experiencing the colors of exotic birds, or watching a male peacock spread its tail feathers in hopes of impressing a female peacock, can be breathtaking. Coloring also provides protection for many birds, as they blend in with the colors of their natural habitat, concealing them from the view of hungry predators.

Most birds regularly *preen* their feathers.

Figure 10-4

This drawing of a feather, with a small section magnified, shows how the barbules link the barbs together.

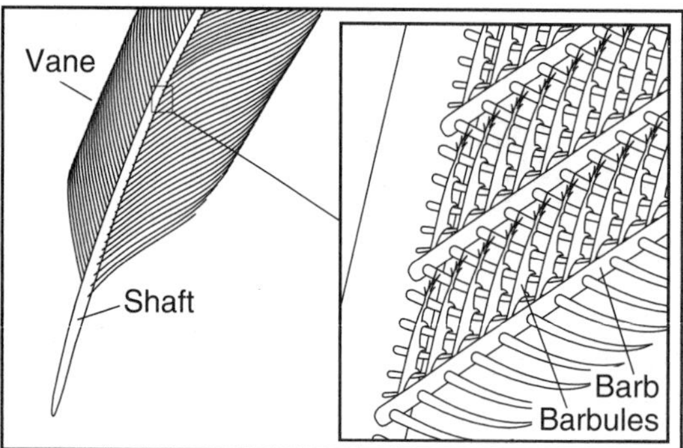

They straighten any feathers that are ruffled, pressing them out and refastening any barbs that might have become detached. This is important for waterproofing and for reducing air resistance in flight. They use the bill to press a drop of oil from a gland that is located just above the tail, then spread the oil over the feathers, providing an attractive sheen and assuring proper protection from water. Thus birds keep their feathers fine-tuned, water-proofed, and ready for both flight and protection from bad weather. Thanks to the oil treatment, ducks can float for long periods of time, effectively protected from water penetration within the feathers.

Beaks and feet

Each species of birds has beaks and feet that seem to be designed well for specialized functions, with broad diversity from one species to another. Figure 10-5 shows some common structures of both beaks and feet. The duck has webbed feet that are useful for swimming, and a spoon-shaped beak that easily scoops up plants and small fish in water. Some beaks are better suited for cracking seeds and some for

Figure 10-5

The beaks and feet of birds come in a variety of forms and sizes.

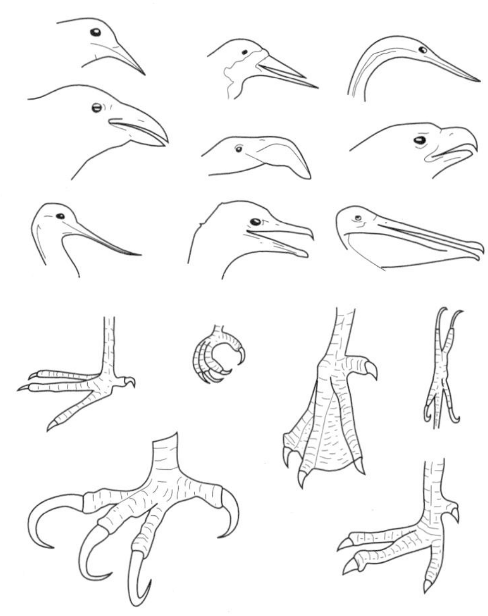

tearing flesh. Some birds' feet have talons that can capture small animals. The sparrow's feet automatically cling to a small limb of a tree or bush—so effectively that the bird can go to sleep without danger of falling.

X. ARTHROPODS

Kingdom	*Animalia*
Phylum	*Arthropoda*

In terms of numbers, the arthropods are by far the largest phylum. All of these animals have *exoskeletons* (skeletons on the outside of their bodies), made of a tough material called *chitin*. Jointed legs and segmented bodies are other characteristics by which the arthropods are known. They range from insects, to spiders, to millipedes and centipedes, to crabs, lobsters, and shrimp. This phylum includes the great majority of all the different kinds of animals in the world. Information follows on just two segments of this voluminous phylum—insects and spiders. Insects comprise an entire class, whereas spiders include only one order of a class of arthropods called arachnids.

Insects

Kingdom	*Animalia*
Phylum	*Arthropoda*
Class	*Insecta*

Few insects live in the oceans, but other than that they live almost everywhere on Earth. They are found from the polar regions to the tropics, and from deserts at elevations below sea level to snow-capped mountain peaks. Some live in total darkness in caves deep within the earth.

These six-legged creatures have some of the most fascinating features and habits of any in the animal kingdom. They use their antennae mostly to smell and to feel; some can even taste and hear with their antennae, and some of these creatures can taste with their feet. Some have sound-sensitive organs on the sides of their bodies and others on their legs. Still others hear by means of hairs on their bodies. They have no voices, but some insects are able to make sounds that can be heard more than 1.5 kilometers (about a mile) away. Some ants serve their colony as food storage tanks, and others keep and care for herds of "cows" (aphids, which provide a sweet liquid food for the ants). A flea can jump more than 100 times its length, and an ant can lift fifty times its own weight. How far could you jump, and how much could you lift if you could do as well?

Insects are the largest class of arthropods. Unlike most members of their phyla, they have three pairs of legs, all of which are attached to the chest, or thorax. Most insects have one or two pairs of wings, also attached to the thorax. Other characteristics which distinguish insects from other arthropods are: three distinct body parts, the head, thorax, and abdomen; and one pair of feelers, or antennae. Most adult insects have both *simple eyes* (one lens) and *compound eyes* (many lenses). They breathe through *spiracles,* which are openings on the sides of the abdomen and thorax.

To say there are more insects than any other class of arthropods, is a gross understatement. Of all the species of animals known and classified at this time (more than 1.5 million), the great majority of them are insects. In addition, scientists discover thousands of new species of insects every year, and it is believed that there are plenty of them yet to be discovered.

Ants, bees, beetles, wasps, houseflies, and butterflies are all insects. If you wrote the names of all known species of insects, with 100 on a page, it would take 8,000 pages. If you could write ten each minute, and if you wrote steadily for eight hours each day, it would take nearly six months to write them all. Furthermore, by then thousands more might have been discovered and you could be busy for hours yet! And on all those pages there wouldn't be the name of even one spider, because spiders are not insects. The major differences between spiders and insects are described in the following section on spiders.

The harm done to people by some insects tends to give all insects a bad name. It works that way with people, too; dastardly deeds done by a few people can give large groups of people a bad reputation. Insects destroy our crops, eat holes in our clothes, eat our food, and infect us with deadly diseases. They bite and sting us, and these can be very painful, and even poisonous.

But that's only one side of the story. The fact is, if there suddenly were no insects it would have very serious consequences for people, for life as we know it could not exist without insects. Insects pollinate many of our food crops, as well as flowers that beautify the landscape. We depend on bees for honey and silk worms for silk to make cloth. They are a necessary part of the diet for fish, birds, and many other animals and even some plants. Some insects eat other insects that damage our gardens and our crops, and still others are scavengers and feed on dead animals and plants, and enrich the soil with their waste products as well as with their own dead bodies.

Sensational survivors

Biologists believe that insects have lived on Earth much longer than humans (about 400 million years, versus 250,000 years for our species) and they have several characteristics that make them champions of survival. First, most insects can fly, which is a great advantage in the constant search for food and in escaping predators. They also have a very keen sense of smell for locating food. They have compound eyes, which gives them wide-angle vision, and many of them are very quick in their escape movements. Their small size makes it easy for them to find shelter from harsh weather and from many predators.

Insects adapt quickly to changing conditions. As a group, they eat almost anything, and some of them have a built-in immunity to many insecticides people use to destroy them. While some insects are killed by the insecticides, resistant individuals live and pass the immunity along to their offspring.

Last, but certainly not least, insects produce new generations rapidly. (This makes them very desirable in biological research; their short life cycles provide quick results in studying hereditary factors and the effects of chemicals.) Being able to fly not only enhances their abilities to find food and escape danger, but also greatly aids in the process of finding a mate.

Queen honeybees and queen ants, after only one mating period, can lay fertile eggs the rest of their lives! Sperm cells are stored in a special chamber in the female's body, to be used as needed. The queen honeybee can fertilize her eggs and produce females, or not fertilize them and produce males. And the females of some species are able to reproduce without mating at all.

While some insects lay only a few dozen eggs in a lifetime, others may lay a billion or more. The prize for the champion egg-layer goes to the female termite, who can produce thousands of eggs a day. She is only about as big as a tiny ant, but her abdomen can be so swollen with eggs that it is about 1,000 times as large as the rest of her body.

Life cycles

All insects develop from eggs, but they do not all go through the same growth pattern as they develop into adults. Most insects go through a *complete metamorphosis,* including egg, larva, pupa, and adult. The egg develops into a larva, a wormlike caterpillar stage. The larva eats almost continuously, and some of them have voracious appetites. It molts (sheds its exoskeleton) several times as it grows, each time growing a new and larger skin. The larva goes into the pupa stage—for a moth, this is called a cocoon; for a butterfly, this is a chrysalis. The moth spins its cocoon of silk, but the chrysalis of the butterfly is a case that forms and hardens around the caterpillar. After a resting period, during which time body tissues change, a fully grown adult insect emerges. The pupa stage varies in length of time from one species of insect to another, but always the transition that takes place during that time is remarkable. Witnessing a beautiful monarch butterfly emerge from a chrysalis, after seeing the former caterpillar, can leave an observer in reverent awe at the miracle of life's processes.

The developmental stages of some insects take a shortcut, with an *incomplete metamorphosis,* which includes three stages: egg, nymph, and adult. An egg of a grasshopper or cricket, for example, does not develop into a caterpillar, but rather hatches as a nymph. The nymph generally resembles the adult, except that it has no wings (or it has short wings) and the body parts are out of proportion, with the head appearing large for the body. It molts several times as it grows, but usually lives in the same surroundings and eats the same food as the adult.

Nymphs of the dragonfly and damsel fly differ more greatly from the adult stage. This particular nymph, often called a *naiad,* lives in the water and breathes with gills. When it has reached its full growth it crawls out of the water and onto a rock or the stem of a plant, molts for the last time, and emerges as a fully winged adult, never to return to the aquatic life.

The simplest pattern in the growth and development of insects occurs in only a few wingless insects, including the silverfish. These insects hatch from the egg looking like miniature adults. The young live in the same surroundings and eat the same food as the adults. They molt several times as they grow, but they change very little in their appearance except to grow larger.

Spiders

Kingdom	*Animalia*
Phylum	*Arthropoda*
Class	*Arachnida*
Order	*Acharina (spider)*

As arthropods, spiders have external skeletons, jointed legs and segmented bodies. Along with scorpions, mites, ticks, and daddy longlegs (or harvestman), they form a special class of arthropods called Arachnida. Characteristics spiders share with other arachnids include two body segments, four pairs of legs, and one to five pairs of simple eyes. Most spiders have eight eyes, arranged in different patterns and providing one of the attributes by which spiders are classified.

Spiders are often mistakenly thought to be insects. The above characteristics clearly separate them from the class of insects, as all insects have three body segments, with distinct head, thorax, and abdomen, whereas with the spider the head and thorax are combined into a single unit called the *cephalothorax.* Insects have only three pairs of legs; spiders have four pairs. Spiders have no compound eyes, no wings, and no antennae.

Another commonly mistaken family relationship, where spiders are concerned, has to do with the harvestman, or daddy longlegs, which is an arachnid along with spiders, scorpions, and so on, but it belongs to a different order, just as scorpions belong to a different order. Although it has four pairs of legs and all the other characteristics common to arachnids, that's where its relationship to the spider ends. The harvestman is as closely related to scorpions as it is to spiders. The harvestman feeds mostly on plant lice and therefore, like the spider, is very useful to gardeners.

There are more than 30,000 known kinds of spiders. Some are smaller than the head of a pin. The South American tarantula, with its legs outstretched, can be up to 25 centimeters (10 inches) long.

Although a few spiders can inflict poisonous bites, and their creepy crawly appearance makes it very difficult for them to win warm human friendships, they really are our allies in the struggle for survival on this planet. They do not eat the food we eat, and the insects that do eat our food provide many a meal for our friends the spiders. In fact, insects make up the major part of the spider's menu, so if we have spiders around the house, it is because we have insects, and the spiders serve us as a battalion standing guard against six-legged intruders. Many of the insects that spiders kill are pests to humans.

A spider does not actually eat an insect, but bites it and injects a poison that paralyzes it, then the spider sucks the juices out of the insect. In fact, spiders do not have chewing mouth parts, so they eat only liquids. However, sometimes a spider will eat some of the solid tissues of its prey by *predigesting* it. The spider sprays strong digestive juices on the tissue. The juices dissolve the tissue, and the material can then be drawn up, by sucking action, into the spider's mouth.

Spider silk is the strongest natural fiber known. It consists of protein and is produced in silk glands in the spider's abdomen. Most spiders have at least five different kinds of silk glands. Some silk glands produce a silk that dries when it contacts the air; other glands produce a silk that remains sticky. The liquid silk flows through tubes from the silk glands to *spinnerets* located at the rear of the abdomen. There the silk is released in the form of very fine threads. The exceptionally fine thread of silk from the black widow spider has been used as cross-hairs on gun sites, bomb sites, and survey instruments.

Some spiders do not spin webs, but webs are only one of this eight-legged creature's uses for silk. Spiders use silk to entangle and wrap up their prey, sometimes storing it for a later meal. The female also makes her nest or cocoon for eggs out of silk. They use it as a dragline to swing to the ground from high places, or just hang from it until danger is past, then climb back up the dragline and continue on their way or return to their nest. Some spiders hitchhike a ride on the wind by spinning a long strand of silk when the wind is blowing. The wind carries them away, with the silk thread acting as a parachute. The bolas spider spins a line of silk with a drop of sticky silk at the end, then swings the line at an insect, snagging its prey with the sticky ball.

With spiders that do spin webs, the shape and pattern of the web is genetically determined.

Crustaceans

Kingdom	*Animalia*
Phylum	*Arthropoda*
Class	*Crustacea*

The crustaceans include such well-known animals as lobsters, crabs, shrimp, and crayfish. Barnacles, wood lice, and water fleas are also crustaceans. Barnacles attach themselves to the hulls of ships and become a nuisance, slowing the ships and reducing their efficiency in moving through water. Removing the barnacles can be a costly and time-consuming task.

Many of the smaller crustaceans eat diatoms and other tiny food-producing plants. The crustaceans, in turn, are consumed by krill, fish, and other larger aquatic animals. These provide food for even larger animals—some whales live largely on krill. Thus crustaceans form a major link in the aquatic food chain.

Like other arthropods, crustaceans grow by shedding their exoskeleton (molting). If a crustacean loses an appendage, such as a claw, a leg, or an antenna, as in a battle with a predator, a new limb may grow in its place. Some crustaceans can even release the limb voluntarily, if necessary for escape.

Most of the 30,000 or so species of crustaceans live in saltwater. Some live in freshwater, however, and a few live on land. Pill bugs and sowbugs are land dwellers but they prefer moist places, such as under a rock or a board.

XI. ANIMAL ADAPTATIONS

The idea of adaptation was treated in the section on birds, earlier in this chapter. Suffice it to say here that other forms of life adapt in similar ways to those that were implied for birds. The term "adaptation" is sometimes used to mean a state of being adjusted to the environment. In this sense, every living organism is adapted. From another perspective, adaptation implies a process of change over time, often in response to shifting environmental conditions, such as weather or food supply. The migrations of the Arctic tern, the elk, and many other animals suggest seasonal adaptations, as do the heavier coats of furry animals in the autumn, or the shedding that occurs to lighten the coat in the springtime. Squirrels instinctively store nuts for the winter as one way of adapting to the inevitable hard times. Evidence abounds also for evolutionary changes that occur so subtly and over such long periods of time as to go unnoticed by the casual observer.

XII. IN CLOSING

The nature of this book limits its scope on any one topic, and nowhere in the book is this limitation felt more than in this chapter on animals. Our intent has been to spotlight some of the animals of greatest interest to children, and to emphasize some of the animal characteristics, similarities and differences that are appropriate for the elementary school curriculum.

LIST OF RESOURCES

"Animals," *World Book Encyclopedia* (1989).

Curtis, Helena, and N. Sue Barnes, *Invitation to Biology, Fourth Edition* (New York: Worth Publishers, Inc., 1985).

Kramer, David C., *Animals in the Classroom* (Menlo Park, CA: Addison-Wesley Publishing Co., 1989).

Tolman, Marvin N., and James O. Morton, *Life Science Activities for Grades 2–8* (West Nyack, NY: Parker Publishing Co., 1986).

Victor, Edward, *Science for the Elementary School, Sixth Edition* (New York: Macmillan Publishing Co., 1989).

CHAPTER

ANIMALS

ACTIVITIES

II. LIVING ORGANISMS

ACTIVITY 10-1: HOW MANY ANIMALS CAN YOU FIND?

Materials Needed:

Magazines and old books with animal pictures that can be cut out
Any pictures of animals
Scissors

Procedure:

1. Make a collection of pictures of animals. A small group or the whole class can work on this project. Ask for help from friends and family.
2. Look through the pictures and talk about them.
   a. Which of the animals in your collection are you familiar with?
      Where did you see them?
   b. Which ones have you never seen before?
   c. Which ones would you like to see?
   d. Of all the animals in the collection, which is your favorite?
   e. Which of the animals in your collection did you think were not even animals?
   f. Share with each other what you know about the animals.

For Problem Solvers:

Find someone who has lived in a different part of the world, and ask them to come to class and tell about animals in the pictures that are common in that part of the world. That person might be in your own class or school or neighborhood. Perhaps your friend will add new animal pictures to your collection.

If you have extra pictures left that you don't need for your collection, create your own picture and include one or more of them in it. You might even use several of them and make a collage.

Teacher Information:

The purpose of this activity is to get students thinking about animals, talking about them, and sharing what they know and the experiences they have had with animals. Don't limit the collection to certain kinds of animals—encourage students to bring pictures of any organism that is an animal. Have students write their names on the back of each picture so they can get their own back. Although they may not think they will want them back, some will become attached to their pictures before they are finished sharing them together.

Give the class several days to collect the pictures and encourage them to get help from family and friends. If a bulletin board is available, let students pin up their animals. If you're lucky, the collection will eventually include insects, spiders, and other creatures that some students might not have realized are animals. Wouldn't it be exciting if someone even brought a picture of an ameba or some other microscopic animal? I wonder if there will be any pictures of humans?

Don't discourage any natural tendencies to begin grouping the pictures, but if that interest starts to show up, consider the following activities and others that you know of that get into classification.

Keep the collection of animal pictures for use with other activities throughout this unit. Encourage students to continue adding to the collection.

Integrating: Social studies, art

Skills: Observing, communicating

III. CLASSIFICATION OF ANIMALS

ACTIVITY 10-2:

WHAT IS DIFFERENT ABOUT US, AND WHAT IS THE SAME?

(Class activity)

Materials Needed:

One class of charming students

Procedure:

1. Divide the class into several small groups.
2. Ask one group to stand at the front of the class. We'll call them Group 1.
3. Assign a second group (Group 2) to arrange Group 1 into two smaller groups, based on something they see about the people in Group 1.
4. When Group 2 is finished with their task, others in the room are to try to guess what characteristic Group 2 used to divide Group 1.
5. After the strategy used by Group 2 has been guessed, another group should have a chance to rearrange Group 1 according to some other visible characteristic and see if they can stump the rest of the class.

Teacher Information:

One of the best ways to begin teaching classification skills is to involve students in classifying students. It would be a good idea to have each group clear their classification criteria with you before they actually rearrange the groups. This will avoid any group using characteristics that would embarrass someone. You could even have each group classify themselves instead of one group classifying another, further reducing the likelihood of embarrassing someone. Students can use any of a number of attributes for classifying, such as those with shoelaces or without, those who are wearing red and those who are not, long hair and short hair, and so on. With such characteristics as long hair and short hair, students will have to agree on a way of determining what is long.

Integrating: Social studies, language arts

Skills: Observing, classifying

ACTIVITY 10-3:
HOW SHALL WE CLASSIFY OUR ANIMALS?

Materials Needed:

Collection of animal pictures (such as from Activity 10-1)

Procedure:

1. Look at the animal pictures, or some of them, and think about what is the same or different.
2. Put the set of pictures in two groups. Be sure that in each group there is something the same about all of the animals in that group, and that no animal in the other group has that particular characteristic.
3. Have someone else look at your groups of pictures and try to guess what criteria you used to group the animals.
4. Change roles and have your friend group the animals. Then you try to decide what criteria was used.
5. Think of another way to sort the animals into two groups and repeat the process.
6. Discuss what you did and what you were thinking. Talk about some other ways the animals could be classified.

For Problem Solvers:

After you get the animal pictures sorted into two groups, think of a way to sort each group into two more groups. Can you do it again with each of those groups? How far can you go with it and still find likenesses and differences?

Do some research on the ways that scientists classify animals. In some ways, your ideas might be just as good as theirs, but try to find out why animals are classified the way they are. Is the same classification scheme used by scientists worldwide? Should it be? Why or why not? Learn what you can and share it with your group.

Teacher Information:

In order to be able to communicate about animals and study them in an organized way, scientists need to agree on criteria for classifying them and on a name for each one. The current system used for classifying living things provides for such communication. Students might begin by grouping the animals according to color, number of legs, size, or how fast they think the animals can move. This experience will give them insight into the need for agreeing on a common, systematic classification scheme. Some of the characteristics they select might be the same as some of those used scientifically.

At the elementary level, the experience of thinking through a variety of ways to group the animals, and explaining the logic in the criteria they select, is more important than it is to learn about the scheme used by scientists for classifying animals. Those who choose to pursue the extension for problem solvers, however, might be intrigued by learning the logic by which animals are classified by scientists. Certainly, the research will provide challenge, insights, and growth for motivated students.

Integrating: Reading, social studies

Skills: Observing, inferring, classifying, communicating

IV. VERTEBRATES AND INVERTEBRATES

ACTIVITY 10-4:

WHAT ARE VERTEBRATES AND INVERTEBRATES?

Materials Needed:

Textbooks

Dictionary

Encyclopedias

Trade books about animals

Collection of animal pictures

Procedure:

1. Use the books that are available and find out what vertebrates are. You could use the dictionary or look up the word in the index of other references.
2. Find out what invertebrates are.
3. In your own words, describe how vertebrates and invertebrates are different.
4. From what you know, is a mouse a vertebrate? An elephant? A worm? A snake? A grasshopper? A snail?
5. Go to your collection of animal pictures and find some vertebrates and some invertebrates.
6. Sort the pictures into two groups: those that are vertebrates and those that are invertebrates.
7. Make a list of vertebrates and invertebrates that people use for food.
8. Make a list of vertebrates and invertebrates that people use for pets, for clothing, or for some other use.
9. Share your information with your group. Do all of you agree about which animals are vertebrates and which ones are invertebrates?
10. Are you a vertebrate or an invertebrate?

Teacher Information:

This exercise will help students to form the concept of what vertebrates and invertebrates are. Encourage them to study skeletons and identify vertebrae in several vertebrate animals, then compare the anatomy of an insect, a spider, and a jellyfish.

Integrating: Reading

Skills: Observing, inferring, classifying, communicating, researching

V. MAMMALS

ACTIVITY 10-5:

HOW ARE MAMMALS DIFFERENT FROM OTHER ANIMALS?

Materials Needed:

Textbooks

Dictionary

Encyclopedias

Trade books about animals

Collection of animal pictures

Procedure:

1. Use the books that are available and find out what mammals are. How are they different from all other animals?
2. From what you know, is a mouse a mammal? An elephant? A bird? A snake? An alligator? A dog?
3. Go to your collection of animal pictures and find some mammals.
4. Sort the pictures into two groups: those

that are mammals and those that are not mammals.

5. Make a list of mammals that people use for food, for clothing, or for some other use.
6. Now sort the pictures again: those that are commonly used for pets, and those that are not commonly used for pets.
7. Examine the two groups. How many common pets are in the group of mammals? How many common pets are in the group of nonmammals?
8. Discuss your information with your group. Do all of you agree about which animals are mammals and which ones are nonmammals?
9. Which group are you a part of—mammals or nonmammals?

For Problem Solvers:

Get permission from your teacher to conduct a contest for class members to find out who can run the fastest, who can jump the farthest, and who can hold their breath the longest. Add other skills if you'd like, and if your teacher approves them. Before the contest begins, predict how well people will do. Predict the average and the high score for each skill. Compute an average and also identify the best score for each category. Then compare these winners with the winners among mammals. Do some research to learn who is the champion among mammals in these skills. How well do humans compete?

Select a person who seems to be about average size for humans and compare the size of this person to the size of the blue whale.

Discuss these questions: Can you think of anything people can do better than any other mammal? Why do you think humans are able to dominate the animal kingdom?

Teacher Information:

This activity should help students recognize the unique characteristics of mammals and why humans are classified as mammals. Those who accept the challenge for problem solvers will enjoy gathering data on several skills of people and comparing them with the skills of various animals. They will find that most of the things we do physically can be done better by certain animals. Humans dominate the animal kingdom because of our ability to think and reason and because of our opposing thumb, which enables us to grasp objects, including weapons.

Among the skills students might consider, here are some of the champions of the animal kingdom: the cheetah can run over 100 kilometers (60 milies) per hour; some kangaroos can jump more than 12 meters (40 feet); and the sperm whale can hold its breath for well over an hour. And while students are comparing humans to other animals, it might also be interesting to add the weight of all persons in the class (be very careful how this is handled, as it can be a very sensitive issue) and compare to the blue whale, which may weigh more than 135 metric tonnes (150 tons).

Integrating: Reading, social studies, math

Skills: Observing, inferring, classifying, measuring, predicting, communicating, formulating hypotheses

ACTIVITY 10-6:
SO I HAVE AN OPPOSING THUMB—SO WHAT?
(Class activity)

Materials Needed:

Wide masking tape

Ribbon for each team, long enough to tie into a bow

Coin for each team

Chair for each team

Procedure:

1. Using the masking tape, tape down the thumbs on both hands of each person in the class. The fingers should be left free to move, but it is important that the thumb is not usable at all.
2. Divide the class into teams for a relay race.
3. Place a chair at the front of the room in front of each team, providing a separate chair for each team.
4. Place a ribbon and a coin on the table for each team.
5. The first person in each line is to do the following:
   a. Take a ribbon and a coin.
   b. Run to the chair.
   c. Put the coin flat on the floor beside the chair.
   d. Tie the ribbon into a bow somewhere on the chair.
   e. Pick the coin up with one hand.
   f. Remove the ribbon from the chair.
   g. Take the ribbon and the coin to the next person in line.

Teacher Information:

The objective of this experience is to give the students a new appreciation for role of the opposing thumb in being able to grasp and manipulate objects. Dogs, cats, horses, and so on are able to use their "hands" for walking and that's about all. They rely on their mouth for defense. Even in eating, they must get their mouth to the food source, while we use our hands to bring food to the mouth as well as for so many, many more things we do.

A trip to the zoo would provide a wonderful opportunity for students to observe animals, with a specific objective in mind. Have them take paper and pencil and write down everything they see animals do with their feet. Be sure the tour includes monkeys. Again, students will discover new insights into the advantage of the opposing thumb.

Integrating: Math

Skills: Observing, inferring, measuring, communicating

VI. FISH

ACTIVITY 10-7:
WHAT IS UNIQUE ABOUT A FISH?

Materials Needed:

Textbooks

Dictionary

Encyclopedias

Trade books about fish

Collection of animal pictures

Procedure:

1. Use the books that are available and find out what makes a fish a fish. How are they different from all other animals?

2. From what you know, is a whale a fish? What about a shark? A penguin? Is an eel a type of fish?
3. Go to your collection of animal pictures and find some fish.
4. Sort the pictures into two groups: those that are fish and those that are not fish.
5. Of those in your "not fish" group, which ones are often mistaken for fish?
6. Go back to your reference books and learn all of the interesting facts about fish that you can find. Make lists of things like these:
   a. Strange-looking fish and what is different about them.
   b. Surprising things fish do to get food.
   c. Amazing ways fish avoid predators.
   d. Unusual places where fish live.
7. Compare your information with others in your group and discuss your ideas about fish.

Teacher Information:

Students have had many opportunities to use their picture collections already. Hopefully they learn and grow each time they use them with minds and eyes focused on a particular type of animal. By examining and comparing pictures, along with reading and researching and comparing and discussing information and ideas with others, students are learning about different types of animals, but even more importantly they are learning how to learn. The interesting facts they learn in this activity will fascinate them, and heighten their awareness and appreciation for this part of the natural world, but as they perform the research activities they stretch their ability to learn more and more about the world around them. Since we're dealing with fish here, this is an excellent setting to use for reinforcing the lesson of the famous Chinese Proverb, "Give a man a fish and you feed him for a day. Teach him how to fish and you feed him for a lifetime."

Integrating: Reading

Skills: Observing, inferring, communicating, researching

ACTIVITY 10-8:
WHAT DO WE NEED TO KEEP PETS IN AN AQUARIUM?
(Class project)

Materials Needed:

10-gallon (or larger) aquarium, glass cover, and stand

Aquarium heater

Aquarium thermometer

Air pump

Clean gravel

Sand

Water plants

Water

Snails

Fish

Fish food

Rocks of various sizes and shapes (clean rocks)

Small fish net

Procedure:

1. An aquarium is a place in your classroom for aquatic animals (see Figure 10A-1). With your teacher's help you can make the aquarium into a comfortable home. Place the aquarium in a sunny, protected place in the room.
2. Decide on the variety of fish you will want to live in your aquarium.

Freshwater fish (goldfish varieties) can usually live comfortably without a special heater in most classrooms. Tropical and exotic fish need a carefully controlled environment, so you will need a heater and thermometer. If you choose saltwater fish and don't live near an ocean, your pet store may have salt you can add to freshwater. However, such aquariums are difficult to maintain.

3. Put 3 centimeters (1 inch) of clean gravel in the bottom of the aquarium, sloping upward from front to back. Add assorted rocks near the back.
4. Spread 3 centimeters (1 inch) of clean sand over the gravel slope.
5. Slowly add water (so as not to stir the sand) up to 5 centimeters (2 inches) of the top.
6. Add green water plants (a variety of six or more). These can be purchased at a pet store and will depend on the kind of fish you choose to keep.
7. If you have chosen to make a freshwater aquarium, all you need to do is add several fish and freshwater snails to keep the tank clean. Put the lid on top. If you have chosen tropical fish, you will need to continue with the following steps.
8. Install the heater and thermometer and wait for the water to reach the desired temperature. (Note: Some heaters come with thermostats, but a thermometer is still helpful as a safety check.)
9. Secure the hose from the air pump to a rock on the bottom of the aquarium. Turn it on.
10. Put the tropical fish in your aquarium. Instead of snails you may need to purchase special fish with suction mouths to keep the tank clean. The pet store can provide special instructions for testing the water and feeding fish.

For Problem Solvers:

Using an encyclopedia or other references, see what you can learn about the fish and other animals that live in your aquarium. Are they natives of your country? If not, where are they from? Do people keep them as pets there?

Measure the size of the fish in your

Figure 10A-1

This aquarium is equipped with a heater and an air pump to regulate the aquatic environment.

aquarium. Keep track of their growth on a graph. Give each one a name, and refer to them by name on your records.

Teacher Information:

If you have never constructed an aquarium before, talk to a pet store owner or someone else about the special needs of tropical fish. You may need additional equipment to maintain it properly.

Aquariums with tropical fish are very attractive and interesting but freshwater or saltwater aquariums (near the ocean) are more representative of water life as it exists. There are several additional advantages to a freshwater aquarium. If it is 10 gallons or larger, it will be nearly balanced and will not require an air pump. "Balanced" means that the plants produce about the same amount of oxygen as the animals use. The animals in turn release enough carbon dioxide for the plants. If you match your fish, snails, and plants properly (this usually takes time), the fish will get food from the plants. The plants will use the waste products of the fish for food to produce new growth, and the snails will keep the whole area tidy and clean.

Occasionally, you should remove the glass lid to permit air to get in (or leave a ventilating space), and you may want to add a little fish food to give your pets a treat. An aquarium that is nearly in balance will need a change of water about twice a year (add pond water occasionally to replace evaporated water). When the water is changed, you will need to start at the beginning with fresh, clean gravel, sand, and rocks. Again use fresh pond water. The same plant and animal life can be retained.

Periodically have the students assist you in checking the "health" of your aquarium. Usually conditions will let you know if you need more plants, animals, or snails.

Don't be concerned if a green slimy film develops on the top of the water. This is a sign of a healthy aquarium. Probably plants and animals too small to see with the naked eye are also living in the tank.

Freshwater aquariums can also provide a home for tadpoles. When they begin to grow legs, simply transfer them to a combined environment of pond water and land and watch them develop into frogs. Use shallow water and tilt the tank so part of the tank floor is not covered with water. This will assure that the tadpoles can get air when their lungs begin to develop.

Integrating: Social studies, reading, math

Skills: Observing, inferring, measuring, communicating, researching

(Except for the addition of the sections "For Problem Solvers," "Integrating," and "Skills," this activity was reprinted with only slight modification from Activity 56, "What Do We Need to Keep Pets in an Aquarium?" in Tolman and Morton, 1986.)

ACTIVITY 10-9:

HOW CAN WE KEEP AMPHIBIANS IN OUR CLASSROOM?

(Class project)

Materials Needed:

Transparent plastic box

Pond water

Dipping net

Tadpoles

Procedure:

1. Tadpoles begin their lives resembling fish in many ways and gradually develop into

adult land animals (see Figure 10A-2). To do this, they must have an environment that combines land and water. Compare your live tadpoles with the ones in this drawing. Find the animal that resembles your tadpoles.

2. Place your plastic box on a flat surface and raise one end of it by placing something under one end, such as cardboard, a wood block, or an old book.
3. Add pond water until more than most, but not all, of the bottom is covered. Your pond water may have a green scum and tiny pieces of material in it. These are healthy signs, so don't remove them.
4. Your aquarium is now ready for the tadpoles. Do not put a lid on the box.
5. Change the pond water about every two weeks. Young tadpoles can eat small amounts of boiled spinach. After a few weeks they can eat spinach without boiling. Don't overfeed them. Once or twice a week is enough.

For Problem Solvers:

Using an encyclopedia or other references, see what you can learn about other amphibians. Are there others that grow through the stages of metamorphosis like frogs do? Make a list of all the amphibians that you can find. Write notes about them, describing ways they are alike and ways they are different. See how many of them you can find in your picture collection of animals. If some of the amphibians in your list are missing from the picture collection, try to find pictures of them and add to the collection.

Find out why amphibians are called amphibians.

Make a journal. Add drawings and notes about your tadpoles every week. Make a graph that shows how long your animals are, and add new information to the graph each week.

Teacher Information:

In nature, animals often lay many eggs so that a few will survive to adult stage. With careful feeding and excellent care, you can expect some tadpoles to advance through several stages of metamorphosis.

Tilting the plastic box so that shallow water and land are available is important, as the tadpoles lose their gills and become lung breathers. This is usually at about the time

Figure 10A-2

Frogs begin the life cycle as aquatic animals and end as amphibians.

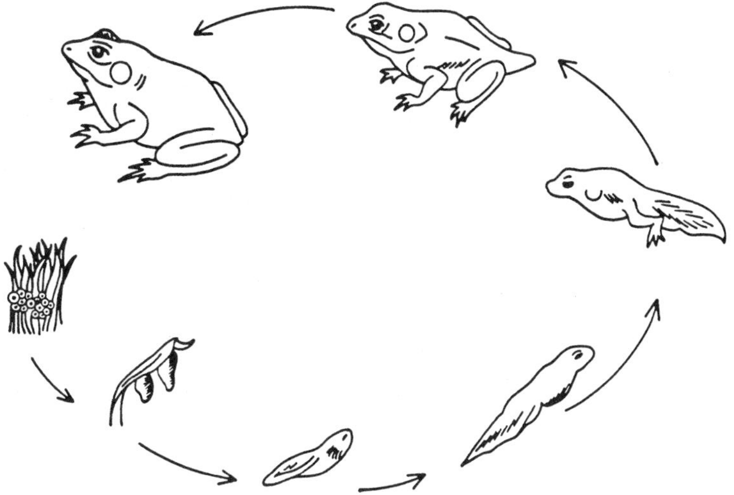

the front legs begin to develop. Without shallow water, many will drown.

If pond water is not readily available, try to obtain some from a high school or college biology department or see your local pet store.

After the tadpoles are in the box, put them in a shady place in the room and set up a feeding and water-changing schedule. Use the dipping net to remove any dead specimens daily. Discuss the tadpoles as observable changes appear. Remind the children that they, too, take a long time to grow and change.

Integrating: Reading, math

Skills: Observing, inferring, measuring, communicating, researching

(Adapted from Activity 67, "What Is a Good Environment for Tadpoles?" in Tolman and Morton, 1986.)

VIII. REPTILES

ACTIVITY 10-10:
HOW CAN WE KEEP REPTILES IN OUR CLASSROOM?
(Class project)

Materials Needed:

Fish tank (at least 20-gallon size) with heavy wire screen cover

Clean gravel

Clean sand

Assorted rocks

Small pieces of wood

Small, shallow plastic pan

Small turtles, snakes, and/or lizards

Procedure:

1. You can keep small reptiles in your classroom if they have a comfortable place to live. Find a warm, sunny, protected place in your room as a permanent location for your terrarium. Although you may use a container that was intended as an aquarium, *aquarium* means "water home" and *terrarium* means "land home".
2. Choose the kind of reptiles that are available and appropriate for your classroom.
3. Use resource books to learn about the reptiles you have chosen and plan a comfortable environment for them. Include plants that are appropriate for your animals.
4. Put about 3 centimeters (1 inch) of gravel in the bottom of your terrarium. Add a similar amount of sand on top. Arrange the rocks and pieces of wood to provide privacy and shade.
5. Locate the shallow plastic pan near one side. Put one or more flat rocks in it so the animals will have a place to climb out and "sun." Be sure the pan is easy to remove, as you will need to clean it regularly.
6. Before you put your reptiles in their new home, be sure you have a heavy wire covering over the top so they cannot climb out.
7. Your terrarium cannot be "balanced" as a freshwater aquarium can be; therefore, your animals will need fresh food and water regularly. The plants will need varying amounts of moisture, too.
8. Put your animals in their new home and observe them.

For Problem Solvers:

Using an encyclopedia or other references, see what you can learn about these and other reptiles. Make a list of all the reptiles that you can find. Write notes about them, describing ways they are alike and ways they are different. See how many of them you can find in your picture collection of animals. If some of the reptiles in your list are missing from the picture collection, try to find pictures of them and add to the collection.

Find out what characteristics of reptiles make them different from other animals. What makes a reptile a reptile?

Teacher Information:

If a fish tank is not available, a cardboard or wooden box with the top and one side covered with heavy plastic can be used. Be sure to provide plenty of air holes covered with screen. Use a sieve to clean the sand about once a week. Commercially produced cages are excellent for temporary housing. They are easy to clean and they will probably reduce the amount of care required.

Live reptiles and food can be obtained from pet stores and science supply houses if they cannot be collected locally.

When animals are kept in the classroom, some are likely to die there. Be aware of the sensitivity of this issue with children. Some animals will eat each other, perhaps even eat their own young, and some naturally have a high mortality rate as they progress through their life stages. Handled properly, these can be valuable learning experiences for children as they observe life's natural processes.

Integrating: Reading

Skills: Observing, inferring, communicating, researching

(Adapted from Activity 57, "How Can We Keep Small Animals in Our Classroom?" in Tolman and Morton, 1986.)

IX. BIRDS

ACTIVITY 10-11:
WHAT CAN WE LEARN ABOUT BIRDS WHILE WE FEED THEM?

Materials Needed:

Plastic plates

String

Different types of birdseed

Procedure:

1. Use the plastic plate as a simple bird feeder.
2. Make three holes near the edge of the plate, equally spaced around the edge of the plate.
3. Tie a string in each hole and use the string to hang your bird feeder in a tree or some other available location.
4. Put birdseed on the feeder and observe the birds that come to eat the seeds.
5. Talk about the birds that come to your feeder. How big are they? What colors do they have? Draw pictures of them and color them the way the birds are colored.

For Problem Solvers:

Do an experiment to find out which type of seeds birds like best. Use several bird feeders at once and put a different type of seed on each feeder. Measure about 30 grams (1 ounce) of seed for each feeder. Observe the feeder frequently to see how well birds seem to like each type of seed. Keep track of how many days each type of seed lasts. As soon as one type runs out, measure out another 30 grams and put it on the feeder. Keep record of how much of each type of seed you use. See if you can decide which type of seed the birds in your area like best. Before you begin, think about what you think birds might prefer and write your hypothesis. What variables are you dealing with? Share your information with your group and talk about what you learned. If observations are made at regular intervals (at specific times of the day), you can also gather information about preferred feeding times. Record the number and types of birds you see.

Do another experiment to find out if certain types of birds prefer certain types of seeds. Repeat what you did for the first experiment, but this time use your identification manual and identify the birds that come to eat. Keep record of the number of birds of each type that come to feed on each type of birdseed. Write your hypothesis before you begin. Also write your variables. What are your conclusions? Are there any birds that seem to like only one type of seed? Are there any seed types that attract only one type of bird? Do you have any seeds that no birds seem to like?

Listen for the song of the birds that come to visit your bird feeders. Try to find a recording of bird songs, and listen to see if you can match the bird songs you hear with the songs on the recordings.

Do you think the same types of birds would visit your feeders at a different season of the year? Write your predictions. Then return to these activities in about three months, try them again, and compare your information with the first time you did the activities.

Design different types of bird feeders. Try using milk cartons, plastic bottles, wooden trays, and so on. Get creative. Do birds seem to be attracted more to one type of feeder than another if all of the feeders have the same type of seeds? If you paint and decorate a feeder, are they any more or less attracted to it than they are to the same type of feeder that is decorated differently or not at all?

Is there someone in your class that has lived in another part of the country or another part of the world, or who has a particular interest in another location? Ask that person to help you find some information about birds in that area. Maybe together you could share your information with your class.

Teacher Information:

This activity begins with a very simple activity that encourages students to provide some bird seed for wild birds, then observe the birds. Students who continue with the extension for problem solvers will experiment with different types of birdseed. They will also try their skills at designing different types of bird feeders, then investigate to see if birds prefer any particular type of feeder. Throughout these experiences, students are building their skills of recognizing and identifying types of birds, and finding out if certain types of birds have unique feeding preferences.

Students are also encouraged to predict whether they will see the same birds at a different time of the year, then return to these activities at a later time.

Finally, students are encouraged to find out about birds that are unique to other areas of the world where one or more students has lived or for some reason has a particular interest in.

Integrating: Reading, writing, social studies, math, art, music

Skills: Observing, inferring, classifying, measuring, predicting, communicating, using space-time relationships, formulating and controlling variables, experimenting, researching

ACTIVITY 10-12:

WHAT TYPES OF HOUSES DO BIRDS LIKE TO LIVE IN?

Materials Needed:

Variety of materials, such as string, straw, grass, small sticks, and so on

Procedure:

1. Find a bird nest. Look around in trees, under eves of buildings, and so on, until you find a bird nest.
2. Important: Do not disturb the nest. Don't climb up to it or try to touch it. It

is against the law to disturb bird nests in the wild.

3. Look at the nest, study it, and draw a picture of it. Notice its size, its shape, and what it seems to be made of. Write all the information you can about the nest.
4. Bring your notes back to the classroom and try to find a picture of the nest in an encyclopedia or some other book. Learn all you can about it, including the kind of bird that built the nest.
5. Draw and color a picture of the bird that built the nest.
6. Try to find some materials like the materials the nest is made of.
7. Make a nest like the one you found, using the same materials. Make your nest the same size and shape, as near as you can.
8. Share your nest with the class and compare it with the one made by real birds. Was it easy to make?
9. Talk about what a difficult task it is to build a good nest, and how skilled and patient birds seem to be in constructing their nests.

For Problem Solvers:

Build one or more birdhouses. Use milk cartons, plastic bottles, wood, or whatever materials you have available. Be creative. Decorate it as you like, with materials that are available to you. Predict what type of bird in your area might be interested in your birdhouse. Find a good place to put your birdhouse outdoors, and see if you have any renters move in and set up housekeeping! Try to pick a place where it will be protected from cats and other animals that might bother the birds.

Teacher Information:

If it is not possible for students to go in search of nests, invite them to find pictures of nests in encyclopedias, trade books, and magazines. They can still do the activity.

Integrating: Reading, writing, social studies, math, art

Skills: Observing, inferring, classifying, measuring, predicting, communicating, using space-time relationships, researching

ACTIVITY 10-13:
HOW DO BIRDS' BONES HELP THEM TO FLY?
(Teacher-supervised activity)

Materials Needed:

Chicken bones, including wing bones

Bones of a mammal, such as sheep, pig, rabbit, or cow

Saw

Procedure:

1. Saw through both types of bones.
2. Examine the structure of the bones. Compare their size, weight, thickness of walls, and whatever other characteristics you notice that are similar or different.
3. Which bones seem to be heaviest for their size?
4. Which bones seem to be lightest for their size?
5. What is there about the chicken bones that really makes them different?
6. Talk about your ideas.

Teacher Information:

The bones you need can be found on the dinner table in many homes. Boil them to remove all the meat, then dry them in the oven. In examining the bones students should notice that the chicken bones are hollow and that they are lighter for their size. Notice also that the wing bone has an inner support structure that gives it strength without adding very much weight.

Integrating: Reading, writing

Skills: Observing, inferring

ACTIVITY 10-14: HOW DO BIRDS' BEAKS HELP THEM TO EAT?

Materials Needed:

Variety of tools, such as:

- pliers
- tweezers
- spoons
- clothespins
- tongue depressors
- scissors
- soda straws
- eyedroppers
- tongs

Variety of "bird food," such as:

- marbles
- jellybeans
- rice
- walnuts or hazelnuts (in the shell)
- short pieces of string
- bowl of water (nectar)

Procedure:

1. Each student may choose one tool.
2. Place the different "foods" at different stations.
3. The tool you chose is your beak.
4. A person assigned as the timer allows each person only a few seconds at each station, to gather food items. They may use only their "beak."
5. Discuss the results. Decide which beak type was best suited for each food item.
6. Discuss your ideas about why each bird seems to have certain preferences for food types.

Teacher Information:

Be sure students note that even though the tongs could pick up the hard-shelled nuts, it was of no use because the tongs couldn't crack them open. Like the pliers, sparrows and other stout-beaked birds are able to crack the shells. The pieces of string might represent worms; some bird beaks are much better adapted for catching them than are others. A hummingbird has no way to eat a fish and a pelican would be very inept at trying to extract nectar from a flower. Compare other types of beaks with types of food birds eat.

Skills: Observing, inferring

X. ARTHROPODS

ACTIVITY 10-15: WHAT AFFECTS THE MOVEMENTS OF ANIMALS?

Materials Needed:

Pill bug (let's call it "Speedy")

Shallow box (shoe box lid or slightly larger)

Paper towels

Lamp with low-wattage bulb (15 to 40 watts) or flashlight

Small garlic clove

Small piece of damp wood

Paper and pencil

Clock with second-hand

Colored pencils

Procedure:

1. Divide the box into fourths by drawing two black lines that cross at the center. Mark the center point with a large dot and label it START (see Figure 10A-3).
2. Draw similar lines on your paper. Again, mark and label the starting point.
3. Place Speedy at START. The box is now Speedy's cage.
4. At the top of the paper, write a prediction that Speedy will move toward the light, that he will move away from the light, or that he will ignore the light.
5. Using a red pencil, put an X on your paper at START, to mark Speedy's starting position. For the rest of this activity, consider your paper to be a representation of Speedy's cage. You will mark your paper to show Speedy's movements in the cage.
6. Put the lamp at one end of the cage, so the light bulb is only a few inches from the cage.
7. For the next ten minutes, put an X on your paper every fifteen seconds to show Speedy's position. Label the first X as #1, the second X as #2, and so on, so you have a good record of Speedy's movements.
8. Move the light to the other end of the box and place Speedy back at START.
9. Use a green pencil this time to make an X on your paper every fifteen seconds for another ten minutes to mark Speedy's movements in the cage. Again number the X's in sequence.
10. With your record of Speedy's movements, you should now be able to tell whether the pill bug is attracted to the light, avoids the light, or is unaffected by the light.
11. Was your prediction accurate?
12. Can you measure Speedy's trail? How far did he travel in the first trial? How far in the second? How far altogether?
13. Discuss with your group how Speedy behaved and what you learned. Try it again if you'd like, perhaps using another pill bug.

Figure 10A-3

You can use this pattern for the box and record sheet when you work with pill bugs.

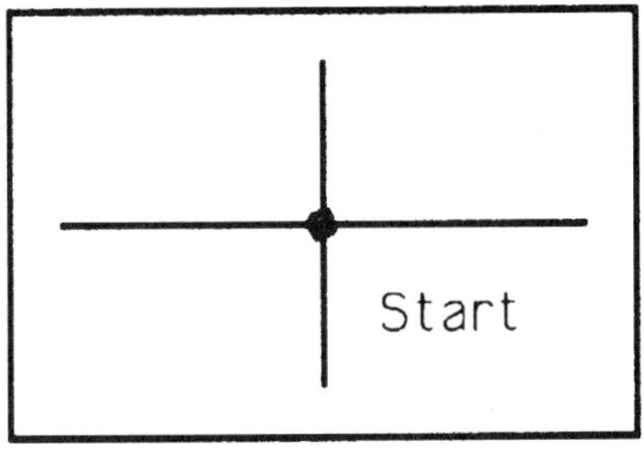

For Problem Solvers:

From what you have learned about pill bugs, think about how they might react to the odor of garlic. Write your hypothesis on a new paper. Prepare the paper with the black dividing lines and the START position at the center. Label this paper "Garlic."

Place the garlic clove inside the box at one end. Put Speedy at START and again mark his position on your paper every fifteen seconds for ten minutes, using a red pencil. Place the garlic clove at the other end of the box and repeat the process for ten minutes using a green pencil. Was your hypothesis accurate?

Now cover the bottom of the box with paper towels. The paper towel on one half of the box should be dry and on the other half the paper towel should be damp. Write your hypothesis regarding Speedy's reaction to moisture. Get a third paper, draw the black dividing lines, mark the START position, and label the paper "Moisture." Again use red and green pencils for the two ten-minute trials. Examine your record and consider your hypothesis.

Share with your group what you have learned about the reactions of pill bugs. Also discuss what you have learned about how to keep record of animal movements. What variables did you use in your experiment with the pill bugs?

Design a similar experiment to determine the effect of certain stimuli (conditions) on the movements of another animal. You might consider using mealworms, crickets, hamsters, birds, or most any animal that you can keep in your classroom or that is where you can observe it regularly. Decide what variables you will use, how you will record the animal's movements, and so on. Do not experiment with conditions that will harm the animal.

See if you can turn your record of animal movements into an artistic design.

Teacher Information:

Students will enjoy studying the movements of pill bugs and other animals, and noting their reactions to different stimuli. This is a valuable learning experience for students who continue with the extension for problem solvers, as they apply their investigative skills to animals.

Integrating: Math, art

Skills: Observing, inferring, measuring, predicting, communicating, using space-time relationships, formulating hypotheses, identifying and controlling variables, experimenting

ACTIVITY 10-16:
HOW CAN YOU CAPTURE AND PRESERVE A SPIDERWEB?
(Teacher-supervised activity)

Materials Needed:

Heavy paper

Spray paint (the paint and paper should be contrasting colors)

Spiderweb

Procedure:

1. Have an adult help you with this activity. Although most spiders are our friends, some are poisonous. You are looking for a web, not a spider, but don't take chances.
2. Find a deserted spiderweb.
3. Spray some paint lightly on the web. You only need enough to make the web wet and make it show up well.
4. Before the paint has time to dry, hold the paper behind the web, then lift the paper so the web lies nicely on the paper.
5. Break or cut the anchor strands on the web.
6. Let the paint dry.
7. Display your spiderweb where it can be seen.

For Problem Solvers:

Do some research on spiderwebs in encyclopedias and trade books. Find out what types of webs different spiders make. Write questions you have about spiders and try to answer them with your research. Here are some to get you started. Why don't spiders stick to their own webs? Are spiders insects? Why or why not? How many eyes do spiders have. What are the characteristics that make a spider a spider? Where does the black widow get its name? Are there male black widows? (Does that make sense?)

Make a collection of spider webs, using the technique described in the above activity.

Classify them according to the web type and try to identify the kind of spider that made it.

Teacher Information:

While spiders are rather creepy-crawly, and they give many people the jitters, they are also fascinating creatures. A battle between a spider and an unfortunate wasp that is caught in the spider's web, can hold even the observer captive for a long time. If spiders are among the animals that live in a classroom terrarium, experiences with them should include the use of magnifiers, allowing students to study their eyes and other body features.

Integrating: Reading, writing

Skills: Observing, inferring

ACTIVITY 10-17: HOW CAN WE OBSERVE AN ANT COLONY?

Materials Needed:

1-gallon glass jar, with lid

Small shovel

Ant hill

Procedure:

1. Find an ant hill and fill the jar about two-thirds full of the soil the hill is made of, being sure that many ants are included.
2. By digging around carefully you might find the queen; she will be clearly larger than the other ants.
3. Put the lid on the jar and punch a few tiny holes in it.
4. Keep the ant colony in a darkened area or else cover it with black paper, exposing it to light only for observation.
5. Feed the ants by placing different foods on the surface of the soil. You will be able to tell what they like to eat. Try sugar, bread crumbs, leaves, and so on.
6. Keep a log of your observations—what the ants do or do not like to eat, where they dig chambers next to the glass, what they seem to do in the chambers, and other things you see that interest you.
7. Read about ants in encyclopedias and trade books. Learn about how they work together. Try to find out why it's best to have a queen ant in your ant colony.
8. Talk about your observations—tell others what you learn about ants.

Teacher Information:

Many hours of enjoyment and learning can be spent in observing a colony of ants. An ant farm made with two glass panels is better than the gallon jar, because it has more observation surface. Its long, thin shape also assures that more of the ants' tunnels and chambers will be dug next to the glass where they can be observed.

Without the queen, the colony will still provide a good observation experience for some time, but the colony is not complete without the queen and it cannot survive over a long period of time without her, as she is the only egg-laying member of the colony.

By trying different foods, children will soon find out what the ants prefer to eat.

Integrating: Reading, writing

Skills: Observing, inferring

ACTIVITY 10-18: WHAT DO MEALWORMS BECOME?

Materials Needed:

Cornmeal, oatmeal, or bran

Large clear glass jar, with screened lid and layer of soil

Mealworms

Apple or potato

Procedure:

1. If you have a container of flour or cereal that is infected by mealworms, you already have the start for your colony. If not, purchase a few mealworms from a pet store.
2. Place your colony in a large jar with a nice, thick layer of cornmeal, oatmeal, or bran.
3. Add a slice of potato or apple to provide moisture. The mealworms will nibble on this and get the moisture they need.
4. Cover the jar with a fine-mesh screening material or netting. The larvae (mealworms) will change into pupae, then into adults (beetles).
5. Provide small pieces of raw vegetables for the beetles. The adults will lay tiny eggs and within a few days these will hatch into a new generation of mealworms.

For Problem Solvers:

Read about metamorphosis in your encyclopedia or trade books. Learn about some insects and what they look like as they go through the stages of metamorphosis. Make a drawing of these stages for one or more insects. Share with others your art work and what you learned about insects and about metamorphosis. Do mealworms go through complete or incomplete metamorphosis?

Study about Monarch butterflies. See if you can find a Monarch caterpillar to observe in the classroom. Be sure you know what it needs to eat and that you take care of it properly. Who knows—maybe you'll see it turn into a butterfly.

Teacher Information:

In this activity, students will learn about metamorphosis in the most exciting way—by experiencing the complete life cycle of an insect. Those who are interested in the problem-solving extension can do some research and prepare for keeping one or more caterpillars in the classroom in addition to the mealworms.

Monitor students as they study and as they search for caterpillars. When capturing caterpillars, they need to notice the type of plant it is on and get a few twigs and several leaves from that plant. Place the caterpillar, twigs, and leaves in a jar with a screened lid. The bottom of the jar should be covered with a layer of soil. Students should check the jar daily and be sure the caterpillar has a constant fresh supply of the same type of leaves. Many caterpillars are very particular about their diet. When the caterpillar is ready to pupate (form a chrysalis or spin a cocoon), some will attach themselves to a twig and others will burrow into the soil. In cold climates many caterpillars require cold temperatures to trigger certain chemical reactions that continue the process of metamorphosis, so as the weather cools off in the fall, place the jar in a protected area outdoors so the pupa will be exposed to the natural temperature changes of the local climate. Frequent observation will assure that students will know when the adult has formed. If timing is right, they might even experience the miraculous moment, as the adult emerges from its prison, unfolds its wings, air-dries them, and flies away when the lid is removed—without a single flying lesson!

Integrating: Reading, writing

Skills: Observing, inferring, research

XI. ANIMAL ADAPTATIONS

ACTIVITY 10-19:
HOW DO LIVING THINGS ADAPT TO CHANGING CONDITIONS?
(Group discussion)

Materials Needed:

Pictures of people living, working, and playing in different climates

Magazines

Other sources of pictures of plants and animals in varying conditions

Procedure:

1. Find a picture of deciduous trees in the summer and a picture of deciduous trees in the winter. How are the trees different? What do they do to survive cold winters? What would happen to these trees if temperatures became extremely cold while the trees were still leafed out? What does the tree do to *adapt* before the extremely cold temperatures come?
2. Find a picture of a bear in its natural summer range and a picture of a bear hibernating. What does the bear do to adapt and survive the winter when temperatures are cold and food supplies are scarce?
3. What do we do to keep ourselves comfortable as the seasons change? How do people in very cold regions adapt? How do people in very warm regions adapt?

For Problem Solvers:

Do some research in encyclopedias and trade books and find out about migrating animals. What are some animals that are known to migrate? Why do they migrate? What animal migrates the farthest? Do people ever migrate?

In what ways have animals made more permanent adaptations with changing conditions? The woodpecker has developed adaptations that enable it to search out insects and grubs under the bark of a tree. Read about the woodpecker and find out what these adaptations are. The flying squirrel has developed adaptations that enable it to glide from high places to lower places. Find out what those adaptations are.

Learn about adaptations that other animals have made as their species has developed, which enables them to do certain things that others cannot do. Make a list of these and share your information with your group.

Teacher Information:

Every species of animal has special adaptations that enable it to do what it does and to live where it lives. Some animals migrate to warmer regions in the winter, others grow warm coverings, while still others hide in a protected location and hibernate as the cold weather passes by. Some animals eat meat, some eat plants, and some eat both. These differences involve more than just differences in food-gathering habits, and more than whether the animal can run fast or whether it has sharp claws or teeth. It also involves differences in digestive systems that have adapted to process certain types of foods.

While many animals have developed the ability to adapt to only a relatively narrow range of climatic conditions, some adapt from season to season and remain very active in broadly varying conditions. Humans do not undergo physical changes that enable them survive extreme temperature changes, yet humans are able to adapt by changing their immediate surroundings. Thus they can survive most challenges that weather, climate, and local food source limitations can offer.

Integrating: Reading, writing, social studies

Skills: Observing, inferring, classifying, using space-time relationships, research

CHAPTER

PLANTS

CHAPTER OUTLINE:

- INTRODUCTION
- SOME MAJOR GROUPS OF PLANTS
  - The Simple Plants
  - The Vascular Plants
  - Evergreen Plants (Conifers)
    - Needles and Scales
  - Deciduous Plants
- FLOWERING PLANTS
  - Seeds
    - Seed Dispersal
  - Roots
  - Stems
  - Leaves
    - Leaf structure
    - Photosynthesis
    - Transpirtation
    - Color changes in leaves
  - Flowers
    - Reproduction
    - Flowers are phototropic
    - Fruit
- SOME PLANTS CAN REPRODUCE WITHOUT SEEDS
  - Cuttings
  - Stems and Bulbs
- USES
  - Seeds
  - Fruit
  - Roots
  - Stems
  - Leaves
  - Flowers
- HOW LONG DO PLANTS LIVE?
- IN CLOSING
- LIST OF RESOURCES
- ACTIVITIES

I WONDER . . .

What is the vascular system of a plant?
What are angiosperms?
What moves water to the top of a tree?
How can you tell the age of a tree?
Is a girdled tree healthy, sick, or just in a "tight squeeze"?
Green plants manufacture their own food? So where's the factory?
What? Do plants *use* oxygen?
Do leaves get new colors in the autumn, or do they just show colors they've had hidden throughout the growing season?

I. INTRODUCTION

Plants usually rank quite high among the favorite science topics for the elementary grades. They present many opportunities for students to watch the growth and development of living things, with a fascinating diversity of size, structure, and color. In terms of cuddliness, plants don't compete well with pets; but feeding and caring for them is a relatively easy task, and when clean-up time comes, plants are sure to gain favor.

Like animals, plants are made of organic tissue, the most basic parts of which are called *cells*. Each type of plant is able to reproduce its kind, passing on the characteristics that make a rose a rose, a radish a radish, and a redwood tree a redwood tree, with traits that distinguish each one as unique in the world of living things.

This chapter provides a brief description of the plant kingdom. Information is given about a few major groups of plants, plus some additional points that are of interest to the elementary grades. The reader should review the section on Living Organisms at the beginning of chapter 10, Animals, for preliminary information.

II. SOME MAJOR GROUPS OF PLANTS

The *common name* of a plant is the name by which the plant is commonly known. These names are usually different from one country to another, and many plants have multiple common names even in the same language and within the same country.

Scientists classify plants according to certain characteristics and assign a scientific name to each plant. These are all Latin, or latinized, names and the system is standardized worldwide, making it possible for scientists to communicate clearly about them in different parts of the world. Such a classification scheme makes it possible for the name of any particular plant to account for the likenesses and differences of that plant, as compared with other organisms.

All plants belong to the plant *(plantae)* kingdom. Similar to the hierarchy used in classifying animals, the plant kingdom is separated into *divisions*, which are further separated into *classes*, then *orders*, then *families*, *genera*, and *species*.

The Simple Plants

The first division in the plant kingdom is called *Bryophyta*. These are mostly small plants, and the majority of them are mosses and liverworts. Very few bryophytes are more than 2 centimeters (3/4 inch) in length. They live in most areas of the world, from the tropics to the polar regions, but they are always in areas where there is liquid water at some time of the year, as water is necessary in their reproductive process. Bryophytes thrive in the moist regions of the tropics and in the temperate zones, and they are the most abundant of all plants in both the Arctic and the Antarctic. Plants in this division have simple, leaf-like structures, but they do not have true leaves, roots, and stems, nor do they produce flowers, fruits, and seeds. They also have no *vascular system* to transport water and nutrients.

The Vascular Plants

The second major division of the plant kingdom, *Tracheophyta,* includes all of the vascular plants, or those having a vascular system. A vascular system consists of tiny tube-like structures that transport water and nutrients from soil to various parts of the plant. This division includes all trees, shrubs, flowers, grasses—in fact, nearly all of the organisms that most of us think of as plants. The remainder of this chapter will consider a few groups and characteristics of the vascular plants.

Evergreen Plants (Conifers)

The *evergreens,* also called *conifers,* are cone-bearing plants (see Figure 11-1). Their most obvious distinguishing characteristics include their scaly cone (the fruit—the reproductive unit—of the conifer), which contains seeds. Conifers are also recognized for their soft wood and for the production of a sticky substance called *resin.* Well-known evergreens include redwood, spruce, fir, cedar, and pine. These trees are often used for lumber, and some of them are used for making paper as well.

Figure 11-1

Evergreens (top) bear cones, while deciduous trees (bottom) do not.

Needles and scales

The leaves of conifers are either in the form of needles or flat scales, and they usually stay on the plant through the winter, which is the reason they are called "evergreens." Cedars and junipers have scale-like leaves, while the pine, spruce, and fir have leaves that are long and thin, like needles. An easy way to distinguish between pine, spruce, and fir is to remember the following:

1. *Pine needles are **p**ointed, and they are arranged in bundles or **p**ackages of one, two, three, five, or eight (see Figure 11-2) (**P**ine = **p**ointed, **p**ackages).*
2. *Spruce needles are **s**harp, and they are **s**eparate or **s**ingle on the twig. They also feel **s**quare when you roll them between your fingers (see Figure 11-3) (**S**pruce = **s**harp, **s**ingle, **s**quare).*
3. ***F**ir tree needles are **f**lexible and **f**lat—try to roll them between your fingers and they will not roll (see Figure 11-4) (**F**ir = **f**lexible, **f**lat).*

Figure 11-2

Pine needles are pointed and arranged in bundles.

Figure 11-3

Spruce needles are sharp, and they are separate on the twig.

Figure 11-4

Fir needles are flexible and flat.

Deciduous Plants

The word *deciduous* comes from a Latin word that means "to fall." It describes trees that drop their leaves in the autumn and go into a period

Figure 11-5

Deciduous plants drop their leaves in the fall.

of dormancy for the winter (see Figure 11-5). Many flowering plants are deciduous.

III. FLOWERING PLANTS

Flowering plants form fruits that contain seeds. In addition to roses, gardenias, pansies, carnations, orchids, and many other plants that are commonly known as "flowers," flowering plants include trees that lose their leaves in the autumn, such as maples, poplars, elms, fruit trees, and others. Grasses and grains are also among the flowering plants, as are many shrubs. Flowering plants are called *angiosperms*.

The main parts of flowering plants are seeds, roots, stems, leaves, and flowers. Let's consider these separately.

Seeds

A seed is produced in the fruit of a flowering plant. It has the ability to grow into a new plant—always the same kind of plant as the one that produced the seed.

All seeds have three parts: seed coat, embryo, and stored food (see Figure 11-6). The *seed coat* is a tough covering, providing protection for the seed. The *embryo* is the tiny new plant, complete with the beginnings of the root, stem, and leaves. The embryo remains dormant until temperature and moisture conditions are right; then it begins to grow. The *stored food* provides nourishment for the new plant until leaves are formed and ready to make food. You can see these parts rather easily in a peanut, or in a bean that has been soaked in water for three or four days.

Most seeds grow best in temperatures of about 15 to 25 degrees Celsius (60 to 80 degrees Fahrenheit). Seeds must have air and water in order to sprout, or *germinate* (see Figure 11-7). Water causes the seed to swell, and the seed coat to soften, making it possible for the new plant to grow out through it. Under proper temperature and moisture conditions, the cells of the embryo begin to divide and the embryo starts to grow. After leaves begin to form and the supply of stored food in the seed is used up, the new plant must have soil, air, and sunlight in order to manufacture food, in addition to continued moisture and appropriate temperature.

Figure 11-6

All seeds have three parts: seed coat, embryo, and stored food.

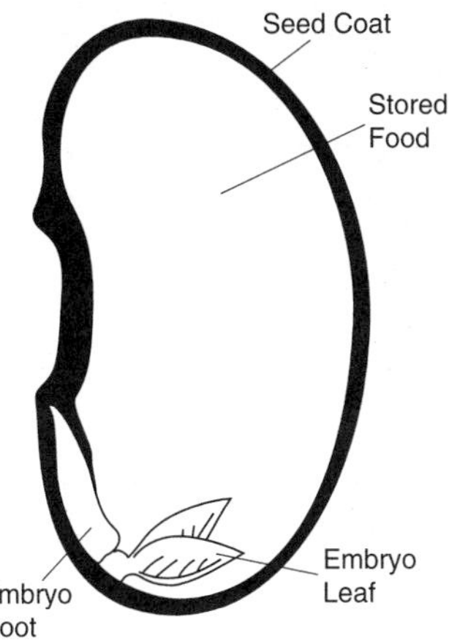

Figure 11-7

A seed sprouts, and eventually grows into a plant

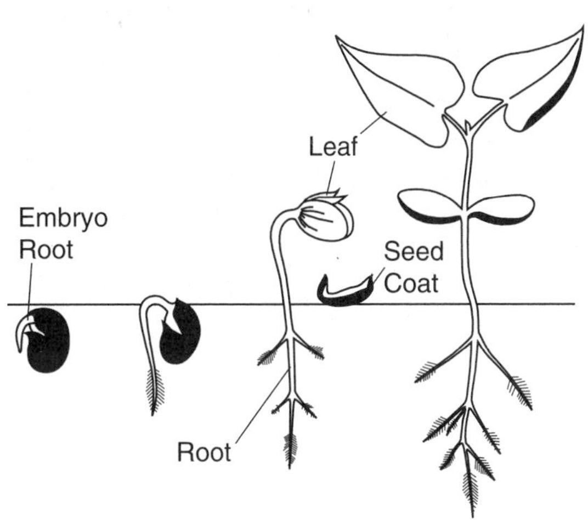

Seed dispersal

Seeds have interesting ways of getting around (see Figure 11-8). Dandelion, milkweed, and cottonwood seeds are attached to parachutes of fine hairs, and are blown in all directions by the wind. Others, such as maple and elm seeds, have wing-like structures that act as sails, and they are also carried by the wind. Still others have hooks, spines, or sticky coats that cling to the fur of animals, the feathers of birds, or the clothing of people. Some seeds are eaten by animals and have hard seed coats, which lets them pass through the animals' digestive systems without being digested. They can be deposited some distance from the mother plant, still able to germinate and grow into new plants. Many seeds are scattered by water, either being washed short distances by rainwater, or carried long distances by streams, rivers, or ocean currents. The thick, buoyant seed coat of the coconut allows it to travel thousands of miles by ocean current before being washed ashore on some remote beach. There it germinates and grows into a new palm tree, sometimes bringing the seed of life to a new island.

Figure 11-8

Parachute seeds, wing-like seeds, and burrs are just a few of the variety of seed forms.

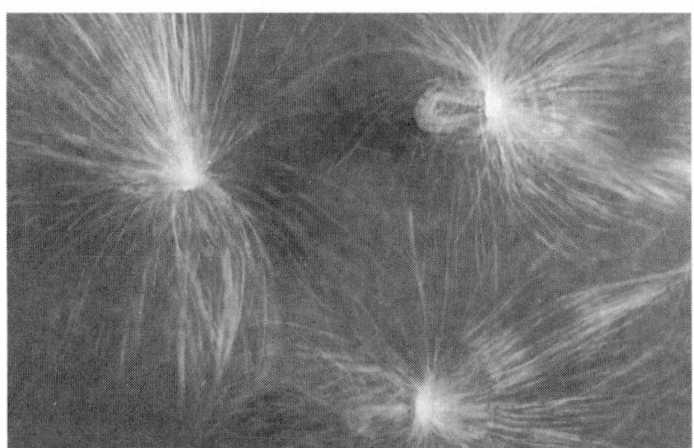

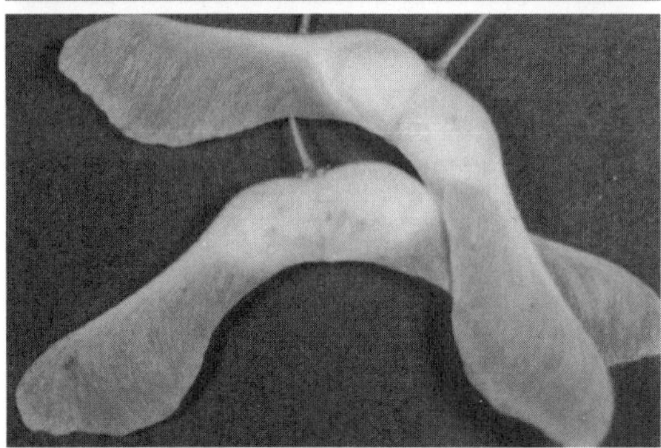

Roots

Somehow—partly in response to gravity—roots always sense which way is down. Regardless of what position the seed is in when it germinates, special hormones in the root tips cause the roots to always grow downward into the soil. This natural tendency is called *geotropism.* With some plants, a main large root *(taproot)* goes down, with small roots extending from it. Other plants send roots out in all directions. The large roots branch out into smaller and smaller ones, including microscopic root hairs. The root system anchors the plant to the ground. The root hairs absorb water and minerals from the soil, and the larger roots store excess food for future needs.

Stems

The stem of a plant extends from the roots to the leaves and flowers, providing support for both. Tiny tubes in the stem carry water and minerals from the soil to be distributed to the leaves, and they carry food manufactured by the leaves, to the roots and other parts of the plant.

Water comes up the stem through the tiny tubes of a tissue called *xylem*. Defying the force of gravity, water and minerals are moved up through the stem—even to the tops of tall trees—by a system of remarkable engineering design. The process begins at the roots, where water is absorbed and moved from cell to cell by *osmosis*. This movement of water into the roots creates a mild pressure called *root pressure*. Osmosis is the natural tendency of cells to maintain an equal concentration of water on both sides of the cell wall. *Transpiration*, the evaporation of water through the stomata of the leaves, plays a major role in moving water up the stem. The heat energy of the sun causes water to evaporate from the leaves and creates a water shortage in the upper cells. This causes water to move into the leaves from the cells below. The continuous upward movement of water through the plant is called *transpirational pull*, because of the role of transpiration in creating a constant shortage of water in the upper cells of the plant.

The process of moisture moving upward through the vascular system of a plant can be shown by placing a stalk of celery or the stem of a carnation in a jar of water to which food coloring has been added. If you try this, cut a slice off the base of the stem just before placing it in the water (see Figure 11-9). This process is explained as an activity at the end of this chapter.

A second type of tubular tissue, called *phloem*, transports manufactured food to all parts of the plant, including the roots.

In trees the xylem tissue (which carries water and minerals from the roots to the leaves) is the sapwood, which is the outer layer of the hard, woody trunk (or stem) of the tree. The phloem, which carries sugar to all parts of the tree, lines the inner bark. A thin layer of dividing cells, called the *cambium*, lies between the xylem and the phloem, adding new cells to both. New growth occurs more

Figure 11-9

Place a piece of celery and a carnation in jars of colored water to demonstrate how moisture moves upward through plants.

rapidly during the best part of the growing season, and more slowly or not at all when the weather turns cold or dry, resulting in a ring-like effect that is easily visible in a cross-section of a tree. Dark rings in the wood indicate a time of slow growth (smaller, more compact cells) and lighter color indicates more rapid growth (larger cells). A light ring and a dark ring together usually represent the growth of the tree during one year. The approximate age of the tree (or of a particular branch) can therefore be determined by counting the growth rings. Climatic conditions throughout the years of the tree's life can be inferred by the width of the rings, as the tree will usually grow more during a year with plenty of rainfall and favorable temperatures than during a dry, cold year (see Figure 11-10).

Knowing the location and role of the xylem and phloem, you can easily understand that the bark of a tree, and the tender layers of tissue just beneath the bark, are vital to the life and health of the tree. A tree that has lost a significant section of bark is seriously wounded. When a tree is *girdled*—that is, when a ring of

Figure 11-10

This cross-section of a tree shows the parts and growth rings.

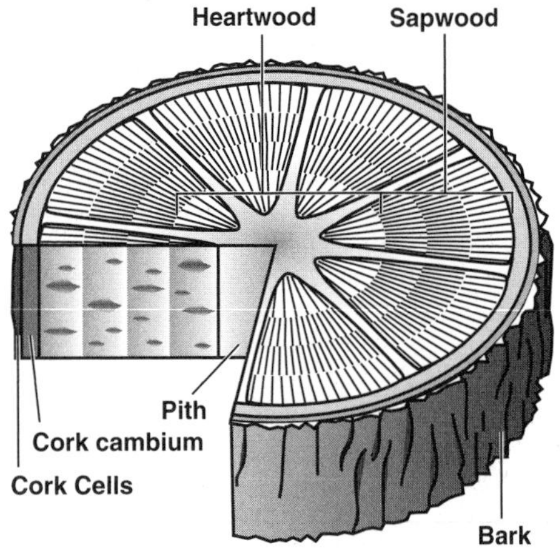

bark is removed all the way around the trunk—the tree will die (see Figure 11-11).

Like roots, stem tips respond to gravity. But while roots grow down with the pull of gravity (positive geotropism), stems usually grow up, against the pull of gravity (negative geotropism) (see Figure 11-12).

Figure 11-11

If the tree is completely girdled, it will die.

Figure 11-12

The plant on top is growing upward normally; the second photo shows how the stem bends to grow after the plant has been tipped to the side and allowed to continue growing in that position.

Leaves

Leaves are a very important, often beautiful part of a plant. The main function of leaves is to make food for the plant. Special processes in the leaves change the food into energy for the plant and help remove waste materials. Structural features of leaves provide some of the most recognizable distinguishing characteristics for plant identification. Leaves tend to turn toward the light. This behavior is called *phototropism.*

Leaf structure

The flat part of a leaf is called the *blade.* Most leaves also have a *petiole,* which is the stalk of the leaf and is attached to the stem of the plant. Some leaves have no petiole and fasten directly to the stem at the base of the leaf (see Figure 11-13).

Figure 11-13

Each leaf in the top photo fastens directly to the stem with no petiole; the Ginko leaf at the bottom has a distinct petiole.

In the leaf blade are *veins,* which provide the transport system for life-sustaining materials. The veins contain an intricate network of tiny, hollow tubes. Through the veins, water and minerals are brought in and distributed throughout the leaf, and food (sugar) that is made by the leaf is carried away for dissemination to all parts of the plant.

Vein Patterns.

Leaf veins are generally arranged in one of three patterns: *pinnate, palmate,* or *parallel.* The pinnate vein pattern, such as that of the willow, somewhat resembles a feather. A large vein, called a *midrib,* extends full length through the middle of the blade, with smaller veins branching off on each side all along the way. The palmate vein pattern resembles a hand, having several (usually five) large veins extending out from the base, like fingers, and smaller veins branching off to all parts of the leaf. The maple is a well-known example of a palmate leaf. Grasses are common examples of the parallel leaf pattern, as is also the beautiful iris. In these plants, many larger veins run side by side from the base of the leaf to its tip, with tiny veins branching off at the sides (see Figure 11-14).

Figure 11-14

These leaves exemplify pinnate, palmate, and parallel leaf patterns.

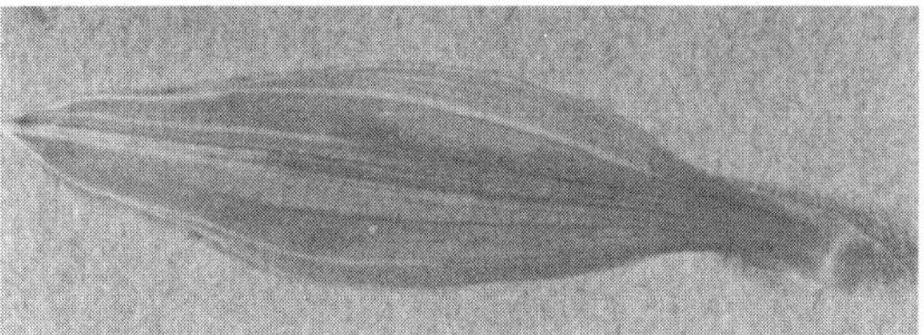

Shape and Edges.

In addition to vein pattern, leaves are characterized by their shape and the nature of their edges. The edges of some leaves are quite smooth. Others are jagged or toothed, and still others, such as the maple, have finger-like projections. Leaves with parallel vein patterns are usually long and narrow, those that are pinnate are relatively wider and shorter, and palmate leaves are quite broad.

Simple or Compound.

Leaves are also recognized as either *simple* or *compound.* If the leaf is all in one piece it is called a simple leaf, even if it is deeply lobed, as are leaves of the maple and the oak. If the leaf is divided into separate parts, it is called a compound leaf. Clover and horse chestnut leaves branch out at the base and are called *palmately compound* leaves. With the pea, leaflets are arranged opposite each other on each side of the midrib; such leaves are *pinnately compound leaves* (see Figure 11-15).

Photosynthesis

Plants manufacture their own food—and here's the factory. The most important function of the leaf is to make food for the plant. Called *photosynthesis,* this process requires water and carbon dioxide, and it can be performed only in the presence of chlorophyll and light. The word photosynthesis implies that something is put together (synthesized) with the help of light (photo). Water comes to the leaf from the soil through the roots and stem of the plant, and carbon dioxide is obtained from the air through tiny openings in the leaf, called *stomata.* Chlorophyll, which gives the leaf its green color, must be present in order for photosynthesis to occur (see Figure 11-16). A simple

Figure 11-16

Photosynthesis is possible because of the chlorophyll in the leaf.

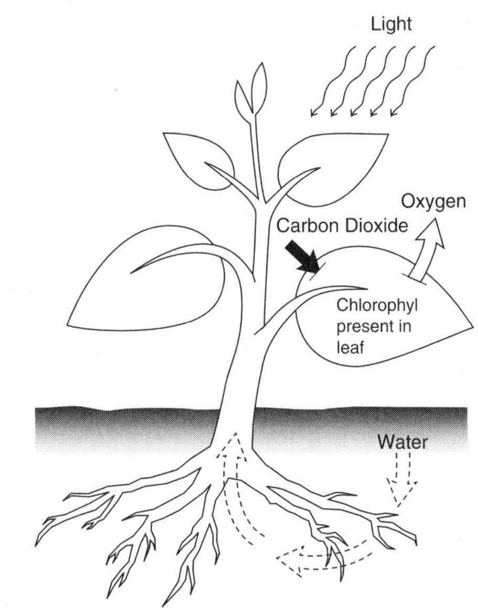

Figure 11-15 ***These leaves demonstrate simple, pinnately compound, and palmately compound leaf patterns.***

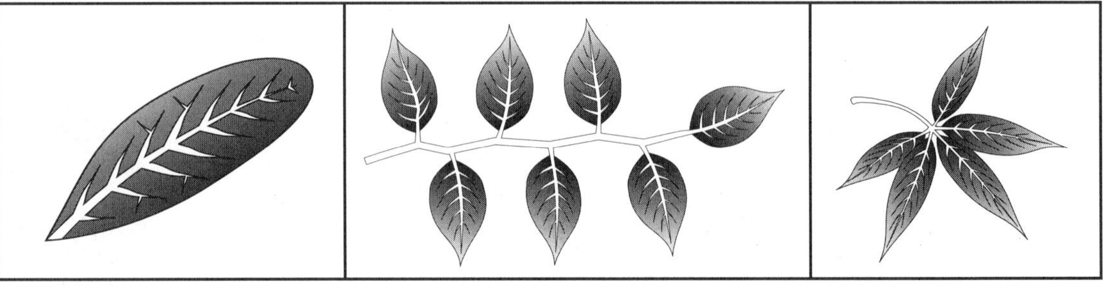

equation for the chemical changes that occur in photosynthesis is: energy + 6 CO_2 + 6 H_2O ——> $C_6H_{12}O_6$ + 6 O_2. For clarification, the formula is repeated with labels in parentheses: energy (sunlight) + 6 CO_2 (carbon dioxide) + 6 H_2O (water) ——> $C_6H_{12}O_6$ (sugar) + 6 O_2 (oxygen). During photosynthesis, oxygen is given off by the plant, through the stomata, as a waste product.

Delivery and Storage.

Newly manufactured food (sugar) is delivered throughout the plant, including the roots, to nourish it and provide energy and raw materials to build new cells needed for growth. Some of the food is stored, with the amount and method of storage varying from plant to plant. Most roots store food to some extent. Carrots, beets, and potatoes have roots or underground stems that are highly specialized for food storage.

Interdependence.

Plants and animals have a symbiotic (interdependent) relationship with respect to oxygen and carbon dioxide. Animals use oxygen and give off carbon dioxide as a waste product. Plants use carbon dioxide and give off oxygen as a waste product. One of the concerns about the destruction of vast amounts of tropical rain forests in recent years is the significant contribution of those forests to the world's supply of oxygen in the atmosphere.

Wait—Plants Use Oxygen Too.

To say that plants take in carbon dioxide and give off oxygen is an oversimplification. Plants do use carbon dioxide and produce oxygen during photosynthesis. However, food (sugar) manufactured by the leaf is carried throughout the plant and used to maintain the plant and produce new cells. Just like animals, plants use oxygen and give off carbon dioxide in the process of utilizing the food. In fact, the act of using up the food is called *oxidation*. Fortunately for humans and other animals, green plants produce more oxygen in photosynthesis than they use up in oxidizing food, and they use up more carbon dioxide in photosynthesis than they give off in the oxidation process.

Transpiration

As water brought up from the roots is used in making food, excess water must be allowed to leave the plant. Herein lies a third function of the stomata. In addition to taking in carbon dioxide and releasing oxygen into the air, the stomata also provide a system to control the amount of water in the plant. Tiny *guard cells* around the stomata control the size of the opening in the stomata according to current moisture conditions. Normally, the stomata are kept wide open so that as much carbon dioxide as is needed can enter the plant. This also allows for the free evaporation of water from the leaf. If the water supply to the roots is limited, however, or the plant is losing water too rapidly (such as on very hot days), the guard cells will narrow, or even close the stomatal openings, thereby conserving water (see Figure 11-17).

Figure 11-17

In this close-up enlargement of a leaf section, you can see stomata and guard cells in both open and closed conditions.

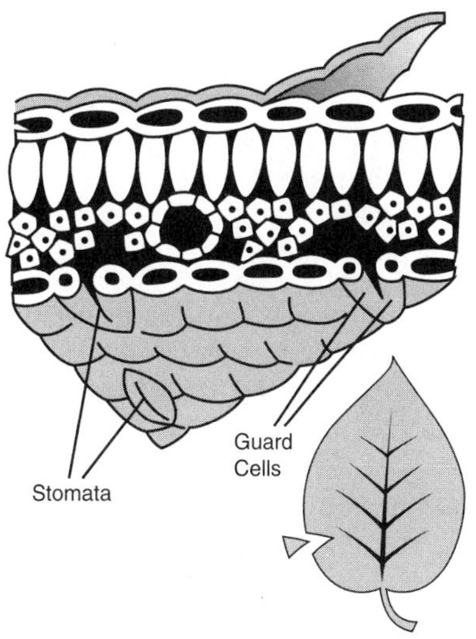

Color changes in leaves

The beautiful colors we see in the leaves of deciduous trees and bushes in the fall of the year are always there. During the growing season, however, these colors are hidden by the green color of chlorophyll. When the plant comes to the end of its growing season and stops producing chlorophyll, the hidden colors appear. Leaves also produce more pigment at this time of the year, enhancing the colorful displays that we see.

Flowers

In flowering plants, the flower itself is the reproductive organ. It produces seeds, often in a protective covering of fruit. Flowers have four parts: *sepals, petals, pistil(s),* and *stamens.* A flower that has all four of these parts is called a *complete flower* (see Figure 11-18). A flower that lacks one or more of these parts is an *incomplete flower.* The sepals cover and protect the flower bud. They are usually green, but with some flowers, such as the tulip, the sepals are the same color as the petals. When the bud opens, the sepals fold back as the petals spread out their colorful display. At the base of the petals are usually small pockets of *nectar,* a sweet liquid that attracts hummingbirds, as well as bees and other insects.

Reproduction

Female Parts of a Flower.

The pistil is the female part of the flower. It is located at the center of the flower. Its parts include a thin stalk *(style)* with a sticky top *(stigma)* and a swollen base called the *ovary.* Inside the ovary are tiny *ovules* (one to many), each containing an egg nucleus that, if fertilized, can become an embryo (seed), capable of producing a new plant.

Male Parts of a Flower.

The stamens are the male part of the flower. They are inside the petals, usually in a ring-like arrangement around the pistil (see Figure 11-19). The stamens, which are quite tall in some flowers and short in others, have two main

Figure 11-18

A complete flower has four parts: sepals, petals, pistils, and stamens.

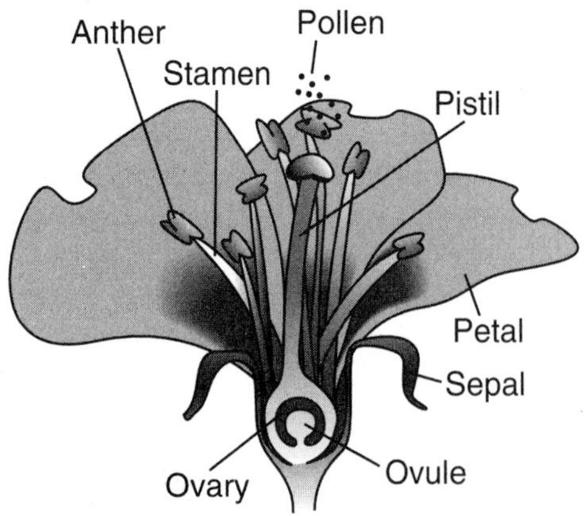

Figure 11-19

The stamens form a ring-like arrangement around the pistil.

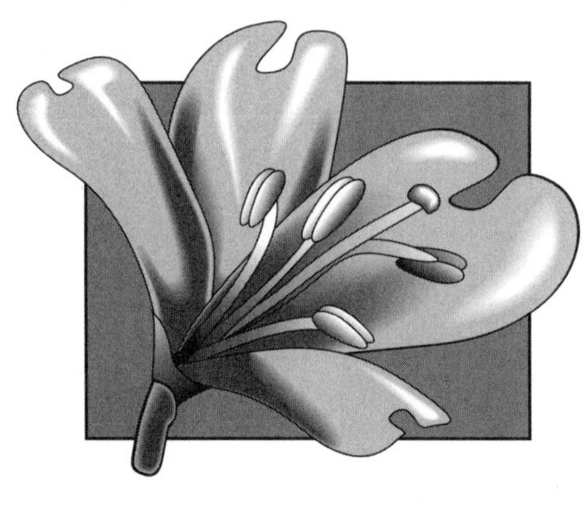

parts—a thin stalk called the *filament,* and a knobby tip called the *anther,* which produces a powdery substance called *pollen.* Each pollen grain contains a sperm nucleus that can unite with, or fertilize, an egg nucleus inside the plant ovary.

Fertilization.

For a seed to form, the egg inside the ovule must be *fertilized.* In this way, reproduction of flowering plants is similar to reproduction of mammals; an egg is fertilized by a sperm, making it possible for offspring to form. When a pollen grain attaches to the sticky stigma, a tube begins to grow down through the pistil, preparing a passage for the sperm nucleus to make its way to the ovary, where it enters the ovule and joins with (fertilizes) the egg. Other ovules in the ovary may be similarly fertilized by additional pollen grains.

Pollination.

Sometimes pollen is moved from an anther to the stigma of the same plant. Usually, however, pollen is transferred from one flower to another by the wind or by insects as they gather nectar. Pollen will stick to the hairy legs and body of an insect; then, as the insect gathers nectar, some of the pollen is brushed off on the stigma of other flowers. Hummingbirds pollinate flowers in the same way. If an egg is fertilized by pollen from the same flower, or from another flower on the same plant, the process is called *self-pollination.* If the pollen comes from another plant, the process is called *cross-pollination.* An egg can only be fertilized by pollen from the same variety of plant.

Flowers are phototropic

Like leaves, some flowers are also phototropic and turn toward the light. Flowers that do this, such as the sunflower, are called compass plants.

Fruit

After the ovules have been fertilized, the wall of the ovary develops into the fruit. In some species, such as peas, beans, poppies, and iris, the ovary wall becomes hard and dry as the seeds ripen. In other species, the ovary wall becomes increasingly fleshy and soft as the seed matures. Some of these fleshy fruits, such as peaches, cherries, and plums, are delicious to eat. The fruit, then, is the ripened ovary containing the seed(s) (see Figure 11-20).

The banana produces seedless fruit. What

Figure 11-20

A seed is produced in a ripening ovary.

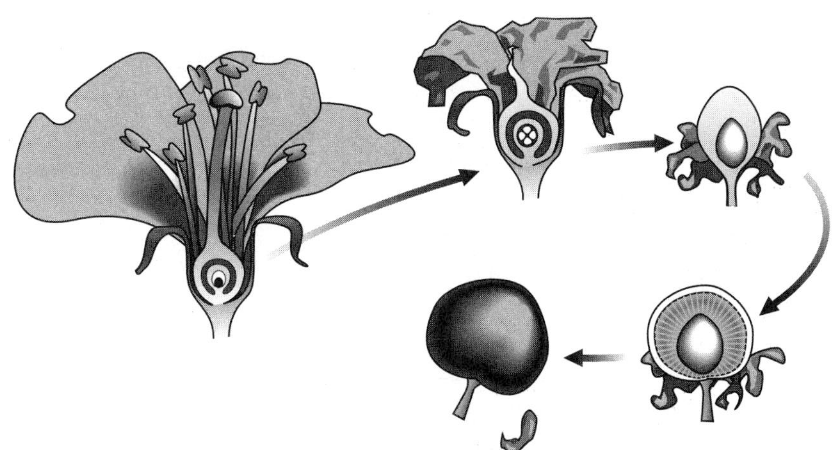

looks like seeds in the banana are unfertilized ovules. New plants grow up from the roots each season, and their flowers produce new bananas without being fertilized. New plants of seedless oranges (and certain other seedless fruits) are produced by grafting parts of seedless trees onto the roots and stems of ordinary fruit trees.

IV. SOME PLANTS CAN REPRODUCE WITHOUT SEEDS

Some plants reproduce without forming seeds. This process is called *asexual reproduction.*

Cuttings

Begonias, coleus, and many other plants can reproduce from *cuttings,* and the process can be as simple as placing a piece of stem (with leaves on it) in water or in moist sand or soil. In a few days, roots begin to grow at the base of the leaf and a new plant develops. To start an African violet, you need only to place a leaf in a container of water in such a way that the petiole (leaf stalk) is actually in the water.

Stems and Bulbs

Tulips are an example of another method of reproduction. Enlarged portions of underground stems, called *bulbs,* will begin to grow and form new plants when placed in proper conditions of moisture and temperature. White potatoes are enlarged underground stem tips, called *tubers.* Tubers contain stored food and, with proper moisture and temperature, can grow into new plants. Potatoes can even be cut into smaller pieces before being planted, as long as each planted piece has at least one bud, or eye. The bud is where new growth occurs.

V. USES

People could not survive without plants. We depend on them for oxygen, food, clothing, shelter, and for many other needs. Here are a few examples of ways we use plants.

Seeds

Some of the most common foods worldwide are seeds, including corn, wheat, barley, oats, rice, peas, beans, and nuts of various kinds. Some cooking oil comes from seeds, including peanut oil and cottonseed oil. Chocolate and cocoa come from the cocoa bean, and coffee comes from the coffee bean. Seeds of mustard, pepper, and nutmeg are used as spices. Fibers that are attached to the cotton seed are used for making cotton cloth.

Fruit

In addition to eating the seeds produced inside the fruit, we also eat the fleshy material surrounding the seeds. Such fruits as cherries, peaches, apples, cantaloupe, apricots, and plums are included in this category, as are several fruits that are customarily thought of as vegetables, such as squash, tomatoes, pumpkin, and cucumbers. There is an easy way to remember whether a food item is a fruit or vegetable: If it forms from a flower, it is a fruit. If it comes from some other part of the plant, it is a vegetable.

Roots

Yes, we even eat roots, including carrots, radishes, beets, and turnips. Horseradish and certain other roots are used as seasonings.

Roots of some plants are used in making candy and medicine; the licorice root is used for both.

Stems

We use stems of plants for food, clothing, shelter, and for many other purposes. We eat the stems of asparagus and potatoes (enlarged, underground stem). Linen is made from the stem of flax. Fibers from the stems of hemp and other plants are used in making rope and twine. Wood from the stems of trees is used for making furniture, in the construction of our homes, and for many other uses including fuel for heating and cooking.

Leaves

Leaves have many uses. Large leaves, such as palm leaves, have long been used to cover roofs of homes in tropical areas of the world. Many leaves are used for food, including lettuce, cabbage, parsley, spinach, and celery. (The celery stalk that we eat is actually the petiole of the leaf. The stem is only the bulb-like base, where the petioles come together.) Tea is made from tea leaves, and tobacco leaves are used for smoking.

Flowers

Probably the best known use of flowers is for decoration. Flowers are also used in making perfumes. We eat the flower of the artichoke and the buds of cauliflower and broccoli. In addition, flowers attract pollinaters to the plant.

VI. HOW LONG DO PLANTS LIVE?

Most flowers and some vegetables grown around the home are *annuals,* meaning that they grow from seed, bloom, produce new seeds, and die in one growing season. *Biennials,* including carrots and hollyhocks, do not produce seeds in the first growing season; but if left in the ground, they will grow the next year and produce seeds in the second season, requiring two growing seasons to complete their life cycle. Many plants, including all trees and most shrubs, continue to live for three or more growing seasons. These plants are called *perennials,* and many of them, such as the redwood tree, often live much longer than we do.

VII. IN CLOSING

Plants bring beauty and variety to the earth. They also play a vital role in our lives. Your students will almost assuredly increase their appreciation for plants as they learn more about them. Children should have many experiences in growing and observing plants, noting likenesses and differences, and in developing their own classification schemes based on observed characteristics. They will also develop better understanding of the contributions of plants as they learn about the many and varied ways we use plants for food, clothing, shelter, fuel, and so on.

LIST OF RESOURCES

Capon, Brian, *Botany for Gardeners: An Introduction and Guide* (Portland, OR: Timber Press, 1990).

Curtis, Helena, and N. Sue Barnes, *Invitation to Biology, Fourth Edition* (New York: Worth Publishers, 1985).

Raven, Peter H., and George B. Johnson, *Understanding Biology* (St. Louis, MO: Times Mirror/Mosby College Publishing, 1988).

Tolman, Marvin N., and James O. Morton, *Life Science Activities for Grades 2–8* (West Nyack, NY: Parker Publishing Co., 1986).

Victor, Edward, *Science for the Elementary School, Sixth Edition* (New York: Macmillan Publishing Co., 1989).

World Book Encyclopedia, 1989.

CHAPTER

PLANTS

ACTIVITIES

II. SOME MAJOR GROUPS OF PLANTS

ACTIVITY 11-1: HOW WOULD YOU CLASSIFY THESE PLANTS?

Materials Needed:

Variety of whole plants (washed), including root structure

Old newspapers or other table cover

Work table

Procedure:

1. Cover the table with newspapers or other protection, as available.
2. Lay the plants out on the table.
3. Examine the plants. Think about some ways the plants are alike and some ways they are different.
4. Separate the plants into two groups, based on their likenesses and differences. Don't tell anyone yet what your criteria is for grouping the plants.
5. Have another person or group try to figure out your criteria.
6. After the other person or group has guessed your criteria, let them regroup the plants, then you try to figure out their criteria.
7. Repeat the activity as long as interest is high.
8. Discuss other ways you could classify the plants, based on their likenesses and differences.

For Problem Solvers:

What is one criterion you think scientists might use to classify plants? Write your ideas on paper. Find the article on plants in an encyclopedia or other reference, or read some trade books about plants. Learn what you can about how scientists classify plants. Can you find anything about the criteria you selected? Do you think your criteria might be as good as theirs? Why or why not? Explain why it is important to have a standardized classification system—a system that everybody agrees on. Write your ideas.

When you are finished with the plants for this activity, find a box, some paper, and some glue. Use parts of these plants, along with other materials you find, to construct a diorama of an outdoor scene that you like. Share it with your group. Take it home and tell others about it and about classifying plants.

Teacher Information:

In order for students to eventually acquire an understanding of the scientific classification of living things, it is very important that they have many experiences in classifying objects based on their own reasoning. Students might decide to classify the plants by size, color, or whether or not they are wilted, but that's okay. They also might compare leaves or flowers and divide their groups based on those characteristics, perhaps using some of the same attributes that are used by scientists. Either way, be accepting and supportive of their logic. The objective at this point isn't to learn the scientific classification of plants, but to discern likenesses and differences and begin developing the ability to classify, based on the characteristics they observe.

Integrating: Reading, writing, art

Skills: Observing, inferring, classifying, communicating

III. FLOWERING PLANTS

ACTIVITY 11-2:

WHAT KINDS OF SEEDS ARE AROUND US?

Materials Needed:

A neighborhood

Procedure:

1. Gather seeds from around your school and neighborhood. Try to get several different kinds of seeds from weeds, trees, and so on. Combine your collections as a group and see how many different kinds you have.
2. Examine your collection of seeds. Divide them into groups according to the ways you think the seeds travel.
3. Label each group of seeds with the words representing ways you think they travel in nature, such as "wind," "animals," and so on.
4. Talk about each seed. Explain why you put it in the group that you did. What is there about the seed that caused you to make that decision? Do others agree?
5. After sharing your ideas, rearrange the groups if you want to.

For Problem Solvers:

Find opportunities to go to other places and gather seeds to add to your collection. See how many different kinds of seeds you can find that are carried by the wind, how many kinds you can find that stick to furry animals, and so on. Use encyclopedias or other books and identify as many of your seeds as you can. You might want to put them in separate envelopes or plastic bags with their names on them.

Make a graph of the different types of seeds collected by the group. Glue seeds to the graph to represent each kind of seed and the number you collected. According to how many seeds of each kind you have, decide whether to let one seed on the graph represent five seeds gathered, ten seeds gathered, and so on. Display the graph where people can see it. Your graph will probably show which seeds are most plentiful in the neighborhood, and which ones are relatively scarce.

You could even prepare one graph for the school grounds and another for the neighborhood outside the school grounds, then compare the two.

Ask a friend who lives in another town or another state to do the same thing, then share information by writing letters to each other—perhaps you can even trade pictures of your graphs, or send samples of the seeds.

Share your information with your class.

Write a song, a poem, or a story about your seeds.

Make a collage with extra seeds you have gathered.

Teacher Information:

Do this activity in the fall of the year and again in the late spring. Have students keep their first collection and compare it with their second collection. Different plants mature and produce seeds at different times of the season. If some students continue with the extension for problem solvers, everyone will be enlightened by learning about the different types of seeds that are in different areas. They might also be surprised to find out how many of them are the same.

Integrating: Reading, writing, art, music, social studies, math

Skills: Observing, inferring, classifying, communicating

ACTIVITY 11-3: WHAT IS INSIDE A SEED?

Materials Needed:

A variety of seeds (include beans, peas, and raw peanuts)

Paper towels

Zip-closed plastic bags

Hand lenses or low-power microscopes

Procedure:

1. Put a wet paper towel in each of several zip-closed plastic bags.
2. In each bag, place several seeds (six to ten) on the paper towel. Put only one kind of seed in each bag.
3. On the second day, open each bag and remove one seed.
4. Split the seeds open.
5. Examine the inside of the seeds and compare them. Use the magnifiers to examine them carefully.
6. What parts do you see in each seed?
7. Discuss your observations.
8. Draw your seeds and write a description of what has happened to the seeds.
9. On the fourth day, remove another seed from each bag. Repeat the examination and share your observations with your group. What has changed in the past two days? Draw the seeds and write about what has happened to them.
10. On the sixth day, repeat step 8.
11. Continue to observe your plants for several more days. Examine all of the parts with your magnifier. Do you see a stem? Do you see roots? What do the roots look like?
12. Examine the roots very carefully with the magnifier. Draw what you see.
13. Discuss the changes you see in your plants. Draw them, and write about them.

For Problem Solvers:

Fill two petri dishes loosely with damp paper towel or cotton. Put two or three corn seeds or bean seeds inside each petri dish. (Decide which kind of seed to use, and put the same kind in each dish.) Tape the lids on the petri dishes and stand them on their edge in a place where they are in the light and where they will not be disturbed. Label one of the dishes "A" and the other one "B." Let the dishes stay in the same position until at least one of the seeds in each dish has sprouted and has roots and stem. Take the lids off and remove all but one of the plants in each dish, leaving the healthiest one. Draw what you see and write notes about your observations.

Notice the direction the roots and stems

are growing. Rotate dish A 90 degrees. Do not disturb dish B. Write about what effect you think the rotation will have on the plant, if any.

In two days, rotate dish A again. Again, do not disturb dish B. Compare the roots and stems in the two petri dishes. Draw what you see and add to your notes. Share your observations with your group.

Now let's test your knowledge of experimentation. Answer these questions on paper:

Which is your experimental plant?

Which plant is the control?

What is the variable you are working with?

What was your hypothesis?

What is your conclusion?

Take your paper to your teacher or someone else who will know, and ask them to check your answers.

Teacher Information:

Students should observe the embryo in the soaked seeds. They might call this a baby plant, and that's okay. Help them to notice the seed coat and to identify the rest of the seed as plant food that is provided for the new plant to live on until it can grow leaves and produce its own food. Subsequent observations will find the embryo getting larger and sprouting. If they leave their new plants in the bags too many days, one of their observations will be that the plants get rotten and stop growing. An excellent extension of the activity would be to transplant the new plants into cups filled with potting soil, then to larger containers when needed, and encourage students to continue caring for and raising their plants.

Students who do the extension for problem solvers should discover geotropism through experimentation, as they observe that plant A, the experimental plant, continues to send the roots down and the stem up. Students are also asked to identify the elements of their experiment.

Integrating: Writing, art

Skills: Observing, inferring, communicating, formulating hypotheses, identifying and controlling variables, experimenting

ACTIVITY 11-4:
HOW DOES WATER TRAVEL IN A PLANT?

Materials Needed:

Celery stalk

Pint jar

Water

Red or blue food coloring

Procedure:

1. Fill the pint jar about two-thirds full of water.
2. Add several drops of food coloring to the water.
3. Cut about 1 centimeter (1/2 inch) off the bottom of the celery stalk, and immediately place the celery stalk in the water.
4. Observe for several days.
5. What happened? Draw a picture of the celery stalk and color it.
6. Discuss your observations.

For Problem Solvers:

Try this activity with a carnation instead of celery. Split the stem part way up and put each half in separate jars, one with red water and the other with blue water. Try some other plants.

How do you think the water gets up into the plants? Write your best explanation. Do some research to find out how the colored water gets up the stem and into the parts of the plant. Does the plant have some kind of pump in it? To pump water as high as a giant redwood tree is tall would require quite a powerful pump, yet those parts of the tree could not live and grow without water. Find out how the tree gets water up there. Is it the same way the colored water went up the celery stalk?

Share your information with your group.

Teacher Information:

Plants must transport water and nutrients to all of its parts in order for those parts to live and grow. In doing this activity, students will observe evidence that water really does move throughout the plant. Students who do the extension for problem solvers will find out the role of capillary action in this process.

Integrating: Reading, writing, art

Skills: Observing, inferring, communicating, formulating hypotheses

(Adapted from Activity 17, "How Does Water Travel in a Plant?" in Tolman and Morton, 1986.)

ACTIVITY 11-5:
HOW ARE LEAVES ALIKE AND HOW ARE THEY DIFFERENT?

Materials Needed:

Collection of tree leaves

Newspaper

Procedure:

1. In collecting leaves, take only one or two from each tree. Trees must have their leaves in order to live.
2. Cover the table with newspaper.
3. Spread your leaf collection out on the newspaper.
4. Examine the leaves. What is alike about them? What is different?
5. Separate the leaves into two groups, based on your observations.
6. Write a description of your criterion.
7. Have someone else examine your groups and try to figure out what criterion you used.
8. Trade roles; have the other person or group separate the leaves, and you try to decide what their criterion was.
9. Change roles and do it again if you have time.
10. Talk about other ways you could group the leaves.
11. Write a list of the ways you can see that the leaves are different.
12. Compare your list with others and talk about your ideas.

For Problem Solvers:

Get a book about leaves and find out what characteristics of leaves are usually used in classifying them. Write a list of these attributes. Are they a lot like the ones you used? What new ideas did you learn?

Find a book that tells about drying and preserving leaves. Try at least one of these ideas with your leaves. Show your preserved leaves to your group. Explain how you preserved your leaves and tell them about any other method you have learned about but haven't tried yet. Help someone else dry some leaves if they want you to. This could be someone in your class, at home, or somewhere else.

Teacher Information:

As with other classification activities we have done, the objective at the elementary level is to encourage students to observe and discern characteristics. As they decide what attributes to use in grouping the leaves, they will probably use some of the same criteria that professionals use—for example, basic shapes and vein patterns of the leaves.

Those who continue with the problem-solving extension will research to find out what characteristics are typically used in leaf classification and compare these attributes to the ones they used. They will also find out how leaves can be dried and preserved. An easy way to dry leaves is to place them between two absorbent surfaces, then press them for a few days. Corrugated cardboard, paper towels, or newspapers work fine as absorbent surfaces. Pressure can be applied by stacking two or three books on top of the leaf sandwich. Put something between the books and the rest of the material to protect the books from moisture coming from the leaves. A piece of plastic, a board, or another layer or two of cardboard will work well.

Integrating: Reading, writing

Skills: Observing, inferring, classifying, communicating

ACTIVITY 11-6:
WHAT ARE THE PARTS OF A FLOWER?

Materials Needed:

Flowers collected on a field trip, large flowers brought from home, or large flowers purchased at a store

Transparent tape

Magnifying glasses

White paper

Pictures of a complete flower

Procedure:

1. Put your flower on a sheet of white paper and examine it carefully.
2. Compare your flower to the one in the picture. Can you find the same parts? You may need a magnifying glass to help you.
3. Carefully take your flower apart. First find the petals, then the sepals (if there are any), and then the pistil. Next find the stamens and the anther.
4. Use transparent tape to tape the parts to your sheet of white paper.
5. Ask your teacher to help you find out why each part of a flower is important.

For Problem Solvers:

Make a collection of pictures of flowers and prepare a bulletin board. Group the flowers in ways that seem logical to you.

Study about flower arranging and learn what colors and what types of plants seem to go well together, as well as other qualities of a flower arrangement that make it appealing to the eye.

Using reference books or trade books, find out the purpose and function of the flower of a plant, other than its beauty. What does it do for the plant? Write a report on what you learn. Share your information with your group. If you'd like, ask your teacher to let you report orally to the class. Find other ways to share what you have learned.

Teacher Information:

Typical flowers have four sets of parts: sepals; petals; stamens; and one or more pistil, which includes the ovary and the stigma. Pollen comes from the anthers attached to the top of the stamens, which are supported by thin filaments. When the ovary is ready to be fertilized, the top of the pistil, called the stigma, will become sticky to collect pollen from the air or spread by insects. When a flower has all four parts it is said to be complete. Flowers lacking any of the four parts are generally classified as incomplete.

This is an excellent individual or small-group activity. Extensions include collecting flowers and pictures for bulletin boards, studying flower arranging, and learning the purpose and function of flowers in nature. Flowers should be appreciated for their beauty. Memorizing the names of flower parts is of little value in the elementary school, but careful observation and firsthand experience will increase children's awareness of plants and enhance appreciation for their beauty.

Integrating: Reading, writing, art

Skills: Observing, inferring, communicating

(Except for addition of the sections "For Problem Solvers," "Integrating," and "Skills," this activity was reprinted with slight modification from Activity 24, "What Are the Parts of a Flower?" in Tolman and Morton, 1986.)

IV. SOME PLANTS CAN REPRODUCE WITHOUT SEEDS

ACTIVITY 11-7: HOW CAN PLANTS REPRODUCE WITHOUT SEEDS?

Materials Needed:

African violet

Small cup or drinking glass

Water

Procedure:

1. Cut a leaf from the African violet.
2. Put water in the cup.
3. Place the leaf in the cup. Find a way to support the leaf so the tip of the leaf is in the water and the rest of the leaf is out of the water. (For instance, spread plastic wrap over the top of the cup and secure with a rubber band.) Then insert the leaf tip into the water through a small hole in the plastic.
4. Observe the leaf for several days. Add water if necessary to keep the leaf tip in water (if plastic is used, adding water probably won't be necessary).
5. When the leaf grows roots, transplant it into a cup of potting soil.
6. Continue to observe and care for your new African violet.

For Problem Solvers:

The leaf, in this activity, is called a "cutting." Try to grow new plants from other plant cuttings. See if you can find any that will grow roots. Do some research to learn about plants that can be grown from plant parts other than seeds or cuttings. Study about them and try some of them. Keep notes and drawings of any changes in the plants as you work with them. Measure the growth of any plants that grow, and keep record of their progress. Make a graph showing the growth. With each trial, write your hypothesis before you begin. Report your results to your group.

Teacher Information:

Students will enjoy seeing their African violet leaf become a new plant. In addition to African violets, Philodendrons and several other plants can be grown from cuttings, including geraniums, coleus, ivy, and others. Carrots will grow if put in water, as will potatoes, sweet potatoes, onions, and beets. The willow is an example of a tree that will do this.

Integrating: Reading, writing, math

Skills: Observing, inferring, communicating, measuring, graphing, predicting, using space-time relationships, formulating hypotheses

USES

ACTIVITY 11-8:
HOW DO PLANTS HELP PEOPLE?

Materials Needed:

Tables or cabinets for student displays

Poster paper

Markers

Procedure:

1. Bring to school an article of clothing that is made from plant parts.
2. Prepare a small poster that identifies the clothing, what material it is made of, and what plant or plant part the material came from, either directly or indirectly. If you can't bring the clothing article, that's okay—just describe it on your poster. If you wear the article, that's okay too.
3. Be prepared to tell the class about the article of clothing that you brought or that is described on your poster.
4. Find a time to share information with others.

For Problem Solvers:

How many others brought clothing that is like yours in some way? Can you classify them as you did the ones in step 2 above? Try it. How many ways can you think of to classify the clothing items? Make a list of them.

Although you might not be allowed to eat food brought from home by other students, you could make a collection of small samples of food items that come from plants. Would you include meat in your collection? If you do, be sure you can explain how it came from plants. Classify the edible plant parts you bring as seeds, roots, fruits, stems, leaves, or flowers.

Do some research and make a list of other ways we use plants.

Teacher Information:

This activity might bring in a lot of cotton shirts, but that's okay. You will probably also get some silk. Someone may bring wool and some leather, and you can explain that these came indirectly from grasses, grains, and weeds eaten by the animals that grew them. Maybe someone will bring nylon, and you can trace it back to oil, which came from the plants that fed the animals whose bodies formed the oil. By doing a bit of geneology on the material from which clothing is made, students should be able to identify plants as the ultimate source of the material. That should raise their respect for plants!

A collection of foods we get from plants could be interesting. Be sure they are in proper containers, so they won't spill or smell up the room. They probably should be discarded or taken back home the same day.

Other uses of plants are many, from building material to fuel. Fuel for automobiles is made these days from corn. Again, take a liberal approach and let students include any item that comes directly from plants or that they can trace back to plants. This could even include motor oil and road tar. Wow! We really do depend on plants!

Integrating: Reading, writing

Skills: Observing, inferring, communicating, using space-time relationships

VI. HOW LONG DO PLANTS LIVE?

ACTIVITY 11-9: HOW LONG DO PLANTS LIVE?

Materials Needed:

Paper and pencil

Procedure:

1. Take a walk around the school building and school yard. Write a list of all of the plants you can find.
2. In a second column, beside each plant on your list, write the name of the plant if you know it or if you can find it. Otherwise, just describe the plant and tell where it is located.
3. Do you remember if any of these plants were planted this year? Do you remember if any of the plants were there last year (if you were here last year)?
4. Now use a third column on your paper. If you think the plant lives only one year, then it dies and must be replanted, put a "1" in the third column. If you think this type of plant usually lives for three or more years, put a "3" in the third column. Try to find someone who knows a lot about plants, and discuss your answers to this part with them.
5. Compare your information with others in your group. If you made your list with a group, compare your information with another group.

For Problem Solvers:

Find an encyclopedia or other reference book on plants, and find out the meaning of the words "annual," "biennial," and "perennial." Go back and check your list. Make corrections in your numbers in the third column if needed. Now that you know what "biennial" means, write "2" beside the names of any plants that are biennials. Share your information with your group.

Of all the plants on the school grounds, which do you think is the oldest? Write it on your paper, then figure out a way to find out how old it is. Is this plant an annual, a biennial, or a perennial? Try to find out what kinds of plants often live longer than people do. What kind of plant is it? What plant holds the record for living the most years?

Find out what is the oldest plant in your town. Check with one or more old-timers and find out what the town was like when that plant began to grow. About what year was it? How many years ago was it? Find out what kind of music was popular at that time. Get some examples and maybe learn the songs, or have someone else sing them for the class.

Teacher Information:

This activity should at least make students aware that some plants have a one-year life cycle, some plants have a two-year life cycle, and some plants live for three or more years. Here's an opportunity to build vocabulary if you want to. If students are already on a terminology overdose, be satisfied with the numbers for the third column.

Integrating: Reading, writing, social studies, math, music

Skills: Observing, inferring, communicating, using space-time relationships, research

CHAPTER

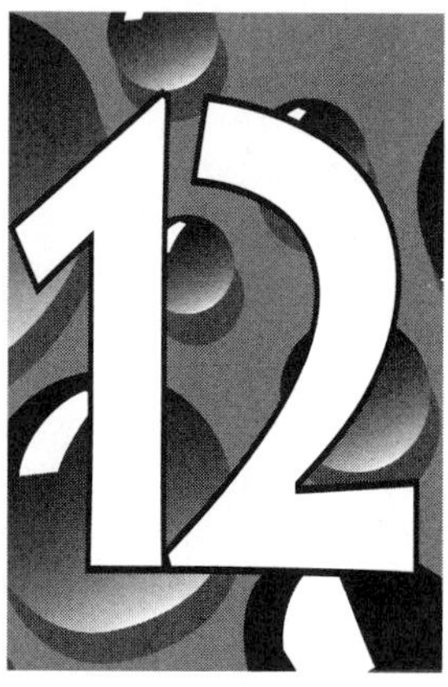

MICRO-WORLDS

CHAPTER OUTLINE:

I WONDER . . .

Why did microorganisms create such dilemmas for scientists regarding the classification system, and what was done to resolve them?

What are some protozoans we can study in the elementary classroom?

How can you measure the length of such a tiny organism?

Do you eat moldy food?

Are bacteria helpful to humans, or are they harmful?

Am I unhappy when food gets rotten? Should I be? What else would be different if that didn't happen?

I. INTRODUCTION

Humankind has always been intrigued by the unknown, and especially beckoned by the realms of nature that are particularly difficult to explore. Curiosities about the vastness of space, and things too far away to be seen by the unaided eye, led to the development of the telescope, and later to space travel.

Similar unbridled curiosities concerning *small* things led to the development of the microscope. In the 1600s, after hundreds of years in development, the instrument revealed a living world never before seen. Anton van Leeuwenhoek, an early Dutch scientist, was the first person to observe microorganisms and record his observations. As it becomes more sophisticated, the microscope continues to reveal more and more of the vastness of worlds too small to be seen by the unaided eye. Chapter 14 mentions the scanning tunneling microscope (STM), which recently brought atoms into view for the first time. This chapter deals with life forms that are too small to be seen with the naked eye. Such organisms are called *microorganisms*, or *microbes*.

In classifying these very tiny living things, scientists struggled for many years as to whether to consider them as plants or animals—the only two kingdoms in the classification system at that time. Many microbes lack certain characteristics that would clearly link them with either plants or animals. Others had both animal-like characteristics and plant-like characteristics, yet they did not really fit into either kingdom. The dilemma resulted in the development of a third kingdom—*protista*. The great diversity of microscopic life led to the more recent five-kingdom system proposed by Robert Whitaker, a biologist at Cornell University. There will continue to be modifications in the classification system as we learn more and more about living things.

In addition to the kingdoms animalia and plantae, the Whitaker system recognizes the kingdoms protista (protozoans and diatoms), monera (bacteria and blue-green algae), and fungi (mushrooms, yeast, and mold). Thousands of different types of organisms are represented in these three kingdoms. Since microscopic life is studied only at an introductory level in elementary science, this chapter is limited to a brief description of protozoans, mold, and bacteria, one example from each of the three new kingdoms.

II. PROTOZOANS

Protozoans include more than 30,000 species of one-celled organisms. They live in moist places, including freshwater, saltwater, and soil. They also live in plants and in animals. Protozoans may have plant-like or animal-like characteristics. For many years, they were classified as animals because most of them move about on their own power. The appropriateness of this classification was questioned, however, because the bodies of some protozoans contain chlorophyll, which enables them to make their own food; this is a characteristic of plants. You can quickly see the dilemma scientists faced, and why it was necessary to break the barriers posed by the system that forced all living things to be considered either plants or animals.

Protozoans eat large amounts of bacteria that are harmful to people. They also serve as food for fish and other aquatic animals. Some of them carry diseases, however (dysentery, malaria, and sleeping sickness, for example), so protozoans can be both helpful and harmful to people.

Based on how they move, protozoans can be thought of in four groups. The first, *apicomplexans,* move by gliding. The second, *sarcodines,* move by extending fingerlike projections called *pseudopods,* or false feet. The third group of protozoans, called *flagellates,* have one or more long hair-like projection called *flagella.* Flagellates move by whipping the flagella about. The last group, *ciliates,* are covered with fine, hair-like *cilia,* which move back and forth, propelling the organism through the water. Three of these four groups of protozoans are described below. Sarcodines, flagellates, and ciliates are represented here by the ameba, euglena, and paramecium, respectively.

Most protozoans, including ameba, euglena, and paramecium, reproduce by fission, or dividing in half. The nucleus divides first, and the halves move to opposite ends of the cell. Then the cell narrows in the middle and separates into two new cells.

Ameba

The ameba, like other sarcodines, has no definite shape (see Figure 12-1). In fact, its shape keeps changing as it moves. It sends out pseudopods (false feet), then the rest of its body flows into the pseudopods. The ameba eats other tiny organisms, such as algae or bacteria, by surrounding them and digesting them. Inside its cell are vacuoles and a cell nucleus. The vacuoles are tiny spaces that collect and expel excess water. Food also goes into vacuoles and is digested there.

Amebas exist in many places, including inside the bodies of animals and at the bottom of ponds.

Figure 12-1

The ameba has no definite shape.

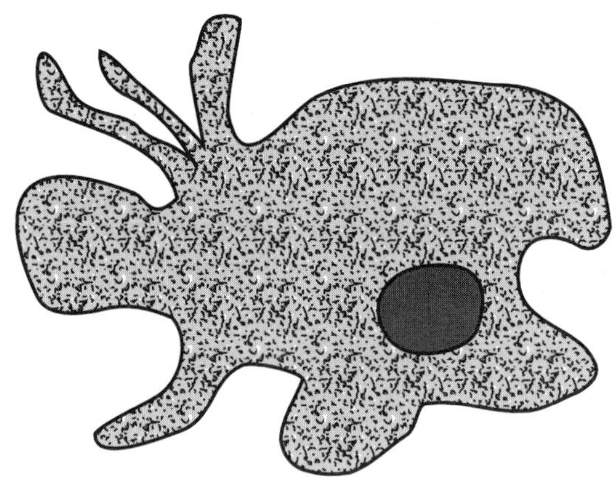

Euglena

The euglena is a flagellate, and it commonly lives in freshwater ponds and streams. Somewhat pear-shaped, it has a hair-like whip, or flagella, on the rounded end (see Figure 12-2). The euglena propels itself through the water by moving the flagella in a somewhat spiral motion. An interesting characteristic of this little creature is that it has chlorophyll, and when in the presence of light it carries on photosynthesis and makes its own food. When light diminishes, the euglena eats bacteria and material from decaying plants and animals.

Figure 12-2

The euglena propels itself by moving the hair-like flagella in a somewhat spiral motion.

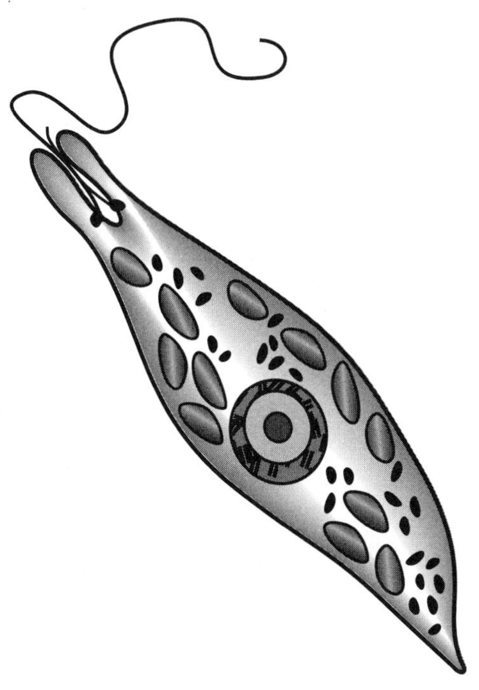

Paramecium

The paramecium is a ciliate. Covered with fine hair-like projections, called cilia, the paramecium resembles the sole of a shoe or slipper (see Figure 12-3). The cilia move back and forth constantly like tiny oars, propelling the organism forward or backward through the water. The paramecium eats other microscopic organisms, such as bacteria, algae, and other protists. Food is swept into a small opening by the cilia and passes through a tube into vacuoles, where it is digested. Paramecium can be found in the scum that forms on the surface of quiet ponds.

Figure 12-3

The paramecium is propelled by the movement of its cilia.

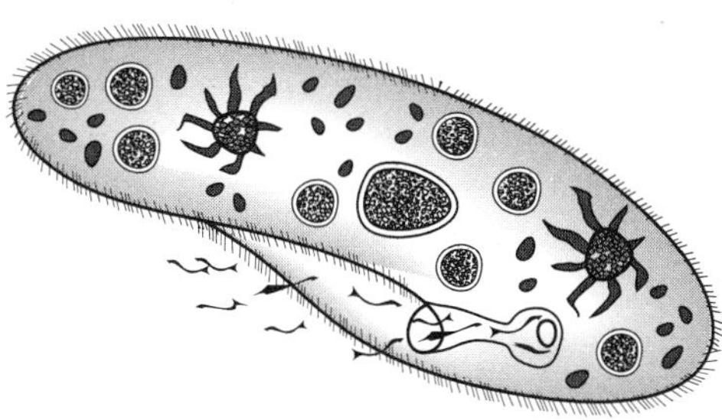

III. MOLD

There are many different kinds of mold, all of which are a part of the *fungi* family. Some of them grow on bread, cheese, and other foods. As the mold matures, it produces spore cases, each about the size of a pinhead, and each containing thousands of tiny spores. Under a microscope, parts can be seen that resemble roots and stems, with the spore cases being at the tops of the stems. When the spore case matures, it breaks open and the spores are released and carried away by air currents. These spores are very plentiful in the air, not a pleasant thought for people who are alergic to them. Those that settle on damp food can grow, mature, and produce more spore cases.

Molds are both harmful and helpful. Many foods must be discarded when molds grow on them. Some cheeses, however, are famous because of special types of mold that grow on them, giving the cheese a flavor that many people enjoy and other people find totally unpalatable. One type of mold produces the drug penicillin. Molds, like bacteria, break down organic matter and help to prepare it to return to the soil. This action not only gets rid of dead organisms and other organic wastes, but it also fertilizes the soil. This is an important process in the ecological system.

Molds can be grown easily. They thrive in dark, warm, moist conditions. Since they are almost everywhere in the air and grow on most any organic surface they land on, little effort is required to grow them on a slice of bread, a slice of potato, or a piece of fruit. Experiences with molds can provide elementary students with valuable opportunities to observe and experiment. A few suggestions are explained in the activities at end of this chapter. Care should be taken to avoid inhaling molds because of allergies and other possible harmful effects.

IV. BACTERIA

There are thousands of different kinds of bacteria. They live almost everywhere, and some of them are less than one ten-thousandth of an inch (one four-thousandth of a centimeter) in diameter. Certain species exist in large numbers on and in the bodies of humans and other animals, especially on the skin, in the mouth, and in the respiratory and digestive tracts.

Many bacteria are helpful—even necessary to human life. Sewage treatment plants use bacteria to purify water, and bacteria are used in making cheese, yogurt, certain other foods, and some drugs. Bacteria are a necessary element in the digestive systems of humans and other animals. They also help to decompose animal wastes, as well as the remains of dead plants and animals, playing a vital role in the important processes of recycling organic material and building soil. Other bacteria are harmful to humans, causing diseases (such as typhoid fever, gastroenteritis, and meningitis), producing toxins, and destroying healthy cells. Still others seem to play their part in the scheme of life with no apparent effect on humans, good or bad.

If you see shiny, round, white or dark bumps on a potato, you are probably looking at a type of bacteria, at work performing its role in nature. If you examine it under a microscope, you will not see parts that look like stems or roots. They will probably look like tiny balls, or like rods, or like spirals.

All bacteria reproduce by fission.

V. IN CLOSING

The study of microorganisms is only a surface exposure in the elementary school; but if hand lenses and simple microscopes are available, a look at the world of small things can establish readiness in these young minds for later study at greater depths. A major objective of elementary science is to heighten curiosity about the natural world by exposing students to science at a very high level of interest. Children (and adults) are fascinated with the new worlds they can see in a microscope.

LIST OF RESOURCES

McLaren, James E., and Lissa Rotundo, *Heath Biology* (Lexington, MA: D. C. Heath and Co., 1985).

Tolman, Marvin N., and James O. Morton, *Life Science Activities for Grades 2–8* (West Nyack, NY: Parker Publishing Co., 1986).

Victor, Edward, *Science for the Elementary School, Sixth Edition* (New York: Macmillan, 1989).

World Book Encyclopedia, 1989.

CHAPTER

MICRO-WORLDS

ACTIVITIES

II. PROTOZOANS

ACTIVITY 12-1:
WHAT TINY ANIMALS LIVE IN POND WATER?

Materials Needed:

Pond water (or water from the surface of a freshwater aquarium)

Droppers

Microscope

Microscope slide

Cotton

Paper and pencil

Procedure:

1. Place a drop of pond water on a microscope slide and put it under the microscope.
2. Search carefully and patiently for any tiny creatures in the water that are moving. You might find one that looks something like these (see Figure 12A-1), but they also might look very different.
3. If you find some thing that moves, observe it carefully and get to know it a bit, like a new friend.
4. If your new friend moves around so fast that you can't keep it within your view in the microscope, remove the slide and drop a tiny bit of cotton on the drop of water. Put the slide back on the microscope and find the little creature again.

Figure 12A-1

An ameba, a paramecium, and a euglena, as they might appear through your microscope.

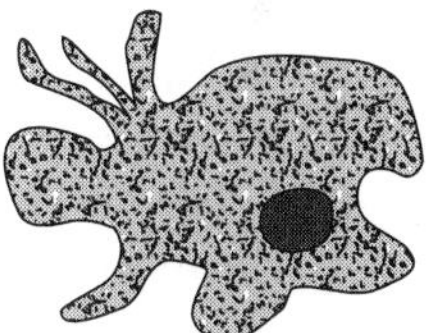

Ameba

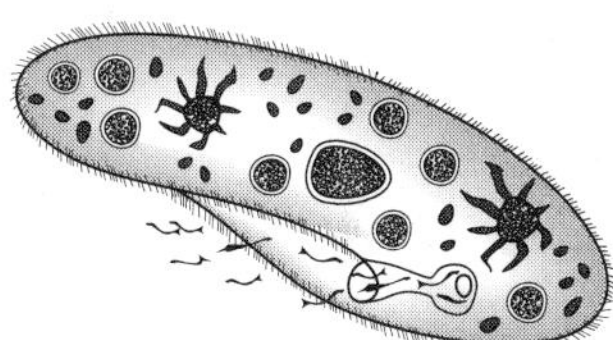

Paramecium

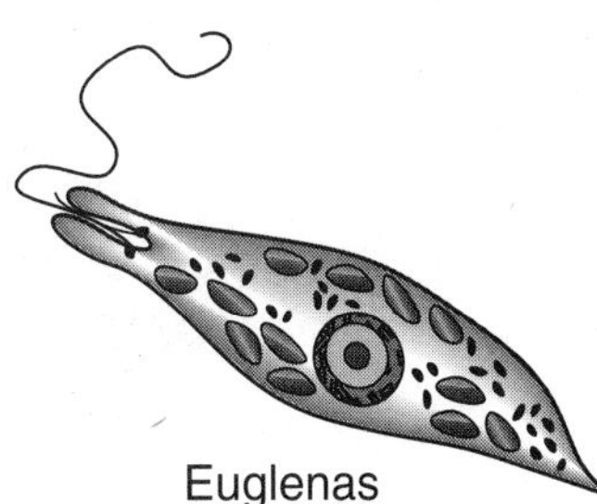

Euglenas

This time it should be in a "cage" within the cotton fibers.

5. When you have observed long enough that you are acquainted with what your friend looks like and how it moves, draw it on your paper. Write about how it moves, and anything else you think is interesting about it. What do you think would be an interesting name for it?
6. Keep looking for other little creatures that move, in the same drop of water or in other drops.
7. Compare your drawings and information with others.

For Problem Solvers:

Do some research and learn what you can about microorganisms. Find out what "protists" are. Why did scientists have a difficult time classifying these organisms when they tried to group them as either plants or animals? Study other tiny organisms that you can find with a microscope.

See if you can figure out a way to measure the actual length of one of the tiny organisms that you find in the pond water. Be sure that it's one that you can't see without the microscope. Hint: Consider using graph paper.

Teacher Information:

Microorganisms are usually fairly plentiful in pond water. The objective of this activity for elementary students is not to use scientific criteria for classification or to learn the scientific names of these little creatures, but for students to find out firsthand that they do exist and that there are many different kinds. This experience will likely spark an interest in some students to continue with such independent studies as those suggested in the extension for problem solvers.

You might choose to invite a biologist into your classroom to share information and activities with your students. It is important that the experience be designed for high interest and geared to the level of your students, to assure a result of greater interest and curiosity to learn more. Stimulating interest is far more important for elementary students than facts learned about this topic.

A copy of graph paper with very fine grid, copied onto transparency film, should provide the creative student with a way to measure the length of a paramecium, and so on. They can put the grid under the microscope slide.

Integrating: Reading, writing, art

Skills: Observing, inferring, measuring, communicating

III. MOLD

ACTIVITY 12-2:

WHAT'S THIS STUFF ON MY BREAD?

Materials Needed:

Plastic bag that can be closed tight

Bread

Hand lens

Paper and pencil

Procedure:

1. Sprinkle a little bit of water on a slice of bread, put the bread in the bag, and seal the bag.
2. Put the bag in a cupboard and leave it there for three or four days.
3. Examine the bread. Is anything on it that wasn't there when you put it in the cupboard? If not, put it back in the cupboard for another two or three days.
4. When you see something strange on the bread, draw carefully what you see.

5. Examine the material carefully with a hand lens. Draw on your paper what you see.
6. Share your information with your group. Did anyone notice things that others did not notice? If so, use the hand lens to examine the bread again. Do your observations verify what your group member saw?

Teacher Information:

Mold should grow readily on moist bread. There are many types of mold, and this experience will expose your students to one of them. There will be plenty of opportunities to study and observe mold further at a later date. At this point, students will learn some of the characteristics of mold, at least that it exists. They should also note that the mold looks and feels fuzzy—somewhat like cotton—and that with the hand lens they can see parts that resemble stems and roots.

Bread that is purchased from health food stores is usually best for such activities because these loaves do not have preservatives.

Caution: Students shouldn't taste or smell materials they are not sure are safe. This is one of those materials to avoid because of possible allergies.

Skills: Observing, inferring, communicating

ACTIVITY 12-3: HOW CAN WE LEARN MORE ABOUT MOLD?

Materials Needed:

Plastic bags that can be tightly closed

Two oranges with mold on them

Two lemons

Moldy bread from previous activity

Hand lens

Marking pens

Procedure:

1. If you do not have oranges with mold, just leave two oranges out of the refrigerator for a few days.
2. Put one orange and one lemon in a bag. Seal the bag and set it aside for a couple of days. Be sure the lemon is touching the orange.
3. Put another orange and another lemon in a second bag and seal the bag. Put the bag aside for a couple of days. Be sure the two fruits in this bag do not touch each other.
4. Look at the oranges and the lemons. What do you see? How does the lemon that was touching the orange look compared to the lemon that was not touching the orange? Draw what you see.
5. Examine the pairs of fruits with the hand lens. Keep one pair of fruits separated from the other pair. Observe very carefully. What do you see? Draw it.
6. Compare the mold on the fruit with the mold on the bread. Observe very carefully. It is exactly the same?
7. Draw what you see.
8. Share your information with your group. What did you learn about mold?

For Problem Solvers:

If a microscope is available, use it to learn more detail about the material you are studying.

Try putting a piece of moldy fruit in bag with a piece of bread. Put one in with a piece of celery. Does the mold that is on the fruit grow on other things that are not fruit?

Design an experiment to find out what conditions mold prefers. Does mold grow better on materials that are moist or materials that are dry? What about temperature conditions? Does it make any difference whether it is in the light or in the dark? Does sunlight affect mold differently than artificial light does? Think of other questions about mold that you could answer by experimenting. Are you using a control as you test your variables?

As you set up each experiment, write on paper what your variables are, write your hypothesis, and decide how you will keep a record of your findings so you can show others what you learned.

Teacher Information:

Here's an opportunity for students to show their stuff with their experimentation skills. Considering all of the options suggested for study and experimentation could be rather overwhelming for some students. If needed, help them to select one question for study. After a time, they might like to try a second question from those suggested, or to pursue a question of their own.

Many experiences with identifying variables and finding ways to control them will help students to feel comfortable in using these elements of experimentation. Similarly, they will improve their skills in formulating hypotheses as they do it over and over again. Be sure students have adequate opportunities to collaborate in designing their experiments and to share their findings with others.

Skills: Observing, inferring, communicating, using space-time relationships, formulating hypotheses, identifying and controlling variables, experimenting

IV. BACTERIA

ACTIVITY 12-4:
HOW DO BACTERIA COMPARE WITH MOLD?

Materials Needed:

Potato

Bread

Two fruit jars (or plastic bags that seal)

Hand lens

Microscope

Procedure:

1. Put a piece of bread and a slice of potato in separate fruit jars. Sprinkle enough water on the bread to make it moist.
2. Leave the lids off both jars for one day.
3. Being sure the bread is moist, seal both jars with their lids (or seal each in bag).
4. Mold spores and bacteria are in the air, and they will collect on the bread and potato.
5. Look at the bread and potato every day.
6. Any fuzzy growth you get is mold. If you also get a dark, shiny substance forming on the potato, you have bacteria growing there.
7. Place a small amount of each type of growth on separate slides and examine them under a hand lens and under a microscope.
8. Compare color, shape, size, and any other attributes you notice as you examine the two types of growths.
9. Draw what you see, being as careful and accurate as you can.
10. Talk about the two types of growth. Share your information and your ideas. How are bacteria and mold alike, and how are they different?

For Problem Solvers:

Think of some other foods that you might grow mold or bacteria on. Try it. Examine the new growths, draw them, and compare them with your earlier drawings. Do they look the same? If not, how are they different?

Teacher Information:

These are exciting investigations for students who are bitten with the curiosity bug. There are many different types of bacteria and many different types of mold. Encourage students to see how many they can find, being careful to notice and record likenesses and differences.

Integrating: Reading, writing, art

Skills: Observing, inferring, communicating, using space-time relationships, formulating hypotheses, identifying and controlling variables, experimenting

ACTIVITY 12-5:
HOW CAN YOU PREPARE A PETRI DISH?
(Teacher-supervised activity)

Materials Needed:

Petri dishes

Water

Gelatin

Beef bouillon cube

Sugar

Baking soda

Saucepan and lid

Hotplate

Procedure:

In this activity you will prepare gelatin and petri dishes for growing bacteria. Be sure you have an adult to help you.

Preparing the gelatin:

1. Combine in the saucepan 500 milliliters (1 pint) of water, 60 milliters (about 4 tablespoons) of gelatin, one beef bouillon cube, 5 milliliters (1 teaspoon) of sugar, and a pinch of baking soda.
2. Bring the solution to a boil for fifteen minutes.
3. Cover the pan with a lid and allow the solution to cool.

Preparing the petri dishes:

1. Put several petri dishes in the oven for one hour at about 107 to 121 degrees Celsius (225 to 250 degrees Fahrenheit).
2. Remove the petri dishes and allow them to cool to room temperature. Keep the dishes covered except when you are filling them or deliberately exposing them to certain planned conditions.
3. Pour gelatin about 5 to 6 millimeters (1/4 inch) deep in each petri dish.
4. Your petri dishes are now ready to use. Remember to keep them covered.

Teacher Information:

This activity is not an investigation, but only to help you and your students prepare petri dishes for future activities in growing bacteria.

ACTIVITY 12-6: WHAT CAN WE LEARN ABOUT BACTERIA?

Materials Needed:

Prepared petri dishes

Procedure:

1. Decide what to expose your petri dishes to, as you prepare to grow bacteria. For example, you might sneeze or cough on one of them, touch a finger to another, a freshly washed finger to another, kiss one, place hair or fingernail clippings on one, and so on.
2. Be sure to keep each dish covered except just long enough to make the planned exposure.
3. If you choose to expose one petri dish to the air, leave the lid off of that one for ten minutes or so.
4. Label your dishes so you will know later what each dish was exposed to.
5. Place your experimental dishes in a warm, dark place.
6. Put one nonexposed petri dish, as a control, with the experimental dishes.
7. Look at your petri dishes every day. If some spots appear, you know bacteria are beginning to grow. Let them grow for a few days.
8. When you think your dishes are ready, examine and compare them. Do all of them have bacterial growth? Are they the same color? How do they look under a hand lens?
9. Put a small amount of each on a slide and examine each specimen under a microscope. Do they look the same under a microscope? How are they the same? How are they different?
10. Draw and describe what you see.
11. Does your control have bacterial growth? If so, try to decide what it might have been exposed to. When? How? What information does your control provide for you as you examine the experimental dishes?

For Problem Solvers:

Select one technique for exposing gelatin to bacteria, then prepare several petri dishes using that same technique. Design an experiment to find out what conditions bacteria grow best in. Find out whether bacteria grow best in light or in the dark, in warm temperatures or cooler temperatures, and so on. Think of conditions that you would like to compare, and make the comparisons. Observe carefully for several days and record your results. Why is it important that you use the same exposure technique for all of the petri dishes you use for this experiment?

Looking back to your experience with mold, would you say the ideal conditions for growing bacteria are the same as the ideal conditions for growing mold?

Design another experiment to determine what things are most effective in slowing or stopping the growth of bacteria. Consider such things as Lysol, tincture of iodine, sunlight, penicillin or other antibiotic (ask an adult to help you find a pill with one of these in it), aspirin, and any other substance you would like to test. Be sure to leave at least one dish covered and sterile for your control. Examine your results, make drawings, explain, prepare charts, or whatever will help you communicate your results to others.

What variables did you work with? What were your hypotheses? What are your conclusions?

Do some research in textbooks, encyclopedias, and other reference books to find out how bacteria are helpful to humans and how they are harmful. Make a list of these, then report, compare, and discuss them with your group.

Go to encyclopedias and other reference books and find information about some of the pioneers in the field of controlling harmful bacteria. Report and discuss their names, their efforts, and their contributions to society.

Teacher Information:

Your problem solvers should be having a heyday. Some very fine science fair projects could result from these experiences. Stay in close communication with students and help them to make these experiences meaningful, to make "connections" between experiments. Challenge them to think of some situation in life wherein answers to important questions could be found by using the techniques they are using here.

Integrating: Reading, writing, social studies, art

Skills: Observing, inferring, communicating, using space-time relationships, formulating hypotheses, identifying and controlling variables, experimenting

CHAPTER

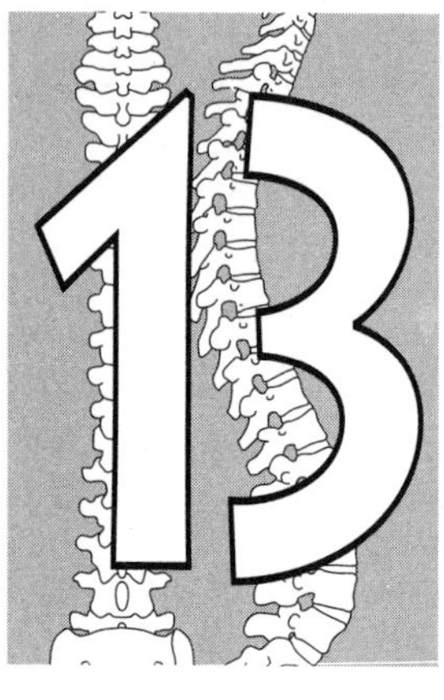

THE HUMAN BODY

CHAPTER OUTLINE:

- INTRODUCTION
- BUILDING BLOCKS OF THE BODY
- THE SKIN
- THE SKELETAL SYSTEM
  - The Skull
  - The Spinal Column
  - The Rib Cage
  - The Arms and Legs
  - The Joints
- THE MUSCULAR SYSTEM
  - The Voluntary and Involuntary Muscles
    - The involuntary muscles
    - The voluntary muscles
- THE CIRCULATORY SYSTEM
  - The Heart
  - The Blood Vessels
  - The Blood
    - Plasma
    - Red blood cells
    - White blood cells
    - Platelets
    - The trip through the body
  - The Lymphatic System
    - The importance of muscular action in circulation
    - The lymph nodes
- THE RESPIRATORY SYSTEM
  - The Nose and Nasal Passages
  - The Larynx
  - The Lungs
  - The Breathing Mechanism
  - The Breathing Control Center
- THE DIGESTIVE SYSTEM
  - The Mouth
  - The Stomach
  - The Small Intestine
  - The Large Intestine
  - Misplaced Credits
  - Effect of Emotions
- THE NERVOUS SYSTEM
  - The Brain
  - The Spinal Cord
  - The Nerves
- THE FIVE SENSES
  - The Sense of Sight
    - Functions of the eye
    - Peculiarities
  - The Sense of Hearing
  - The Sense of Taste
  - The Sense of Smell
  - The Sense of Touch
- IN CLOSING
- LIST OF RESOURCES
- ACTIVITIES

I WONDER . . .

What does the skin do for me, other than to cover me up and hold me together?
Which parts of the body have the most bones?
What types of joints are there to allow the bones to move?
What would happen if all muscles were voluntary muscles?
Why must many muscles work in pairs?
How is the circulatory system like a highway system?
Other than the heart, how do muscles help with circulation?
How does the lymphatic system fit in with the circulatory system?
What does atmospheric pressure have to do with the breathing process?
Why does the stomach get a bad rap?
If most digestion doesn't take place in the stomach, then where does it happen?
How is the nervous system like the electrical system of a car?
How do our eyes and our nose mislead us when they get tired?
Do we really see with our eyes and hear with our ears?
How do chemicals produced by the body affect our moods and emotions?

I. INTRODUCTION

Of all the wonders of nature, none surpasses the human body as a masterpiece of structure and design. No other creature has the ability to think and reason to the extent that humans can. Nothing else on Earth has such capacity to create or such power to destroy. A greater understanding of the body and how to care for it can increase the quality of life, and few science topics surpass that of the human body in capturing the interest of children, especially in the intermediate grades. The objective of this chapter is not to produce physiologists, but simply to provide an introductory glimpse of the structure, the function, and the marvels of the human body.

In this chapter, we will discuss building blocks of the body, the skin, the skeletal system, the muscular system, the circulatory system, the lymphatic system, the respiratory system, the digestive system, the nervous system, and the five senses. For some students, the preliminary information we deal with at the elementary level will kindle a curiosity that will lead to a lifetime of study. For others, follow-up study will be limited to the health and science courses required by the public schools. But all should gain a foundation for making better-informed decisions in caring for their bodies.

II. BUILDING BLOCKS OF THE BODY

The body can be thought of as a busy and productive factory, with many functions and many products that enable us to live pleasant and useful lives. Like a factory, the body is made up of many different kinds of materials. The smallest unit of living tissue is called a *cell.* The average adult human body is made up of some 60 trillion cells, which vary greatly in size, shape, and function. Groupings of similar cells form *tissues.*

There are four main types of tissue in the body:

1. **Muscle tissue,** *which forms all the muscles of the body.*
2. **Connective tissue,** *which supports body parts and holds them together, including bone, blood, tendons, ligaments, and cartilage.*
3. **Nerve tissue,** *which includes the brain, the spinal cord, and all nerves.*
4. **Epithelial tissue,** *which forms the outer skin and lines body cavities, such as the mouth, nose, stomach, intestines, and heart.*

Tissues are the basic material from which the more complex body parts and systems are formed. A group of tissues working together to perform a body function make up an *organ.* The human body has many organs, including the skin, heart, lungs, liver, eyes, and so on. Organs that are part of the same general function combine to form *systems,* such as the skeletal system, the digestive system, and the circulatory system. Several organs and systems are described in the following sections.

III. THE SKIN

The most obvious and visible organ of the body is perhaps one of the least recognized and appreciated for what it does. The skin is not just a sausage wrapper that demands much care and gives little in service. Although it is thin and flexible, the skin is the body's outer security system. Its glands, nerves, blood vessels, and even fatty tissues perform functions that are necessary to the preservation of our lives. For external protection, it provides a waterproof covering for the body, keeping inside moisture in and outside moisture out—a service that is necessary for life. In addition to protecting the body from the invasion of unwelcome moisture, the skin protects it from being invaded by a horde of potentially harmful bacteria, many of which even live on the skin. As a part of its protective function, the skin is a significant communications network. Its complex nervous system provides the sense of touch, which warns the body of danger and enables it to experience important input from the outside world.

Altogether the skin is about 3 millimeters (1/8 inch) thick, and it covers the entire body. It consists of two layers: the *epidermis* and the *dermis* (see Figure 13-1). The epidermis is a paper-thin outer layer with a protective covering of dead skin cells. As new epidermal cells are produced, the older ones are pushed up, become flat, hard, and dry, and eventually flake off. In fact, millions of dead skin cells flake off each day—the epidermis is completely replaced approximately once a month. Dead cells are washed away in the shower and rubbed away by clothing and bedding.

There are no blood vessels in the epidermis, but live cells are nourished by *diffusion* from below. (Diffusion is the random movement of molecules to regions of lower concentration, resulting in uniform distribution of the molecules.) A callus is a protective, thickened layer of epidermal tissue, formed in response to a rubbing or wearing action on the surface of the skin. The thin skin covering water blisters is also epidermal tissue, with the blisters forming between the layers of skin.

The strong, elastic connective tissue that lies just beneath the epidermis is the dermis. This layer is much thicker than the epidermis, and it contains an elaborate collection of nerves, blood vessels, glands, and cells that produce hair. Beneath the dermis is a layer of fatty tissue that binds the skin to the flesh. A significant portion of the body's air-conditioning system is contained in the dermis. On a hot day, dermal

Figure 13-1

The skin has two layers and many components.

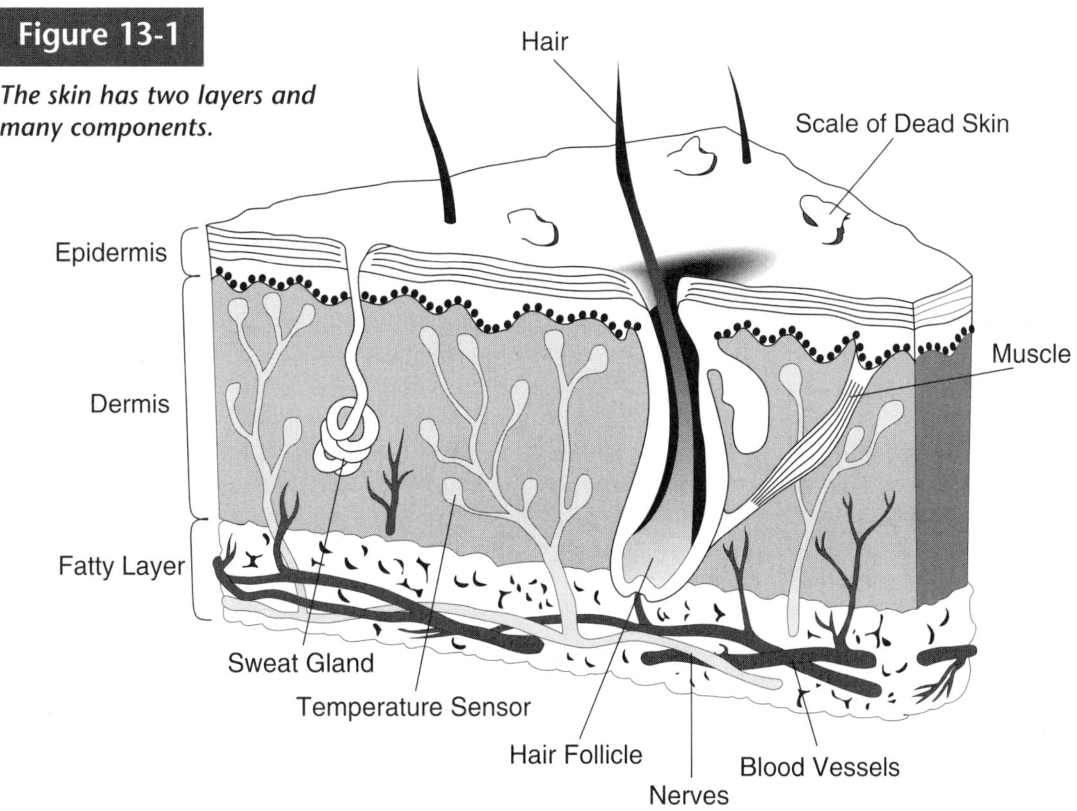

blood vessels dilate, bringing more blood near the surface for cooling and giving the skin a flushed appearance. The same reaction can be triggered by emotion, such as anger or embarrassment. In cooler temperatures, the surface blood vessels contract, forcing more blood to the interior of the body and conserving heat. The contracting mechanism can also be triggered by emotion; "cold feet" from fear are very real. The response of the skin to changes in external temperatures, in an effort to maintain constant body temperature, is an example of *homeostasis,* which is the maintenance of constant physiological conditions within the body.

Sweat glands assist the dilated blood vessels in cooling the body surface, secreting moisture when it is needed. Hundreds of these glands are contained in each square inch of dermal tissue—roughly 2 million on the surface of the body. Evaporation is a cooling process; the molecules with greatest energy (heat) escape into the air first, leaving those with less energy behind. The body is cooled as moisture evaporates on the surface of the skin. Evaporative coolers on homes, popular in dry climates, operate on this same principle.

The role of sweat glands extends beyond the air-conditioning system; they also help to take out the garbage, and they continue to function even on cool days. The water in sweat takes with it excess salt and other wastes from the blood. Even when a person is not aware of sweating, the sweat glands put off about $^1/_4$ liter (1 cup) of water, along with waste products, during one day of moderate temperatures. On a hot day, they may secrete several times that amount. The secretion of the sweat glands can be stimulated by emotions such as anxiety and fear, just as the dilation of blood vessels can be. This reaction commonly causes moist palms, as palms have an abundance of sweat glands.

The pigment *melanin,* which is produced by cells in the skin, determines the color of eyes, hair, and skin. Freckles are concentrations of melanin. Exposure to the sun causes pigment granules to rise from the lower part of the epidermis to the surface, providing a protective tan as the body tries to defend itself against ultraviolet rays. Despite warnings about the risk of skin cancer and premature skin aging from overexposure to the sun, many people consider getting a beautiful dark tan one of the most important events of the summer. Some of these people continue tanning throughout the year by using artificial tanning systems when that method is more accessible or more desirable than using the sun. As important as the skin is, some people care more about its temporary appeal than about its lasting fitness and healthy appearance.

IV. THE SKELETAL SYSTEM

The human skeleton, which provides the structural framework for the body, consists of bones that are cushioned by cartilage. Although the bones are made up of cells, there is a hard material, consisting mostly of calcium phosphate, between the cells that make bones rigid. Many bones are hollow and are filled with a soft tissue called *marrow,* which manufactures red blood cells. Cartilage has a material between its cells that is flexible but tough. The skeleton of the human fetus is mostly cartilage, but as the body matures to adulthood, cartilage cells are replaced by bone cells. The adult skeleton still includes cartilage, however. The ends of long bones are padded with a layer of this tough material. Also, cartilage discs provide cushions between the vertebrae of the spinal column. The ears and the end of the nose are made of a different kind of cartilage, which provides both form and flexibility.

The Skull

There are more than 200 bones in the body. The *skull* consists of the cheek, nose, and jaw bones, plus several plate-like bones that together form the *cranium,* which surrounds and protects the brain. In children, the bones that encase the brain are rather loosely joined together, allowing growth of individual plates. As a person matures to adulthood, these plates fuse solidly together.

The Spinal Column

The *spinal column* (see Figure 13-2) consists of a series of thirty-three vertebrae, which support the torso and the head and allow both to bend and turn. A second major role of the spinal column is to provide a protective channel for the spinal cord. Each vertebrae has a donut-hole center, and the spinal cord, attached to the base of the brain, extends down through the spinal column. Nerves branch out from the spinal column, supplying the conduit for chemical-electrical signals between the brain and the various parts of the body.

Figure 13-2

The vertebrae that make up the spinal column support the torso and the head, and allow both to bend and turn.

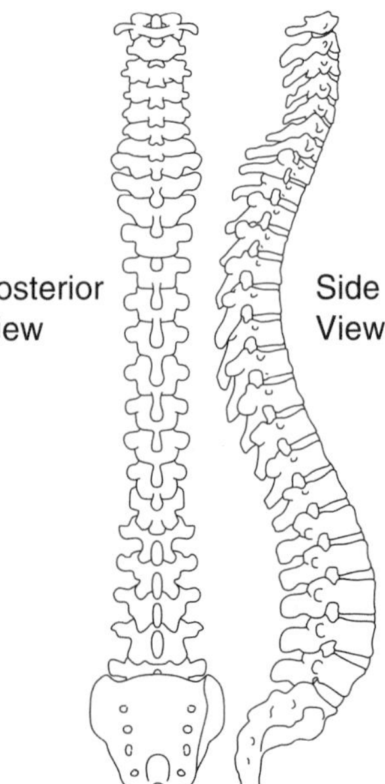

The Rib Cage

The *rib cage,* consisting of the *sternum* (breast bone) and *ribs,* surrounds and protects the heart, lungs, liver, and spleen. The rib cage contains twenty-four ribs, symmetrically arranged in twelve matching pairs. All ribs connect to the spinal column, and the top seven pairs connect also in front to the sternum. Together, they provide a protective enclosure for the heart and lungs. The rib cage has some flexibility, and with the help of muscles it aids breathing by expanding and contracting.

The Arms and Legs

The arms attach to the *pectoral girdle,* which makes up the shoulders, and the legs attach to the *pelvic girdle,* which attaches to the lower part of the spinal column and forms the hips. Long bones extend the hands and feet far enough from the torso to allow the movement necessary for walking and reaching. Many small bones form the framework of the feet and toes, providing support and balance in standing, walking, and running. Other small bones form the framework of the hands and fingers, allowing the continuous and varied movement needed in using the hands. Approximately half of all the bones in the body are located in the feet and hands.

The Joints

Any point where two bones meet is called a *joint. Ball-and-socket joints,* such as at the shoulders and hips, allow bones to move in many different directions. *Pivot joints,* like those of the neck, wrists, and ankles, allow movement back and forth, along with limited radial movement; but they provide less range and freedom than the ball-and-socket joints. *Hinge joints* allow free movement back and forth, similar to the hinge on a door. Examples of hinge joints are those of the knees, elbows, fingers, and toes. Wherever bones meet at movable joints, the bones are held together by strong bands of connective tissue called *ligaments.* Without ligaments, joints would not be strong, and many would slip easily out of place.

V. THE MUSCULAR SYSTEM

Muscles are the labor force of the body; all body movement is caused by contracting muscles. Running, lifting an arm, and even blinking your eyes require working muscles. Altogether, there are more than 400 different muscles in the human body; each one is either a *voluntary muscle,* an *involuntary muscle,* or both voluntary and involuntary.

The Voluntary and Involuntary Muscles

All of the movements already mentioned are movements that you control. You run, walk, and blink your eyes when you decide to do those things. Movements that you consciously control are caused by voluntary muscles.

But wait—what about the blinking of the eyes? You have the ability to blink them when you want to, but sometimes you blink without doing it deliberately. Your eyes blink—like it or not—when an object comes quickly near them or when dust particles get in them. They also blink quite frequently, without any conscious effort being applied, in a constant process of keeping the eyeballs clean and lubricated. The eyelid muscles are both voluntary and involuntary. The diaphragm is that way, too. You can stop breathing briefly and stop the up-and-down movement of the diaphragm; but unless it is deliberately stopped, the diaphragm continues the breathing action, assuring a constant intake of oxygen and elimination of carbon dioxide. Parents need not worry about tantrum-throwing children harming themselves by holding their breath. When a person deliberately stops breathing, the involuntary action very soon overpowers the voluntary action, and automatic breathing begins again. When the oxygen supply is short, the muscles that control breathing no longer respond to voluntary commands. This is another example of homeostasis, as the body maintains constant internal conditions that are necessary for life.

The involuntary muscles

Some muscles are totally involuntary. You cannot stop your heart from beating just by deciding that it will stop. You would not even know what to do to consciously start the muscle actions that assist with the movement of food through the digestive system, or those in the walls of blood vessels that assist the heart in forcing blood through the body.

The muscles that are the most critical in keeping the body alive are controlled automatically by the brain and the rest of the nervous system. Schools don't teach children how to breathe, how to manage the circulatory system, or how to digest food; each person's "computer" is preprogrammed to do those things. And isn't it a good thing—you would need to be competent chemists to know how to digest food, and even then you would be so busy mixing chemicals and turning valves on and off that you wouldn't get anything else done. Then if you had to deliberately cause the lungs to breathe and the heart to beat you would really be in trouble. There would certainly be no time for sleeping!

The voluntary muscles

Voluntary muscles usually work in pairs (see Figure 13-3). *Skeletal muscles* (those that move the body frame) are attached to bones by their tough, white cords of connective tissue called *tendons.* The tendons are actually considered to be a part of the muscle. The muscles on the front of the upper leg bone that cause the leg to straighten are matched by muscles on the back of the leg, ready to pull the lower leg back again. The *biceps muscle* on the front of the upper arm that contracts to raise the lower arm in a lifting action is matched by the *triceps muscle* on the back of the upper arm that can cause the arm to straighten. For all two-way movements of the skeleton, pairs of muscles can be identified. Muscles can only pull—they cannot push. They contract and then relax, and are lengthened by the contracting of the muscle(s) on the opposite side of the bone.

Figure 13-3

Voluntary muscles usually work in pairs.

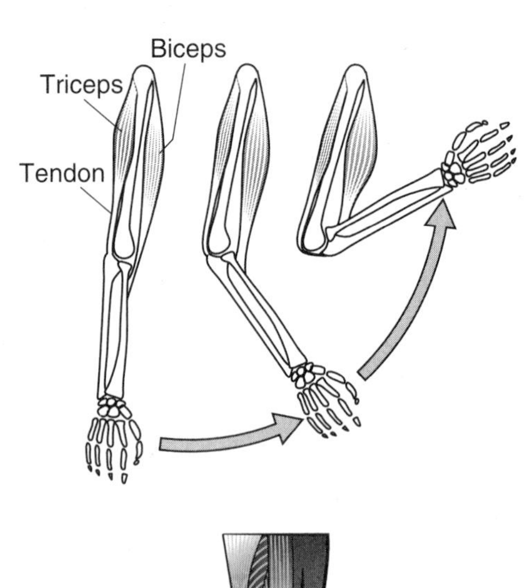

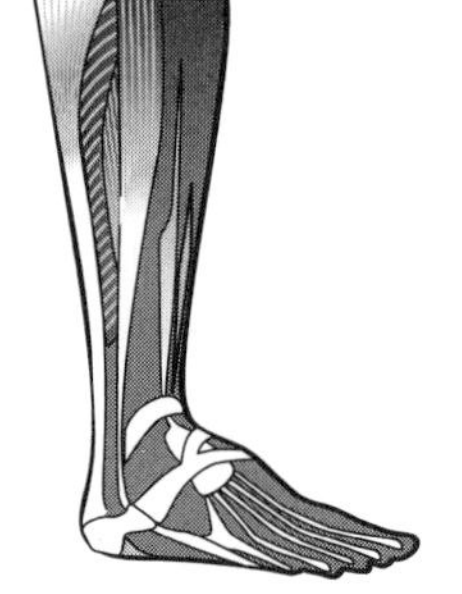

VI. THE CIRCULATORY SYSTEM

If the body is thought of as a factory, with the skin providing the external security system, the skeletal system forming the framework, and the muscles supplying the labor force, the circulatory system is the transportation mechanism that performs the function of moving goods in and out. The circulatory system consists of the heart, which generates the power; the blood, which carries the materials; and blood vessels, which provide the highways through which the blood flows. Nutrients and oxygen are the raw materials needed for producing energy and replacing cells. The blood transports both of these materials throughout the body. Blood also carries waste products, including carbon dioxide and dead cells, to organs that remove them from the body. The lymphatic system supports the work of the circulatory system and is sometimes considered to be a part of it. The lymphatic system is described within this section as a part of the circulatory system.

The Heart

The heart, which is a mass of muscle designed as a pump, keeps blood flowing through the blood vessels. About the size of one's fist, the heart is located in the middle of the chest, to the left of center, protected by the rib cage. The heart pumps blood through a network of blood vessels that totals approximately 75,000 miles, and every pound of excess body fat increases the workload for the heart by adding about 200 miles of capillaries. The adult heart pumps enough blood to fill a 4,000-gallon container every day. Amazingly, it continues faithfully for many years, and usually with very little complaint.

The human heart has four pumping chambers—two above, called *auricles,* and two below, called *ventricles* (see Figure 13-4). Blood flows from large veins into the auricles, which contract to force it into the ventricles. When the ventricles contract, blood is forced out through large arteries to begin its journey. The two auricles are separated by a divider called a *septum,* as are the two ventricles, so the heart is actually a double pump, with the left and right sides forming completely separate blood paths. The right side of the heart takes blood from the body and pumps it to the lungs; the left side takes blood from the lungs and pumps it to the body. Valves in the heart and veins prevent blood from moving in the wrong direction as the heart alternately pumps and relaxes.

Figure 13-4

This cross-section of the human heart shows the four chambers.

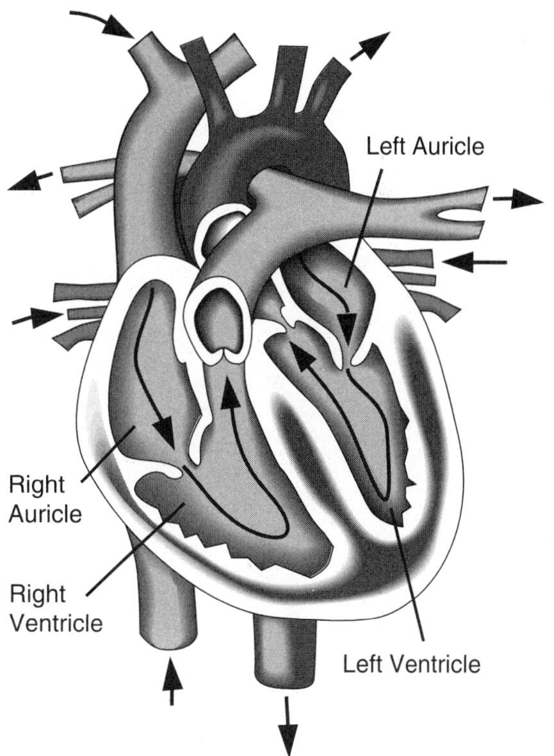

The Blood Vessels

The system of blood vessels includes *arteries, veins,* and *capillaries.* Arteries transport blood away from the heart, and veins bring blood toward the heart. Blood moves from the right side of the heart to the lungs through the *pulmonary arteries* and returns to the left side of the heart through the *pulmonary veins* (see Figure 13-5). The left side of the heart pumps the blood into an artery called the *aorta,* which leads to other arteries that branch out into smaller and smaller arteries, somewhat like highways that move outward from the capital city into smaller cities, then to towns and finally into the smallest villages.

Capillaries, the smallest of the blood vessels, are at the end of the supply line; they receive and distribute the goods. Microscopic in size, they pass between the cells of the body tissues. They are so small that red blood cells must squeeze through in single file. Capillary walls are so thin that molecules of oxygen and nutrients pass right through into the cells, and molecules of carbon dioxide and other waste products pass from the cells into the blood. This happens by diffusion. After making its delivery and taking on a new load of waste products, blood flows into tiny veins, which in turn lead to larger and larger veins on the return trip to the heart. The larger veins have valves that prevent blood from moving in the wrong direction.

Figure 13-5

Blood moves from the right side of the heart to the lungs through the pulmonary arteries.

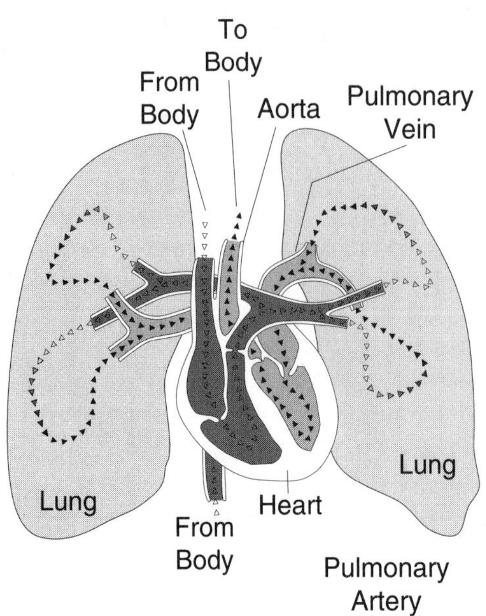

The Blood

The main performer in this drama is the blood, which consists of a liquid called *plasma,* plus solid material, including *red cells, white cells,* and *platelets.*

Plasma

The plasma brings nutrients to the cells and carries away waste materials. It also contains chemicals called *hormones,* which control many activities in the body, and *fibrinogen,* which helps the blood to clot.

Red blood cells

Red blood cells are the most abundant solid material in human blood, with about 5 million of them in each milliliter (0.03 ounce). Magnified, they look like discs with depressed centers, somewhat resembling donuts with centers pressed in instead of removed. Red blood cells pick up oxygen from the lungs, deliver it to the cells of the body where it is exchanged for carbon dioxide, and return the carbon dioxide to the lungs to be exhaled. Blood gets its red color from an iron compound called *hemo-*

globin, which is contained in the red blood cells and which is responsible for their ability to transport oxygen.

Each red blood cell has a lifespan of about 120 days, and during that time it makes approximately 75,000 round trips from the heart to other parts of the body. Each second, about 1.2 million of them are discarded and replaced by new red blood cells, which are manufactured in bone marrow—mostly in the ribs, skull, and vertebrae.

White blood cells

White blood cells are larger but much less numerous than red blood cells. Colorless and somewhat spherical in shape, with irregular protrusions, these little soldiers defend the body against infection and disease. They can pass through capillary walls and move among the cells of the body, destroying harmful bacteria and other disease-causing agents or organisms.

Platelets

Platelets are colorless, irregularly shaped, and even smaller than the red blood cells. They give off a chemical that reacts with fibrinogen in plasma to cause clotting when exposed to the air at a wound site.

The trip through the body

Along its journey through the body, the blood has many tasks to perform. After leaving the heart it goes directly to the lungs, where it discards carbon dioxide and takes on a fresh supply of oxygen, then back to the heart for another trip throughout the body. When blood gets a fresh supply of oxygen, it takes on a bright red color. As oxygen in the blood is exchanged for carbon dioxide, during its life-maintaining journey through the body, the bright red color turns to dark red. Skin has a yellow pigment that causes the dark red blood in veins to appear blue when seen through the skin.

As it moves through the body, the blood passes through the digestive system and picks up absorbed nutrients. It circulates among body cells, leaving oxygen and nutrients and picking up carbon dioxide and other waste materials, and cleanses the body of harmful materials and organisms, such as disease-causing bacteria. The blood also moves through the urinary system, depositing waste products, and goes through the liver and spleen, where bacteria and worn-out blood cells are filtered out and removed.

The Lymphatic System

The *lymphatic system* works very closely with the circulatory system of the blood, but it is less commonly understood. Sometimes it is considered a part of the circulatory system, and sometimes the circulatory system is described without mention of it, treating this important system as though it were a forgotten stepchild.

It was stated above that as blood moves through capillaries around the body cells, white blood cells pass through the capillary walls and move among the cells, collecting harmful bacteria and other disease-causing organisms. However, the white blood cells do not pass alone through the capillary walls. Some of the blood plasma seeps through and flows freely among the cells, bathing them with nutrients and picking up waste materials; some white cells go along with other matter in the plasma. Part of the plasma seeps back through the capillary walls and into the bloodstream, but some of it does not. Plasma that has passed through the capillary walls to flow among the cells, and does not pass back through the capillary walls and into the bloodstream, flows into a separate system of tiny tubules that connect to larger and larger tubes. This system is called the lymphatic system, and the fluid material in its vessels is called lymph.

The importance of muscular action in circulation

The heart does not pump lymph through the lymphatic system. Instead, lymph is moved by the massaging action of body muscles. Lymph vessels have valves that prevent the fluid from flowing backward; and as muscles contract, the lymph is squeezed through the vessels. The transparent, straw-colored liquid that fills blisters, or which appears when the skin is scraped, is lymph.

The lymph nodes

In certain locations of the body, especially at the neck, in the armpits, and near the groin, the lymph vessels enlarge to form *lymph nodes*. At the nodes is a concentration of white blood cells that kill harmful bacteria that might have been picked up from the cells by the lymph. Thus the lymph is filtered and purified before being returned to the blood. Lymph is directed into large lymph vessels, which empty into large blood veins just below the neck, returning the lymph to the bloodstream.

VII. THE RESPIRATORY SYSTEM

The major function of the respiratory system is to supply the body with oxygen and to discard carbon dioxide, which is produced as a by-product of cells. Blood transports oxygen from the lungs to the cells of the body and transports carbon dioxide back to the lungs to be exhaled. The actual exchange of carbon dioxide for a fresh supply of oxygen is called *respiration,* which takes place in tiny air sacs in the lungs, but all of the body parts that help to get those gases in and out of the body are part of the respiratory system. These parts include the *nose, nasal passages, throat, larynx, trachea, bronchial tubes,* and *lungs.*

The Nose and Nasal Passages

Incoming air passes first through the nose and nasal passages, where it is cleaned, warmed, and moistened, an important conditioning process in preparing air to be used by the lungs. Hairs in the nose filter out some of the foreign material, such as dust and bacteria, from the air. More of such particles are trapped by a sticky *mucus* (produced by *mucous glands)* that lines the nasal passages. To keep it from becoming stale, the mucus is replaced about every twenty minutes. Tiny hair-like structures *(cilia)* in the nasal passages are constantly moving back and forth, directing the mucus down the throat to be swallowed or coughed up.

Sometimes, especially when a person has a cold or flu, enough mucus builds up to cause discomfort in breathing. Usually, the excess mucus can be expelled by blowing the nose, but care must be taken because blowing can force bacteria from an infected throat into the *auditory (Eustachian) tubes* leading to the inner ears, sometimes causing further problems there. While nasal passages are blocked, a person must breathe through the mouth, which usually causes dryness in the mouth and throat that can be quite uncomfortable. Bypassing the nose also deprives the lungs of the assistance normally provided by the nasal passages—cleaning, warming, and moistening the air.

The Larynx

The *larynx,* or voice box, is conveniently located above the trachea, taking advantage of the movement of air to produce sound, enabling us to communicate with the voice. A flap of tissue called the *epiglottis,* which covers the opening into the larynx whenever you swallow, prevents food and water from entering the trachea and directing such material down the *esophagus* into the stomach. When the swallowing action is finished, the epiglottis lifts and opens the larynx, allowing breathing to resume.

The Lungs

Air next enters the bronchial tubes, which direct it into the lungs. There the bronchial tubes branch out into smaller and smaller tubes, the smallest ending with grape-like bunches of tiny air sacs called *alveoli,* which are surrounded by "cobwebs" of capillaries (see Figure 13-6). There are millions of alveoli in each lung. Oxygen passes through the capillary walls and is picked up by the red blood cells. Carbon dioxide passes from the red blood cells, through the capillary walls, and into the alve-

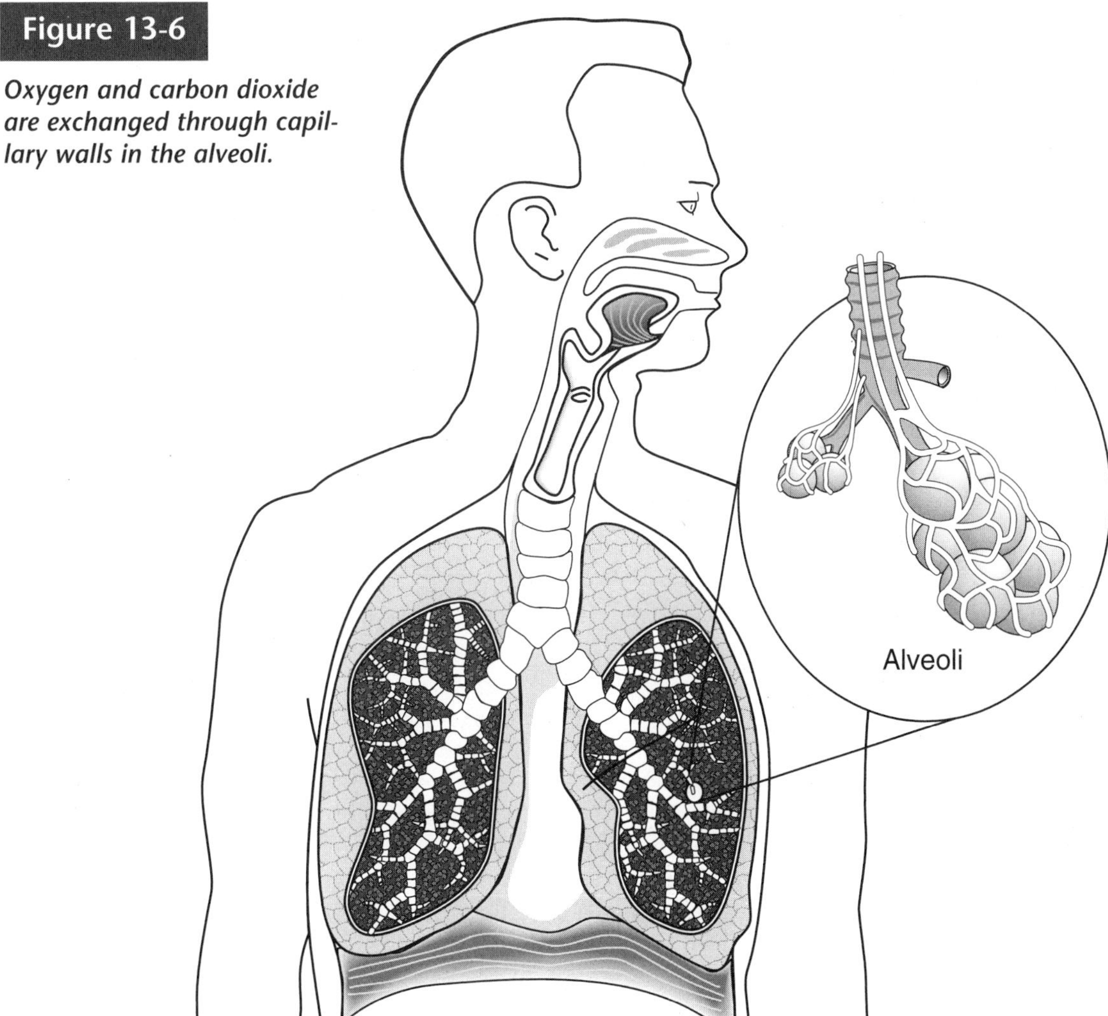

Figure 13-6

Oxygen and carbon dioxide are exchanged through capillary walls in the alveoli.

oli. From there it is discharged from the body as the used air is exhaled.

The Breathing Mechanism

The lungs have no muscle tissue, so they rely on other muscles to move air in and out. A strong sheet of muscle, called the *diaphragm*, located between the abdomen and the chest cavity, works in harmony with rib muscles as we breathe. When the muscles of the diaphragm contract, the diaphragm is pulled downward. At the same time, the rib muscles pull the rib cage outward. Both of these actions expand the chest cavity, which decreases air pressure in the lungs. Air pressure in the lungs is then less than atmospheric pressure, and air is forced into the lungs.

Next the diaphragm and rib muscles both relax, allowing the chest cavity to decrease in volume. This increases the air pressure inside the lungs. Air pressure inside the lungs is then greater than atmospheric pressure, and air flows out of the lungs. Muscles inside the rib cage are capable of forcing air out of the lungs, thus speeding up the breathing process. This can be done voluntarily, or if a person is short of breath, it will happen automatically.

The Breathing Control Center

These complex operations must be accurately coordinated and controlled. Breathing rate is controlled by the medulla oblongata—the lower part of the brain that attaches to the spinal cord. As long as energy is being used by the body at a normal rate, a normal supply of oxygen is needed at the cells to produce energy and heat from nutrients in digested food. Responding to this input, the medulla oblongata signals the respiratory system to continue breathing processes at a normal rate. Exercise increases the need for energy and therefore the need for oxygen. As these needs increase, the brain signals the heart to beat faster and blood flows faster through the lungs. As more oxygen is needed to supply the increased blood flow, the diaphragm and rib muscles are stimulated to increase breathing rate. When the need for increased oxygen is past, both heart rate and breathing rate slow again to normal.

The effect of the breathing control center of the brain, including the immediate response of the muscles used in breathing, can be experienced by taking two or three consecutive deep breaths, then relaxing. Responding to a momentary over-supply of oxygen in the lungs, breathing will stop for several seconds, then resume at the normal rate.

VIII. THE DIGESTIVE SYSTEM

The digestive system includes all of the organs through which food passes as it is processed through the body, beginning at the mouth and ending at the large intestine, where waste is discharged from the body. Although food passes through the throat, esophagus, and large intestines, the organs most directly involved in the actual digestion process are the mouth, stomach, and small intestine, with the small intestine playing the major role. In addition to these organs, digestive glands, such as the salivary glands, gastric glands, intestinal glands, liver, and pancreas, are vital in the process of preparing food for use by the cells of the body. Without the chemicals produced by these glands, the digestive organs would be ineffective caverns of tissue.

Food undergoes both mechanical digestion and chemical digestion as it passes through the body. Mechanical digestion includes the processes that break up the food and mix it. Chemical digestion results from the many chemicals that are added to the food by the digestive system. Mechanical and chemical digestion processes both begin in the mouth.

Food is moved through the digestive system by peristalsis, as involuntary muscles in the system contract and relax, massaging the food and moving it through the digestive tract. Peristalsis occurs in the stomach, as well as in the intestines.

The Mouth

Digestion begins at the moment food enters the mouth. Here it is chewed into small pieces and mixed with saliva. This process is very important in preparing food for the next stage of digestion, which takes place in the stomach. Saliva, produced by salivary glands located in the jaw under the mouth cavity, moistens and softens the food, making it easy to swallow. In addition, it contains chemical substances that change starch to sugars that can be used by the body. Swallowing is a very important next step in the digestion process, as it moves food from the mouth into the stomach.

The Stomach

The stomach is a pear-shaped, muscular pouch located toward the left side of the body below the diaphragm. Food may stay in the stomach from a few minutes to several hours, depending on the amount and type of food. Other conditions, including the emotional state of the person, also affect this timing. One important role of the stomach is that of storage pouch, making it possible for a person to go several hours between meals. Here the food is also prepared for the small intestine, where most of the digestion takes place. In the stomach, the food is mixed with hydrochloric acid and other gastric juices produced by *gastric glands.* Powerful involuntary stomach muscles contract and relax over and over, in a churning action that further breaks up the partly digested food and mixes it thoroughly with the gastric juices. Many undesirable bacteria that may have entered the stomach with food, are killed by the hydrochloric acid. The lining of the stomach is protected from the acidic environment by a mucus coating and by a small amount of ammonia that is secreted in the lining of the stomach; otherwise the stomach would digest itself.

When the stomach has finished its part in the digestion process, the food is moved into the small intestine through an opening at the bottom of the stomach called the *pyloric valve.*

The Small Intestine

The food is not yet prepared for use by the cells. In fact, the major digestion processes take place in the small intestine. Food is let out of the stomach in small amounts into the *duodenum*—the upper part of the small intestine. The acid in the food is immediately neutralized by chemicals in the duodenum. If food mixed with acid comes too fast, the hydrochloric acid will eat into the wall of the duodenum, the cause (and the most common site) of ulcers. The primary contributing factor to the development of ulcers here is a decrease in the production of protective mucus in the lining of the duodenum.

Although the small intestine is only about 2.5 centimeters (1 inch) or so wide, it is about 7 meters (23 feet) long, coiling back and forth inside the abdomen. Here the food is mixed with pancreatic juice (produced by the pancreas), bile (produced by the liver), and intestinal juice (produced by glands in the lining of the small intestine). As food moves through the small intestine, the muscular intestinal walls continue to massage it, and the digestion process is completed. The food material that is useful to the body is now in liquid form and is absorbed through the thin wall of the intestine into blood capillaries and carried by the bloodstream to the cells of the body. Each cell absorbs the nutrients that it needs and gives back waste products no longer useful to the cell, to be carried away by the bloodstream for disposal.

Technically, swallowed food is not within the body until and unless it is absorbed into the bloodstream. Any material that is swallowed, passes through the system, and is discharged by the body without being absorbed is not considered to be within the body.

The Large Intestine

Food that cannot be digested by the small intestine, along with countless millions of dead bacteria, continues as waste material through the small intestine and into the *large intestine.* About twice the diameter of the small intestine but only about 1.5 meters (5 feet) long, the large intestine is a waste and recycling facility. Here most of the water is removed from the waste material and returned to the bloodstream to be recycled and used by the body. This guards against dehydration, which would otherwise surely result, as the body uses about 2 gallons of fluid daily in the production of digestive juices. The waste material normally has a fairly solid consistency by the time it reaches the end of the large intestine, where it is discharged from the body.

Misplaced Credits

While the stomach often gets credit for work done by the small intestine (digestion), it also takes the blame for embarrassing rumbles made from time to time by the small intestine. When we hear our "stomach growling," the noise is usually coming from the small intestine. And the burning sensation often called "heartburn" or "sour stomach" ironically doesn't happen in either the heart or the stomach. Instead, poor eating (or sometimes drinking) habits cause a gas bubble to form in the stomach; it rises, carrying with it hydrochloric acid, into the lower esophagus—the real location of the burning sensation.

Effect of Emotions

The secretion of digestive juices and the action of muscles lining the stomach and small intestines are affected by emotions. Excitement, anger, depression, and stress can upset the digestive process and cause considerable discomfort.

IX. THE NERVOUS SYSTEM

Many of the functions of a modern automobile are controlled by computerized equipment. Wires lead from the computer to a *wiring harness,* which is a bundle of wires leading from under the dashboard to the engine compartment, with individual wires branching off all along the way to the lights, ignition system, charging system, air-conditioner, and various other systems and parts that work together to make the vehicle function properly (see Figure 13-7). This system is somewhat analogous to

Figure 13-7

Wires branch out from the trunk of an automobile wiring harness to provide electrical energy to various parts of an automobile.

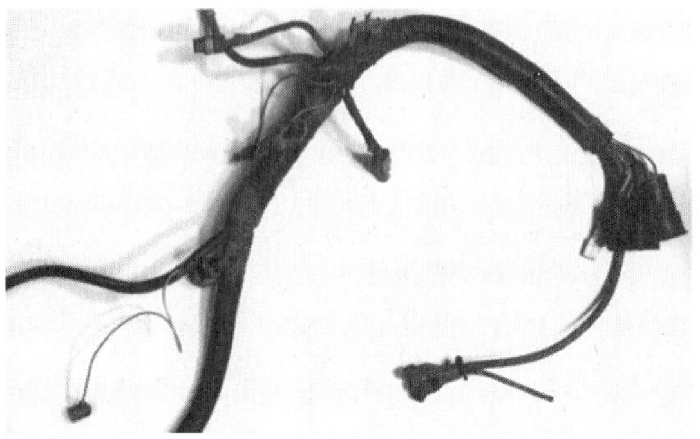

the nervous system, which consists of the brain, the spinal cord, and nerves that run throughout the body. Like the computer in the car, the brain is the central control mechanism. The spinal cord is the main trunk of the wiring harness—a bundle of nerves that attaches at the base of the brain and runs through a channel in the spinal column. Along the way, nerves branch off to every part of the body (see Figure 13-8).

Figure 13-8

Nerves branch out from the spinal cord to take impulses to various parts of the body.

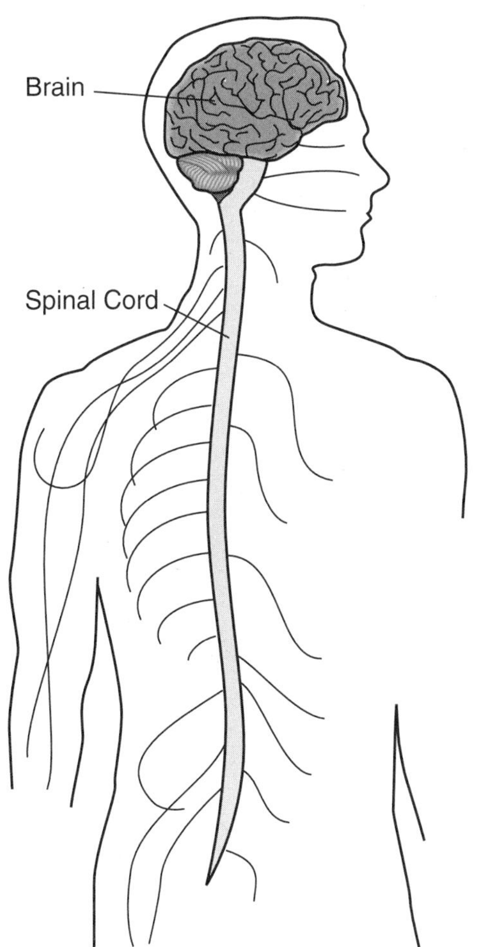

The Brain

The brain is the master computer that monitors and controls the functions of all the organs and systems of the body. As the control center for the body, the brain gets about 20 percent of the body's blood flow and uses about 20 percent of the body's oxygen supply. The brain constantly monitors the oxygen level within the blood and sends signals to the muscles that control breathing, adjusting breathing rate as needed. Receiving input on the current requirements for energy and oxygen in the cells, the brain adjusts the heart rate, sending regular impulses to the heart muscles that cause them to repeatedly contract and relax, keeping blood flowing through the body according to the body's needs. In warm weather, the brain turns on the body's air-conditioning system by causing perspiration to flow through pores of the skin, which then cools the body by the natural cooling effect of evaporation.

The brain receives input from the eyes, ears, skin, and other sense organs, and interprets those messages in ways that we perceive as sight, sound, smell, and so on. Hence, technically speaking, we don't see with the eyes or hear with the ears. And when a part of the body is injured, the brain receives the information and initiates the body functions that begin the healing process. These and hundreds of other body functions are constantly monitored and controlled by the brain, including the way we feel and how well we learn and remember. Each of these processes takes place in one of three major sections of the brain: the *medulla oblongata*, the *cerebellum*, and the *cerebrum* (see Figure 13-9).

The medulla oblongata is located at the base of the brain, joining the top of the spinal cord. It controls the involuntary functions of the body, such as breathing, digesting food, and pumping blood. It also controls sneezing and coughing.

The cerebellum is just above the medulla oblongata, and among its tasks are those of

Figure 13-9

The main sections of the brain are the cerebrum, the cerebellum, and the medulla oblongata, which is contained within the brain stem.

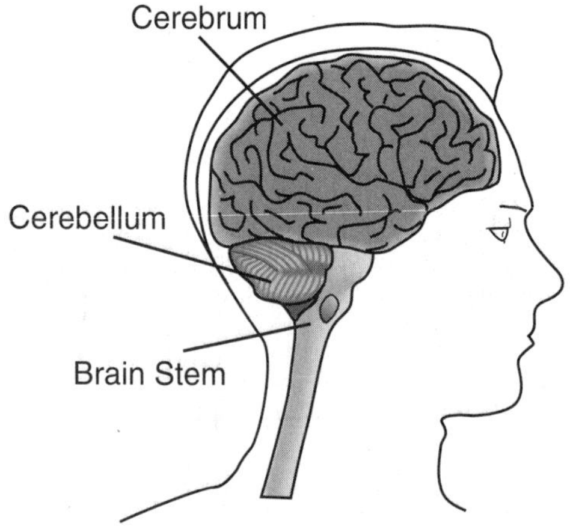

keeping the sense of balance and coordinating muscle movements for smooth operation.

At the front of the brain is the largest section—the *cerebrum.* Among its many important functions is the control of learning, reasoning, thinking, imagination, and memory. This part of the brain also receives and interprets messages from the sense organs. The cerebrum is divided into two sections, which control the voluntary muscles of the body: The left side of the brain controls muscles on the right side of the body, and the right side of the brain controls the movements of the left side. The two halves of the brain are believed to function differently in their effect on learning and reasoning: The left side of the brain seems to have more influence on writing, mathematics, and abstract reasoning, and the right side appears to control spatial judgments and concrete learning processes. It is believed that the way people learn best depends in part on which side of their brain is dominant.

The Spinal Cord

The spinal cord attaches to the brain stem through an opening in the base of the skull. An intricate communication network, it extends down the body within the spinal column and includes thirty-one pairs of nerves that branch off to all parts of the body below the head, including the heart, lungs, arms, legs, and so on. When the spinal cord is damaged, the functions of nerves below the point of damage will be impaired or terminated.

The Nerves

Nerves run throughout the body. Like wires in the electrical system of the automobile, they stand ready to carry messages to and from the various working parts. This analogy has double meaning: First, the nerve serves as the channel through which signals travel, and second, nerve impulses are actually electrical-chemical signals. Each time you lift an arm, wiggle a toe, clear your throat, blink your eyes, hear a bird sing, or smell the aroma of a flower, it is because of impulses that travel on nerves between the brain and other parts of the body. When nerves are damaged, some body function is impaired.

X. THE FIVE SENSES

While the brain is the control center for all body functions, it relies heavily on the sense organs to provide input to guide its function. Indeed, much of what we think, say, and do is based on information coming from the sense organs. Information from *receptor cells* (specialized sensory neurons) is sent to *sensory centers* within the brain for interpretation (perception) or automatic response.

The receptor cells are found in specialized organs, most of which perform multiple functions. For example, the tongue contains receptor cells for taste, but the tongue also moves food around in the mouth for chewing and to the back of the throat for swallowing, and it plays a major role in the process of forming sounds when we talk. The nose is an important part of the respiratory system, but it also contains the receptor cells for the sense of smell. The skin performs vital functions as the covering for the body, and it also includes the system of nerves that provides the sense of touch. The inner ear contains three tubes that are shaped like semicircles, called the *semicircular canals,* which give us our sense of balance; in addition the inner ear contains organs that are vital to the sense of hearing. The eyes do not seem to perform a role beyond providing the sense of sight; but that sense, although not crucial to the preservation of life, is certainly important to learning, and to the quality of life. The mechanisms that provide the senses often referred to as the *five senses* are considered in this section.

The Sense of Sight

The eyes are the organs that provide the sense of sight (see Figure 13-10). Eyes are delicate instruments resting in protective sockets at the front of the skull. The front of the eyeball is constantly bathed with a watery liquid, commonly referred to as *tears,* which comes from *tear glands.* The *eyelids,* like small windshield wipers, spread this fluid over the eyeballs with a frequent blinking action, keeping the eyeballs clean and moist. This liquid contains chemicals that kill harmful bacteria that may be present. Normally, tears drain through tiny tubules into the nasal cavity. Sometimes the tear glands are stimulated, either by emotion or by a speck of dust or other foreign particle in the eye, to produce more liquid than can be drained off. At such times, tears overflow the tiny drainage system and run down the face. Malfunctioning tubules sometimes result in a similar cheek-wetting experience.

Figure 13-10

The eye is a delicate instrument.

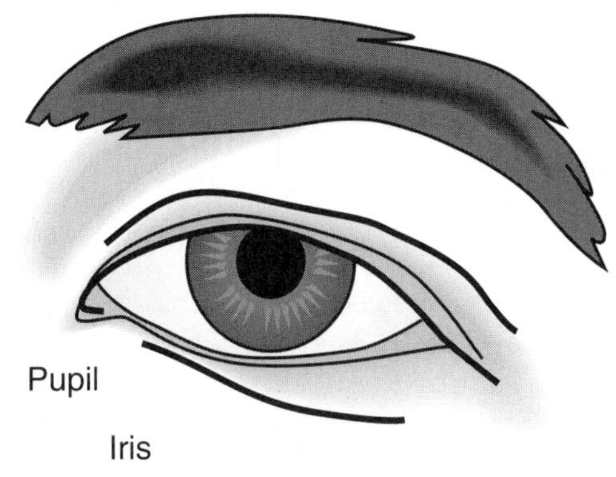

Functions of the eye

The eye is a video camera that is constantly supplying the brain with pictures of everything that is in front of it. The outside of the eyeball is a white, opaque material, except for a transparent window at the front, called the *cornea.*

Behind the thin, clear covering is the *iris,* which is the colored part of the eye that opens and closes like the diaphragm of a camera. Immediately behind the iris is a convex *lens.* The opening in the center of the iris is called the *pupil.* It appears black because of the dark cavern inside the eyeball. The iris automatically adjusts the size of the pupil in response to current light conditions, making the pupil larger as light becomes dimmer, and smaller as light becomes brighter. This both increases our viewing pleasure and protects the eye against damage from bright light. The iris opens wide in darkness.

Light passes through the lens, which bends the light and focuses it onto the back of the eyeball. The inside of the eyeball is filled with a clear, jellylike material.

The lining of the back of the eyeball, called the *retina,* is filled with light-sensitive nerve endings that are connected to the *optic nerve.* When light strikes the retina, the tiny nerve endings send impulses to the optic nerve, which carries the impulses to the brain. The brain converts these impulses to images and we experience sight. Thus, *we see with the brain,* not with the eyes.

The retina contains two kinds of photo receptor cells, *rods* and *cones.* The cones respond to color and objects in bright light. The rods respond to objects in dim light, but they do not respond to color, which explains why the things we see in dim light appear only in shades of black and white. In the eyes of some people there are too few cones, or the cones are defective; these people do not detect certain colors clearly. We say these people are *color blind.* More men than women are color blind. The term "color blindness" deceivingly implies that such a person lives in a black and white world, which rarely is the case.

Peculiarities

Some interesting peculiarities are associated with the sense of sight. First, the eye retains an image for a brief period of time. Because of this, when we see a series of still pictures in rapid succession, we get the illusion of motion. This principle is utilized in making motion pictures.

Second, the rods and cones become tired. This can be demonstrated by staring at a colored object for fifteen seconds or so, and then looking at a blank wall. The image will appear briefly in its complimentary colors, while the rods and cones that have been used to see the object rest.

Third, since an inverted image is produced by a convex lens, images we see are focused upside down on the retina, yet we see them right side up. Scientists are still puzzling over the process that turns the image right side up in our minds.

Another peculiarity is the existence of a blind spot in our vision. This occurs because an incomplete image is formed on the retina due to the position of the optic nerve. At the point where the optic nerve joins the retina, there are no rods or cones to sense the image. One of the activities at the end of this chapter demonstrates the blind spot.

And last, each eyeball contains tens of millions of electrical connections, and can handle about 1.5 million messages simultaneously. The eye is more sensitive than the finest video camera.

The Sense of Hearing

We commonly refer to the flaps of skin and supporting cartilage on the sides of the head as the *ears.* Granted, their function of collecting sound waves and sending them into the *auditory canal* (ear channel) is important. And the significance of the auditory canal must not be overlooked, either, because in a distance of about 2.5 centimeters (1 inch) there are myriads of hairs and about 4,000 wax glands that protect the inner parts from intrusion by dust, insects, and other uninvited guests. The wax also protects against infection, and should not be removed with toothpicks or other instruments. Excess wax is shed naturally, and only rarely needs to be removed. This should be done only by a physician, as efforts to pick out the wax can damage the eardrum.

But the process of hearing really takes place *inside* the head. In addition to the *outer* ear, the body's auditory apparatus (see Figure 13-11) includes structures within the *middle ear,* and the *inner ear.* The middle ear consists of the *ear drum* and three small bones, called the *hammer,* the *anvil,* and the *stirrup.* The hammer is connected to the inside of the ear drum, and as sound waves cause the ear drum to vibrate, the hammer vibrates also. The higher the pitch, the faster the vibrations; the louder the sound, the stronger the vibrations. Vibrations are transferred from the hammer through the anvil to the stirrup, which, in turn, vibrates against an oval window leading to the *cochlea.* Shaped somewhat like a snail shell, the cochlea is filled with a fluid and thousands of sensitive nerve

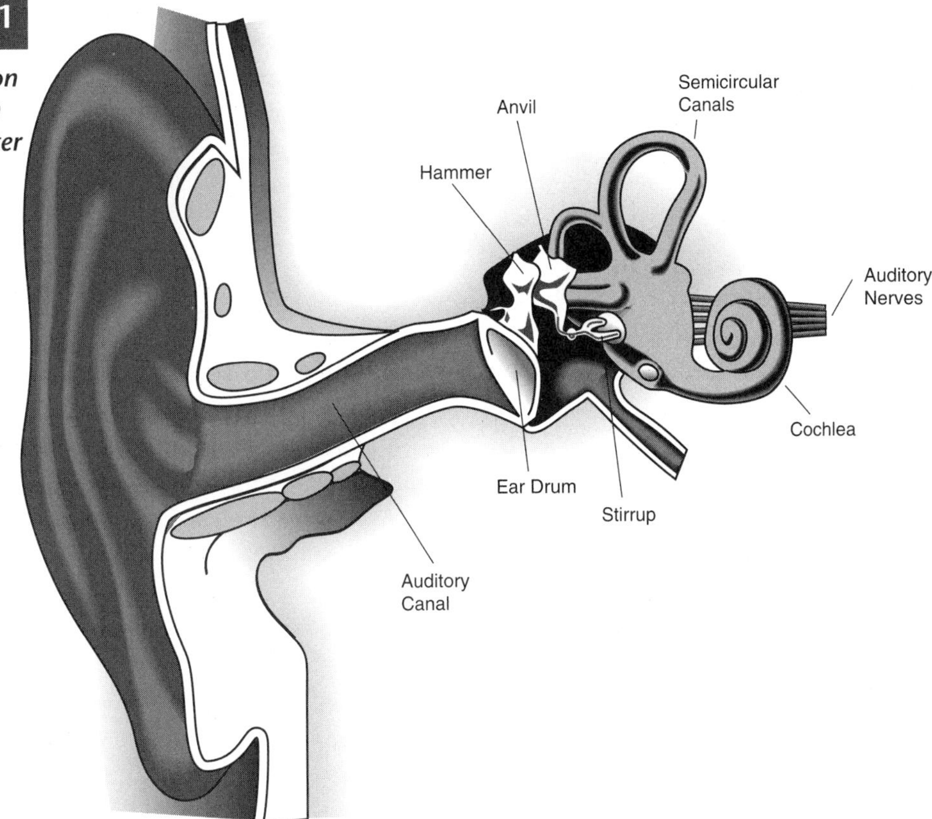

Figure 13-11

This cross-section shows the main parts of the outer ear, the middle ear, and the inner ear.

endings that detect the vibrations and send impulses through the *auditory nerve* to the brain. These impulses are interpreted by the brain as the perception we call sound. The inner ear has more than 30,000 electrical circuits—enough to provide phone service to a small city!

Sound going through the hammer, anvil, and stirrup may appear to be an inefficient system. Why don't the vibrations bypass these bones and go directly to the sensitive nerve endings? The bones do more than relay vibrations; they also serve to amplify the effect of the sound waves.

Sounds produced inside the head are conducted directly to the inner ear through bone. When we chew on nuts or celery, we hear the chewing, but these sounds are not usually heard by others. When we speak, we hear ourselves both from air vibrations entering the auditory canal, and from sound conducted through the bones of the head. For this reason, our voice doesn't sound quite the same to us as it does to someone else, and most of us think our own voice sounds strange on a tape recorder.

With the current popularity of loud music, it is important to consider the vulnerability of the very sensitive mechanisms in the ears. Sound is measured in units called *decibels.* A soft whisper is measured at about 20 decibels, and normal conversation at about 60 decibels. The intensity of sound from a rock band is about 120 decibels. Numbers alone would give the impression that the rock band is about twice as loud as normal conversation, but a jump of 20 points on the decibel scale represents a hundredfold increase in intensity. Therefore, increasing volume from 60 to 80 decibels (100 times), then to 100 decibels (10,000 times), and finally to 120 decibels, places loud rock music at *1 million* times the intensity of normal conversation. Considering this, it is easy to understand why sustained loud noise—whether it comes from rock music, from the roar of a nearby jet engine, or from any other source—is responsible for damage to the hearing of many people today. Sustained high-pitched sounds are particularly damaging to the ear. You might think of it as being somewhat like walking over a grassy area—the fine grass blades are eventually destroyed. The sensitive nerves can also be destroyed through repeated abuse by loud noise.

Figure 13-12

The tongue's primary taste centers are bitter, sour, salty, and sweet.

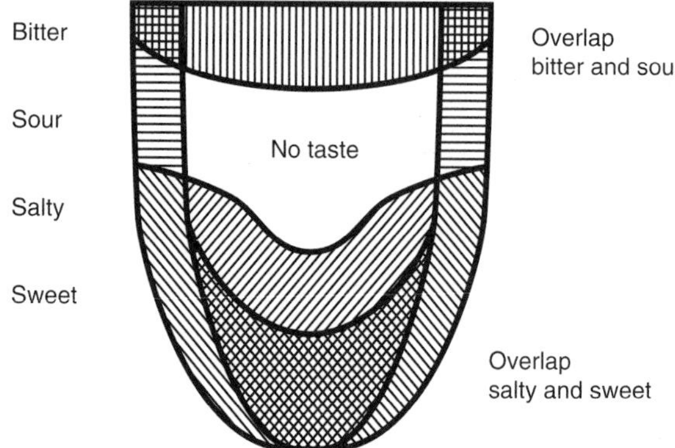

The Sense of Taste

The body has an intricate and selective detection center conveniently located where a variety of substances enter it—in the mouth. Nerve endings that are sensitive to taste are located in *taste buds,* which are in several areas of concentration on the tongue (see Figure 13-12) and in some other parts of the mouth. When chemicals in food are dissolved in saliva, they flow around the taste buds, and we experience the sensation of taste. Taste buds recognize only four flavors: sweet, salty, sour, and bitter. However, like primary colors on an artist's palate, these few flavors can blend together to produce thousands of different savory sensations.

Each type of taste bud is specialized for only certain tastes. The taste buds at the tip of the tongue are sensitive to sweet and salty flavors; they add great pleasure to the act of eating. The taste buds that recognize sour flavors are grouped along the sides of the tongue; taste buds that are sensitive to bitter flavors are located at the back of the tongue. Taste buds that recognize sour and bitter are also located in the roof of the mouth. Many foods have more than one flavor, blending together to form large numbers of different flavors. The taste buds work together in subtle ways. While eating, a person cannot tell which flavors are being sensed by which parts of the tongue. And the tongue receives a little outside help; odors from food enter the nasal passages as we eat, and the flavors we think we are just tasting actually come from a combination of taste and smell.

The sense of taste seems to remain rather constant throughout life, but not all people taste exactly the same flavors from any particular food. In fact, tastes can vary greatly; the same food can taste delicious to one person and horrid to another. There's no point in arguing whether blue cheese dressing is tasty or nasty, for example, because when two people claim different flavors for the same food, they are probably both right.

The Sense of Smell

At the roof of the nasal cavity is a patch of tissue smaller than a postage stamp. The patch contains millions of cells that are sensitive to odors (chemical molecules), an additional detection system that helps us appreciate, understand, and react to our world. Molecules in the air we breathe contact these cells. Anything we can smell throws off molecules of scent, whether it is perfume, a banana, or freshly cut grass. These molecules contact the sensitive cells, and sensations are carried through nerves to the brain; otherwise we would not smell these things. Although less sensitive than the sense of smell of many animals, the human nose can detect thousands of odors. The keenness of this sense usually sharpens with those who lose their eyesight or hearing, partially compensating for the absence of information from other senses.

When we are exposed to an odor for a few minutes, the nerve endings begin to lose their sensitivity to that particular odor. This can be a distinct advantage to those who work in places with unpleasant odors. The disadvantage is that our homes, or even our own bodies, can emit odors that are unpleasant to others without our being aware of it.

The Sense of Touch

In addition to providing the body's protective shelter, the skin is part of its system of detection and communication. A versatile member of the detection team, the skin is sensitive to touch, pressure, heat, cold, and pain. Nerve endings that are responsible for these sensations are located in the dermal layer of the skin. Nerve endings in the skin are not spread evenly over the body. The tips of the fingers are much more sensitive than most locations on the surface of the body because the nerve endings are much more concentrated there, with thousands of them in each fingertip.

Sometimes sensations that result from the sensors in the skin are not appreciated. We enjoy the warm and pleasurable sensations, but we'd rather not be bothered with such sensations as pain or discomfort from the cold. It is important to recognize that these sensations are protective signals—survival mechanisms. If we had to rely only on thermometers and our sense of reason to keep the body away from extreme temperatures, there would be much more injury, sickness, and death from such exposure. You would be much more likely to pick up a hot pan, put your hand in hot water, or go skiing without adequate protective clothing, if these things didn't hurt. The fact that we feel pain when the body is injured helps us to avoid many causes of bodily abuse. Closely related, discomforts inside the body can also provide critical information. Even if the body had other ways to warn us of an infected appendix or stomach ulcers, if that information was not accompanied with discomfort and pain, we would be far less likely to respond and get help quickly.

XI. IN CLOSING

While there are problems and processes surrounding the human body that still puzzle even scientists and doctors, a great deal can be studied and learned about the body by elementary students. Increased understanding of their own body prepares students to live a healthier, safer, and happier life.

LIST OF RESOURCES

Caselli, Giovanni, *The Human Body and How It Works* (New York: Grosset & Dunlap, 1987).

Curtis, Helena, and N. Sue Barnes, *Invitation to Biology* (New York: Worth Publishers, Inc., 1985).

Raven, Peter H., and George B. Johnson, *Understanding Biology* (St. Louis, MO: Times Mirror/Mosby College Publishing, 1988).

Tolman, Marvin N., and James O. Morton, *Life Science Activities for Grades 2–8* (West Nyack, NY: Parker Publishing Co., 1986).

Victor, Edward, *Science for the Elementary School, Sixth Edition* (New York: Macmillan Publishing Co., 1989).

World Book Encyclopedia, 1989.

CHAPTER

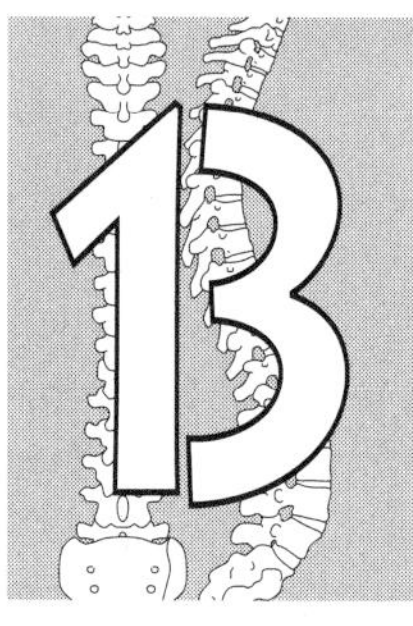

THE HUMAN BODY

ACTIVITIES

II. BUILDING BLOCKS OF THE BODY

ACTIVITY 13-1: WHAT IS A CELL?

Materials Needed:

Microscope
Microscope slide
Toothpick
Tincture of iodine

Procedure:

1. Use the toothpick to scrape off a small amount of material from the inside of your cheek.
2. Put the material on the slide and put a tiny amount of tincture of iodine on it.
3. Examine the material with the microscope.
3. What do you see?
4. Draw what you see and compare it with the drawings others make from the same activity.
5. Talk about your observations with your group.

For Problem Solvers:

Go to your encyclopedias and other reference books and learn all you can about cells. What are they made of? How do your cheek cells compare with the cells of a plant? What is the outside of the cell called if it is a plant cell? What is it called if it is an animal cell? Study with the microscope as well as from books. Draw what you see in the microscope and compare your drawing with others. You might want to look at other tissues, including blood.

Teacher Information:

In this activity, students will see epithelial cells, which are the type of tissue that covers the body and lines the mouth, the stomach, and other body cavities. Students are fascinated with microscopes, and in using microscopes to see what otherwise evades the eye. This activity gives them a chance to look at a part of themselves that they probably didn't even know was there, as they will examine some of the body's most basic building blocks—cells.

Integrating: Reading, writing, art

Skills: Observing, inferring, communicating, researching

ACTIVITY 13-2:
HOW DO THE BODY SYSTEMS WORK TOGETHER?

Materials Needed:

Bicycle

Picture of body showing internal organs

Procedure:

1. Examine the bicycle and explain how it works. For each part that moves, tell what makes it move. How do the different parts depend on each other?
2. Look at your body and tell what parts you think depend on other parts.
3. Bend down and pick something off the floor. How did your hand depend on your arm, your arm depend on your shoulders, your shoulders depend on your back, your back depend on your legs, and your legs depend on your feet?
4. Compare the ways your body parts depend on each other with the way the bicycle parts depend on each other.
5. Look at the picture of the body's internal organs. Can you add to your explanation of parts of the body that depend on each other?

Teacher Information:

If you feel that your students are ready for it, this discussion could be expanded to include dependence of the body parts mentioned above on the nervous system, the digestive system, and so on. The intent of this activity is to help students understand that the body has many parts and systems that depend on each other for proper functioning of the body. No one system is independent.

Integrating: Physical education

Skills: Observing, inferring, researching

(This activity was reprinted from Activity 86, "How Do the Body Systems Work Together?" in Tolman and Morton, 1986.)

III. THE SKIN

ACTIVITY 13-3:
WHAT DOES MY SKIN DO FOR ME?

Materials Needed:

None

Procedure:

1. Blow on the back of your hand.
2. Describe what the moving air feels like on the back of your hand.
3. Wet the back of your hand and blow on it again.
4. What did it feel like this time? Did it feel the same?
5. If the blowing felt different the second time, describe the difference.

For Problem Solvers:

If you have a fan available, turn the fan on and stand in front of it. Describe how it feels the best you can. Next, do some strenuous exercise for several minutes—pushups, pull-ups, run up and down a set of stairs several times, or if it's a hot day run around outdoors. When you feel very tired, and moisture appears on your arms and face, stand in front of the fan again. How does it feel, compared to the way it felt before exercising? Spray water on your face and stand in front of the fan. Talk about it with your group. What do you think makes the difference? See if you can find out why.

Do some research in encyclopedias or other references and learn all you can about the skin. What does it do to provide air-conditioning for our bodies? Find out about evaporative coolers that are used in homes, and compare them with the way the skin keeps us cool. What does it do to help keep us warm on a cool day? How does it help take garbage out of our bodies? How does it respond when we get too much sunshine? Is it wise to expose the skin to a lot of time in the sunshine or use of tanning lamps? Why? What else can you learn about the skin?

Teacher Information:

The skin is a remarkable organ. Students will experience its role as an air-conditioner. Those who continue on with the problem-solving activity will learn that the skin does far more than it usually gets credit for, and that keeping the skin healthy is very important. It really doesn't deserve to be abused by overexposure to the sun and to the artificial tanning that it is often required to endure.

Integrating: Reading, writing, physical education

Skills: Observing, inferring, researching, communicating

IV. THE SKELETAL SYSTEM

ACTIVITY 13-4: WHAT HOLDS BONES TOGETHER, AND WHAT MAKES THEM MOVE?

Materials Needed:

Chicken leg (or turkey leg), complete with foot

Knee joint of a sheep (or calf or pig)

Procedure:

1. Examine the knee joint. Try to determine what holds the two bones together.
2. Can you find a white substance on the ends of the bones? Is it harder than the bone itself, or softer?
3. Get a book about bones and find out what the white material is.
4. Examine the chicken leg. Locate a cord that extends out the top.
5. Pull on the cord and watch the toes. What did they do? Look in your book and find out what this cord is called.
6. Feel the back of your own leg, just above the heel. Can you find a similar cord? With your hand on the cord, move your foot and compare the way the cord works with the operation of the cord of the chicken leg.
7. Can you find more of these cords on your feet? Your hands? Other parts of your body?

For Problem Solvers:

Find out more about bones. Be creative in your search. Feel your own bones and draw your skeleton the best you can on a piece of paper. How many bones can you count in your body? Compare your drawing with a diagram of a human skeleton in an encyclopedia or a library book about the body. Which of your bones do you think is the largest? Which do you think is the smallest? Find out, and check your answer. Were you right? What animals have the smallest bones? What animal has the largest bones? What is the largest bone ever seen? Would you say your bones are quite large, or quite small?

Teacher Information:

Students will become more aware of the skeletal system and what makes it work. Animal bones can usually be obtained at a meat market. For examining cartilage and ligaments, calf bones will also do fine. Chicken and turkey bones work especially well for experiencing the function of tendons, because the legs are small and light and it's easy to operate the toes by pulling on tendons.

Integrating: Reading, writing, physical education, art, math

Skills: Observing, inferring, communicating, researching

V. THE MUSCULAR SYSTEM

ACTIVITY 13-5:
HOW DO MUSCLES COOPERATE?

Materials Needed:

None

Procedure:

1. Raise and lower one of your arms several times.
2. Using your other hand, find the muscle that raises the arm.
3. Put one hand on a table, with your arm still bent. Push against the table while you try to straighten your arm.
4. Find the muscle that causes the arm to straighten. Is it the same muscle that bends the arm?
5. Talk to others who are doing this activity and compare what you learned.

For Problem Solvers:

In this activity, you should have found a pair of muscles that move your arm—one of the muscles bends the arm and the other straightens it. Try to find other pairs of muscles on your body that work together.

Which muscles work when you want them to work? Make a list of these. Next, make a list of the muscles you have no control over. Now make a list of those you have some control over, but not all the time. When you have finished your lists, compare them with your group. Find out what these types of muscles are called.

Teacher Information:

In addition to locating the pair of muscles that bend and straighten the arm, students should be able to find similar pairs of muscles for the legs, fingers, toes, and others. Those who continue with the extension for problem solvers should enjoy the challenge of finding and classifying the voluntary muscles, the involuntary muscles, and those that are both voluntary and involuntary. Using trade books and other references, they should easily be able to find the names "voluntary muscles" and "involuntary muscles." Students should include the breathing muscles (diaphragm and rib muscles) and the eyelids among those that are both voluntary and involuntary.

Integrating: Reading, writing, physical education

Skills: Observing, inferring, communicating, researching

VI. THE CIRCULATORY SYSTEM

ACTIVITY 13-6:
HOW HARD DOES THE HEART WORK?

Materials Needed:

Firm rubber ball (a tennis ball is fine)

Procedure:

1. Put the ball in one hand.
2. Squeeze the ball.
3. Squeeze it again.
4. Keep squeezing the ball.
5. Watch the second-hand on the clock. Squeeze the ball about once each second.
6. Keep squeezing the ball. It's okay. Your hand rests each time it relaxes between pumps. But keep up with the clock—one squeeze per second.
7. How long can you keep this up? Is your hand getting tired?
8. Now stop and think about your heart. How many times did you squeeze your hand? How long did you keep doing it?
9. How long has your heart been squeezing? What would happen if it stopped for a five-minute rest?

For Problem Solvers:

What is your heart rate? How many times does your heart beat in one minute? How many times does it beat in one hour? In one day? Let's keep going—about how many times has your heart beat since you were born?

From what you know about your own heart rate, predict the average heart rate for the class, then set up a project to test your prediction.

Do some research and find out about how much blood your heart pumps each time it pumps. How much blood does it pump each day? How much blood has your heart pumped since you were born? If you put all of that blood in one tank, how large would the tank be? Would it fit inside your classroom?

Teacher Information:

Here's a chance for students to find out just how untiring their heart really is. They won't be able to keep squeezing on the ball very long. Their heart keeps pumping day and night without stopping. The heart rests between pumps, but students will find that relaxing their hand between squeezes doesn't provide much of a break. Students who can handle the research and mathematics will be challenged by the extension for problem solvers, as they compute the number of times their heart beats over an extended period of time and how much blood it really does pump.

Integrating: Reading, writing, physical education, math

Skills: Observing, inferring, measuring, predicting, communicating, researching, using space-time relationships

ACTIVITY 13-7: WHAT DOES THE CIRCULATORY SYSTEM DO?

Materials Needed:

Colored pencils

U.S. map

Outline of the human body

Procedure:

1. Get some information about a trucking company. Where to their trucks go as they deliver various products? Where do they get the products from?
2. On your map, mark the cities the company takes products to, and draw lines showing the routes trucks might take to get there. Draw their return trip on a different route and with a different color of pencil.
3. On the outline of the human body, draw the heart and lungs, and show where some of the main arteries and veins are.
4. Talk about how your circulatory system is like the trucking company. Talk about it with your group and share your ideas.

For Problem Solvers:

Explaining one thing by comparing it with another is often called an "analogy." This activity uses an analogy that compares the body's circulatory system with a trucking company. Learn all you can about the blood and the circulatory system from books that are available. From the information you have, and from your own creative thinking, answer these questions: What are the products the circulatory system delivers? What parts of your body supply those products? In this analogy, what parts of the circulatory system could you compare with the freeways, highways, streets, and roads used by the trucks? In the circulatory system, where are the trucks? What provides the power to move the trucks along?

Teacher Information:

This activity presents an analogy between the operation of a trucking company and the task the circulatory system performs for the body. Get involved in the discussions and be sure the point of the analogy is clear, and that students learn about the role of the circulatory system in supplying nutrients to the many locations throughout the body. The trucking company does not manufacture products, but it provides a very important service in picking up the products from factories and delivering them to many different locations of need. Similarly, the heart does not produce nutrients that are needed by the cells of the body. Oxygen is acquired by our lungs from the air we breathe. Nutrients are prepared by the digestive system from food we eat. Neither the lungs nor the digestive system is equipped to deliver their products to the cells, so a separate delivery system is needed. This is the role of the circulatory system. Continuing the analogy, the arteries, capillaries, and veins are the highways and roads. The blood represents the trucks, as it carries the necessary oxygen and nutrients to the cells of the body. However, the "trucks" cannot move on their own power. The heart provides the force that moves the blood along.

Integrating: Reading, writing, art, social studies

Skills: Observing, inferring, measuring, communicating, researching, using space-time relationships

VII. THE RESPIRATORY SYSTEM

ACTIVITY 13-8:
HOW CAN YOU MAKE A LUNG MODEL?

Materials Needed:

Clear plastic cup (must be made of a plastic that does not shatter easily—use one of the better brands)

Soda straw

Large balloon (9 inches or larger)

Small balloon

Small rubber band (or tape)

Procedure:

1. Drill a small hole in the bottom of the plastic cup, in the center, using a knife or the point of a pair of scissors. The hole should be just the right size for the soda straw to fit through snugly.
2. Insert the soda straw through the hole in the bottom of the cup.
3. Slide the small balloon over the bottom end of the straw (the end that is inside the cup) and secure the balloon around the straw with the small rubber band (or tape).
4. Cut the neck off the large balloon. Stretch the balloon over the opening of the cup. You might need to ask someone to hold the cup while you do this. This is the diaphragm.
5. Your lung model is now complete (see Figure 13A-1). Pinch the diaphragm between your fingers and pull down, then push the diaphragm up. Do that several times, as you observe the "lung."
6. Discuss how the lung model works and how it shows the action of your lungs.

Figure 13A-1

The completed lung model shows how the lungs work.

For Problem Solvers:

Try to explain why air goes into, and out of, the small balloon of your lung model. It happens for the same reason that air goes into and out of your own lungs. Where is your diaphragm? Why is it necessary? What is its job? Talk about air pressure, and how the actions of the diaphragm help you to breathe. Use your lung model to help you explain the action of the lungs to others.

Teacher Information:

The breathing mechanism relies on atmospheric pressure to operate. Air flows from regions of high pressure to regions of low pressure, and the diaphragm creates pressure differences. Muscles that expand and contract the rib cage also affect the pressure. As the diaphragm is pulled down and the rib cage expands, the volume of the chest cavity increases. This has the effect of lowering the air pressure inside the lungs and, with air passages open, atmospheric pressure, now greater than the air pressure inside the lungs, forces air into the lungs until pressure is equalized inside and outside the lungs. As muscle action decreases the size of the chest cavity, air pressure inside the lungs increases, exceeding atmospheric pressure, and air flows from the lungs into the atmosphere. While the air is in the lungs, an exchange of carbon dioxide for oxygen occurs.

The lung model students make in this activity shows the action of the diaphragm in creating pressure differences, causing air to flow into and out of the "lung."

Integrating: Art, language arts

Skills: Observing, inferring, communicating

ACTIVITY 13-9:
HOW CAN YOU MEASURE YOUR LUNG CAPACITY?

Materials Needed:

1-gallon jug

Sink (large pan or fish tank will do fine)

Flexible plastic 1/4-inch tubing, about 50 centimeters (20 inches) long

Soda straws

Masking tape

Water

Procedure:

1. Put water in the sink, about half full.
2. Cut off a short segment of soda straw for each person to use as a mouthpiece. Each person should have his or her own mouthpiece.
3. Place the jug in the sink, fill the jug with water, and turn it upside down in the water in the sink. Although the bottom of the jug is now out of the water, the water should stay in the jug.
4. Hand the end of the tubing to the person whose lung capacity is to be measured.
5. The person should insert his or her piece of soda straw into the end of the tubing.
6. Put the other end of the tubing in the water and hold it under the mouth of the jug.
7. The person predicts, by pointing to a position on the jug, where the water level in the jug will be when he or she stops blowing, then the person takes a deep breath and blows, emptying the lungs as much as possible.
8. What happened to the air in the jug?
9. Put a mark on the jug to show the water level after the person stopped blowing. You might want to number the mark to help you remember which one belongs to who.
10. Continue with the next person, being sure that each person uses his or her own mouthpiece.

For Problem Solvers:

Figure out a way to measure, in liters (quarts), the lung capacity of each person. Predict what you think is the average lung capacity of the class, then test your prediction by involving everyone in the activity.

Do you think lung capacity would be different after five minutes of strenuous exercise? Write your hypothesis. Then test your hypothesis by involving several people in similar exercise. Be sure you measure their lung capacity both before and immediately after exercising. Do you think age makes a difference? How about comparing males and females? How about comparing people who exercise regularly with those who don't? Write each hypothesis, then do the experiment, to test these and other variables you might choose to use. Do not use variables that will embarrass people, such as weight. Height is sometimes a sensitive measure as well, especially for tall girls and short boys.

Why does the water stay in the jug when the jug is upside down, the mouth of the jug is under the water, and the bottom of the jug is above the water level? And why does the water come out of the jug when someone blows on the tube?

Teacher Information:

Soda straws do come in different sizes, but the size that seems to be most standard is 1/4 inch in diameter and fits just right when inserted into the end of the 1/4-inch tubing. By using a separate segment of soda straw as a mouthpiece for each person, the same tubing can be reused as needed. Plenty of challenge is offered for the problem solvers, as they predict, measure, and compute averages.

The suggested experimenting offers an opportunity for real scientific investigation, as students formulate hypotheses regarding the effect of specific variables, and test their hypotheses. The variables that are suggested above should be fairly straightforward and easy to test. This activity, including the experimenting, can usually be done at home if students choose to do so. Potentially sensitive variables, such as weight and smoking habits, must be treated carefully—perhaps left alone.

Integrating: Math, social studies, physical education

Skills: Observing, inferring, predicting, measuring, communicating, using space-time relationships, formulating hypotheses, identifying and controlling variables, experimenting, researching

(Adapted from Activity 87, "What Is Your Lung Capacity?" in Tolman and Morton, 1986.)

VIII. THE DIGESTIVE SYSTEM

ACTIVITY 13-10: HOW LONG IS THE DIGESTIVE SYSTEM?

Materials Needed:

Rope or cord, about 9 meters (30 feet) long

Four short pieces of ribbon

Meter stick or measuring tape

Procedure:

1. From one end of the rope, measure enough length to represent what you think is the length of your mouth and throat together and tie a ribbon around the rope.
2. Tie a second ribbon, leaving enough length to represent your esophagus and stomach.
3. Measure another 7 meters (23 feet) and tie a third ribbon around the rope. This section represents your small intestine.
4. Measure about 1.5 meters (5 feet) from the third ribbon and tie a fourth ribbon around the rope. This section represents your large intestine.
5. Ask a partner to hold one end of the rope while you hold the other end. Stretch the rope out full length. This is approximately the length of the digestive system of an adult.
6. What do you think about it? Discuss it with your group and share your impressions and ideas.

For Problem Solvers:

Find a library book on the digestive system, or go to encyclopedias or your science textbook. Learn about the digestive system. Where does digestion begin? Does all digestion take place in the stomach? Does most digestion take place in the stomach?

Teacher Information:

It's quite enlightening to see a representation of the digestive system stretched out full length. Few people would suspect that it really is that long. Another surprise comes when we learn that most digestion occurs outside the stomach. Most of us think that the stomach digests our food. The major player in the digestion process is actually the small intestine.

Integrating: Reading, math

Skills: Observing, inferring, communicating, researching

IX. THE NERVOUS SYSTEM

ACTIVITY 13-11:

HOW ARE THE PARTS OF THE BODY CONNECTED TO THE BRAIN?

Materials Needed:

String—several colors

Automotive wiring harness

Pencils

Crayons

Large outline of the human form

Outline of the human body, showing internal organs

Procedure:

1. Draw and color the organs of the body on the large human form. You may look at the outline that shows the organs in deciding where to draw them on the large form. Be sure to include the brain.
2. Lay the automotive wiring harness out on the large form, with the main part of the harness on the spine.
3. Pull the sections of wires toward the main organs of the body and tape them down. These represent large bundles of nerves.
4. Tape the individual wires in areas that will show the nerve connections to the hands, feet, and to all parts of the body. If you run out of wires, use string to finish.
5. If the wiring harness is not available, do all of the nerves with colored string.
6. How do you think the wires are like the body's nervous system? Talk about it with your group. Where do the signals come from that control all of the parts of the body?

For Problem Solvers:

Find out which parts of the brain control certain parts of the body. Be sure those parts are connected to the correct part of the brain on your large model.

Write on paper any questions you have about the nerves and the nervous system. Read about the nervous system in an encyclopedia or a library book. Try to find answers to your questions. How do the nerves carry signals? Are these electrical impulses?

Teacher Information:

There are plenty of examples that could be used to show systems that involve a central command unit that branches out into smaller and more far-reaching segments of the system. Many social structures are designed that way. Local school systems usually have superintendents who are in charge of individual systems, with principals and supervisors as communication links with teachers, then students. Governments are organized similarly, as are military systems, corporations, and professional organizations.

The electrical system of today's automobile has a computer at the command post, with major trunks of wiring extending to the charging system, the ignition system, and so on. If one can be obtained, as from an auto salvage yard, let students use it in "wiring" the human body. Within the ignition system, the wires branch out to the distributor, the coil, the spark plugs, and so on, each of which plays its own important part in the function of the automobile, and similar branching occurs within each of the other major components of the system.

The automotive electrical system uses a wiring harness, which is especially meaningful in its likeness to the nervous system of the body. The spinal cord is the main trunk in the "wiring harness" of the body, attaching to the brain (the computer) at the base of the skull. This wiring harness branches out at various points as it extends down through its protective shaft in the spinal column, then more and more branches are involved as the system serves body system, organs, and the various parts that allow us to eat, transform food into energy, walk, talk, and the myriad other functions that the human body performs.

Students will perceive the nervous system of the body more clearly as they experience the process of "wiring" the system. If an automotive wiring harness is available, use it as the basis of the system as students go through the process of connecting the brain to the various body parts. If not, students could make their own nerve harness with colored string and tape.

Integrating: Reading, writing, art, physical education

Skills: Observing, inferring, communicating, researching

X. THE FIVE SENSES

ACTIVITY 13-12:

WHAT HAPPENS TO THE IRIS AS LIGHT CHANGES?

Materials Needed:

Mirror

Procedure:

1. Hold the mirror close enough to your face so that you can easily see the iris (colored part) of your eyes.
2. Look at the iris of one eye carefully and see if you can detect any movement.
3. Hold one hand up to the side of your eye to shade the light. As you do, watch the iris carefully.
4. Remove your hand from the eye, still watching the iris.
5. Close one eye or put your hand over it to shut out the light. When you open it, observe the iris immediately.
6. What happens to the iris as you change the amount of light around it? Why do you think this happens?

For Problem Solvers:

Find someone who will show you how the diaphragm of a camera works. Learn about the F-stop and the shutter speed. Ask to see these mechanisms operate with the back of the camera open, so you can be looking through the lens as they work.

Do some research in encyclopedias and library books to learn more about the functions of the eye. What do we mean by peripheral vision? How good is yours? Think of a way to compare your peripheral vision with that of some other people, and see if it's the same for everybody. Remember to write your hypothesis first. Also find out how we judge depth with our eyes, and how well you can judge depth with one eye.

Teacher Information:

The iris opens and closes to adjust the amount of light entering the eye through the pupil. The diaphragm of a camera operates much the same way.

You might pair students up and have them observe the iris in each other's eyes as light conditions change. Caution them not to shine bright light in their eyes or look directly at bright lights. The movement of the iris is easily observed in room light by closing the eyes or temporarily shading with the hand.

As students get into the extension for problem solvers, care must be taken to assure safety of the camera. Perhaps you know someone who is a camera buff and would come as a resource person to help your students learn about the operation of a camera and make connections with the functions of the eye. Many cameras today (if not most) have light-sensing mechanisms that automatically adjust the camera diaphragm. Be sure students recognize that the eye had that act perfected long ago.

Integrating: Reading, writing, art, physical education

Skills: Observing, inferring, communicating, formulating hypotheses, identifying and controlling variables, experimenting, researching

(Except for addition of the sections "For Problem Solvers," "Integrating," and "Skills," this activity was reprinted from Activity 123, "What Happens to the Iris As Light Changes?" in Tolman and Morton, 1986.)

ACTIVITY 13-13: WHAT IS THE EAR MADE OF?

Materials Needed:

Paper

Colored pencils (or crayons)

Reference books, including encyclopedias and trade books

Procedure:

1. Find a picture that shows the parts of the ear.
2. Draw your own picture of the ear. Label and color the parts.
3. Find out about the ears of many different animals.
4. Make a list of animals that have ears on their heads that you can see, like we do.
5. What are some animals that have ears that are quite different from ours? Do snakes have ears?
6. Can some insects hear? Do they have ears on their heads?
7. Share your information with your group. Did anyone learn something different about ears than you did?

For Problem Solvers:

Do more research and learn all you can about the human ear, how it works, and what we need to do to take care of it.

Find out how sounds are measured for loudness. What is a decibel? How many decibels is normal conversation measured at? What about a whisper? A shout? Loud rock music? A jet engine? Can loud sounds damage your ears, if you are around them a lot?

What are the main parts of the ear? How do they work? Make a model of the ear that has an ear channel and an ear drum. Make your model show how these parts affect the parts of the middle ear.

Where does ear wax come from? Does it do any good? Should you dig it out with a toothpick?

Teacher Information:

Students will become more aware that there is more to the ear than the flap of cartilage that we see on the side of the head. Drawing and labeling the parts will help them remember what the parts are and where they are located. Students will also begin to realize that nature has created many different designs of sound-sensitive mechanisms as they learn about the ears of different types of animals. Those who have an interest in continuing with the extensions for problem solvers will continue learning about the functions of the ear. They will learn that the ears can be damaged by excessive exposure to loud sounds, or by probing into the ear channel with toothpicks or other instruments.

Integrating: Reading, writing, art, physical education, math

Skills: Observing, inferring, communicating, researching

ACTIVITY 13-14: WHICH PART OF THE TONGUE IS MOST SENSITIVE TO TASTE?

Materials Needed:

Variety of food samples

Paper cups (one for each type of food)

Box of toothpicks

Blindfold

Water

Chart paper

Markers

Procedure:

1. Find a partner to do this activity with you.
2. Blindfold your partner.
3. Using a toothpick, place a small amount of one type of food on the region of the tongue identified as "1" in the illustration (see Figure 13A-2). Your partner is to judge the taste with his or her mouth still open so the food sample is not spread to other regions of the tongue. The taste judgment this time is to indicate strength as well as type of taste: strong sweet, weak sweet, strong salty, weak salty, strong sour, weak sour, strong bitter, or weak bitter.
4. Record your partner's judgment of taste, have him or her rinse mouth with water, then place the same type of food on region 2, then 3, then 4, then 5. Record the taste judgment each time. Be sure the mouth is rinsed with water between tastes.
5. When you have placed the first food type on all five regions of the tongue and recorded your partner's judgment of taste, do the same with the next food type.
6. After recording your partner's taste judgment of each type of food, trade places

Figure 13A-2

The taste regions of the tongue are labeled here to help you test your sense of taste.

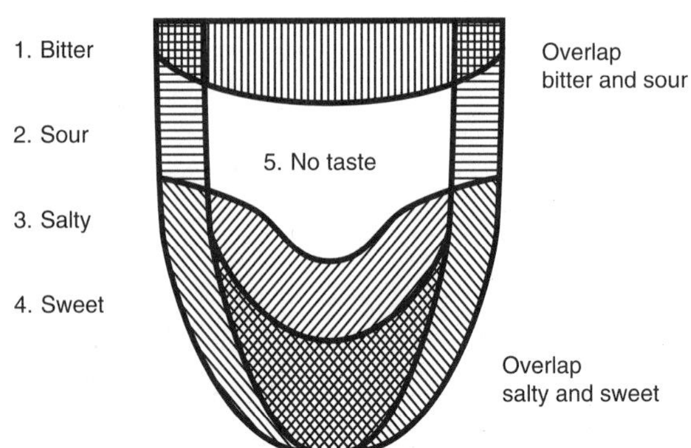

and have your partner give you the same taste tests.

7. Analyze the information you have collected in this activity and see if some regions of the tongue seem to be more sensitive to certain tastes than other regions. Make a chart showing your findings.

For Problem Solvers:

Are tastes affected by smell? Set up an experiment to find out. Before you begin, describe in writing the variable you will deal with and write your hypothesis. When you finish, make notes indicating whether your hypothesis was right, and what else you learned.

Teacher Information:

Certain regions of the tongue are known to be more sensitive to certain tastes. These are shown in the illustration. Results of the above investigations should approximate this information. Have students share and compare their findings. Where differences are found, encourage students to try to identify reasons for the differences. Possible factors include not placing the food sample in the exact same locations, closing the mouth, or spreading the food sample to other parts of the tongue. Also consider differences in taste sensitivities from one person to another, or simply the subjectivity of the judgment.

Integrating: Reading, writing, physical education

Skills: Observing, inferring, communicating, formulating hypotheses, identifying and controlling variables, experimenting, researching

(Except for addition of the sections "For Problem Solvers," "Integrating," and "Skills," this activity was reprinted from Activity 110, "Which Part of the Tongue Is Most Sensitive to Taste?" in Tolman and Morton, 1986.)

ACTIVITY 13-15:
WHERE IS YOUR SENSE OF SMELL REALLY LOCATED?

Materials Needed:

References, including encyclopedias and trade books

Procedure:

1. Find a book about the sense of smell.
2. Find out where the sense of smell really is. Is it all over inside the nose?
3. Draw a picture of the inside of the nose and show where the sense of smell is located.
4. Look up information about the sense of smell of other animals. Do all animals have a sense of smell? Do some animals have a better sense of smell than we do?
5. Compare your information with others who do this activity. What did you learn from your group that you hadn't learned from the books you used?

For Problem Solvers:

Do snakes have a sense of smell? How does it work? Find out about other animals having a sense of smell that works different than ours does.

Teacher Information:

The human sense of smell is really located in a postage-stamp-size patch at the roof of each of the two nasal passages. Each patch contains cells that are sensitive to scent. Molecules are given off by things around us and they enter our nose with the air we breath. When they contact these patches, messages are sent to our brain which we experience as the sensation we call "smell." Nerve endings that are sensitive to a particular smell often lose their sensitivity after we are exposed to that odor for a few minutes. Many animals, including dogs, have a keener sense of smell than we do.

With some animals, the sense of smell functions differently. Snakes have a unique mechanism called the Jacobson's organ, which detects smell from molecules brought into the mouth by the tongue.

Integrating: Reading, writing, physical education

Skills: Observing, inferring, communicating, researching

ACTIVITY 13-16:
WHERE IS YOUR SENSE OF TOUCH MOST SENSITIVE?

Materials Needed:

None

Procedure:

1. Do this activity with a partner.
2. Ask your partner to close his or her eyes.
3. Place the tips of three of your fingers, about 3 centimeters (1 inch) apart on your partner's back. Ask your partner to tell you how many fingers are touching his or her back.
4. Touch the palm of your partner's hand with one finger, then two. See if your partner can tell without looking how many fingers you are using.
5. Do the same on the shoulder, the forearm, the neck, the forehead, and the back.
6. In what areas is your partner able to tell with the most accuracy how many fingers you are using?
7. Trade places and have your partner test your sense of touch in the same manner.
8. Compare the results. Is your sense of touch the most sensitive in the same areas as that of your partner?

Teacher Information:

Sometimes it is surprising to find out how little sensitivity we have on some parts of the body. Students usually find that on their hands, fingers, and face they can tell quite accurately how many fingers are touching. On the back and arms the sense of touch is noticeably less sensitive. They might like to discuss times when they have noticed that injuries are much more painful in some places than in others.

Integrating: Physical education

Skills: Observing, inferring

(Except for addition of the sections "For Problem Solvers," "Integrating," and "Skills," this activity was reprinted from Activity 129, "Where Is Your Sense of Touch Most Sensitive?" in Tolman and Morton, 1986.)

CHAPTER

ENERGY AND THE NATURE OF MATTER

CHAPTER OUTLINE:

I WONDER . . .

What is *work*?
What is the difference between kinetic energy and potential energy?
What causes gravity? Does anyone know?
How are energy and matter related?
Are *mass* and *weight* synonymous terms? If not, how do they differ?
What can we do to illustrate the effect of inertia in the classroom?
How can a boat be powered by a drop of soap?
How does a water strider walk on water?
What do cohesion and adhesion have to do with a blood test?
Why could you and every other person be considered a "space case"?

I. INTRODUCTION

Other than energy and matter, what else is there? Actually, nothing; for the entire universe consists of matter and energy in many different forms and combinations. The idea of matter is easy to grasp. It is stuff. It is everything that has mass and occupies space. We can usually see it, feel it, taste it, or smell it, and some forms of matter can be detected by all of these senses. Energy is more difficult to comprehend. We see only the evidence that it exists as it does work. Energy is sometimes defined as the ability to do work, but it is more than that. Before we get into that, though, let's define *work.*

For science applications, *work* is usually defined in terms of motion of an object over a distance and the force on the object. When a shoe is picked up off the floor, work is done on the shoe. When an ant drags a tiny leaf across the sidewalk, work is done on the leaf. But if a man pushes on a brick wall, no matter how hard he strains or how much he perspires, if the wall doesn't move, no work is done on the wall. Work is done on the man's body, as it moves and contorts in an effort to shift the wall, but no work is done on the wall unless the wall moves. (Many of us prefer a broader definition of work, for even to think requires effort and energy and can make us feel tired. To those of us who take this position, perhaps any activity that requires effort and makes us feel tired is considered work.)

In this chapter, we describe kinetic and potential energy, the conservation and transformation of energy, and the relationship between energy and matter. Next, matter is defined and discussed in terms of its properties, including the relationship between weight, mass, and inertia; physical and chemical changes; cohesion and adhesion; surface tension; and capillary action. Finally, we consider the building blocks of matter, atoms and molecules, as well as the combining of these to make elements, compounds, mixtures, and solutions.

II. ENERGY

The above definition of energy is too simplistic because other events, such as chemical changes, also require energy, while often no movement is apparent. When a flashlight is turned on, energy is required to light the bulb, but we don't see anything move. So energy must be more than the ability to cause movement. Let's redefine energy, then, as the ability to do work *or* to produce a chemical change.

Most of the energy on the earth comes from the sun, although some forms of energy are stored within the earth itself, such as heat, nuclear energy, and gravitational potential energy. We feel the sun's energy as heat. Plants capture it and use it in making the food we eat. Ultimately, energy manifests itself in many forms, including light, sound, magnetism, and so on. Some of these forms of energy are dealt with in separate chapters of this book. At this time let's consider two major classes of energy: *kinetic energy,* which is energy due to movement; and *potential energy,* which is energy due to position or condition.

Kinetic Energy

Kinetic energy is the energy of motion—energy that an object has because it is moving. Motion, hence kinetic energy, can result when gunpowder explodes and sends a bullet speeding toward its target, when water rushes down from a dam, or from any other event in which an object moves. A rock falling from a cliff has kinetic energy, as does a moving bicycle, a flying arrow, a baseball speeding toward a bat, and a bat swinging toward the ball.

Potential Energy

Potential energy can be thought of as *stored energy.* When a ball is placed at the edge of a table, energy is stored in the ball in the form of its potential to fall. A tree has potential energy, because it will fall if something should cut through its trunk or destroy the roots that hold it in place. When the string of a hunting bow is pulled back, the bow has potential energy because its stretched fibers have a natural tendency to return to their relaxed position. If an arrow is placed on the string, and the string is released, the bow will transfer its energy to the string, the string will transfer the energy to the arrow, and the arrow will go zipping through the air. But the bow will do no work unless its potential energy is unleashed by releasing the string. Potential energy exists in water above a dam, in wound-up springs, and in stretched rubber bands. Energy that is stored, and is held in readiness to do work, is potential energy.

The force of gravity

Gravity, quite literally, keeps our feet on the ground. But it does more than that. Gravity is a central and vitally important force. Without it, rain would not fall. In fact, there would be neither air to breathe nor water to drink, for the molecules of air and water would move out into space, with nothing to hold them to the earth's surface. The moon cannot have an atmosphere because its gravitational force is too weak to hold the necessary amounts of air molecules. If a huge supply of air were transported to the moon, it would soon dissipate out into space for lack of sufficient gravity to hold the molecules captive at the surface.

We tend to think of gravity only as a force that attracts objects to the earth and to other large heavenly bodies, but Sir Isaac Newton, in his *law of gravitation,* stated that all bodies, from the largest star in the universe to the smallest particle of matter, attract each other. Even small objects, such as the human body, have a gravitational attraction for all other objects; however it is extremely weak. The gravitational force is strong enough to be noticed only when huge objects, such as planets, are involved. The greater the mass of an object (the amount of material the object consists of), the stronger is its gravity. Also, the farther apart two bodies are, the weaker is their gravitational attraction for each other.

In his law of gravitation, Newton made no attempt to explain why the earth and all other masses exert a gravitational force on each other, but his theory of gravity explains many of the behaviors of nature. We have learned ways to use gravity to our advantage and ways to avoid its potentially destructive effects. We build safety rails around high stairways, so we won't fall and get hurt. We build huge retaining walls along highways that pass around mountains or along hillsides, so soil and rock won't slide down onto the highways.

Gravitational potential energy

Gravity provides *gravitational potential energy* to a ball resting at the edge of a table, to a rock at the edge of a cliff, to a raindrop forming in a cloud, or to any other object that is in a position to fall from its current elevation to a lower level. We store great amounts of water behind a dam, then let the gravitational potential energy of the water change to kinetic energy and produce electricity as the water falls through turbines that turn generators (see Figure 14-1). We also use gravity to bring water from reservoirs to irrigate our crops at lower elevations.

Acceleration of gravity

As an object falls toward the earth, it increases its rate of descent (assuming no air resistance or other interference) by 32 feet per second per second. In other words, each second the object falls, it is traveling 32 feet per second faster than it was traveling the previous second. At the end of the first second of fall, the object is falling at the rate of 32 feet per second. At the end of two seconds, the rate of descent is 64 feet per second, at the end of the third second the rate of fall is 96 feet per second, and so on. A steel ball and a feather, if dropped simultaneously in a vacuum, would fall at the same rate, because without air there would be no resistance; the feather would not flutter to the ground, but instead would fall at the same rate as the steel ball. This experiment was performed on the moon with a hammer and a feather during an *Apollo* mission.

Figure 14-1

This gravity-fed turbine turns generators to produce electricity, using gravitational potential energy.

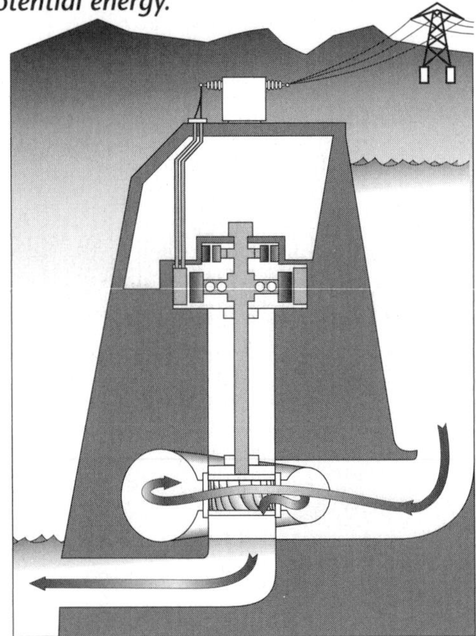

If a broad object that has a lot of surface area compared to its weight, such as a feather or a sheet of paper, is dropped from above the ground on the earth, air resistance will have a noticeable effect in slowing the fall. (That's why parachutes are used.) If the object that is dropped is quite compact, the effect of air resistance is minimal. If you drop a large steel ball and a small rubber ball simultaneously, from the same height, they will reach the ground together.

Internal Energy

Actually, energy forms go far beyond the obvious. We feel heat radiating from a hot plate as the random molecular motion is speeded up within the plate. The motions of electrons produce both light and electricity, although we don't see them move because they are so extremely small. Still, their motion is a form of energy. Such forms of energy as electrical energy and chemical energy, which involve microscopic particles, are called *internal* energy. Internal energy is the sum of all kinetic and potential energy of all molecules of a substance.

"When a moving object slows down because of friction, the energy of the object is not lost but can be accounted for in the total energy of the individual molecules of the object and its surroundings" (Baliff, 1972). When a driver slams on the brakes of a car, the loss of kinetic energy can be accounted for in increased energy of the molecules within the brake system, the tires, and the road; the increase in temperature is sometimes easily noticed by touching the tire, or especially by touching the metal of the brake system.

Conservation and Transformation of Energy

Energy can neither be created nor destroyed. It can be transferred from place to place, and even transformed from one form to another, but the total amount of energy existing in the universe does not change. This is the *law of conservation of energy.*

While the total amount of energy remains the same, it is constantly being changed from one form to another. If such transformation could not happen, plants could not make food from nutrients and sunlight, water would not evaporate, and any number of natural processes could not occur. Come to think of it, no energy would be produced by the sun, and no one would be around to worry about whether energy could be transformed or not.

In addition to the countless natural processes that change energy from one form to another, people have learned to cause many such transformations to take place to their advantage. The energy in fossil fuels powers our automobiles and makes our homes more comfortable as it is changed to thermal energy. The same energy may be transformed into electrical energy, as is the kinetic energy of water falling from a dam. In turn, electrical energy is carried to homes, factories, and so on, and there it is transformed into still other forms of energy, including light and mechanical energy. Just think of all the energy needs that have been filled by converting fossil fuels (coal and oil) into electrical energy. The list of examples of energy transformation, both in nature and those caused by humans, could go on almost endlessly.

III. CONSERVATION OF MASS AND THE RELATIONSHIP BETWEEN ENERGY AND MATTER

Closely related to the law of conservation of energy is a law of *conservation of mass,* which states that mass can neither be created nor destroyed. When chemical changes occur, such as in the burning of wood, atoms are rearranged and form molecules of carbon and gases, but the total mass (amount of matter) does not change measurably.

Early in the twentieth century, Albert Einstein suggested that matter and energy are more interrelated than scientists previously thought. Einstein proposed that it is possible for matter to change to energy and for energy to change to matter. Scientists have since found evidence that Einstein's theory was right. When certain atoms are broken into simpler atoms, some mass is lost while a tremendous amount of energy is given off. Also, when energy is added to a substance, the mass of the substance is increased, though usually the change is not large enough to measure.

These findings have resulted in combining the laws of conservation of mass and conservation of energy into a *law of conservation of mass and energy*. The new law suggests that mass can be changed into energy and energy can be changed into mass, but the total amount of mass and energy in the universe is constant. At the elementary school level, however, there is little cause to be concerned with the transfer of energy to mass and mass to energy.

IV. THE NATURE OF MATTER

A long time ago the curiosity of people gave birth to questions about what matter really is. The ancient Greeks thought all matter was made of four elements—earth, air, fire, and water. History gives credit to Aristotle as being one of the scientists who reached that conclusion. As more information was acquired through an increased study of metals over a period of hundreds of years, Aristotle's theory was abandoned. Eventually, medieval philosopher-scientists called alchemists directed their efforts toward an unsuccessful attempt to turn various metals into gold. History has continued to be a great teacher, and humankind has acquired vast amounts of information about the nature of matter. As we progress, we must look over our shoulders with respect, however, rather than criticism, because the persistence of those people over the centuries laid the foundations that made possible today's scientific knowledge. Consider also that we are still asking questions about what matter really is, and the time will likely come when the current level of scientific knowledge will be perceived as being rather primitive.

We note our former definition that matter is anything that has mass and occupies space. This includes air, water, soil, stone, metal, animals, plants, planets, and so on. Some things consist of many different substances. The human body is an example; air is another. Material that is made up of only one kind of matter is called a *pure substance.*

Matter can be in any of three states—*solid, liquid,* or *gas.* Solids can be hard or soft, but they have a definite size and shape, like rock, cotton, or wood, for example. A liquid, such as water, has a definite size, but it has no definite shape and therefore takes the shape of its container. A gas has neither a definite size nor a definite shape; it assumes both the size and shape of its container. At room temperature, oxygen and carbon dioxide are common examples of gases. Even these can change form at extremely low temperatures; dry ice (solid carbon dioxide) and liquid oxygen are formed by cooling and compressing these gases.

Most substances can change from one state to another, given the necessary temperatures, but water is the only common substance that exists in nature in all three states. Most water on the earth is in liquid form, but at temperatures of 0 degrees Celsius (32 degrees Fahrenheit) or lower it becomes a solid (ice). Massive amounts of water evaporate into a gaseous state in the atmosphere every day. The rate at which water evaporates speeds up as temperatures increase, and slows down as temperatures decrease.

Properties of Matter

All substances have certain properties, or characteristics, that distinguish them from all other substances. Some of these are *physical properties* and some are *chemical properties.*

Physical properties include size, shape, color, texture, and so on. Melting, boiling, and freezing temperatures are also physical properties, as are the ability of a material to conduct heat and electricity, and its tendency to dissolve in water and other liquids. Each type of substance has some physical properties that are different from those of all other substances.

Characteristics that have to do with the chemical makeup of a substance, or how it reacts with other substances, are its chemical properties. When water and vinegar are added to separate portions of baking soda, evidence of different chemical properties can be observed as carbon dioxide begins to bubble up from the baking soda mixed with vinegar but not from the portion to which water has been added. When iron gets wet, rust (iron oxide) soon begins to form, but stainless steel is much more resistant to the formation of rust, indicating different chemical properties. A substance (such as iron) that reacts readily with other substances is said to be *active,* while a substance (such as helium) that does not is said to be *inert.*

Weight, Mass, and Inertia

All objects that are at or near the earth's surface are pulled toward the center of the earth by the force of gravity. The gravitational force on an object is called its *weight.* The force of gravity on an object is stronger the nearer the object is to the center of the earth. Therefore, an object weighs slightly less at the top of a high mountain than it does at a low elevation. The higher an airplane flies, the less it and its passengers weigh. An astronaut is affected less and less by the earth's gravity as the spacecraft gets farther and farther from the center of the earth.

Frequently mass and weight are confused as being synonymous terms. They are not, but weight is proportional to mass. While weight is the gravitational force on an object, the term *mass* refers to the amount of material the object consists of. Weight changes with distance from the center of the earth, while mass remains constant. An astronaut weighs less on the moon than on the earth (about one-sixth as much), but the astronaut's mass is the same.

Inertia can be defined as a tendency to remain at rest or in uniform motion in a straight line unless acted upon by some external force. Stated another way, inertia is a resistance to change in speed and direction. This idea is credited to Isaac Newton as his *First Law of Motion.* It explains why a heavily loaded cart is difficult to get moving even though it is on wheels. Inertia is directly related to mass—the greater the mass, the harder it is to start an object moving or to change its speed or direction. Due to its great mass, much force is required to start a freight train moving down the track *and* much force is required to get it stopped. Because of the relationship between mass and inertia, physicists usually define mass as a measure of inertia, or even consider the two terms to be synonymous. At the elementary level, let's stay with the definition stated above and remember that inertia is directly related to mass.

The earth maintains its forward motion in space because of inertia. The sun's gravity prevents the earth from traveling in a straight line but rather holds it in a near-circular orbit around the sun. No *force* is needed to *keep* it moving, but gravity forces its change of direction. The earth continues in orbit because there is no force opposing its forward movement. It acquired its position and motion when it was formed.

Physical and Chemical Changes in Matter

When the physical properties of a substance change, such as size, shape, or color, this indicates that a *physical change* has taken place. A change in state from a liquid to a solid or to a gas is a physical change. Adding heat to water can change the water to steam; removing heat can change water to ice. When a *chemical change* occurs, a new substance is formed, with chemical properties that are different from those of the original substance. Chemical changes are not easily reversible; in fact, reversing chemical changes is often impossible. When wood burns, for example, much of the material escapes into the air as a gas, while carbon remains behind as a black solid. Neither the material given off into the air nor the material left behind is wood. As iron rusts, a chemical change takes place, and the red powdery substance that is left is not iron, but iron oxide. Iron can be recovered from iron oxide by inducing additional chemical changes, but wood can never be reformed from the carbon and gases that are produced as wood burns. Most chemical changes are irreversible.

It is important to note, however, that even when a chemical change occurs, the same elements exist; they are just combined in different ways. If we could gather the materials and recombine the elements as they were before, the original substance could be formed. Although we can't take the carbon and gases that result from wood burning and produce wood again, the elements that formed the wood still exist, just in different forms. This is consistent with the law of conservation of mass, discussed earlier in this chapter.

Cohesion and Adhesion

Due to electrical attractions at the microscopic level, the molecules of a substance have an affinity for each other; in other words, they stick together. Water molecules stick to water molecules and iron molecules stick to iron molecules. The tendency of like molecules to cling to each other is called *cohesion*. The molecules of a solid have a much stronger cohesive attraction than do those of a liquid. The molecules of a liquid remain in close proximity to each other, but they move around relatively freely, allowing the liquid to flow into the shape of the container. Those of a solid hold a more rigid formation with each other, thus the solid maintains its shape. Gas molecules seem not to have much cohesion, as they freely move away from each other, limited only by the size of their container.

The molecules of most substances also have an attraction for molecules of certain other substances. This attraction is called *adhesion*. Water molecules, for instance, have an adhesive attraction with many other materials, including wood and glass, leaving such surfaces wet if water comes in contact with them. Adhesion makes it possible for two different substances to stick together. Some substances have an unusually strong adhesive attraction for certain other materials and are used as glue, or *adhesive*, for that particular material. In fact, much research is done to develop substances that have an especially strong adhesion with materials that commonly need to be repaired, such as wood and plastic.

Surface Tension

The cohesive force of liquid molecules has an interesting effect at the surface of the liquid. This effect is commonly noticed with water when a cup is filled level full, then more water is added. A water molecule that is beneath the surface is attracted in all directions by the cohesive effect of other water molecules around it. A molecule that is on the surface, however, is attracted by other water molecules below and to the side, in every direction except upward, because there are no other water molecules above. The attraction of the surface molecules to each other creates a skin-like effect on the surface of the water, called *surface tension*.

Let's illustrate surface tension with a game that has been popular among children for many years, "Red Rover." Two teams line up facing each other. We'll call them Teams A and B. Team A is spread out in a line, with hands locked. On a signal from Team A ("Red Rover, Red Rover, send Julie right over"), the designated person from Team B runs to Team A and tries to break through one of the hand-grips. If the person does not get through, he or she becomes a part of Team A. If successful in breaking the grip, the runner takes one of the two people who couldn't hold the grip back to join Team B. Next, Team B gives the signal and Team A sends a runner. And so goes the game until one team is left without two people to run between.

Think of the molecules of water at the surface as playing Red Rover with hands locked. The reluctance of these molecules to release their grip from each other is evidenced as a cup is filled, then more water added until the surface is heaped up. Water molecules cling together until they are heaped up enough that their cohesive attraction is overpowered by the force of gravity, and water spills over the edge of the cup. You can also see the effect of surface tension if you carefully lay a sewing needle or a double-edged razor blade on a pan of water (see Figure 14-2). The sewing needle or razor blade will float, supported by surface tension, showing the reluctance of water molecules to release their grip on each other. Water striders (water skeeters) and some other tiny animals are able to literally walk on water because of surface tension (see Figure 14-3).

If you place a bit of powdered soap, or a drop of liquid detergent, on the surface of the overfilled cup, water will quickly spill over the edge. As soap molecules dissolve into the water, they move between the water molecules, causing them to release each other. We say the soap breaks the surface tension. Try to float a double-edged razor blade on a pan of water after soap has been added, or add soap after the razor blade is already floating.

Figure 14-2

This razor blade can float on the surface of the water because of surface tension.

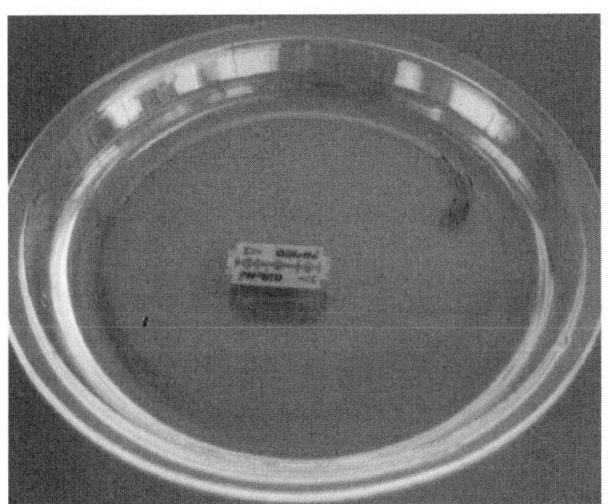

Figure 14-3

Water striders are easily supported on water by surface tension.

Capillary Action

You have probably had the experience of a blood test. The nurse pricks your finger with a sharp instrument (ouch!), then squeezes out a big, red drop of blood. Next she places one end of a thin glass tube (usually called a capillary tube) on the drop of blood, with the tube pointing down so the blood can run down into it. Right? Wrong! The nurse holds the glass tube at an upward angle and blood rushes up into it in an instant, against the force of gravity! How is that possible? Weren't you just dying with curiosity? (Dying, but not with curiosity, right?)

The force that causes the blood to flow upward against the force of gravity is called *capillary action,* and it happens because of a combination of the forces of adhesion and cohesion. Blood molecules literally climb the wall of the tube in their attraction for glass molecules (adhesion). Other blood molecules cling to those blood molecules (cohesion) and are carried up with them.

You could also compare capillary action to a group of prisoners trying to escape by climbing over a prison wall. As one prisoner scales the wall, another, seeing what is happening, grabs the leg of the first in hopes of going along. Think of the second prisoner as a hitchhiker. The blood molecules that are in contact with the glass wall of the tube are like the first prisoner climbing the wall. Other blood molecules (hitchhikers) cling to the first, and together they move up into the tube. But the first prisoner can pull only a few hitchhikers up the wall. For this reason, the tube that the nurse uses for the blood test has a very fine opening, greatly limiting the number of hitchhikers and increasing the proportion of molecules in contact with the walls of the tube, thus increasing the adhesive effect.

Compare this effect with what you see on the sides of a drinking glass that is only partly filled with water. If you look carefully, you will notice that the liquid seems to be trying to climb the sides of the glass. The water is sloped up where it touches the side of the glass. Chemists call this sloped region the *meniscus* (see Figure 14-4). The slope is there because of the adhesive attraction of water molecules for the glass wall, combined with the cohesive attraction between water molecules. The size of the opening creates the different effect in the drinking glass that results in a meniscus, and in the capillary tube that results in a liquid flowing upward. Liquid will rise in the tube until the force of gravity on the rising liquid equals the force of the capillary action; the smaller the tube, the higher the liquid will rise (see Figure 14-5).

Figure 14-4

Water slopes up where it meets the side of a container, and the sloped region is called the meniscus.

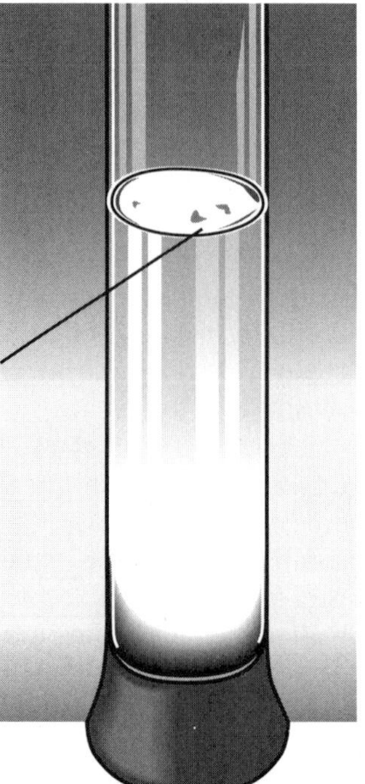

Figure 14-5

These tubes of varying diameters show how liquid rises higher in smaller tubes.

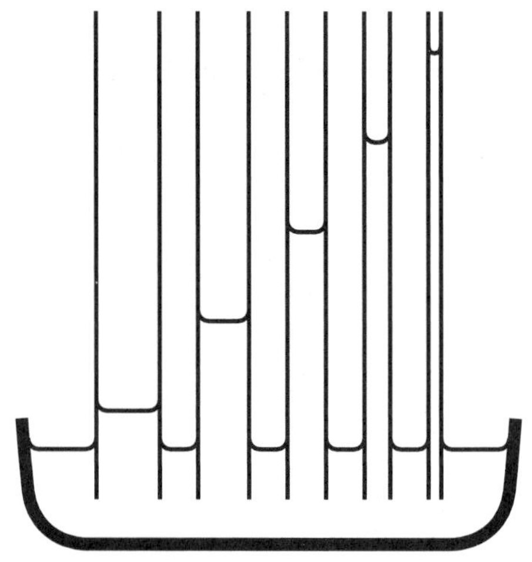

The idea of using a capillary tube to draw blood is an ingenious one, but like so many other great ideas, nature thought of it first. When we water a houseplant by placing water in a plate under the plant, we rely on capillary action to carry water up through the soil to the plant. Also, if a paint brush is dipped into water, the water will rise up into the narrow spaces between the bristles by capillary action. Oil soaks upward into a lamp wick and water into a towel, if one end is in the respective liquid. All of these things happen by capillary action.

The Building Blocks of Matter

Atoms

All matter is made of tiny particles, called atoms. As tiny as atoms are, scientists tell us they consist of three types of still smaller particles called *protons, neutrons,* and *electrons.* The protons and neutrons form a *nucleus* at the center of the atom. Electrons have only a very small fraction of the mass of protons and neutrons, and they move very rapidly. The mass of a proton or neutron is over 1,800 times that of an electron. The mass of electrons is therefore usually ignored when considering the mass of atoms.

All protons, neutrons, and electrons are like all other protons, neutrons, and electrons, except for the numbers of them that are combined in an atom. That, along with the combining of different atoms together in forming molecules, is what makes any particular substance different from all other substances.

Electrons move around the nucleus, and each has a negative electrical charge. The proton has a positive electrical charge, and the neutron is neutral. Usually, each atom has the same number of electrons as protons, and we say the atom is neutral.

Negative charges and positive charges attract each other, while positive charges repel each other and negative charges repel each other. Still, the protons of an atom are very tightly packed, together with the neutrons, in the center of the atom (the nucleus). A powerful force (sometimes called the strong nuclear force) holds these parts together in the nucleus, overcoming the tendency of the protons to repel each other.

Electrons move around the nucleus in definite energy levels, or shells. They were once thought to orbit the nucleus somewhat like planets orbit the sun, but scientists have come to think electrons are more like bees buzzing around a hive, occupying a given space, moving very rapidly, and maintaining their definite configuration of energy levels, or shells, but not necessarily in particular orbits.

What Are You Made of? Space!

An old children's rhyme states that little boys are made of "frogs and snails and puppy-dog tails." Scientists say, no, they are mostly space, and so are little girls, and so is everything else.

It is just as difficult to envision the minute size of atomic particles as to visualize the immense dimensions of outer space. Actually, the nature of atoms is often compared with the solar system. The nucleus of any given atom is kept relatively far away from any other nucleus by the rapidly moving electrons. The result is that the vast majority of matter is empty space. Indeed, the proportion of empty space within an atom is much greater than the proportion of empty space in the solar system. If a material could be compressed to the point that nuclei were close together, eliminating the empty space between them, a thimbleful of that material would weigh thousands of tons. The nucleus has a diameter about one hundred-thousandth the diameter of the atom. In that proportion, if a nucleus were 1 centimeter across, the atom would be wider than the length of ten football fields end to end! The vast majority of matter is empty space.

A First Look at Atoms

Only recently have scientists seen atoms. They appear as fuzzy little balls, which is what scientists have been saying for a long time that they would look like if we could see them. The instrument responsible for this very significant scientific advancement is the scanning tunneling microscope (STM). This microscope was one of the most important inventions of this century, providing unprecedented images of the unseen world (Fisher, 1989).

Molecules

Atoms combine to form molecules. In some cases, the molecule consists of only one kind of atom. Each molecule of oxygen gas, for instance, consists of two oxygen atoms. However, a water molecule has two hydrogen atoms combined with one oxygen atom. A *molecule* is the smallest particle of a substance that has all of the properties of the substance.

All substances are made up of molecules, which are so tiny that only the largest of them can be seen with the powerful electron microscope. Billions of water molecules are contained in a single drop of water. All molecules of a substance are alike, and they are different from the molecules of any other substance. If a small amount of salt and a small amount of sugar were ground to the finest possible powder, each tiny particle of salt would still be salt and each tiny particle of sugar would still be sugar.

All molecules are constantly moving and striking other molecules. Gas molecules move very rapidly and they are far apart. In a liquid, the molecules move more slowly and are much closer together, but still move around relatively freely. The molecules of a solid seem to just move back and forth, or vibrate, in place (see Figure 14-6).

Elements, Compounds, Mixtures, and Solutions

Elements

Elements are often called the building blocks of matter. An atom is the smallest particle of an element that has the properties of the element. All atoms are made of protons, neutrons, and electrons, but there are many different kinds of atoms. The atoms of each element are different from those of all other elements due to the numbers of protons and electrons that make up the atom.

There are currently 109 known elements. About ninety (chemists do not totally agree on this number) of these occur in nature and the rest are made by scientists. The atoms of one element can combine with the atoms of other elements to form different substances. All of the thousands upon thousands of natural substances on the earth are made of the ninety or so natural elements.

For easier communication about the elements, especially in using chemical formulas, scientists have assigned a one- or two-letter symbol to each one. For some elements, the

Figure 14-6 ***These drawings show the comparative proximity of molecules of a solid, a liquid, and a gas. (Science and Children Feb. 1989)***

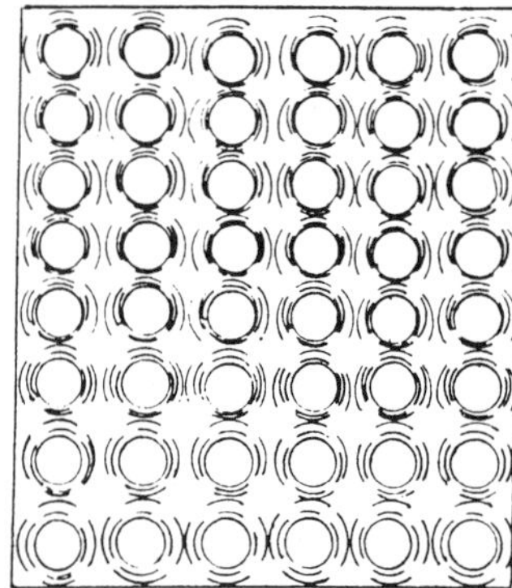

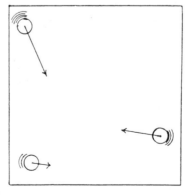

Molecules (or atoms) in a solid: With heat coming from the bottom, molecules there are further apart with larger amplitude oscillations.

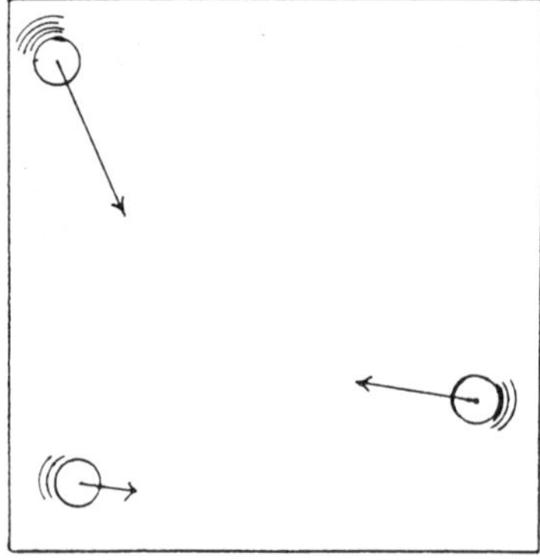

Molecules (or atoms) in a gas: The average distance between molecules is 10 molecular diameters.

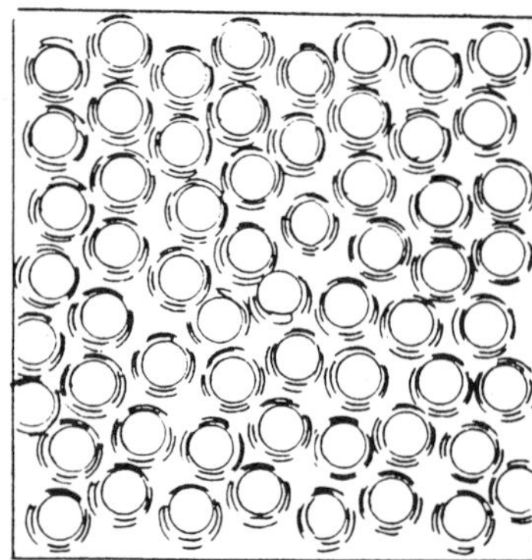

Molecules (or atoms) in a liquid: Spacing is similar to a solid, but the organization of the array slowly changes as molecules migrate.

symbol is taken from its common name, and for others it represents the Latin name.

The Periodic Table of the Elements lists all of the known elements. The position of any particular element on the Periodic Table is based on certain characteristics of the element, and is meaningful to the student of chemistry. Columns of elements in the Periodic Table, for instance, have similar chemical properties. The number of neutrons in an element can vary. Table 14-1 lists the first ten elements of the Periodic Table, along with the symbol of each element and its number of protons, electrons, and the most common number of neutrons.

Another interesting sampling of the elements is shown in Table 14-2. This list shows the eight most common elements in the earth's crust and the percent of the total weight each represents. Notice that these eight elements account for 98 percent of the total weight of the earth's crust, and that 75 percent of the crust is accounted for with just the first two, oxygen and silicon.

Table 14-1 *The First Ten Elements of the Periodic Table*

Element	Symbol	No. of Protons	Most Common No. of Neutrons	No. of Electrons
Hydrogen	H	1	0	1
Helium	He	2	2	2
Lithium	Li	3	4	3
Beryllium	Be	4	5	4
Boron	B	5	6	5
Carbon	C	6	6	6
Nitrogen	N	7	7	7
Oxygen	O	8	8	8
Fluorine	F	9	10	9
Neon	Ne	10	10	10

Table 14-2

Eight Most Common Elements in the Earth's Crust

Element	Symbol	Percent of weight
Oxygen	O	47.3
Silicon	Si	27.7
Aluminum	Al	7.9
Iron	Fe	4.5
Calcium	Ca	3.5
Sodium	Na	2.5
Potassium	K	2.5
Magnesium	Mg	2.2

Compounds, mixtures, and solutions

When two or more different kinds of atoms chemically combine to form a new substance, that substance is called a *compound.* A compound has its own physical and chemical properties, different from those of the elements from which it was formed. For example, hydrogen and oxygen both exist in nature as gases, but when two hydrogen atoms combine with one oxygen atom, a chemical change takes place; the result is the compound water. Hydrogen gas is extremely explosive, and oxygen gas supports combustion; together, however, they form a substance that is used to put fire out. That's incredible!

Sometimes two or more elements or compounds coexist without combining chemically. Such a material is called a *mixture.* Salt and sand could be put together to form a mixture. Although it may be very difficult to separate them visually, each tiny salt crystal would remain a salt crystal and each grain of sand would still be sand. A common example of a mixture is the air we breathe. Air is mostly nitrogen gas and oxygen gas, but the two elements remain separate and distinct, and each retains its own unique physical and chemical properties. Other substances in the air, such as water vapor and carbon dioxide, likewise retain their unique properties.

When a mixture of two substances results in the molecules of one substance being spread out evenly and equally between the molecules of the other substance, the mixture is called a *solution.* This can happen when two liquids are combined together (such as alcohol mixed with water), or when a gas is combined with a liquid (such as carbon dioxide mixed in water to make soda water). Many common solutions involve a solid dissolved in a liquid. Salt, for example, will dissolve in water to form a salt-water solution. In such cases, the solid is called a *solute* and the liquid is called a *solvent;* the solute dissolves into the solvent.

V. IN CLOSING

One of the goals of elementary science is to help children acquire a greater interest in, and appreciation for, the world around them. And after all, the world *is* matter and energy. All that we see, all that we are, consists of these two things in all their varieties and forms. As we study these topics we get a glimpse of the building blocks and the workings of the natural world. As we study all other topics of science, we deal with the many varieties and forms of matter and energy.

LIST OF RESOURCES

Ballif, Jae R., and William E. Dibble, *Physics: Fundamentals & Frontiers* (New York: John Wiley & Sons, 1972), 172.

Fisher, Arthur, "Seeing Atoms," *Popular Science* (April 1989): 102–7.

Mason, Grant W., *et al., Physical Science Concepts* (Provo, UT: Soundprint, 1989).

Tolman, Marvin N., and James O. Morton, *Physical Science Activities for Grades 2–8* (West Nyack, NY: Parker Publishing Co., 1986).

Victor, Edward, *Science for the Elementary School, Sixth Edition* (New York: Macmillan Publishing Co., 1989).

CHAPTER

ENERGY AND THE NATURE OF MATTER

ACTIVITIES

II. ENERGY

ACTIVITY 14-1:
HOW CAN YOU MEASURE WORK?

Materials Needed:

1-pound weight

Ruler

Procedure:

1. Stand the ruler on the table.
2. Raise the 1-pound weight to the top of the ruler. To raise 1 pound a distance of 1 foot, you did 1 foot-pound of work.
3. Raise the 1-pound weight 6 inches. How much work did you do?
4. Raise the weight 2 feet. How much work did you do this time?

For Problem Solvers:

Try to determine the amount of work required to raise various objects different distances. Climb a set of stairs. How much work did you do to get to the top? Can you compute the amount of work done in dragging a heavy object 3 feet across the floor? Put the object on a wheeled cart and compare the amount of work required to move it 3 feet.

Teacher Information:

The foot-pound is a standard unit for measuring work. A force of 1 pound moved a distance of 1 foot is 1 foot-pound. Therefore, if a 1-pound weight is lifted 1 foot, 1 foot-pound of work has been done. Lifting the same weight 3 feet requires 3 foot-pounds of work. A 1-pound weight pulled 1 foot across the floor doesn't necessarily represent 1 foot-pound of work. Some device (perhaps a spring scale) is needed to measure the force being applied while the weight is being pulled across the floor. It may be that several pounds of weight could be pulled with a force of 1 pound, depending on the friction between the weight and the surface.

A student climbing a set of stairs needs to consider his or her weight and the *vertical distance* moved, in determining the amount of work done in the process of climbing the stairs. A 100-pound body moved a vertical distance of 10 feet requires 1,000 foot-pounds of work.

Integrating: Math

Skills: Measuring

(Adapted from Activity 34, "How Is Work Measured?" in Tolman and Morton, 1986.)

ACTIVITY 14-2: IN WHAT WAYS IS ENERGY USED IN OUR NEIGHBORHOOD?

Materials Needed:

Paper (divided into two columns)
Pencil

Procedure:

1. Go for a walk around the school yard. Watch for indications of energy being used.
2. In the lefthand column of your paper, describe anything you see happening that uses some form of energy.
3. In the righthand column of your paper, beside the event, write what you think is the form of energy being used.
4. Share your information with the class and discuss your observations.

For Problem Solvers:

In addition to the events you observe that are using energy at the time, look for clues that energy has been used or will probably be used. Use a separate two-column paper. Describe the event you think has used energy or will yet use energy, but is not now using energy. Also identify the type of energy involved.

Teacher Information:

In this activity, students are looking for events that use some form of energy, such as lights burning or fans running. For each event they find, they are to write what form of energy they think is being used—electricity, gasoline, and so on. Be liberal in accepting student responses as they share their observations. Remember: If something moves, energy is being used, even if it is just a leaf blowing in a breeze. It will be interesting to see if students include on their list the chemical energy they use in taking the walk, writing their notes, and so on.

The extension of the activity for problem solvers should trigger the imaginations of your students. A parked automobile could be included on this list, as could the bricks used to build a home (energy was used in making the bricks, as well as in transporting them and placing them in the wall), the boards in a fence, or leaves lying on the ground.

Integrating: Language arts

Skills: Observing, inferring, predicting, communicating, using space-time relationships

ACTIVITY 14-3: IN WHAT WAYS DO WE BENEFIT FROM SOLAR ENERGY?

Materials Needed:

Paper (divided into two columns)
Pencil

Procedure:

1. Go for a walk around the school yard. Watch for clues that solar energy is either being used or has been used in the past.
2. In the lefthand column of your paper, describe anything you see that you think involves solar energy.
3. In the righthand column of your paper, describe how you think solar energy is involved with the thing or the event that you described at the left.
4. Share your information with the class and discuss your observations.

For Problem Solvers:

In addition to the things and events you observe that involve solar energy, consider your list of energy-users from the previous activity and try to trace all of the energy sources back to the sun.

Teacher Information:

Student observations might include such things as a solar-powered calculator, light and heat coming from the sun through the windows, or a solar collector seen on the roof of a house.

In the problem-solving extension, students should consider all energy types and trace them to the sun. For example, gasoline comes from oil, which was formed from organic matter of long ago. The organic matter could not have existed without energy from the sun. From this activity, students should conclude that almost all energy comes ultimately from the sun. Even wind energy results from the heating of air masses by the sun.

Integrating: Language arts

Skills: Observing, inferring, communicating, using space-time relationships

ACTIVITY 14-4:
HOW CAN YOU GET THE MOST ENERGY FROM THE SUN?

Materials Needed:

Three identical jars

Paper and pencil

Black paper

Aluminum foil

Tape

Three thermometers

Sand

Procedure:

1. Fill the three jars with sand.
2. Cover one jar with black paper, including the top, and tape the paper in place.
3. Cover the second jar with aluminum foil, including the top, and tape the foil in place.
4. Leave the third jar uncovered.
5. Record the temperature on the thermometers. Be sure all three indicate the same temperature.
6. Insert one thermometer into the sand of each jar. With the two covered jars, puncture a hole in the top covering and insert the thermometer through the hole.
7. Place all three jars in the sunlight. All should receive the same direct sunlight.
8. Check and record the temperature of the three thermometers every fifteen minutes for about two hours.
9. How do the temperatures compare? What can you say about the effect of a black surface and a shiny surface on absorption of energy from the sun?
10. Remove the jars from the sunlight and continue to record the temperatures of the three thermometers for two more hours.
11. How do the temperature changes compare? What can you say about the effect of a black surface and a shiny surface on heat loss?

For Problem Solvers:

Would the effect of the colored paper be the same with red, blue, or other colors, as with black? Is the effect of the foil the same with the dull side out as with the shiny side out? Devise a way to test these questions, then carry out your plan and report your results to your teacher. Are the effects the same at different times of the day? What materials would help to hold the heat in the jar at night? Try to think of other questions you could investigate with this activity. What implications does your information have for using solar energy in heating water? In heating homes? Ask your teacher to help you find a way to share your information with others.

Teacher Information:

The uncovered jar of sand will provide a control to help students observe the effect of both the black and the shiny surface. The temperature of the jar with the black surface should increase noticeably faster than that of the other two. The foil will reflect heat, and the temperature increase of the sand covered by it should be very slow.

Astronauts wear reflective clothing to help protect them from the direct rays of the sun.

Integrating: Social studies

Skills: Observing, inferring, measuring, communicating, using space-time relationships, formulating hypotheses, identifying and controlling variables, experimenting

(Except for the sections "For Problem Solvers," "Integrating," and "Skills," this activity was reprinted from Activity 36, "How Can You Get the Most Energy from the Sun," in Tolman and Morton, 1986.)

ACTIVITY 14-5:
HOW CAN YOU COOK A HOT DOG IN THE SUN?

Materials Needed:

Shoe box

Poster paper

Aluminum foil

Clear plastic wrap

Coat hanger

Tape

Hot dog

One sunny day!

Procedure:

1. Cut a piece of poster paper the right size to nest in the shoe box, forming a half circle.
2. Nest the poster paper in the shoe box and tape it in place.
3. Cut a section of the coat hanger about 10 centimeters (4 inches) longer than the shoe box. This is your skewer.
4. Bend the skewer at a right angle about 5 centimeters (2 inches) from one end. Bend another right angle about 3 centimeters (1 inch) from the same end. The end that's bent should now be in the form of a crank, resembling the handle of a pencil sharpener (see Figure 14A-1).

Figure 14A-1

This is how your wire should look after you have bent it twice.

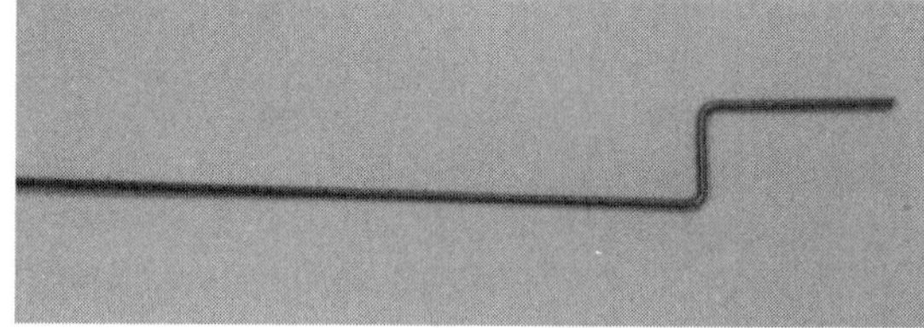

5. Insert the skewer through the shoe box, piercing both ends of the box at about 5 centimeters (1 inch) from the upper edge.
6. Remove the skewer and line the box with aluminum foil. Be careful to keep the surface of the foil as wrinkle-free as possible.
7. Reinsert the skewer in the box, this time pushing it through the hot dog, so the

hot dog is in the middle of the cooker (see Figure 14A-2).

Figure 14A-2

Here is your solar cooker, complete with hot dog!

8. Cover the open face of the cooker with clear plastic wrap.
9. Prop the cooker in such a position that it is aimed toward the sun, and wait while your lunch is cooked!

For Problem Solvers:

Examine the design of the solar cooker. Consider what there is about the cooker that makes it work. What variables could you change to improve it or to accomplish the same thing with a different design? Design your own solar cooker. Does the covering of clear plastic wrap affect the efficiency of your cooker? Would a second layer of plastic wrap help, or hinder? Does it work better in the morning, midday, early afternoon, or evening? What else can you cook in your cooker?

Teacher Information:

An oatmeal box, cut in half lengthwise, could make a fine substitute for the shoe box and poster paper. The purpose of the clear plastic wrap is to take advantage of the greenhouse effect to trap heat within the cooker.

Consider having a contest with the cookers. One possible competition would be to insert the bulb of a thermometer in the hot dog and time the cooking to a predetermined temperature. Those who do the problem-solving extension could have a similar contest using their own designs.

Integrating: Math

Skills: Observing, inferring, measuring, communicating, using space-time relationships, formulating hypotheses, identifying and controlling variables, experimenting

ACTIVITY 14-6: HOW CAN YOU COOK AN APPLE IN A PLASTIC CUP?

Materials Needed:

Clear plastic cup

Styrofoam cup (the plastic cup should nest inside the foam cup)

Thin slices of peeled apple

Tape

Black construction paper (8 1/2 by 11 inches)

Clear plastic wrap

Aluminum foil

Procedure:

1. Place three or four slices of apple inside the clear cup.
2. Cover the top of the clear cup with plastic wrap. Secure the plastic wrap with tape.
3. Line the interior of the foam cup with black construction paper.
4. Place the clear cup inside the foam cup.

5. Form a tall, broad funnel shape with the foil (shiny side in) and place the cups at the bottom of the funnel. Secure the funnel with tape as necessary to maintain its shape (see Figure 14A-3).
6. Your cooker is now ready to use. Prop it up in the sunshine, with the funnel aimed toward the sun. Allow about an hour to cook, but check on it every few minutes, as cooking time will vary greatly, according to such factors as sky conditions, time of day, and outdoor temperature.

For Problem Solvers:

Think of ways to redesign the cooker and make it better. Does the Styrofoam cup fill any useful purpose? Is the plastic wrap needed? What happens if you put the dull side of the foil inside instead of the shiny side? Would larger cups work better? What about smaller cups? Think about other variables you might change to investigate with this activity. What else can you cook in your cooker?

Teacher Information:

Here's another design of a solar cooker for students to experiment with. You could invite them to sprinkle some cinnamon and sugar on their apple slices. The Styrofoam cup is intended to provide insulation. The plastic wrap provides a trapped enclosure to take advantage of the greenhouse effect. Students who do the extension for problem solvers might want to have a contest to see who has the more efficient design.

Integrating: Math

Skills: Observing, inferring, measuring, communicating, using space-time relationships, formulating hypotheses, identifying and controlling variables, experimenting

Figure 14A-3 *This solar cooker, made with a plastic cup and foil, will really cook these apples.*

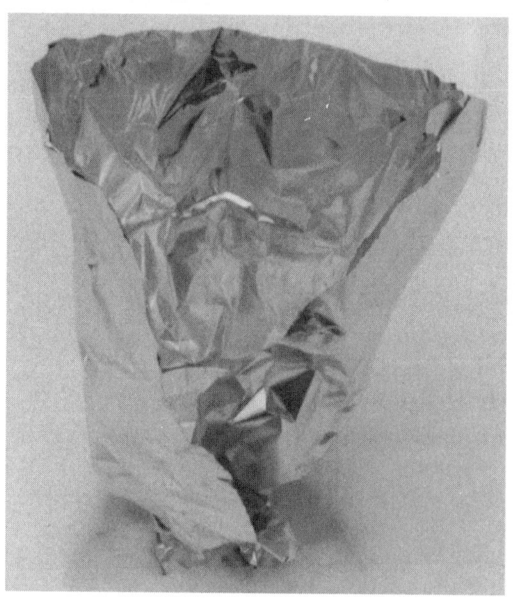

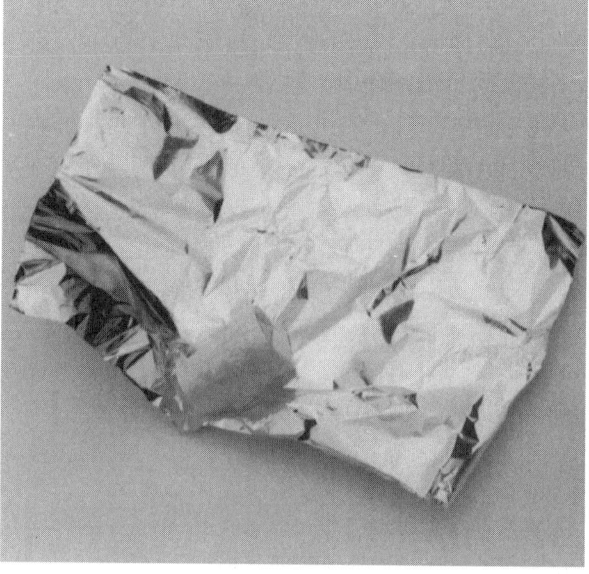

ACTIVITY 14-7: HOW CAN YOU SHOW THE DIFFERENCE BETWEEN KINETIC AND POTENTIAL ENERGY?

Materials Needed:

Rubber band

Procedure:

1. Stretch the rubber band, then release it and let it fly.
2. Describe the rubber band in terms of its kinetic and potential energy at each of the following points:
   a. As it was lying on the table
   b. As you held it in a stretched position, before you released it
   c. While it was flying through the air
   d. After it stopped
3. Find other things in your room—a book on the shelf, a ball, a fan—and describe them in terms of their kinetic and potential energy.

Teacher Information:

Any object at rest has neither potential nor kinetic energy, unless the object is in a position to fall, in which case it has potential energy. A stretched rubber band has potential energy. When the rubber band is released, it has energy of motion, or kinetic energy. After it stops at rest on the floor, it has neither potential nor kinetic energy. Students will be challenged by the final instruction. Those who really know what kinetic and potential energy are should be able to follow a ball through the stages of bouncing and identify the cycle of kinetic energy and potential energy.

Skills: Observing, inferring, communicating

ACTIVITY 14-8: HOW DOES GRAVITY AFFECT HEAVY AND LIGHT OBJECTS?

Materials Needed:

Large book
Small book
Wadded paper
Pencil
Eraser
Paper clip
Paper

Procedure:

1. Take the large book in one hand and the small book in the other. Hold the two books at exactly the same height.
2. Drop both books at the same time. Have someone watch to see which book hits the floor first.
3. Repeat the book drop three times to be sure of your results.
4. Which book falls faster, the large one or the small one?
5. Compare the pencil and the paper in the same way. First predict which you think will fall faster.
6. Compare the various objects, two at a time. In each case, predict which will fall faster, then compare with three drops to test your prediction.
7. Of all the materials you tried, which falls fastest? Which falls more slowly?
8. Explain how the force of gravity compares with objects that are large, small, heavy, and light, according to your findings. How do the falling speeds compare?

9. Compare the falling speed of the wadded paper with that of a flat sheet of paper dropped horizontally.
10. Compare the falling speeds of two flat sheets of paper, one dropped vertically and the other horizontally.
11. Compare the falling speed of the wad of paper with that of a flat sheet of paper dropped vertically.

Teacher Information:

The force of gravity pulls all objects to the earth at the same rate, regardless of the size or weight of the object. Air resistance can slow the rate of fall, so the flat paper, held in horizontal position, will fall more slowly. Except for the factor of air resistance, the rate of fall is equal. In a vacuum, a rock and a feather will fall at the same speed.

Skills: Observing, inferring, measuring, communicating

(This activity was reprinted from Activity 45, "How Does Gravity Affect Heavy and Light Objects?" in Tolman and Morton, 1986.)

III. CONSERVATION OF MASS AND THE RELATIONSHIP BETWEEN ENERGY AND MATTER

ACTIVITY 14-9: WHAT CAN I DO TO HELP CONSERVE ENERGY?

Materials Needed:

Notepaper (two columns)

Pencil

Procedure:

1. Make a list of all the ways you can find that energy is used at school. Write these things in the lefthand column of your paper.
2. In the righthand column, across from each energy-user, write one or more things that you think could be done to decrease the amount of energy used on that thing.
3. Compare your notes with others and discuss them.
4. Make a similar list of energy users at home, including your ideas for decreasing energy usage.
5. Discuss your home energy list with your parent or guardian.

For Problem Solvers:

Okay, problem solvers, let's get serious about it. Go back to your lists of energy users and the ideas you wrote for decreasing energy usage. Study this list and identify at least one or two that you think you could really make a difference with and think of a plan. Write your plan and discuss it with your teacher. Then carry out your plan. Try to include some computed estimates of potential energy savings. If you need to get a group of students and meet with the school principal or custodian, or meet with the teachers in faculty meeting, do it. If it means you need to request a family council to discuss your ideas, do it. Report the results of your efforts to your teacher.

Teacher Information:

The efforts of a few students have been known to get attention for a conservation need when adults couldn't. Encourage any students who choose to pursue the extension for problem solvers. Help them to be sure their plan is reasonable, then help them find a way to be heard. In cases where there are successes to report, be sure they have opportunities to share their successes with others—it might even be a time to invite the media to consider reporting the project to the public. If nothing else, success in such efforts will, in the least, leave the students more aware of conservation needs and more committed to doing their part.

Integrating: Language arts, social studies, math

Skills: Observing, inferring, measuring, predicting, communicating, using space-time relationships, identifying and controlling variables

IV. THE NATURE OF MATTER

ACTIVITY 14-10: WHAT IS INERTIA?

Materials Needed:

Two chairs

Broom

Four lengths of cotton thread, about 40 to 50 centimeters (1.5 feet) each

Two rocks or other weights, about 1 kilogram (2 pounds) each

Procedure:

1. Lay the broom across the backs of two chairs (or other supports).
2. Tie two pieces of thread to the broom handle, several inches apart.
3. Tie one of the rocks to each of the threads attached to the broom handle. The rocks should hang down several inches from the broom handle.
4. Tie each of the other two threads to one of the rocks. These threads should hang freely from the rocks.
5. Hold tightly to one of the lower threads and pull down slowly but firmly until a thread breaks.
6. Hold tightly to the other lower thread and jerk quickly, breaking a thread.
7. Which thread broke when you pulled slowly? Which one broke when you jerked? Explain.
8. Get some new thread and repeat the activity to verify your results.

Teacher Information:

As a lower thread is pulled slowly, the force of the pull is equal on both the upper and lower thread. In addition, the upper thread is supporting the weight of the rock (pull of gravity). Thus, the upper thread will usually break if the two threads are identical.

Newton's first law of motion states that an object at rest tends to remain at rest, and an object in motion tends to remain in motion in the same direction and at the same speed unless it is acted upon by an outside force. This is sometimes referred to as the law of *inertia*. Inertia is the resistance to change referred to in Newton's first law. The rock, in this case, is an object at rest. As the lower thread is given a quick jerk in step 6, the resistance, or inertia, of the rock protects the upper thread from receiving the full impact of the downward force. Thus greater force is applied to the lower thread than to the upper thread, and the lower thread will break.

Integrating: Math

Skills: Observing, inferring, measuring, communicating

(This activity was reprinted from Activity 49, "What Is Inertia?" in Tolman and Morton, 1986.)

ACTIVITY 14-11: IS AIR REAL?

Materials Needed:

Plastic bag

Procedure:

1. Blow up the bag and tie the top.
2. Do you see anything in the bag?
3. Try to roll the bag up. Can you do it?
4. Is the bag empty? Explain what is happening.

Teacher Information:

In doing this activity students will quickly notice that although the bag appears to be empty, because there is nothing visible inside, it really is full of air and air is real. It is matter and all matter takes up space, which is the point of this activity—air takes up space.

Skills: Observing, inferring

ACTIVITY 14-12: HOW STRONG IS AIR?

Materials Needed:

Several plastic bags (about the size of bread sacks or small garbage bags)

Two tables, same size

Procedure:

1. Place a book on a plastic bag.
2. Do you think you can lift the book by blowing air into the bag? Make a prediction.
3. Test your prediction by blowing air into the bag.
4. Put several books on the same bag and predict whether you can lift all of the books by blowing air into the bag.
5. Again, test your prediction by blowing air into the bag.
6. Now lay several bags out on the table, each with the opening at the edge of the table. Next, turn one table upside down on the other. Get volunteers to come up—one for each bag.
7. Together, predict whether you can lift the table by blowing air into the bags.
8. Instruct the participants to blow, all at the same time, when you give the signal.
9. Do it one more time—but this time place a chair on the upside-down table and get a volunteer to sit on the chair.
10. Predict whether you can lift the chair and person, as well as the table.
11. Test your prediction.
12. What do you have to say about this?

Teacher Information:

This activity is a clincher. The purpose of this activity is to make the point that matter takes up space, using air as an example of matter. Those who participate will remember forever that air is matter—that it is real and takes up space. If you want to really give your students a thrill, you can be the one to sit on the chair in the last part of the activity. If you have eight or ten upper elementary students around the table, each with a bag to blow on, they should be able to lift you.

Skills: Observing, inferring, predicting

ACTIVITY 14-13:
IS PERFUME A LIQUID OR A GAS?

Materials Needed:

Bowl

Perfume

Procedure:

1. Pour a few drops of perfume into the bowl.
2. Ask the rest of the group to raise their hands as soon as they smell the perfume.
3. Where were the students sitting who smelled the perfume first? Where were those sitting who smelled it last?
4. What did you learn from this activity?

Teacher Information:

Some students will have a more acute sense of smell than others, but in general students nearer the perfume will smell it first and those farthest away will be the last to smell it. The aroma will fill the room in a short time, giving evidence that the liquid in the bowl changes to a gas. The objective of this activity is to show that materials can change from one state to another—in this case, from a liquid to a gas.

Skills: Observing, inferring, predicting, using space-time relationships

ACTIVITY 14-14:
HOW CAN A SOLID BECOME A LIQUID?

Materials Needed:

Bowl with about 250 milliliters (1 cup) of water

Soup spoon

Sugar (one spoonful)

Procedure:

1. Put one spoonful of sugar into the water and stir it in. Continue to stir until the sugar is completely dissolved into the water.
2. Set the bowl aside where it will not be disturbed.
3. Leave the bowl alone for several days—until the water evaporates.
4. When the water is gone, examine the substance that is left in the bowl.
5. Taste the white substance.
6. What is it? Explain what you think happened.

Teacher Information:

In this activity, students have an experience with sugar dissolving in water, then returning to solid form as the water evaporates. The sugar undergoes a physical change. It dissolves into the water, but no chemical change occurs, as verified by the fact that after the water evaporates, the material in the bowl is sugar. The sugar remained sugar even while it was dissolved in the liquid.

Skills: Observing, inferring

ACTIVITY 14-15:
HOW CAN A SOLID AND A LIQUID MAKE A GAS?

Materials Needed:

Alka-Seltzer tablet

Two empty film cans

Water

Procedure:

1. Place 1/2 Alka-Seltzer tablet in a film can.
2. Put a small amount of water in the second can (about one-eighth full).
3. Pour the water from the second can into the first can. Immediately snap the lid on tight and stand back.
4. What happened?
5. Does this show a physical change or a chemical change? How can you tell?
6. Discuss your observations with your group and compare your ideas.

Teacher Information:

You might choose to use this activity as a demonstration to add an element of surprise, instead of providing the materials and student instructions above. If you do this, pulverize the Alka-Seltzer tablet so that it is not recognizable (mystery powder) and put the equivalent of about 1/2 tablet in a film can (A) before giving the can to students. Give students a second can (B) that contains a small amount of water. Instruct students to leave the lids on the cans until you give the signal, then remove both lids, pour the water from can B into can A, and immediately snap can A lid on tight. Be prepared for a bit of excitement as the lids begin to pop off and go flying through the air. If students put the lids right back on, the process will probably repeat itself three or four times.

Film cans come in opaque black plastic and in translucent plastic. Consider doing this activity twice—once with the opaque can to provide the element of surprise, then with the translucent can so students can see the bubbling action as the liquid and solid react together to form a gas.

Have paper towels on hand for this activity. When both lids and kids are gathered up (good luck!), talk about chemical changes and the fact that in this case a solid combined with a liquid produced a gas (carbon dioxide).

You can do a similar activity to show an example of physical changes by using a small amount of baking soda and vinegar instead of Alka-Seltzer and water. (Another option is to use a small piece of dry ice in the film cans. Recognize, however, that dry ice isn't as harmless as it appears. If dry ice is used, take precautions to see that students do not misuse it, such as by putting it in their mouth or in a glass jar with the lid on.)

Integrating: Language arts

Skills: Observing, inferring, communicating

ACTIVITY 14-16:

IS BURNED SUGAR STILL SUGAR?

(Teacher-supervised activity)

Materials Needed:

Aluminum foil

Sugar

Candle

Match

Hand lens

Procedure:

1. Tear off a piece of aluminum foil, about 15 by 15 centimeters (6 by 6 inches).
2. Put a small amount of sugar in the middle of the foil—1 milliliter of sugar (about the amount that is in a sugar cube) is plenty.
3. Place the candle on another piece of foil and light the candle with the match.
4. Pick up the first piece of foil by the edges and carefully hold the sugar over the flame until some of the sugar turns black.

5. Remove the foil from the flame, set it aside to cool, and blow out the candle.
6. When the burned sugar is cool, examine it carefully. Crumble some of it up. Examine it with a hand lens and compare it with sugar that didn't get burned. Taste a little bit of it. Does it taste like sugar?
7. Was this a physical change or a chemical change?
8. Discuss your observations with your group and share your ideas.

Teacher Information:

Use caution with this activity, both in letting students work with a flame and in asking them to taste the burned sugar. You should be sure students have no food allergies before asking them to taste anything.

This activity will show an example of chemical change. The burned material left on the foil is not sugar, but carbon. Most of the hydrogen and oxygen that were in the sugar have gone into the air as gases. Students should recognize that they cannot retrieve the hydrogen and oxygen and combine them with the carbon again to restore the materials as sugar. It is also important that students understand that nothing has been lost or destroyed except the sugar. The materials that were in the sugar have only been chemically changed to new forms in the process of burning, but all of the carbon, hydrogen, and oxygen atoms that were in the sugar still exist, and those same atoms will likely become a part of many other substances in the future. What a marvelous recycling plan!

Integrating: Language arts

Skills: Observing, inferring, measuring, communicating

ACTIVITY 14-17:
WHAT IS SURFACE TENSION?

Materials Needed:

Small plastic cups of different sizes

Eyedropper

Water

Procedure:

1. Fill one of the small cups level full with water. To be sure it is level full—no more and no less—lay your pencil across the top of the cup and pour in water until the water *barely* touches the pencil. Pour very slowly and carefully when the water level gets near the pencil.
2. Look at the cup that is now level full with water, and estimate how many drops of water you can put on it, using the eyedropper, without spilling over. Each person should make his or her own estimate, and write the number before adding any drops of water.
3. After everyone has written their estimate, begin adding drops and counting. Add the drops carefully—your challenge now is to put as many drops on the cup as you can, without spilling over the side of the cup.
4. How many drops of water were you able to put on the cup that was already level full with water?
5. Are you surprised? Talk about your observations and your ideas.
6. Repeat the entire process, using a cup of a different size.
7. What are you learning about water?

Teacher Information:

This activity is almost a sure thing to bring some surprises, and it will capture student interest for three or four rounds if the cups are not large. A cup with a top diameter the size of a regular drinking glass will hold several hundred drops of water after it is already level full. Smaller cups are best, so students don't become weary of counting. Even a one-ounce pill cup will usually hold about 100 drops, beginning level full. Students will learn as much from smaller cups without spending so much of their time counting drops.

From doing this activity, students should learn something about surface tension. As explained in the content section of this chapter, surface tension is the skin-like effect at the surface of the water that results from cohesion—the attraction of water molecules for each other (applies to other substances as well).

This is also an excellent activity for developing and reinforcing the skill of estimating. The experience of estimating multiple times in a series of similar activities, such as the number of drops of water that can be put on the top of an already-full cup, helps to reinforce this skill. The experience can be extended to related activities, such as estimating the number of drops of water that can be put on coins of different sizes or the number of paper clips, pennies, or nails that can be put in a level-full cup (larger cup). The eyes get bigger as students fill a cup with objects after the cup was already level full with water.

If your students are ready to deal with averages, have them compute the average number estimated by their group and/or the class. After the counting is complete, averages can be computed again.

Integrating: Language arts, math

Skills: Observing, inferring, measuring, predicting, communicating

---

ACTIVITY 14-18:
WHAT ARE MIXTURES AND SOLUTIONS?

Materials Needed:

Two glass jars

Spoons (or stirrers)

Sugar

Water

Marbles or small rocks

Paper clips

Toothpicks

Bits of paper

Paper and pencil

Procedure:

1. Fill each jar about half full of water.
2. Put the marbles, paper clips, toothpicks, and bits of paper in one jar and a spoonful of sugar in the other jar.
3. Stir both jars and observe what happens to the materials in the water.
4. Compare the results in the two jars. One is a mixture and the other is a solution.
5. Try other substances in water, such as sand, powdered milk, or powdered chocolate. Make a list of those you think produce a mixture and those that produce a solution. Explain the differences you observe.

Teacher Information:

A mixture consists of two or more substances that retain their separate identities when mixed together. Solutions result when the substance placed in a liquid seems to become part of the liquid. A solution is really a special kind of mixture—one in which the particles are all molecular in size.

Materials listed can easily be substituted or supplemented with other soluble and nonsoluble materials.

Skills: Observing, inferring, predicting

(This activity was reprinted from Activity 15, "What Are Mixtures and Solutions?" in Tolman and Morton, 1986.)

CHAPTER

HEAT

CHAPTER OUTLINE:

I WONDER . . .

What is "thermal energy"?
How do the words "heat" and "temperature" relate to each other?
What makes an ice skater's skates slick?
What are some ways that energy can be transformed?
What does pressure do to temperature?
What is our main source of heat?
Why are sidewalks made with joints?
Why do many people run hot water over the ring of a fruit jar?
Does water expand when it gets warm as other materials do?
What do impurities do to boiling point and freezing point?
If water did not expand as it freezes, would that be good, or bad? Why?
What are the advantages and disadvantages of evaporative coolers, compared to refrigeration air-conditioners?

I. INTRODUCTION

Few factors affect our lives, in terms of comfort level, where we live, and what we wear, more than does heat and our ability to control it. We place a great deal of importance on keeping ourselves in comfortable temperature conditions, and we expend enormous amounts of resources in that effort. The better we understand what heat really is, and how it can be controlled, the more efficient we can be in our efforts to accomplish that goal.

This chapter defines heat and describes its effects on materials. It also discusses ways heat is transferred, and some of the things people do to control temperatures in their surroundings in an effort to be more comfortable.

II. WHAT IS HEAT?

We often use the term *heat* rather loosely, whether we are referring to warm air coming from a furnace ("The furnace is blowing heat into the room") or the amount of energy in molten iron. Air is *heated* by the furnace and a bar of iron can be heated until it melts. The total amount of energy within either of these materials, however, is more properly referred to as *thermal energy*, and is determined by the movement of molecules (see the discussion of Internal Energy in chapter 14). Heat is actually the *transfer* of thermal energy.

The previous chapter defined kinetic energy as the energy of motion. Thermal energy is a form of kinetic energy. We cannot see the motion involved because it is the motion of molecules. We can, however, see evidence of it, and we can feel its effect. Molecules are always moving, and *temperature* is a measure of how fast they move (on the average). The faster they move the warmer the material is, and the slower they move the cooler it becomes. *Cold* is not a form of energy, but only a term used to describe a condition of low levels of thermal energy.

Temperature and *thermal energy* are not synonymous. Temperature is a *measure of the average kinetic energy of molecules,* whereas thermal energy refers to the *total energy of a substance.* If a cup of water in one container and a gallon of water in another container have the same temperature, the gallon has more thermal energy because there is more of it. You could get burned by a tub of hot water and yet be unharmed by a spark; even though the spark may have much higher temperature than the water, the water has more thermal energy.

Figure 15-1

Rubbing your hands together will produce heat.

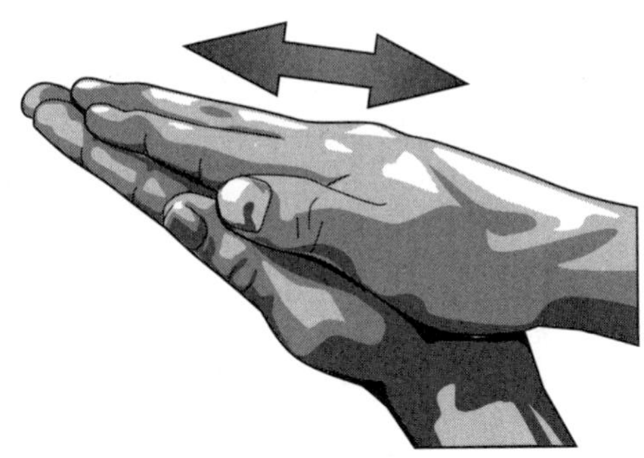

III. ENERGY TRANSFORMATION

Since temperature is a measure of the average kinetic energy of molecules, anything that causes a change in the speed of molecules causes a change in temperature. Molecules are energized by many things, including friction, pressure, percussion, and chemical reactions. These events, and all others that increase molecular movement, increase temperature.

When two surfaces are rubbed together, molecules are energized (their speed increases), and temperatures are increased. Rubbing your hands together briskly for just a few seconds will produce a noticeable increase in the temperature of the skin (see Figure 15-1). The friction involved causes molecules in the skin to move faster, and we feel the result. Try it again after applying some hand lotion. The hand lotion acts as a lubricant and reduces friction, resulting in less change in temperature.

When a gas is compressed, molecules are energized and the temperature rises. That is one of the reasons that weather is typically warmer at lower elevations and colder at higher elevations. At lower elevations, the thickness of the atmosphere is greater, which increases atmospheric pressure. This pressure causes air molecules to move more rapidly, resulting in higher temperatures. With lower pressure at higher elevations, molecules move more slowly, resulting in lower temperatures.

Another example of the effect of pressure on the temperature of a substance has to do with ice skaters. Ice skaters do not really skate on ice, but on a thin layer of water. The pressure of the skate's blades increases the temperature of the ice enough to melt under the blade, and the skater glides along on a very thin lubricating layer of water. Extremely cold temperatures make skating more difficult because the ice does not melt as readily under the pressure of the skate.

Percussion is a form of sudden pressure. When a piece of metal is struck sharply with a hammer, molecules are energized and the metal becomes warmer. After repeated strikes on a thin piece of metal, the temperature change is easily noticeable to the touch.

Chemical reactions frequently produce heat. Such reactions are called *exothermic reactions,* which means that heat is given off. For example, when wood, coal, gasoline, or other fuels burn, heat-producing chemical reactions occur. Exothermic reactions cause molecules to move faster. We see evidence of increased molecular movement in the form of increased temperatures.

When an electric current flows through a wire, resistance of the wire to the flow of electrons produces thermal energy in the wire. By selecting the right size and type of wire, the energy produced can be controlled and used to toast bread, heat homes, and so on. Some materials glow brightly when they are heated by electric current. Light bulb filaments are made of such materials.

Other sources of thermal energy include *solar* energy and *nuclear* energy. The main source of energy on the earth is solar energy. Nuclear energy, either from splitting heavy atomic nuclei (fission) or fusing light nuclei together, is a potential source of tremendous amounts of energy. Nuclear fusion reactions, in fact, are the source of the sun's energy.

IV. TEMPERATURE AND THE STATES OF MATTER

Water can easily be changed from one state to another by changing its temperature. *Freezing point* is the temperature at which a liquid becomes a solid. *Melting point* is the temperature at which a solid becomes a liquid. For water, freezing point and melting point are both at 0 degrees Celsius (32 degrees Fahrenheit). If energy is being added, the water is melting; if energy is being removed, the water is freezing.

Almost all substances have a melting point and a freezing point (always the same temperature for any given substance). For iron the melting point is very high, but even iron will melt if the temperature is high enough. Some materials, depending upon the pressure, change directly from solid to gas without becoming liquid at all. Dry ice (solid carbon dioxide) is such a substance; at room temperature and normal atmospheric pressure, dry ice changes from solid to gas without becoming a liquid. Perhaps surprisingly, even water behaves this way under certain conditions. If the temperature is below 0 degrees Celsius ice can evaporate directly into water vapor, and water vapor can change to ice, without becoming a liquid. This commonly happens when frost forms and evaporates in a freezer.

A liquid becomes a gas as the liquid evaporates and molecules escape into the air. The higher the temperature, the more rapid the evaporation. Evaporation normally occurs at the surface, but if water is heated to a certain point, it can take place within the liquid. When this happens, bubbles form beneath the surface, usually at or near the heat source, and rise to the surface, and we say the water is *boiling*. The temperature at which this happens is called the *boiling point* (see Boiling and Freezing Points, below).

Gas molecules have a lot of energy; they move rapidly and are far apart. Molecules of solids have much less energy and seem to almost vibrate in place, continuously moving but maintaining a regular formation. The molecules of a liquid have less energy than those of a gas, but more than those of a solid (see Figure 14-6). They remain close together, yet are relatively free to move, giving the liquid the property of being able to flow to the shape of its container. (See chapter 14 for information about relative molecular cohesive force of solids, liquids, and gases.)

As energy is added to a substance, the molecules move more rapidly and can result in a solid being changed to a liquid or a liquid to a gas. As energy is removed from a substance, the molecules move more slowly, and can result in a gas being changed to a liquid or a liquid to a solid. As a solid is heated to its melting point, considerable energy must be added to actually change it to a liquid—which happens without increasing temperature (this is called "latent" heat). Only when the material is all melted will the temperature rise further. Something similar happens at the boiling point; after the boiling point is reached, additional energy is required to make the substance actually boil, but temperature does not increase.

V. HEAT CAUSES EXPANSION

Changes occur in materials as energy is added or removed, even if the material does not change from one state to another. In any given state of matter, materials generally expand when heated and contract when cooled.

Even with a solid, the molecules that are vibrating in place vibrate faster when energy is added, causing the material to expand slightly. Liquids expand and contract more than do solids with similar temperature changes. Gases expand and contract much more dramatically than do either solids or liquids.

People have learned to make certain adjustments to compensate for the expansion and contraction that occurs as materials change in temperature; in some cases, they have even learned to use this phenomenon to their advantage. For example, blocks of cement are usually spaced to allow them to expand and contract without buckling or breaking. You have probably noticed expansion joints in sidewalks. If you observe carefully enough during the year, you will notice that the spaces are wider during the winter than during the summer. Telephone lines and power lines are installed with more sag if they are installed in hot weather, so they can contract without breaking and without putting excessive stress on the lines and poles as temperatures drop. Railroad rails are even laid with spaces between the ends to allow the steel to expand and contract as temperatures change.

When a person attempts to open a jar of home-canned fruit, they often find that the jar ring is very difficult to remove. This can be puzzling to those who canned the fruit because they know they did not put it on that tight. Most people learn that the ring is much easier to remove if hot water is first run over it. Some people just do that because someone suggested it and it works. Others know that heating causes the jar ring to expand, loosening its tension around the jar.

Now for the puzzle: Why is the ring so much tighter now than when it was first put on the jar? Consider the temperature of the ring at the time it was put on. It was probably hot, and whoever did the canning likely put the lid on the jar about as tightly as they could. Well, nature did the rest. As the ring cooled, it contracted, becoming tighter and tighter. Heating the ring reverses that process and the ring becomes easier to remove.

Liquids also expand and contract with changes in temperature. A liquid thermometer is made by placing a liquid (alcohol or mercury) in a sealed glass tube with a narrow channel. The channel is called the *bore,* and it is sometimes as fine as a human hair, or finer. As the liquid expands because of increased temperature, it is forced up the tube; as the liquid contracts it comes down the tube again. A scale on the tube indicates the current temperature.

A different type of thermometer is made by laminating strips of two unlike metals together, face to face (see Figure 15-2). This is called a bi-

Figure 15-2

The two metals in a bi-metal thermometer expand and contract at different rates.

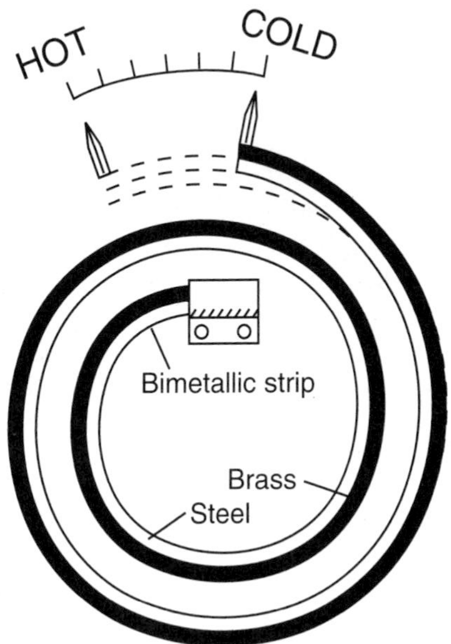

metal (meaning two metals) strip. The two metals expand and contract at different rates, forcing the strip to bend as the temperature changes. The laminated metal strip is connected to a needle that indicates temperature on a scale.

The same device can be used to open and close a switch. In this application it is called a *thermostat,* and it is installed in the electrical circuit of a furnace, refrigerator, or other appliance, to automatically turn the appliance on and off in response to temperature changes.

VI. TEMPERATURE SCALES

The United States is almost alone in its use of the Fahrenheit temperature scale because it is the only major country in the world still not fully using the metric system. The rest of the world, and all scientists including those in the United States, use the Celsius scale. Although our progress is slow in metric implementation, the United States has officially accepted the metric system and we are moving in the direction of compliance with it.

One of the advantages of the metric system is simplicity. For example, consider two basic numbers that students usually memorize when dealing with temperature—freezing point and boiling point of water. On the Celsius scale, these are round numbers, 0 degrees and 100 degrees, which are much easier to remember than the numbers 32 degrees and 212 degrees on the Fahrenheit scale. Although it is generally recommended that students use a conversion chart (see Figure 15-3) rather than take extra time to convert temperatures mathematically, it is helpful to know what to do if a conversion chart is not available. Temperatures can be converted easily by using the following standard formulas (C = Celsius temperature, F = Fahrenheit temperature).

$$C = (5/9)(F - 32)$$

$$F = (9/5)C + 32$$

Figure 15-3

Use this temperature conversion chart to convert Fahrenheit to Celsius.

Fahrenheit to Celsius Degrees
(*Increments of 5 degrees Celsius)

°F	°C	°F	°C	°F	°C
-49	-45 *				
-40	-40 *	36	2	76	24
-31	-35 *	37	3	77	25*
-22	-30 *	38	3	78	26
-13	-25 *	39	4	79	26
-4	-20 *	40	4	80	27
1	-17	41	5*	81	27
2	-17	42	6	82	28
3	-16	43	6	83	28
4	-16	44	7	84	29
5	-15 *	45	7	85	29
6	-14	46	8	86	30*
7	-14	47	8	87	31
8	-13	48	9	88	31
9	-13	49	9	89	32
10	-12	50	10 *	90	32
11	-12	51	11	91	33
12	-11	52	11	92	33
13	-11	53	12	93	34
14	-10 *	54	12	94	34
15	-9	55	13	95	35*
16	-9	56	13	96	36
17	-8	57	14	97	36
18	-8	58	14	98	37
19	-7	59	15 *	99	37
20	-7	60	16	100	38
21	-6	61	16	104	40*
22	-6	62	17	113	45*
23	-5 *	63	17	122	50*
24	-4	64	18	131	55*
25	-4	65	18	140	60*
26	-3	66	19	149	65*
27	-3	67	19	158	70*
28	-2	68	20 *	167	75*
29	-2	69	21	176	80*
30	-1	70	21	185	85*
				194	90*
31	-1	71	22	203	95*
32	0 *	72	22	212	100*
33	1	73	23		
34	1	74	23		
35	2	75	24		

VII. BOILING AND FREEZING POINTS

Boiling point is significantly affected by atmospheric pressure, and therefore by altitude. This fact explains why cooking times are different at different altitudes, why we use pressure cookers, and why we put pressure caps on automobile radiators. When we speak of boiling point being 100 degrees Celsius (212 degrees Fahrenheit), we always specify "at sea level." (For an explanation of the effect of air pressure on boiling point, see chapter 14) Freezing point is lowered by increased pressure, but so slightly that it is not appreciably affected by altitude changes of only a few thousand feet. Water freezes essentially at 0 degrees Celsius (32 degrees Fahrenheit) whether it is at the top of Mt. Everest or at sea level.

Both freezing point and boiling point are affected by impurities. Impurities raise the boiling point *and* lower the freezing point. Antifreeze is added to automobile cooling systems to protect them from damage in very cold temperatures. Sugar or salt, as impurities added to the water, would also offer protection from cold temperatures. We use rock salt on icy sidewalks because it lowers the freezing point of water. However, sugar and salt are corrosive and would ruin an automobile engine. Commercial antifreeze (usually ethylene glycol) will not corrode the engine and is safe for use as the needed impurity in water for winter protection. Many people don't realize that antifreeze is also needed in the summer. While the impurity lowers freezing point, protecting the engine from cold temperatures, it also raises the boiling point, thereby protecting the engine from hot summer temperatures as well. (Antifreeze also usually contains a rust inhibitor, which is needed year-round for protection to the engine and cooling system.)

Water is famous as an exception to the rule of expansion and contraction given above. At most temperatures, water expands and contracts as energy is added or removed, respectively, just as other materials do. However, as temperature decreases toward the freezing point, a strange thing happens. Beginning at about 4 degrees Celsius (39 degrees Fahrenheit), water reverses itself and begins to expand. It continues to expand until freezing point (0 degrees Celsius/32 degrees Fahrenheit) is reached. Actually, the change in density that occurs between 4 degrees Celsius and 0 degrees Celsius is so slight as to be almost undetectable; the change in density occurs upon freezing. Total expansion is nearly 10 percent. (At 0 degrees Celsius the density of ice is 0.917 grams per cubic centimeter; at 0 degrees Celsius, the density of water is 1.000 grams per cubic centimeter.) This happens due to a peculiar characteristic in the structure of the water molecule. As water approaches freezing point, the molecules realign themselves in such a way that they take up more space.

Although this may seem to be a strange twist in nature, you should be very glad that it happens. As water gets colder, it contracts, gets heavier, and sinks toward the bottom of the body of water. But as it gets colder still and approaches freezing temperature, it expands and rises to the top, trapping slightly warmer water below and protecting aquatic life from freezing temperatures. In fact, if water suddenly did not do that any more, it would have very serious consequences for life on this planet. If water continued to contract as it freezes, it would stay at the bottom of a body of water. Lakes and oceans would freeze from the bottom up instead of from the top down. Harsh winters could freeze some bodies of water solid, killing fish and most other forms of life. Thawing of the same bodies of water in the spring and summer would be very slow, and those in colder climates would never thaw completely. Ice caps of the earth would grow and climates would get colder. As it is, ice floats on top of a body of water, offering an insulating cover, preventing rapid loss of heat from water below. In addition, since the ice is on top, it is exposed to the sunshine, so it melts relatively quickly as the weather warms up.

Even so, the expansion of water as it approaches freezing point has both advantages and disadvantages. While that strange twist of nature keeps ice afloat and exposed to the melting powers of the sun, it also breaks water pipes, radiators, and automobile engine blocks. It damages roads, causing "frost heaves" as underlying material freezes, expands, and lifts. As water molecules realign themselves while freezing, they are relentless in their insistence to take up more space, and they do it with seemingly limitless force. This force breaks solid rock with apparent ease, but we'll leave that to the chapter that deals with geology. Suffice it to say here that the expansion of water as it freezes is both a bane and a benefit to humankind.

VIII. HEAT TRANSFER

Having discussed some of the effects of energy transfer, let's consider how thermal energy moves from one place to another. Energy travels by any of three methods: conduction (heat flow), convection, and radiation. Let's discuss these one at a time.

Conduction

Since molecules are constantly moving, they are also constantly bumping into each other. As molecules are energized, or take on more energy, they move faster. We say they have more thermal energy. They bump into other molecules at higher speeds, and the increased kinetic energy is passed on to other molecules, then to still others, in a chain reaction that continues on and on.

The process of molecules bumping into molecules, transferring thermal energy from one to another throughout a substance, is called *conduction* or *heat flow*. Some materials are better heat conductors than others. Materials that are good conductors of heat are usually also good conductors of electricity. Copper, silver, aluminum, iron, and steel are all excellent conductors. Metal cups are not very desirable for hot drinks because heat is conducted so quickly through the metal. In this case, conduction has two negative effects: It burns the hand and it dissipates heat quickly from the liquid. Cooking pans usually have handles covered with wood or a type of plastic to provide insulation from the hot metal when the pan needs to be picked up.

Convection

Convection is a transfer of energy as energy is carried in moving liquids or gases. Materials expand when heated (molecules move faster and spread farther apart), resulting in a reduction of density. As air gets warmer, the heated portion expands; it becomes lighter than the surrounding cooler air, so it rises. The result is that whenever temperature differences exist within a pocket of air, the air will circulate with continuous currents of rising and falling air as the warmer air rises and the cooler air, which is heavier than warmer air, flows in to take its place. The same process takes place in water or in any other liquid or gas. The movement of a fluid due to temperature differences is called a *convection current*. Such currents, on a large scale, are responsible for winds in the atmosphere and for ocean currents. Convection cannot occur in an empty vacuum chamber, because it involves moving molecules of air or other fluid.

Radiation

Heat can also move by *radiation*, which is a transfer of energy by means of electromagnetic waves. This process has nothing to do with moving molecules and therefore can occur within a vacuum. The sun radiates enormous amounts of energy through space, so much that with only one two-billionth of it entering the earth's atmosphere, there is plenty to supply the energy needs of this planet. We are quite fortunate that energy can transfer by radiation, because there are very few molecules in space and the sun's energy could not get to us by either conduction or convection, as both of these processes require matter.

Radiant energy from a freshly started fire in a fireplace works quickly, but conduction is slow because air is a poor conductor and convection currents are weak until air near the fireplace is quite warm. Therefore, you feel the heat immediately on the side of you that is toward the fireplace, but the opposite side of you might still feel cold. Radiant energy from the fire immediately begins to be absorbed by the walls, furniture, and so on. The air in the room is slowly heated by these objects and by convection currents as warm air near the fireplace rises and cooler air moves in from below.

When radiant energy, such as that which comes from the sun, strikes a solid, opaque object, the energy is absorbed and the molecules of the object move faster, so the object becomes warmer. The air is then warmed by the surfaces of such objects. Radiant energy has then been transformed into thermal energy.

The amount of radiant energy that becomes thermal energy depends on the type of material it strikes. Dark, rough materials absorb energy quickly, and the temperatures of such materials increase accordingly. Light-colored, smooth materials reflect much of the radiant energy that strikes them, with relatively little temperature change.

Transparent materials, such as air and glass, allow radiant energy to pass through with little effect. However, energy reemitted (reflected) from objects is in the form of longer, slower-vibrating waves, which do not pass through transparent materials easily. For this reason, an automobile standing in the sun gets very warm inside if the windows are left closed on a hot, sunny day. Indeed, it can get quite warm even if the air temperature outdoors is quite cool. Greenhouses take advantage of this effect; in fact, this phenomenon is called the *greenhouse effect*.

IX. INSULATION

People have a very low tolerance for change in temperature. Within a range of just a few degrees, we reach for a sweater or a fan, for a heater or an air-conditioner. Thus we often have need to control the transfer of energy, to keep it where we want it and to keep it away from where we don't want it to be. Knowing how to accomplish this not only helps us to remain comfortable, but it helps us to preserve our food and protect computers and other equipment that require controlled temperatures. Since energy is transferred by conduction, convection, and radiation, our challenge in temperature control includes being able to block these three processes. To do that we use *insulation* (materials that can be used to stop the conduction of heat).

Metals are good conductors and therefore poor insulators. Wood is a very poor conductor and therefore a good heat insulator. Glass, rubber, and most other nonmetals are also good insulators. Gases (including air) are especially good insulators, if convection currents can be kept low, because the molecules are so far apart, greatly slowing the transfer of kinetic energy. Gas molecules collide with other gas molecules much less frequently than do molecules of solids or liquids. Most nonmetals containing numerous small air spaces are good insulators. These include such materials as wood, cork, wool, and plastic foam. A vacuum space is still more effective as an insulator; it cannot conduct heat because there are no molecules to transfer the energy, so radiation is the only heat-transfer mechanism possible.

Clothing

We insulate our bodies from the cold by wearing clothing that holds in the energy our bodies produce. Our bodies are designed to maintain a temperature of 37 degrees Celsius (98.6 degrees Fahrenheit). All we need to do to stay warm in cold weather is trap that energy, so it doesn't escape into the atmosphere.

Fabric is a poor heat conductor, as is air, so a fabric that has numerous trapped air spaces, frequently called "dead air spaces," is excellent for making cold-weather clothing. Wool is especially good for this purpose because of countless dead air spaces. Goose down is used as an insulating layer between layers of fabric for the same reason, as are some synthetic materials, including foam padding. It is important that while trapping body heat, the clothing also allows moisture to dissipate, so body perspiration can escape.

Dark colors tend to absorb energy from sunlight, which makes them warm, while light colors reflect sunlight. Therefore dark colors are usually best for cold-weather clothing and light colors are usually preferred for warm weather.

Most of us think of insulated clothing only in terms of protecting us from cold weather. When we get uncomfortably warm, we wear light clothing or we take some of it off (be careful, not too much!). But some parts of the world are so warm that clothing must actually be worn to insulate from the heat. The people of Arabian countries, for instance, have long been known to wear extra clothing to protect them on a hot day.

Homes and Other Buildings

Homes, schools, and offices can be extremely expensive to heat during cold weather and to cool during hot weather unless measures are taken to minimize the transfer of heat energy through the walls. Even in moderate climates, furnaces and air-conditioners are often needed at certain times of the year. Both cost and comfort level can be far more tolerable if buildings are well insulated.

The same principles we discussed regarding clothing apply to protecting buildings from temperatures that are too warm or too cold for comfort. Light colors are more inclined to reflect sunlight, and dark colors absorb sunlight better. This presents more of a dilemma for buildings than for clothing, because the color of buildings can't be changed from day to day or from season to season. In moderate climates, the colors of buildings are probably more often selected for aesthetics than for temperature control, because in those climates both light and dark colors have their advantages at different times of the year. In very warm climates, light colors are more often used (see Figure 15-4).

Homes and other buildings are insulated by installing fiberglass, rock wool, plastic foam, or other insulating material between inner and outer walls and above ceilings. Weather-stripping can be used to prevent air leakage (convection) around doors and windows. Double window panes are often used because the dead air space between them greatly reduces the amount of heat transfer; or a sealed vacuum space between the panes is still more effective. Insulated doors can also be used. Outside walls are often made of poor heat-conducting material, thus adding insulating qualities to the walls. Such materials include wood, brick, cinderblock, and in some locations adobe, which has excellent insulating qualities. Compacted earth, another material with superb insulating value, is used in a type of architecture called "rammed earth."

X. HEATING AND COOLING OUR HOMES

There was a time when many groups of people migrated from season to season, like birds, to warmer and cooler climates, in order to live in

Figure 15-4

This school is painted white to reflect the desert's heat.

tolerable temperature conditions throughout the year. Without adequate means of protecting themselves from severe temperatures, these groups were quite limited as to the regions where they could set up housekeeping. Today, facilities and equipment are available to combat the weather of almost any climate, allowing people to live in most any area that appeals to them.

Heating

Except in very warm climates, homes are typically heated with central furnaces fueled by natural gas, oil, propane, or electricity. Most heating systems either heat the air directly, circulating the heated air throughout the house or else they use a hot-water system. In a hot-water system, the furnace is used for heating water; the water is then circulated through radiators located throughout the house. The radiators heat the rooms by radiation and by air-convection currents.

Cooling

Since temperature is a measure of the average kinetic energy of molecules, cooling is a process of removing heat, or causing molecules to slow down. Whatever can be done to slow the movement of molecules in a substance will remove heat from that substance.

Evaporative coolers

Again, Mother Nature thought of it first, but many homes in dry climates are cooled by *evaporative coolers.* Evaporation is a cooling (energy-removing) process. As water evaporates, the molecules of highest energy are the ones that escape into the air, leaving behind those of lesser energy. Our bodies use this principle through perspiration to help regulate body temperature. In an evaporative cooler, water is circulated through filters. Air is forced through the wet filters, speeding the evaporation process and cooling the air as it passes through the filters. The same fan that forces air through the filters blows the cooled air into the house, offering welcome relief to its inhabitants. (See chapter 21 for a discussion of the cooling effect of evaporation.)

Evaporative coolers have certain limitations. Evaporation is not fully controlled by a switch on the wall, nor can the temperature inside a home that uses an evaporative cooler be thus controlled. Effective evaporation is dependent on certain atmospheric conditions, namely heat and low relative humidity. As is explained in chapter 21, evaporation slows down as relative humidity increases. Evaporative coolers are therefore not effective in humid climates. Even in dry climates, where they perform at their best, they take a back seat to refrigeration systems in terms of precise control of temperature in a room or building. Evaporative coolers also pump a lot of moisture into the air, which may be desirable in a dry climate.

Refrigeration

Homes cooled by *refrigeration systems* do not depend on certain atmospheric conditions in order for the air conditioning to function properly. This method of cooling also has the advantage of precise temperature control. While evaporative coolers can definitely cool the air on a hot, dry day, refrigeration systems can control cooling within a degree or two of a specified temperature; set a thermostat on the wall to the desired temperature, and that's the temperature you get. Perhaps the difference could be compared with the results of using a wood stove and using a central furnace during cold weather: The wood stove has the ability to warm the home; but with a central furnace, one can set a thermostat to the desired temperature and expect that temperature to be maintained. Evaporative coolers can provide cool air, but a refrigeration system can keep temperatures constant by thermostatic control.

Another factor that often influences decisions of which cooling system to install is cost. Evaporative coolers are relatively inexpensive to install and they operate on very little energy. Electricity is needed to operate the fan that forces air through the filters and into the home, and a small electric motor is also used to pump water and keep the filters wet. The refrigeration system is much more costly, both to install and to operate.

Actually, refrigeration systems are a type of evaporative cooler. They use the principle of evaporation as a cooling process, but instead of water they use a liquid refrigerant, such as Freon, that evaporates at a much faster rate than does water. The refrigerant is circulated through a system of sealed tubes within the air conditioner (or within the walls of the freezing compartment of a refrigerator). The fluid evaporates as it circulates, rapidly absorbing heat energy from the surrounding air. Sealed inside the tubes, the refrigerant is then compressed under great pressure, which transforms the refrigerant back into liquid form, and it continues this cycle. The liquid refrigerant circulates through the cooling system, evaporating within its chamber of sealed tubes and drawing heat energy from its surroundings, then being compressed and returned to liquid form. As the refrigerant is compressed, the heat that it absorbed while evaporating is emitted into the air in a location outside the building or, in the case of the food refrigerator, out into the room air. (Because of this emission of heat, one should not place a refrigerator in a room that one is trying to keep cold.) The major operation cost with a refrigeration system is in the energy required to operate the compressor.

Energy Sources for Heating and Cooling

Heating and cooling buildings uses huge amounts of energy. Unfortunately, the lion's share of that energy currently comes from fossil fuels (coal, oil, and natural gas), which are limited and will eventually expire. Other forms of energy are available and must be developed to assume a major role in these and other processes that consume so much energy. For instance, nuclear energy can already heat and cool homes in areas where nuclear power plants have been allowed, although many people are nervous about the very existence of nuclear plants. Also, more efficient ways of using solar energy are being developed; this unlimited source of energy promises many exciting possibilities for future heating and cooling of our homes and other buildings.

XI. IN CLOSING

As students better understand the ways that thermal energy is used and controlled, they will perceive more clearly the ways in which they can personally help in the effort to use energy resources wisely. With a knowledge of the role of various heat-control factors, such as color, dead air spaces, and convection currents, they will have increased insight regarding the effect of building designs. They will also be better prepared to make appropriate selections of personal articles, such as clothing and sleeping bags.

LIST OF RESOURCES

Ballif, Jae R., and William E. Dibble, *Physics: Fundamentals and Frontiers* (New York: John Wiley & Sons, 1972).

"Heat," *World Book Encyclopedia*, 1989.

Tolman, Marvin N., and James O. Morton, *Physical Science Activities for Grades 2–8* (West Nyack, NY: Parker Publishing Co., 1986).

Victor, Edward, *Science for the Elementary School, Sixth Edition* (New York: Macmillan Publishing Co., 1989).

CHAPTER

HEAT

ACTIVITIES

II. WHAT IS HEAT?

ACTIVITY 15-1:

HOW DOES TEMPERATURE CHANGE AFFECT MOLECULES?

Materials Needed:

None

Procedure:

1. Students should get into a group and move around slowly, not together but in random movement. They represent molecules in this activity.
2. Assign one student to be the caller. He or she will control the "temperature" simply by calling out "Raise the temperature" or "Lower the temperature."
3. All "molecules" should move more quickly when the temperature is raised. They should slow down when the temperature is lowered.
4. The caller should raise and lower the temperature several times, lowering it until the molecules almost stop moving, and raising it until they are running around.

Teacher Information:

Students represent molecules in this activity, which is best done outdoors. We are not dealing yet with the differences in molecular movements of solids, liquids, and gases, but only showing that molecules increase in energy (move faster) when heat is added to a system and they decrease in energy as heat is removed. This activity works well with small children. Older children can discuss changes in molecular movement, but may or may not feel comfortable in acting it out.

Integrating: Language arts, physical education

Skills: Observing, inferring, communicating

III. ENERGY TRANSFORMATION

ACTIVITY 15-2: WHAT DOES FRICTION DO TO TEMPERATURE?

Materials Needed:

Hand lotion

Procedure:

1. Rub your hands together for a few seconds.
2. What do you feel?
3. Put hand lotion on your hands, then rub them together again.
4. What is different this time?
5. Share your ideas. Talk about what happened.

For Problem Solvers:

Get a hammer, a nail, and a board. Drive the nail into the board. Pull the nail out of the board with the hammer, then feel the nail. Share with others what happened. Find other ways to use friction to generate heat.

Teacher Information:

Friction transforms mechanical energy into heat, and it will be easily noticed by students as they rub their hands together. This is a good time for your students to practice tracing the source of energy back to the sun: (1) plants use solar energy to make food; (2) we eat the plants (or animals eat the plants and we eat the animals); (3) our bodies get chemical energy from the plants or animals we eat; (4) our muscles transform some of the chemical energy (food energy) into mechanical energy as we rub our hands together; (5) in rubbing our hands together we create friction; (6) friction transforms some of the mechanical energy into heat.

If hand lotion is not convenient for students to use for this activity, water also works quite well as a lubricant for a short time. Students who do the extension for problem solvers will think of other ways to use friction to generate heat.

Integrating: Language arts

Skills: Observing, inferring, communicating, experimenting

ACTIVITY 15-3: WHAT DOES PRESSURE DO TO TEMPERATURE?

Materials Needed:

Hammer

Piece of metal

Procedure:

1. Strike the piece of metal with the hammer several times.
2. Feel the metal. What has happened to it?
3. Talk about it. Share your ideas with your group.

For Problem Solvers:

Do some research and see what you can learn about what pressure does to temperature. Find out what "percussion" means and figure out how it relates to the above activity. Study about ice skaters and find out why their skates glide along on the ice and why the skates don't work as well in extremely cold temperatures.

Teacher Information:

Pressure increases temperature. Striking the metal with a hammer is *percussion*, which is a form of sudden temperature. Students who do the extension for problem solvers might be interested learning about such tools as air wrenches and jackhammers. Perhaps they could talk to someone who uses these tools and ask about the heat generated from using them. Jackhammers are often used in construction, and air tools of various kinds are used in mechanic shops and auto body shops. Tools used in these shops include air-powered chisels, which are something like a miniature jackhammer.

It would also be of interest for these students to talk to an expert ice skater and learn about the role of pressure in melting the ice, which enables the skate to glide along on a thin, lubricating layer of water.

Integrating: Language arts

Skills: Observing, inferring, communicating, research

ACTIVITY 15-4: HOW CAN CHEMICALS CREATE HEAT?

Materials Needed:

Pint jar

Plastic spoon

Thermometer

Calcium chloride

Water

Procedure:

1. Put about 250 milliliters (1 cup) of water into the jar. The temperature of the water will be fine just as it comes out of the tap.
2. Measure the temperature of the water and record the temperature.
3. Add 1 spoonful of calcium chloride to the water and stir it in.
4. As soon as the calcium chloride has dissolved, measure and record the temperature again.
5. Has the temperature changed? Which direction, and how much?
6. Try it again, this time adding 2 spoonfuls of calcium chloride.
7. What do you think about this? Discuss your results.

For Problem Solvers:

What do you think would happen if you used 3 spoonfuls of calcium chloride? Four? Set up an experiment to find out how much effect calcium chloride really does have on the temperature of water. Identify your variables and include a control. Write your hypothesis. Ask your teacher to approve your plan before you actually begin the experiment. Make a graph of your results. Share your findings with others.

Teacher Information:

Combining calcium chloride with water produces an exothermic reaction, meaning that it gives off heat. Students will find that the heat produced is both measurable and predictable. This activity provides an excellent opportunity for motivated students to do actual scientific experimentation.

Integrating: Math

Skills: Observing, inferring, measuring, predicting, communicating, formulating hypotheses, identifying and controlling variables, experimenting

IV. TEMPERATURE AND THE STATES OF MATTER

ACTIVITY 15-5: WHAT ARE SOLIDS, LIQUIDS, AND GASES?

Materials Needed:

Ice cube

Plate

Hand lens

Sunshine

Procedure:

1. Place the ice cube on the plate.
2. Is the ice cube a solid, a liquid, or a gas?
3. With the lens, examine the ice cube very carefully, especially where it is melting. Watch the ice crystals become liquid.
4. Separate one small drop from the rest of the water on the plate.
5. Put the plate on a window sill in warm sunlight.
6. Examine the small drop of water with the lens for several minutes.
7. What happened to the liquid? What is it now? Explain what you saw the best you can.

Teacher Information:

Water exists abundantly in nature as a solid, a liquid, and a gas. This activity gives students an experience with water in all three states. If they are patient enough to observe the ice cube in the process of melting and the drop in the process of evaporating, the concept of the states of matter will be reinforced in their minds. With a hand lens, it's really quite interesting to watch the changes take place. Try it yourself if you get a chance.

Skills: Observing, inferring

ACTIVITY 15-6: HOW CLOSE ARE MOLECULES IN SOLIDS, LIQUIDS, AND GASES?

Materials Needed:

None

Procedure:

1. Get in a group on the playground, without very much space between people—just elbow room. All of you are now molecules.
2. Students should turn back and forth and move their feet, but stay in their place and not move around in the group. This represents a solid substance. Each molecule moves constantly but stays in place.
3. Now the ice is beginning to melt. Everyone should move around in the group, but without the group getting any larger. This represents a liquid. Molecules are constantly moving, and they flow past each other easily, but the volume of the substance doesn't increase appreciably.
4. Now the water is beginning to evaporate. Everyone should begin to move faster and faster, without trying to stay within the same boundaries. This represents a gas. Notice that the molecules are moving much faster than they were, and the volume of the substance increased dramatically.
5. Discuss the experience in terms of the solid, liquid, and gaseous forms of water that you saw in the previous activity.

Teacher Information:

This activity takes off from Activity 15-1, but goes a step further to illustrate that molecules move differently in solids, liquids, and gases. Young children enjoy acting out the movements of molecules. If your students don't feel comfortable with dramatizing the movements, you might just prepare a transparency of Figure 15-4 and discuss it. Perhaps if you asked students to try to think of a way to illustrate the concept, they would be out on the playground acting it out as an idea of their own.

Integrating: Physical education

Skills: Observing, inferring, using space-time relationships

V. HEAT CAUSES EXPANSION

ACTIVITY 15-7:

WHAT HAPPENS TO SOLIDS AS THEY ARE HEATED AND COOLED?

(Teacher-supervised activity)

Materials Needed:

Wire, about 1 meter (1 yard) long

Large nail or small bolt

Candle

Match

Procedure:

1. Wrap one end of the wire around the nail and anchor the other end to a support. Adjust the wire so the nail swings freely but barely misses the table or floor.
2. Light the candle and heat the wire.
3. Observe the nail. What happened?
4. Remove the candle and allow the wire to cool.
5. Observe the nail. What happened?
6. What can you say about the effect of heat on solids?

Teacher Information:

Caution: This activity uses open flame, necessitating close supervision.

As the wire is heated by the candle, it will expand, and the nail, which was swinging freely above the surface, will drag. As it cools, the wire will contract and the nail will swing freely again. Other solids expand and contract similarly when heated and cooled.

If students have had experience with home-canned fruit, ask what they do when they can't get the ring off of the fruit jar. Most people learn, at some time, to run hot water over the ring, but many people do not know why the technique works. An excellent application for what has been learned would be to challenge students to explain why people run hot water over the ring. If they can explain this, they should be able to explain how the ring became so tight in the first place.

Skills: Observing, inferring

(This activity was reprinted from Activity 39, "What Happens to Solids as They Are Heated and Cooled?" in Tolman and Morton, 1986.)

ACTIVITY 15-8:

WHAT HAPPENS TO LIQUIDS AS THEY ARE HEATED AND COOLED?

Materials Needed:

Narrow-necked juice bottle or soda bottle

One-hole rubber stopper to fit the bottle

Balloon stick

Water

Food coloring

Bowl

Procedure:

1. Fill the bottle with water.
2. Put several drops of food coloring into the water.
3. Insert the tube (balloon stick) through the top of the stopper until it extends slightly out the bottom of the stopper.
4. Press the stopper into the jar of colored water until the water is forced part way up into the tube.
5. Mark the tube at the water level.
6. Place the bottle in the bowl in case colored water comes out the top of the tube.
7. Find a way to warm and cool the water. To warm it, you could put it near a heater, place it in the sunshine, or just wrap your hands around it for a few minutes.
8. What happens to the water level in the tube as the water temperature goes up?
9. What happens to the water level in the tube as the water temperature goes down?
10. Discuss your ideas about what is really happening.

For Problem Solvers:

The device you just made can become a thermometer. Place it on a table, next to the wall, and put a paper behind it that you can write on. Make a mark on the paper at the water level in the tube. Read the current temperature from a commercial thermometer and write the temperature beside the mark. As the temperature changes, record the temperatures on your paper. Then put the commercial thermometer aside and use your homemade thermometer to check the temperatures each day. Do you think your thermometer will respond as rapidly to temperature changes as the commercial thermometer does? Why or why not?

Teacher Information:

In doing this activity, students make a thermometer. Although its use is limited to the range of mild temperatures, this thermometer can be calibrated and then used to determine atmospheric temperature with considerable accuracy. It will be relatively slow to respond to temperature changes because of the relatively large amount of liquid involved. Students who do the extension for problem solvers should note that their commercial thermometer has only a tiny bulb of liquid (usually alcohol) and therefore adjusts quite quickly to changes in air temperature.

Balloon sticks are available from party supply stores. For this activity, the solid white color is preferable to the colorful patterns that are available, because the colored water in the tube shows through more distinctly.

This activity is repeated in the chapter on weather, as one of several homemade weather instruments students can construct and use. The purpose of the activity at this point is to illustrate that liquids expand when heated and contract when cooled. Using water to represent liquids will help to dispel misconceptions that water is an exception to the rule of expansion and contraction. Although water expands as it freezes, unlike other substances, at higher temperatures it behaves similar to other substances in that it expands with increasing temperature and contracts with decreasing temperature.

Integrating: Math

Skills: Observing, inferring, measuring

(Adapted from Activity 40, "What Happens to Liquids as They Are Heated and Cooled?" in Tolman and Morton, 1986.)

ACTIVITY 15-9:

WHAT HAPPENS TO GASES AS THEY ARE HEATED AND COOLED?

Materials Needed:

Narrow-necked juice bottle or soda bottle

One-hole rubber stopper to fit the bottle

Balloon stick

Water

Food coloring

Bowl

Procedure:

1. Put about 2 to 3 centimeters (1 inch) of water in the jar.
2. Put a few drops of food coloring into the water.
3. Insert the tube (balloon stick) through the top of the stopper until it extends about 1 centimeter (1/2 inch) or so out the bottom of the stopper.
4. Press the stopper into the bottle. Do not try to force water part way up into the tube.
5. Place the bottle in the bowl in case water overflows out the top of the tube.
6. Predict whether the water level will change more or less, with changes in temperature, than with the device you made in the last activity that you filled all the way up with water.
7. Find a way to warm the bottle. You could put it near a heater, place it in the sunshine, or just wrap your hands around it for a few minutes.
8. What happens to the water level in the tube as the air temperature in the bottle goes up?
9. What happens to the water level in the tube as the air temperature goes down?
10. How do the changes compare with the changes from the previous activity? Why?
11. Discuss your ideas about what is happening.

For Problem Solvers:

See if you can make this device become a thermometer. Consider the differences between this device and the one you made in the previous activity. What are the major differences? Which one is most useful as a thermometer? Why?

Teacher Information:

At first glance, this might appear to be a repetition of the previous activity—and it is, in fact, very similar. In the previous activity, the bottle was filled with water, whereas this activity includes only enough water to provide an indicator of change. The bottle is mostly filled with air this time—and that's an important difference. Changes noted in the liquid level in the tube will result from expansion and contraction of air, which will be much more dramatic than the changes noted from expansion and contraction of water in the previous activity. And that's the point: Gases expand and contract much more with a given change in temperature than do liquids or solids.

Another difference your problem solvers might deduce is that this device will be affected by changes in atmospheric pressure, as well as by changes in temperature.

Integrating: Math, language arts

Skills: Observing, inferring, predicting, measuring, formulating hypotheses

(Adapted from Activity 41, "What Happens to Gases as They Are Heated and Cooled?" in Tolman and Morton, 1986.)

ACTIVITY 15-10:
WHY DO SIDEWALKS HAVE JOINTS?

Materials Needed:

Paper
Pencil
Ruler
Lots of patience

Procedure:

1. You will do part of this activity now and part of it later, when the weather changes.
2. On a warm day, find four sidewalk joints that you are sure you can find again later on. Find a way to number them 1, 2, 3, and 4.
3. Measure the spaces between the blocks of concrete.
4. Record on your paper the widths of joint 1, joint 2, joint 3, and joint 4.
5. Predict what the same widths will be on a cold day. Write your predictions.
6. On a cold day, measure those same spaces again and record the widths of the joints again.
7. How do the widths of the joints on a warm day compare with the widths of the same joints on a cold day?
8. Review your predictions. How accurate were they?
9. What seems to be happening? From what you have learned, explain why.

For Problem Solvers:

Think about the way you compared sidewalk joints on warm and cold days. Find a way to also compare the sag in power lines on warm and cold days. Think about what you expect to happen, based on what you already know, and write your hypothesis. What are the variables involved?

Try to arrange to interview a building contractor, a cement contractor, or a power company line worker. Before you meet with the person, write down some questions you might ask about what their people do to allow for changes in temperature. It's okay if you think of more questions during the interview. Report what you learn.

Teacher Information:

The instructions suggest taking the first measurement on a warm day and the follow-up measurement on a cold day. That sequence could be reversed and have the same result. On a long-term basis, you might consider taking some photographs of sidewalk joints and power lines on hot days and very cold days. Be sure the photographs are paired to compare the same locations. You might try to arrange for a visit to your class by a building contractor, cement worker, line worker, or other person who has insight regarding compensating for extreme temperature changes. The class could prepare questions together for the visitor and conduct a group interview.

Integrating: Language arts, social studies

Skills: Observing, inferring, measuring, predicting, communicating, using space-time relationships, formulating hypotheses, identifying variables

VI. TEMPERATURE SCALES

ACTIVITY 15-11:

HOW DO CELSIUS AND FAHRENHEIT TEMPERATURE SCALES COMPARE?

Materials Needed:

Thermometer with both Celsius and Fahrenheit scales

Paper

Pencil

Ruler

Procedure:

1. Make five columns on your paper. In the first column, make a list of several different locations in and near the building, where you will measure the temperature. If possible, at least one of these should be in the sunshine and one in the shade. Also, try to get permission to check the temperature inside someone's car.
2. Beside the first location on your list, in the second column, write your estimate of the temperature in degrees Celsius.
3. In the fourth column, write your estimate of the temperature in degrees Fahrenheit for the first location.
4. Now take your thermometer and check your estimate for the first location by measuring the temperature at that location. Record the actual reading of degrees Celsius in column 3 and degrees Fahrenheit in column 5.
5. Compare your estimates with the actual temperature readings.
6. Next write your estimates for the second location, then measure the temperature for that location.
7. Continue in this way through your list of locations. Each time, be sure you check the accuracy of your last estimates, then write your estimates for the next location before you measure the temperature at that location.
8. Are your estimates becoming more accurate?
9. Compare notes with others. Discuss your results.

For Problem Solvers:

Think of other things you could do to become well acquainted with both of the temperature scales. Also find some other ways to develop your estimating skills.

Teacher Information:

This activity should help students feel better acquainted with the two temperature scales. For the foreseeable future, they will need to be competent with both. The instructions to the problem solvers also suggest that they think of ways to further develop their estimating skills. Help them think of this in terms of identifying a series of similar activities in order that they can write an estimate, check their estimate, write another, check it, and so on, getting immediate feedback each time on the accuracy of their estimates, and hopefully improving as they go.

Integrating: Math

Skills: Observing, inferring, measuring, estimating

VII. BOILING AND FREEZING POINTS

ACTIVITY 15-12:

HOW CAN YOU DISCOVER THE BOILING POINT OF WATER?

(Teacher-supervised activity)

Materials Needed:

Celsius thermometer

Saucepan

Hotplate

Water

Procedure:

1. Put about 2 to 3 centimeters (1 inch) of water in the saucepan.
2. Predict how hot you will be able to get the water when you put the pan on the hotplate. Write your prediction.
3. Put your thermometer in the water, put the pan on the hotplate, and get the water as hot as you can. Get permission from your teacher before you begin, and be very careful.
4. Check the temperature of the water as it is heating. When you think it is as hot as it can get, write the temperature.
5. Compare the temperature of the water with your predicted temperature.
6. Talk about what you learned. Do you think you could get the water hotter on a bigger stove? What if you used a larger pan, with more water—could you get it hotter?

For Problem Solvers:

After you get the water as hot as you can get it, add some salt. Don't put in more salt than will dissolve into the water. Continue heating, stirring, and checking the temperature. Does the salt seem to make any difference in the maximum temperature? If so, do some research and see if you can find out why.

If you would like to pursue this further, try adding something else to the water instead of salt, such as sugar or anything that will dissolve into the water. Compare the results—experiment with the different materials and try to determine what has the greatest effect. Each time you try a new substance, think about what you have learned and write a hypothesis stating what you think will happen, based on what you already know. Can you predict the change in boiling point based on the amount of water and the amount of substance added to the water? Do you think antifreeze in the cooling systems of automobiles has any value in the summer?

Teacher Information:

Boiling point is 100 degrees Celsius if it is pure water at sea level. Boiling point is affected by altitude and it is affected by impurities. With this activity, students will discover the boiling point of tap water at their altitude, and they will discover that they cannot raise the temperature of water beyond the boiling point. Those who care to pursue the extension for problem solvers will also discover that boiling point is affected by impurities. They will experiment with different substances as additives and compare the effect, based on the substance added and the amount.

Integrating: Math

Skills: Observing, inferring, measuring, predicting, formulating hypotheses, identifying and controlling variables, experimenting

ACTIVITY 15-13:
HOW CAN YOU DISCOVER THE FREEZING POINT OF WATER?

Materials Needed:

Celsius thermometer

Saucepan

Ice

Water

Procedure:

1. Put about 2 to 3 centimeters (1 inch) of tap water in the saucepan.
2. Predict the temperature of tap water. Check the temperature of the water with your thermometer.
3. Predict how cold you will be able to get the water by adding ice to it. Write your prediction.
4. Put your thermometer in the water, add some ice, and get the water as cold as you can.
5. Check the temperature of the water as it cools. When you think it is as cold as you can get it, record the temperature.
6. Compare the temperature of the water with your predicted temperature.
7. Talk about what you learned. Do you think you could get the water colder with more ice? Bigger pieces? Smaller pieces? By stirring?

For Problem Solvers:

After you get the water as cold as you can get it, add some salt. Don't put in more salt than will dissolve into the water. Continue cooling, stirring, and checking the temperature. Does the salt seem to make any difference in the minimum temperature? If so, do some research and see if you can find out why.

If you would like to pursue this further, try adding something else to the water instead of salt, such as sugar, rubbing alcohol, or anything that will dissolve into the water. Compare the results—experiment with the different materials and try to determine what has the greatest effect. Each time you try a new substance, think about what you have learned and write a hypothesis stating what you think will happen, based on what you already know. Can you predict the change in freezing point based on the amount of water and the amount of substance added to the water? Antifreeze is mostly alcohol. Would any other substance help to protect your car's engine against freezing? Why do you suppose alcohol is used?

Teacher Information:

Freezing point is 0 degrees Celsius if it is pure water. Like boiling point, freezing point is affected by impurities. Unlike boiling point, freezing isn't affected by altitude—because it is not affected by air pressure. With this activity, students will discover the approximate freezing point of tap water. It might not quite reach freezing point but it will come very close. Those who care to pursue the extension for problem solvers will also discover that freezing point is affected by impurities. They will experiment with different substances as additives and compare the effect, based on the substance added and the amount.

Integrating: Math

Skills: Observing, inferring, measuring, predicting, formulating hypotheses, identifying and controlling variables, experimenting

VIII. HEAT TRANSFER

ACTIVITY 15-14:
WHAT IS CONDUCTION?
(Teacher-supervised activity)

Materials Needed:

Iron rod

Six marbles

Wax

Candle (large)

Match

Clock or watch with second hand

Procedure:

1. Using a small wad of wax, stick the six marbles on the iron rod, at positions 1, 2, 3, 5, 6, and 7, as shown in Figure 15A-1. Let position 4 be at the center of the rod and measure 5 centimeters (2 inches) between positions.
2. Support the ends of the rod on stacks of books and place the candle under position 4.
3. You are going to heat the rod at the center. Predict what will happen and write your prediction on your paper. Write the numbers of the marbles in the order that you think they will fall.
4. Light the candle and note the position of the second-hand on the clock.

Figure 15A-1

The marbles are mounted to the metal rod with wax.

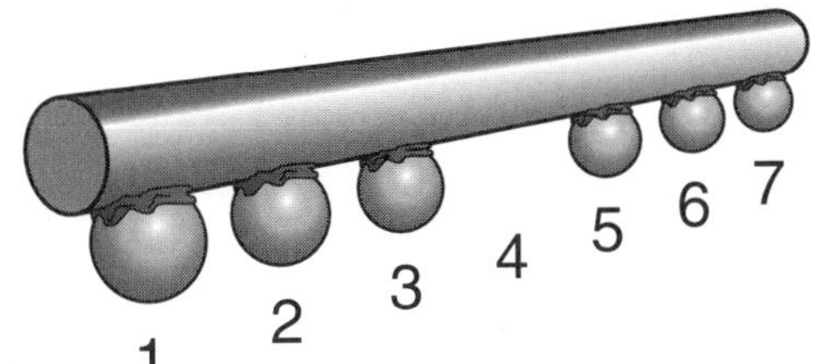

5. Heat the rod for three minutes. As each marble falls, record the position of the marble and the amount of time since you started heating the rod with the candle.
6. Which marbles fell first?
7. Which marbles fell last?
8. Why do you think it happened in that order? Discuss your ideas.
9. Were your predictions accurate?

For Problem Solvers:

Get an aluminum rod and a glass rod, preferably the same diameter and length as the iron rod. For each of these, repeat the above process. Before you begin, think about how you expect the aluminum and glass to compare with the iron rod and write your hypothesis. Predict the amount of time you think it will take for each marble to fall. Then test your ideas by doing the activity with the aluminum and glass rods.

If you can find a copper rod the same size, compare it with the others. Remember to write your hypothesis before you begin. Be very careful to not burn yourself by touching the rods while they are hot.

Teacher Information:

The major purpose of this activity is to show that heat moves through materials by conduction. This will be evident as the marbles closest to the heat source fall first. Students who do the extension for problem solvers will use rods made of various materials. They will discover that some materials are better heat conductors than others. They will likely find that the glass rod doesn't conduct heat as well as the metal rods do.

Integrating: Math

Skills: Observing, inferring, measuring, predicting, using space-time relationships, formulating hypotheses, identifying and controlling variables, experimenting

ACTIVITY 15-15:
WHAT IS CONVECTION?

Materials Needed:

Fish tank (or deep dishpan, or the like)

Water

Ice

Plastic bag

Food coloring

Tape

Procedure:

1. Fill the tank about two-thirds full of water. Give the water time to settle before continuing the activity.
2. Put several ice cubes in the plastic bag and seal the bag.
3. Lay the bag of ice cubes in the water at one end of the tank, being careful to disturb the water as little as possible.
4. Anchor the bag with tape to assure that it will remain in place.
5. Add several drops of food coloring to the water near the ice.
6. Observe the food coloring.
7. What is the food coloring doing?
8. Share your ideas and discuss what is happening.

For Problem Solvers:

Add to the above system a heat lamp, or just a light bulb, at the end opposite the ice. You will probably need a fresh supply of ice. You will also need to either have fresh, clean water or else use a different color of food coloring than has already been put into the water, in order to observe the movements of the water. How do you think the water movements with the heat lamp added to the system will compare to the water movements without the heat lamp? Write your hypothesis, then try it. Talk about what you observe—share your ideas. What implications does this have for the oceans?

Do you think air moves in similar patterns as it warms and cools? Design an experiment to find out. Clear your plan with your teacher and try it.

Teacher Information:

Movement of the food coloring will reveal that the water is circulating, with cold water moving down and across the bottom while warmer water moves up and across the top. These are convection currents, and they occur within any fluid (water, air, and so on) when temperature differences occur within the body of the fluid. Such convection currents in the atmosphere produce winds. They also occur constantly in the oceans.

Skills: Observing, inferring, measuring, predicting, using space-time relationships, formulating hypotheses, identifying and controlling variables, experimenting

ACTIVITY 15-16:
WHAT IS HEAT RADIATION?

Materials Needed:

A cool, sunny day

Procedure:

1. Take a friend to do this activity with you.
2. On a cool, sunny day, go outdoors and stand in one position, facing the sunshine.
3. How does the front of you feel? How does the back of you feel?
4. Turn around with your back to the sunshine.

5. Now how does the front of you feel? How does the back of you feel?
6. Stand in the shade and answer the same questions.
7. Talk about what you did and how you felt. Can you feel warm when the air is still cool? Discuss your ideas.

For Problem Solvers:

How much do you think the sunny side of the building is affecting the temperature of the air nearby? Get a thermometer. Predict the temperature of the air: (1) near the building on the sunny side, (2) in the shade of the building, and (3) away from the building. Now measure and compare these temperatures. For part 3, shade the thermometer with your hand to be sure you are measuring air temperature without the influence of sunlight striking the thermometer directly. How did you do with your predictions? Share your findings with your group.

What is the variable you are working with in this activity?

Teacher Information:

When the air around you is heated by convection currents, you probably feel about the same amount of warmth all over. Radiant energy, as from the sun (or from a stove), passes through the air with little effect, but warms the objects that it strikes. The air is then heated by those objects. Sometimes one of those objects is you. The person doing this activity will feel warmth from the sun on the side that is turned toward the sun, while the other side is affected only by the air, which is still quite cool.

Integrating: Math

Skills: Observing, inferring, measuring, predicting, using space-time relationships, formulating hypotheses, identifying and controlling variables

ACTIVITY 15-17:
WHAT IS THE GREENHOUSE EFFECT?

Materials Needed:

A sunny day

Two thermometers

Two small pieces of cardboard

Clear plastic bag

Procedure:

1. On a sunny day, predict the temperature of the air in the sunlight near the ground.
2. Test your prediction by placing a thermometer on a small piece of cardboard and laying it on the ground in the sunlight.
3. Put the other thermometer in the clear plastic bag.
4. Blow up the bag with air and place it on a second piece of cardboard beside the first thermometer.
5. Predict what the two temperatures will be in two minutes. Write your prediction.
6. Watch the two thermometers for two minutes. Check and record the temperatures.
7. How close was your prediction?
8. How much difference was there between the two temperatures? Which was warmer? Why?
9. Discuss your observations and ideas.
10. What suggestions do you have for people who leave pets locked in cars during hot weather?

For Problem Solvers:

Obtain permission to measure the temperature inside someone's car that is nearby. Select a car that is facing the sun. Predict the temperature inside the car on the dashboard, with windows up. Make a second prediction of the temperature in a place that is inside the car but not in the sunlight. Record your predictions.

Test your predictions by placing two thermometers side by side in the car. Do not have the car door open longer than necessary. Leave the thermometers in place for two to three minutes, then read the thermometers, record the temperatures, and compare them with your predictions. How did you do?

Do some research on the *greenhouse effect.* Find out what it means and why it is called that. Share your information with your group and relate it with your findings in this activity.

Teacher Information:

Radiant energy passes through transparent material quite readily. The energy waves then reflect from other objects as longer waves, however, and cannot pass through the transparent material as easily. So the sun's energy passes through the windshield of a car, but as the energy reflects off seats and other objects, the rebounding waves remain trapped inside the car, and heat energy accumulates.

Integrating: Math, social studies

Skills: Observing, inferring, measuring, predicting, using space-time relationships, formulating hypotheses, researching

IX. INSULATION

ACTIVITY 15-18:

WHERE AND WHY DO WE USE INSULATION?

Materials Needed:

Two thermometers

Small piece of wool cloth

Small piece of nylon cloth, same size as the wool

Refrigerator (or ice chest with ice)

Procedure:

1. Check to be sure the two thermometers show the same temperature.
2. Wrap one thermometer with the wool cloth and the other with the nylon cloth.
3. Place both thermometers in the refrigerator.
4. Predict the temperatures that will show on the two thermometers after five minutes in the refrigerator. Record your predictions.
5. After five minutes, remove the thermometers and read the temperatures.
6. Which thermometer seemed to be most protected from the cold temperature of the refrigerator? Compare the temperatures with your predictions.
7. Think about your findings and discuss your ideas. On a cold day, would you prefer to wear a nylon shirt or a wool shirt? Why?

For Problem Solvers:

Design an experiment to find out what materials have the best insulation value. Consider comparing either some fabrics that are commonly used for clothing, or some materials used to insulate houses, or both. Perhaps even compare materials commonly used in constructing homes, such as brick and lumber. List the materials you are comparing, describe your procedure, and clear your project with your teacher. Think about what you expect to find, and write your hypothesis. What are your variables? What can you use as a control?

Do some research and find out what kinds of clothing are worn in the very warm and very cold climates. What parts of the world are most concerned about having buildings well insulated, and what materials do they use? Do they use the most effective insulating material, or do they settle for material that is less effective because of cost? Think of other related questions to include in your study of insulation.

Share your findings with your group when you are finished.

Teacher Information:

This begins as a simple activity by which students can discover that some materials provide better insulating value than others. Students who do the extension for problem solvers will move from there into a full-fledged experiment, comparing various materials and finding out which provide the best insulation.

Review students' experience with the earlier activity that used an iron rod to discover that heat can be conducted through materials. While the objective of that activity was to discover the idea of heat conduction, those who did the extended activity compared rods made of different materials to determine which materials conducted heat best. A connection needs to be made between that activity and the concept of insulation. The poorest heat *conductors* are the best heat *insulators*.

Integrating: Math, social studies

Skills: Observing, inferring, measuring, predicting, using space-time relationships, formulating hypotheses, researching

X. HEATING AND COOLING OUR HOMES

ACTIVITY 15-19:

HOW DO PEOPLE HEAT AND COOL THEIR HOMES?

Materials Needed:

Pencil and paper

Procedure:

1. Conduct a survey of the class or school to find out what types of heating systems are used in homes locally. Find out how many homes have a central heating system, what type of systems (forced air, hot water, and so on) are used, and what type of fuel is used.
2. Graph the results, showing the types of heating systems and fuel types.
3. Share your information with your group.

For Problem Solvers:

Do some research and find out what areas of the world commonly use central heating systems in their homes, the types of heating systems, and fuel types most commonly used. What areas of the world need heating systems in their homes but do not commonly use them because of cost? Report your findings to your group.

Now consider the needs people have for cooling their homes. What type of equipment is commonly used in your area? In other areas of the world? What type of energy is used? Use the ideas given above to answer these questions, as well as other questions you'd like to add.

Check your home for energy efficiency. Does it need more insulation? Storm windows? Storm doors? Caulking around windows? Try to identify one or more ways to maintain more comfortable temperatures in your home with less energy usage.

Teacher Information:

Very likely, some students don't even know what type of heating system or fuel type is used in their own home. This is a good time for them to ask some questions and find out. This activity will help students learn more about fuels we typically use for heating our homes and the variety of options and preferences. Those who do the extension for problem solvers will gain insights regarding the varying needs for heating systems in different climates, as well as some of the needs that are not being met.

Integrating: Math, social studies

Skills: Communicating, researching

CHAPTER

LIGHT AND ELECTROMAGNETIC WAVES

CHAPTER OUTLINE:

- INTRODUCTION
- WHAT IS LIGHT?
- SOURCES OF LIGHT
- TRANSPARENT, TRANSLUCENT, AND OPAQUE MATERIALS
- LIGHT TRAVELS FAST AND IN STRAIGHT LINES
- SHADOWS
- REFLECTION
  - Law of Reflection
  - Scattering Light Deliberately
  - Types and Uses of Mirrors
- REFRACTION
  - Lenses
    - Types of lenses
    - Uses of lenses
- COLOR
  - Separation of Colors
  - Primary, Secondary, and Complementary Colors
  - Mixing Colored Lights
  - Mixing Colored Pigments
  - Colors of the Sky and Sea
- IN CLOSING
- LIST OF RESOURCES
- ACTIVITIES

I WONDER . . .

What is light?
How fast does light travel?
Why are shadows sometimes lighter around the edges?
How can light reflection be effectively demonstrated?
What does refraction have to do with magnifiers?
Why do we see colors?
How does a prism work?
Why are the primary colors of light different from the primary colors of paint?
Why do the sky and sea both look blue?

I. INTRODUCTION

Do you see the light? Actually, the only thing you ever really see is light, and there are only a few things that give off their own light. Light sources include burning candles, the glowing filament of a light bulb, and our primary source of light—the sun. When you look at trees, mountains, a beautiful flower, or a friend, all you see is light that comes from somewhere else and is reflected by those things.

Light is much more important than just for seeing; there would be no life without it. Plants cannot live without light, and we depend on plants for food, and even for the oxygen we breathe. But wait—just what *is* light?

II. WHAT IS LIGHT?

Light is a member of a group of waves, called *electromagnetic waves.* Others in the group include radio waves, infrared rays, X-rays, and gamma rays. All of these are part of the *electromagnetic spectrum* (see Figure 16-1). Visible light, which is only a narrow band within the electromagnetic spectrum, includes all of the colors we see. All electromagnetic waves, including light, travel at a speed of 299,792 kilometers (186,282 miles) per second. For practical purposes, these numbers are usually rounded to 300,000 kilometers (186,000 miles).

Each form of electromagnetic wave has its own unique *wavelength* and *frequency.* A wavelength is the distance from one crest (high point) or trough (low point) to the next crest or trough, or the distance between any two successive parts of a wave. Frequency refers to the number of waves that pass by a given point in one second, or the number of vibrations per second. As shown in Figure 16-2, long wavelengths are associated with low frequencies and short wavelengths are associated with

Figure 16-1 *Visible light is only a narrow band within the electromagnetic spectrum.*

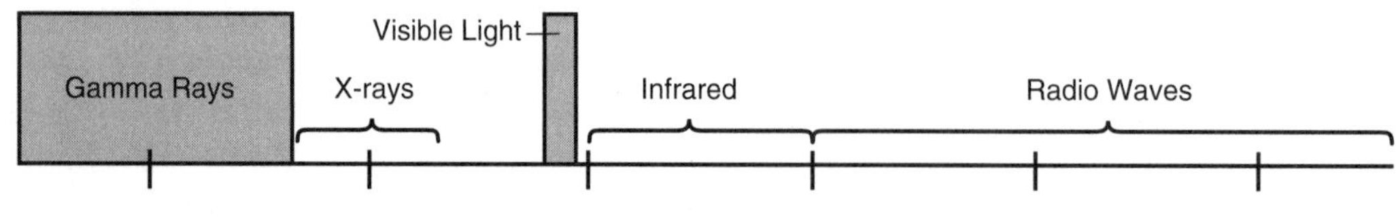

Figure 16-2 *This chart of the electromagnetic spectrum shows wavelength: the distance from one crest or trough to another crest or trough.*

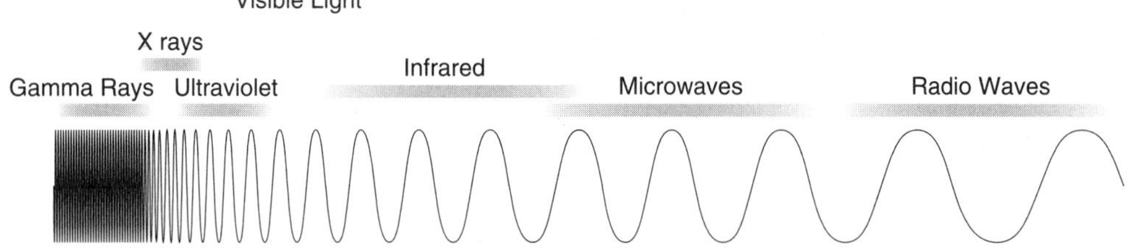

high frequencies. The energy travels at the same speed; so with shorter wavelengths more of them are crowded into the same amount of space, therefore more of them pass by a given point in one second. Radio waves, for example, have long wavelengths and low frequencies; X-rays and gamma rays have shorter wavelengths and higher frequencies. This is reflected in a simple formula: speed = wavelength X frequency. This is known as a relation of inverse proportions. That is, as wavelength or frequency increases, the other decreases proportionately, thus speed remains constant.

Scientists know a great deal about these waves, how they behave, how to use them, and how to produce them. They have found that light originates from the accelerated motion of electrons. Still, no one knows exactly what light is, and no one has ever seen an electron. The purpose of this chapter is not to speculate about the unknown aspects of the nature of light, but to explore some of the exciting known characteristics of this form of energy.

III. SOURCES OF LIGHT

All light sources are either *natural* or *artificial.* Until relatively recently, people got by with natural sources of light. The primary source of light, then and now, is the sun. While stars produce light, our sun is the only star that is close enough to the earth to be a significant source of light. Still, we are fascinated by the stars that decorate the night sky, and seagoing vessels have for centuries relied on them for direction, as do aircraft today. Although the moon shines in the sky and even provides enough light for us to see our way around at night when it is bright and full, it is not a light source. It only *reflects* the sun's light. Other natural sources of light include fire and, yes, even the firefly, though it would be most difficult to read by one.

Until the invention of the light bulb, fire was the only portable and controllable source of light. By experimenting with available fuels and different materials for wicks and styles of lamps, people developed the ability to provide light where light was needed. Continued efforts for greater convenience led to the development of the artificial light sources of today, providing a myriad of types and colors of light, available in the most decorative forms imaginable. Such artificial light sources include the light bulb, or incandescent light, which uses a thin tungsten filament that gets hot and glows brightly when electricity flows through it. The light bulb is filled with an inert gas, such as nitrogen or argon. Air is sealed out because the oxygen in air would cause the filament to burn away too quickly.

The fluorescent light tube burns cooler and gives off more light, for the amount of energy it uses, than does the incandescent light bulb. The tube is coated with chemicals called *phosphors.* A small amount of mercury in the tube is vaporized when electricity passes through small tungsten filaments at each end of the tube. As electricity flows through the mercury vapor, invisible ultraviolet rays are given off, which strike the phosphors coating the inside of the tube and the phosphors glow brightly.

IV. TRANSPARENT, TRANSLUCENT, AND OPAQUE MATERIALS

When light strikes an object, the light either passes through the object, or it is reflected, or it is absorbed and converted into heat. With transparent material, such as air, water, and clear glass, almost all light passes through; very little is absorbed and very little is reflected. Translucent materials reflect some light and absorb some light, but they allow most of the light to pass through. However, as light passes through translucent material, it is scattered (reflected in many directions). We say the material is not clear, meaning we cannot see objects through it clearly. Translucent glass or plastic is commonly used for bathroom windows and for other locations where light is desirable but visibility is not. Opaque materials do not allow light to pass through. All of the energy from the light is either reflected or absorbed and converted to heat energy. Examples of opaque materials include wooden boards, the metal part of car doors, books, and any other material that does not allow light to pass through. Plastics can be transparent (food wrap or clear plastic windows), translucent (plastic windows made for use in bathrooms), or opaque (most plastic boxes and equipment cases).

V. LIGHT TRAVELS FAST AND IN STRAIGHT LINES

Light travels so fast that we see things happen around us essentially at the instant they occur. At a speed of 300,000 kilometers (186,000 miles) per second, it takes light about eight minutes to travel from the sun to the earth. Its speed is equivalent to traveling around the earth about seven times in one second. Even at that speed, distances in space are measured in *light-years* because distances in space are so great. One light-year is the distance light travels in one year, or about 9.5 trillion kilometers (6 trillion miles). Proxima Centauri, the nearest star to the earth other than the sun, is over four light-years away. If you traveled at 30,000 kilometers (18,500 miles) per hour, the approximate speed of a space shuttle as it orbits the earth, it would take you more than 148,000 years to reach this "nearby" star.

Although light can be reflected and refracted, as discussed in the following sections, it travels in straight lines. It doesn't curve around objects. If that was not so, part of you might be missing—your shadow.

VI. SHADOWS

When light is blocked from a portion of a lighted surface by an opaque object, an image of the object appears on the surface. The image is darker than the surrounding surface because light has been blocked by the object. We call the image a *shadow.* Shadows are formed because light always travels in straight lines.

Sometimes shadows are darker in the middle and lighter around the edges. This does not imply that light is bending somewhat, but only that the edge of the object is not blocking the light from the entire light source. If the light source is broad, light rays approach the object from different angles (see Figure 16-3). Some, but not all, of the light rays are blocked at the edge, resulting in less light being cast on the surface; thus, a lighter shadow. The shadow is darker where all light rays from the light source are blocked. The darker part of the shadow, in the middle, is called the *umbra,* and the lighter outer part is called the *penumbra*.

Figure 16-3

The ball on the left is lighted by a narrow light source, and the ball on the right is lighted by a broad light source. Notice that the left ball casts a sharper shadow.

VII. REFLECTION

When you look at a lighted lamp bulb, you see the bulb because rays of light are being emitted from the bulb to your eyes. The same is true when you see the burning flame of a candle or any other light source. (You should never look directly at the sun, as it can easily damage your eyes in just a few seconds.) However, if you see a light bulb when the lamp is turned off, what you actually see is light that is coming from another source and is being reflected by the bulb. In order for you to see any object that does not give off its own light, three conditions must exist: there must be a light source, the light must strike the object, and light must be reflected from the object to your eyes.

All objects that do not give off their own light either reflect light, absorb light, or allow light to pass through them. Some materials are transparent, some are translucent, and some are opaque. Even most transparent materials absorb and reflect some light. If you see a piece of clear glass, you know that some light is being reflected by it; otherwise you wouldn't see it.

Opaque materials differ greatly in the amount of light they reflect and how much they absorb. In general, dark, rough objects absorb more light, while light, smooth objects reflect more light.

Law of Reflection

Reflected light always leaves the reflecting surface at the same angle as it strikes the surface. Stated precisely, the *angle of incidence* equals the *angle of reflection.* This is called the *law of reflection.*

To visualize the angle of incidence and angle of reflection, consider the way a ball bounces. If you drop a basketball straight down on the floor, it bounces straight up. If you throw the ball on the floor at a slight angle, it bounces up at a slight angle, then curves downward because of gravity. Try it, and notice. Then throw the ball at more of an angle. As you continue, you will notice that each time you throw the ball, it leaves the floor at the same angle that it approaches the floor, then it curves downward because of gravity (see Figure 16-4).

To make the analogy complete, you need to use a bit of imagination and consider what the ball would do if it were exempt from the force

Figure 16-4

Notice the path of a ball, as it bounces at an angle, then curves: The angle of incidence and the angle of reflection are equal until gravity interferes.

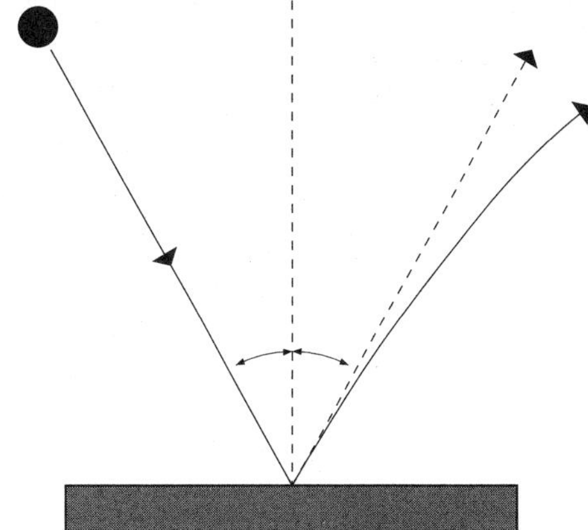

of gravity—a "magic" ball. As you "throw" the ball in your mind, the motion of the ball will not curve. After you throw the ball, it continues in the same direction until it strikes something, then it reflects and continues in one direction until it strikes something else. With such a ball you would notice that if you threw it at a 45-degree angle, it would reflect at a 45-degree angle; and if you threw it at a 10-degree angle, it would reflect at a 10-degree angle (see Figure 16-5).

You can achieve this effect by rolling a ball across a floor or table top and bouncing it off the wall. Since the ball is rolling on a surface, gravity does not interfere with its line of travel. This assumes that the surface is perfectly level and perfectly smooth, of course.

The angle at which you throw the ball against the floor is the *angle of incidence.* The angle at which the ball bounces from the floor is the *angle of reflection.* Those two angles are always equal; and without the influence of gravity, the ball would always travel in straight lines.

For our purposes, we can consider light to be exempt from the law of gravity; it behaves in a similar way to the magic ball. It always travels in straight lines, and the angle of incidence always equals the angle of reflection. Perhaps for light this principle is easiest to perceive with a mirror. The mirror is shiny because it reflects almost all light that strikes it, and it reflects all light rays at the same angle. If you place a mirror on the floor and shine a flashlight straight down into it, the light reflects straight up. If you aim the flashlight at a slight angle to the mirror, it will reflect at a slight angle.

Figure 16-5

The "magic" ball, not affected by gravity, continues at the angle of reflection.

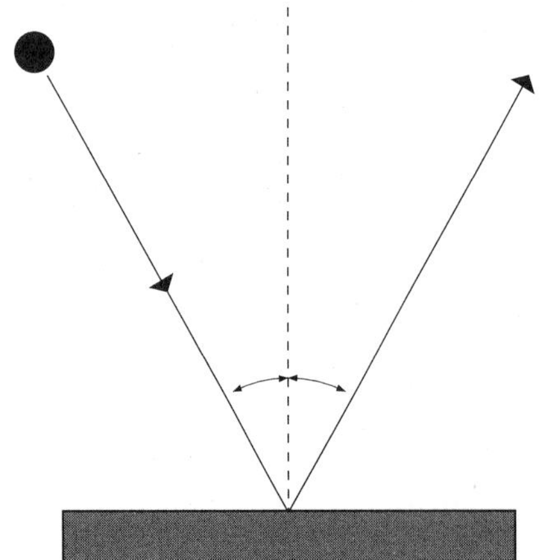

Tap two chalkboard erasers together over the mirror, so the beam of light from the flashlight has to go through the chalk dust in the air, and you will be able to see the angle of the beam of light. The angle of incidence will always equal the angle of reflection. Other suggestions to help you see the beam of light are given in the activities section at the end of this chapter.

With the shiny surface of a mirror, it is easy to see that light always travels in straight lines and that the angle of incidence equals the angle of reflection. Even on dull or rough surfaces, however, the law of reflection still holds true. Think back again to the magic ball that is not affected by gravity. Imagine throwing the ball on a rough surface, such as a rocky or graveled road. Each time you throw the ball, it will bounce off in a different direction because each time the ball is thrown, it strikes a surface that lies at a different angle. If you could see the small part of the rock the ball strikes each time, you would find that the angle of incidence and the angle of reflection are, in fact, equal every time. And remember, our magic ball always moves in straight lines because it is not affected by gravity.

If you threw several magic balls at the rocky surface at one time, the balls would all bounce off in different directions, because each one strikes a part of the surface that is at a different angle. That's the way it is when light strikes a rough surface. Each narrow light ray is like the magic ball, and shining a flashlight on a rough surface is like throwing many magic balls on a rocky surface; they scatter in many different directions (see Figure 16-6).

What about a surface that feels smooth and looks smooth, but is dull instead of shiny? Examine that surface with a hand lens or microscope, and you will find that it isn't smooth at all; the variations in the surface are tiny, but the light rays that strike the surface are still reflected in many different directions. For each light ray, the angles of incidence and reflection are equal, and each light ray travels in straight lines, consistent with the principles that govern light.

Types and Uses of Mirrors

Most of us usually think of a mirror as being a flat piece of glass with a reflective backing. We probably use this type of mirror more than any other, although curved mirrors also have many uses.

If a mirror surface is slightly *concave*, or curved inward, objects reflected by it appear larger than normal. Such magnifying mirrors are sometimes used for shaving or for applying makeup. (However, if a concave mirror is curved too much, the image will appear smaller and upside down.)

Figure 16-6 *Light is scattered as it reflects from a rough surface.*

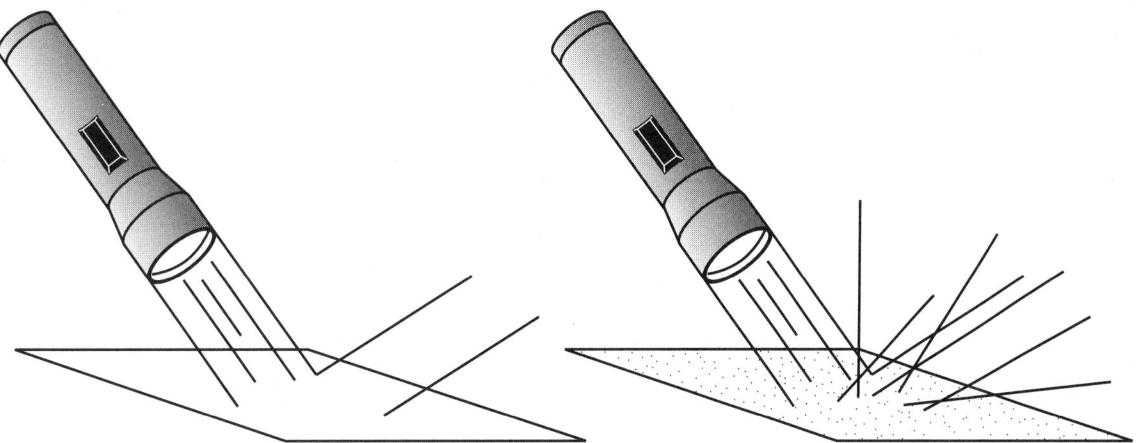

Scattering Light Deliberately

In lighting homes, offices, and so on, fixtures are often used that scatter light in order to reduce glare. Translucent bulbs or tubes are often used. Sometimes indirect lighting techniques are used, placing the lights behind opaque shades and reflecting the light toward the ceiling or the floor. The light is then reflected into the room by the ceiling and walls. These surfaces are usually dull and scatter the light, minimizing glare and making the area more pleasant.

Concave mirrors are used in flashlights and automobile headlights. They are also used in astronomical telescopes to gather light from stars and make the stars appear closer. A mirror designed for use in a telescope is curved just the right way so that all of the light that strikes its surface is reflected and comes together at one point. This point is called the *focus* (or the *focal point*). The mirror of a flashlight or headlight is similarly curved and has a light bulb at the focus, and a beam of light is reflected from the mirror in the intended direction.

A *convex* mirror surface, which is curved

outward, has the opposite effect. Convex mirrors are sometimes used as outside mirrors on automobiles because, while objects appear smaller, the field of vision is increased so that the driver can see what is at the side of the vehicle. Such mirrors are often used on the passenger side of cars so the driver can see automobiles at the side that are otherwise in a "blind spot." The mirror increases safety when the driver changes lanes. These mirrors often have a message printed on them to warn the driver, "Objects in mirror are closer than they appear." Many trucks have a small, round convex mirror at the bottom of a large rectangular flat mirror, to give drivers the advantage of the broadened field of vision while maintaining the true perspective (including sense of distance) offered by the flat mirror (see Figure 16-7).

Figure 16-7

The reflection of a car shows up in the convex mirror, but it does not show up in the flat mirror.

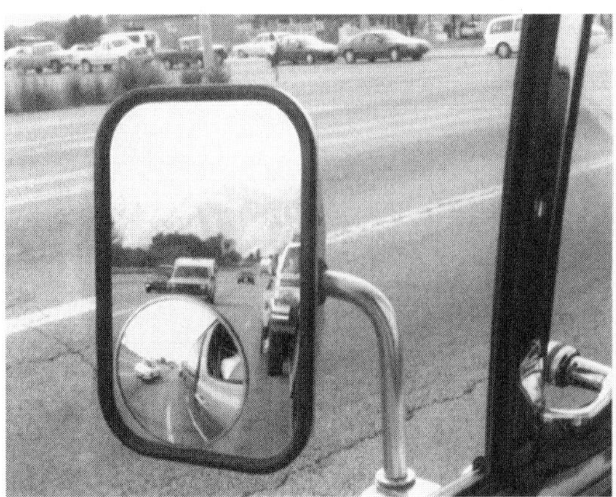

With a flat mirror (also called a plane mirror), the image appears in its true size, but the image appears to be behind the mirror. What you really see is a reflection of objects in front of the mirror. They appear to be as far behind the mirror as the objects actually are in front of it. The image is also reversed. If you look at yourself in the mirror and raise your left arm, the image appears to raise its right arm. If you touch your right ear, the image appears to touch its left ear.

VIII. REFRACTION

Light travels in straight lines, but it bends as it passes at an angle from one medium to another (from one transparent material to another type of transparent material). This happens because light moves at different speeds through different materials. Earlier in this chapter, we stated that light travels at a speed of 300,000 kilometers (186,000 miles) per second. That is the speed light travels through air; it travels slightly faster through a vacuum, but the difference in speed is insignificant. The speed of light slows as the density of the medium increases. Water is more dense than air, and glass is more dense than water. Light travels approximately three-fourths as fast through water as through air, and about two-thirds as fast through glass as through air. The difference in speed causes light to bend if it passes at an angle from one medium to another. This effect is called *refraction*.

To visualize the effect of refraction, think of a group of soldiers marching in a straight line across a hard, flat surface (see Figure 16-8). As they march along, they come to a large rectangular sandpit. All soldiers reach the sandpit at the same time. They slow down as they march through the sand, but all soldiers march at equal speed and their direction does not change. As they leave the sand together, they walk faster, but still at an equal speed and still their direction does not change. As they approach the next sandpit, however, the left end of the line reaches the sandpit first. All soldiers must still keep marching in a straight line. As the first soldier steps into the sand, he slows down a bit because the sand makes walking more difficult. With each successive step, more soldiers enter the sand and slow their pace. All soldiers walk at an equal pace through the sand, and all soldiers walk at an equal pace on the hard surface, but they walk more slowly through the sand than across the hard surface. The result is that as soon as the first soldier enters the sand, the line of soldiers begins to bend in the direction of the first soldier.

Figure 16-8

This diagram of soldiers marching into rectangular sandpits, one straight on and the other at an angle, shows how light bends as it passes from one medium to another.

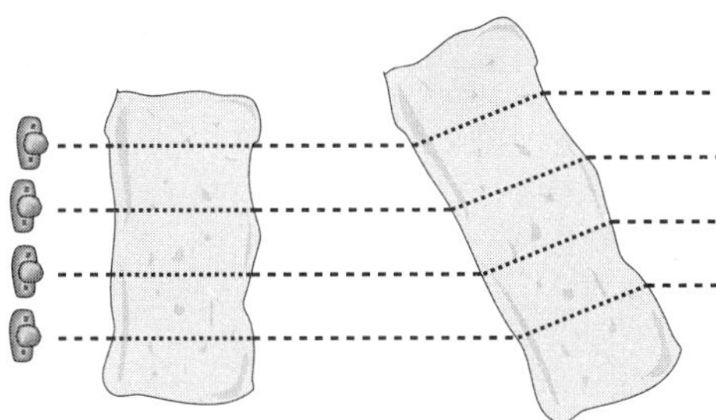

Notice in the diagram that the soldier on the left end of the line steps out of the sandpit first and begins to speed up as soon as he reaches the hard surface. As he does, the line begins to bend back to the right. By the time all soldiers are on the hard surface again, the line is moving in the same direction as before they came to the sandpit, but their path is shifted slightly to one side. Although light rays are not soldiers, and light rays do not walk through sandpits, this analogy should add meaning to the notion of the refraction, or bending, of light as it passes at an angle from one transparent material to another of different density.

Refraction is easy to see with an aquarium that is filled with water. Add a small amount of milk to the water (begin with just a few drops), then shine a flashlight into the aquarium (be sure there are no fish in the aquarium!). As shown in Figure 16-9, if you aim the light beam straight in from the side or from the top, at a right angle to the surface, you will notice that the light does not bend. This is similar to the group of soldiers as they approached the first sandpit all at the same time. However, if you shine the flashlight into the aquarium at an angle, the light will noticeably bend as it enters the milky water. (The presence of milk does not affect the bending of light as it enters the water; it just makes the light more visible.)

Try putting a spoon in a clear drinking glass filled with water, and you will notice that the spoon appears to be broken at the surface of the

Figure 16-9

If the light enters the water at an angle, it is refracted, or bent.

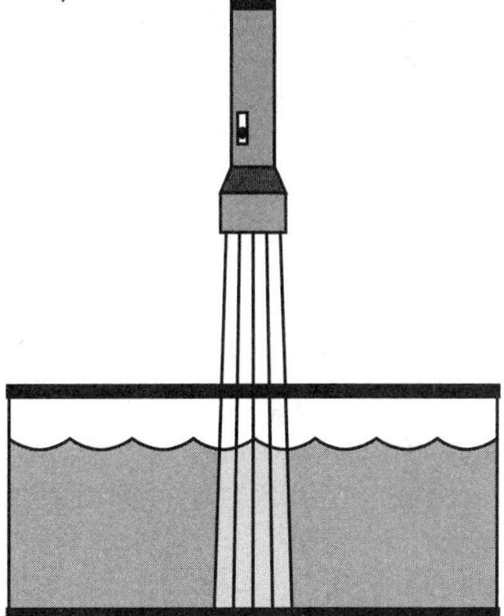

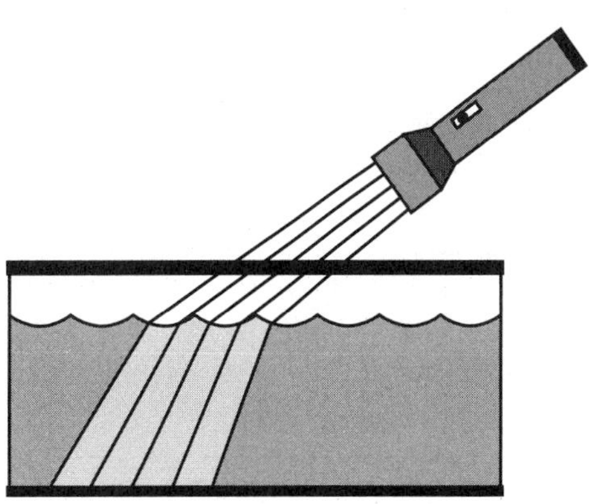

Figure 16-10

Note that the spoon appears to be broken at the surface of the water.

water (see Figure 16-10). This effect is due to the refraction of light. Notice that the spoon is not exactly where it appears to be as you peer through the side of the glass. Likewise, when you see a fish in a lake, the fish is not exactly where it appears to be. Bears, eagles, and other land and air predators of fish seem to know about light refraction; they are not fooled by the bending of light rays (see Figure 16-11).

Lenses

When light rays pass into a more dense material at an angle, they bend inward. When they pass into a less dense material at an angle, they bend outward. Without the discovery of refraction of light, we would not have eyeglasses, contact lenses, microscopes, binoculars, or telescopes. Even the reflecting telescopes mentioned above use lenses in addition to mirrors.

There is no magic in a pair of eyeglasses or in a telescope. These devices use lenses, which apply the principle that light refracts. A lens is a piece of curved glass or other transparent material. Even water can become a lens. Place a drop of water on the print of a magazine page, and you will easily see the magnifying effect of the drop of water as the light reflected from the page is refracted when passing from water into air. The domed surface of the water results in a magnifying effect, and the water drop becomes a lens. Lenses may be curved on one side and flat on the other, or they may be curved on both sides, depending on the desired effect. They are used to bend, or refract, light rays.

As light rays pass through a lens, they always bend toward the thickest part of the lens. As you look at a lens and try to determine which direction the light rays will bend, think about the line of soldiers and the sandpit. As light passes from air into the lens, then back into air, it will bend in the same direction as the line of soldiers marching from a hard, smooth surface into a sandpit and back to a hard, smooth surface.

Figure 16-11

When you look at fish underwater, the fish is not exactly where it appears to be.

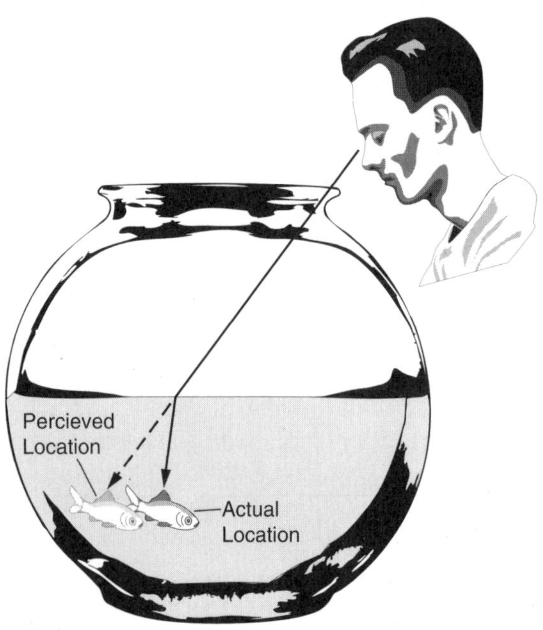

Types of lenses

Earlier in this chapter we discussed two types of mirrors: concave and convex. The same terms are used in describing lenses. In general, those that curve inward are called *concave lenses,* and those that curve outward are called *convex lenses.*

A concave lens is thin in the middle and thick at the edges. Light rays always bend toward the thicker part of the lens, so as they pass through a concave lens, they spread out. The image always appears smaller and right-side up. The more the lens is curved, the smaller the image will appear (see Figure 16-12).

The opposite effect is achieved with a convex lens, which is thick in the middle and thin at the edges. Light rays passing through a convex lens bend toward the middle (always toward the thicker part of the lens) and come together at a point somewhere beyond the lens. The point at which the light rays come together is called the *focus* (often called *focal point)* of the lens (see Figure 16-13). The distance from the lens to the focus is called the *focal length,* and is determined by the amount of curvature of the lens. If you compare two convex lenses of the same diameter but different thickness, you will find that the one that is thicker in the middle will have a shorter focal length. The human eye contains a flexible convex lens that adjusts, by muscles reshaping the lens, to focus on objects at different distances.

A convex lens placed between a burning candle and a screen results in an inverted image on the screen. Try it with a lamp or a flashlight (see Figure 16-14).

If you place a convex lens between an object and your eye, the image will appear larger and right side up. The lens is now a magnifier. An easy example of this effect is the water drop on the magazine page suggested in the discussion of Lenses, above. If the distance between the

Figure 16-12

The image seen through a concave lens is smaller than the actual object, and right-side up.

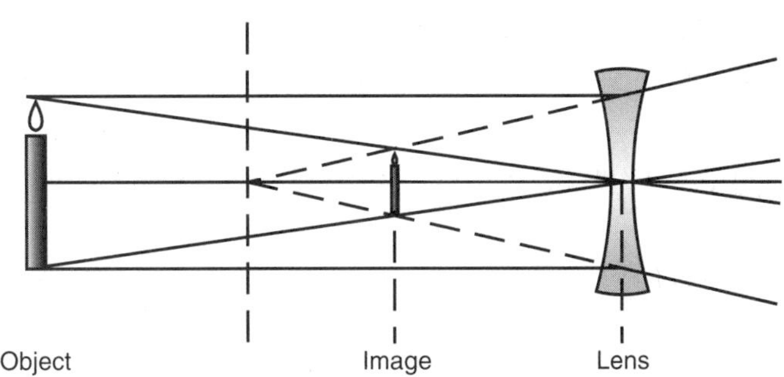

Figure 16-13

***The point at which light rays come together after passing through a convex lens is called the* focus, *and the distance from the lens to the focus is the* focal length.**

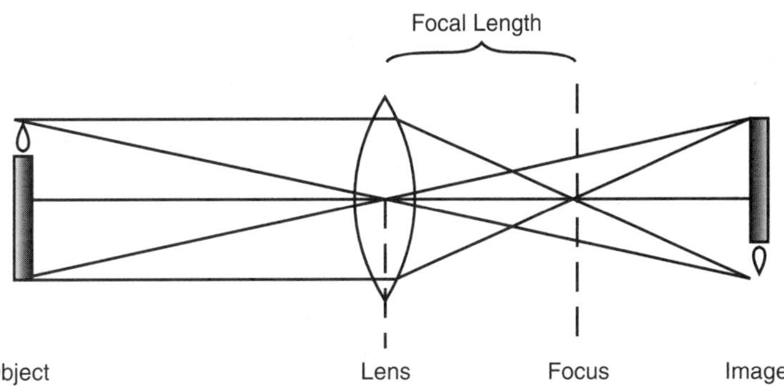

Figure 16-14

Through a convex lens, the image of the flame is upside down.

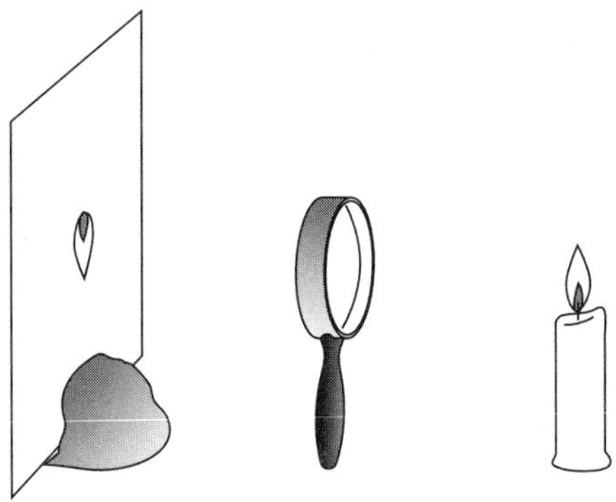

object and the lens is greater than the focal length of the lens, the image is inverted.

Uses of lenses

A *camera* uses a convex lens to bring the image of the subject into focus on the film, which is placed at the back of the camera. The farther away the subject is from the camera, the closer the lens must be to the film for the subject to be in sharp focus. Because of this, cameras are usually designed with lenses that can be moved in and out to adjust the distance between lens and film. Cameras that have no focus feature have immovable lenses, and anything closer than about 2 meters (6.5 feet) from the camera is out of focus.

Eyeglasses use one lens in front of each eye, each lens designed according to the need of the eye. These lenses are shaped and positioned to assist the natural lens of the eye in focusing the image sharply on the back of the retina.

Projectors use one or more convex lenses to focus on a screen an enlarged image from a small transparent film. This is done by passing a strong light through the film. The film is placed in the camera upside down, so the image will be right-side up on the screen.

A *microscope* uses two convex lenses at opposite ends of a light-tight tube. Light rays reflected from an object pass through the lower lens, called the objective, which enlarges the image. The light rays then pass through the upper lens, called the eyepiece, which magnifies the image still further. The tube containing the lenses can be moved up and down to place the object at the focal point of the objective lens.

Distant objects are observed by either reflecting or refracting *telescopes.* A reflecting telescope uses a large mirror to gather light from a distant object and focus it onto a small convex lens, which magnifies the image and focuses it onto the eye. The basic function of a refracting telescope is similar to that of a microscope, only it uses a much larger objective lens to gather light from a distant object. The large lens focuses the light onto a small convex lens (the eyepiece), which further magnifies the image.

IX. COLOR

Visible light is composed of light of a range of wavelengths, each color of light having its own unique wavelength. Seven colors are traditionally identified in the color spectrum: red, orange, yellow, green, blue, indigo, and violet. The first letters of these colors are commonly used as an acronym forming the name ROY G. BIV, to aid in the learning of the color sequence of the visible spectrum. White light is a composite of all the visible wavelengths. Black is the absence of them.

To the artist, color is a characteristic of an object. To the physicist, "color" is neither in the object nor in the light emitted or reflected by the object. It is, instead, a physiological experience. One might say that color is "in the eye of the beholder." Certain physical characteristics of materials cause the material to absorb or reflect electromagnetic waves of specific wavelengths. The cones in human eyes, and those of some other animals, are selectively sensitive to certain electromagnetic waves. Some cones are stimulated by low-frequency waves, others by high-frequency waves, and still others are more sensitive to waves of medium frequency. Different signals are sent to the brain by the cones, according to the frequency of the waves involved. The brain responds to signals from the cones by "seeing" different colors.

Perhaps the effect could be compared to alphabetic characters on the screen of a computer monitor. As a key is pressed on the keyboard, a certain combination of electrical impulses goes through the machine, and the computer responds by causing an image to appear on the screen. The electrical impulses do not contain images of alphabetic characters, but the computer responds to those impulses by producing certain images on the screen. The image is not a *characteristic* of the signal, but is created by the machine *in response to the signal*. Similarly, "color" is not a characteristic of electromagnetic waves reflected by an object, but only *the mind's interpretation* of certain impulses.

Separation of Colors

Because light is refracted, or bent, when it passes from one medium to another, it displays itself as a spectrum of color as it passes at a slant through a *prism*—a triangular piece of transparent material, such as glass or plastic. Since each color of light has its own unique wavelength, each one is refracted differently. Short light waves are bent more than long light waves, resulting in a separation of the colors in a pattern that extends from violet (shortest wavelength) to red (longest wavelength) (see Figure 16-15). When the rays of colored light coming from a prism are focused into a second prism, the pattern of colored light combines to form white light again, verifying that white light is a mixture of the various colors of light.

Yes, light can be divided into a pattern of its component colors by a piece of glass, but again, guess who thought of it first? You guessed it, nature did. People never grow too old to be enchanted by the beauty of a rainbow. Rainbows are sometimes associated with romance. Poems are written about them, songs are sung about them, and numerous stories are told of ever-elusive treasures that lie at the "rainbow's end." Truly one of nature's more appreciated beauties, the phenomenon of the rainbow is sunlight's way of showing its true colors. During, or immediately after, an early morning or late afternoon rain shower, drops of water in the air act as tiny prisms and break sunlight into a spectrum of color in the form of a large, beautiful arch. With the morning or afternoon sun low in the sky, you may sometimes see small rainbows in the spray of a sprinkler from a garden hose.

Figure 16-15

When light passes through a prism, it displays itself as a color spectrum.

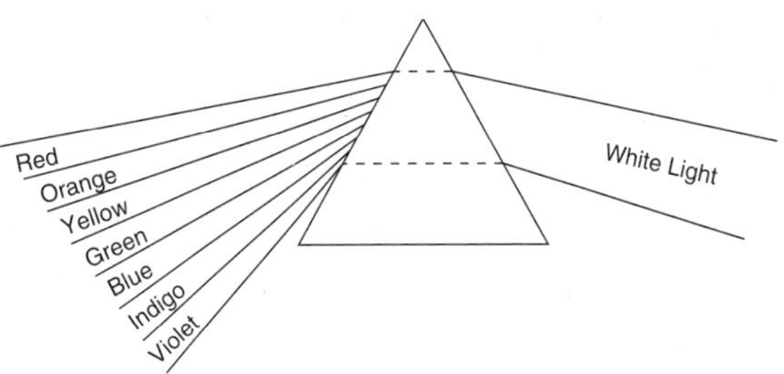

Primary, Secondary, and Complementary Colors

The topic of primary, secondary, and complementary colors can be confusing, because they are different for light and for pigment (paint). Primary colors are the colors that together can produce any color in the spectrum. When colored lights shine on a screen, the colors combine. This is an *additive* process. Paints do not produce color, but instead reflect color. Each color of paint reflects the color we see and absorbs, or subtracts, the rest. This is a *subtrac-*

tive process. In dealing with primary colors, then, we must consider colors of light and colors of paints (pigments) separately.

Mixing Colored Lights

The primary colors of light are red, blue, and green. These three colors, in different combinations and different amounts, can produce the entire color spectrum. Red, blue, and green are called the *additive primary colors.* The three of them combined produce white. As seen in Figure 16-16, combinations of these colors in pairs produce yellow, magenta, and cyan, which are called the *additive secondary colors.*

Looking at the overlapping circles of color produced by the primary colors of light, each opposing pair, a primary color and a secondary color, when put together will produce white. These are called *complementary colors.* The additive complementary colors are green and magenta, blue and yellow, and red and cyan.

Figure 16-16

Combinations of the additive primary colors produce the additive secondary colors.

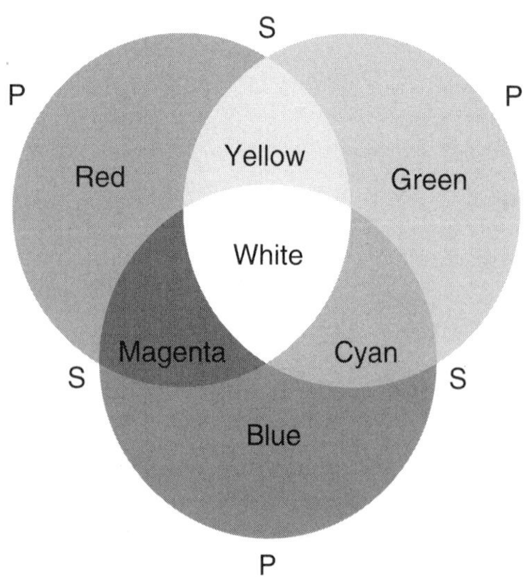

Mixing Colored Pigments

Mixing pigments is a different process from mixing colors of light. Green, blue, and red lights combine to make white light, but green, blue, and red paint do not produce white paint. Similarly, red paint mixed with green paint does not produce yellow paint. While mixing lights is an additive process, paint mixing is a subtractive process. Red paint absorbs all colors except red, or we may say it *subtracts* all colors except red. It reflects red, so we see it as red—that's the color that is reflected back to our eyes. Green paint absorbs all colors except green, blue paint absorbs all except blue, and so on. When red and green paint are mixed, the result is black, because all colors are absorbed. (Actually, the result is more of a muddy, dark brown, because the colors are not perfect and absorption is less than complete.)

The primary colors of paint are magenta, yellow, and cyan. These three colors, mixed in different combinations and different amounts, can produce the entire color spectrum. Cyan, magenta, and yellow are called the *subtractive primary colors.* The primary colors of paint are often stated as red, yellow, and blue, but that is a loose reference to magenta, yellow, and cyan. As shown in Figure 16-17, combinations of these colors in pairs produce red, green, and blue, the *subtractive secondary colors.* Notice the subtractive secondary colors are the additive primary colors, and the subtractive primary colors are the additive secondary colors.

Colors of the Sky and Sea

As sunlight passes through the atmosphere, some light waves are scattered by molecules of air, and by dust and smoke particles. The shorter light waves (violet and blue) are scattered by very tiny particles, even by atoms and air molecules. On a clear day, the sky appears blue because of the scattering of these high-frequency light waves. When an abundance of smoke

Figure 16-17

The subtractive primary colors are the additive secondary colors, and the subtractive secondary colors are the additive primary colors.

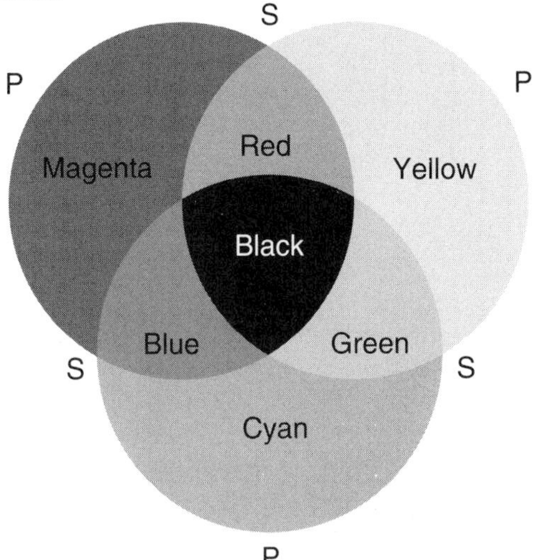

Figure 16-18

Sunlight passes through more miles of atmosphere in the morning and evening than in the middle of the day.

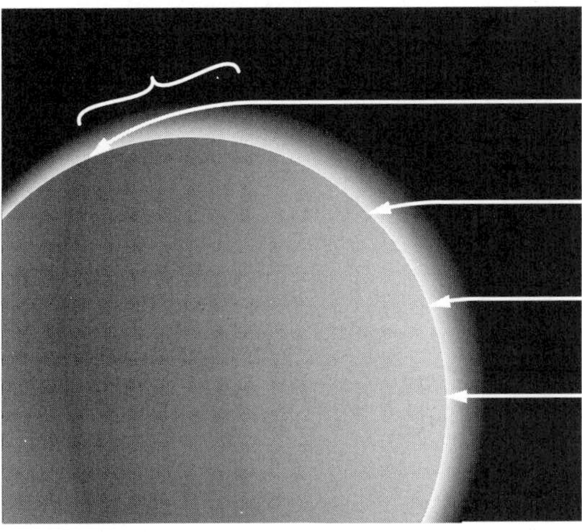

and dust particles are in the air, the longer light waves (yellow, orange, red) are also scattered and the sky takes on more of a grayish or whitish color. After a heavy rainstorm, when much of the dust and smoke has been washed out of the atmosphere, the sky becomes a deeper blue.

In the morning and evening, sunlight must pass through more atmosphere to reach the earth's surface (see Figure 16-18). So much blue light is scattered by the thicker atmosphere that only lower frequencies of light (yellow, orange, red) survive to reach the surface, resulting in the beautiful display that we see from nature's paintbrush, in the sunrise and sunset.

As you look across a large body of water and see a deep blue color, what you really see is a reflection of the blue sky, rather than the color of the water itself. Water molecules tend to absorb red light. Very little red light penetrates deeper than 30 meters (98 feet) of water. As red is removed by the water, the complementary color of red, which is cyan or bluish-green, remains. Looking down into the ocean or a lake, one sees a bluish-green color.

X. IN CLOSING

Light plays many important roles in our lives, including enabling us to simply see our way around. Our ability to use light is enhanced as we learn more and better ways to create it and to control it. We see more clearly into space, and we view the depths of microscopic worlds, as we learn to control light better. Indeed, much of our learning and much of our enjoyment in life come through visual media, and are enhanced as we learn more about the nature of light.

LIST OF RESOURCES

Ballif, Jae R., and William E. Dibble, *Physics: Fundamentals and Frontiers* (New York: John Wiley & Sons, 1972).

Hewitt, Paul G., *Conceptual Physics* (Glenview, IL: Scott, Foresman and Co., 1989).

LHS GEMS, *More Than Magnifiers* (Berkeley, CA: Lawrence Hall of Science, University of California, 1988).

LHS GEMS, *Color Analyzers* (Berkeley, CA: Lawrence Hall of Science, University of California, 1989).

"Light," *World Book Encyclopedia*, 1989.

Tolman, Marvin N., and James O. Morton, *Physical Science Activities for Grades 2–8* (West Nyack, NY: Parker Publishing Co., 1986).

Victor, Edward, *Science for the Elementary School, Sixth Edition* (New York: Macmillan Publishing Co., 1989).

CHAPTER

LIGHT AND ELECTROMAGNETIC WAVES

ACTIVITIES

II. WHAT IS LIGHT?

ACTIVITY 16-1: HOW DOES LIGHT ENERGY TRAVEL?

Materials Needed:

Jump rope (a fairly long rope will work better than a short one)

Procedure:

1. Have a friend hold one end of the rope while you hold the other end.
2. Hold the rope about waist high and stretch it out quite tight.
3. While your friend holds the other end steady, give your end a short, quick flip and watch the movements of the rope carefully.
4. Ask your friend if he or she felt anything at the other end of the rope.
5. Now you hold your end steady and ask your friend to give the rope a short, quick flip. Again, observe the rope movement.
6. What did you see? What did you feel?
7. Did you feel energy come to you from your friend? Did the rope really travel, or just the energy?
8. Think about it and talk about what happened. Describe the movements of the rope.

Teacher Information:

In doing this activity, students should conclude that energy moved along the rope, but the rope really didn't go anywhere. Although we can't see it happening with light energy, this demonstrates a characteristic of wave energy, of which there are many forms. Energy from earthquakes, for instance, can be felt many miles away from the area where the shifting of rock layers actually occurred, yet nothing visibly traveled the distance of those miles. Wave energy can also be observed easily in a pond (or pan) of water, by simply dropping something into the water and watching the waves move across the pond. If a leaf, a twig, or a duck is floating on the water, it doesn't move along with the wave, but simply moves up and down as the wave moves across the pond, showing that the water doesn't travel as the energy is transferred. Light is a form of wave energy.

Skills: Observing, inferring, communicating

III. SOURCES OF LIGHT

ACTIVITY 16-2:

HOW IS REFLECTED LIGHT DIFFERENT FROM SOURCE LIGHT?

Materials Needed:

Flashlight

Procedure:

1. Take a flashlight into a dark room.
2. Turn the flashlight on and shine it on some object that is in the room.
3. You can now see both the flashlight and the object that the light is shining on.
4. Turn the flashlight off. Do you still see the object?
5. Turn the flashlight back on. Do you see both the flashlight and the object again?
6. Which of these (the flashlight or the object) is a light source and which do you see because of reflected light only?
7. Discuss this and see if you agree.

Teacher Information:

You see things either because they produce light, or because light is reflected from them. Light that comes from an electric lamp, a fire, the sun, or from other sources that produce light is called source light. For anything you see that does not produce its own light, you see it because of reflected light—light comes from some light source and reflects off the object to your eye. If that didn't happen, you wouldn't see the object at all.

Skills: Observing, inferring

IV. TRANSPARENT, TRANSLUCENT, AND OPAQUE MATERIALS

ACTIVITY 16-3:

WHAT DO THE WORDS TRANSPARENT, TRANSLUCENT, AND OPAQUE MEAN?

Materials Needed:

Variety of transparent, translucent, and opaque items

Procedure:

1. Sort the items into groups A, B, and C as follows.
   a. If you can see light through the item, but you can't see objects on the other side of it clearly, put the item in Group A.
   b. If you can see through the item and see objects on the other side clearly, put the item in Group B.
   c. If you can't see any light through the item at all, put the item in Group C.
2. Label the groups "Transparent," "Translucent," and "Opaque," according to which you think is correct for each group.
3. Discuss your labels with your group. Do they agree with your labels and with the items you have in each group?
4. Ask your teacher, or someone assigned by your teacher, to check your labels.
5. Ask a friend to say the words for you and you write them on paper. Then you can use this paper to check your spelling.

6. Now look around your classroom, the school, your home, and so on, and make a list of transparent, translucent, and opaque materials. Be sure to include your bathroom windows—which list will you put them in?
7. Share your lists and discuss what you learned.

Teacher Information:

The first part of this is activity is a vocabulary exercise. For most students, the challenge won't be in dividing the items into three groups, but only in assigning the labels. For those who need it, this will help them to remember the correct vocabulary. Students will enjoy making their lists of examples of the three types of materials, and sharing them.

Integrating: Spelling, vocabulary

Skills: Observing, classifying

V. LIGHT TRAVELS FAST AND IN STRAIGHT LINES

ACTIVITY 16-4:
WHAT PATH DOES LIGHT TRAVEL?

Materials Needed:

Four 3 by 5 inch cards

Paper punch

Clay

Flashlight

Procedure:

1. Stack three of the cards.
2. With the paper punch, reach as far toward the center of the cards as you can and punch a hole in the three cards.
3. Pinch off three small pieces of clay and stand one of the three cards in each piece of clay. Place the cards about 10 centimeters (4 inches) apart. We'll call these cards 1, 2, and 3.
4. Using another small piece of clay, stand card 4 (not punched) behind the three punched cards (see Figure 16A-1).
5. Now shine the flashlight through the hole in card 1. Line up cards 2 and 3 so that the light goes through all three and forms a bright circle on card 4.
6. Move card 2 slightly to one side and shine the flashlight through the holes again.

Figure 16A-1 *This is how the four cards should look.*

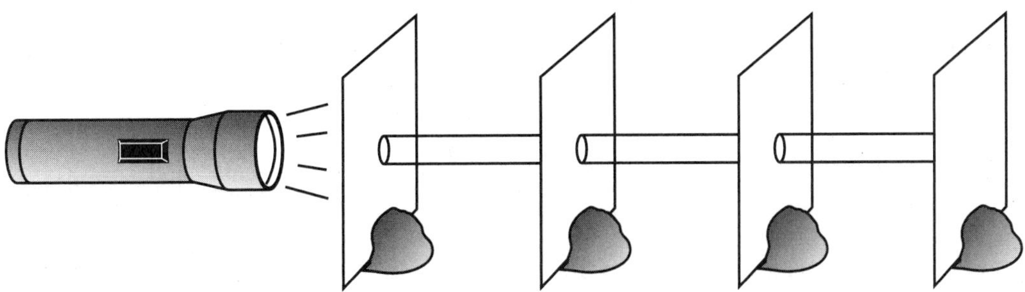

7. What happened? What does this tell you about the path light travels?

Teacher Information:

In doing this activity, students will discover that light travels in a straight line. The cards must be positioned with the holes perfectly lined up in order to form a complete circle of light on card 4.

Integrating: Math

Skills: Observing, inferring, measuring

(Adapted from Activity 54, "What Path Does Light Follow?" in Tolman and Morton, 1986.)

VI. SHADOWS

ACTIVITY 16-5:
HOW DOES YOUR SHADOW CHANGE?

Materials Needed:

Butcher paper

Crayon (or chalk)

Procedure:

1. Mid-morning is a very good time to do this activity. You need to do it outdoors.
2. Work with one or two partners—more than that if your teacher says it's okay.
3. Each person needs a piece of butcher paper that is a little bit longer than the person is tall.
4. One person at a time will have his or her shadow drawn by the others. The person should lay the paper on the ground and stand on one end of the paper, so the entire shadow is on the paper.
5. Draw the shadow when you are ready. Record the time of day.
6. Find a way to remember exactly where your paper was at the time your shadow was drawn, so you can bring the paper back later and put it in exactly the same place. Record the time of day that each shadow outline is finished.
7. When the shadows are all drawn on the papers, lay down on your shadow and see if it fits your body. Did it? If not, try to decide why. Talk about it with your group.
8. Take your paper with you and find a place to put it away.
9. About an hour later, bring your paper back and put it in exactly the same place that it was when your shadow was drawn.
10. Stand the way you were when your shadow was drawn.
11. Does your new shadow fit your old one? Move around and try to make it fit. Has something changed? What is it? Why? Talk about your ideas with the others.
12. Come back later in the day and try it again.

For Problem Solvers:

After someone draws your shadow in the middle of the morning, think about how your shadow might look one hour later. Draw your predicted shadow with a different color of crayon. Use a third color and draw what you think your shadow will look like in two more hours.

On a different day, have someone draw your shadow again. Do it at the same time of day as you did before. When it's finished this time, predict what your shadow will look like in the middle of the afternoon. Be sure that when you come back to check it out, you put your paper in the exact same place it was in earlier and that you stand exactly as you stood when the shadow was drawn.

Now, here's a challenge for you. Go to your Earth globe and select a spot on the globe that is at a different latitude than you are. Then draw your shadow as you think it would be right now if you were there. Try the same thing using your latitude but a different longitude.

What variables are you dealing with in this activity?

Teacher Information:

Encourage students to experiment with their shadows. It will only take a few minutes for their shadow to begin to look different on the paper. The experience will help them to be more aware of what shadows are, the sun's constant movement, and how the sun's position in the sky affects shapes and positions of shadows.

Students who do the extension for problem solvers will have fun with the predictions. Notice whether they draw their predicted afternoon shadow in the opposite direction from their feet as their morning shadow was. They will also have an interesting challenge with the task of mentally placing themselves at a different latitude or longitude and drawing the shadow they would have if they were there.

Integrating: Art, social studies

Skills: Observing, inferring, predicting, communicating, using space-time relationships, identifying variables

VII. REFLECTION

ACTIVITY 16-6: HOW DOES LIGHT BOUNCE?

Materials Needed:

Table

Rubber ball (a tennis ball or racquet ball will work fine)

Mirror

Flashlight

Chalkboard eraser

Procedure:

1. Place the table next to a wall.
2. Stand the mirror on the table and against the wall. Tape the mirror to the wall, or fasten it in some other way so that it is flat against the wall and won't fall over.
3. Roll the ball across the table toward the mirror. Notice the angle of the path of the ball as the ball approaches the mirror and as it bounces off of the mirror.
4. Roll the ball several times, changing the position and each time comparing the angles of the ball as it approaches the wall and as it reflects off the wall.
5. Discuss your observations.
6. Lay the flashlight on the table and aim it at the mirror. Can you see the beam of light as it approaches the mirror and as it reflects off of the mirror? If not, tap a chalkboard eraser over the table—the dust should cause the light beam to show up clearly. Turn the room lights off if necessary.
7. When you can see the flashlight beam clearly, roll the ball along the light beam toward the mirror. Does it stay with the reflected light beam as it bounces off of the mirror?
8. Talk about the angles of the light beam. Measure the angle between the approaching light beam and the wall and the angle between the reflected light beam and the wall. How do they compare?
9. What can you say about the angles of light beams and bouncing balls?

For Problem Solvers:

From what you now know about the angles of light reflections, stand a small mirror on a table (clay works well to stand the mirrors in). Lay your flashlight on the table—don't turn it on yet. Pick a target on the wall. Now place the mirror where you think it will reflect the light to the target when the flashlight is turned on. Turn the flashlight on and test it. If it missed your target, adjust the mirror and the flashlight as necessary to hit the target. Practice your skill by trying several targets.

When you feel confident with this, try two mirrors. Reflect the light from one mirror to another, then to the target. See if you can do it with three mirrors. What have you learned about the angles of light being reflected from a surface?

Get some paper and crayons or colored pencils and create a design that uses only pairs of angles that are the same as they approach and "reflect" from the edge of the paper.

Teacher Information:

With reflected light, as with the bounce of a ball, the angle of incidence equals the angle of reflection. This is called the law of reflection. You may or may not care to use those terms with your students, depending on their level of readiness, but by doing this activity students should learn the concept. The extension for problem solvers will help students to apply and reinforce the concept, and they will have fun in the process.

Integrating: Art, math

Skills: Observing, inferring, predicting

VIII. REFRACTION

ACTIVITY 16-7: HOW DO YOU SPEAR A FISH?

Materials Needed:

Plastic dishpan

Coin

Two meter sticks

Tape

Metal rod (straightened coat hanger will do)

Procedure:

1. Fill the dishpan about two-thirds full with water.
2. Place a coin at the bottom of the pan. (This is your "fish!")
3. Make a V-shaped trough by taping two meter sticks together.
4. Hold one end of the trough at the edge of the pan, above the water, and try to spear the "fish" by aiming with the trough and sliding the metal rod down the trough.
5. Did you hit the fish? How close did you come?
6. What happened? Did the fish swim away? Do you need glasses?
7. Practice and see if you can improve your accuracy.
8. Discuss what you had to do to hit the fish. Talk about your ideas.

For Problem Solvers:

Place a coin in an empty bowl. Stand in such a position that the coin is just hidden from your view by the edge of the bowl. Without shifting your position, have someone pour water in the bowl, being careful not to disturb the coin. What happened? Relate this to the experience with the "fish" in the above activity. Go home and try this on your family and friends.

Do some research and see if you can find out why this happens.

Teacher Information:

If students keep the end of the trough out of the water, they will most likely miss the coin considerably on the first try. With practice they will learn that the coin isn't where it appears to be, and they will compensate and increase their accuracy. This experience will provide an effective introduction to the concept of refraction of light and the optical illusions that refraction causes.

Skills: Observing, inferring, predicting, researching

ACTIVITY 16-8: HOW CAN YOU MAKE A WET LENS?

Materials Needed:

Water

Magazine

Procedure:

1. Place a drop of water on the print of a magazine page.
2. Notice the letters under the water drop. How do they compare with the letters that are not under the water?
3. Share your observations. Talk about what you learned about water. Why do you think this happens?

For Problem Solvers:

Make a portable lens by putting a drop of water on a small sheet of acetate. Put it over the print of a book page and over various other objects.

Find a piece of copper wire and make a small loop in one end. The rest of the wire will provide a handle. Put a drop of water in the loop and use this device as a magnifier. Experiment with different materials, such as a different size wire, different size loop, and so on. You might even try using a liquid other than water. Make a list of the variables you work with. Share what you learn with others, and see if together you can think of any other variables to change to see if there would be a different result.

Teacher Information:

Refraction of light has the effect of magnifying anything that is seen through a clear, dome-shaped material. For the problem solvers, the drop of water on a sheet of acetate or in a wire loop will provide a portable lens. As they experiment they will discover the effect of varying the size of the drop. They should notice the effect of the flattening of the water dome as they try to use a larger drop on acetate, and of the elongation of the dome as they try to use a larger drop in the wire loop. Experimenting with the liquid, such as adding food coloring or using cooking oil, will produce some interesting effects.

Skills: Observing, inferring, identifying and controlling variables, experimenting

ACTIVITY 16-9: HOW DOES A LENS AFFECT THE WAY LIGHT TRAVELS? (Teacher-supervised activity)

Materials Needed:

Candle

Match

White cardboard

Magnifying glass

Pan

Procedure:

1. Prop the cardboard on a table.
2. Stand the candle in a pan or other non-flammable container about 60 to 90 centimeters (2 to 3 feet) away from the cardboard.
3. Light the candle.
4. Hold the magnifying glass near the cardboard. Move it slowly toward the flame until a clear image of the candle appears on the cardboard (see Figure 16A-2).
5. Do you see anything strange about the flame? What effect do you think the magnifying glass has on what you see?

Figure 16A-2

Move the lens toward the candle until the image appears on the cardboard.

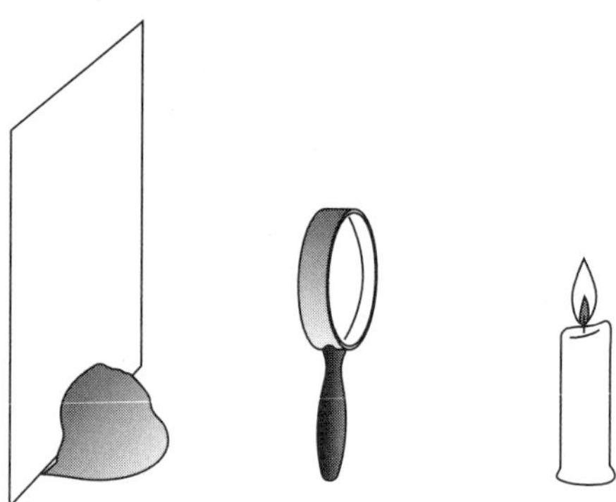

For Problem Solvers:

Experiment with variables such as lens type (if other lenses are available) and distances between the lens, the card, and the candle. What differences did these changes make? Share your findings with your group.

Teacher Information:

The bending of light through refraction results in an inverse image of the flame as it is projected onto the cardboard. The same thing happens to the eye. Images are projected onto the back of the eye upside down, but they are reversed to their true perspective as they are interpreted by the mind.

Integrating: Math

Skills: Observing, inferring, identifying and controlling variables, experimenting

(Except for the sections "For Problem Solvers," "Integrating," and "Skills," this activity was reprinted from Activity 64, "How Does a Lens Affect the Way Light Travels?" in Tolman and Morton, 1986.)

ACTIVITY 16-10:
WHAT ARE CONVEX AND CONCAVE LENSES?

Materials Needed:

Flashlight

Convex lens

Concave lens

Sheet of glass

Procedure:

1. Shine the flashlight toward a white, flat surface.
2. Now shine the flashlight through the clear glass toward the same surface.
3. Do you see a difference in the lighted surface with or without the glass?
4. Shine the light through the convex lens toward the same surface. What differences do you see?
5. Shine the light through the concave lens

toward the same surface. What difference does it make?

For Problem Solvers:

Experiment with different lenses, if other lenses are available. In addition to noticing differences in the light of the flashlight, use the lenses to examine different objects. Write notes that tell the object you examined, the type of lens you used, and what the lens did to the appearance of the object. In general, what do convex lenses do? What do concave lenses do? Share your findings with your group. Talk about what you learned.

Do some research on different types of lenses. Find out what the *focal length* is.

Make a list of all the applications for lenses that you can find (where they are used). Share your information with your group.

Teacher Information:

Students will notice that the clear glass did not affect the appearance of the lighted surface appreciably, while the convex lens bends light inward, concentrating the light and causing it to appear brighter on the white surface. The concave lens bends the light outward, spreading it over a larger surface and causing it to appear less bright. Those who do the extension for problem solvers will learn that convex lenses magnify and that they are thicker in the middle than on the edges; and that concave lenses make things appear smaller, and that they are thinner in the middle than on the edges.

In their search for applications, students should include such things as cameras, eye glasses, contact lenses, microscopes, telescopes, and projectors.

Skills: Observing, inferring, identifying and controlling variables

IX. COLOR

ACTIVITY 16-11: WHAT IS A PRISM?

Materials Needed:

Flashlight (or projector)

Prism

Procedure:

1. Shine the flashlight through the prism and onto a blank wall or a white sheet of paper.
2. What do you see?
3. If you see any colors, write the colors in the order that they appear. Turn the room lights off and see if the colors show up any better.
4. Where do you think the colors come from? Discuss what you think about it.
5. Have you ever seen colors like these before? If so, where?

For Problem Solvers:

Fill a fish tank with water (about two-thirds full is enough). Put the tank in the sunlight. Look for colors on the walls and ceiling, and in the tank itself. Change your position and look from a different angle. Change the position of the tank and keep looking for colors on the walls, ceiling, and in the tank. If you find colors, write down the pattern of colors you see, in the order that they appear. Compare the order of the colors wherever you see them.

Place a mirror tile inside the tank. Stand it at the bottom, leaning against one side. Repeat the search for colors. Be sure the tank is in the sunlight. Compare the order of the colors again. Is the pattern always the same? Is it the same as you saw when you used the glass prism at the beginning of this activity?

Put the mirror in a dishpan full of water, with the mirror leaning at an angle as before. Shine light through the water and onto the mirror, either with a flashlight or, better yet, use sunlight. Discuss with your group what you have learned from this activity.

Identify one variable you manipulated in doing this activity. Talk to your group and see if they agree.

Teacher Information:

As students use the prism, they will notice a band of colors in this order: violet, indigo, blue, green, yellow, orange, and red. Sometimes the blue and indigo are considered as one color. These are the colors contained within white light, which is a combination of all colors. Each color has its own wavelength and is bent to a different degree as light passes from air to glass and back to air. When light passes through a prism, the light is bent enough to actually separate the colors.

When conditions are right, water droplets in the air can act as a prism, creating a rainbow. The prism effect can easily be produced with homemade prisms using water and a mirror tile, as some students will experience as they do the extension for problem solvers.

Skills: Observing, inferring, identifying and controlling variables

ACTIVITY 16-12: WHAT COLOR IS WHITE?

Materials Needed:

White posterboard
Compass
String 1 meter (1 yard) long
Crayons
Scissors

Procedure:

1. With your compass, draw a circle 15 centimeter (6 inches) in diameter on the posterboard.
2. Cut out the circle with the scissors.
3. Draw three equal pie-shaped sections on the posterboard and color them red, green, and blue.
4. Make two small holes near the center of the circle (see Figure 16A-3).
5. Thread the string through the holes (in one end and out the other) and tie the ends of the string together, forming a loop that passes through the two holes of the disk.
6. Center the disk on the string loop and make the disk spin by alternately stretching and relaxing the string.
7. As the disk spins, watch the colored side.
8. What happens to the colors? Why do you think this happens?

Figure 16A-3

Your circle should look like this after step 4.

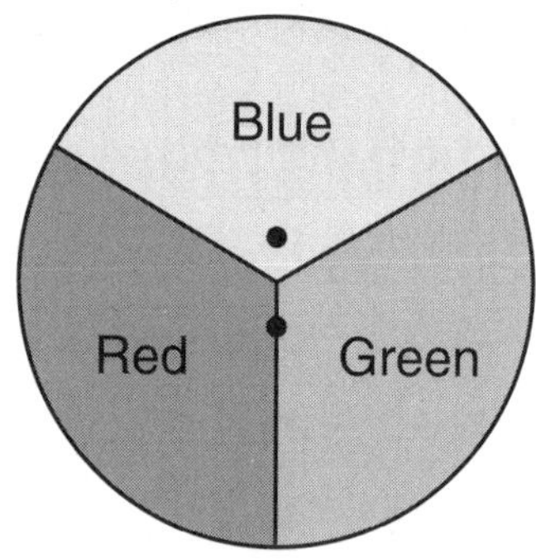

For Problem Solvers:

Try the same thing with another disk and different colors. Expand the activity with other ideas; for example, use only two sections and color them with complementary colors, such as yellow and blue. Each time you try a new color combination, make a prediction of what you will see as the disk spins. Share and discuss your results.

Teacher Information:

As the primary colors spin, they should blend together to form a grayish white. If one of the colors seems to dominate, some of that color should be replaced with more of the other two colors. Blue might need a bit more than its share. Students will enjoy experimenting with various color combinations and testing their predictions of the resulting blends.

The disk may spin better if its weight is increased by doubling the thickness of posterboard or pasting the disk onto cardboard. Another option is to mount the disk onto a sanding pad designed for a quarter-inch drill. The drill could then be used to spin the disk. If a drill is used, the disk must be secured well, as it could fly off and cause injury. This is less likely to happen if you use a drill with a variable-speed switch and keep it at low speed.

Integrating: Art, math

Skills: Observing, inferring, measuring, predicting, identifying and controlling variables

(Except for the sections "For Problem Solvers," "Integrating," and "Skills," and additional slight modification, this activity was reprinted from Activity 65, "What Color Is White?" in Tolman and Morton, 1986.)

CHAPTER

SOUND

CHAPTER OUTLINE:

I WONDER . . .

What happens to sound when the air gets thinner?
How much noise can be made with a string?
How a megaphone is like a flashlight?
How music is stored on a phonograph record?
If a phonograph record can be played without the phonograph?
How sympathetic are sympathetic vibrations?
What in the world is a Triple-T Kazoo?

I. INTRODUCTION

Even with the sense of sight and the ability to enjoy the visible wonders of nature, the world would be dull without sound. Although some people are unable to hear and yet get by, most of us can't even imagine what life would be like without music, the rustle of wind in the trees, the roar of a waterfall, the clapping and rolling of thunder, the song of a bird, or the laughter of a child, to say nothing of the role sound plays in enabling us to talk and communicate with each other. We even depend on sound to warn us of dangers, as with fire alarms, automobile horns, and the hair-raising sound of a rattlesnake.

Sound shares some commonalities with light; in other ways its nature is very different. Both are waves and both carry energy. However, light is a vibration of nonmaterial electromagnetic fields, while sound is conducted only through a medium of material substance—solid, liquid, or gas. Without substance to vibrate, there is no sound. Actually, the source of all waves is something that vibrates, but for light the vibrations are of electrons in atoms. For sound it can be the prongs of a tuning fork, and we can frequently see and feel the vibrations, as well as hear them.

If a tree falls in a forest and there is no ear to hear, is there sound? If a rock falls from a cliff far from any living thing, is there sound? Such questions have been debated for a long time; their answers hinge on the definition of sound. Is it a property of a vibrating object, or is it an interpretation of those vibrations by the brain? People do not all agree on the definition of sound because some consider it to be a physical wave, while others define sound as the physiological and psychological effects on a person or other organism. This chapter will discuss sound in terms of waves that carry energy, which occurs whether or not there is an ear close enough to detect it. In that sense, the sounds created by the fall of a tree in a forest or by the tumbling of a rock from a cliff are independent of the presence of any organism or sound-sensing device.

II. WHAT IS SOUND?

Sound is produced when materials vibrate. Energy in sound waves can be transmitted from one substance to another. A tuning fork struck by a rubber hammer vibrates and causes the air around it to vibrate. The movement of air molecules, in turn, can cause other objects to vibrate, such as an eardrum, or even another tuning fork. When an eardrum is struck by vibrating air molecules, the eardrum vibrates at the same frequency. Behind the eardrum are some small bones that are caused to vibrate by the rapid movement of the eardrum. These bones are attached to a sensing mechanism that sends electrical impulses through the auditory nerve to the brain, which gives the sensation we call sound (see Figure 13-11).

Because we have two ears, we can even tell which direction a sound is coming from. If a sound is coming from directly in front of the listener, it reaches both ears at the same time. If the sound source is to one side or the other, the sound reaches one ear before it does the other. With this information, the brain can automatically determine the direction of the source.

III. HOW SOUND TRAVELS

As a tuning fork, guitar string, or other object vibrates, the rapid back and forth movement causes surrounding air molecules to move. As illustrated in Figure 17-1, the air molecules are pressed together when the vibrating object moves forward and pushes against them. When the object moves back, air molecules spread out. The position where the molecules are pressed close together is called a *compression;* where the molecules are spread out it is called a *rarefaction.* One compression and one rarefaction together make up one *wavelength.* As air molecules vibrate, they bump into other air molecules, which bump into still others, and sound waves thus spread out in all directions from the vibrating object, like ripples of water when a pebble is tossed into a pond.

Figure 17-2 shows a slinky used as a model for sound waves. Notice the compressions and rarefactions in the slinky. Of course, sound waves do not move in a line like the waves that ripple down the length of a slinky; they spread out in all directions from the source of the sound. Thus you hear a sound whether it comes from above you, below you, or from the side.

Sound travels approximately 1 kilometer in three seconds (about 1 mile in five seconds) through air at room temperature. It moves slightly faster in warmer air and slightly slower in cooler air because as molecules get warmer, they move faster; they bump into each other more often and with increased energy. Although sound moves very fast, compared to speeds of most familiar objects, it is very slow when compared to the speed of light. For this reason, as you watch a parade from a distance, the marchers seem to be out of time with the music and the drums. You see the movement of the marchers instantly, but it takes a moment for the sound to reach your ear. If you ever saw a person pounding on something from a distance, you probably noticed that the sounds and motions do not match up. You see the movement instantly (at the speed of light), but the sound lags behind, depending on how far

Figure 17-1

A tuning fork creates compressions/ rarefactions of air molecules as it vibrates.

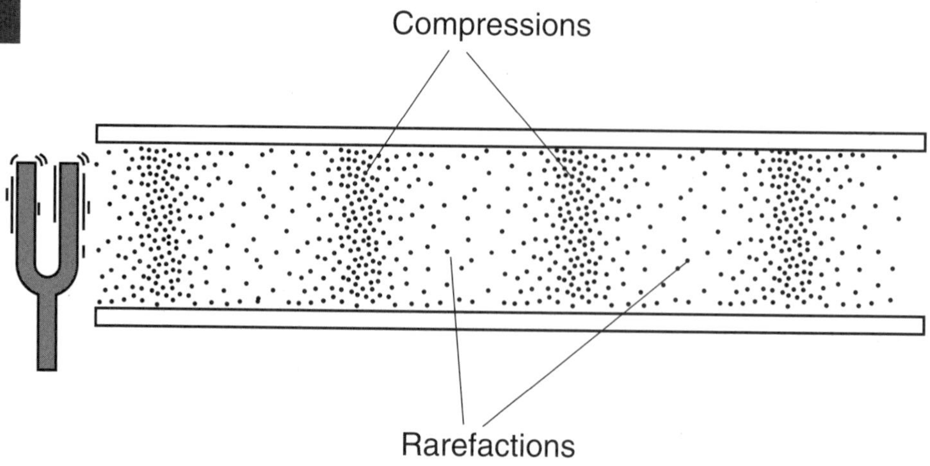

Compressions

Rarefactions

Figure 17-2 *This slinky shows compressions and rarefactions.*

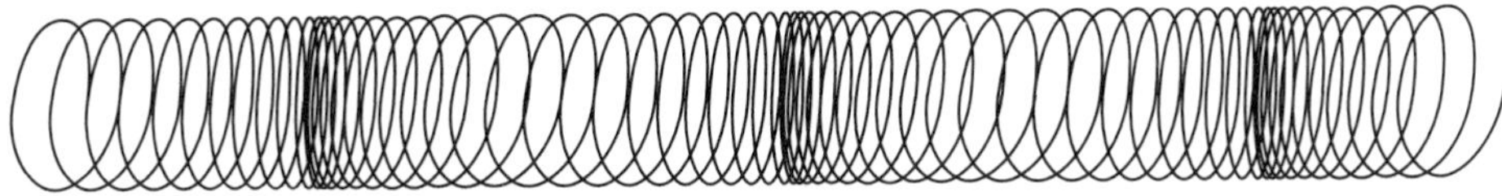

away the pounding is from you. For the same reason, the sound of thunder lags behind the lightning that causes it.

Sound travels faster through liquids than through gases, and faster through solids than through liquids or gases. The closer the molecules are in a substance, the faster sound travels through that substance. Sound travels about four times faster through water than through air, and about fifteen times faster through steel than through air. A train can be heard from miles away by a person whose ear is against the rail. Early Native Americans put their ears to the ground to listen for distant hoofbeats.

Sound travels faster through air at sea level than it does at high altitudes because the molecules of air are closer together at sea level than at higher altitudes. Sound cannot travel in a vacuum, as there are no molecules to transfer the vibrations. If a doorbell is hung in a bell jar, and the air is pumped out of the jar with a vacuum pump, for example, the vibrating motion of the ringing bell can be seen but cannot be heard, for there is no medium to transmit the sound. Astronauts on the moon communicate by radio. Without air, it is impossible to speak to each other as we normally do—through sound waves. Radio, like light, uses electromagnetic energy and can travel through space; it does not need molecules in order to travel.

IV. CHARACTERISTICS OF SOUND

Sounds differ from each other in pitch, intensity, and quality. We hear a great variety of sounds due to differences in these three characteristics.

The term *pitch* refers to the highness or lowness of sounds as we hear them. Pitch varies with *frequency*—the number of vibrations per second. Frequency is a physical parameter, while pitch refers to a physiological/psychological perception. The faster an object vibrates, the higher the pitch; the slower the object vibrates, the lower the pitch. The normal human ear is able to hear sounds with a frequency range of about 16 to 20,000 vibrations per second. This varies somewhat from person to person, and the range usually narrows with age. Some animals, including dogs, can hear sounds of still higher frequency. Sounds of higher frequency than can be detected by the human ear are called *ultrasonic* sounds.

Frequency (thus pitch) is affected by the nature of the vibrating object. Vibrations of objects that are smaller, shorter, or stretched more tightly (as with a rubber band) produce a higher pitch than do those of objects that are larger or longer. A piccolo, for instance, produces a higher pitch than a flute, and the pitch of a violin, guitar, or other stringed instrument goes up as the string is tightened or as it is made shorter by pressing it against the neck of the instrument with a finger.

Another interesting fact is that the speed of a sound wave is independent of its frequency. Otherwise, listening to a concert would be a very unpleasant experience for all listeners except those sitting at the front of the auditorium, because the high and low sounds from an orchestra would arrive at the back of the auditorium at different times. Fortunately, sound waves of various frequencies travel through air at the same speed.

Intensity is related to loudness or softness of sound and indicates how strongly the object vibrates. The stronger an object vibrates, the more energy the sound waves have and the larger and louder the sound waves are. Sounds can also be made louder, or *amplified*, by causing the sound waves to move more air. A large speaker moves more air than does a small speaker. If the base of a vibrating tuning fork is placed against a table, the table will also vibrate and move more air with its large surface, and the sound will be louder.

Actually, intensity is a physical property of sound waves, while loudness refers to the way we perceive sounds. If the ears are not working properly, even an intense sound might not sound very loud. Sound intensity can be accurately and consistently measured by an electronic device designed to detect sound. The unit of measure used is the *decibel*. Whispering registers about 20 decibels, normal conversation about 60 decibels, noise from busy street traffic about 70 decibels, thunder about 110 decibels, and a jet plane from a distance of 30 meters (33 yards) about 140 decibels.

Two people can speak or sing at the same frequency and intensity, yet their voices sound very different. Strike a note at the same pitch and intensity on a banjo and a violin, and a person acquainted with the stringed instruments can distinguish one instrument from the other. These differences are due to sound *quality*. Vibrating objects actually vibrate in multiple frequencies, the lowest of which is called the *fundamental tone*, while the others are called *overtones*. The overtones can vary greatly, as they are affected by the size, shape, and material of the vibrating object. These differences are responsible for the differences in sound quality.

V. REFLECTION OF SOUND WAVES

Another similarity between sound and light is that the energy from both can be reflected or absorbed by materials they strike. If sound waves strike large, hard surfaces, such as a cliff or the wall of a building, the waves are reflected back in unison and can produce an *echo*. Most people can hear the echo as separate from the original sound if the two are separated by about a tenth of a second. With less separation in time, the original sound and the echo blend together and our ears are fooled into thinking they are one, in much the same way that our eyes are fooled by the rapid sequence of still pictures in a movie, which we interpret as continuous motion.

Sound travels about 33 meters in 0.1 second. If you stand about 16.5 meters (55 feet) from a reflecting surface and shout, the sound will get to the wall and reflect back to you in about 0.1 second. If the reflecting surface is less than 16.5 meters from the source of the sound, the reflected sound waves blend in with the original sound and make it louder. If the reflecting surface is more than 16.5 meters from the source, the reflected waves are separate and seem to come from a distant source. Since sound travels about one kilometer (0.621 mile) in three seconds, if the cliff is 250 meters (1,320 feet) away, the echo will occur about 1.5 seconds after the sound is made—the time required for the sound to get there and back.

Sometimes sound bounces off many surfaces and produces a series of echoes. This effect is experienced in thunderstorms when the echoes of thunder are heard to roll across the sky as sounds reflect between cloud and ground and among air layers of different densities.

Sounds can be very annoying in a large auditorium that is not designed to control echo. If the auditorium is filled with people, the problem is reduced because much of the sound is absorbed by bodies and clothing. These facilities are sometimes partially lined with acoustic tile or other material that is rough and has many small holes in it. Such materials break up sound waves by absorbing some of them and reflecting others in many directions (somewhat like light is diffused by a translucent material). This prevents the echo effect of a concentration of sound waves reflected together. A good auditorium is designed for a pleasant balance between absorption and appropriate reflection of sounds.

Sounds can be both broadcast and gathered. Megaphones are used by cheerleaders at ball games to direct sound waves in a given direction. Speakers used on sound equipment project sound in the direction of the target audience. Outdoor theaters often have a large shell-like structure behind and over the performers that directs the sound out toward the audience.

The same technique used to direct sound waves is also used to gather them. If you hold the small end of a megaphone up to your ear, sounds will be amplified as they are gathered and reflected by the cone toward the ear. The outer ear is shaped in such a way that it gathers sounds and directs them into the ear channel. Some people increase the effect of the outer ear by cupping the hand over the ear, causing more sound waves to be directed into the ear. Horses, rabbits, dogs, and many other animals can turn their ears, focusing them in the direction of the sound.

In the past, speaking tubes have been used in buildings and in ships. Sound reflects back and forth as it is directed down the tube, even around corners, allowing communication that would otherwise have been impossible, through walls and from one floor to another. Even today the heating and ventilation systems of some homes can be used as intercoms, by shouting into a vent. Children sometimes use a garden hose in the same way; it works quite well and for surprising distances.

VI. THE HUMAN VOICE

Your voice box, or *larynx,* has two thin, strong bands of tissue stretched over it (see Figure 17-3). These are called *vocal cords* or *folds.* The vocal cords of men are usually longer and thicker than those of women. Air passes freely by the vocal cords as you breathe. However, the vocal cords have muscles attached to them that allow you to tighten them. When you do this, and force air past them, the vocal cords vibrate similar to the way stretched rubber bands vibrate in a stream of air, and sounds are made. If you place your fingers on your throat and hum, you will feel your vocal cords vibrating. By tightening the muscles attached to your vocal cords, you can stretch them tighter and they vibrate faster, or loosen them and they vibrate more slowly, thus producing sounds of higher and lower pitch. Like thicker and longer rubber bands, thicker and longer vocal cords produce lower pitch, which explains why men usually have lower voices than women and why there is a wide variety of higher and lower voices, even within each of these groups. Sound quality of the voice is affected by many factors, including air passages in the throat, mouth, and nose, the position and shape of lips, tongue, and teeth, and the shape and condition of sinus cavities, which act as resonating chambers.

Figure 17-3

This diagram of the larynx shows the vocal cords.

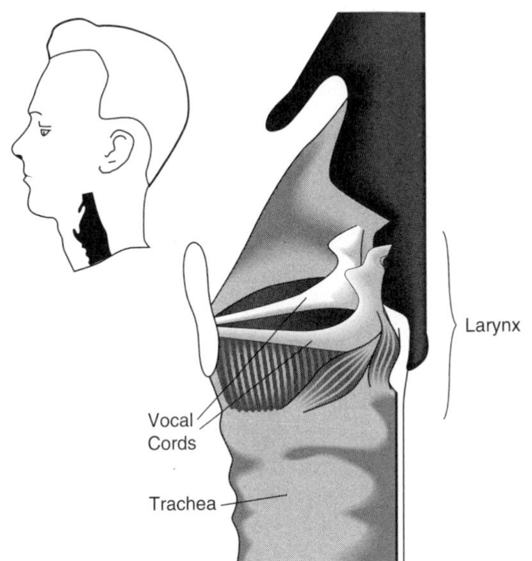

VII. MUSIC

Generally speaking, music consists of sounds that are pleasant and are produced by regular vibrations, while those that are unpleasant and caused by irregular vibrations are usually considered *noise*. However, just as we do not all have the same taste for food, we also differ in our preferences for music. What is music to one person might well be considered unpleasant noise by another. Most people would consider sound coming from the traffic of a busy street to be noise. Some people enjoy rock and roll music, however, while others consider much of it to be nothing but noise, and do not enjoy it at all. Your favorite music may be classical, country western, or folk; others might not like any of these.

The ability to create musical sounds has taken on a whole new meaning with the electronic age. While electronically produced sounds add to, and even quite effectively duplicate, the sounds of conventional musical instruments, the traditional tools of music show no signs of being completely replaced by new technology in musical sound. Conventional musical instruments are typically classified into three groups: stringed instruments, wind instruments (woodwinds and brass), and percussion instruments.

Stringed Instruments

In a stringed instrument, the vibration of strings is transferred to a sounding board, then to the air. With some instruments, such as the violin and the cello, strings are stroked with a bow. With other instruments, strings are plucked. These include the guitar, ukulele, banjo, and harp. The strings of a piano are struck by padded hammers.

Frequency is controlled by tightness, length, and thickness of the strings. The pitch is lower if the string is looser, longer, or thicker, and it can be made higher by tightening the string or by using a shorter or thinner string. The effect of these variables (thickness, length, and tightness) can easily be shown with a variety of sizes of rubber bands, as suggested in the activities section of this chapter. Most stringed instruments have only a few strings, and the musician changes the pitch by pressing the strings with the fingers, thereby changing the length of the vibrating portion of the string. The piano has many strings, each preset for a particular pitch (see Percussion Instruments, below). The harp also has many strings, but the pitch can be raised by pressing a pedal.

Although the sound begins at the string, the shape and construction of the instrument are very important. When the strings vibrate, the entire instrument (or soundboard, as with the piano) vibrates at the same frequency and produces the quality of the tones for that instrument. One instrument can be of superior quality and very costly, while another is of poor quality and relatively inexpensive, because of the construction of the vibrating parts of the instruments—even if the two instruments have identical strings.

Woodwind Instruments

With the piccolo and the flute, a stream of air is blown across a hole near one end of the instrument, and the column of air inside the instrument vibrates. Most woodwinds, including the clarinet, the oboe, and the saxophone, use a mouthpiece with a reed, which is usually a thin piece of cane. When air is blown into the mouthpiece, the reed vibrates and makes the air column in the instrument vibrate. The musician changes the pitch by pressing and releasing pads that close and open small holes along the length of the instrument, having the effect of changing the length of the vibrating air column.

Brass Instruments

Brass instruments, including the trumpet, cornet, bugle, French horn, tuba, and trombone, get their name because they are made of brass. The column of air inside the instrument is made to vibrate by pressing the lips against a metal mouthpiece and vibrating the lips while blowing into the mouthpiece. The pitch is controlled by changing the tightness of the lips and by making the vibrating air column longer or shorter. With most brass instruments, the length of the air column is changed by pressing and releasing valves, which add or delete segments of tubing the air flows through.

Some brass instruments have no valves to change the length of the vibrating air column. The bugle player controls the pitch strictly by the tightness of the lips and by how hard air is blown into the instrument. The trombone has a slide that moves in and out to change the length of the air column.

Percussion Instruments

Percussion instruments work by striking a surface to produce sound. Some percussion instruments are made of a solid material, such as wood or metal. These include the cymbals, chimes, bells, wood block, and castanets. Others have a diaphragm (membrane) stretched over a hollow container, and include the tambourine and a variety of drums. The piano has strings, but musicians usually consider it a percussion instrument because the strings are struck by small, padded hammers to produce sound.

Percussion instruments vibrate when they are struck by the hand or by a mallet or other object. For those that have a diaphragm stretched over a hollow container, the pitch can be altered by tightening or loosening the diaphragm. Tightening the diaphragm raises the pitch and loosening the diaphragm lowers the pitch. The thickness of the material the diaphragm is made of also affects the pitch; thinner material produces a higher pitch. In addition, the smaller the diaphragm, the higher the pitch.

Electronic Musical Instruments

Electronic musical instruments are very different from conventional musical instruments. Instead of strings, diaphragms, and air columns, they use electronics to produce vibrations in loudspeakers. These instruments can produce unique tones, and they can duplicate the sounds of conventional musical instruments. Such versatility provides the musician with a powerful new tool.

VIII. EAR DAMAGE FROM SOUND

Sound can be the source of pleasure and important information. It can also damage the organ designed to detect it. Just as the sense of sight can be damaged by exposure to intense light, the sense of hearing can be damaged by exposure to very loud sounds. The extent of hearing damage depends on how near, how loud, how long, and how often the ear is subjected to the sound. Just as you should protect your eyes from exposure to intense light, you should also protect your ears from exposure to intense sound. (See also "The Sense of Hearing" in Chapter 13.)

IX. DOPPLER EFFECT

As a boat on a lake begins to move, waves move out from it in all directions. The boat moves toward the last wave sent out, so when the next wave is sent, it is closer than normal—thus the wavelength is shorter (see Figure 17-4). Sound

Figure 17-4

As this boat moves, the waves are shorter in front of the boat and longer behind it.

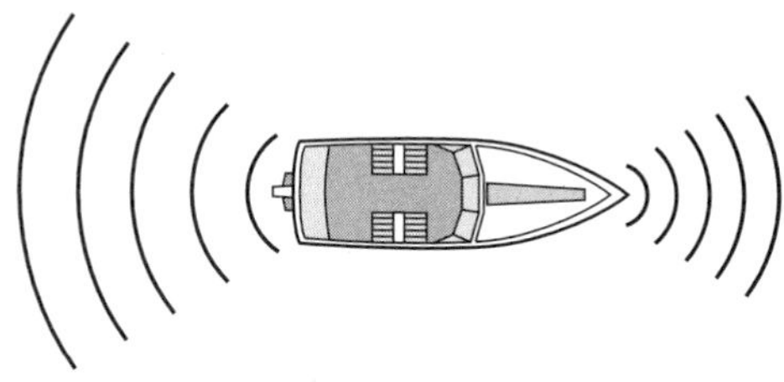

waves behave similarly. Anyone who has heard an automobile or train go by with its horn blasting might have noticed that the pitch changes as the vehicle passes by. As the sound approaches rapidly, the pitch is higher than if the source is standing still. As it passes by, the pitch lowers noticeably. This is known as the Doppler effect. Sound travels out in all directions, and as the vehicle moves, it pushes into the sound waves, having the effect of shortening the sound waves in the direction of the vehicle's movement and lengthening them behind it, similar to the waves of water from the boat (see Figure 17-5). Shorter sound waves produce a higher pitch and longer sound waves produce a lower pitch, so as the vehicle speeds by, the pitch drops.

Figure 17-5

When the car is in motion, sound waves are compressed in front of it and lengthened behind it.

X. SONIC BOOM

Consider the Doppler effect with the vehicle moving faster and faster. The sound waves in front of the vehicle get shorter and shorter until the vehicle reaches the speed of sound. At that point, the sound waves only spread out to the side and behind the vehicle. They do not spread out in front of the vehicle because the vehicle is moving as fast as sound waves move. When a jet airplane approaches the speed of sound, compressed sound waves and compressed air actually act as a barrier in front of the airplane.

Remember the boat on the lake; as it starts out and increases its speed, waves in front of it get shorter and appear to pile up. The driver must increase the power in order to push over the barrier of waves, then the water ahead is smooth. In order for the airplane to go faster than sound, it must push through a barrier of compressed air. This not only requires more power, but pushing through the sound barrier produces a shock that can severely stress the structure of the aircraft. Once through that barrier, it is easier for the aircraft to go still faster, but from the moment of breaking the sound barrier, the shock wave (sonic boom) follows along with the airplane, in a cone-shaped pattern, and is heard and felt by those on the ground as the airplane passes overhead (see Figure 17-6). The effect is greatly diminished if the aircraft is flying at high altitude. With improved construction materials, technology, and design, modern aircraft are able to withstand the stress of pushing through the sound barrier much better than earlier designs.

Many people have the mistaken notion that the sonic boom is a sudden, momentary explosion that occurs at the moment that the airplane surpasses the speed of sound, and then it's over. Not so; the shock wave continues with the airplane until the airplane slows its speed below the speed of sound. We usually think of the speed of sound as about 1,200 kilometers

Figure 17-6

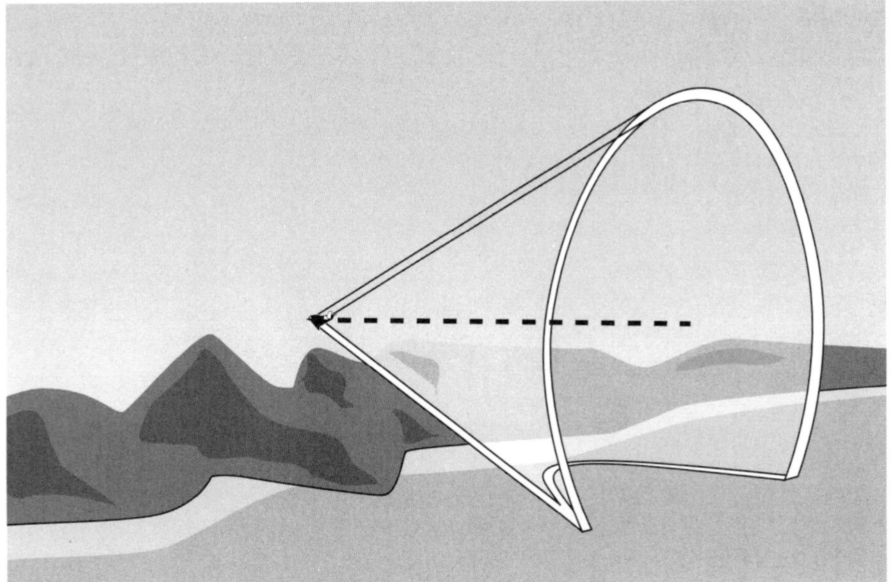

This jet airplane has broken the sound barrier, and the cone-shaped shock wave follows behind it.

(750 miles) per hour, though it varies somewhat with differing temperature and altitude.

XI. SYMPATHETIC AND FORCED VIBRATIONS

All solid objects have a natural frequency of vibration. Sound waves from one object vibrating at the natural frequency of a second object can cause the second object to vibrate. Sound waves from one vibrating tuning fork can cause another tuning fork to vibrate if the two are identical. Compressions and rarefactions of vibrations from the first tuning fork have the effect of pushing and pulling on the second tuning fork. Such responding vibrations are called *sympathetic vibrations.*

Sympathetic vibrations can be compared to a father pushing a child in a swing. The swing has a natural frequency that is determined by the length of the ropes. If Dad pushes on the swing at that frequency, the swing can be made to go higher and higher (intensity is increased), but it will continue at the same frequency. Sound waves become stronger with increased intensity (loudness), but the frequency at a given pitch remains the same.

If Dad pushes at a different frequency, that is, if he pushes on the swing before it completes its cycle, the effort will decrease, not increase, the distance the swing travels. Similarly, a sound at a frequency other than the natural frequency of a vibrating tuning fork or other vibrating object tends to deaden, rather than intensify, the motion of the vibrating object. Sympathetic vibrations will occur in a second tuning fork only if the first vibrates at the natural frequency of the second.

Windows vibrate in response to the sounds from a truck or low-flying airplane passing by. Fine crystal (or a common drinking glass) can vibrate sympathetically to sounds from a radio or from a singer if the pitch is the same as the natural frequency of the crystal. In fact, if the sound is loud and sustained at the natural frequency of the crystal, the crystal can actually shatter from intense sympathetic vibrations. In 1940 the newly constructed Tacoma Narrows bridge in the state of Washington was destroyed in a similar way. A mild gale caused the bridge to swing and twist at its natural frequency with increasing intensity until the

Figure 17-7

The Tacoma Narrows bridge was destroyed by sympathetic vibrations.

Washington State Historical Society, Tacoma, WA

bridge collapsed (see Figure 17-7). A standing order in the military is to break step when crossing a bridge, to avoid setting up movements of the bridge of its natural frequency, which could increase to the point of damaging the bridge.

If the base of a vibrating tuning fork is placed on a table, the sound gets louder because the table is caused to vibrate at the same frequency as the tuning fork. Such vibrations are called *forced vibrations,* and usually occur when a vibrating solid object is placed in direct contact with another solid object.

XII. DETECTING OBJECTS WITH SOUND

Geophysicists use sound to examine formations in the earth's crust. One technique used is to set off a small explosion at or near the earth's surface. By noting the nature of resulting echoes they can determine the type and thickness of rock layers and possible locations of mineral and oil deposits. Bats and dolphins use similar techniques to monitor their surroundings, locating both predators and prey through echoes of sounds they make themselves.

A device called *sonar* (acronym for SOund Navigation And Ranging) uses sound waves to locate underwater objects. Sound waves are sent out and reflections are detected from any direction. Navy ships use this device to detect submarines and underwater obstructions. Fishing vessels use the same technique to detect schools of fish.

Ultrasound (sound with frequencies above the range of normal human hearing) is used to test materials such as metals and plastics. It is also used to clean delicate instruments, including watches. A relatively recent application of this technique is to check the development of a human fetus, as it is much safer than X-ray.

XIII. IN CLOSING

Sound has been an important source of information for organisms that have roamed the earth since long before this planet was inhabited by people. We are still learning about the characteristics of sound, ways it is used by the animal kingdom, and about new applications for this form of energy. Medical researchers will continue to search for more and more information about how sound vibrations are transmitted to the brain, and how to restore the sense of hearing to people who suffer from partial or total hearing loss. Considering the many ways we rely on sound, including for information and enjoyment, most of us can't imagine what life would be without sound.

LIST OF RESOURCES

Ballif, Jae R., and William E. Dibble, *Physics: Fundamentals & Frontiers* (New York: John Wiley & Sons, 1972).

"Sound," *World Book Encyclopedia*, 1989.

Strong, William J., and George R. Plitnik, *Music, Speech, High-Fidelity, Second Edition* (Provo, UT: Soundprint, 1983).

Tolman, Marvin N., and James O. Morton, *Physical Science Activities for Grades 2–8* (West Nyack, NY: Parker Publishing Co., 1986).

Victor, Edward, *Science for the Elementary School, Sixth Edition* (New York: Macmillan Publishing Co., 1989).

CHAPTER

SOUND

ACTIVITIES

WHAT IS SOUND?

ACTIVITY 17-1: WHAT NEW SOUNDS CAN YOU HEAR?

Materials Needed:

Paper and pencil

Procedure:

1. Sit quietly and listen for two minutes. Write a list of all the sounds you hear.
2. Put a mark beside each sound that you haven't noticed in your classroom before. Why do you think you don't usually notice these sounds?

Teacher Information:

People often become accustomed to background noises that are common in their environment, and ignore them. Thus we can be unaware of certain sounds around us. This is an opportunity to talk about listening skills, and about the difference between listening and really hearing. A discussion of how it feels to really be quiet can lead to an art or creative-writing activity.

Skills: Observing

(Adapted from Activity 78, "What Is Sound?" in Tolman and Morton, 1986.)

ACTIVITY 17-2: HOW ARE SOUNDS PRODUCED?

Materials Needed:

Meter stick

Foot ruler

Tongue depressor

Procedure:

1. Place the meter stick on a table, with part of it extending over the edge of the table.
2. Hold the stick firmly on the table with one hand. With the other hand, flip the other end of the meter stick by pushing it down and then releasing it quickly.
3. What do you hear? Why?
4. Try the meter stick in different positions, with different lengths extending over the edge of the table.
5. What happens to the sound as the vibrating part of the stick gets longer?
6. As the vibrating part of the stick gets

longer, does the speed of vibration change? In what way?

7. Repeat steps 1 through 4 using the foot ruler and the tongue depressor. What happens to the sound as the stick gets smaller?

For Problem Solvers:

Continue this investigation by using plastic rulers, different types of sticks, and other materials. Predict the result before trying the new material.

Teacher Information:

This activity can be done with any grade level, though the level of discussion and discovery will vary greatly from grade to grade. If a sound is heard, something is vibrating. This is an excellent activity to help students to associate sounds with vibrating objects, because the vibrations are observable. Even younger students should make this connection as they perform the activity. As their perceptions become more keen, students will notice that when they shorten the vibrating portion of the object, the pitch goes up, and as the vibrating portion of the object becomes longer, the pitch goes down. They will also notice that as the vibrating object gets smaller, such as progressing from the meter stick to the foot ruler to the tongue depressor, the pitch goes up. For each object, however, both pitch and speed of vibration are affected by changing the length of the vibrating part of the stick.

Skills: Observing, inferring, predicting, controlling variables

ACTIVITY 17-3: WHERE CAN YOU FIND SOUND?

Materials Needed:

Paper and Pencil

Procedure:

1. Go for a walk around the building or playground. As you do this, make a list of all the sounds you hear. If possible, do this during break time when many people are around, and then do it again when the halls and playground are relatively quiet.
2. Stop frequently and listen for any sounds that you don't usually hear.
3. Share and discuss your list with others in the class. Did some people hear sounds that others didn't hear?
4. Compare the break-time list with the list made when other people were in class. Which sounds are on one list but not the other? Why?
5. What sounds were occurring during break time but were not heard at that time? Why?
6. Now go back to your lists and write, for each sound, what you think was vibrating to produce the sound.

Teacher Information:

Sounds often go unnoticed because we become accustomed to them, or perhaps because we are thinking about something and we tend to turn our minds off to other things. Sometimes sounds are drowned out by other sounds that are louder and more dominating, just as a flashlight would go unnoticed in a brightly lighted room even though the flashlight is turned on. This activity ends by focusing student attention on the main idea of this series of activities—sounds are caused by vibrating objects. Identifying exactly what vibrates to produce sounds is often an intriguing challenge.

Integrating: Language arts

Skills: Observing, inferring, classifying, communicating

III. HOW SOUND TRAVELS

ACTIVITY 17-4:
HOW CAN YOU MAKE A TELEPHONE?

Materials Needed:

Two paper cups or plastic cups (or tin cans)

String, at least 3 meters (10 feet) long

Two toothpicks

Procedure:

1. Punch a small hole in the bottom of each of the two cups, using one of the toothpicks or a pair of scissors.
2. Insert one end of the string through the hole in the bottom of one cup. Tie the end of the string around one toothpick. The toothpick should be inside the cup; this is to keep the string from pulling back out through the hole. If the toothpick is too long to fit in the bottom of the cup, break some of it off (see Figure 17A-1).
3. Attach the other end of the string to the other cup in the same way.

Figure 17A-1

Your cup, string, and toothpick should be set up like this.

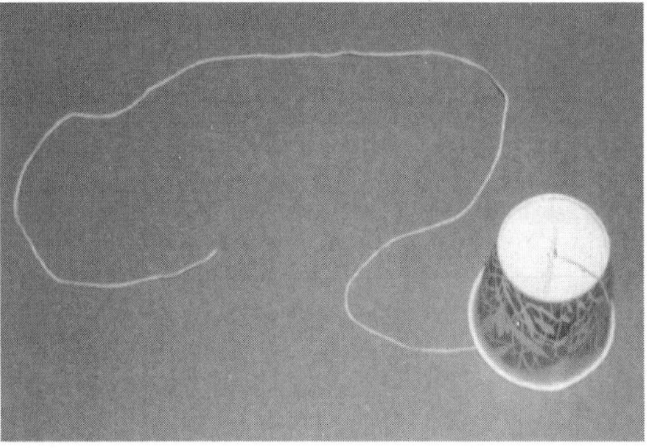

4. Get a friend to take one cup while you take the other. Stretch the string until it is tight.
5. One person should hold the open end of the cup to one ear while the other person talks into the other cup. Take turns talking and listening.
6. Describe what is happening and why.

For Problem Solvers:

Try using tin cans instead of cups. Try replacing the string with fishing line, wire, dental floss, or heavier and lighter string. Try empty cans in place of the cups. Try larger or smaller cups. Each time you try something new, talk about it and predict what the difference will be before you test the change. What other investigations can you think of for the homemade telephone? Do you know what a party line is? If not, find out what it is and see if you can make a party line with homemade telephones.

Teacher Information:

Students of all ages will enjoy building homemade telephones and investigating with different materials. They have learned that whenever sounds are heard, something is vibrating. Therefore there must be a "medium," or something for the sound to travel through to get to our ear. That material is the medium, and in this case is the string (and cup). They begin to learn, now, that sound travels through solids (such as string) as well as gases (such as air). Their investigations might include touching the string while using the telephones. If not, you could touch the string as students are talking through the device; this stops the vibration of the string and cuts the communication. A party line can be made with two pairs of telephones by wrapping the string of one pair around the string of the other; now one person can talk to three people at once (see

Figure17A-2

These two pairs of paper-cup telephones have been set up as a party line.

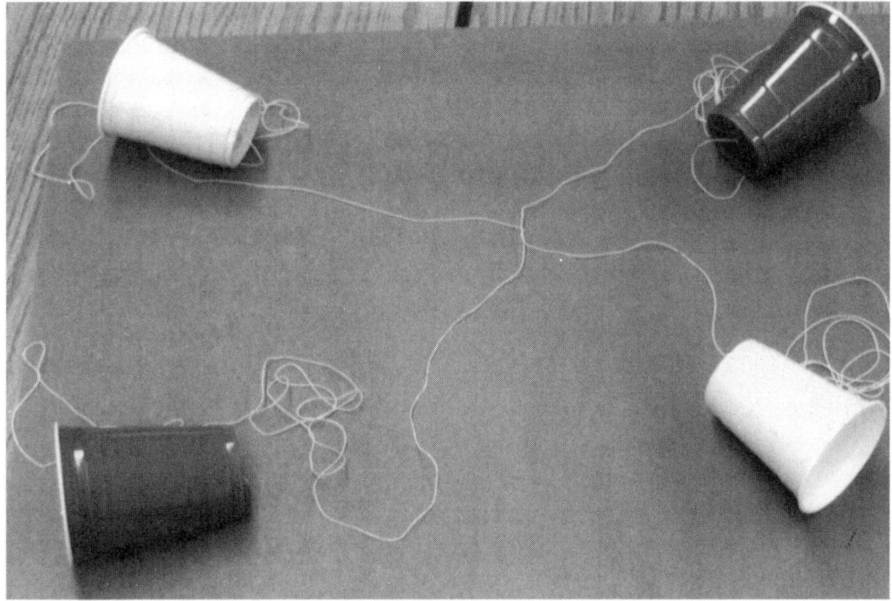

Figure 17A-2). Have students try adding more pairs to the system.

Integrating: Language arts

Skills: Inferring, predicting, communicating, formulating hypotheses, identifying and controlling variables, experimenting

ACTIVITY 17-5: WHAT HAPPENS TO SOUND WHEN THERE ARE FEWER MOLECULES? (Teacher-supervised activity)

Materials Needed:

4- to 8-ounce jar with tightly sealing lid

Thread or string

Hot (not boiling) water

Small bell

Tape

Procedure:

1. Use the string to suspend the bell in the jar by taping it to the inside of the lid. Be sure the bell does not touch the sides or bottom of the jar (see Figure 17A-3).
2. Gently shake the jar and listen to the bell.
3. Remove the lid with the bell attached and carefully pour about 2 to 3 centimeters (1 inch) of hot water into the jar.
4. Allow the jar to stand for about 30 seconds and then replace the lid. Be sure the bell does not touch the water.
5. Let the jar cool, then gently shake it again and listen to the bell.
6. What happened? What can you say about this?

Teacher Information:

Before hot water is poured into the jar, the children should be able to hear the bell clearly. Hot water in the jar will cause the air to expand and force some of the molecules out. With fewer air molecules in the bottle,

Figure 17A-3

The bell is suspended from the lid of the jar.

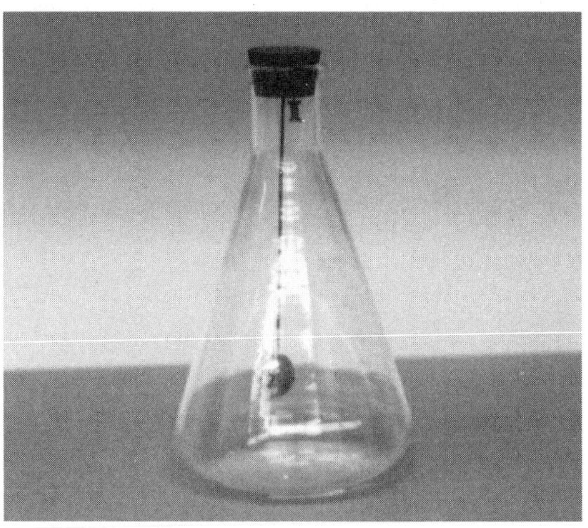

sound vibrations will not travel as easily, so the bell will not sound as loud. The difference will be greater after the jar has cooled and the water vapor has condensed into liquid.

Discuss the problem of communication on the moon, where there is no air to carry sound vibrations.

Skills: Observing, inferring

(Reprinted from Activity 97, "What Happens to Sound When There Are Fewer Molecules?" in Tolman and Morton, 1986.)

ACTIVITY 17-6: CAN YOU MAKE CHIMES WITH A COAT HANGER?

Materials Needed:

Wire coat hanger

Two pieces of string, about 50 centimeters (20 inches) each

Procedure:

1. Tie the two strings to the bottom of the coat hanger.
2. Holding the ends of the strings, suspend the hanger upside down. Slide the strings to opposite ends of the hanger so it hangs evenly (see Figure 17A-4).
3. Wrap the end of one string around the index finger of one hand. Do the same with the other string and the other hand.
4. Now lean over, put your index fingers in your ears, and sway the hanger to tap it on a desk, chair, or other solid object.
5. What do you hear? What is vibrating?

Figure 17A-4

Attach the strings to the bottom of the coat hanger.

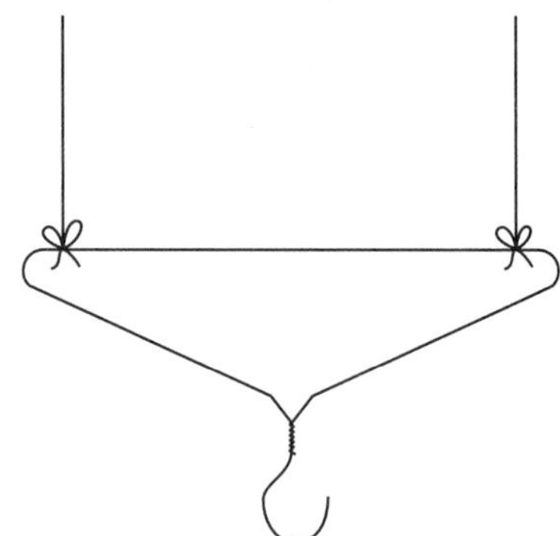

For Problem Solvers:

Experiment with different coat hangers, as well as spoons, forks, scissors, and other objects in place of the coat hanger. Try replacing the string with different types of string, thread, dental floss, wire. Remember to predict what the result will be before you try each new change. Try to think of other variables you can change as you investigate with this activity.

Teacher Information:

Students should be able to identify the string and coat hanger as the vibrating materials. If they do not immediately recognize that the fingers are also vibrating, guide them to that idea by asking leading questions.

When struck without the fingers in the ears, the hanger will sound flat and metallic. With fingers in the ears, the sound is usually a pleasing gong, and louder—demonstrating that sound travels better through solids (the string) than through the air.

Investigations should include replacing the hanger with a variety of metal and nonmetal objects to compare the difference. Students should also try tapping the hanger against a variety of objects that are hard, soft, metal, nonmetal, and so on.

Skills: Observing, inferring, predicting, communicating, formulating hypotheses, identifying and controlling variables, experimenting

(Adapted from Activity 93, "How Does Sound Travel? (Part III)," in Tolman and Morton, 1986.)

ACTIVITY 17-7: HOW MUCH NOISE CAN YOU MAKE WITH STRING?

Materials Needed:

One piece of string, about 50 centimeters (20 inches) long

Plastic cup

Toothpick

Procedure:

1. Punch a hole in the base of the cup.
2. Attach the string to the cup, using the toothpick to hold the string, similar to the way you attached strings to cups for the paper cup telephone. This time it doesn't really matter whether the string extends from inside the cup or from outside the cup.
3. Hold the cup in one hand and grip the string with the thumb and index finger of the other hand.
4. Pull on the cup and see if you can make a noise as the string is drawn through the fingers of the other hand.
5. Wet the string and try it again. See how many different sounds you can make.

For Problem Solvers:

Try using different materials. Predict what will happen if you use a plastic cup. What about different size cups? Try something else in place of the cup. Does length of string or size of string affect the sound? What other variables can you change as you investigate different effects?

Teacher Information:

Be prepared for a noisy activity with this one. This is a good activity to end the day with. Students can continue their investigations at home. In discussions, have students identify the materials that are vibrating. Reinforce the meaning of the term "medium," with respect to sound. In this case the medium is air—sound travels through air to get from the vibrating object to our ears.

The cup can be outfitted with a beak, feathers, and eyes to become a "Yellow Chicken," "Red Hen," or whatever (see Figure 17A-5). This adds to the fun of the

Figure 17A-5

A cup decorated as a "Red Hen."

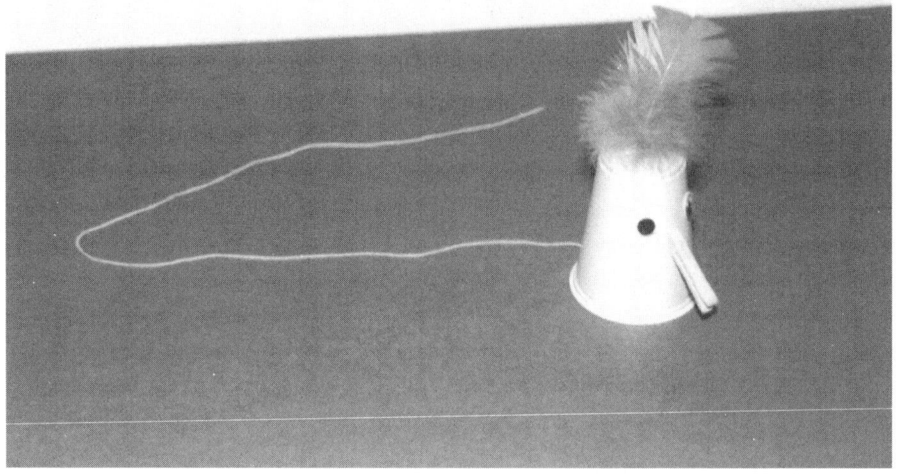

activity, applies artistic talents, and gives students a chance to be creative.

Skills: Observing, inferring, predicting, communicating, formulating hypotheses, identifying and controlling variables, experimenting

ACTIVITY 17-8: HOW FAST DOES SOUND TRAVEL?

Materials Needed:

Drum, cymbals, large metal lid or something else that will make a loud sound when visibly struck

Stick to strike object

Procedure:

1. Take your drum or other object out on the school grounds. Ask other members of the class to go with you.
2. Move at least 100 meters (approximately 105 yards) away from the other students.
3. Strike the object several times so the others can see the movement of your arm and hear the sound.
4. Remember, when you see an object move at a distance, you are seeing reflected light travel. When you hear the sound, you are hearing sound vibrations.
5. Have the students tell you what they observed. What can you say about the speed of light and the speed of sound?
6. Discuss these questions:
   a. Would altitude affect the speed of sound?
   b. Would sound travel more easily during the day or night?
   c. Would sound travel better on a cold or a hot day?

Teacher Information:

Light travels at about 300,000 kilometers (over 186,000 miles) per second. By comparison, sound is a slowpoke, moving at approximately 1,200 kilometers (about 750 miles) per hour at sea level. (Speed of sound is affected by wind, temperature, humidity, and density of the air, and therefore varies slightly as these conditions change.) Even at the short distance of 100 meters, it will be possible to see the child strike the drum before the sound is heard. Children who have been to athletic events in a large stadium may have noticed that sounds made on the playing field by athletes or bands are seen before they are heard. Airplanes, especially fast jets, are sometimes difficult to locate in the sky by their sound because the sound is traveling so much more slowly that by the time it arrives, the plane has moved to a new position.

Children should be able to answer the questions in step 6 if they remember that sound travels better in air when there are more molecules. Higher altitudes have *thinner air*, fewer molecules per cubic centimeter. Cold air contains more molecules and is *heavier*. Therefore, sound would travel better at night or on a cold day.

Integrating: Language arts

Skills: Observing, measuring, communicating, using space-time relationships

IV. CHARACTERISTICS OF SOUND

ACTIVITY 17-9: DO YOU HEAR WHAT I HEAR?

Materials Needed:

Tape recorder

Audio tape with a variety of sounds recorded at school, at home, and so on, preferably sounds the child hears at least occasionally

Blank tape

Procedure:

1. Turn on the tape recorder and listen to the first sound, then turn the machine off and write what you think made the sound you heard.
2. Repeat step 1 for each of the other sounds on the tape.
3. Think about and discuss the differences you hear in the sounds. Try to use descriptive words, such as high, low, loud, soft, squeaky, gruff, and so on.
4. Use the tape recorder and blank tape to record some sounds of your own for others to listen to and identify. Try to locate or create some unusual sounds.

Teacher Information:

This is a good opportunity for children to build vocabulary and extend their ability to verbally express their thoughts, as they describe the recorded sounds. In the recording, include several sounds that are familiar to the students. These can be sounds from around the school, such as a swinging door, children at play, copy machine running, or telephone ringing. They can be sounds outdoors or around the home. They should include some animal sounds, especially for young children. And yes, the sound of a flushing toilet is a must for such recordings.

The experience of recording new sounds provides an opportunity for cooperative groups to work together. Students enjoy finding and creating sounds to be identified by other students and perhaps see if they can even fool the teacher.

Integrating: Language arts

Skills: Observing, inferring, communicating

ACTIVITY 17-10: CAN YOU DESCRIBE OBJECTS FROM THEIR SOUNDS?

Materials Needed:

Several film cans or other opaque containers with lids to serve as rattle cans

Each rattle can should have something

different in it, such as a metal washer, a small block of wood, a marble, a few grains of wheat, a cottonball, a small rubber stopper or cork stopper, or a small amount of sugar.

Procedure:

1. Pick up one of the containers, shake it gently, and listen.
2. Describe what is inside. Use as many descriptive words as you can, such as hard, soft, flat, round, and so on. Is there just one of them, two or three, or many? About how big is it?
3. Do the same with each of the other containers.
4. Compare your observations with others. Listen to their descriptions and see if you agree. Work together and see how many ways you can describe what is inside the container.
5. Find one or more empty containers with lids. Put an object in each one and see if your friends can describe the objects by listening to the sounds they make.

Teacher Information:

This activity provides an excellent opportunity for students to work together in cooperative groups, as they listen, observe, share their observations, and select items for additional rattle cans. The object of this activity is not to guess exactly what item is in the container, but to practice skills of observation by listening and skills of verbal expression.

If desired, you could request that students also try to guess what the actual item is. A risk associated with this is that students might do a great job of describing the object as flat, thin, hard, and about 2 or 3 centimeters wide, then feel that they were wrong because they guessed the item as a quarter, only to find out that it was a metal washer. The descriptors were accurate and the response should be considered correct, because that is the object of the activity.

An interesting adaptation to consider for this activity is to prepare pairs of identical rattle cans—two with wheat, two with marbles, and so on—and have students match them up in pairs, based on the sounds made from rattling the contents. Several pairs should be prepared. The containers could be numbered randomly with a list of numbers and contents for self-checking or group-checking of accuracy. This is an excellent activity to use at a party or other event to mix people up and get them acquainted. Give each person one rattle can and instruct each to find his or her partner by listening to the rattle cans.

Integrating: Language arts

Skills: Observing, inferring, communicating

ACTIVITY 17-11: WHAT CAUSES SOUND?

Materials Needed:

About 50 centimeters (20 inches) of fishing line or string

Three short wooden dowels or pencils (about 5 to 10 centimeters, or 2 to 4 inches)

Shoe box with lid

Pencil

Procedure:

1. Make a hole in one end of the box with your pencil.
2. Insert one end of the fish line through the hole and tie it to one of the dowels. The dowel should be inside the box, with the remainder of the fish line on the outside (see Figure 17A-6).
3. Tie a second dowel to the other end of the fish line.

Figure 17A-6

The shoe box, with fish line and two dowels, should look like this.

Figure 17A-7

The homemade guitar is ready to be plucked.

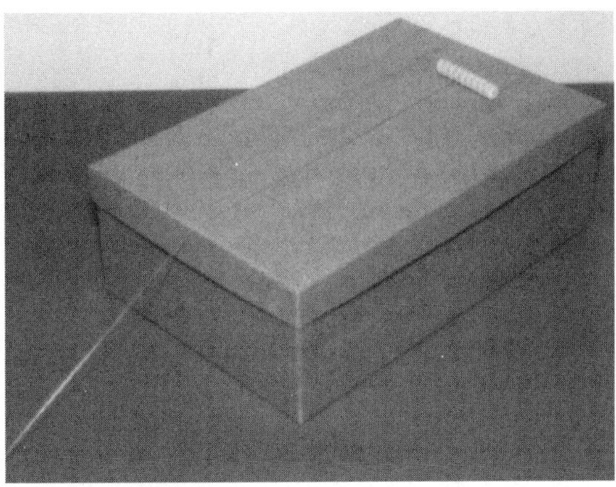

4. Place the lid on the box and lay the fish line over the top of the box. Put the third dowel under the fish line near one end of the box, as shown in Figure 17A-7.
5. Using the dowel on the free end of the fish line as a handle, tighten the line. The line that is now across the top of the box will behave much like a guitar string.
6. Pluck the string as you hold it tight by pulling on the dowel. Pull tighter and pluck the string again.
7. Continue plucking the string as you change the tension.
8. Describe what you observe. Compare your findings with others.
9. Try to play a melody on your one-string homemade guitar.

For Problem Solvers:

Try using different materials, such as boxes of different sizes, different types of string, and perhaps a board instead of a box. Before you make any change, think about it and predict the result in terms of any change in the sound that you expect to occur, then try your idea and test your prediction. You might try a totally different design—be creative. Can you make a similar instrument by using rubber bands?

Teacher Information:

The purpose of using this activity at this point is to deal with the characteristics of sound, namely that pitch goes up as the string is tightened and the pitch goes down as the string is loosened. Refer back to the earlier activity with the meter stick, the foot ruler, and the tongue depressor. At that time students learned that sounds are associated with vibrations and that the length and size of the vibrating object affects the pitch that is produced. This activity adds the effect of tightness of the vibrating object.

The dowel on the top of the lid serves as a bridge to keep the string elevated enough to vibrate freely. Guitars, violins, and other stringed instruments use this principle.

Integrating: Music, language arts

Skills: Observing, inferring, predicting, communicating, formulating hypotheses, identifying and controlling variables, experimenting

(Adapted from Activity 82, "What Causes Sound?" in Tolman and Morton, 1986.)

V. REFLECTION OF SOUND WAVES

ACTIVITY 17-12: HOW CAN SOUND BE REFLECTED?

Materials Needed:

Two megaphones (can be just large paper cones)

Procedure:

1. Have a friend go to the playground with you. Move far enough apart that you have to shout to hear each other.
2. Speak to each other without using the megaphones.
3. Hold the megaphone or cone up to your mouth, pointed in the direction of your friend, and speak to your friend again. Try to speak about as loud as you did without the megaphone.
4. Take turns speaking to each other with and without the megaphones.
5. Move farther apart and continue speaking to each other with and without the megaphones.
6. Talk about your observations. Was it easier to hear each other with or without using the megaphone?

For Problem Solvers:

Find a flashlight, a separate flashlight bulb and two flashlight batteries. You will also need a piece of wire about three times as long as a battery. First, be sure the flashlight works and that you can hook up the bulb, wire, and batteries in the right way to make the light shine; we'll call this your homemade flashlight. Next, take these materials into a dark room or outdoors at night. Turn on the flashlight and shine it on an object in front of you. Now turn off the flashlight and use your other homemade flashlight to light up the same object. Discuss the results with a friend. Examine the flashlight and see if you can tell what made the difference. The reason the flashlight lights up the object better than your homemade flashlight does is very much like the reason that a megaphone makes it easier to hear a person's voice. Now, here's the tough question—what is the reason? Discuss your ideas. Search available resource books to find the answer. If necessary ask your teacher.

Teacher Information:

Megaphones are shaped to reflect sound and focus it forward, similar to the way a flashlight reflector focuses light forward. Many speakers are cone-shaped for more effective projection of sound. Students who do the activity "For Problem Solvers" should recognize that the megaphone serves as a reflector for sound, thereby performing a similar function to that of the reflector of a flashlight.

Integrating: Reading, spelling

Skills: Observing, inferring, predicting, research

ACTIVITY 17-13: HOW CAN SOUND BE GATHERED?

Materials Needed:

Megaphones from the previous activity

Procedure:

1. Have a friend go to the playground with you. Move far enough apart that you have to shout to hear each other.
2. Speak to each other without using the megaphones.

3. Hold the megaphone or cone with the small end up to your ear and the open end pointed in the direction of your friend, and ask your friend to speak to you. Try to speak about as loud as you did without the megaphone.
4. Take turns speaking to each other with and without the megaphones (small end to your ear).
5. Move farther apart and continue speaking to each other with and without the megaphones.
6. Talk about your observations. Was it easier to hear each other with or without using the megaphone? Why?

Teacher Information:

Incoming sound waves are reflected inward toward the small end of the megaphone. This action might be compared to the function of a funnel; as water is poured into the open end (large end) of a funnel, it flows toward the small end. As sound enters the large end of a megaphone, it is reflected inward toward the small end.

Integrating: Language arts

Skills: Observing, inferring, communicating

VI. THE HUMAN VOICE

ACTIVITY 17-14:
HOW DOES THE VOICE MAKE SOUNDS?

Materials Needed:

Rubber bands—variety of sizes

Procedure:

1. Select a medium-size rubber band. Stretch it out and blow hard on it.
2. Does the rubber band make any sound when you blow on it?
3. Stretch the same rubber band tighter and blow on it again. What happened to the sound?
4. Let the rubber band relax a bit and blow on it again. What happened to the sound?
5. Select a thicker rubber band and repeat the above steps. How do the sounds compare with the sounds of the first rubber band?
6. Select a thinner rubber band and repeat the steps again. How do the sounds compare this time?
7. Hold your fingers on your throat and hum. What do you feel?
8. Now just relax and breath normally, keeping your fingers on your throat. Discuss your findings.
9. Compare what you observed with the rubber bands to what you think is happening in the throat as you make sounds with your voice.

Teacher Information:

The vocal chords consist of two thin, strong bands of tissue. These can be tightened by muscles in the throat. When they are tightened and air is forced rapidly through them, the vocal chords vibrate and sounds are made. When they relax for normal breathing, air just passes over them. Just as students will find is true of rubber bands, vocal chords that are long and thick produce lower sounds, while those that are shorter or thinner produce higher-pitched sounds. Vocal chords of men are usually longer and thicker than those of women.

Sound quality of the voice is affected by many factors, including air passages (throat, mouth, nose), and the position and shape of the lips, tongue, and teeth, and the shape and condition of the sinus cavities.

Integrating: Language arts

Skills: Observing, inferring, communicating

VII. MUSIC

ACTIVITY 17-15:

HOW CAN YOU PRODUCE SOUND WITH A SEWING NEEDLE?

(Teacher-assisted activity)

Materials Needed:

Phonograph

Discarded phonograph record

Paper cup (medium size)

Sewing needle (medium-size)

Procedure:

1. Very carefully push the sewing needle through the bottom edge of the paper cup (see Figure 17A-8).
2. Put the phonograph record on the revolving turntable of the phonograph.

Figure 17A-8

Push the needle through the paper cup in this way.

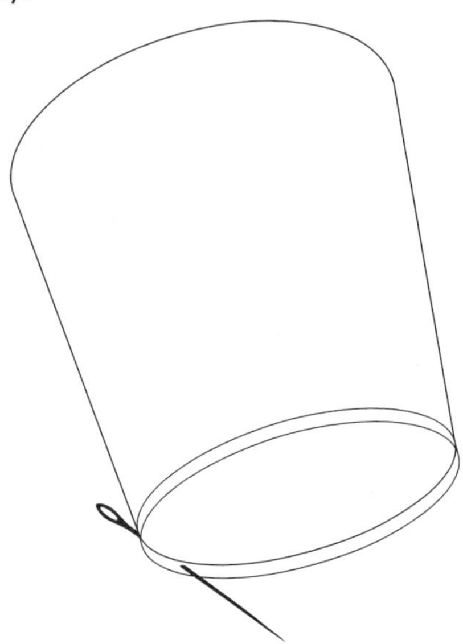

3. Hold the cup with just two fingers and gently rest the needle on the grooves of the record. The needle should be slanted away from the direction of turn of the record, so it doesn't dig into the record, but instead rides smoothly in the groove (see Figure 17A-9).
4. What do you hear? What is vibrating, and why? Discuss what's happening.

Figure 17A-9

You can use a paper cup and a sewing needle to play a record.

For Problem Solvers:

Here are two tasks for you. First, get a hand lens or a microscope and examine the record. You already know that sounds come from vibrations. Figure out what causes the vibrations, and what causes the pitch to go up and down.

Your second task is to investigate further with this activity using different materials. Identify variables that are involved, change them one at a time, and see what happens. State what you think will happen each time before you try something new, then test your idea. For instance, try cups of different sizes, both paper and plastic. Must it be a cup? Try a paper cone, or just a sheet of paper. Insert the needle through the eraser of a pencil, then as the needle rides the record lean over with your ear near the pencil (be careful not to put the pencil inside your ear). Would a different size needle change the sound? Would a straight pin work as well? Do you need the phonograph at all, or can you figure out another way to turn the record?

Teacher Information:

Some of us used to think there was something magic about a phonograph, but I sure don't see anything magic about a paper cup or a sewing needle. Yet these simple materials produce music and voice from a phonograph record. Those who do the activities for problem solvers will examine the record with a hand lens or a microscope. They will find that the grooves in the record are not smooth, but bumpy. These bumps cause the needle to vibrate, which in turn causes the cup or paper cone to vibrate, and the cup or paper cone amplifies the sound. The problem solvers should also notice that the bumps are not evenly spaced—some are close together and others are farther apart. These little sharpies (the students, that is, not the needle) will probably reason that the closer together the bumps are the faster the needle vibrates, making the pitch go up, with the inverse being true where the bumps are farther apart.

Students will also enjoy investigating with this activity using a variety of materials and techniques. If there are still doubters about the phonograph adding a touch of magic to the event, they might devise a way to spin the record on a kitchen turntable.

Now, after students figure out what makes the pitch go up and down, they might discuss their ideas about how all of the other qualities of sound are captured in those bumps and grooves to produce all of the sounds of an orchestra, and even the distinct sound qualities of a particular human voice. Let's not get carried away, though, or we'll all be back to calling it magic again.

Integrating: Language arts, music

Skills: Observing, inferring, predicting, communicating, formulating hypotheses, identifying and controlling variables, experimenting

(Adapted from Activity 101, "What Are Some Ways to Use Sound?" in Tolman and Morton, 1986.)

ACTIVITY 17-16:
HOW CAN YOU MAKE A BUGLE FROM A DRINKING STRAW?

Materials Needed:

Supply of soda straws

Scissors

Procedure:

1. Flatten about 2 to 3 centimeters (1 inch) of one end of a soda straw with your teeth or your fingers.
2. Cut the flattened tip to a point (see Figure 17A-10).
3. Put the pointed end of the soda straw in your mouth and blow. See how much noise you can make.
4. Blow on the soda straw again. As you blow, snip a piece off the end of the straw with your scissors. Be careful, don't clip your nose!
5. What happened to the pitch when you snipped off a piece of the soda straw? Explain.

For Problem Solvers:

Prepare a series of snipped straws of different lengths, each having a different pitch. Can you play a tune with them?

As a second challenge, find a pair of soda straws, one of which will fit inside the other.

Figure 17A-10 *Here's how your soda straw should look with its end cut.*

Now use the two of them together to make a trombone. Can you play a tune with your trombone?

Here's a third challenge—try making a flute out of a single soda straw, by cutting finger holes along the length of the straw. See if you can tune it to a piano or other instrument. You might need to try several soda straws before you're satisfied with your masterpiece. Play some tunes with it. Can you think of other ways you could change variables and try a new idea?

Teacher Information:

In this activity students reinforce what they have learned earlier about sound, and they use their knowledge in the actual construction of musical instruments. Those who take on the challenge of the activities for problem solvers will make three different instruments that can be used to play tunes, or at least to drive the teacher up the wall. The instruments might not qualify for the symphony, but they will be capable of producing several pitches, using what students know about how the length of the vibrating object and its effect on pitch.

Integrating: Language arts, music

Skills: Observing, Inferring, predicting, communicating, formulating hypotheses, identifying and controlling variables, experimenting

ACTIVITY 17-17: HOW CAN YOU MAKE A TRIPLE-T KAZOO?

Materials Needed:

Toilet tissue tube

Waxed paper or tissue paper (large enough to wrap around the end of the tube)

Scissors

Paper punch

Procedure:

1. Using the paper punch, punch a hole at one end of the toilet tissue tube. Reach in as far from the end of the tube as a standard punch will reach.
2. Wrap a small piece of waxed paper or tissue paper over one end of the tube and secure the paper with a rubber band. Do not cover the punched hole with the paper.
3. Hum into the open end of the tube, and shazam—you have just made a Triple-T kazoo!
4. Have you figured out yet where it gets the name Triple-T?
5. Play your favorite tunes with your kazoo by humming into the open end.

Teacher Information:

Humming into the open end of the Triple-T (that is, toilet tissue tube) causes the paper on the other end to vibrate at the same frequency as the voice, thus producing the same pitch as the one that is hummed. You can make an instrument that is easy to play using materials that would otherwise be discarded. Anyone who can hum a tune can play the Triple-T kazoo.

Integrating: Music

Skills: Observing

ACTIVITY 17-18: CAN SODA BOTTLES PLAY A TUNE?

Materials Needed:

Three glass soda bottles of the same size and shape

Water

Paper slips numbered 1 through 8

Pencil

Procedure:

1. Pour water in the bottles, each a little bit fuller than the last.
2. Blow gently across the top of one of the bottles until a sound is produced. Practice this until you become proficient at producing a sound, then try to blow sound out of the rest of the bottles as well.
3. Adjust the water level in each bottle until you have a musical scale as you blow across the series of bottles.
4. Number the papers 1 through 8 and put them under the bottles, in sequence. If you can tune your bottles to a piano, you might want to write the musical notes on the papers as well as the numbers.
5. What is vibrating to make the sounds, as you blow across the tops of the bottles?
6. Play a tune with your bottles. You might want to have two or three people involved, with each person assigned to designated bottles.

For Problem Solvers:

Tap the bottles on the side, near the top, with a pencil or other hard object. Do all of the bottles sound the same? Why or why not? What vibrates to produce sound when you blow across the top of the bottles? What vibrates to produce sound when you tap the bottles? What will happen to the pitch as water temperature changes? What will happen to the pitch as water evaporates?

Teacher Information:

Blowing across the tops of one of these bottles causes the air column in the bottle to vibrate. The shorter the vibrating column of air, the higher the pitch, consistent with what our students have learned about sound. Therefore, as more water is added, the pitch from blowing goes up. When the bottles are tapped on the side, it's the glass that vibrates to produce sound. Water slows the vibration of the glass, so the pitch from tapping the bottle goes down as water is added, while at the same time the added water makes the pitch from blowing go up.

Of course, evaporation will change the pitch. Change in temperature can also change the pitch due to expansion and contraction of the water.

Integrating: Music, math

Skills: Observing, inferring, measuring, predicting, communicating, controlling variables

(Adapted from Activity 85, "How Can Sounds Be Produced? (Part I)," in Tolman and Morton, 1986.)

ACTIVITY 17-19:

CAN WE CREATE A CLASSROOM ORCHESTRA?

(Note: This entire activity is for Problem Solvers)

Materials Needed:

A variety of materials students can bring to class, such as wooden blocks, tin cans, paper cups, sticks, tubes, soda bottles, sandpaper, conduit, boxes, rubber bands, string, and so on

Procedure:

1. In groups, examine the materials brought from home by the group.
2. Brainstorm and list ways these materials could be used to make sound.
3. Each group should select one or more items and form an orchestra with rhythm instruments, kazoos, and whatever else is produced by the groups.
4. Students could be allowed to borrow and exchange materials from group to group, as it becomes apparent that they have needs as well as extras.

Teacher Information:

For thousands of years, people have made and played musical instruments. This activity will provide a fun time for students to use their creativity and their knowledge of sound, to create a homemade orchestra as a class. Students could also be encouraged to extend the effort at home if they have ideas for making other instruments that they want to pursue further.

Integrating: Music, art

Skills: Observing, inferring, classifying, predicting, communicating, identifying and controlling variables

VIII. EAR DAMAGE FROM SOUND

ACTIVITY 17-20:

CAN SOUND BE UNPLEASANT OR EVEN DAMAGE HEARING?

Materials Needed:

None

Procedure:

Allow students to share any experiences they have had with discomfort from sound, whether it be from being around extremely loud equipment, rock music, or simply sounds that are unpleasant to them. The constant hum of a motor, for instance, can be very annoying to some people, or a certain style of music, or the constant drip, drip from a leaking faucet.

Teacher Information:

Some of this discussion will get into areas other than hearing damage, but such dialog gives students an opportunity to share their experiences with sound. Some of these experiences will relate to actual pain from loud sounds, and some of them will reflect personal preferences.

Sound is measured in decibels. Normal conversation is typically about 60 decibels, while jet engines can register higher than 140 decibels even from half a football field away. Extended exposure to loud sounds, including loud rock music, can cause hearing damage.

Integrating: Music, language arts

Skills: Communicating

IX. DOPPLER EFFECT

ACTIVITY 17-21:
HOW CAN YOU CHANGE THE PITCH OF A HORN?

Materials Needed:

Tape recorder

Blank audio tape

Automobile

Procedure:

1. Assign a responsible student to operate the tape recorder.
2. Have a group of students stand beside a road near the school. They can stand back well away from the road and they should, of course, be well supervised.
3. Arrange for a responsible adult to drive a car past the group. The driver should begin honking the horn about a block away and not let off the horn until the car is about a block past the group.
4. The person with the tape recorder should put it on the "record" mode before the horn begins to honk and continue recording until after the horn has stopped.
5. Discuss the experience as a group. What changes did you notice in the sound of the horn as the car went by?
6. Review the experience during the discussion by listening to the recording. Discuss what causes the pitch changes that are heard.

Teacher Information:

If it is not convenient to include students as spectators during the recording of the horn-blasting, second best would be to record it outside of school and just let them hear the recording. The live experience is, of course, more meaningful. The faster the car is moving as it passes the observers, the more dramatic will be the change in pitch with the Doppler effect.

If a sound source is moving rapidly, as it approaches you it pushes into the sound waves, having the effect of shortening the waves and raising the pitch. As the sound source retreats, it has the effect of lengthening the sound waves and lowering the pitch. See the section on Doppler Effect in this chapter for illustrations that compare the Doppler effect with waves from a moving boat.

Integrating: Language arts

Skills: Inferring, communicating

X. SONIC BOOM

ACTIVITY 17-22:
WHAT IS A SONIC BOOM?

Materials Needed:

None

Procedure:

Discuss any experiences students recall with regard to a sonic boom.

Teacher Information:

The discussion should include an attempt to clarify misconceptions students might have that the "boom" occurs only at the moment that an aircraft accelerates past the speed of sound. The effect actually follows the aircraft as long as it is traveling at speeds in excess of the speed of sound.

Try to get a pilot, or other expert in supersonic sound, to come in and speak to the class, especially about what the sonic boom is, its effect on people, and rules of flight that relate to it.

Integrating: Language arts, social studies

Skills: Communicating

XI. SYMPATHETIC AND FORCED VIBRATIONS

ACTIVITY 17-23: WHAT ARE SYMPATHETIC VIBRATIONS?

Materials Needed:

Two identical tuning forks

Two guitars, freshly tuned

Procedure:

1. Strike one of the tuning forks against the heel of your shoe, then immediately hold the two tuning forks side by side.
2. After just a few seconds, touch the first tuning fork (the one that struck the shoe) with your finger to stop its vibration.
3. Listen carefully and you will probably hear the second tuning fork vibrating.
4. Stand two guitars on the floor near each other, face to face but not touching each other.
5. Pluck one string of one guitar, then touch it and stop its vibration.
6. Listen carefully and you will probably hear the sound made by the same string of the other guitar.

Teacher Information:

Each vibrating object has a natural frequency, the frequency at which it normally vibrates. When two objects having the same natural frequency are placed near each other, if one of the objects is caused to vibrate, the sound waves moving through the air will often cause the second object to vibrate. This would be a good time to discuss the notorious demise of the Tacoma Narrows bridge (see Figure 17-7).

Integrating: Language arts

Skills: Observing, communicating

ACTIVITY 17-24: WHAT ARE FORCED VIBRATIONS?

Materials Needed:

Tuning fork

Table (preferably solid wood construction)

Procedure:

1. Strike the tuning fork on the heel of your shoe, then immediately place the base of the tuning fork on the table and listen carefully.
2. Did the sound get louder? What do you think is happening?

Teacher Information:

Often when a vibrating solid object comes in contact with another solid object, the second object vibrates at the same frequency as the first, even though the two objects have different natural frequencies. This is called forced vibration. In this activity, the wooden table will probably vibrate at the frequency of the tuning fork. Since the table has such a large mass to vibrate, it amplifies the sound.

Skills: Observing, inferring

XII. DETECTING OBJECTS WITH SOUND

ACTIVITY 17-25: WHAT IS SONAR?

Materials Needed:

Encyclopedias

Other books and resources as available

Procedure:

1. Go to encyclopedias and other available resources and do some research to find out about *sonar.*
2. Prepare a report on your findings.
3. Report to the class and compare information with others who did the same research.

Teacher Information:

Sonar is used in many ways to detect objects. It is a form of echo-location. A sound is emitted and if it strikes an object it is echoed back. The distance of the object is computed from the time that lapses after the sound is emitted and before the echo returns. Bats use sonar to detect the location of insects in the air with extreme accuracy. The bat emits a high-pitched sound, which bounces off the insect and is reflected back to the bat. Dolphins also use sonar to locate objects and edibles in the ocean. Relatively recently, people have discovered sonar and use it today in a variety of ways.

For additional information for discussion, see the section on Detecting Objects with Sound in this chapter.

Integrating: Language arts

Skills: Communicating

CHAPTER

ELECTRICITY AND MAGNETISM

CHAPTER OUTLINE:

I WONDER . . .

What is static electricity?
Is lightning static electricity?
Why does clothing sometimes cling?
What are magnetic materials, and why are they attracted by magnets?
How does a magnetic compass work?
What are open and closed circuits?
What are parallel and series circuits?
How do magnetism and electricity relate to each other?
How does a power plant get electricity out of water?

I. INTRODUCTION

This chapter deals with three topics: static electricity, magnetism, and electric current. These topics are so interrelated, and in some ways interdependent, that even the question of which is the most logical order of presentation can be debated. We've decided to treat static electricity first, followed by magnetism, then electric current. We placed the latter two topics together because of the special relationship between them: Each can be used to produce the other.

An argument could be raised as to whether static electricity and magnetism should be taught together or kept widely separated. Confusion often results from the similarity of behaviors in these two natural phenomena—like charges repel and unlike charges attract, just as like poles repel and unlike poles attract —and it is usually a good idea to keep such potentially interfering notions separated. Madeline Hunter explains that concepts are like paint—if you want them to mix, put them together; if you don't want them to mix, keep them apart (Hunter, 1978). Static electricity is often thought to be a magnetic force, but it is not; they are two different forces. And as common as the confusions between static electricity and magnetism are, perhaps it is best to bring them together and tackle the problem head-on. To use an analogy, if a learner investigating the characteristics of mammals looks separately at a mule deer and an antelope, he or she might easily conclude that they are of the same species; but if the two are seen together, careful comparison will reveal that they have distinctly different features. By similarly examining static electricity and magnetism together, the likenesses and differences might be more clearly distinguished.

II. STATIC ELECTRICITY

Static electricity is to current electricity as a parking lot full of trucks is to a convoy of the rigs traveling down a freeway. At one moment the parking lot might be filled with the same trucks that later on are moving along the freeway, but in the parking lot they are stationary and on the freeway they are moving. The word "static" means stationary, still, or not moving. Ordinary electric currents in wires are moving streams of electrons, while *static electricity* is an imbalance of positive and negative charges. When you scuff your feet across a carpet that has not been treated to prevent static electricity, you build up an electrostatic charge, but when you reach out to a doorknob the charge is drained off.

All matter is composed of very tiny particles, called molecules. Molecules are so small that electron microscopes are required to see some of the larger ones. As tiny as they are, molecules are made of smaller particles, called atoms. Only in recent years have scientists "seen" atoms for the first time, by use of special instruments (Fisher, 1989). They look like fuzzy little balls, just as scientists have been saying for a long time they would probably appear if we could see them (see Figure 18-1).

Figure 18-1

Images of atoms, as produced by the STM, look like fuzzy balls.

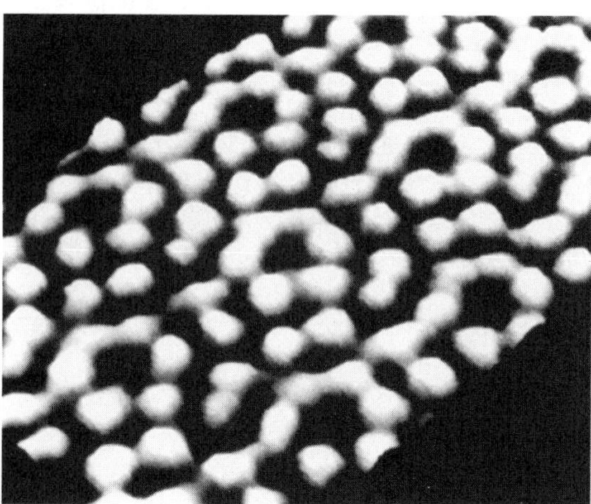

Courtesy of IBM Research.

The atom is composed of still smaller particles, called protons, neutrons, and electrons. The protons and neutrons form a very small but massive nucleus at the center of the atom, and to separate them requires a great amount of energy. The electrons are outside the nucleus; they move very rapidly, and the outermost ones do not always stay with the same nucleus, but may move from atom to atom.

Each proton has a positive electrical charge and each electron has an equal negative charge. The total electrical charge on a neutron is zero. Normally the same number of electrons are associated with an atom as there are protons in its nucleus. Therefore the atom is neither positively nor negatively charged; we say it is neutral.

Friction can cause electrons to transfer from one material to another. Some materials have a greater affinity for electrons than others do. When two materials are rubbed together, electrons can be transferred from the material with lesser affinity for electrons to the material that has a greater affinity for them. The materials are no longer neutral, but instead both now have an *electrostatic* charge. The material that acquired additional electrons has a negative charge (more electrons than protons). The other material has a positive charge because it now has fewer electrons than protons.

In this list of common materials, the ones at the top have a greater affinity for electrons; the ones at the bottom have a lower affinity.

- **Plastic**
- **Rubber**
- **Nylon**
- **Glass**
- **Wool**

In general, when a material on the list is rubbed with another material higher on the list, the former material gives up electrons to the latter. The material lower on the list becomes positively charged and the material higher on the list becomes negatively charged. When a hard rubber comb is rubbed with wool cloth, for example, electrons transfer from the wool to the rubber comb. The comb now has more electrons (negative charges) than protons (positive charges), so the comb is said to be negatively charged. The wool is positively charged, having given up some of its electrons to the rubber comb (see Figure 18-2).

Figure 18-2

The comb is negatively charged, and the wool cloth is positively charged.

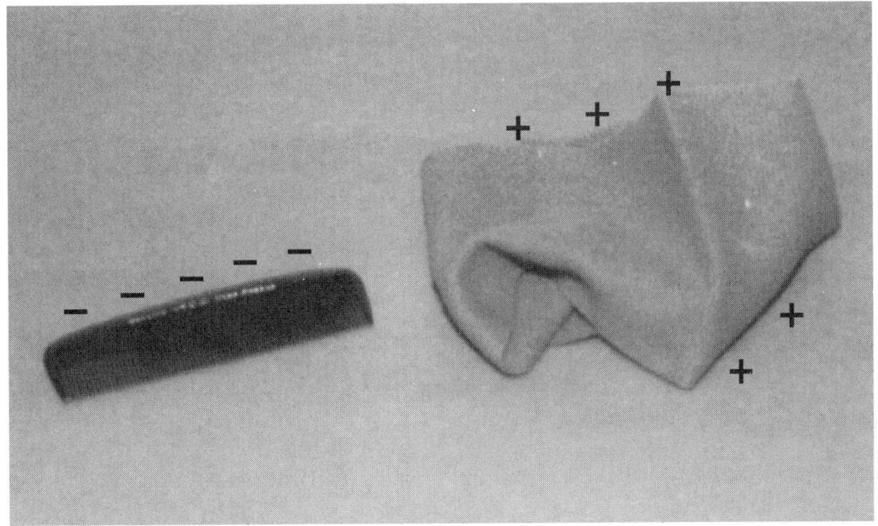

The transfer of electrons can be greatly impeded if the materials involved are not clean or if they are treated with certain substances. A freshly emptied plastic bread bag will usually not build up a charge of static electricity when rubbed on a sheet of glass, because of an oily film on the bag. Materials are available commercially to put in clothes dryers to reduce or eliminate "static cling," which results from static electricity that builds up as clothes tumble in the dryers. Antistatic chemicals are sprayed on carpet to avoid the nuisance of static electricity as people walk across the carpet. This same treatment helps to keep the carpet clean, because any buildup of static electricity in the carpet attracts dust.

Materials will remain charged only until they have a chance to neutralize. If you scuff your feet across an untreated carpet and then touch a doorknob, a spark jumps between your finger and the doorknob. The spark is a stream of electrons moving to neutralize the electrical charge. Sometimes you can feel the spark, and in the dark you can even see it, as electrons move from finger to doorknob. Before you touched the doorknob (or someone's nose!), there was an electrostatic charge—a buildup of electrons—on you (think about the trucks in the parking lot). When the spark occurred, electrons flowed—current electricity (think about the trucks moving down the freeway).

Now, a word about real trucks. Older gasoline tankers had a chain attached beneath them that dragged on the ground. Friction from the fuel sloshing in the tank can build up an electrostatic charge. The charge was constantly drained off into the ground by the chain to avoid a possible spark, which might ignite the fuel. Today's trucks are internally grounded to avoid the possibility of a spark without the need of a chain dragging on the ground, but ground cables are attached to the truck while

Figure 18-3

This gasoline tanker uses a ground cable hook-up while loading fuel to avoid sparking.

loading fuel to avoid any possibility of a spark from static electricity (see Figure 18-3).

The Law of Electrostatic Attraction and Repulsion

When two negatively charged objects are brought together, they repel each other. The same is true of two positive charges. However, unlike charges attract each other. The law of electrostatic attraction and repulsion states that unlike charges attract and like charges repel (see Figure 18-4).

Figure 18-4

The balloons on top repel each other because they have like charges, and the bottom pair attract each other with opposite charges.

Electrostatic Induction

If a blown-up balloon that has been rubbed with wool or cotton cloth is brought near a small piece of paper, the paper will usually be attracted to the balloon. It is easy to understand that the balloon was charged, because it was rubbed with wool; but the paper was not rubbed—why was the paper attracted to the balloon? Because a neutral object (the piece of paper) is attracted to a negatively charged material (balloon) (see Figure 18-5). But wait—if a glass rod is positively charged by rubbing it with a plastic bag, the paper will also be attracted to the glass rod, just as it was to the balloon. The paper is attracted to a negatively charged balloon *and* it is also attracted to a positively charged glass rod (see Figure 18-6). This is very strange.

Figure 18-5

Bits of paper are attracted to a negatively charged balloon.

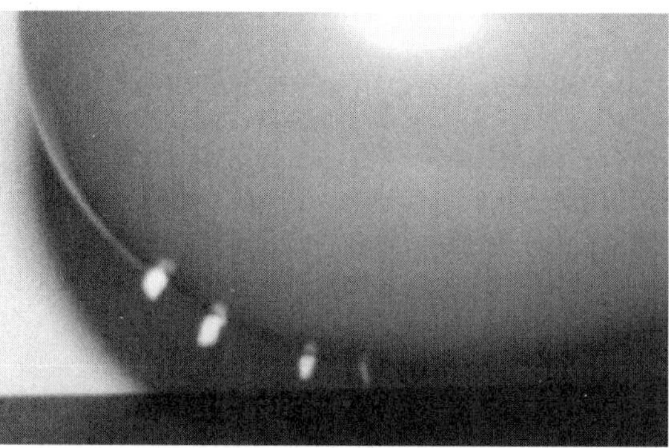

It appears that neutral objects are attracted to charged objects. That isn't quite true. Actually, a charge is *induced* in the neutral object by the charged object. The induced charge is always opposite that of the charged object. So neutral objects are attracted to charged objects, but only after a charge is induced at the surface of the neutral objects. (The object is still neutral, but the charges are redistributed.)

Figure 18-6

Bits of paper are attracted to a positively charged glass rod.

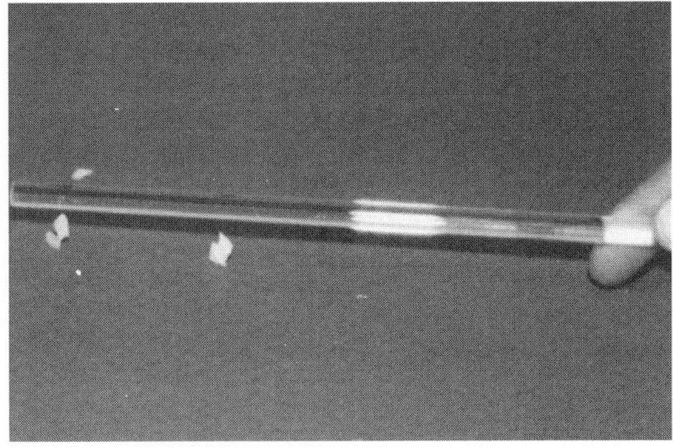

Here's what happens. As the negatively charged balloon approaches the neutral paper, the electrons at the surface of the paper are repelled and recede slightly, leaving the surface of the paper with a positive charge. This is called an induced charge, as no electrons actually transferred from one material to another. With an induced positive charge near the negative balloon, the paper is attracted to the balloon.

A secondary effect now occurs; as the paper rests on the balloon, some of the excess electrons on the balloon drain onto the paper. The paper now has a negative charge and it is repelled by the negatively charged balloon. (Try it and you'll find that the paper is actually ejected.) With the paper on the table again, the excess electrons acquired by the paper from the balloon drain off the paper into the table top, leaving the paper neutral. If the charged balloon is held just above the bits of paper, the paper will usually dance up and down as the process occurs over and over again, sometimes in rapid succession.

A charge can also be induced in the neutral paper when it is approached by the positively charged rubber rod. As the rod approaches the paper, electrons are drawn slightly toward the surface, producing a negative charge at the surface of the paper. The paper is now attracted to the positively charged rod. With the paper in contact with the rod, some electrons transfer from the paper to the rod. This results in the paper having a positive charge, and it is repelled by the rod.

Lightning and Thunder

Lightning is an electric current, but it is usually considered along with the topic of static electricity because it results from an electrostatic charge.

Lightning is a huge electric spark produced by static electricity. We have already discussed induced charges and charges produced by friction. Lightning involves both. As turbulent air swirls, friction between air currents and clouds and friction between air currents results in huge numbers of electrons being transferred and creates a build-up of powerful charges of static electricity. Clouds can either gain or lose electrons and therefore can become either positively or negatively charged. It is even possible for one end of a cloud to be charged positively while the other end of the same cloud has a negative charge.

A charged cloud can impose an induced charge on the surface of the ground. If the cloud has a positive charge, electrons will be drawn slightly toward the surface of the ground; thus the ground surface is charged negatively. If the cloud has a negative charge, electrons at the surface of the ground are repelled and recede slightly into the surface, leaving an induced positive charge at the surface of the ground.

The natural condition of materials is neutral, and the natural tendency of any charged substance is to become neutralized. When you scuff your feet across a carpet and become negatively charged, the charge immediately drains off as you reach out to touch a doorknob. Actually, the spark occurs just before you touch the doorknob—as soon as your finger gets close enough to the doorknob that the electrons can jump across the air gap between your finger and the doorknob. Air is an insulator to electricity, however, so that weak spark can jump only a very short distance through air space.

Similarly, electrostatic charges build up in the clouds until the charge is great enough to cross the air space. A path of positive and negative charges is created in the air, then a giant spark occurs, which we call lightning. Lightning can strike from cloud to ground if the cloud has a negative charge, or from ground to cloud if the cloud has a positive charge. Remember, it is the electrons that move, so the spark will move from a negatively charged area to a positively charged area. Lightning can also strike from cloud to cloud, or within a cloud.

Lightning is always very powerful. When we think of lightning, we think of a force that can kill, or that can explode trees, start forest fires, or burn buildings. It is important to remember that air is an insulator to electricity. A tremendous charge is required to jump across hundreds of feet of airspace, which lightning frequently does. Actually, millions of volts of electricity are involved—sometimes hundreds of millions of volts.

Lightning follows a zig-zag path. It is easier for lightning to pass through moist air than through dry air. It seeks out the path of least resistance, and in the process of seeking out the moist air pockets, its path is jagged.

Tall objects standing up from the ground provide an easier path for lightning because they are closer to the cloud. Such objects as trees and buildings are not good electrical conductors, but they are better conductors than is air, so lightning is more likely to strike if tall objects are in its path. Much damage can occur to those objects, as tremendous heat is generated in the path of a lightning bolt.

People often put a lightning rod at the end of a building, with one end buried in the ground and the other end extending above the building. The lightning rod not only becomes the tallest object, but it is made of metal and is an excellent conductor; so if lightning is inclined to strike nearby, it will be attracted to the lightning rod and drain off harmlessly into the ground, saving the building from possible damage. Actually, the lightning rod often provides a constant drainage of the electrostatic charge in the air, so the rod does more than just attract lightning strikes; it tends to provide a continuous neutralizing influence.

The human body isn't an especially good conductor, but lightning passes far more easily through the body than through a few more feet of air space. Therefore, to be the tallest object around during an electrical storm is to volunteer as a human lightning rod. Not only should you avoid being the tallest object in the area during a lightning storm, but you should stay away from tall objects, such as trees, that might attract lightning. If possible, go into a building and get into an interior room on the lowest floor. Stay away from windows, outside walls, water pipes and fixtures, and electrical appliances. If you are out in the open, it is recommended that you roll up in a ball, making yourself as small as possible, with only the balls of your feet touching the ground. This is thought to be more effective than lying flat on the ground; in a flat position you increase your surface area. Being in a low area, such as in a dry ditch, also reduces the chance of being struck by lightning.

As lightning passes through air, the air is heated very rapidly—to temperatures hotter than those at the surface of the sun! With the rapid increase in temperature comes a sudden expansion of the air, resulting in an explosion, not unlike that which occurs on a smaller scale from a firecracker or a stick of dynamite. The explosion we hear from lightning is called thunder. For a more complete description of thunder, see chapter 21.

III. MAGNETISM

Magnetism is one of the most "attractive" topics in elementary science. In fact, it has passed the test of time in being able to capture the curiosity of children of all ages, from one to 100—at least!

What Is a Magnet?

A magnet attracts magnetic materials. There are four well-known strongly magnetic materials—iron, steel, nickel, and cobalt. Iron, nickel, and cobalt are elements, while the various types of steel are alloys (mixtures) of iron, with carbon and certain other materials included. Objects that are attracted to a magnet commonly contain one or more of these four materials.

Magnets are either natural or manufactured. Natural magnets are commonly called *lodestone,* and they contain a type of iron ore called *magnetite.* Magnetite is magnetic (attracted by magnets), but a lodestone *is* a magnet. Lodestones are irregularly shaped rocks. Manufactured magnets are made of special combinations of metals, but must include one or more of the magnetic materials. Aluminum is often included to make the material light in weight but still very effective. A popular material for making magnets is alnico, a combination of aluminum, nickel, and cobalt.

In recent years, ceramic magnets have been broadly used. These magnets are usually formed from strontium ferrite or barium ferrite, and are shaped in a die under pressure. They are usually less costly than alnico magnets, which gives them a distinct advantage for classroom use (Barrow, 1990).

Magnets are often named according to their shape. Such is true of horseshoe magnets, rod magnets, disc magnets, and bar magnets.

Law of Magnetic Attraction and Repulsion

When the north-seeking pole of one magnet is brought near the south-seeking pole of another magnet, they attract each other. If like poles are brought together, they repel each other. This is called the *law of magnetic attraction and repulsion.*

What Is Magnetism?

Many theories have been proposed over the years in an effort to explain the behavior of magnets. The theory that has emerged as the most widely accepted explains magnetism in terms of *domains* of atoms. In magnetic materials, atoms arrange themselves in clusters, or domains, and within these domains most of the electrons spin in the same direction, whereas in nonmagnetic materials, electrons spin in a random order. Each spinning electron acts as a tiny magnet. Domains of atoms with electrons spinning in a common direction add to the magnetic effect.

Each domain behaves as a magnet, with a north pole and a south pole. Even so, in their natural state the domains are randomly arranged (see Figure 18-7) and the material does not behave as a magnet. When an object made of magnetic material, such as an iron nail, is placed in a magnetic field, the domains of atoms arrange themselves with north and south poles lined up together (see Figure 18-8). The nail becomes a magnet, and will attract other magnetic materials, such as paper clips or other nails. When the nail is removed from the magnetic field, the domains of atoms tend to resume their random arrangement and the nail is no longer a magnet. This is also true of straight pins and many other objects that are made of magnetic material.

When a sewing needle is brought into a magnetic field, domains line up together, as do those of the nail. However, they do not resume their random arrangement when removed

Figure 18-7

In the natural state, domains are randomly arranged.

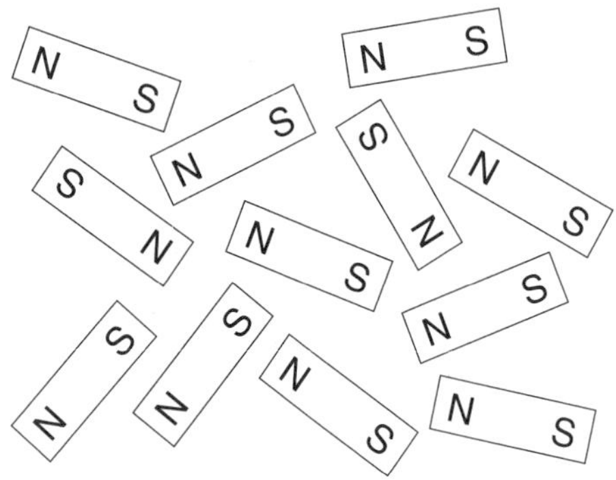

Figure 18-8

When a magnetic material is placed in a magnetic field, the domains line up in order.

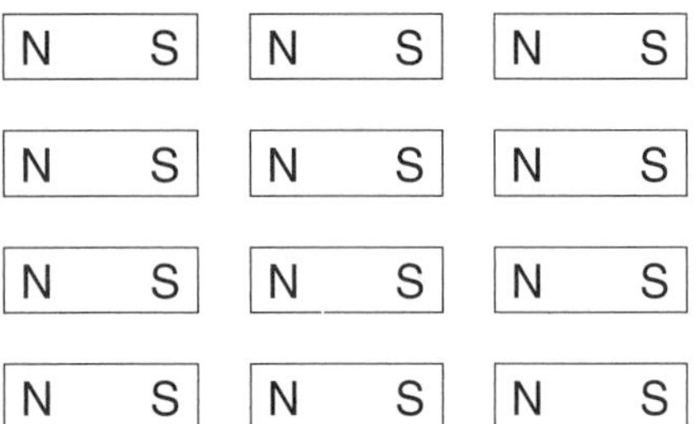

from the magnetic field, and the needle becomes a permanent magnet with a magnetic field of its own. Tool steel, like the steel sewing needles are made of, can become permanently magnetized. This is true also of alnico, mentioned above, and of certain other mixes of magnetic materials. Many screwdrivers, scissors, and other tools can be permanently magnetized, as can certain other types of very hard steel. Hardness seems to be a factor, but not all steel can be permanently magnetized. A screwdriver or other such item can be magnetized by stroking it several times across one pole of a strong permanent magnet. For best results, the screwdriver should be stroked across the same pole of the permanent magnet several times in the same direction. Old bar magnets that have become weak can be given new life in the same way.

Another way to make a permanent magnet is to use the shank of a screwdriver, or other appropriate material, as the core of an electromagnet. (See the section Electricity Can Produce Magnetism, later in this chapter.)

Magnetic Fields

Magnets are strongest at the poles. *Magnetic lines of force* go out in all directions from the poles, and the space they occupy is called the *magnetic field*. Magnetic materials that are within the magnetic field are attracted to the magnet. You san see the pattern of the magnetic field by laying a card (or sheet of glass) over a magnet and sprinkling iron filings on the card (see Figure 18-9). Of course, the pattern of iron filings on the card only shows the lines of force in one plane, whereas the lines actually go out from the poles in all directions. You can see a three-dimensional pattern by using a jar, a bar magnet, and a tube, as is demonstrated in Activity 18-4 at the end of this chapter (see Figure 18-10).

Figure 18-9

The iron filings on this card reveal the magnetic field of the magnet that is under the card.

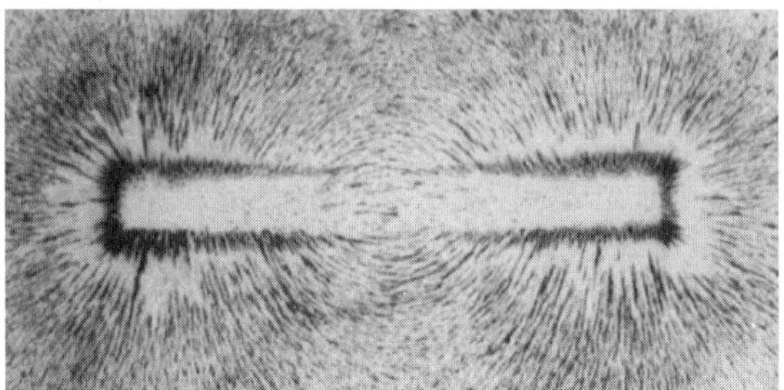

Figure 18-10

The jar with tube, magnet, and iron filings shows a three-dimensional pattern of the magnetic field.

Magnetic fields are disturbed by the presence of any magnetic material. Figure 18-11a shows an iron-filings pattern of the magnetic field of a bar magnet. Figure 18-11b shows the same field with a small iron bolt at one end of the magnet. The same pattern is shown in Figure 18-11c with a plastic pen cap at the other end of the magnet. Notice the lines of force are distorted by the bolt but undisturbed by the pen cap. Magnetic lines of force pass through nonmagnetic materials and they seem to be unaffected by the presence of such materials.

Caring for Magnets

You can weaken a magnet by striking it with a hard object, such as a hammer, or by dropping it on a hard surface, such as concrete. Extreme heat, as from a torch, can effectively demagnetize a permanent magnet. Improper storage, such as tossing magnets together in a drawer, or with the like poles of two bar magnets placed together, is a third way to weaken permanent magnets. A weak magnet stored in contact with a strong magnet can result in rearranging the poles of the weak magnet.

It follows that to properly care for magnets you should avoid striking or dropping them, you should keep them away from extreme heat, and you should store them properly. Bar

Figure 18-11a

Iron filings reveal the pattern of the magnetic field of a bar magnet.

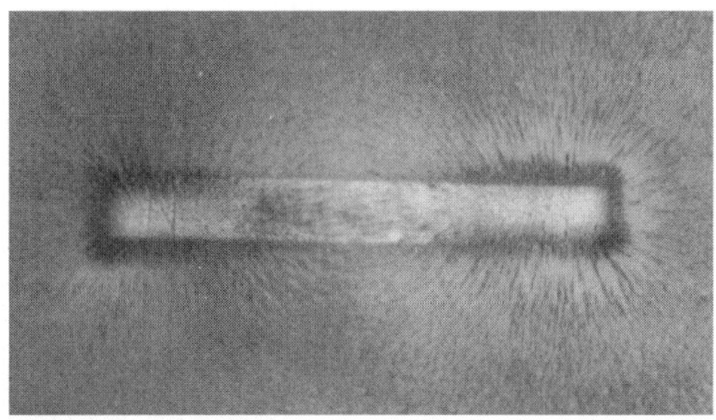

Figure 18-11b

The same field, with a small iron bolt at one end of the magnet. The magnetic field is distorted by the bolt.

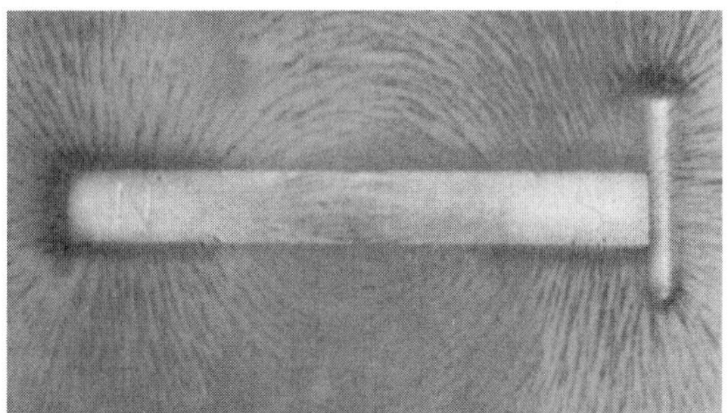

Figure 18-11c

The same field, with a plastic pen cap at the other end of the magnet. The plastic does not disturb the magnetic field.

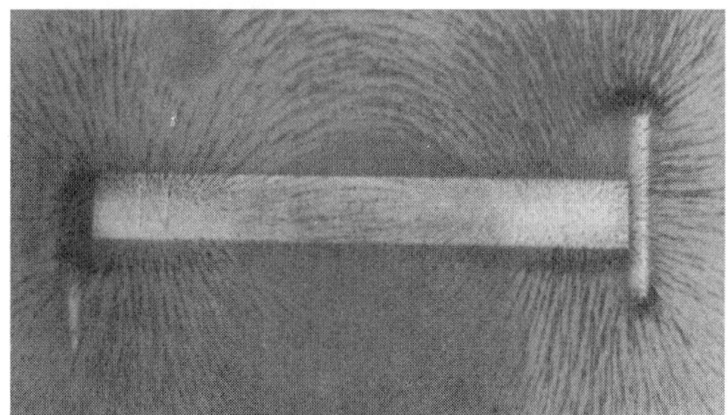

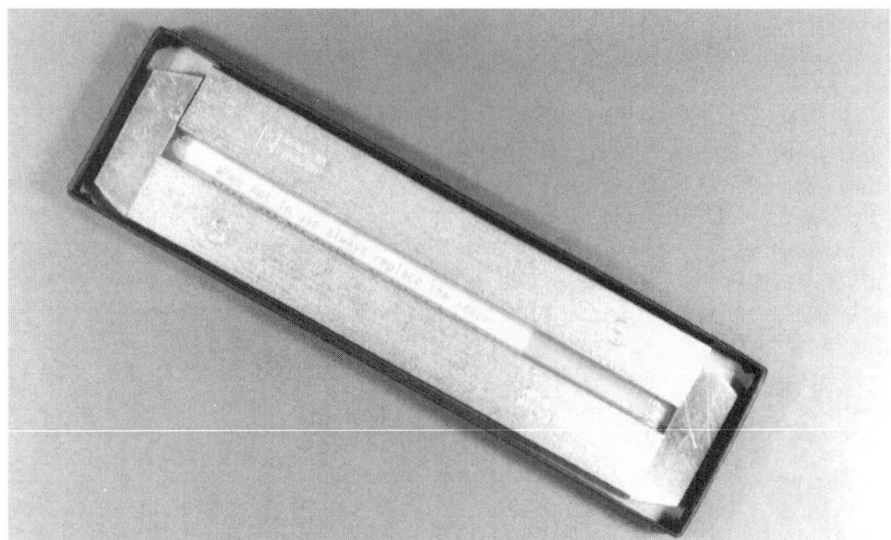

Figure 18-12

A bar magnet, properly stored, will retain its strength better than if it is stored improperly.

magnets should be stored in pairs, with unlike poles together and a spacer between them. Place a *keeper* (a piece of soft iron—even a paper clip) across the poles at each end (see Figure 18-12). Horseshoe magnets should be stored either in pairs with poles together, or with a keeper across the two poles. For disc magnets, use iron washers as keepers and put one on each side of the magnet, or just store the disc magnets in pairs.

Finding Directions with a Magnet

Finding directions is made easy by the fact that the earth behaves as a huge, though weak, magnet. Like other magnets, the earth has poles. The magnetic north and south poles are slightly to one side from the geographic north and south poles of the earth. If a bar magnet is freely suspended in space, such as cradled and hanging from a thread or suspended on a free-moving pivot, the bar magnet will line up within the magnetic lines of force, with its north pole pointing in the general direction of the earth's magnetic north pole and its south pole pointing toward the earth's magnetic south pole. If a magnetized needle or small bar magnet is floated on a piece of wood or cork in a bowl of water or on a pond (away from magnetic materials), the magnet will line up with the magnetic poles of the earth. If you think this contradicts the law of magnetic attraction and repulsion because the *north* pole of the magnet is attracted to the *north* pole of the earth, you're right, but only because the poles of magnets were named before their effect with the earth was really understood. To avoid confusion, the poles of magnets are now commonly referred to as the *north-seeking* pole and the *south-seeking* pole. Another way to explain this apparent dilemma is that the magnetic pole of the earth in the northern hemisphere is a *magnetic south pole* (Halliday & Resnick, 1988).

A magnet used to find directions on the earth is called a *compass.* Of course, there must be no other magnet or magnetic material nearby or the compass needle will be attracted by those things and will not function accurately as a compass. This is true of any magnetic compass.

A field compass uses a magnetized needle in a small case that can be easily carried. This is much more convenient for the user than suspending a bar magnet from a thread or floating a magnetized needle on a pond of water. It is important to understand, though, that functionally they are the same. The compass needle is simply a magnetized needle freely suspended on a pivot so it can respond to the magnetic field of the earth, aligning itself with the magnetic north and south poles. Most compass needles are marked, making it easy to remember which end points north, and each one usually includes a printed pattern that assists in making precise readings of directions in degrees.

When a compass is brought near a magnet, the compass needle responds to the magnetic field of the magnet. The north pole of the compass needle is attracted to the south pole of the magnet, and the south pole of the needle is attracted to the magnet's north pole. Thus a compass can be used to identify the poles of an unmarked magnet.

IV. ELECTRIC CURRENT

Electric current is an electric charge in motion. As stated earlier, even lightning is electric current. Though it results from static electricity, the lightning bolt is a flow of electrons. We usually think of electric current as a controlled current contained within electrical wiring.

Conductors and Insulators

Some materials allow electrons to flow easily through them. Such materials are called *conductors* of electricity. Other materials resist the flow of electrons and are called nonconductors, or *insulators*. Both conductors and insulators are needed in using current electricity. Still other materials are not particularly effective, either as conductors or insulators. Copper, silver, aluminum, iron, and most other metals are good conductors. Graphite (a form of carbon) is an example of a nonmetal that is a good conductor of electricity.

Effective insulators include glass, rubber, wood, and dry air. Varnish, cloth, and plastics are also good insulators, and are often used as coatings for electrical wires. Such insulation helps prevent electrical shock to someone who touches a wire that is carrying an electric current, though a shock can still sometimes occur, depending on the size of the wire, the thickness of the insulation, and the voltage. These coatings keep the flow of electrons confined within a wire and prevent it from taking undesired paths. Without coverings of insulation, coils of wire in generators and motors would be useless; the electric current would flow across the coil instead of around and around the wire within the coil, which is necessary in order for the coil to function as intended.

Closed Circuits and Open Circuits

Electricity must have a complete path from the power source, through the circuit, and back to the source. If this path is broken the circuit is incomplete. An *incomplete circuit* is called an *open circuit*. Electricity cannot flow unless the circuit is complete. A *complete circuit* is called a *closed circuit*. This is easy to see with the simple circuit shown in Figures 18-13 and 18-14. As illustrated, switches are commonly used to make it easy to open and close a circuit.

Series and Parallel Circuits

Widespread public recognition of the difference between series and parallel circuits could bring an end to a common marketing deceit. It is amazing that every year people buy thousands upon thousands of sets of miniature Christmas lights that are most likely—and totally unnecessarily—doomed for a short life of use. The string of lights might have 120 miniature bulbs, and if any one of them burns out, works loose, or in any way goes bad, the entire set goes out. You are

Figure 18-13

This circuit—battery, bulb, wires, and switch in open position—is incomplete.

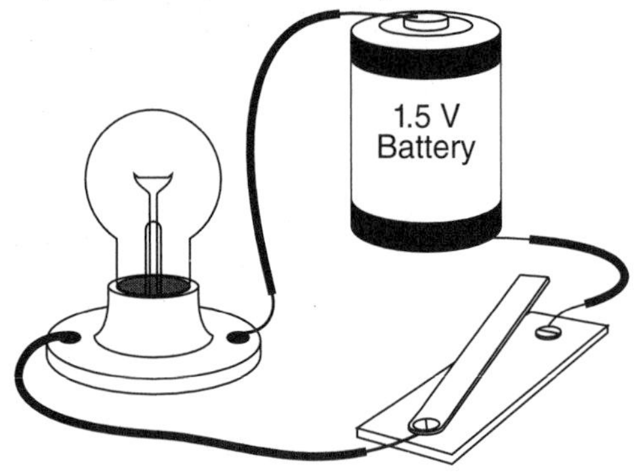

Figure 18-14

This circuit—battery, bulb, wires, and switch in closed position—is complete.

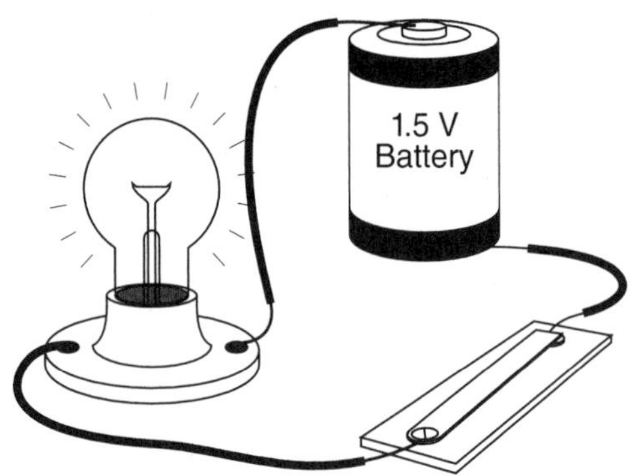

comforted by the information printed on the box that lets you know that several spare bulbs are included with the set. If the lights go out, here's what you do: Starting at one end of the line, replace the first bulb with one from the package of spare bulbs; if the set comes back on, you know you found the faulty bulb; if not, go to the next bulb, repeating the replacement process until the lights come on again. No problem—there are only 120 of the little beasts to try! The reassurance of the replacement instructions on the box will likely last only until the first bulb burns out.

Anyone who has had this experience knows that it can be a major frustration. Most people will replace strings of lights that don't light up, because it just isn't worth the time and inconvenience required to do the troubleshooting. Oh, and speaking of troubleshooting, you might have spent all that time fraying your nerves for nothing. You see, it's possible that the string has a faulty plug, a broken wire, or that you have simply lost current to the outlet, and you might have replaced the entire set of 120 bulbs before it occurred to you that the bulbs might not be responsible for the problem. On the other hand, what if the new bulb you took out of the package was flawed—or perhaps you or someone else absentmindedly dropped a spent bulb into the package last time a bulb was replaced? You could go insane trying to find the problem.

You are willing to replace your sets of Christmas lights every year or two, rather than hassle with them, and the manufacturers know it. A very simple alteration in manufacturing—wiring the lights in parallel—relieves you of the great majority of the troubleshooting effort, with very little increase in manufacturing cost. As long as the public is willing to buy the strings of lights with built-in demise, manufacturers are willing to continue making them, and stores are willing to continue selling them.

The difference is really rather simple, once you see it in operation. With series wiring, the lights are connected in such a way that the electric current must pass through one bulb before it can get to the next. Parallel wiring is done in such a way that each bulb receives the current independent of the other bulbs. Figure 18-15 shows two light bulbs wired in series and Figure 18-16 shows two bulbs with parallel wiring. As students construct and test both of these circuits, they will quickly notice the difference when one bulb is removed or loosened on each setup.

Now let's go back to the troubleshooting process. With parallel-wired Christmas lights, if the entire set goes out, you know

Figure 18-15

These two light bulbs are wired in series.

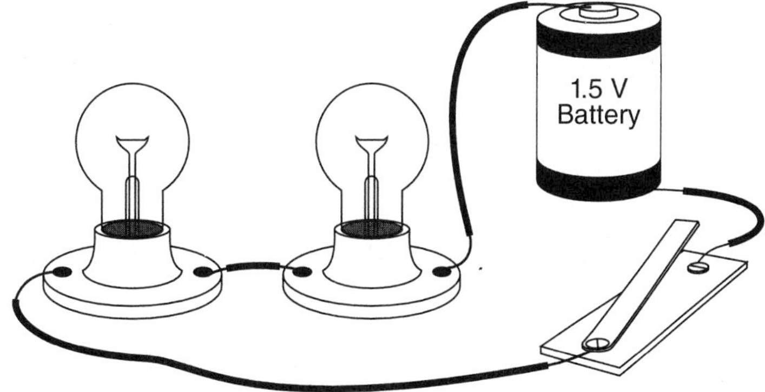

Figure 18-16

These two light bulbs are wired in parallel.

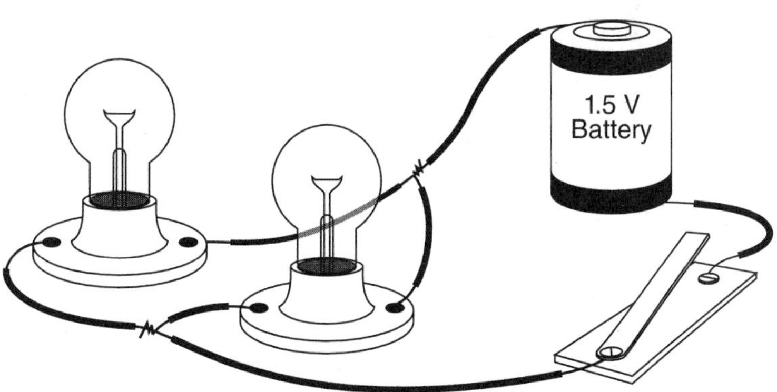

right away that the problem *is not* the bulbs. Most likely you have lost power to the outlet; otherwise, your set probably has a faulty plug or a broken wire. When a bulb does go out, the rest of the bulbs still glow, and you know immediately which bulb to replace. Perhaps student insight in the difference between parallel and series wiring will be communicated at home, ultimately saving lots of families from one of the most common Christmas headaches. Come to think of it, I wonder if the manufacturers of headache remedies are in on the scheme!

Relationship Between Magnetism and Electricity

The introduction of this chapter stated that magnetism and current electricity have an interesting relationship, in that either one can produce the other. Let's discuss that now.

Electricity can produce magnetism

Whenever an electric current flows through a wire, a magnetic field exists around the wire.

This fact makes electromagnets possible. The magnetic field around a single strand of wire is weak at any given point, but it accumulates as many parts of the wire are brought together when insulated wire is wound into a coil. If an iron core is placed in the center of the coil, the core is magnetized whenever electricity flows through the wire. The magnetic field of the iron core is now much greater than the magnetic field of the coil alone.

Iron is used as the core of an electromagnet because iron easily becomes magnetized in the presence of a magnetic field; and when the electricity is turned off, it loses its magnetic effect very quickly. For a small electromagnet, an iron bolt works very well as the core. One of the advantages of electromagnets over permanent magnets is that they can be turned on and off at will. In many applications, such as a crane handling scrap metal, permanent magnets are not useful because they cannot be turned off. If a crane used permanent magnets to lift scrap metal, it would not be able to release its load.

A second difference between electromagnets and permanent magnets is that the strength of electromagnets can easily be increased or decreased. Electromagnets can be strengthened by increasing the number of windings in the coil of wire or by increasing the electric current flowing through the wire (see Figure 18-17).

A third difference between electromagnets and permanent magnets is that the polarity of an electromagnet can easily be reversed. If the direction of electron flow through the wire is reversed, the pole that has been the north pole becomes the south pole, and the pole that was the south pole becomes the north pole. Standard battery-powered electric motors could not operate without the ability to quickly reverse the poles of electromagnets.

The poles of an electromagnet, like those of a permanent magnet, can be identified by bringing a magnetic compass nearby.

One of the early broad-scale uses of electromagnets was the telegraph. Today electromagnets are used in numerous applications, including electrical switches, doorbells, television, radio, and telephones. Generators and electric motors of all kinds use electromagnets.

Figure 18-17

Adding a battery to this electromagnet clearly increases its strength.

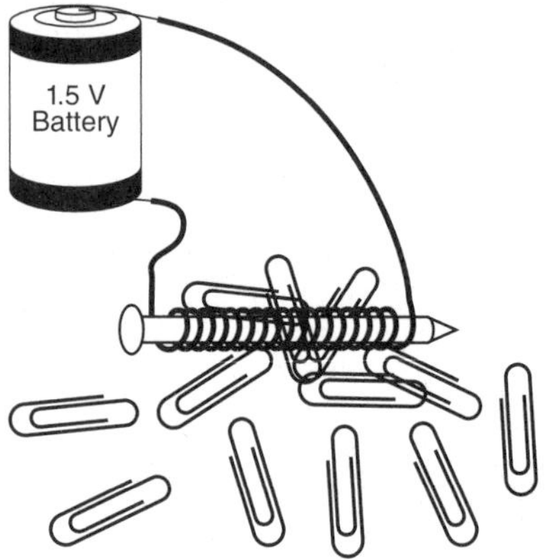

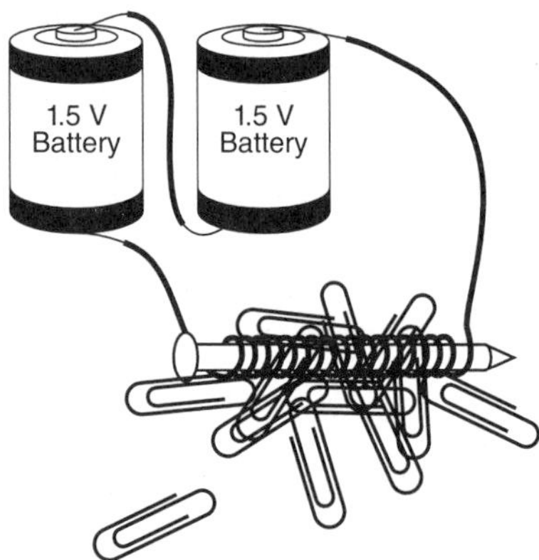

Magnetism can produce electricity

When a coil of wire passes through a magnetic field, electrons in the wire receive a force that starts them moving, in a particular direction, through the wire. This assumes that the two ends of the wire are connected in some way, either directly or indirectly. The direction of the electron flow in the wire can be changed by changing the direction the coil moves through the magnetic field. But wait—we learned earlier in this chapter that whenever electricity flows through a wire, the wire is surrounded by a magnetic field. Then electricity can produce magnetism *and* magnetism can produce electricity. (It is important to note that the coil must be moving through the magnetic field in order to cause electrons to flow. The electron flow is not produced as a coil of wire simply sits in an unchanging magnetic field.)

This explains the secret of hydroelectric power plants, which seem to magically take electricity out of water. Water behind a dam is not filled with electricity waiting to be extracted, but it does have gravitational potential energy. The potential energy is used by channeling falling water through turbines. The turbines have thousands of miles of insulated wire in coils that spin within powerful magnetic fields as the turbines are turned by the force of the falling water (see Figure 18-18). The resulting flow of electrons through the wire is carried to homes, factories, and other areas of need, sometimes many hundreds of miles from the power plant.

Figure 18-18

In a hydroelectric power plant, huge coils of wire are turned within magnetic fields by the force of falling water.

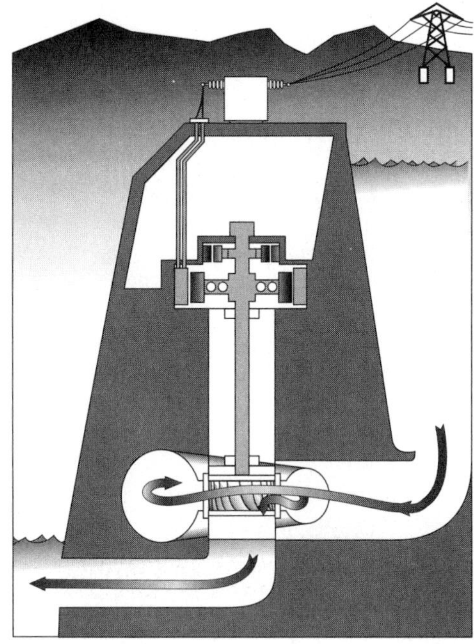

Any force that can spin a coil of wire within a magnetic field thus can generate electricity. Many power plants burn coal or natural gas to produce steam, then use the steam power to spin coils of wire within magnetic fields. These plants use up enormous amounts of fossil fuels. Hydroelectric plants use only falling water as the power source, instead of using precious nonrenewable natural resources. Clean-air advantages of this method of producing electricity are significant. Nuclear energy, despite its drawbacks of nuclear waste and fear of radiation from possible malfunctions, is becoming more popular as a source of energy for electrical power plants around the world.

On a smaller scale, each automobile has its own electrical power plant. Called an alternator, it is powered by the engine and, like the huge hydroelectric plant, it spins coils of wire within a magnetic field. Electrical energy from the alternator provides power for headlights and other lights, for windshield wipers, stereos, and for numerous other devices in the automobile that require electricity. In addition, it keeps the storage battery charged. The battery then provides energy for the starter motor and for other electrical needs when the engine is not running and turning the alternator.

Small electrical generators are available for bicycle lights. This generator has a small wheel that rubs on the bicycle tire and spins a coil of wire within a magnetic field. Handheld flashlights are also available, which have generators that are turned by repeatedly squeezing the hand. When the user stops the repeated squeezing action, the light goes out.

V. IN CLOSING

Galvani, Franklin, Edison, and other electrical pioneers had no way of knowing the extent of the influence their investigations would have on humankind. In fact, few things have had greater impact on society than has electricity. Electricity influences our lives in many ways every day. And we must not ignore the role magnetism plays; not only is magnetism at work in every electric motor and in many other devices, but electricity could not be produced in the most common conventional ways without magnetism. Magnetic force and electrical energy are indispensable in today's society.

LIST OF RESOURCES

Barrow, Lloyd H., "Ceramic Magnets Pass the Bar," *Science and Children* 27, no. 7 (April 1990): 14–16.

Fisher, Arthur, "Seeing Atoms," *Popular Science* (April 1989): 102–7.

Halliday, David, and Robert Resnick, *Fundamentals of Physics* (New York: John Wiley & Sons, 1988), 690.

Hewitt, Paul G., *Conceptual Physics* (Glenview, IL: Scott Foresman & Co., 1989).

Hunter, Madeline, Workshop on evaluation of teaching, UCLA, November 1978.

Mason, Grant W., et al., *Physical Science Concepts* (Provo, UT: Soundprint, 1989).

Tolman, Marvin N., and James O. Morton, *Physical Science Activities for Grades 2–8* (West Nyack, NY: Parker Publishing Co., 1986).

Victor, Edward, *Science for the Elementary School, Sixth Edition* (New York: Macmillan Publishing Co., 1989).

World Book Encyclopedia, 1989.

CHAPTER

ELECTRICITY AND MAGNETISM

ACTIVITIES

II. STATIC ELECTRICITY

ACTIVITY 18-1: WHAT DOES A BALLOON FIND ATTRACTIVE?

Materials Needed:

Balloon

Wool cloth (or cotton)

Several small bits of paper

Puffed rice

Pieces of plastic foam

Procedure:

1. Blow up the balloon and tie the neck.
2. Rub the balloon with the cloth.
3. Bring the balloon near the bits of paper.
4. What happened?
5. Predict what will happen if you bring the balloon near other small, light objects, such as the puffed rice and the plastic foam pieces.
6. Test your prediction by bringing the balloon near the puffed rice and the plastic foam pieces.
7. What happened? Was your prediction accurate?
8. Talk about your observations with your group.

For Problem Solvers:

Do some research and learn all you can about static electricity. Is lightning static electricity? What makes the paper, puffed rice, and other things react the way they do with the balloon?

Continue your research by reading about the law of electrostatic attraction and repulsion. Now, before you really decide why the bits of paper and other things reacted the way they did, find out about materials being charged by induction. Include this information in your explanation.

Teacher Information:

Static electricity is a most fascinating topic to study. Students will learn about it as they read, as well as by working with materials.

Lightning is often mistakenly used as an example of static electricity. Although it is caused by static electricity, lightning itself is actually current electricity.

When a charged object approaches a neutral object, the neutral object becomes charged by induction. At first glance it might appear that the law of electrostatic attraction and repulsion is violated as the bits of paper, which have not been charged by rubbing, are attracted to the charged balloon.

Actually, the near side of the bits of paper are charged, by induction, with the opposite charge as the balloon. Thus charged, the bits of paper are attracted to the balloon.

Additional information about electrostatic induction is given in this chapter.

Integrating: Reading, writing, math, art

Skills: Communicating, researching

III. MAGNETISM

ACTIVITY 18-2:

WHAT MATERIALS ARE ATTRACTED TO A MAGNET?

Materials Needed:

Nail

Bolt

Paper clip

Brass screw

U.S. coins

Canadian nickel (pre-1988)

Other magnetic and nonmagnetic objects

Magnet

Paper and pencil

Procedure:

1. Sort the objects into two groups. In one group, put all of the objects that you think will be attracted to the magnet. Call this the Yes group. Put all of the objects that you think will not be attracted to the magnet in the other pile, and call this the No group.
2. Now use the magnet and test your predictions. Set aside the ones you did not have right, so you can find out why and learn from the activity.
3. Are all of the objects in the Yes group metal, and all of the objects in the No group nonmetal?
4. Were there any surprises for you?
5. Talk to your group about what you learned, and about what you would still like to learn about magnetism.

For Problem Solvers:

Do some research and find out what materials are attracted to a magnet. There are only four. I'll bet you can list some of them already. Find out what the others are.

From doing the activity, what do you know about the Canadian coin? What about the U.S. coins? See if you can find other coins, from the U.S. and from foreign countries, and test them to see if they are magnetic. Test older coins and newer coins. Make a list of the ones you test. Each time, make a prediction based on what you know, before you test the coin.

Teacher Information:

A common perception is that metals are attracted to magnets and nonmetals are not. There are many metals that are not magnetic, including copper and brass. Actually, there are only four materials that are magnetic: iron, steel, nickel, and cobalt. All materials that are attracted to a magnet have at least one of these four materials in them.

Pre-1988 Canadian nickels are magnetic. One of these always makes a fun addition to the collection of items used for this activity. They can be obtained from a coin shop if there is not a more suitable source available.

Note: Be sure students understand that magnets should be kept away from wrist watches, calculators, computers, audio tapes, video tapes, and computer disks.

Integrating: Reading, writing, social studies

Skills: Observing, inferring, classifying, predicting, researching

ACTIVITY 18-3: HOW DO MAGNETS REACT TO EACH OTHER?

Materials Needed:

Two bar magnets

Piece of wire about 15 centimeters (6 inches) long

Pliers

Stack of books

Ruler

Thread

Procedure:

1. Make a cradle for the bar magnet, something like the one shown in Figure 18A-1.

Figure 18A-1

Make a cradle for the magnet.

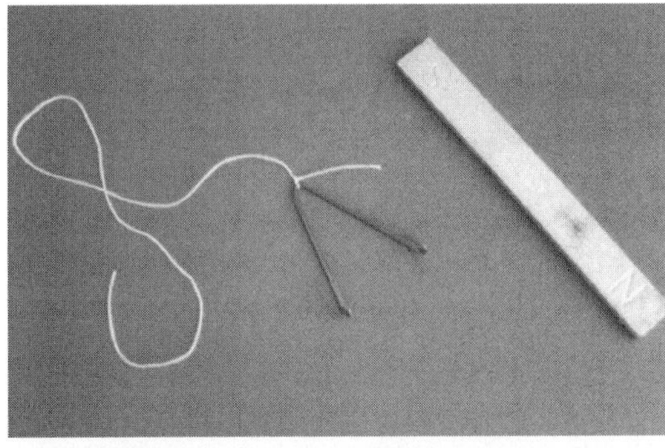

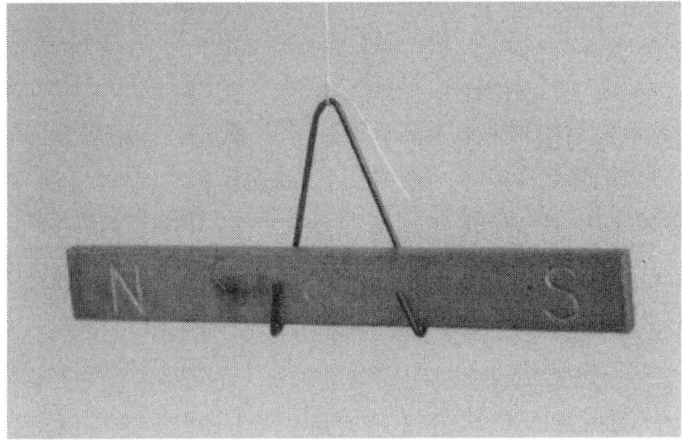

2. Rest the magnet in the cradle and tie the thread to the top of the cradle.
3. Hold the bar magnet in the air so it can turn freely.
4 Bring each end of the other bar magnet near the one that is suspended from the thread.
5. What happened?
6. Turn the bar magnet around and bring it near again.
7. What happened? Why? Discuss your ideas with your group.

For Problem Solvers:

Try floating a magnet on a piece of wood in a large bowl of water. What happens? What is the magnet now? Explain how a compass works. Look it up in a book if you need to.

Teacher Information:

A compass is simply a magnetized needle that is freely suspended, with minimal friction. This allows the needle to respond to the magnetic field of the earth, thus it aligns itself with the earth's north and south poles. A compass must not be near any magnetic materials during use, or it will be attracted to those materials and will not give a true reading as a compass.

Any bar magnet that is properly magnetized and freely suspended will behave as a compass. The magnet that is suspended on a thread or the magnet that floats in a bowl of water are both effective compasses. If a metal pan is used for the bowl of water, it must be aluminum. If the pan has iron in it, the magnet will be attracted to the pan and will not act as a compass.

Integrating: Reading, writing, math, art

Skills: Communicating, researching

ACTIVITY 18-4:
WHAT DOES A MAGNETIC FIELD LOOK LIKE?

Materials Needed:

Iron filings

Cylinder-shaped magnet (bar magnet can be used)

Jar with mouth slightly larger than the diameter of the magnet

Sheet of acetate (or sheet of paper)

Tape

Paper towel (or cotton ball)

Procedure:

1. Roll the sheet of acetate into a tube and secure it with tape. The magnet should fit inside the tube and the tube should fit inside the jar.
2. Pour some iron filings into the jar.
3. Insert the tube into the jar.
4. Put a wad of paper towel in the tube and slide it down to the bottom of the tube.
5. Slide the magnet into the tube.
6. Shake the bottle, then observe the iron filings.
7. What do you notice about the iron filings? Why did this happen? Discuss your ideas with your group.

For Problem Solvers:

For another experience with magnetic lines of force, get some iron filings and a card. Put a magnet on a table and lay the card over the magnet. Sprinkle a few iron filings on the card. Tap the card lightly. Explain what happened. Find information in a book to help you. Try the same thing with a different magnet, or with two magnets together. For each new magnet or new combination of magnets, predict what the magnetic field will look like, based on what you know.

You can make a permanent picture of your magnetic field if you spray the iron filings lightly with paint or with spray adhesive. How do you think the picture sprayed with adhesive will be different from the picture sprayed with paint? *Caution*: Before paint or adhesive is sprayed, be sure the card used is large enough to protect the magnets from the spray, that the floor or ground surface is properly covered with paper, and precautions are taken to protect clothing. To keep iron filings and spray from getting directly on the magnet, put the magnet in a plastic bag.

Teacher Information:

For the 3-D model of a magnetic field, cow magnets work very well because of their cylindrical shape. Others can be used, too. Select a magnet and a jar that will work out together. Although the magnetic field around a magnet is invisible, it is not imaginary. The magnetic lines of force are very real, and they can be seen as the iron filings line up within them. This model shows that the magnetic field is three dimensional and that the magnetic lines of force go out in all directions from the poles.

A very interesting bulletin board can be made from the pictures of magnetic fields, as students get creative with the extension for problem solvers. Let them use magnets of different shapes and sizes. They can use magnets singly or combine them side by side, end to end, or in various combinations to make faces and other designs. Students are instructed to take precautions for protection of surroundings before spraying with paint or adhesive. You will need to follow through to see that they understand and follow the precautions.

Integrating: Reading, writing, art

Skills: Observing, inferring, predicting, researching

IV. ELECTRIC CURRENT

ACTIVITY 18-5: WHAT IS A COMPLETE CIRCUIT?

Materials Needed:

Flashlight bulb

Flashlight cell

Strip of aluminum foil

Procedure:

1. Using the bulb, the flashlight cell, and the aluminum foil, make the light turn on.
2. If the first thing you try doesn't work, try something else.
3. When you get the light to turn on, show your teacher. Don't help your neighbor until your neighbor has had plenty of time to struggle with it.
4. Explain to each other in your group what you had to do to make the light turn on.
5. You made a complete circuit. Talk about what that means.

For Problem Solvers:

Get some light bulbs, bulb holders, and insulated wire, and set up a complete circuit, using the flashlight cell as a power source. When it's complete, and the light bulb is on, it's also called a closed circuit. If you disconnect one wire it will be an open circuit. Try it. Does the light bulb glow in an open circuit?

Do some research and find out what series and parallel circuits are. Set up two bulbs wired in series and then set them up wired in parallel. Explain what the difference is. Do most sets of Christmas lights use series wiring or parallel wiring? Why do you think they do that? Talk about it with your group, with your teacher, and with your parents. Which kind of Christmas light sets will you want to buy in the future?

Look closely at an unfrosted light bulb. Can you trace the path the current follows through the bulb? What happens if the filament breaks?

Make a switch to use with your circuits.

What is a short circuit? Find out, and demonstrate one.

What are conductors and insulators? Use your circuit to test several different materials to find out if they're conductors or insulators. For each item, predict which it is and write your prediction.

Teacher Information:

The heavy-duty foil wrapper of a candy bar works well for this activity. You can just give students the light bulb, flashlight cell, and a candy bar, and tell them to make the light turn on, using nothing other than those materials. Chewing gum wrappers sometimes work, but they are usually made of lighter foil and you need to try it out first to be sure it will work. In this activity, don't be too quick to help students who don't make the light turn on with their first try. Let them struggle—that's what problem solving is all about. When they finally realize what "complete circuit" means, very important lights will come on inside their heads as well as in their hands!

Students who continue with the extension, making series and parallel circuits, will have more of a challenge. When two bulbs are wired in series, if one goes out, the other one will go out, too. This is the way most sets of Christmas lights are wired. When two bulbs are wired in parallel, they operate independently of each other. More information about series and parallel wiring is provided within this chapter.

Motivated students will continue with their study to find out about short circuits and devise a way to show what that means. They will also test various materials to determine whether they are conductors or insulators.

Integrating: Reading, writing, art

Skills: Observing, inferring, predicting, researching

CHAPTER

MACHINES

CHAPTER OUTLINE:

I WONDER . . .

What are the simplest forms of machines?
Do the simple machines have anything to do with the complex machines of today?
How can friction be of help?
How can we determine the mechanical advantage of a machine?
What relationship does the screw have to the inclined plane?
What type of lever is a fishing pole?
How can a bicycle wheel be thought of as a lever?
What kind of simple machine is a block-and-tackle? What is it used for?

I. INTRODUCTION

Whenever you visit a clothing factory, a farm, or a steel mill, you see machines all around: sewing machines and presses; tractors and harvesters; or huge presses, rollers, and forklifts. Today the world has been transformed by electronics, and a closer look will reveal that computers are often a part of the tractor, the forklift, and yes, even the sewing machine. For our purposes, however, we'll focus on the mechanical aspects of machines. And we don't need to go to the farm or the factory to see machines, for virtually every home in modern society has a broad variety of them (see Figure 19-1).

Not only are tractors and forklifts machines, but so are the scissors at the clothing factory, and so is the farmer's pitchfork. And when we take a close look at the tractor, we find that it is made of many simple machines. The brake pedal, for instance, is a machine, as is the accelerator, and even the steering wheel.

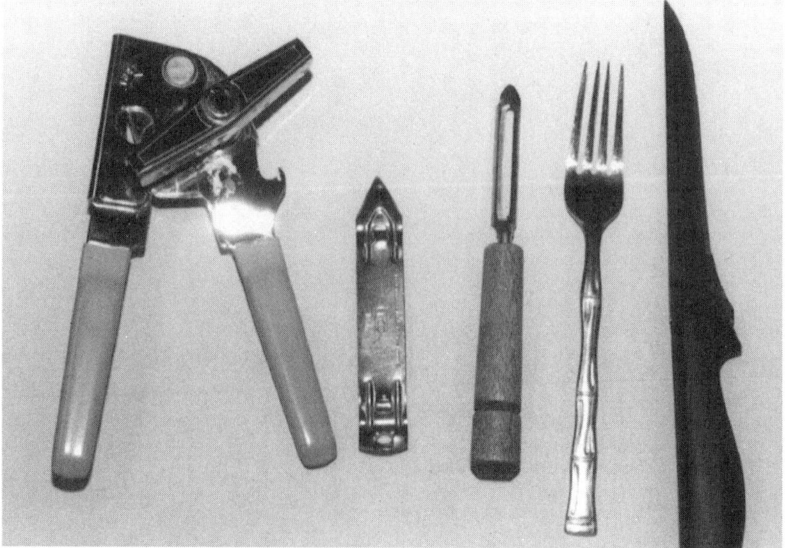

Figure 19-1

Simple machines can be found in any home.

The sewing machine actually incorporates many simple machines, and so do most other machines. Even the pencil sitting on the table beside the sewing machine is a machine, too. Specific types of machines are described later in this chapter, but first let's consider some related topics, including what a machine is and how it helps us, and how friction affects the efficiency of a machine.

II. WHAT IS A MACHINE AND HOW DOES IT HELP US?

A machine is a device that helps make work easier. Some type of force must be applied to the machine to cause it to do work. Sometimes the force comes from muscles, and sometimes from burning gasoline, electricity, wind, steam, gravity, or springs. Scientists usually define *work* as moving an object through some distance by applying a force. Work involves a transfer of energy. Whether a 10-ton boulder is hauled away by a truck, or a grain of sand is moved a distance of 1 millimeter by a tiny ant, work is done if something moves under the influence of a force. If you struggle to move the 10-ton boulder by hand, you might get very tired and expend a great amount of energy, but no work is done on the boulder unless the boulder moves. If a boulder floats through outer space under the influence of no forces, no work is done on it. Both motion and force must be present for work to be done. We'll use this definition here as we consider work done by machines.

Machines can help us in four ways. They can (1) increase the amount of force applied to an object, (2) increase the distance and speed an object moves, (3) transfer a force from one place to another, and (4) change the direction of a force. No machine can increase both force and distance at the same time. That would violate the law of *conservation of energy*, which cannot be done. You can increase the force applied by a simple machine by decreasing the distance the load is moved as the effort is moved a given distance. Increasing the distance the load is moved decreases the force applied on the load. If either force or distance is increased, the other must be decreased by at least the same amount.

III. THE ROLE OF FRICTION

Whenever one material slides against another, there is a resistance caused by the irregularities in the surfaces of the materials. Sometimes the material feels rough to the touch, but even a surface that feels smooth to the touch has tiny irregularities that can be seen under a microscope as little bumps and hollows. If the material feels rough to the touch, the unevenness of the surface is greatly exaggerated under a microscope or a hand lens. The resistance that results when irregular surfaces rub together is called *friction*.

In addition to making it more difficult to slide one material across another, friction produces heat (transforms kinetic energy into heat energy). The greater the friction, the greater the amount of heat produced. An easy way to experience heat produced by friction is to rub your hands together rapidly for a few seconds. Generally, with machines, heat produced by friction is undesirable, because it increases the rate at which parts wear out, and sometimes fires even start from the heat of friction. Friction also increases the amount of force necessary to move one material across another. In order for motors and other equipment to operate efficiently, friction must be minimized. Those who design machines try to reduce friction.

The amount of surface area between two objects does not affect friction if the amount of force pressing the two surfaces together is the same. As that force increases, however, friction becomes greater.

Sliding friction is less than *starting friction*. It takes more force to start an object sliding across a surface than it does to keep it sliding once it has started. *Rolling friction* is much less than sliding friction, because bumps and hollows on the two surfaces roll over each other and do not catch on each other. This is why wheels are usually mounted under heavy appliances that need to be moved frequently. This is also why ball bearings and roller bearings are used between wheels and axles.

Friction can be reduced by smoothing the surfaces involved and by using a *lubricant* between them. When a lubricant is used between two surfaces, the surfaces slide on the lubricant instead of against each other. Many materials are used as lubricants, including oil, grease, wax, graphite, and water.

While friction is usually an enemy in the operation of a machine, it is also beneficial in some ways. A vehicle would not be able to stay on the road without friction, and brakes depend on friction to stop a car. Without friction we wouldn't be able to walk without slipping and sliding. Writing with a pencil would be impossible. Friction holds the pencil between our fingers and it rubs graphite (commonly called the "lead" of a pencil) onto the paper as the pencil slides across the paper. Nails and screws hold wooden and metal parts together because of friction; without friction the nails and screws would slip out. While friction makes work more difficult, and we struggle to devise ways to overcome friction, it is sometimes necessary.

IV. MECHANICAL ADVANTAGE

When a machine makes work easier we say the machine gives us a *mechanical advantage.* The mechanical advantage can be determined by dividing the load by the effort. If, for example, by using a machine we can lift a 400-pound load with a force of only 100 pounds, the machine is providing a mechanical advantage of four (load/effort = 400/100 = 4). That is the *actual mechanical advantage,* and can always be determined by dividing the load, or resistance, by the effort that is required to move the load. Because of friction, the actual mechanical advantage in most systems is somewhat less than the *ideal mechanical advantage.* See the discussion of Block and Tackle later in this section for an example comparing ideal and actual mechanical advantage.

V. THE SIX SIMPLE MACHINES

All mechanical devices consist of one or more of six *simple machines:* the inclined plane, the screw, the wedge, the lever, the wheel-and-axle, and the pulley. The machines are often separated into two groups. The screw and wedge are really forms of the inclined plane, so they are included in the *inclined plane family.* The wheel-and-axle and the pulley are forms of the lever and are combined with the *lever family.* The six simple machines are considered below in these two related groups.

Group 1: The Inclined Plane Family

The simplest form of this group is the *inclined plane.* While the other two—the screw and the wedge—are identified with different names and have their own functions, you will easily recognize them as forms of the inclined plane.

The inclined plane

The inclined plane is a slope, or a slanting surface, usually used to connect a lower level with a higher level. When a barrel is too heavy to lift up to a platform, it can be rolled up a ramp (see Figure 19-2). The ramp is an inclined plane. Less force is required to roll the barrel up the inclined plane than to lift it directly up to the platform. We recall that when a machine increases force, it does so at a cost of distance. The distance up the ramp is greater than the distance straight up from the ground to the platform. Longer and longer ramps can be used to further reduce the force needed to move the barrel, but the distance the barrel must be moved to attain the same altitude continues to increase as the inclined plane is lengthened.

A road that goes up a hillside is an inclined plane. A stairway and the sloping floor of a theater are other common examples.

Figure 19-2

A ramp is a simple machine.

The wedge

The wedge is an inclined plane that is designed to move into or under something. The woodcutter's wedge is used to split logs. A nail has a wedge point to help it spread fibers apart as it passes through wood (see Figure 19-3). The tip of a hand truck is wedge-shaped to make it easier to force it under a box or other load. The incisor teeth at the front of your mouth are wedges. With a wedge, friction can help or hinder. If we consider a log-splitting wedge, for instance, it is easy to see that friction makes it very difficult to drive the wedge into a log, yet without friction the wedge would not stay in the log to await the next blow from the ax. The blade of the ax is another example of a wedge. A knife blade is also a wedge.

Figure 19-3

The wedge point of the nail aids in forcing the nail into the board.

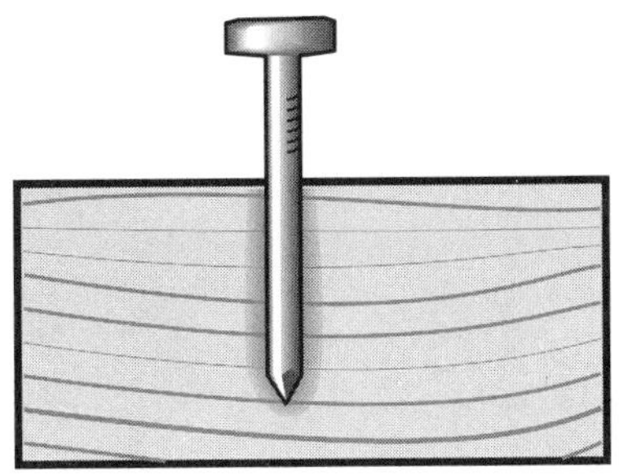

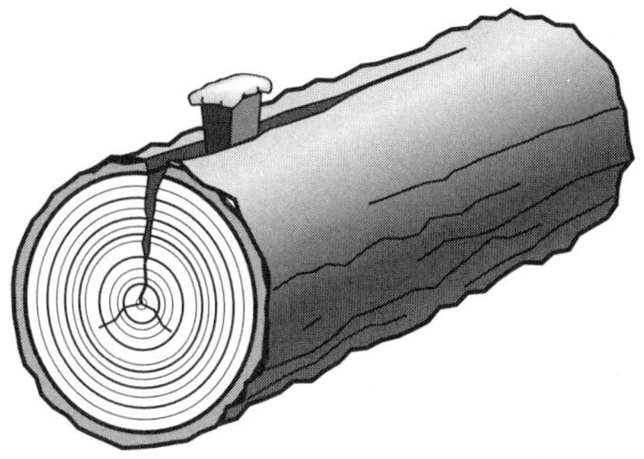

The screw

Perhaps the most obvious example of the screw is the fastener that is known by that name—*the screw*. A screw has a ridge that winds around and around its center in a spiral (see Figure 19-4). The spiraling ridge is called a *thread*. Examine a screw and you will see that the thread is only a spiral-shaped inclined plane. You can wind a triangular-shaped paper around a pencil (see Figure 19-5) and transform an inclined plane into a screw. Other applications of the screw as an inclined plane include the thread of a bolt, jar lid, adjustable piano stool, screw-type jack, vise, and the base of a light bulb.

Figure 19-4

The threads on these screws are spiral-shaped inclined planes.

Group 2: The Lever Family

The second group of simple machines consists of three classes of levers, the wheel-and-axle, and the pulley. Although the wheel-and-axle and the pulley are not usually thought of as levers, they really are forms of levers, and they are considered here as part of the lever family.

Levers are all around us—from spoons to brooms to toilet handles. In fact, not only are they all around us; they are also a part of us, in the form of arms, legs, fingers, toes, and jaw. Mobiles are made of levers, too, and what fun students have constructing them and making them balance. This is an excellent way to learn about levers and bring the world of science together with the world of art.

Three classes of levers

When a farmer finds a large rock in his field, he usually moves it to avoid damage to plows and

Figure 19-5

You can wrap a triangular-shaped paper around a pencil to transform the paper into a screw-shaped inclined plane.

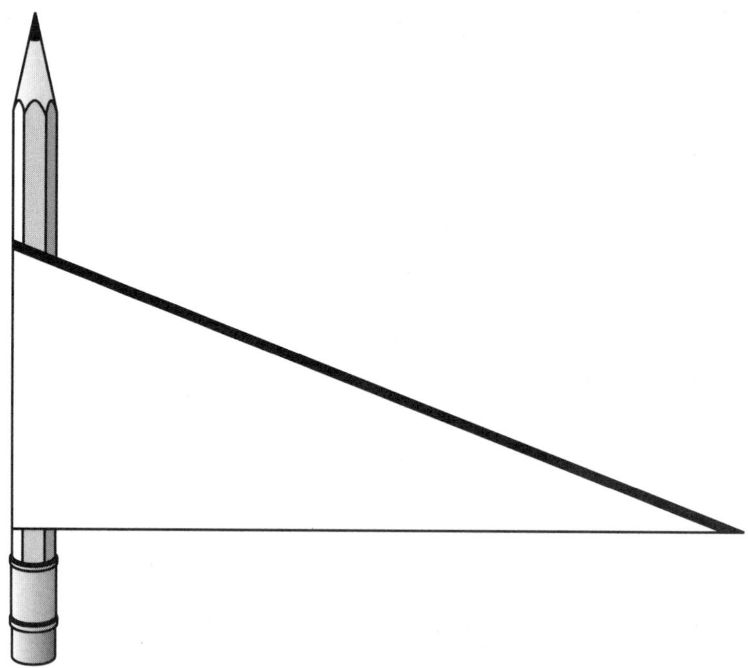

other equipment. If the rock cannot be moved by hand—perhaps it is wedged against another rock—the farmer will sometimes use a long bar of steel, or a wooden plank, to pry the rock loose. The bar is called a pry-bar or *lever.* A lever is any rigid bar that rests on a fixed point and is used to move something or to put pressure against something. The object the lever is moving or putting pressure against—in this case, the rock—is called the *load* or *resistance.* The fixed point the lever rests against, for the farmer perhaps a ridge of solid ground or another rock, is called the *fulcrum.* The force exerted on the lever is called the *effort.* The distance from the fulcrum to the point on the lever where the effort is exerted is called the *effort arm.* The distance from the fulcrum to the point where the load contacts the lever is called the *load arm* or *resistance arm.*

Like other simple machines, the lever is used to provide some form of mechanical advantage, which varies according to the position of the fulcrum relative to that of the effort and the load. In general, the closer the fulcrum is to the load, the less effort is necessary to move the load, but the effort will have to move farther to move the load a given distance. The relative positions of the load, fulcrum, and effort also determine whether the lever is a *first-class, second-class,* or *third-class* lever.

The First-Class Lever.

With the first-class lever, *the fulcrum is between the load and the effort.* A pry-bar used by the farmer in the above example is a first-class lever (see Figure 19-6). The shorter the load arm and the longer the effort arm, the less force

Figure 19-6

The fulcrum of a first-class lever is between the effort and the load.

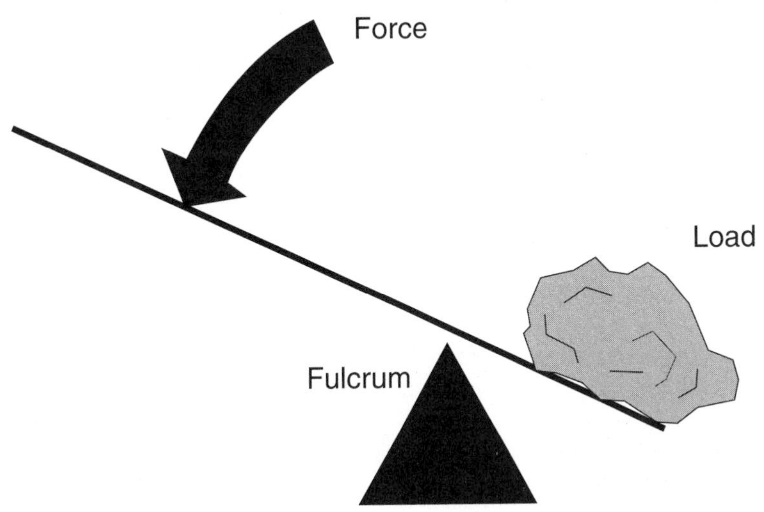

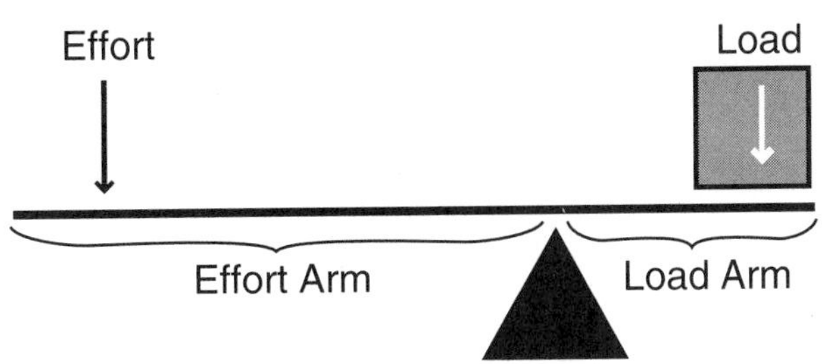

required to move the load. However, as the effort arm gets longer and the load arm gets shorter, the effort must move farther to move the load a given distance. Moving the fulcrum closer to the effort increases the length of the load arm and decreases the length of the effort arm, thus increasing the force needed to move the load, but the load will move farther and faster relative to the distance and speed the effort moves. The trade-off is always force for distance and speed. As long as the fulcrum is closer to the load than it is to the effort, there is a mechanical advantage of force, with the first-class lever. If the fulcrum is halfway between load and effort, there is no mechanical advantage, but only a change in direction. If the fulcrum is closer to the effort arm, the mechanical advantage is in distance and speed.

With a first-class lever, the load always moves in the opposite direction from the effort. The see-saw, or teeter-totter, is probably the best example. Most children are familiar with it and have discovered how to work with it to give one side or the other a mechanical advantage before they are taught formally about levers. Scissors and pliers are double first-class levers.

The Second-Class Lever.

A second-class lever is one in which *the load is between the fulcrum and the effort.* The load arm is always shorter than the effort arm, so there is always a gain in force. The effort and load move in the same direction with a second-class lever. A wheelbarrow, a nutcracker, and the oar of a rowboat are all examples of second-class levers (see Figure 19-7). With the oar out of the water it appears to be a first-class lever with the fulcrum in the middle where the oar rests on the boat. In operation, however, it is easy to see that the fulcrum is the water and the load is the point at which the oar is attached to the boat; remember, it's the boat you're trying to move—not the water.

The Third-Class Lever.

With the third-class lever *the effort is between the load and the fulcrum.* The effort arm is always shorter than the load arm, so there is always a loss in force but a gain in distance and speed. The load always moves farther and faster than the effort. A fishing pole is an example of a third-class lever. As the angler casts the line, the fulcrum is at or near the base of the pole, the effort is only a few centimeters from the fulcrum, and the load is at the tip of the pole (Figure 19-8). The end of the pole swishes through the air with only a relatively slight action by the wrist and arm. You are trading force for distance and speed. To bring in a fish of a few pounds on the end of the line can require a terrific amount of force at the handle

Figure 19-7 ***The wheelbarrow, the nutcracker, and the oars of a rowboat are all second-class levers.***

Figure 19-8

The fishing pole is a third-class lever. The effort arm and the load arm are both measured from the fulcrum.

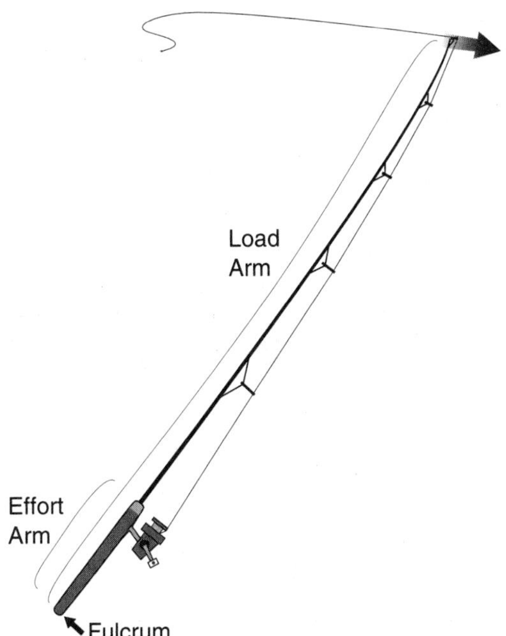

Figure 19-9

The human arm is a third-class lever.

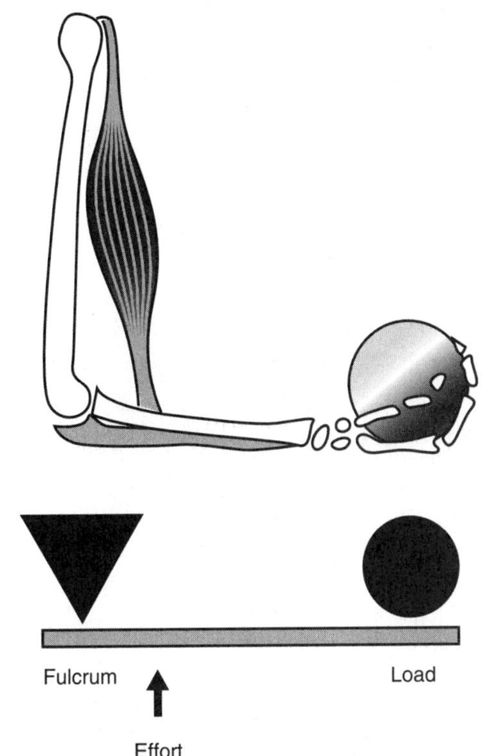

of the fishing pole. A third-class lever does not change the direction of the force; both load and effort move in the same direction. Both the load arm and the effort arm are measured from the fulcrum. Brooms and shovels are third-class levers, and so are your arms and legs (see Figure 19-9).

The wheel-and-axle

The well was a common source of water long before the pump was invented. Water was obtained by lowering a bucket, tied to a rope, into the well. The other end of the rope was tied to a *windlass*. The windlass (see Figure 19-10) was one of the early machines devised by humankind, and it holds a place at the heart of world history. Poems and songs have been written about the windlass and the "old oaken bucket." Most people have seen pictures of such a well and heard about the importance of the windlass, the bucket, and the well as a source of water for the people.

You can think of the windlass as a continuous first-class lever that goes around and around (see Figure 19-11). The fulcrum is at the center of the axle (shaft) that is being turned. The load arm is the radius of the axle. The effort arm is the length of the lever from the center of the shaft to the handle where force is applied.

Let's create a new design for the windlass. Instead of holding a single handle and moving the hand in a circular motion to turn the shaft, let's install three more levers. We'll turn the shaft one-quarter of a turn with one lever, then take the next lever and turn the shaft another

Figure 19-10

The windlass moves the bucket (the load) in the well.

Figure 19-11

The windlass is a continuous first-class lever.

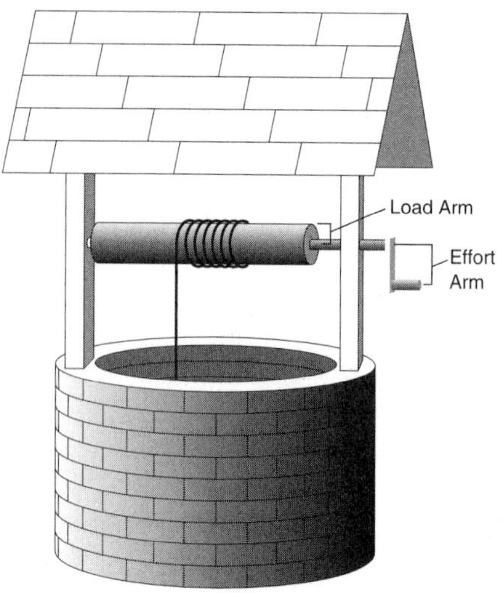

Figure 19-12

The windlass with four handles facilitates moving the load from more positions.

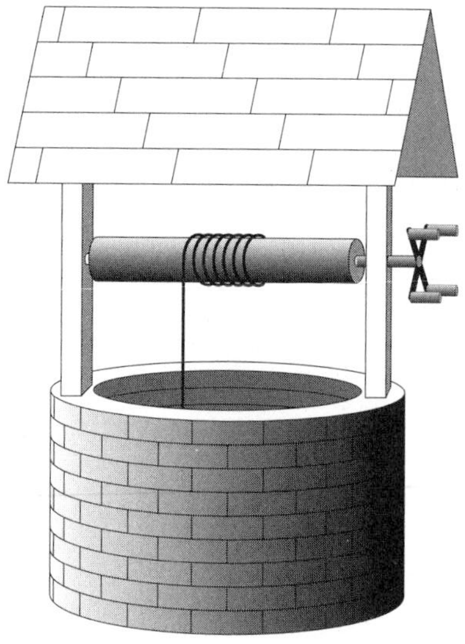

quarter of a turn. We can cause the shaft to go around and around by moving the hand back and forth, switching from lever to lever (see Figure 19-12).

Now let's replace the levers with a wheel. The wheel gives us the advantage that we can hold any point on the wheel and move it to turn the shaft (see Figure 19-13). It is as though we have an infinite number of levers attached to the shaft, and we can turn the shaft with any one of them. Alas! We have just designed a wheel-and-axle! The wheel-and-axle is like a continuous first-class lever that is made up of an infinite number of levers attached to an axle: The fulcrum is at the center of the axle; the load arm is the radius of the axle; and the effort arm is the radius of the wheel (length of the lever from the fulcrum to the effort position).

Notice that with a wheel-and-axle the wheel is attached to the axle, so if the wheel turns, so does the axle, and if the axle turns, so does the wheel. A mechanical advantage of force can be gained by using the wheel to turn the axle, as with the windlass and the steering wheel of a

Figure 19-13

The windlass with wheel in place of the handle is really a wheel-and-axle.

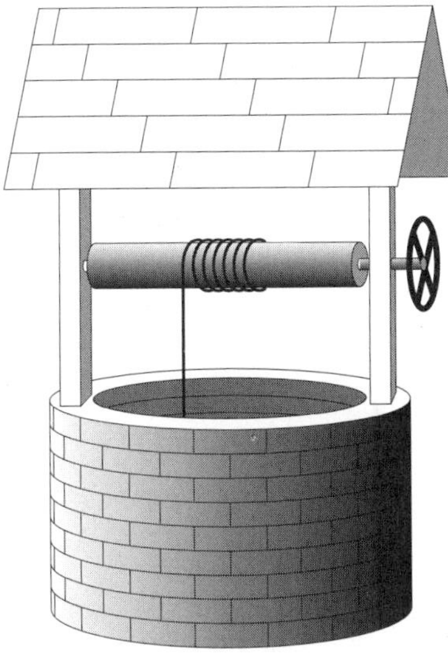

car. A mechanical advantage of speed and distance can be achieved by using the axle to turn the wheel, such as with the rear wheel of a bicycle or the drive wheels of a car. In this application, the wheel-and-axle is a third-class lever. Doorknobs and screwdrivers are other applications of the wheel-and-axle, but notice that the with these, the wheel turns the axle. Doorknobs and screwdrivers are designed to increase force in the turning of the shaft, and they are first-class levers. But remember, the wheel doesn't have to be a complete wheel; the windlass with a single handle is really a form of the wheel-and-axle. Other examples include the pencil sharpener, the egg beater, and the crank that was used to start the automobile engine many years ago.

The pulley

One major difference between the wheel-and-axle and the pulley is that with the wheel-and-axle, the wheel is attached to the axle, whereas the pulley is a wheel that turns on a stationary axle. There is usually a groove in the pulley to hold a rope, a cable, or a belt in place around it.

Pulleys are sometimes mounted in a stationary or fixed position. These are called *fixed pulleys*. If a box on the floor needs to be raised to a higher level, a rope from an overhead pulley can be attached to the box, then pulling down on the rope raises the box. The fixed pulley does not provide a mechanical advantage by decreasing the force needed to lift the box, and it does not increase speed and distance of movement. It simply changes the direction of the force. Pulling down on the rope causes the load to go up (see Figure 19-14).

Figure 19-14

The fixed pulley: Pulling down on the rope causes the load to go up.

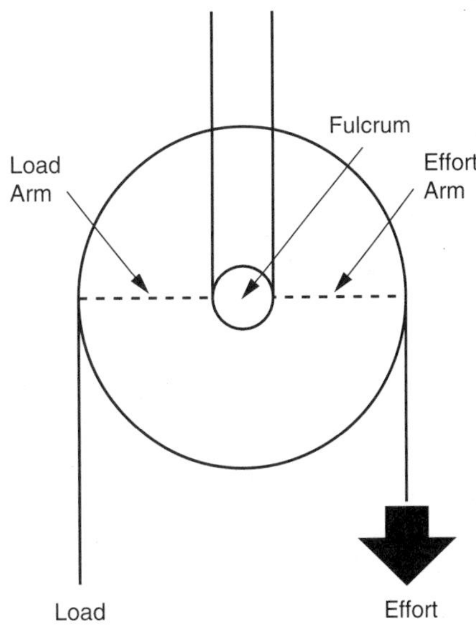

The fixed pulley acts like a continuous first-class lever, with the fulcrum at the center of the axle, the force at one rim of the wheel, and the resistance or load at the other rim. Fixed pulleys are used for flag poles, curtain rods, and many other applications. During the construction of tall buildings, some form of device using a fixed pulley is often used to lift building materials to upper levels of the structure.

Movable pulleys are attached to the load with one end of the rope being attached in a fixed position. When a force is applied to the other end of the rope, the pulley moves with the load. Because the pulley moves, the load travels only half as far as the effort and requires only half as much force to move it. The movable pulley is like a turning second-class lever, with the fulcrum at one rim of the wheel, the load at the axle, and the effort at the other rim of the wheel. It does not change the direction of the force because the movable pulley moves with the load (see Figure 19-15).

Figure 19-15

The moveable pulley requires half as much force as the fixed pulley.

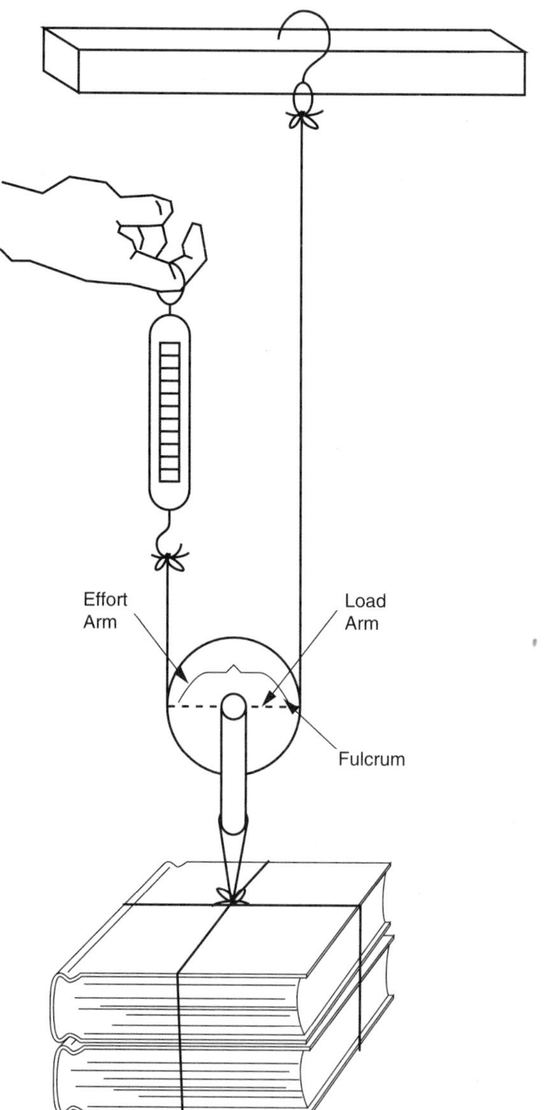

The block and tackle

A fixed pulley can be combined with a movable pulley to change direction and gain force at the same time. This device is called a *block and tackle* (see Figure 19-16). Two or more fixed pulleys can be combined with two or more movable pulleys, making it possible for one person to lift very heavy loads with ease. One movable pulley doubles the force applied to the load but also doubles the distance the effort must travel. Using two movable pulleys results in four times the force and the effort travels four times as far as the load. A load of 100 pounds can be lifted with only 25 pounds of force if two movable pulleys are used. That, of course, considers the *ideal mechanical advantage.* The ideal mechanical advantage of a system of movable pulleys can be found by simply counting the number of ropes supporting the movable pulleys. One pulley has two ropes coming from it, two pulleys have four, three pulleys have six, and four pulleys have eight. The ideal mechanical advantage with four movable pulleys, then, is eight; the load is distributed evenly over eight ropes. Because of friction in the system the actual mechanical advantage is somewhat less. The actual mechanical advantage can be found by dividing the resistance, or weight of the load, by the effort. The actual mechanical advantage can vary from one set of pulleys to another because of a difference in friction.

Figure 19-16

A block and tackle can use multiple pulleys.

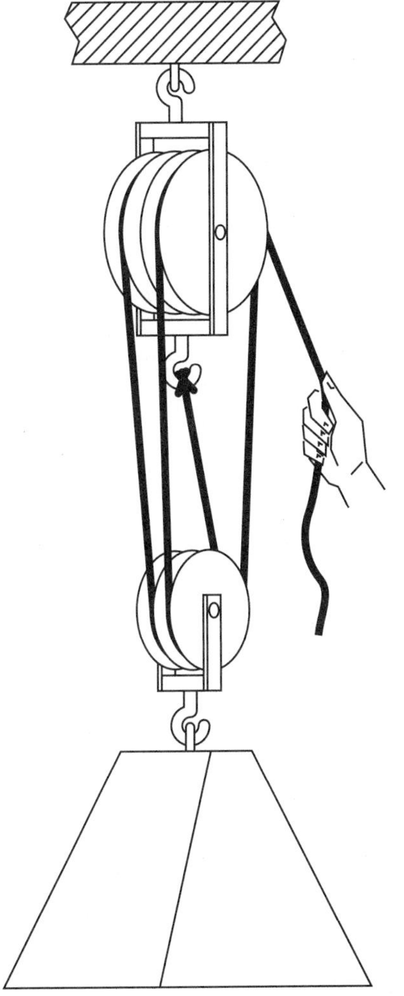

Compound Machines

When two or more simple machines are combined, the resulting device is called a *compound machine*. Most of the machines we use are compound machines. An automobile engine is a compound machine; in fact, the automobile itself is a compound machine, as it contains many simple machines in addition to those that make up the engine. A pair of scissors is another compound machine, as is a wheel-type can opener and a host of other common tools and appliances. For example, the handle of an ax is a *lever* and the blade is a *wedge;* thus, the ax is a compound machine. The handle of a pencil sharpener, like a windlass, is part of a *wheel-and-axle;* it turns two *screws* that have sharp, *wedge*-shaped edges that sharpen the pencil. And the list of commonly used compound machines goes on to include screwdrivers, egg-beaters, and many more.

VI. IN CLOSING

Even in the modern world of electronics and computers, we continue to use more and more machines. In fact, one of the growing uses of computers in the home, on the highway, and in the factory, is to control the functions of machines, usually resulting in greater efficiency of the machines' productive potential as well as greater convenience for humans.

LIST OF RESOURCES

Ballif, Jae R., and William E. Dibble, *Physics: Fundamentals and Frontiers* (New York: John Wiley & Sons, 1972).

Tolman, Marvin N., and James O. Morton, *Physical Science Activities for Grades 2–8* (West Nyack, NY: Parker Publishing Co., 1986).

Victor, Edward, *Science for the Elementary School, Sixth Edition* (New York: Macmillan Publishing Co., 1989).

CHAPTER

MACHINES

ACTIVITIES

II. WHAT IS A MACHINE AND HOW DOES IT HELP US?

ACTIVITY 19-1:

WHAT IS A MACHINE?
(Group activity)

Materials Needed:

None

Procedure:

1. Discuss the question, "What is a machine?" Accept all answers at this point. Answers will likely be mostly examples—tractor, car, sewing machine, and so on. Make a list.
2. Help the group notice that all of the things on the list help us do something more easily than we could do them otherwise. That's what machines are for.
3. Ask for additional ideas about smaller, simpler things. Suggest that a hammer is a machine, and so is a knife, and so is a screwdriver. Add to the list.
4. Now have everyone look around the room and find things we use to make work easier. Add to the list—scissors, letter openers, thumb tacks, straight pins, staple pullers, staplers, pencil sharpeners, door knobs, and even light switches are machines. What else?
5. Go through the list again. This time have the group tell something that each machine on the list does.
6. Find some of the items on the list that are in the classroom. Decide what we do with these things and try to do that task without the machine. For instance, bat a ball without a bat, sharpen a pencil without a pencil sharpener, cut a slice of bread without a knife, and so on.

For Problem Solvers:

Read a library book about simple machines, or read about simple machines in the encyclopedia. Find out what the simple machines are, how they work, and the things they do for us.

Find examples of the simple machines in your life. Can you make models of some of them?

Design a machine that will do some simple task.

Teacher Information:

The purpose of this activity is to help us to begin thinking about what makes a machine a machine, and to begin recognizing things around us as machines. Do not attempt, yet, to classify them into standard groupings or to give them labels. At some time in this activity, point out that our arms, legs, and fingers are machines.

Integrating: Reading

Skills: Observing, inferring, communicating

III. THE ROLE OF FRICTION

ACTIVITY 19-2:
WHAT DOES FRICTION DO?

Materials Needed:

Water

Procedure:

1. Hold the palms of your hands against your cheeks. How do they feel?
2. Rub your hands together briskly, then hold them against your cheeks again. How do your hands feel now?
3. What do you think made the difference?
4. Dip your hands in water, then rub them together and hold them against your cheeks again.
5. Is there a difference this time? What is it? Why?
6. Discuss your ideas with your group.

For Problem Solvers:

Make a bundle of three or four books by tying a string around them. Put the books on a table and attach the spring scale to the string. Drag the books with the spring scale, noticing the reading on the spring scale. Record the force required to start the books moving and the force required to keep them moving. Put several round pencils under the books and again record the force required to start the books moving and the force required to keep them moving.

Get together with others who are doing this activity and discuss your ideas about starting friction, sliding friction, and rolling friction.

Investigate the question, "Is friction ever good?" Think about it as you read about friction in library books and other resources.

Teacher Information:

When two materials rub together, some of the energy used in sliding them against each other is transformed into heat energy. You can easily detect this by rubbing your hands together and holding them against your cheeks, as in the above activity.

While we usually think of it as a negative, because it makes things hot and wears things out, friction is also a necessary part of our lives. We couldn't walk down a sidewalk and it would be very difficult to even sit on a chair. Life would be impossible without friction.

Integrating: Reading, writing, math

Skills: Observing, inferring, communicating, researching

IV. MECHANICAL ADVANTAGE

ACTIVITY 19-3:
WHAT IS MECHANICAL ADVANTAGE?

Materials Needed:

Bundles of books wrapped with string

Spring scales

Hand truck

Procedure:

1. Attach the spring scales to the string of one of the bundles.
2. Lift the books with the scales and record the weight.
3. Do the same with the other bundles of books, recording the weight each time.
4. Add the weights of the bundles and record the total weight of the books.
5. Lay the hand truck on the floor. Put all of the books on the hand truck.
6. Attach the spring scales to the handle of the hand truck and lift the hand truck with the spring scales.
7. Record the force needed to lift the books with the hand truck. How does this compare with the weight of the books?
8. Divide the force required to lift the books without the hand truck by the force required with the hand truck. The result is called the *mechanical advantage*. What is the mechanical advantage in this case?
9. Compare your information with others who did this activity.

For Problem Solvers:

Shift the books to a different position on the hand truck. Predict the force that will be needed to lift the hand truck at the handle this time. Predict the mechanical advantage. Stand the hand truck up, put the books on it, and predict the force and mechanical advantage in this position. Write your predictions each time, then test them.

Teacher Information:

You should be able to borrow a hand truck from the supply room or from the custodian.

Mechanical advantage is a number that suggests the advantage obtained by using a machine. If an object weighs 400 pounds and it can be lifted by the machine with 100 pounds of force, the mechanical advantage is four. This number is obtained by dividing the force required without the machine by the force required when the machine is used. In the case of this activity, students will get different values according to the weight of their books, the length of the hand truck, and where they place the books on the hand truck. If 50 pounds of force is required to lift the books without the hand truck, and 25 pounds of force is required with the hand truck, the hand truck offered a mechanical advantage of two. It is very important that this value *not* be perceived as a mechanical advantage of hand trucks. It only applies to the way it was used this time. This will become clear as students try the activity multiple times with the books and the hand truck in different positions.

The idea of mechanical advantage will appear in other activities in this chapter. The purpose of this activity is only to begin thinking about what *mechanical advantage* means.

Integrating: Math, writing

Skills: Observing, inferring, measuring, predicting

V. THE SIX SIMPLE MACHINES

ACTIVITY 19-4:

WHAT KIND OF WORK DOES THE INCLINED PLANE DO?

Materials Needed:

Bundle of books

Roller skate (or toy truck)

Spring scale

Board, about 1 meter (3 feet) long

Procedure:

1. Tie the bundle of books to the roller skate. Lift the books and the skate with the spring scale and record the weight.
2. Place the board on the floor. Make a ramp by propping up one end of the board. Put it on a step, on a low stool, or some other object.
3. Place the bundle of books on the roller skate and drag the roller skate, with its load, up the ramp using the spring scale.
4. Record the force required to pull the load up the ramp. Compare this force with the weight of the load.
5. Change the position of the ramp by propping the end higher or lower. Predict the force that will be required to pull the load up the ramp this time. Try it and test your prediction.
6. Predict and test the force required to do the same thing using other ramp positions.
7. Compare your findings with others who are doing the same activity.

For Problem Solvers:

Compute the mechanical advantage of the ramp by dividing the weight of the load by the force required to pull it up the ramp.

Compare the height of the ramp with its length. Compare the weight of the load with the force required to pull the load up the ramp, from several ramp positions. Do you notice any trends? Write a hypothesis about the effect of ramp height compared with ramp length. Compute the mechanical advantage from several more ramp positions and test your hypothesis. Test your hypothesis with a longer board.

Teacher Information:

The ramp, as one of the simple machines, allows us to move a load from one level to another without needing to lift the entire weight of the load. The effect of the ramp slope on mechanical advantage will quickly become evident with this activity. After several attempts, students should become fairly accurate with their predictions of the force that will be required to pull a given load up the ramp with differing ramp heights.

Those who pursue the extension for problem solvers will continue on with computations of actual mechanical advantage at each position. Under ideal conditions the mechanical advantage of the ramp can be calculated by dividing ramp length by the height of the propped-up end. Ideally, then, if a ramp is five times as long as it is high, a 250 kilogram (550 pound) barrel can be rolled up the ramp with 50 kilograms (110 pounds) of force. Friction never allows the ideal mechanical advantage to also be the actual mechanical advantage. The actual mechanical advantage is computed by dividing the weight by the measured force required to pull the load up the ramp. Any inaccurate measurements will also, of course, take their toll on the accuracy of results when computing the mechanical advantage of the ramp.

Every mechanical advantage represents a trade-off. In the case of the ramp, we have the advantage of being able to move the load with less force. The trade-off is that the load must be moved over a greater distance. It is important that students recognize that the total work required is not reduced, but only redistributed.

Integrating: Math

Skills: Observing, inferring, measuring, predicting, formulating hypotheses, identifying and controlling variables, experimenting

ACTIVITY 19-5:
WHAT KIND OF WORK DOES THE WEDGE DO?

Materials Needed:

Stack of books

Door wedge

Procedure:

1. Place the stack of books on the floor.
2. Place the door wedge on the floor with the books, with the point of the wedge barely under the books.
3. Tap the wedge toward the books. Do not let the books slide across the floor.
4. Do the books move? In which direction?

For Problem Solvers:

What uses can you think of for the wedge? Discuss your ideas with others. Read about the wedge in a book about simple machines or in an encyclopedia, and find out some ways the wedge is used in addition to the uses you thought of.

How is a wedge different from an inclined plane?

Teacher Information:

The wedge changes the direction of the movement of a load by forcing two surfaces to separate. If a wedge is driven under something, as with the books, a horizontal movement of the wedge results in an upward movement of the load. A log-splitter's wedge is used to separate two parts, splitting the log.

Some perceptive students will recognize that the wedge is really an inclined plane. When it is used as a ramp the load is moved up the inclined plane. When it is used as a wedge, the "ramp" is forced into or under the load.

Integrating: Reading

Skills: Observing, inferring

ACTIVITY 19-6:
WHAT IS A SCREW?

Materials Needed:

Pencil

Sheet of white paper

Scissors

Black marker

Large wood screw

Procedure:

1. Cut a triangle from a sheet of white paper by cutting diagonally, from corner to corner (see Figure 19A-1).

Figure 19A-1

Cut the rectangular paper diagonally from corner to corner.

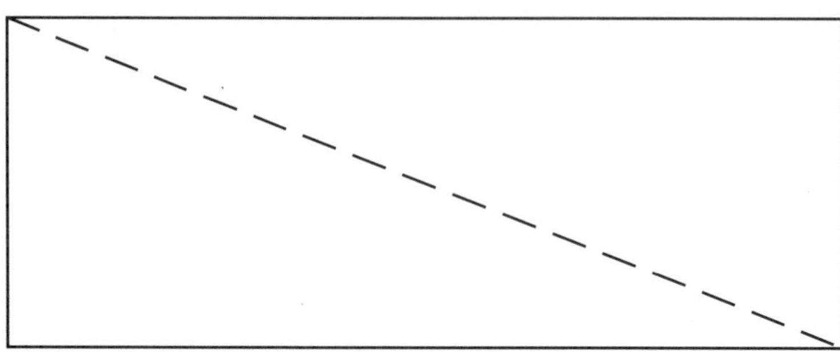

2. Using the marker, make a heavy black line along the hypotenuse (the longest side) (see Figure 19A-2).
3. Hold the triangle upright on top of your table or desk. Which of the simple machines we have already studied does the triangle now look like?
4. Beginning with the short side, wrap the paper triangle around a pencil (see Figure 19A-3).
5. Hold the wrapped pencil side by side with the large wood screw.
6. Does the heavy line of the triangle resemble the threads of the screw?
7. How would you say the threads of a screw compare to an inclined plane? Think about how the triangle with its black edge looked before you wrapped it around the pencil.

For Problem Solvers:

What uses can you think of for the screw other than the type of screw that is used with a screwdriver? Discuss your ideas with others. Read about the screw in a book about simple machines or in an encyclopedia, and find out some ways the screw is used in addition to the uses you thought of.

Figure 19A-2

Darken the hypotenuse of the triangle.

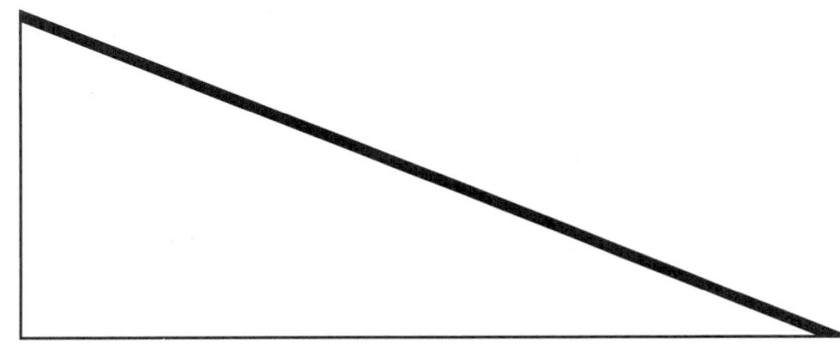

Figure 19A-3

Wrap the triangle around the pencil.

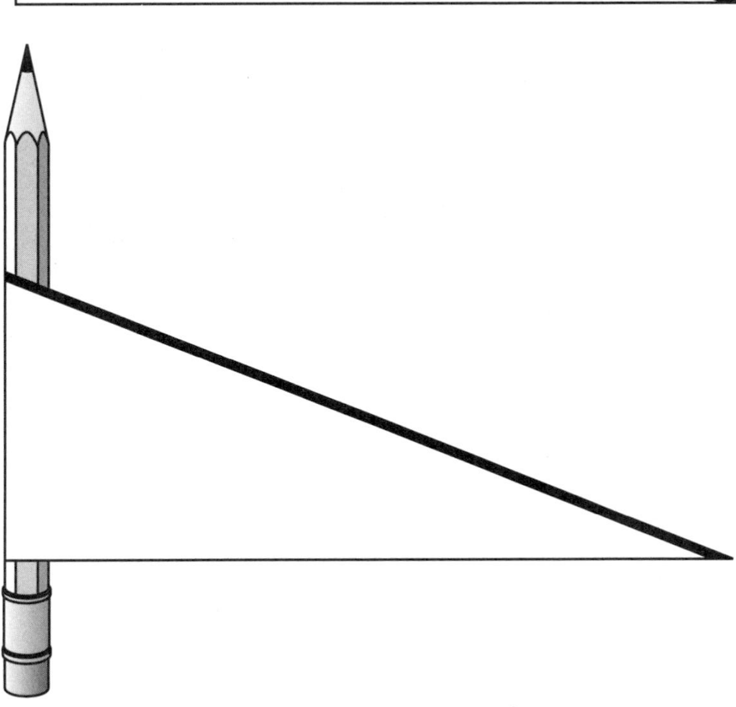

How is a screw different from an inclined plane?

Teacher Information:

The screw is a form of inclined plane that winds around in a spiral. The spiral-shaped ridge around the screw is called the *thread*.

Integrating: Reading

Skills: Observing, inferring

(Except for addition of the sections "For Problem Solvers," "Integrating," and "Skills," this activity was reprinted from Activity 124, "What Is a Screw?" in Tolman and Morton, 1986.)

ACTIVITY 19-7: WHAT IS A FIRST-CLASS LEVER?

Materials Needed:

1-kilogram (2-pound) bag of sand

Heavy-duty meter stick

Spring scale

Fulcrum

Procedure:

1. Weigh the bag of sand (the load) and record the weight.
2. Place the fulcrum under the lever (meter stick) at the center.
3. Place the load on one end of the lever. Pull down on the other end of the lever with the spring scale. Record the force required to lift the load.
4. How does the force required to lift the load compare with the weight of the load?
5. Move the fulcrum halfway between the center and the end the load is on. Lift the load again by pulling down on the lever with the spring scale.
6. How much force was required to lift the load this time?
7. Move the fulcrum halfway between the center of the lever and the end opposite the load. Lift the sand again, using the spring scale. Now how much force is required to lift the load?
8. Discuss your findings with others. What have you learned about a first-class lever? Which direction do you move the end of the lever in order to lift the load? Which direction do you move the fulcrum to make it easier to lift the load?

For Problem Solvers:

The end of the lever the load is on is called the *load arm*. The end you pull on is called the *effort arm*. Which direction does the effort arm need to move in order to move the load up? See if you can find a way to use the same lever to force an object to move down. Which direction will the effort arm need to move?

Move the fulcrum to a new position under the lever. Predict how much effort will be required to lift the load. Record the position of the fulcrum and the amount of force you predicted, then test your prediction. Predict, record, and test another position. Your predictions should be quite accurate by now. Explain how you make your predictions.

Go to a teeter-totter (see-saw) on the playground, if there is one. Examine the teeter-totter and compare it with the first-class lever you have been working with. Select a person for each end of the teeter-totter. Before they get on it, from what you have already learned, make a prediction of where the fulcrum should be for these people to balance on the teeter-totter. Test your prediction. Try it several times, changing at least one person each time.

Teacher Information:

Students need an object of known weight to work with for this activity. The weight does not need to be 1 kilogram and it does not need to be sand. It can be books or a bag of salt, BBs, marbles, rocks, or whatever is convenient. A piece of PVC pipe works well as a fulcrum, but it can be most anything that can be placed under the lever. The fulcrum should have a pointed top or a rounded top so the lever rocks smoothly up and down.

Students learn here about the function of a first-class lever. Those who pursue the extension for problem solvers should be able to place the lever properly in order to lift a given load with a pre-determined amount of force. Students should notice that a first-class lever reverses the direction of the load—the effort arm and load arm move in opposite directions.

If the school has no teeter-totter, a makeshift teeter-totter could be constructed with a plank, using a barrel, a pipe, or some other suitable object as a fulcrum.

Integrating: Math, physical education, writing

Skills: Observing, inferring, predicting, identifying and controlling variables

ACTIVITY 19-8: WHAT IS A SECOND-CLASS LEVER?

Materials Needed:

1-kilogram (2-pound) bag of sand

Heavy-duty meter stick

Spring scale

Fulcrum

Procedure:

1. Weigh the bag of sand and record the weight.
2. Place the load (sand) on the lever about in the middle.
3. Place the fulcrum under one end of the lever and lift on the other end with the spring scale.
4. You now have a second-class lever. Notice that as you lift the books, the load and the effort move in the same direction.
5. Record the amount of force required to lift the load with the load in the middle of the lever and the effort on the end.
6. Predict the force required with the load halfway between the middle and the fulcrum. Record your prediction, then test it.
7. Predict the force required with the load at the same end as the effort. Record your prediction, then test it.
8. What happens to the force required to lift the load as the load moves toward the fulcrum? What happens to the force required to lift the load as the load moves toward the effort? Discuss these questions with others who are doing the same activity.

For Problem Solvers:

Write a statement that compares the first-class lever and the second-class lever. How are they similar? How are they different? Try to find examples of second-class levers.

Teacher Information:

As students investigate with the second-class lever, they will find that as the load is moved toward the fulcrum, less force is required to lift the load. As the force required to lift the load is reduced, the distance the load moves is also reduced.

With a second-class lever the load arm is measured from the fulcrum to the load. The effort arm is measured from the fulcrum to the point on the lever where force is applied.

As with the first-class lever, the force required to lift a load can be predicted by comparing the length of the load arm with the length of the effort arm. With the second-class lever, a mechanical advantage of force can be acquired while the effort and load move in the same direction. A wheelbarrow is a second-class lever.

Integrating: Math, physical education, writing

Skills: Observing, inferring, predicting, identifying and controlling variables

ACTIVITY 19-9: WHAT IS A THIRD-CLASS LEVER?

Materials Needed:

1-kilogram (2-pound) bag of sand

Heavy-duty meter stick

Spring scale

Table

Procedure:

1. Weigh the bag of sand and record the weight.
2. Place the load (sand) on one end of the lever.
3. Place the other end of the lever under the edge of the table, and lift the load by holding the lever in the middle.
4. This is a third-class lever. Notice that as you lift the books the load and the effort move in the same direction. This was also true with the second-class lever.
5. What is the fulcrum now?
6. Record the amount of force required to lift the load with the load in at the end of the lever and the effort in the middle.
7. With the effort between the load and the fulcrum, predict the force required to lift the load as you move the effort to various positions along the lever. Record your prediction each time, then test it.
8. What happens to the force required to lift the load as the load moves toward the fulcrum? What happens to the force required to lift the load as the load moves toward the effort? Discuss these questions with others who are doing the same activity.

For Problem Solvers:

Write a statement that compares the third-class lever with the first-class lever and the second-class lever. How are they similar? How are they different? With the third-class lever, will the effort ever be less than the load? What is gained by using the third-class lever? Try to find examples of third-class levers.

Teacher Information:

As students investigate with the third-class lever, they will find that as the effort is moved toward the fulcrum, more force is required to lift the load. As the force required to lift the load is increased, the distance and speed the load moves is also increased.

With a third-class lever, the load arm is measured from the fulcrum to the load. The effort arm is measured from the fulcrum to the point on the lever where force is applied.

As with the first-class and second-class levers, the force required to lift a load can be predicted by comparing the length of the load arm with the length of the effort arm. With the third-class lever, a mechanical advantage of distance and speed can be acquired while the effort and load move in the same direction. A fishing pole is a second-class lever. Your arms and legs are also third-class levers.

Integrating: Math, physical education, writing

Skills: Observing, inferring, predicting, identifying and controlling variables

ACTIVITY 19-10: WHAT IS THE WHEEL-AND-AXLE?

Materials Needed:

Compass

Stiff paper at least 10 centimeters square

Pencil

Scissors

Tape measure

Procedure:

1. Use the compass to make a circle on the paper.
2. Cut out the circle.
3. Insert the pencil through the center of the circle. You have made a wheel-and-axle (see Figure 19A-4).

Figure 19A-4

Insert the pencil through the center of the paper to make a wheel-and-axle.

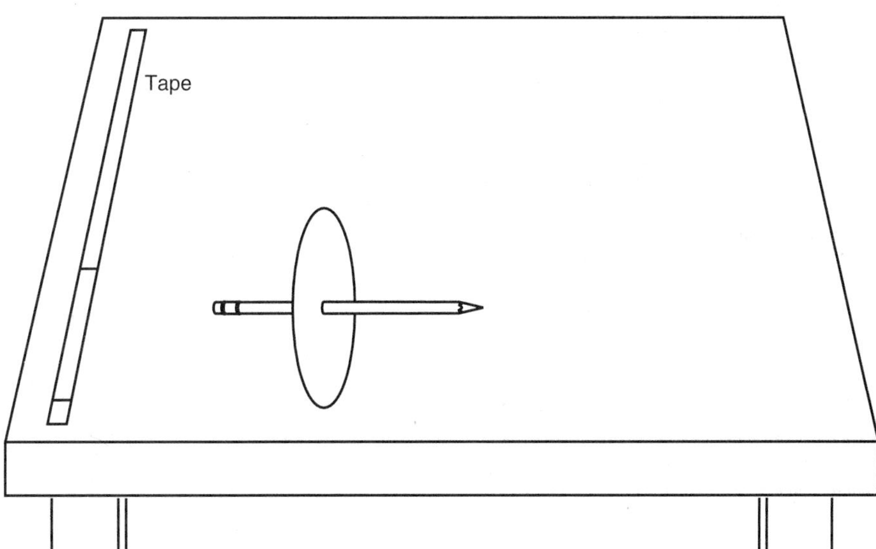

4. Roll your wheel and axle along the tabletop. How many times does the pencil rotate as the wheel rotates once?
5. Measure the distance the wheel traveled in one complete rotation.
6. Remove the pencil from the wheel, place the pencil on the table, and measure the distance it travels in one complete rotation.
7. How far would the pencil travel if rotated ten times?
8. Insert the pencil (axle) back into the wheel. How far does it travel now in ten rotations?
9. Name one advantage of the wheel and axle.

For Problem Solvers:

The wheel-and-axle is really a form of a second-class lever or a form of a third-class lever, depending on how it is used. Try to understand and explain that. Talk to others who are working with the same things.

Examine a pencil sharpener. What types of simple machines are involved in it?

Teacher Information:

The wheel-and-axle is a form of the lever. When the wheel or the axle turns, the other turns also. If the wheel turns around the axle, as on bearings, it is not a wheel-and-axle.

If the wheel is turning the axle, it is a form of second-class lever (see Figure 19A-5). The fulcrum is at the center of the axle. The radius of the wheel is the effort arm of the lever and the radius of the axle is the load arm. There is increased force but less speed and distance.

Figure 19A-5

If the wheel is turning the axle, it is a second-class lever.

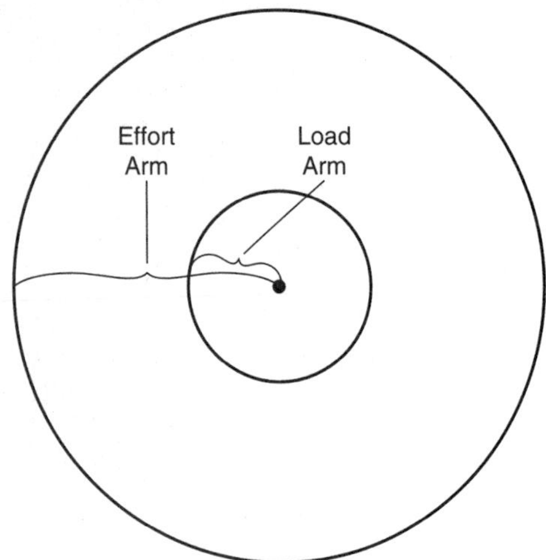

Examples of the wheel-and-axle acting as a second-class lever include the doorknob, the screwdriver, and the steering wheel of an automobile.

If the axle is turning the wheel, it can be thought of as a form of third-class lever. The fulcrum is at the center of the axle. The radius of the wheel is the load arm and the radius of the axle is the effort arm (see Figure 19A-6). The effort arm is shorter than the load arm, so there is a gain in speed and distance but a decrease in force.

Figure 19A-6

If the axle is turning the wheel, it is a form of third-class lever.

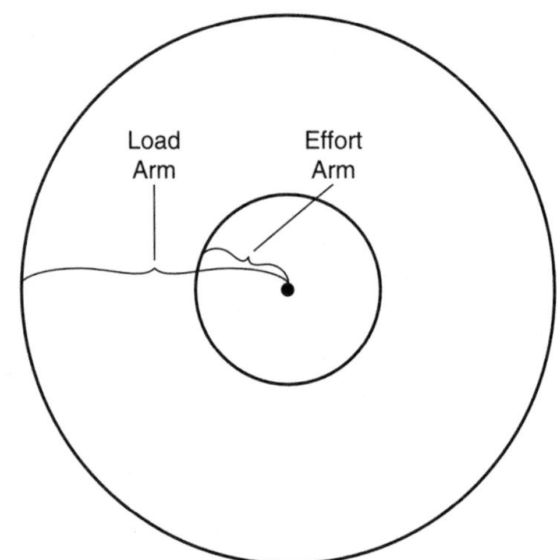

Integrating: Math

Skills: Observing, inferring

(Except for addition of the sections "For Problem Solvers," "Integrating," and "Skills," this activity was reprinted from Activity 117, "What Is the Wheel-and-Axle?" in Tolman and Morton, 1986.)

ACTIVITY 19-11:
WHAT IS A PULLEY?

Materials Needed:

Pulley

Cord

Bundle of books

Spring scale

Cross bar

Procedure:

1. Mount the pulley to the cross bar. This is called a fixed pulley because it is anchored in place.
2. Tie one end of the cord to the bundle of books and put the other end through the pulley.
3. Pull down on the cord. What happens to the books?

4. How does the force required to lift the books compare with the weight of the books?
5. What does a fixed pulley accomplish?
6. Now remove the pulley from the bar and tie the pulley to the bundle of books.
7. Tie one end of the cord to the bar, with the cord still through the pulley.
8. Lift on the other end of the cord. What happens to the books?
9. Now how does the weight of the books compare with the force required to lift the books?
10. This is called a movable pulley, because the pulley moves with the load.
11. Discuss your observations with others who are doing this activity, and talk about your ideas.

For Problem Solvers:

Use both a fixed pulley and a movable pulley. How does the weight of the load compare with the effort (force) required to lift it? Compute the mechanical advantage by dividing weight by force. If you have more pulleys, tie another movable pulley to the load. Predict what the mechanical advantage will be. Write your prediction and test it.

Read about pulleys and about the block and tackle. See if you can find an easy way to estimate the amount of force that will be required to lift a load, simply by knowing the weight of the load and how many movable pulleys are attached to it. Discuss what you are learning with others who are interested in this activity.

Teacher Information:

The cross bar for this activity could be just a bar, a pipe, or a board rested on two tables with work space between.

A fixed pulley offers no mechanical advantage of either force or of speed and distance, but it simply changes the direction of movement. Pulling down on the rope causes the load to go up, but the force required equals the weight of the load.

The movable pulley does not change the direction of force. It cuts in half the force required to lift the load, and doubles the distance the effort moves while the load is moved a given distance.

Imaginations can flourish with this activity, as students continue with the extension for problem solvers. Additional fixed and movable pulleys can be used, and soon they will have a block and tackle. The ideal mechanical advantage of force can be computed by dividing the weight of the load by the number of ropes coming to the load, of which there are two for each pulley that is attached to the load. Actual mechanical advantage can be computed by dividing the weight of the load by the actual force required to lift it. There will be some difference due to loss caused by friction.

Integrating: Reading, writing, math

Skills: Observing, inferring, researching, formulating hypotheses, identifying and controlling variables

CHAPTER

AIR AND WATER

CHAPTER OUTLINE:

I WONDER . . .

How can the atmosphere be compared to an ocean?
What role does the atmosphere play in distributing water around the earth?
What does Bernoulli's principle have to do with airplanes?
What is the water cycle, and what do rocks have to do with it?
How does a steel ship float?

I. INTRODUCTION

Air and water are vital natural resources. Although the majority of the water is on the earth's surface at any given time, it constantly cycles through the atmosphere, which redistributes it around the globe. Therefore, although we think of the atmosphere as a blanket of air, water is inseparably a part of it. Our lives are influenced constantly by what is happening in the atmosphere.

Until recent decades, many people thought Earth's supply of air and water was so vast that it could not be significantly affected by the actions of living creatures. We now know that both of these precious resources are vulnerable to the pollutants that are by-products of our ever-growing demand for goods and services. We are beginning to realize that the quality of life for all inhabitants of this planet depends on the way humans care for the huge, yet fragile supply of air and water that surround it.

II. AIR

You and I live at the bottom of an ocean, just as surely as do fish at the bottom of the sea. Ours is an ocean of air, but it is an ocean just the same. The mixture of gases we call the atmosphere is one of the unique characteristics of this planet, and it contributes in a crucial way to the earth being alone among the planets of this solar system in the support of life as we know it.

One of the important roles the atmosphere plays is to control the amount of heat received and lost by the earth. We might think of it as a great insulating blanket. The atmosphere controls the amount of heat from the sun that reaches the surface of the earth during the day so that we keep warm without frying, and at night it holds enough heat in to keep us from freezing. This protective shield is threatened by the vast amount of pollutants being spewed into the air by many sources, including automobiles and factories.

On the moon, which has no atmosphere, temperatures reach a scorching 127 degrees Celsius (261 degrees Fahrenheit) during the day and dip as low as -173 degrees Celsius (-279 degrees Fahrenheit) at night. Days and nights on the moon are approximately twenty-eight times longer than on the earth, intensifying the heating and cooling periods. Temperatures would be much more extreme on the earth if it were not for the moderating effect of the atmosphere. Even at that, only about one two-billionth of the energy from the sun reaches the earth's atmosphere.

The most abundant gas in air is nitrogen—about 78 percent. Approximately 21 percent of the air we breath is oxygen, a gas that is essential to life. Our bodies burn oxygen as fuel, and a constant supply is so critical that we begin to feel uncomfortable in just a few seconds of being deprived of a fresh supply, and we would die in a few minutes without it.

Oxygen is a very active gas, meaning that it combines easily with many substances. It is necessary in the processes of burning, decay, and corrosion. Sometimes these processes occur at inopportune times and cause untimely destruction, yet they are needed in the natural recycling of the elements and we are learning to control them better for the benefit of the earth and life on it.

The remaining 1 percent of the earth's atmosphere consists of a variety of gases, including carbon dioxide, hydrogen, helium, and others. Although carbon dioxide is present in the air only in very small quantities, it is a very important gas. It causes bread to rise, soda pop to sparkle, and it is a factor in many common chemical reactions. Plants use it in making food, which is then utilized not only by people and other animals, but by the plants themselves, for plants manufacture their own food. As plants use carbon dioxide, they give off oxygen as a waste product; and as animals take in oxygen they emit carbon dioxide, forming a symbiotic relationship that provides an important link in the chain of events that recycles the elements and maintains the critical balance necessary for the support of life on this planet.

The atmosphere is thickest and heaviest near the surface of the earth, because of the weight of the air above, and it grows gradually thinner and thinner at higher altitudes. For convenience of communication and scientific study, the atmosphere is thought of as being layered (see Figure 20-1). The layer next to the surface is called the *troposphere,* and extends to about 10 to 16 kilometers (6 to 10 miles) from the surface. Almost all the water vapor in the atmosphere is in this first layer, thus clouds and storms and almost all weather conditions occur in the troposphere.

Next is the *stratosphere,* extending upward to about 32 kilometers (20 miles) from the surface. The air in this layer is much thinner than that of the troposphere. It is cloudless and has little or no weather conditions.

The *mesosphere* reaches on up to about 80 kilometers (50 miles). This layer contains a special form of oxygen, called *ozone,* which absorbs ultraviolet rays from the sun, protecting our skin from severe burns.

Figure 20-1

We think of the atmosphere as having four layers.

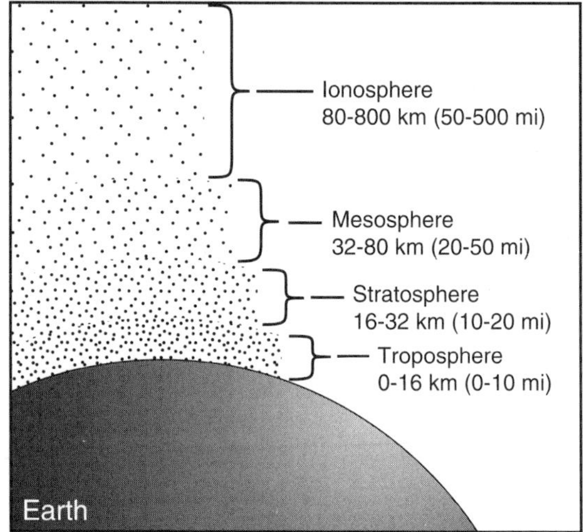

The *ionosphere* continues from the mesosphere to as far as 800 kilometers (500 miles) from the surface of the earth. This layer gets its name from a reaction of ultraviolet rays from the sun with particles of air, forming electrically charged particles called *ions.* The northern lights (aurora borealis) occur as bursts of energy particles from sunspots react with the ionosphere.

The top layer of the atmosphere is called the *exosphere,* and extends from the ionosphere upward until it cannot be distinguished from outer space. (For all practical purposes, "space" can be considered to begin at about 160 kilometers [100 miles] from the earth's surface, as there is almost no air above that point.) In the exosphere is an area of intense radiation, called the *radiation belt.*

Air Pressure

Air is colorless, odorless, and tasteless. Although it is invisible, it is real, it takes up space, it has weight, and it is held to the earth by gravity. At the surface of the earth, 1 liter (1 quart) of air weighs about 1.2 grams. The weight of the air creates pressure on the surface of the earth. *Air pressure,* or *atmospheric pressure,* presses on all surfaces and in all directions. It presses upward and sideways just as hard as it presses downward; this is a characteristic of fluids.

The weight of the air at sea level exerts a pressure of about 1 kilogram per square centimeter (14.7 pounds per square inch). At higher altitudes the pressure decreases because the weight of the layer of air above is less. Moving air (wind) exerts more pressure on surfaces it strikes than does still air, the same as does moving water. The harder the wind blows, the greater the pressure it applies.

Air pressure in a sealed container can increase or decrease as certain conditions change. The pressure is caused by the air molecules inside the container striking against the walls of the container. If the pressure on the inside of the container is equal to the pressure on the outside of the container, the container is said to have zero pressure. Pressure inside the container will increase if more air is added (there are more air molecules striking the same amount of inside wall space), if the air inside the container is heated (the air molecules have increased energy and strike the wall with greater force), or if the size of the container is decreased while the amount of air inside the container stays the same (there are more air molecules per unit of wall space). Pressure inside the container will decrease if some air is removed (there are fewer air molecules striking the same amount of inside wall space), if the air inside the container is cooled (the air molecules have less energy and strike the wall with less force), or if the size of the container is increased but the amount of air inside remains the same (there is more wall space for the same number of air molecules).

A common application of this principle can be shown in the use of an ordinary drinking straw. When a drinking straw is placed in a cup of water, the water rises in the straw to the level of the water in the cup, because air pressure inside the straw is equal to that outside the straw. In use, a person's mouth is placed over the drinking straw and some of the air is drawn out of the straw. The pressure inside the straw is now less than that outside the straw, and water is forced up the straw due to pressure exerted by the atmosphere on the surface of the liquid in the cup.

Bernoulli's Principle

In the eighteenth century, Swiss scientist Daniel Bernoulli discovered a very interesting relationship between the speed and pressure of a fluid. What has become known as *Bernoulli's principle* states that the pressure in a fluid decreases as the speed of the fluid increases. The principle applies to air, water, or any other fluid.

If air, for example, is blown across a strip of paper that is in the form of an airfoil (see Figure 20-2), the paper will rise. With air rushing

Figure 20-2

The paper strip and airplane wing cross-section are both airfoils.

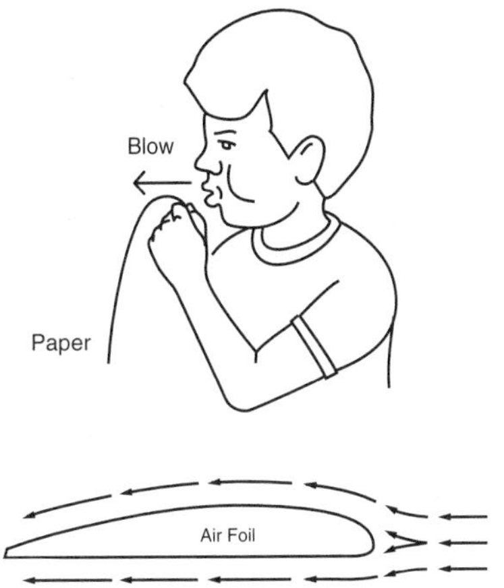

across the top of the paper, air pressure is reduced at that point and the paper is lifted by atmospheric pressure from underneath. Airplane wings are designed with a curved top and a nearly flat bottom to force air to travel faster over the top than across the bottom, reducing the pressure on the top surface, thus providing lift from atmospheric pressure beneath the wing.

A Precious Resource

Unfortunately, our precious atmosphere is being used as a sewer. Years ago, many people thought the atmosphere, being so vast, could absorb the gases produced by factories, automobiles, and so on, with little or no negative effects. Today we know that, even as large as it is, the atmosphere is vulnerable and we must significantly reduce the amount of pollutants spewed into the air.

III. WATER

The most abundant element in the air is nitrogen, but the most abundant element on Earth is oxygen. That may be a surprise to some people, who think of oxygen only as a gas that exists in the air we breathe. Actually, the great majority of the earth's oxygen exists in forms other than oxygen gas, including SiO_2 (sand) and H_2O (water). Water, which contains most of the earth's oxygen, is the most abundant substance on the planet, covering more than 70 percent of the earth's surface. Still, much of the earth suffers from water shortages. Water, like air, is another of the earth's secrets, for no other planet in our solar system seems to have liquid water, which is most crucial in the support of life. In addition to personal needs, huge amounts of water are required for many other processes, including agriculture and the manufacture of goods. Although there is a global abundance of water, getting the right amounts in the right places and in the right form is a constant struggle in many parts of the world.

Have you ever tried to prepare a sealed, self-sustaining terrarium? Getting the right balance of soil, water, plants, and animals (perhaps snails) such that the plants provide enough oxygen for the animals and the animals provide the right amount of carbon dioxide for the plants, so the system can sustain itself for a long period of time, is rather tricky. One of the processes that occurs within the terrarium is the water cycle: Water evaporates into the air, condenses back into liquid on the walls of the container, then drips or runs into the soil and ponds. We can think of the earth as a huge terrarium in which these same actions occur, maintaining a critical balance of the necessary substances.

The Water Cycle

Some people think recycling of natural resources was a new idea when we began stomping on aluminum cans and turning them in to be melted down, in order to save on energy and aluminum. The world's most massive recycling project has been going on for millions of years. It is called the *water cycle*, or *hydrologic* cycle, a process that allows the same water to be used over and over again, year after year after endless year. Indeed, part of the water you drink today could be the same water you bathed in a year ago, or it could be the same water that once stood in an Asian rice paddy, in a mosquito-infested swamp of South Africa, or fell on the Pilgrims at Plymouth Rock. It's okay, though, because each time the water is recycled it is also purified (another of nature's miracles) and made ready for the next user.

Most of the earth's water is in the oceans. In fact, if the world's total water supply could be placed in a 55-gallon drum, the oceans would account for more than 53 gallons of it. The atmosphere would contribute a little more than a pint, and freshwater lakes would represent about half an ounce! Ice caps and glaciers would total more than a gallon. The rest exists as groundwater, saline lakes, and the like.

It's easy to see that if all water stayed in the ocean, life would be very difficult. Seawater is salty, and as such it is not suitable for consumption by humans or for plants or animals that normally live on land or in fresh water. Not only would we have to purify the water we use, but we would also have to transport it to areas where it is needed. Life would be limited to areas very near the oceans. The water cycle does all of that in a spectacular way (see Figure 20-3). Heat from the sun causes water to evaporate into the air from the oceans. As the water evaporates it is purified, because only the water goes into the air, leaving salt and other impurities behind. Air currents carry much of the moist air over land areas. The air cools, and the moisture it contains condenses into water drops or ice crystals, which fall to the ground as rain, snow, or some other form of precipitation.

Even the soil and rock layers on the earth's surface play an important role in the water cycle. Some of the moisture that falls to the ground soon evaporates again and some runs directly into streams and rivers, which make their way to lakes and oceans. That which quickly evaporates or runs off, however, does not provide for the year-round needs of plants and animals on land. Fortunately, much of the moisture soaks into the ground, feeding the roots of plants and often soaking deep into the soil. Given sufficient moisture, it continues to soak through soil, sand, gravel, and all porous, or *permeable* material, including sandstone. Eventually the moisture reaches nonporous, or *impermeable* rock, such as quartzite or granite. Unable to sink further, the water saturates the soil and rock above the impermeable layer. The water in the saturated material is called *groundwater.* The upper level of the groundwater is called the *water table,* which moves up and down as wet and dry seasons come and go. Sometimes the water table reaches the surface and ponds form.

On a slope, such as a hillside, groundwater flows slowly through the soil and rock to lower areas. It sometimes comes to the surface on a hillside, forming a spring. Such water may or

Figure 20-3 ***The natural process of water evaporating, condensing, and precipitating is called the water cycle.***

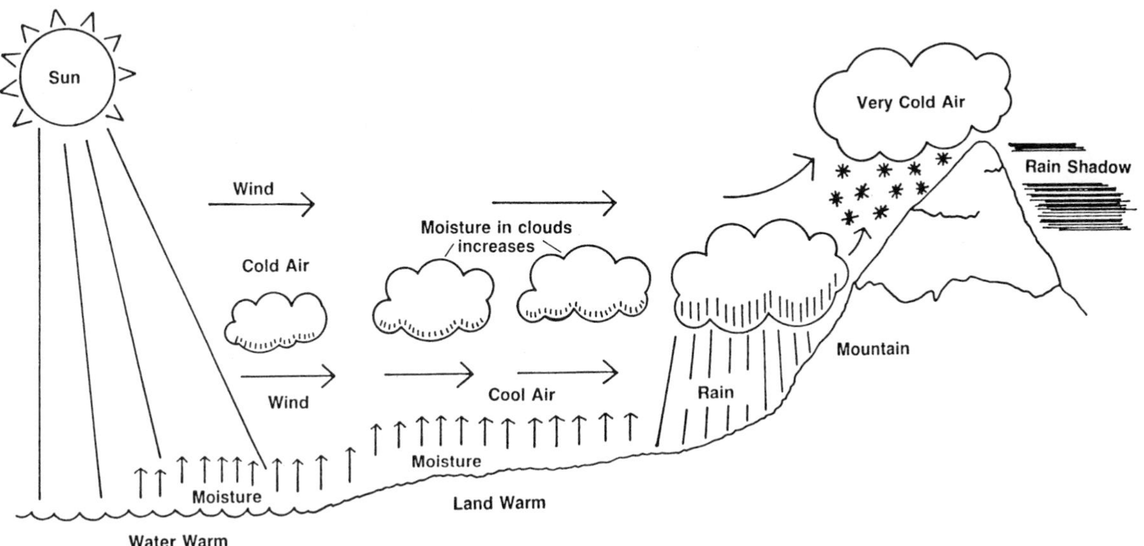

may not be pure and good for drinking, depending on the minerals and other materials that dissolve in it as it moves through the ground. In some areas it comes in contact with hot rock layers underground, producing hot water at the spring.

If a hole is dug or drilled deep enough to penetrate into the groundwater, the water moving through the ground flows into the hole, forming a well. Water can then be pumped out and the well will be constantly replenished as long as the water table is above the bottom of the hole. If a dry season drops the water table below the bottom of the hole, the well runs dry. In some cases, the well can be dug deeper and will provide water again. In many cases, a wetter season will bring sufficient water to raise the water table high enough to supply the once-dry well.

Water Pressure and Buoyancy

Like air, water is a fluid; and as such, it exerts pressure against the surface of its container or against the surface of any object that is in the water. Water pressure increases with depth, and at any given point it is equal in any direction—downward, upward, and sideways. Pressure is not affected by the size or shape of a container, except as depth changes. The pressure against the wall of a container at a given depth is the same whether the container is large or small, wide or narrow.

This is the same principle that causes an object to float. As an object is placed in water, upward pressure is exerted according to the amount of water being displaced, or pushed out of the way. Consider two objects, A and B. If object A weighs less than a volume of water equal to the volume of the object, A will float. If object B weighs more than a volume of water equal to the volume of the object, B will sink. Object A will sink into the water until it has displaced an amount of water equal in weight to the weight of the object itself, then it will stop sinking. Stated another way, an object is buoyed up by a force equal to the weight of the water displaced. The discovery of this principle is credited to Archimedes, and is called the Archimedes principle.

Even though steel is more dense than water and a small piece of steel quickly sinks when placed in a pan of water, a steel ship will float because it is shaped like a hollow bowl and it therefore displaces a lot of water. The ship will sink into the water until it has displaced an amount of water equal to its own weight, then it will stop sinking. At that point, the force of water pushing upward against the bottom of the ship is equal to the force of gravity pulling the ship downward. If cargo is then loaded onto the ship, it will sink further, constantly adjusting to the level at which the weight of the water displaced is equal to the weight of the ship. Since saltwater is heavier than freshwater, the ship will float a little bit higher in the ocean than it will in a river or a freshwater lake. An experienced skipper would not load a ship to the maximum in ocean water, then head up a river.

Oceans

Earth's four large oceans, which together cover more than 70 percent of the earth's surface, are actually all joined as one giant sea. However, just as the forty-eight contiguous states are really a single land mass, and the countries of South America are together but thought of as being separate entities, the oceans are also considered separate to make it easier to communicate about different regions of the earth. The four oceans are called the Pacific, Atlantic, Arctic, and Indian Oceans (see Figure 20-4).

Relative sizes

The *Pacific Ocean* is both largest and deepest, comprising about three-eighths of the total

Figure 20-4

The four large oceans are actually joined as one giant sea.

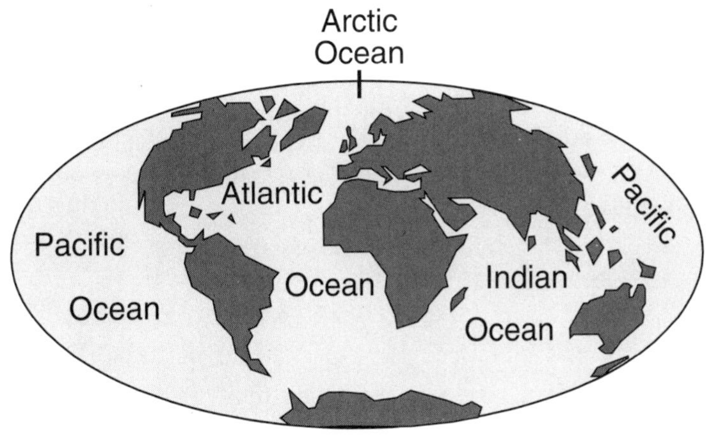

ocean surface and having an average depth of about 3,940 meters (12,900 feet). The Pacific Ocean covers about one-third of the earth's surface. It is large enough to hold all of the continents of the earth! Next largest is the *Atlantic Ocean,* including about one-quarter of the earth's total sea surface and having an average depth of about 3,580 meters (11,700 feet). The *Arctic Ocean* caps the north pole and is almost completely covered with ice. No land mass exists at the north pole. The *Antarctic Ocean* surrounds Antarctica, a land mass that forms the south polar cap. The *Indian Ocean* lies south of Asia and between Africa and Australia and claims about one-eighth of the earth's sea surface.

Continental shelf and continental slope

Generally speaking, the *continental shelf* slopes gradually out from the continent with relatively shallow water, rarely more than 180 meters (590 feet) deep. The slope then becomes much sharper, forming the *continental slope,* extending downward to the ocean floor, which has an average depth of about 4 kilometers (2.5 miles). The deepest part of the ocean, the Marianas trench, lies in the Pacific Ocean southwest of Guam, and is about 11 kilometers (7 miles) deep.

Mountains in the oceans

The ocean floor actually consists of mountains and valleys. Some of these mountains are taller than any found on the continents. Though the tops of most of them are still far beneath the ocean surface, some of them pierce the surface to form islands, such as the Azores, the West Indies, and the Aleutian Islands.

Deposits collect

As rain falls on land, many minerals are dissolved and carried to the oceans by rivers and streams. The continuation of this process over untold thousands of years has resulted in vast quantities of salt, magnesium, gold, and other minerals being dissolved in seawater. Some of these minerals, including magnesium, bromine, and table salt, are commercially extracted. The cost of obtaining gold from seawater is not commercially feasible, but perhaps that will change some day.

Temperatures vary

Seawater varies greatly in temperature, being warmer at the surface and near the equator. Even at the equator, water deep in the ocean can be very cold, at times approaching freezing temperature.

Constant circulation

Water at the ocean surface is constantly moving, due to the force of winds blowing on the water, the rotation of the earth, convection (cold water sinks and warmer water rises), and other factors. These currents of huge masses of water are affected by the outlines of continental shorelines and by the depth and shape of the ocean floor. At the same time surface currents are moving, deep-sea currents are also in motion, sometimes in opposite directions to surface currents. Since cold water is heavier than warm water, the cold waters in the polar regions sink deep and travel across the ocean bottom to the equator. Water that contains more salt is also heavier than water with less salt, thus deep currents are also affected by salt content.

IV. IN CLOSING

Air and water will always be here, but their future quality depends on human care. Today's children are tomorrow's leaders and decision makers. The importance of helping them develop an attitude of understanding, concern, and a determination to preserve the quality of these vital resources cannot be overemphasized.

LIST OF RESOURCES

Ranger Rick's NatureScope: Wild About Weather (National Wildlife Federation, 1986).

Tolman, Marvin N., and James O. Morton, *Earth Science Activities for Grades 2–8* (West Nyack, NY: Parker Publishing Co., 1986).

Victor, Edward, *Science for the Elementary School, Sixth Edition* (New York: Macmillan Publishing Co., 1989).

World Book Encyclopedia, 1989.

CHAPTER

AIR AND WATER

ACTIVITIES

II. AIR

ACTIVITY 20-1: DOES AIR TAKE UP SPACE?

Materials Needed:

Clear plastic cup

Paper towel

Deep bowl filled with water

Procedure:

1. Wad the paper towel up and push it to the bottom of the plastic cup. Test to see that it will stay when the cup is turned upside down. Secure it with a roll of tape in the bottom of the cup if necessary.
2. Holding the cup upside down, push it into the water, all the way to the bottom of the bowl. Then bring it up, still keeping it upside down.
3. Feel the paper towel. It is wet?
4. Explain. Discuss your ideas with your group. Does air take up space?

Teacher Information:

The paper towel will remain dry, giving evidence that air is real and takes up space. With the cup upside down, air is trapped inside the cup, keeping water out.

Skills: Observing, inferring

(Adapted from Activity 24, "How Can You Test to See If Air Is Something?" in Tolman and Morton, 1986.)

ACTIVITY 20-2: HOW CAN WE TELL IF AIR HAS WEIGHT?

Materials Needed:

Wide-mouth jug

Bread sack (or other plastic bag)

Large, heavy-duty rubber band

Procedure:

1. Put your hand into the bag and push the bag down into the jug.
2. Pull the opening of the bag over the lip of the bottle and secure it with the rubber band.
3. Now reach your hand into the bag, grab the bottom of the bag, and pull the bag out of the bottle.

4. What happened? Can you feel something pushing back? What is it?
5. Explain and discuss with your group.

Teacher Information:

Here students learn that air has weight. As students attempt to pull the bag out of the bottle, air pressure in the bottle (between the bottle and the bag) is greatly reduced. The weight that students feel pushing back is the weight of the air in the atmosphere—atmospheric pressure.

Skills: Observing, inferring

ACTIVITY 20-3:
HOW CAN WE TELL IF AIR PRESSURE IS REAL?
(Teacher-supervised activity)

Materials Needed:

Glass jug

Aluminum foil (or large pan, such as a cookie sheet)

Balloon

Water

Tissue (or a half-section of paper towel)

Match

Procedure:

1. Put enough water in the balloon to make it slightly larger than the opening of the bottle. Tie the neck of the balloon.
2. Set the balloon on the bottle, spout up, to be sure that it will stay in that position.
3. Remove the balloon from the bottle.
4. Lay the foil out on the table and put the bottle on the foil. This is to protect the table in case the match or burning tissue should be accidentally dropped.
5. Light the tissue with the match, drop the tissue in the bottle, and immediately rest the water balloon on the bottle. The balloon will probably bounce for a few seconds, so steady it by holding the neck of the balloon.
6. What happened? Explain the best you can.
7. Discuss your ideas with your group.

Teacher Information:

This is a version of the old egg-in-the-bottle trick. The water balloon is easier to use because it is versatile for size and can be adjusted to fit the bottle. As the tissue burns, the air in the bottle is heated and much of it escapes between the lip of the bottle and the water balloon, causing the balloon to dance for a few seconds. When the fire goes out, the air quickly cools and condenses, decreasing the pressure within the bottle. Atmospheric pressure is now greater than the pressure within the bottle, and the water balloon is pushed into the bottle by atmospheric pressure.

Many people make the mistake of thinking that the balloon is drawn in by a force of suction from within the bottle. It is important to recognize that suction is not a force, but only a word we use to describe a lack of air pressure. Lack of pressure does not do work. When air pressure inside the bottle is reduced, atmospheric pressure pushes the balloon inside the bottle.

Skills: Observing, inferring

III. WATER

ACTIVITY 20-4: WHAT HAPPENS TO WATER ON THE SIDEWALK?

Materials Needed:

Spray bottle

Water

A warm, sunny day

Sidewalk

Procedure:

1. Put some water in the spray bottle.
2. Adjust the nozzle to produce quite a narrow spray.
3. Write your initials on the sidewalk with water, using the spray bottle.
4. Look at your initials a few minutes later. What's happening to them?
5. Discuss your ideas with your group.

For Problem Solvers:

Set up an experiment to determine the effect of temperature on evaporation time. You will need to devise a way to be sure you use the same amount of water for each trial, that the surface is the same, and that other conditions are kept constant except temperature. Be sure to write your hypothesis before you begin each trial. Make a graph that shows evaporation time at each temperature.

Do another experiment to determine the effect of type of surface. Does water evaporate at the same rate on asphalt as it does on concrete sidewalks? What about a large rock? Plastic? Wood?

Teacher Information:

Help the group with the discussion of evaporation. Include in the discussion the question of what would happen if water suddenly would no longer evaporate. What effect would that have on the water cycle, and our sources of water for drinking, for watering our crops, and so on?

Those who do the extension for problem solvers will go beyond thinking about the fact that water goes into the air. They will find out how evaporation rate is affected by temperature and by the surface the water is on. Maybe these sharpies will think of other questions to investigate on their own.

Integrating: Math

Skills: Observing, inferring, measuring, communicating, using space-time relationships, identifying and controlling variables, experimenting

ACTIVITY 20-5: HOW DOES THE BOTTLE GET WET?

Materials Needed:

Jar with lid

Ice

Food coloring

White paper

Towel

Procedure:

1. Fill the bottle with ice water.
2. Add a few drops of food coloring.
3. Put the lid on the bottle and dry the outside of the bottle with the towel.
4. Set the bottle on the white paper.
5. Look at the bottle every few minutes.
6. What's happening? Why?

7. Explain the best you can. Discuss your ideas with your group.

Teacher Information:

After a few minutes, the jar will likely be wet on the outside, as the air near the bottle cools and moisture condenses onto the bottle. Students have seen this happen many times with a pitcher of ice water or with other containers of cold drinks. When an open container is used in this activity, it's easy to assume that the water somehow came over the top of the container. This is the reason for the lid. The reason for using food coloring and placing the jar on white paper is to dispel any thoughts that the water might be seeping through the side of the bottle. If this happened, the water on the outside of the jar would be colored, and if it ran down the side of the container and onto the white paper it would be particularly easy to see the color.

Skills: Observing, inferring

ACTIVITY 20-6: WHAT MAKES THE WATER MOVE?

Materials Needed:

Fish tank (or large transparent bowl)

Water

Small bag of ice

Tape

Food coloring

Procedure:

1. Fill the tank about two-thirds full of water. Let the water settle before continuing.
2. Hang the bag of ice over one end of the tank so that the bottom of the bag is in the water. Tape the bag to the tank so that it will remain there without moving.
3. Add two or three drops of food coloring to the water near the ice.
4. Observe patiently.
5. What happens? Discuss what you see and explain the best you can.

For Problem Solvers:

Do some research about convection currents in your library books and encyclopedia. Find out about convection currents that are at work in the ocean. Where do they occur? What keeps them moving? What effect do they have on weather? Write notes on what you learn. Draw the oceans of the world and show the major ocean currents.

What is the water temperature deep in the ocean at the equator? Why?

Try the above activity again, but in addition to having ice on one end, which might represent the ice at the north pole or the south pole, add a sun to the system by placing a heat lamp in a position to shine on the other end of the tank. If a heat lamp isn't available, just use a regular light bulb in a lamp. Predict the effect the sun will have on the convection currents.

Teacher Information:

We hear more about convection currents of air than of water, but they are probably easier to observe in water. The movement of the current can be speeded up by shining a heat lamp on the pan on the opposite end from the bag of ice. A large pan will work fine for showing the convection currents, but if a small fish tank is available it greatly enhances the view.

Students who do the extension for problem solvers will learn about the enormous convection currents that are at work in the oceans. They will find that the same action they see happening in the fish tank happens on a gigantic scale in the oceans, and for the same reasons and more. They will learn that even the varying concentrations of salt in the water affects ocean convection currents.

Integrating: Reading, writing, art

Skills: Observing, inferring, predicting, communicating

CHAPTER

WEATHER, SEASONS, AND CLIMATE

CHAPTER OUTLINE:

- INTRODUCTION
- THE GREENHOUSE EFFECT
- SOME FACTORS THAT AFFECT TEMPERATURE
- WINDS
  - Wind Belts
    - The doldrums
    - Horse latitudes
    - Trade winds and westerlies
    - Easterlies
    - Subpolar lows
  - Jet Streams
  - Monsoons
  - Land-Sea Breezes
  - Mountain-Valley Breezes
- THE WATER CYCLE
  - Evaporation
  - Humidity
  - Condensation
  - Dew Point
  - Dew and Frost
  - Clouds
    - Cirrus
    - Stratus
    - Cumulus
    - Prefixes
    - Fog
  - Precipitation
    - Rain
    - Snow
    - Sleet
    - Ice storms
    - Hail
- ELEMENTS OF WEATHER
  - Air Masses
  - Fronts
  - Highs and Lows
  - Severe Weather
    - Hurricanes
    - Tornadoes
    - Thunderstorms
- FORECASTING THE WEATHER
  - Instruments
    - Temperature
    - Air pressure
    - Wind direction
    - Wind speed
    - Relative humidity
    - Rainfall
    - Snowfall
  - Methods of Gathering Information
    - Radiosonde and dropsonde
    - Weather airplanes
    - Weather satellites
    - Radar
    - Lightning Detection System
  - History of Weather Forecasting
- SEASONS
- CLIMATE
- IN CLOSING
- LIST OF RESOURCES
- ACTIVITIES

I WONDER . . .

What are the basic factors that influence weather?
What's the difference between sleet and hail?
How is hail formed?
What is a weather front?
Why aren't weather forecasts more accurate?
How can moisture in the air be measured?
What is a radiosonde?
What's the difference between *seasons* and *climate?*

I. INTRODUCTION

Weather is the condition of the atmosphere, and it affects our lives in numerous ways. Most everything we do (or perhaps decide not to do) outdoors is affected by the weather. In many cases, the work we do, the way we spend our leisure time, and the clothing we wear depend on the weather. Probably no other aspect of nature is talked about more or has a greater impact on our lives than this phenomenon. The weather may even affect our moods and our health. Studies have shown that people often feel more cheerful on a sunny day and more gloomy if the weather is gloomy, too. *Biometeorology* is the science that studies how weather affects living things.

Factors that affect weather include air temperature, wind direction and speed, and all of the contributing elements of the water cycle. Surface temperature of the ground has a profound effect on air temperature, and uneven heating of the ground results in uneven heating of the air which, in turn, causes winds. The complexity of the system makes prediction of weather very difficult.

II. THE GREENHOUSE EFFECT

Radiant energy from the sun passes through the air with little effect, but it heats objects it strikes, such as buildings, trees, and the land and water surfaces of the earth. The air, in turn, is heated mostly by these surfaces. The atmosphere traps most of the heat that is radiated from the ground and seas at the earth's surface, and prevents it from easily passing back into space. This is called the *greenhouse effect*, and in some very important ways the operation of greenhouses is based on this principle.

Energy from the sun comes mainly in short wavelengths. These easily pass through the atmosphere and through transparent materials such as clear glass or plastic, but the energy is reflected in longer wavelengths that do not easily pass through these materials. Energy that is not absorbed at the earth's surface is radiated back into the air as heat, in longer wavelengths, and is therefore captured by the atmosphere and by transparent enclosures such as greenhouses.

III. SOME FACTORS THAT AFFECT TEMPERATURE

The amount of heat received by the earth's surface depends on several factors, including these:

1. *The curved shape of the earth results in the sun's rays striking different areas of the*

earth at different angles, and therefore with different levels of intensity. Areas near the equator get the most direct, concentrated rays, so they usually absorb the most heat. Polar regions get only indirect, slanted rays, with less heat. Sometimes the sky is overcast, reflecting more of the sun's energy back into the upper atmosphere.

2. *Yet a cloudy sky doesn't necessarily mean temperatures will be lower on the earth.* A cloud cover on a cold night acts as a blanket, absorbing and reflecting heat radiated from the earth's surface, thereby reducing the amount of heat lost through the night.
3. *The air is heated much more during long, hot summer days and more heat is lost during long, cold winter nights.*
4. *Dark and rough land surfaces absorb heat more quickly and radiate it into the air more quickly than do smooth, clear water surfaces.* So when the sun shines equally on land and water surfaces, the land heats more quickly than does the water, thus heating the air above it more quickly. Land also cools more quickly when the sun goes down, while water is much slower to change temperature and its day and night effect on air temperature is therefore more uniform.

IV. WINDS

Since air temperature is mostly affected by surface temperature, the uneven heating of the earth's surface results in uneven heating of the air. Convection currents operate constantly in the atmosphere, in a complex system that includes at least the following factors:

1. Cold air is heavier than warm air, and tends to flow under warm air, causing the warm air to rise.
2. Temperatures at high altitudes are usually colder than temperatures at lower altitudes, so as air rises it cools, becomes heavier, and again sinks beneath warmer air masses.
3. Air in the cool polar regions has a general tendency to flow toward the equator, while the warm air near the equator rises.
4. As the earth spins on its axis, the surface at any given location is warmed by the sun during the day, then it cools at night, in varying degrees according to the many contributing factors.
5. In addition to the general tendency of air masses to flow from the polar regions toward the equator, the uneven heating of the air as it passes over various land and water bodies results in a complex flow of many air masses around the globe, in patterns that are somewhat consistent but only partly predictable.

Wind Belts

Cold air, being heavier than warm air, applies more pressure to the earth's surface. Winds are the convection currents created by shifting air masses due to uneven temperatures, as air from cold, high-pressure areas move to warm, low-pressure areas. Winds are always named for the direction they come *from.* Wind that blows from north to south is a *north wind,* for example.

If the earth did not rotate, the movement of air masses over the earth would be relatively simple, as warm air from the equator would rise and move toward the poles, while the cool polar air would fall and move toward the equator. While that general convective movement does occur, the rotation of the earth greatly complicates the system, deflecting winds and resulting in a series of wind belts that move in a somewhat consistent pattern. The system is further complicated by a shifting of wind belts with the seasons, as the sun's rays affect different parts of the earth differently in summer and winter, due to the tilt of the earth on its axis (see Figure 21-1).

The doldrums

Consistent with the cycle of convection currents, heated air at the equator rises and creates a low pressure area called the *doldrums*, with air movements mostly upward and toward the poles, cooling as it rises higher into the atmosphere.

Horse latitudes

At about 30 degrees latitude, both north and south from the equator, the air has cooled enough to sink toward the earth's surface again, forming a belt of descending, high-pressure air called the *horse latitudes*, an area of mostly calm, but with occasional light, changeable winds.

Trade winds and westerlies

In the northern hemisphere, the winds are deflected to their right by the earth's rotating motion. The sinking air at the horse latitudes forms a high pressure area between two wind belts, one called the *trade winds* (flowing back toward the equator from the east), and the other called *westerlies* (flowing toward the poles from the west). Those flowing toward the equator are called the *northeast trade winds*, and those moving toward the north pole are called the *southwesterlies* because they come from the southwest.

In the southern hemisphere the winds are deflected to their left. Those moving toward the equator are called the *southeast trade winds* and those flowing toward the south pole are called the *northwesterlies* because they come from the northwest.

Easterlies

Cold, heavy air masses at the poles move toward the equator. In the northern hemisphere they move to their right (from east to west) and are called the *polar northeasterlies*. In the southern hemisphere they move to their left (from east to west) and are called the *polar southeasterlies*. These winds are cold and often violent.

Subpolar lows

A second belt of low pressure, called the *subpolar lows*, is created at about 65 degrees latitude, both north and south, a little more than two-thirds of the distance from the equator to the poles. This results as the warm air from the pre-

Figure 21-1

Global winds move in a somewhat consistent pattern.

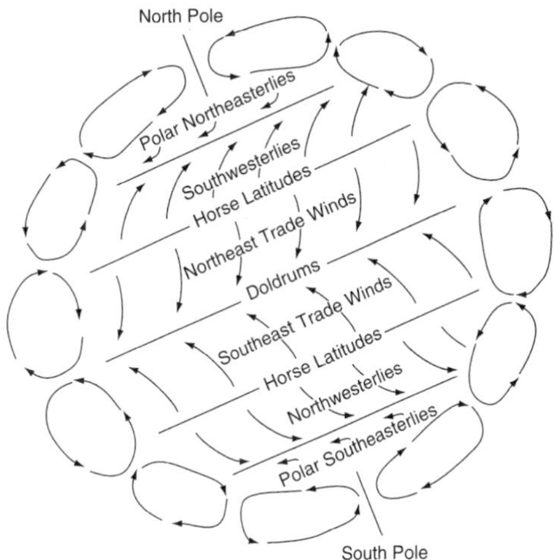

vailing westerlies moving toward the poles is pushed up by cold air from the polar easterlies moving from the poles toward the equator. The upward movement of this warm air produces an area of low pressure.

Jet Streams

There are narrow bands of high-altitude, high-speed winds located in the prevailing westerlies of both the northern and southern hemispheres. These winds, called the *jet stream,* are at about 8 to 16 kilometers (5 to 10 miles) above the earth's surface and travel at speeds up to 640 kilometers (400 miles) per hour. Both the location and speed of the jet stream vary with the seasons. These winds are closer to the poles, higher in altitude, and move at higher speeds in the summer. In the winter, they shift toward the equator, drop to lower altitudes, and move at slower speeds. There is another jet stream in the lower stratosphere of the arctic circle, and still another in the lower stratosphere of the antarctic circle. In the winter, when the jet streams are at the lower altitudes, airplanes take advantage of them as strong tailwinds to reduce flying time.

Monsoons

A *monsoon* is a seasonal wind produced by the difference in heating between oceans and land masses during the summer and winter. Since land temperatures change more readily than ocean temperatures, the land becomes warmer than the ocean in the summer and colder than the ocean in the winter. In the summer, the relatively cool air over the ocean is heavier and moves inland. In the winter, the air over the land is cooler and heavier and moves out to sea. Air masses coming from the ocean in the summer are moist, resulting in a rainy season over land in the summer months. The winter months become a dry season, as the dry overland air moves out to sea and is replaced by still more dry air. Some of the best examples of monsoons are found in India, Australia, Spain, and Portugal.

Land-Sea Breezes

Near oceans and large lakes the effect of temperatures changing at different rates over land and water surfaces brings air movements that change direction on a daily basis. The land warms faster than the water during the day and cools faster than the water at night. The result is somewhat of a daily monsoon on a small scale. As the land warms up during the day, and the warming air over it rises, the relatively cooler and heavier air over the water surface moves inland. The direction is reversed at night as the land cools below the temperature of the water.

Mountain-Valley Breezes

Mountain and valley breezes are akin to land and sea breezes. Being somewhat sheltered, temperature changes occur more slowly in valleys than in the exposed surrounding mountains. This results in wind shifts similar to those described for land and sea. Like the water surface, valleys experience less daytime-nighttime temperature extremes, and breezes blow from valley to mountain during the day and from mountain to valley during the night. Early morning canyon breezes are therefore common in the valley.

V. THE WATER CYCLE

The water cycle and its significance to life on Earth were discussed in the previous chapter.

The process of liquid water evaporating into the atmosphere, moving over the earth, and precipitating back to the surface in liquid form, is a very important part of what weather is all about.

Evaporation

Water evaporation is the process of water changing from a liquid into an invisible gas. When water is heated on a stove, water molecules near the heat source can be energized sufficient to evaporate within the liquid, and form bubbles at the bottom of the container. When water boils, these bubbles form rapidly and rise vigorously to the surface.

In nature, evaporation always takes place at the surface of the water. Molecules are constantly moving, and the faster-moving molecules at the surface reach "escape velocity" and go off into the air, becoming molecules of water vapor. As water temperature increases, the molecules have more energy, they move faster, and they escape into the air at a faster rate, thus the water evaporates more rapidly. The larger the surface of the body of water, the more evaporation will occur; and if the air is dry, water will evaporate faster than if the air already contains a lot of water vapor. The rate of evaporation also increases in windy conditions. Water molecules escape into the air more easily if atmospheric pressure is low; thus, if all else is equal, evaporation will occur more readily on a mountain top than in a nearby valley.

Evaporation is a cooling process. As water evaporates, the molecules of highest energy, or highest temperature, are the ones that escape into the air. Thus, the liquid that is left behind has less energy and lower temperature. When a drop of water gets on your skin, the skin feels cooler at that point until the drop has evaporated away. You feel the cooling effect of evaporation dramatically as you step out of a shower or swimming pool, especially on a dry day. The dryer the air, the faster the evaporation occurs, and the more the cooling effect is felt. Homes and other buildings in dry climates are often cooled with evaporative coolers, using this principle (see chapter 15).

Humidity

The term *humidity* refers to moisture in the air. *Specific humidity* is the actual amount of water vapor present, while *relative humidity*, usually expressed in percent, is a measure of the amount of moisture the air contains compared with the maximum amount it can hold at that temperature. Warm air is capable of absorbing more moisture than cold air. As air cools, the effect is somewhat like lightly squeezing a wet sponge; even though no water is added, the ability of the sponge to hold water is decreased and therefore the "relative humidity" is higher. When the air is saturated, relative humidity is 100 percent.

Condensation

Condensation is the changing of water vapor back into liquid. The same factors that affect the speed of evaporation also affect the speed of condensation, only in reverse. As air is cooled, the molecules of water vapor lose energy, move more slowly and come closer together. If the moisture content (specific humidity) is high enough, the air becomes saturated (100 percent relative humidity). As the air is cooled further, water molecules come together to form water droplets.

Dew Point

The air temperature at which condensation takes place is called the *dew point*. The higher the specific humidity, the higher the dew point will be. Or, stated another way, if more moisture is in the air, dew point will be reached at a higher temperature. Remember the sponge? If more water is in the sponge, you don't need to squeeze it very hard to get water to run out. Inversely, the less water there is in the sponge, the harder you must squeeze to get water from it. Likewise, if specific humidity is lower, the dew point is lower; temperature must drop lower to initiate condensation.

Dew and Frost

Dew and *frost* form as moisture from the air condenses and collects on objects and on the earth's surface. As objects cool at night, the air around them is also cooled. If the air is cooled below its dew point, water vapor in the air condenses on surfaces as droplets of water, called dew. If the dew point is below freezing temperature, condensation occurs in the form of ice crystals, leaving a layer of frost on the surface of the object.

Clouds

When warm air containing water vapor rises high in the air it becomes colder. If the air is cooled below its dew point, the water vapor condenses into tiny droplets, and a cloud is formed. Usually the water vapor condenses around tiny particles in the air, such as dust or smoke. These particles are called *condensation nuclei*. If the air is below freezing temperature, the water vapor condenses as tiny ice crystals. As long as the ice crystals or water droplets are tiny, the slightest air movement keeps them suspended in the air. As more water vapor condenses on them they grow larger and heavier and eventually they fall out of the air as precipitation. Their size when they fall depends largely on the amount of turbulence that holds them suspended in the air.

The shape of a cloud is determined by how it is formed. If the air movement is horizontal, clouds form in layers, and are called *cirrus* or *stratus* clouds. *Cumulus* clouds tend to form in conditions of vertical air movement.

Cirrus

Cirrus clouds are feathery or wispy and are the highest clouds in the sky. They can be from 6.5 to 13 kilometers (4 to 8 miles) high. Because of their altitude they always consist of ice crystals. Even on a hot summer day the air that high is very cold.

Stratus

Stratus clouds form in layers. They are nearest to the earth's surface, often cover the whole sky, and they are usually associated with stormy weather.

Cumulus

If the movement of the cooling air is vertical, clouds form in large, billowy masses, and are called cumulus clouds. If they look like large, smooth cottonballs, they contain ice crystals. If they look more like a head of cauliflower, they contain water vapor. Cumulus clouds are usually flat on the bottom, but they can extend very high. They are usually associated with fair weather, but when they grow large and black, they become thunderclouds and they can bring thunderstorms, heavy rains, and sometimes hail.

Prefixes

The prefix *alto,* added to a cloud name, means "high." Altostratus clouds are stratus clouds that are unusually high. *Nimbo* (prefix) or *numbus* (suffix) can be added to mean "rain." Thus nimbostratus clouds are rain clouds. Cumulonimbus clouds are often called *thunderheads* (see Thunderstorms, in the next section of this chapter).

Fog

Fog is a cloud on the ground.

Precipitation

Precipitation refers to any form of moisture that falls from the atmosphere, including *rain, snow, sleet,* and *hail.*

Rain

As water vapor condenses in the atmosphere and forms tiny droplets, the slightest air movement is enough to keep them from falling to the ground. They move around in the cloud with the air currents. These droplets come together to form larger droplets, which in turn combine to form still larger drops. When a drop of water is large enough that the force of gravity overcomes the effect of the air currents that are keeping the drop suspended in the air, it falls to the earth as *rain.* Therefore the size of a raindrop that falls depends on the turbulence in the air.

Snow

If the air temperature is below freezing, water vapor condenses in the form of ice crystals, which in turn collect to form snowflakes. *Snow,* therefore, is not frozen rain, but collections of ice crystals. As with raindrops, the snowflakes remain in the cloud, stirred around by the air currents, until they become heavy enough that they are pulled away from the air currents by gravity and fall to the ground. Often precipitation begins in the cloud as snowflakes, but melts as it falls through warmer air, and reaches the ground as rain. Each snow crystal has six sides, and it is claimed that no two snowflakes are exactly alike, because there are so many possible shapes that can form as the crystals collect together.

Sleet

Sometimes as raindrops fall from the cloud they pass through colder air and freeze before they reach the ground. This is called *sleet,* which is frozen rain.

Ice storms

Ice storms occur when temperature conditions are such that super-cooled rain freezes on contact with a surface, forming a layer of ice on streets, trees, electrical wires, and other surfaces. Sometimes thick and heavy layers of ice from ice storms result in much damage, as they break tree branches and power lines and make road surfaces extremely hazardous.

Hail

Hail is formed when there are strong upward air currents within a thundercloud, usually during a summer thunderstorm. As raindrops form they are carried high into a layer of very cold air, and the raindrops freeze. Then they fall into the warmer, moist air and a second layer of moisture collects on them. Again they are carried upward by the air currents and the second layer freezes. This can happen over and over again, sometimes collecting many layers of ice and growing to the size of marbles or even golf balls or larger before they are heavy enough to fall from the strong updrafts of air. Hailstones more than 5 inches in diameter and weighing over 1-1/2 pounds have been recorded. Extensive damage can be caused by hailstorms in a very few minutes—crops can be destroyed, roofs of buildings torn up, windows shattered.

VI. ELEMENTS OF WEATHER

Weather is in the air. When the local weather reporter describes the weather, he or she describes conditions of the air, including temperature, humidity, atmospheric pressure, wind direction and speed, and precipitation. When predicting the weather, the forecaster considers information regarding air masses that are moving across the earth's surface. An air mass approaching a particular area brings with it the weather for that area for the next period of time.

Air Masses

An air mass is a huge, homogeneous body of air, and the weather it will bring depends largely on its temperature and moisture conditions and the air masses it interacts with. It can be hundreds, or even thousands, of miles across. The air mass acquires its conditions from the surface over which it forms, usually over a polar or tropical area, where it might sit for days or even weeks. An air mass that forms over Canada will bring cold, dry air as it moves southward, while an air mass that forms over the South Pacific will be warm and moist. As an air mass moves over the earth's surface its conditions change, very slowly because of its size, as it is affected by the conditions of that surface. Before an area can significantly change a moving air mass, the air mass influences the weather of that area.

Fronts

When two air masses meet, the boundary between them is called a *front.* When a heavy, cold air mass pushes a warm air mass, it is called a *cold front* and has a steep frontal boundary (see Figure 21-2). When a warm air

Figure 21-2

A cold front forms when a cold air mass pushes a warm air mass.

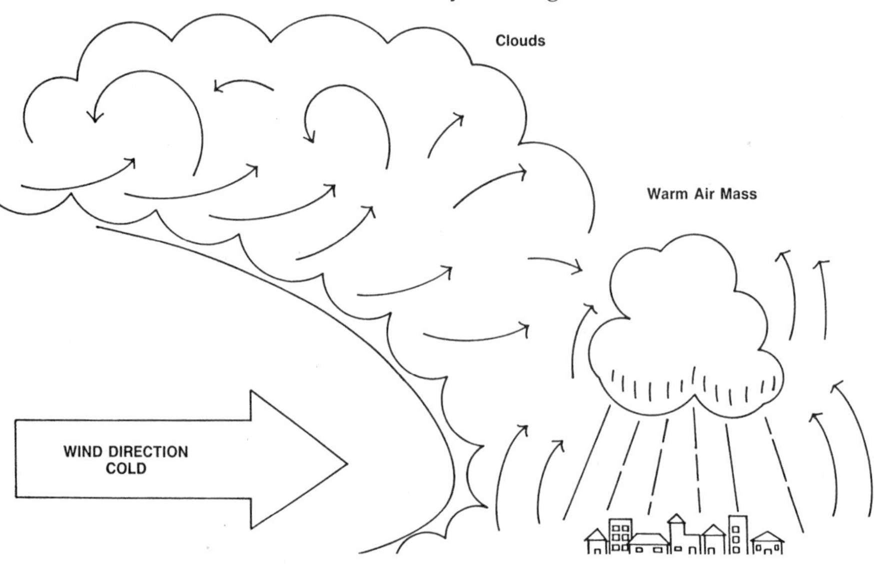

mass follows a retreating cold air mass, it is called a *warm front* and has a shallow, less deep frontal boundary. Precipitation typically accompanies a front.

Highs and Lows

Since cold air is heavier than warm air, cold air masses have higher pressure than do warm air masses. An area of low pressure is called a *low* or *cyclone*. The lowest air pressure in a low is at its center, because of the upward movement of the warm, light air. Air of higher pressure blows inward toward the center of the low and, due to the earth's rotation, the heavier air blowing inward is deflected toward the right, in the northern hemisphere, and travels in a circular, counterclockwise direction. As the warm air of a low-pressure area is pushed up by the colder, heavier air around it, the warm air cools and its capacity to hold moisture is decreased. Clouds and precipitation result. Lows, or cyclones, are usually associated with bad weather.

An area of high pressure is called a *high* or *anticyclone*. The highest air pressure in a high is at its center, with the downward movement of the cool, heavy air. Air blows outward from the center of a high and, because of the earth's rotation, the air travels in a circular, clockwise direction in the northern hemisphere. As the cold, heavy air in a high-pressure area falls toward the earth, it becomes warmer, increases its capacity to hold moisture, and results in bright, clear weather. Highs, or anticyclones, are usually associated with good weather.

Severe Weather

Some of the most feared and destructive events in life are due to severe weather, often in the form of hurricanes, tornadoes, thunderstorms, or a combination of these. Hurricanes are the single greatest natural threat to human life worldwide. An improved warning system has greatly reduced the danger to human life posed by hurricanes in the United States, although property damage can be enormous. In the United States, more human lives are lost to lightning and flash floods. This results, to a great extent, from public ignorance. Many people disregard these dangers. They play golf during thunderstorms, ignore flash flood warnings, and in other ways place themselves in positions vulnerable to these weather-related dangers.

Hurricanes

Hurricanes (called *typhoons* in the western Pacific Ocean and *cyclones* in India) are lows, or cyclones, that form over oceans in the tropics. The period of June through November is called the "hurricane season," as almost all hurricanes form during these months, especially during August, September, and October. At this time of the year the tropics receive a tremendous amount of energy from the sun, causing enormous amounts of ocean water to evaporate. Warm, moist air forms above the surface of the ocean. Huge masses of colder, heavier air move in, forcing the warm, moist air upward and creating violent, whirling movements of air that spiral in toward the center of the storm. With windspeeds of 64 kilometers (40 miles) to 120 kilometers (74 miles) per hour, such a storm is called a "tropical storm." Above that speed the storm is considered a hurricane, and can reach windspeeds of 240 kilometers (150 miles) per hour or more. At the "eye," or center of the hurricane is an area of almost no wind, about 24 kilometers (15 miles) in diameter. The hurricane itself is usually about 480 kilometers (300 miles) wide, but the strongest winds are usually in a narrow ring extending out about 40 kilometers (25 miles) or so from the center.

Hurricane Hugo (see Figure 21-3) struck the

Figure 21-3

Hurricane Hugo, as seen by satellite, struck in September 1989.

Printed with permission of the National Hurricane Center, Coral Gables, FL.

Caribbean and the eastern coast of the United States in September of 1989. The total property damage exceeded 10 billion dollars. The low death toll (relative to other hurricanes of similar intensity) of forty-nine was credited to greatly improved forecasting techniques, making evacuations possible from threatened areas.

In the northern hemisphere, hurricanes generally travel west to northwest, then in a northeasterly direction; however, their paths are rather unpredictable. Their forward motion is usually around 24 kilometers (15 miles) per hour.

Surprisingly, winds are not the greatest threat from hurricanes. The greatest damage is caused by the waves they produce, as a huge mound of raging water, called the *storm surge*, comes ashore. These can be 4.5 meters (15 feet) or more above normal sea level. This problem is accentuated, of course, if it comes at high tide.

The National Hurricane Center, at Coral Gables, Florida, is responsible for forecasting hurricanes and for issuing hurricane warnings for a large portion of the globe. Their task is both important and frustrating. If they over-warn, people soon stop listening, because of the great inconvenience and cost associated with a proper response to a hurricane warning. In 1985, the average shutdown cost (preparation of factories and so on) was estimated by the NWS to be $50 million per 300 miles of coastline. So over-warning does not bring praises and appreciation. However, if they under-warn, lives will likely be lost. Trying to outguess Mother Nature is a very challenging, and often thankless, job.

Giving names to hurricanes has been a practice for hundreds of years. Historically, those in the West Indies were named after the saints' days on which the hurricanes occurred. Some were given female names before the end of the nineteeth century and, for whatever reason, that practice became widespread during World War II. In 1953 the U.S. weather services began naming storms with female names. With increased sensitivity to gender-related issues, the procedure was modified in the late 1970s to include an equal number of male and female names.

Tornadoes

Tornadoes, also called funnel clouds or twisters, are the smallest, most violent, and most short-lived storms. When they occur over a body of water they are called *waterspouts.* There are hundreds of tornadoes each year and they occur almost exclusively in the United States. Although they can occur in any level land area, and all of the forty-eight contiguous states have experienced them, the region most vulnerable to tornadoes seems to begin at Texas and fan out to the east and north from that point through a path called the "tornado belt" (see Figure 21-4).

Figure 21-4

The tornado belt begins at Texas and fans out to the east and north.

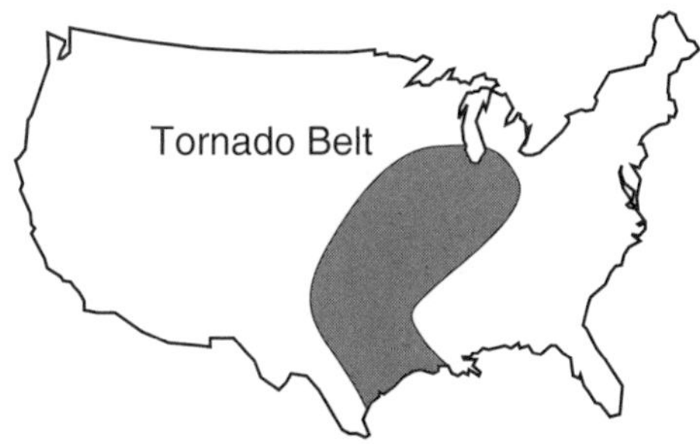

Usually, cold, heavy air pushes its way under warm air masses. Sometimes, however, a layer of cold, dry air is pushed over a layer of warm, moist air. When this happens, the warm, moist air can quickly force its way up through the layer of cold air in a spiral fashion, forming a tornado. The funnel of the tornado may or may not reach the ground, and sometimes it will touch down at one point, lift for a while, then touch down again a short distance away.

A tornado is narrow, but can be as much as 1.6 kilometers (1 mile) wide (see Figure 21-5). It moves in a wandering path at speeds of about 40 to 64 kilometers (25 to 40 miles) per hour. The spinning winds in this powerful updraft can reach speeds up to 800 kilometers (500 miles) per hour. They can uproot trees, rip roofs off buildings and send them soaring, and sometimes the winds take entire buildings. Trailer houses and other light frame structures are especially vulnerable to these fierce winds. Tornadoes usually last only a few minutes.

Figure 21-5

Tornadoes can sweep across the landscape without warning.

NOAA photograph

Thunderstorms

Cumulus clouds are usually fair weather clouds, but they can respond to unstable atmospheric conditions, grow tall and dark, and become cumulonimbus clouds, or *thunderheads. Thunderstorms* come from cumulonimbus clouds, and they are accompanied by lightning, thunder, strong gusts of wind, heavy rain, and sometimes hail. Thunderstorms are associated with strong updrafts of warm, moist air and equally rapid downdrafts of cool air. Water accumulation in a thunderhead can reach 500,000 tons or more.

Lightning.

Turbulence creates friction between air currents, between air and water drops, and between air and ground, resulting in powerful charges of static electricity. With some areas having a shortage of electrons and others an excess of electrons, due to friction (induction also plays a role), the force of electrical attraction between the positively charged areas and the negatively charged areas sometimes becomes so great that a huge spark of electricity travels from the negative to the positive. We call this spark *lightning.*

Although lightning results from a static, or stationary charge, lightning itself is current electricity. Air is a very poor conductor of electricity, therefore a tremendous charge of static electricity is required to cause an electrical spark to pass through hundreds of feet of airspace, as lightning commonly does. The path is made easier by moisture in the air, and lightning follows the path of least resistance. Therefore, lightning moves in a jagged pattern, easily visible in a thunderstorm, as it seeks out the regions of moist air (see Figure 21-6).

The human body is not a good conductor of electricity, but it is a much better conductor than is airspace, and a person can become a human lightning rod. If possible, you are advised to go into a house or other large building. Stay away from swimming pools or other open water, tall trees, water pipes, metal fences, clotheslines, and metal equipment such as golf clubs, motorcycles, and bicycles. If, in a thunderstorm, your hair stands on end or your skin tingles, lightning may be about to strike. Drop to your knees and crouch down. Do not run or lie flat on the ground. More people are killed each year by lightning than by tornadoes. (For a more complete description of lightning and static electricity, induction, lightning rods, and safety, see chapter 18.)

Thunder.

When lightning strikes, the air through which it passes is suddenly heated, causing it to expand very rapidly, or explode. In fact, lightning heats the air along its path to temperatures ranging from 15,000 to 30,000 degrees Celsius (27,000 to 54,000 degrees Fahrenheit)! The resulting violent expansion of the air causes vibrations, which we hear as *thunder.* Thunder, then, can be thought of as the sound from an explosion, and it occurs for the same reason as an explosion from any other cause, including firecrackers, dynamite, a tire blowing out, or a popping balloon. All of these events cause rapid expansion of the air, and the resulting vibrations strike the eardrums very hard. The rumbling of thunder is a series of echoes produced as the sound is reflected back and forth by the clouds.

The sound of thunder is always preceded by lightning, and the delay is a clue to how near or

Figure 21-6

Most of us have witnessed the beautiful fury of lightning.

far away the lightning is. The delay is the difference between the speed of light and the speed of sound. Light travels at about 300,000 kilometers (186,000 miles) per second, equivalent to traveling around the earth approximately seven times in one second. Therefore we see lightning essentially at the instant that it happens. Sound, however, travels much more slowly, requiring about three seconds to travel 1 kilometer (about five seconds to travel 1 mile). By counting the seconds, then, one can determine about how far away the lightning is. If the thunder seems to happen immediately with the lightning, it's much too close for comfort.

We often hear it said that lightning never strikes in the same place twice. Although it would be unusual, that is both an incorrect statement and an unsafe assumption. The probability that lightning will strike at any given location is very low, but that probability remains the same whether or not lightning has struck there before.

VII. FORECASTING THE WEATHER

Almost everyone has free access to the world's largest science laboratory—the atmosphere. As you are getting acquainted with weather, and efforts to predict weather patterns, one of the most effective things to do is to look skyward each day and ask yourself, "What does the sky look like, and what does that tell me about today's weather?" You might want to get your students in the habit of doing that, and sharing their observations and ideas with each other.

Sometimes, knowing in advance what the weather might be is just a convenience, as we decide what clothes to wear, whether to spend our time indoors or outdoors, or whether to go "over the river and through the woods" for Thanksgiving dinner. In many cases weather forecasts have much greater importance. If farmers receive a warning of possible frost, they can sometimes take steps to protect their crops. Accurate predictions of hurricanes, tornadoes, and floods, can often save many lives and significantly reduce property damage. Routing patterns, schedules, and fueling plans for airplanes and ships can be adjusted if the nature, location, and path of severe weather are known, avoiding possible tragedy.

Meteorology is the science that deals with the study of weather, and a person who studies and forecasts the weather is called a *meteorologist.* Since weather is the condition of the atmosphere at a particular time and place, meteorologists describe the weather by observing cloud types and measuring air temperature, air pressure, wind direction and speed, humidity, and the amount and type of precipitation. To forecast the weather for a given location, meteorologists need similar information about air masses that are moving into the area. Such measurements are made with a variety of instruments.

Instruments

Many measurements are required for weather forecasts. These are provided by specialized instruments designed to sense certain atmospheric conditions and changes.

Temperature

To measure temperature, meteorologists use a *thermometer* very similar to the thermometers we use in our homes (see Figure 21-7). The most common type has mercury or other liquid (usually alcohol) in a bulb that has a narrow opening into a glass tube. The liquid expands when it gets warmer, forcing it higher up into the tube, and contracts when it cools, causing the liquid to come back down into the bulb. The amount of expansion and contraction with any given temperature change is consistent for

Figure 21-7

The liquid thermometer is the most common type.

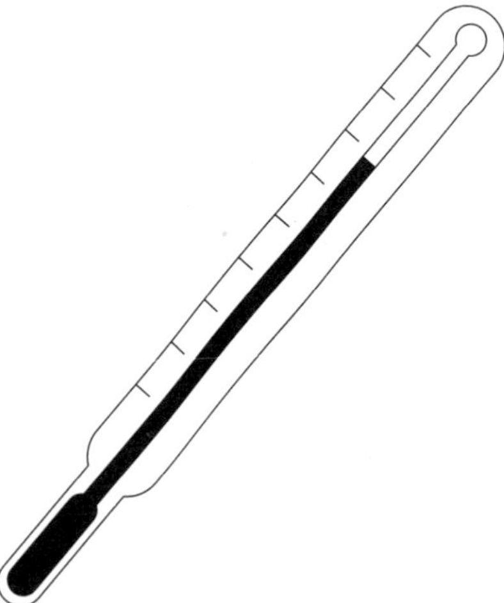

Figure 21-8

The bi-metal thermometer is commonly used in thermostats.

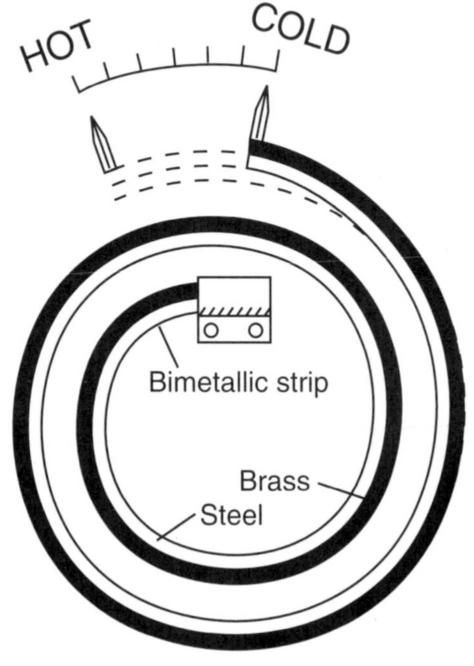

any given liquid, and a scale on the thermometer allows you to read the current temperature. The scale may be in degrees Fahrenheit or degrees Celsius. The United States is the only major country in the world that still commonly uses the Fahrenheit scale. Even the United States is moving toward more common use of the Celsius scale, along with the other elements of the metric measurement system, to be consistent with the rest of the world and because it is an easier system to learn and more efficient to use.

Another type of thermometer is called the bi-metal thermometer (see Figure 21-8). This device involves a strip of two different types of metals that have been laminated together face to face. The two metals expand and contract at different rates, forcing the bi-metal strip to bend as temperatures change. Sometimes the strip is coiled, allowing a longer strip in a small space. A pointer is attached that indicates the current temperature on a scale.

Meteorologists use thermometers that, in addition to providing the current temperature, have special indicators that give the minimum and maximum temperatures for the day (see Figure 21-9). This information is important in establishing day-by-day trends.

Air pressure

Air pressure is measured by *barometers.* A *mercury barometer* (see Figure 21-10) consists of a glass tube that is sealed at one end, filled with mercury, and inverted with the open end in a dish of mercury, in such a way that no air is allowed into the tube. The mercury in the tube will then fall until the weight of mercury in the tube is equal to the force of air pressure on the surface of the mercury in the dish. Air pressure will support about 76 centimeters (30 inches) of mercury. The height of the column of mercury will change slightly as atmospheric pressure

Figure 21-9

The minimum/maximum thermometer indicates its lowest and highest readings since the last time it was reset.

changes, thus providing a constant measure of atmospheric pressure.

A second type of barometer is called an *aneroid barometer* (see Figure 21-11). This instrument is made of an airtight chamber that has flexible walls, and from which some of the air has been extracted. It is very sensitive to changes in atmospheric pressure, and the walls move in and out as atmospheric pressure goes up and down. A pointer is attached, indirectly by levers, to the wall of the aneroid barometer and points to a dial, which is calibrated to indicate pressure in centimeters or inches of mercury.

Some aneroid barometers, called altimeters, are calibrated to measure height above sea level. This is possible because air pressure is greater at lower altitudes and less at higher altitudes. Air pressure changes approximately 2.5 centimeters (1 inch) of mercury with every

Figure 21-10

The mercury barometer measures atmospheric pressure.

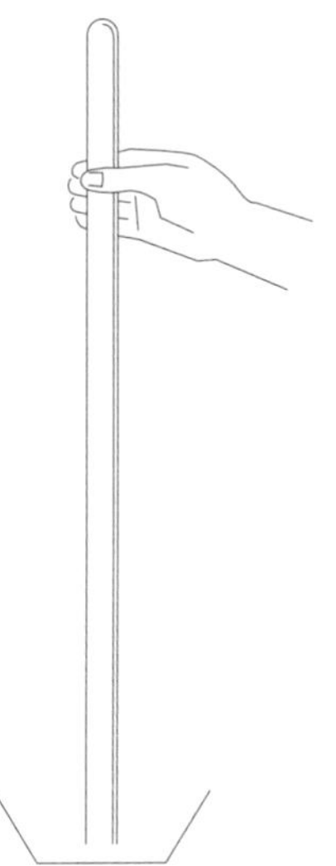

Figure 21-11

The aneroid barometer is made of an airtight chamber with flexible walls.

305 meters (1,000 feet) of change in altitude. The markings on the dial of an altimeter indicate the number of meters (or feet) above sea level instead of centimeters (or inches) of mercury, but the instrument is really a modified barometer.

Wind direction

A *wind vane* is used to indicate wind direction (see Figure 21-12). It is usually constructed in the shape of an arrow with a broad tail and mounted on a pivot, so it is free to move when the wind blows against it. As the wind strikes the broad tail, the arrow turns to point into the wind. Airports often use large wind socks and various other designs of wind vanes for easier visibility from the air.

Wind Speed

Wind speed is measured by an *anemometer,* which is usually constructed with three or four hollow cups mounted on separate arms and facing the same direction, with the system mounted on a low-friction pivot (see Figure 21-13). The wind catches the opening of the cups, causing the anemometer to spin. The number of revolutions per minute of the anemometer is translated to wind speed. The anemometer is calibrated to measure wind velocity in kilometers (or miles) per hour.

Figure 21-12

Wind vanes indicate wind direction.

Figure 21-13

The four-cup anemometer measures wind speed.

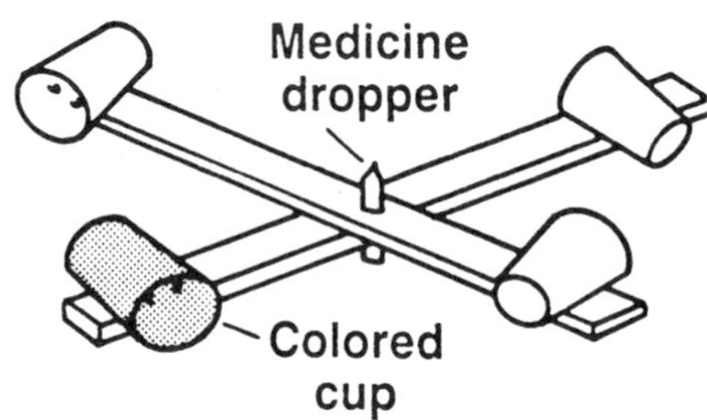

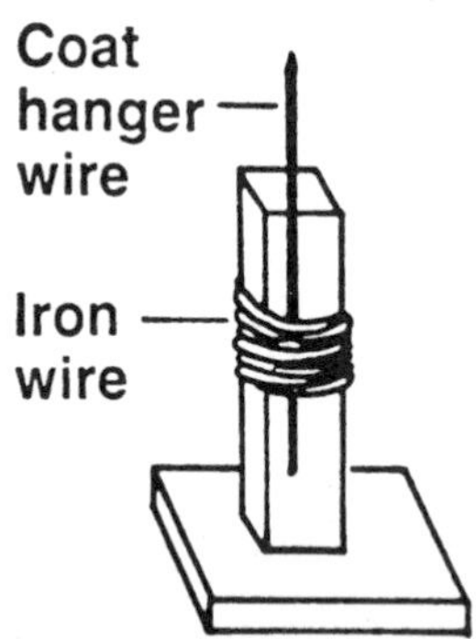

Relative humidity

Relative humidity is measured with a *hygrometer.* A common form of hygrometer is the *wet/dry bulb hygrometer,* commonly called a *psychrometer* (see Figure 21-14). The psychrometer has two thermometers that can be identical except that a cloth is wrapped around the bulb of one of them. In use, the cloth is soaked with water. Since evaporation is a cooling process, the wet bulb is cooled by evaporation of water from the cloth. The dryer the air, the faster evaporation will occur, and the greater the cooling effect on the wet-bulb thermometer. If the air is very humid, little evaporation will occur and the two thermometers will show less temperature difference. Thus dryer air results in a greater difference in the readings of the two thermometers. The meteorologist uses the difference in temperature to find the relative humidity on a relative humidity table (see Figure 21-15). The psychrometer is usually placed in the path of a fan to assure maximum evaporation, therefore maximum cooling.

Figure 21-14

The psychrometer measures relative humidity.

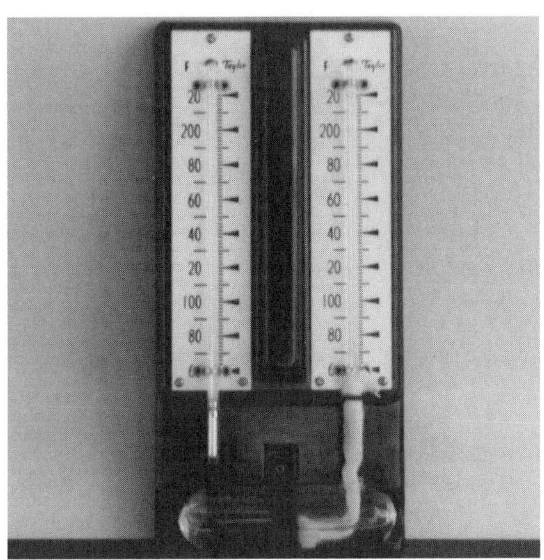

A second type of psychrometer is the *sling psychrometer.* Like the first design, the sling psychrometer has two thermometers, and the bulb of one of them is wrapped with a wet cloth. The two thermometers are mounted to a handle with a pivot connection. Air is then forced past the sling psychrometer by swinging it around by the handle. The effect is the same for both designs of the psychrometer.

Another type of hygrometer is the *hair hygrometer* (see Figure 21-16). Human hair becomes longer when wet and shorter when dry, and is very sensitive to moisture in the air. A small bundle of human hair is attached to a pointer, which moves back and forth across a scale as moisture conditions change.

For a continuous record of relative humidity, the meteorologist uses a *hygrograph,* a hair hygrometer that uses a pen instead of a pointer. The pen rides on a revolving sheet of paper, recording any changes in relative humidity.

Rainfall

Rainfall is measured with a *rain gauge* (see Figure 21-17), which is usually constructed as a narrow cylinder with a funnel-shaped top. Using the funnel results in a taller column of water in the cylinder with a given amount of rainfall, providing a more accurate measurement. With a known funnel-to-cylinder area ratio, the actual amount of rainfall is easily determined. For example, if the ratio is 10:1, the depth of water in the cylinder is divided by 10 to determine the actual rainfall. At this ratio, three inches of water in the rain gauge would indicate three-tenths inch of precipitation.

Snowfall

Snowfall is measured in two ways. First, the depth is measured in an open area with a stick. Second, the amount of water contained in the

Figure 21-15a *Relative humidity table 1*

Wet Bulb Temperature °C	10	11	12	13	14	15	16	17	18	19	20	21	22	23	24	25	2
1	6	1															
2	15	9	4														
3	25	18	12	7	3												
4	34	27	21	15	10	6	2										
5	45	37	30	23	18	13	9	5	1								
6	55	46	39	32	26	21	16	11	7	4	1						
7	66	56	48	41	34	28	23	18	14	10	7	4	1				
8	77	67	58	50	43	36	30	25	20	16	13	9	6	3	1		
9	88	78	68	59	51	44	38	32	27	23	19	15	11	8	6	3	1
10	100	89	78	69	60	53	46	40	34	29	25	21	17	14	11	8	5
11		100	89	80	70	62	54	48	42	36	31	26	22	19	16	13	1
12			100	90	80	71	63	56	49	43	37	32	28	24	21	18	1
13				100	90	80	72	64	57	50	44	39	34	30	26	23	1
14					100	90	81	72	65	58	52	46	41	36	32	28	2
15						100	91	81	73	66	59	53	47	42	37	33	2
16							100	90	82	74	67	60	54	48	43	39	3
17								100	91	82	74	67	61	55	50	45	4
18									100	91	83	75	68	62	56	51	4
19										100	91	83	76	69	63	57	5
20											100	91	83	76	70	63	5
21												100	92	84	77	70	6
22													100	92	84	77	7
23														100	92	85	7
24															100	92	8
25																100	9
26																	1
27																	
28																	
29																	
30																	
31																	
32																	
33																	
34																	
35																	
36																	
37																	
38																	
39																	
40																	
41																	
42																	
43																	
44																	
45																	
	10	11	12	13	14	15	16	17	18	19	20	21	22	23	24	25	2

Dry Bulb Temperature °C

7	28	29	30	31	32	33	34	35	36	37	38	39	40	41	42	43	44	45
	1																	
	5	3	2															
2	9	5	4	4	2	1												
6	14	11	9	7	5	4	2	1										
1	18	15	13	11	9	7	5	4	3	2								
6	23	20	17	15	12	10	9	7	6	4	3	2	1					
1	27	24	21	19	16	14	12	10	9	7	6	4	3	2	1	1		
6	32	29	26	23	20	18	15	13	12	10	8	7	6	5	4	3	2	1
1	37	34	30	27	24	21	19	17	15	13	11	10	8	7	6	5	4	3
7	42	38	35	31	28	25	23	20	18	16	14	13	11	10	8	7	6	5
3	48	44	40	36	33	30	27	24	22	19	17	16	14	12	11	10	8	7
9	54	49	45	41	37	34	31	28	25	23	21	19	17	15	14	12	11	9
5	59	55	50	46	42	38	35	32	29	26	24	22	20	18	16	15	13	12
1	66	60	55	51	47	43	39	36	33	30	28	25	23	21	19	17	16	14
8	72	66	61	56	52	48	44	40	37	34	31	29	26	24	22	20	18	17
5	79	72	67	62	57	52	48	45	41	38	35	32	30	27	25	23	21	19
2	85	79	73	67	62	58	53	49	45	42	39	36	33	31	28	26	24	22
00	93	86	79	73	68	63	58	54	50	46	43	40	37	34	31	29	27	25
	100	93	86	80	74	69	64	59	55	51	47	44	41	38	35	32	30	28
		100	93	86	80	74	69	64	60	55	51	48	44	41	38	36	33	31
			100	93	86	80	75	70	65	60	56	52	49	45	42	39	36	34
				100	93	87	81	75	70	65	61	57	53	49	46	43	40	37
					100	93	87	81	76	70	66	61	57	53	50	47	44	41
						100	93	87	81	76	71	66	62	58	54	51	47	44
							100	93	87	82	76	71	67	62	58	55	51	48
								100	94	87	82	77	72	67	63	59	55	52
									100	94	88	82	77	72	68	63	59	56
										100	94	88	82	77	72	68	64	60
											100	94	88	83	78	73	68	64
												100	94	88	83	78	73	69
													100	94	88	83	78	74
														100	94	88	83	78
															100	94	89	83
																100	94	89
																	100	94
																		100
7	28	29	30	31	32	33	34	35	36	37	38	39	40	41	42	43	44	45

Dry Bulb Temperature °C

Figure 21-15b *Relative humidity table 2*

Wet Bulb Temperature °F \ Dry Bulb Temperature °F	50	51	52	53	54	55	56	57	58	59	60	61	62	63	64	65	66	67	68	69	70	71	72	73	74	75	76	77	78
33	2																												
34	7	4	1																										
35	12	9	6	3																									
36	17	14	10	7	2																								
37	22	19	15	12	9	6	4	1																					
38	28	24	20	17	14	11	8	6	3	1																			
39	33	29	25	22	19	15	12	10	7	5	3	1																	
40	39	35	31	27	23	20	17	14	11	9	6	4	2																
41	44	40	36	32	28	25	21	18	16	13	10	8	6	4	2														
42	50	46	41	37	33	29	26	23	20	17	14	12	10	7	5	3	2												
43	56	51	47	42	38	34	31	27	24	21	18	16	13	11	9	7	5	3	1										
44	62	57	52	48	43	39	35	32	29	25	23	20	17	15	12	10	8	6	5	3	1								
45	68	63	58	53	48	44	40	37	33	30	27	24	21	18	16	14	12	10	8	6	4	3	1						
46	74	69	63	58	54	49	45	41	38	34	31	28	25	22	20	17	15	13	11	9	7	6	4	3	1				
47	80	75	69	64	59	55	50	46	42	39	35	32	29	26	24	21	19	16	14	12	10	9	7	5	4	3	1		
48	87	81	75	70	65	60	55	51	47	43	40	36	33	30	27	25	22	20	18	15	14	12	10	8	7	5	4	3	1
49	93	87	81	76	70	65	61	56	52	48	44	41	37	34	31	28	26	23	21	19	17	15	13	11	9	8	6	5	4
50	100	93	87	82	76	71	66	61	57	53	49	45	42	38	35	32	30	27	24	22	20	18	16	14	12	10	9	8	6
51		100	94	88	82	76	71	66	62	58	54	50	46	43	39	36	33	31	28	26	23	21	19	17	15	13	12	10	9
52			100	94	88	82	77	72	67	63	58	54	50	47	43	40	37	34	32	29	27	24	22	20	18	16	15	13	11
53				100	94	88	82	77	72	68	63	59	55	51	48	44	41	38	35	33	30	28	25	23	21	19	17	16	14
54					100	94	88	83	78	73	68	64	60	56	52	48	45	42	39	36	33	31	29	26	23	22	20	18	17
55						100	94	88	83	78	73	69	64	60	56	53	49	45	43	40	37	34	32	29	27	25	23	21	19
56							100	94	89	83	78	74	69	65	61	57	53	50	47	44	41	38	35	33	30	28	26	24	22
57								100	94	89	84	79	74	70	65	61	58	54	51	47	44	41	39	36	33	31	29	27	25
58									100	94	89	84	79	74	70	66	62	58	55	51	48	45	42	40	37	34	32	30	28
59										100	94	89	84	79	75	70	66	62	59	55	52	49	46	43	40	38	35	33	31
60											100	95	89	84	80	75	71	67	63	59	56	53	50	47	44	41	38	36	34
61												100	95	89	85	80	75	71	67	64	60	57	53	50	47	44	42	39	37
62													100	95	90	85	80	76	72	68	64	60	57	54	51	48	45	42	40
63														100	95	90	85	80	76	72	68	64	61	58	54	51	49	46	43
64															100	95	90	85	81	76	72	69	65	61	58	55	52	49	46
65																100	95	90	85	81	77	73	69	65	62	59	56	53	50
66																	100	95	90	86	81	77	73	69	66	62	59	56	53
67																		100	95	90	86	82	77	74	70	66	63	60	57
68																			100	95	90	86	82	78	74	70	67	63	60
69																				100	95	91	86	82	78	74	71	67	64
70																					100	95	91	86	82	78	74	71	67
71																						100	95	91	87	82	79	75	71
72																							100	95	91	87	83	79	75
73																								100	95	91	87	83	79
74																									100	95	91	87	83
75																										100	96	91	87
76																											100	96	91
77																												100	96
78																													100
79																													
80																													
81																													
82																													
83																													
84																													
85																													
86																													
87																													
88																													
89																													
90																													
91																													
92																													
93																													
94																													
95																													
96																													
97																													
98																													
99																													
100																													
101																													
102																													
103																													
104																													
105																													
106																													
107																													
108																													
109																													
110																													

79	80	81	82	83	84	85	86	87	88	89	90	91	92	93	94	95	96	97	98	99	100	101	102	103	104	105	106	107	108	109	110
3 5 7 10	2 4 6 9	3 5 7	2 4 6	1 3 5	2 4	1 3	2	1																							
12 15 18 20 23	11 14 16 19 21	10 12 15 17 20	8 11 13 16 18	7 9 12 14 16	6 8 10 13 15	5 7 9 11 14	4 6 8 10 12	3 5 7 9 11	2 4 6 8 10	1 3 5 7 9	2 4 6 8	1 3 5 7	1 2 4 6	2 3 4	1 2 3	2 3	1 2	1 2	1												
26 29 32 35 38	24 27 30 32 35	22 25 28 30 33	21 23 26 28 31	19 21 24 27 29	17 20 22 25 27	16 18 21 23 26	15 17 19 22 24	13 15 18 20 22	12 14 16 19 21	11 13 15 17 19	10 12 14 16 18	9 11 13 15 17	8 10 12 14 16	7 9 11 12 14	6 8 10 11 13	5 7 9 10 12	4 5 7 9 10	4 5 7 9 10	3 4 6 8 9	2 4 5 7 8	2 3 5 6 8	1 2 4 5 7	2 3 5 6	1 3 4 5	1 2 3 5	2 3 4	1 2 4	1 2 3	1 2	1 2	2
41 44 47 50 54	38 41 44 48 51	36 39 42 45 48	34 37 40 43 46	32 35 37 40 43	30 33 35 38 41	28 31 33 36 39	26 29 31 34 37	25 27 30 32 35	23 25 28 30 33	22 24 26 29 31	20 22 25 27 29	19 21 23 25 28	18 20 22 24 26	16 18 20 22 25	15 17 19 21 23	14 16 18 20 22	12 14 16 18 20	12 14 16 17 19	11 13 14 16 18	10 12 13 15 17	9 11 13 14 16	8 10 12 13 14	8 9 11 12 13	7 8 10 11 12	6 8 9 11 12	6 7 8 10 11	5 6 8 9 10	4 5 7 8 9	4 5 6 8 9	3 4 6 7 8	3 4 5 6 8
57 61 64 68 72	54 58 61 65 68	51 55 58 61 65	49 52 55 59 62	46 49 53 56 59	44 47 50 53 56	42 45 47 50 54	39 42 45 48 51	37 40 43 46 49	35 38 41 43 46	34 36 39 41 44	32 34 37 39 42	30 32 35 37 40	28 31 33 35 38	27 29 31 34 36	25 27 30 32 34	24 26 28 30 32	22 24 26 28 30	21 23 25 27 29	20 22 24 26 28	19 21 23 24 26	18 19 21 23 25	17 18 20 22 24	16 17 19 21 23	15 16 18 20 21	14 15 17 19 20	13 14 16 18 19	12 13 15 17 18	11 13 14 16 17	10 12 13 15 16	10 11 12 14 15	9 10 12 13 15
75 79 83 87 91	72 76 79 83 87	69 72 76 80 84	65 69 72 76 80	62 66 69 73 76	59 63 66 70 73	57 60 63 66 70	54 57 60 63 67	51 54 58 61 64	49 52 55 58 61	47 50 52 55 58	44 47 50 53 56	42 45 48 50 53	40 43 46 48 51	38 41 43 46 49	37 39 41 44 47	35 37 39 42 44	33 35 37 40 42	32 34 36 38 41	30 32 34 36 39	28 31 33 35 37	27 29 31 33 35	26 28 30 32 34	24 26 28 30 32	23 25 27 29 31	22 24 26 27 29	21 23 24 26 28	20 21 23 25 27	19 20 22 24 26	18 19 21 23 24	17 18 20 22 23	16 17 19 21 22
96 100	92 96 100	88 92 96 100	84 88 92 96 100	80 84 88 92 96	77 80 84 88 92	73 77 81 84 88	70 74 77 81 84	67 70 74 77 81	64 67 71 74 78	61 65 68 71 74	59 62 65 68 71	56 59 62 65 68	54 57 60 62 66	51 54 57 60 63	49 52 55 57 60	47 50 52 55 58	44 47 50 52 55	43 45 48 50 53	41 43 46 48 51	39 42 44 46 49	38 40 42 44 47	36 38 40 43 45	34 36 39 41 43	33 35 37 39 41	31 33 35 37 39	30 32 34 36 38	29 30 32 34 36	27 29 31 33 35	26 28 30 31 33	25 27 28 30 32	24 25 27 29 31
				100	96 100	92 96 100	88 92 96 100	85 88 92 96 100	81 85 88 92 96	78 81 85 89 92	75 78 81 85 89	72 75 78 82 85	69 72 75 78 82	66 69 72 75 79	63 66 69 72 76	61 63 66 69 73	58 61 64 67 70	56 58 61 64 67	53 56 59 62 64	51 54 56 59 62	49 52 54 57 59	47 50 52 55 57	45 48 50 52 55	43 46 48 50 53	42 44 46 48 51	40 42 44 47 49	38 40 43 45 47	37 39 41 43 45	35 37 39 41 43	34 36 38 40 42	32 34 36 38 40
									100	96 100	92 96 100	89 92 96 100	85 89 92 96 100	82 85 89 93 96	79 82 86 89 93	76 79 82 86 89	73 76 79 82 86	70 73 76 79 83	67 70 73 76 80	65 68 71 74 77	62 65 68 71 74	60 63 65 68 71	58 60 63 66 68	55 58 60 63 66	53 56 58 61 63	51 54 56 58 61	49 52 54 56 59	47 50 52 54 57	45 48 50 52 55	44 46 48 50 53	42 44 46 48 51
														100	96 100	93 96 100	89 93 96 100	86 89 93 96 100	83 86 89 93 96	80 83 86 90 93	77 80 83 86 90	74 77 80 83 86	71 74 77 80 83	69 71 74 77 80	66 69 72 75 77	64 66 69 72 75	61 64 67 69 72	59 62 64 67 70	57 59 62 64 67	55 57 60 62 65	53 55 57 60 62
																			100	96 100	93 96 100	90 93 96 100	86 90 93 97 100	83 87 90 93 97	80 84 87 90 93	78 81 84 87 90	75 78 81 84 87	72 75 78 81 84	70 72 75 78 81	67 70 73 75 78	65 68 70 73 76
																								100	97 100	93 97 100	90 93 97 100	87 90 93 97 100	84 87 90 93 97	81 84 87 90 93	78 81 84 87 90
																													100	97 100	94 97 100

Dry Bulb Temperature °F

Figure 21-16

The hair hygrometer is sensitive to moisture in the air.

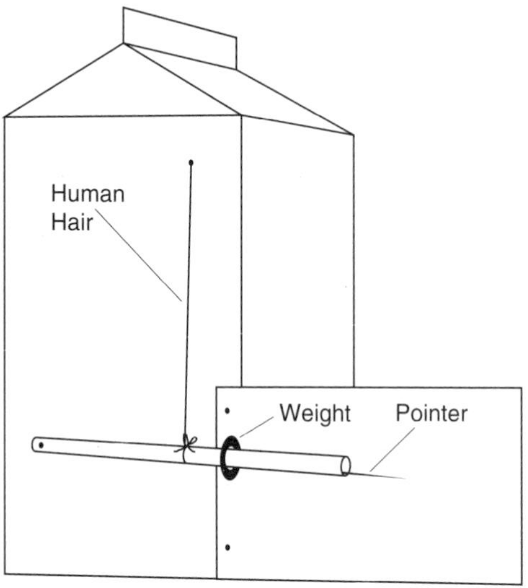

Figure 21-17

We use the rain gauge to measure rainfall.

snow is measured. Snow can be light and fluffy and contain little water, or it can be heavy and wet and contain much more water. To determine water content, a given amount of snow is melted and measured. The average snow-to-water ratio is approximately 10:1. Both rainfall and snowfall are usually measured to the nearest hundredth of a centimeter or inch.

Methods of Gathering Data

A twenty-four-hour forecast for North America requires many, many *millions* of measurements. To provide this data, various forms of the above instruments are used in different ways and at different locations in the United States and throughout the world. Worldwide, over 3,500 *groundstations* (see Figure 21-18) contribute weather data. Adding to surface-level observations are ships and buoys at sea. Some of the buoys are anchored in the water and others drift with the currents.

Radiosonde and dropsonde

In forecasting the weather, surface-level observations are important but not sufficient by themselves. Meteorologists also need to know the atmospheric conditions at high altitudes, as these conditions have an impact on weather near the ground. For many years, the *radiosonde* has played an important role in gathering such information.

This instrument is tied to a weather balloon and sent up into the upper atmosphere. As it rises, it sends information by radio signal to ground stations, including temperature, pressure, and humidity of the air through which it passes, as well as the altitudes at which the measurements are taken. The balloon expands as it ascends to higher and higher altitudes where the atmospheric pressure is lower and lower. At about 27,000 meters (90,000 feet) it

Figure 21-18

These groundstation instruments provide some of the millions of measurements required to make a twenty-four-hour weather forecast for North America.

bursts and the radiosonde, equipped with a parachute, drops safely to the earth. Many of these are returned by people who find them, in response to a message printed on the radiosonde. Those that are returned are refurbished and reused. Radiosondes are launched at exactly the same times of the day, every day, from hundreds of locations throughout the world.

Some radiosondes are dropped from airplanes and take a reverse trip through the atmosphere. Called *dropsondes,* these instruments transmit information as they descend toward the ground by parachute.

Weather airplanes

Weather airplanes also gather data at specific altitudes through certain geographical regions, and they are frequently used to track storms, including hurricanes. By close observations, and sometimes even flying through the hurricane, important data is collected to help scientists know just what the hurricane is doing and to predict its next moves.

Weather satellites

Recent developments in the technology of tracking and forecasting the weather include satellites and radar. *Weather satellites* are put into orbit around the earth. Some of these, called *polar orbiting* satellites, continuously circle the globe in a path over the poles at an altitude of about 800 kilometers (500 miles). They take photographs of the earth, each of which includes about 2 percent of the earth's surface. Since the earth rotates on its axis, these satellites see a different part of the globe at each orbit. Some polar orbiting satellites can photograph the entire earth twice each day.

Some weather satellites (see Figure 21-19) are *geostationary* or *geosynchronous.* These are placed at an altitude of about 35,680 kilometers (22,300 miles). At this altitude, the entire planet can be seen, from horizon to horizon. The time required for this satellite to circle the earth is equal to the time required for the earth to rotate once on its axis, thus the geostationary satellite remains suspended above a certain part of the globe. Four of them, properly placed, can photograph the entire earth.

Weather satellites provide vital weather

Figure 21-19

Four weather satellites can photograph the entire earth.

NOAA photograph

information, including detection and surveillance of hazardous weather conditions, especially hurricanes (see Figure 21-20). They take photographs of the earth that show cloud cover and movement of air masses. In addition to visual imagery, satellites provide infrared imagery, which shows surface temperatures of the earth. An advantage of infrared imagery is that it is just as effective at night as in the daylight hours. Satellites also take measurements of humidity.

Figure 21-20

Satellite photographs show cloud cover and movement of air masses across the earth.

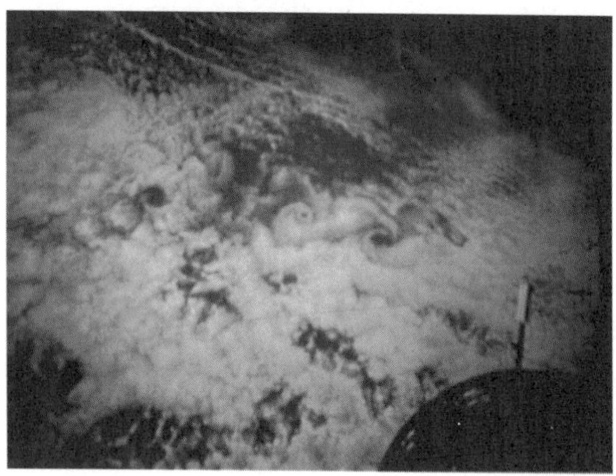

NOAA photograph

Radar

Unlike satellite photographs, *radar* (see Figure 21-21) is not blocked by cloud cover. Operated near ground level, it sends out radio waves, which are reflected by water drops and ice crystals that are large enough to fall out of the cloud as precipitation. So radar detects precipitation, not clouds. The reflected waves can be detected up to a distance of about 400 kilometers (250 miles), and the distance is determined by the time required for the return of the reflected radar waves. Such information is important because it tells where actual storm systems are currently located. *Doppler radar,* relatively new in its implementation with the weather service, can also determine the speed and direction in which storms are moving.

Most land areas around the world have some type of weather observation stations. However, more than two-thirds of the globe is covered by water, and the condition of the atmosphere over large areas of the ocean is rarely observed except by satellite. The numbers of locations of ships and buoys that gather weather data are far too few. Since the weather over land masses is highly impacted by air masses that form in maritime regions, the sparcity of information from water-covered areas greatly handicaps meteorologists in their

Figure 21-21

Radar uses radio waves to detect precipitation.

NOAA photograph

ability to accurately predict what type of weather is moving into many parts of the world.

Lightning detection system

Less well-known is the national Lightning Detection System. Ground-level sensors, designed to detect lightning that strikes between cloud and ground, are placed at sufficient locations throughout the United States to detect all lightning that strikes the earth. With one monitor, a meteorologist can observe all lightning activity across the nation, as it happens. This provides important information as to location of current thunderstorms.

Probably very few occupations are targets of more public criticism and scorn than that of the weather forecaster. Some people are even inclined to blame the weather forcaster for the weather. No one who makes a serious study of weather, however, would likely criticize weather forecasters for faulty predictions. Extensive amounts of time and energy are expended in an effort to outguess Mother Nature. Progress is being made, but the art and science of weather forecasting is very complex and continues to be elusive. The United States and most other countries share weather data freely, to provide the most complete worldwide information possible regarding weather conditions. More information makes possible more accurate weather forecasting.

History of Weather Forecasting

People have tried to predict the weather for a long, long time. More than 4,000 years ago, forecasts were based on the positions of the stars. The rain gauge is thought to have been developed before 300 B.C., and the weather vane about 50 B.C. The thermometer came more than sixteen centuries later, invented by the well-known Italian scientist Galileo in 1593. Just fifty years later, in 1643, a student of Galileo's, Torricelli, invented the barometer. The hair hygrometer was developed in 1783 by Horace Benedict de Saussure of Switzerland.

Weather maps of the early 1800s showed that weather systems move with the prevailing winds. That knowledge could not be used to warn people of approaching storms, however, because reports of weather observations were sent by mail, and the storms arrived before the mail.

The problem of slow communication was partially corrected in 1844, with the development of the telegraph, by Samuel F. B. Morse. Joseph Henry, secretary of the Smithsonian Institution in Washington, D.C., received the first weather report sent by telegraph in the

United States In 1856, France became the first nation to establish a weather service that relied on telegraphed reports, followed by Great Britain in 1860 and Canada in 1871.

The first national weather forecasting agency in the United States was formed in 1870 as part of the Army Signal Service. In 1890 Congress organized the Weather Bureau under the Department of Agriculture. In 1940 it was transferred to the Department of Commerce. Its name was changed to the National Weather Service (NWS) in 1970 and it became a part of the National Oceanic and Atmospheric Administration (NOAA), still under the Department of Commerce.

When the first practical electronic digital computer was developed in the 1940s, the analysis of data was made much faster. The radiosonde came into common use in the 1930s, followed by the first weather radar in the 1940s and the launching of the first U.S. weather satellite in 1959. In 1960 *Tyros I* became the first weather satellite equipped with a TV camera. In 1974 the United States placed its first full-time weather satellite in geostationary orbit.

Today the NWS provides observations, records, and forecasts, regarding weather and certain water resources, such as major rivers, in the United States and its territories. The NWS also issues warnings of hurricanes, tornadoes, severe thunderstorms, flash floods (there is more death and destruction from flooding than from all other natural disasters combined), and other dangerous storms. Special weather information is provided for airplane pilots, mariners, farmers, and fire fighters.

The NWS has headquarters in Washington, D.C., and regional offices at Kansas City, Missouri; Fort Worth, Texas; Long Island, New York; Salt Lake City, Utah; Honolulu, Hawaii; and Anchorage, Alaska. It has full-time staffs at about 300 weather stations in the United States and its possessions.

Facilities of the NWS include the National Hurricane Center in Coral Gables, Florida, which provides forecasts and warnings of tropical storms for the Gulf coast and the East coast. Hurricane centers in San Francisco and Honolulu provide similar information for Pacific areas. The National Severe Storm Forecast Center at Kansas City, Missouri, keeps watch on the entire nation for conditions that may produce severe local storms, such as tornadoes or severe thunderstorms.

Information from the National Weather Service is made available through public radio, television, telephone, and newspapers. Many parts of the country have special weather channels available by television. The Weather Service also broadcasts local weather reports through its own NOAA Weather Radio (NWR). This service is available through the use of a special high-frequency receiver.

VIII. SEASONS

Weather is the condition of the atmosphere at a given time and place. *Season* refers to the regular, repeating pattern of change in weather during the year, including summer, fall, winter, and spring. Although temperatures and amounts of precipitation vary from year to year for any given season at any given location on the globe, the seasonal patterns are distinctly consistent when viewed over a long period of time. Some parts of the globe experience more dramatic changes from season to season, (snow and bitter cold temperatures in the winter followed by hot summers), while other areas are warm all year long and never experience snow, and still other areas are cold year-round. Nevertheless, patterns of change throughout the year for any given area are rather consistent over the long term.

IX. CLIMATE

Climate refers to the average year-round weather of a particular location, established from weather records over a period of many years. Just as weather affects what we wear and the activities we participate in on a daily basis, climate affects our lives on a broader scale, including where we live, the crops we grow, the type of automobile we drive, the construction of our home and the way it is equipped for heating and cooling, and where we spend our vacation. A scientist who studies climate is called a *climatologist*.

The climatologist studies a number of characteristics of the atmosphere, but the two major elements that determine climate are average temperature and average annual precipitation. Temperature and rainfall patterns, in turn, are affected by several factors, including each other, in a very complex system.

Temperature, for example, is affected by latitude, becoming generally colder toward the poles and warmer toward the equator. Near the equator the sun's rays are direct, or nearly so, throughout the year, and the days and nights are equally long, creating warm temperatures year-round. Midway between the equator and either pole, the days are long and the nights are short in the summer, and the sun's rays are direct, making for hot summers. The same regions have long nights and short days in the winter, with slanting rays from the sun, generating cold winters. The polar regions have constant sunlight during the summer months, but the sun stays near the horizon and the summers remain cool. Still, these are mild compared to the winter months when the sun never quite comes up over the horizon.

Other factors affecting temperature trends include altitude, land and water masses, prevailing winds, ocean currents, and terrain. In any given region, temperatures are cooler at high altitudes where the air is light and thin. Sea region temperatures are less extreme than those of land regions, because water yields much more slowly to temperature change. Land masses heat up and cool down more quickly, and are therefore more likely to have hot summers and cold winters. Whether the prevailing winds are bringing warm air from near the equator or cold air from polar regions has a great impact on the temperature trends of any particular region, especially those of mid-latitudes.

Ocean temperatures affect air masses that pass over them, thus they affect the temperatures of land regions that lie in the paths of such air masses. In turn, ocean temperatures are affected not only by latitude, but by ocean currents, which can be warmer or colder than would normally be expected for a given latitude, depending on whether they bring polar water or tropical water.

The terrain, whether mountainous or flat, can stop or slow the movement of an air mass, or provide a relatively unobstructed channel for rapid, far-reaching movement. The high Rocky Mountains obstruct the eastward movement of air masses coming from the mild climate of the west coast, for instance, greatly limiting the effect of those air masses on the Great Plains. At the same time, the Great Plains allow free flow of the cold, polar winds all the way to the Gulf of Mexico, and the hot summer winds from the south move just as freely northward.

Annual precipitation patterns are controlled by most of the same factors that affect annual temperature trends. Like temperature, precipitation is most obviously affected by the nature of air masses that pass over an area. Precipitation is also heavily impacted by the interaction of one air mass with another. Yet the nature of those air masses, their temperature, the moisture they contain, and the probability of precipitation, are controlled by the surface over which they were formed and over which they move. Those that form over water will be moist, while those that form over land masses will be relatively dry. Precipitation is affected by the prevailing winds and by the terrain, as these factors help to determine the paths air masses follow.

All of these factors have a bearing on general weather trends, therefore on the climates of the regions of the world. Even the prevailing winds and ocean currents, which create frequent changes in the daily weather conditions of any given area, contribute to the climate, as they occur in patterns that add to the consistency of overall temperature and rainfall trends year after year.

X. IN CLOSING

Weather, seasons, and climate—these topics are closely interrelated, each having its independent elements, yet none being totally separable from the other. No effort was made in this chapter to deal with the complex aspects of weather forecasting, but only to bring to light the basic nature of weather and to point out some of the main factors used in describing weather and in predicting future weather patterns.

LIST OF RESOURCES

Ranger Rick's NatureScope: Wild About Weather (National Wildlife Federation, 1986).

Tolman, Marvin N., and James O. Morton, *Earth Science Activities for Grades 2–8* (West Nyack, NY: Parker Publishing Co., 1986).

Victor, Edward, *Science for the Elementary School, Sixth Edition* (New York: Macmillan Publishing Co., 1989).

World Book Encyclopedia, 1989.

CHAPTER 21 WEATHER, SEASONS, AND CLIMATE

ACTIVITIES

II. THE GREENHOUSE EFFECT

ACTIVITY 21-1: WHAT IS THE GREENHOUSE EFFECT?

Materials Needed:

Clear plastic bag

Two thermometers

Two pieces of cardboard

A sunny day

Paper and pencil

Procedure:

1. Read the temperature indicated on the thermometers.
2. Write the temperature on your paper.
3. Put one thermometer inside the plastic bag. Blow up the bag with air and seal the opening.
4. Place the two pieces of cardboard in an open area in the sunlight.
5. Place the plastic bag with the thermometer on one piece of cardboard and place the other thermometer on the other piece of cardboard.
6. After one minute, read and record the temperature indicated on each thermometer.
7. Repeat step 6 each minute for several minutes.
8. Compare the temperature changes of the two thermometers. If there is a difference, what do you think might have made the difference? Discuss your ideas with your group.

For Problem Solvers:

Find other places that are in the sunlight but enclosed with transparent material. A car with the windows rolled up is a good example. A jar with a lid on might be another. Can you find others? With each one, check the temperature inside and compare with outside temperature. If you use a car, be sure to get the owner's permission before you get inside.

Consider all of the examples you used and compare them to your experience with the plastic bag. What do you think is happening? Find a way to learn about the operation of a greenhouse (plant nursery). Visit one if you can; otherwise, talk to someone who knows about them or read about them in an encyclopedia or other book.

Teacher Information:

Energy comes from the sun in short wavelengths, which pass easily through transparent materials. It reflects off surfaces in longer wavelengths, which do not pass as easily through the same materials. Thus energy is trapped and the temperature increases. This is called the greenhouse effect. Most people have experienced this effect, especially when cars are left in the sunlight with all windows closed. Temperatures can be very warm inside a car even on a very cool day, due to the greenhouse effect.

Integrating: Math

Skills: Observing, inferring, measuring, using space-time relationships, identifying and controlling variables

III. SOME FACTORS THAT AFFECT TEMPERATURE

ACTIVITY 21-2:

HOW ARE DIRECT LIGHT RAYS DIFFERENT FROM SLANTED LIGHT RAYS?

Materials Needed:

Flashlight

Dark room

Procedure:

1. Stand just a few feet from a wall and shine the flashlight toward the wall directly in front of you. How big is the bright spot from the flashlight?
2. Without changing your position, shine the flashlight up the wall. How big is the bright spot now? Is the bright spot as bright as it was before?
3. What do you think made the difference? Discuss your ideas with your group.

For Problem Solvers:

Learn what you can about the direct and indirect light rays from the sun, as it shines on different parts of the earth. Does the sun shine as directly on southern Alaska as it does on southern Florida? Does it shine in the winter where you live as directly as it does in the summer? What makes the difference? How does it affect temperatures in various areas around the world? Read from books and ask questions of people you think will know, and when you think you know the answers to these questions, discuss your information with your group and report it to your teacher.

Teacher Information:

Students will learn that with slanted rays, the same amount of light and heat are spread over larger surfaces, diluting the effect. Areas near the poles receive only slanted rays from the sun. In areas of moderate climate, winters are cooler than summers because of the difference in directness of the sun's light. Like the flashlight shining on the wall, when a given amount of energy is spread over more surface area, the energy received is less intense.

Skills: Observing, inferring, communicating

IV. WINDS

ACTIVITY 21-3: WHAT ARE CONVECTION CURRENTS? (Teacher-supervised activity)

Materials Needed:

Convection box

Two chimneys

Pan of ice

Candle

Matches

Metal pan

Procedure:

1. Place one chimney over each of the two small openings in the top of the convection box.
2. Place the pan of ice inside the box under one of the chimneys.
3. Place the metal pan under the other chimney.
4. Stand the candle in the metal pan and light the candle with a match.
5. Observe the movement of the smoke. Discuss your observations with your group.
6. Reverse the positions of the ice and the candle and repeat the process. What changes did you observe? Explain why you think this happened.

For Problem Solvers:

Fill an aquarium or dishpan with tapwater. Fill a small plastic bag with ice, place the bag in the water at one end of the tank, and tape the bag to the tank. Place a lamp at the other end of the tank, positioned so that the lighted bulb is near the tank to provide heat to the water.

Allow the system to remain undisturbed for several minutes, then carefully add a few drops of food coloring to the water at each end of the tank. Observe the movement of the food coloring in the water. Explain what happens and compare it with the action you observed when you used the convection box.

Teacher Information:

The activity should be done as a teacher demonstration or with close supervision, since flame is involved.

An aquarium with a cardboard cover makes a good convection box. A cardboard box also works just fine. If a cardboard box is used, cut a door in one end, cutting only on three sides and leaving the door hinged on the fourth side. The door must be large enough for moving the candle and pans in and out. Cut out one side of the box and cover it with clear plastic to provide a transparent viewing area.

Cut two holes in the top of the convection box; the chimneys will be placed over these holes. The chimneys can be lamp chimneys or they can be tall metal cans with both ends removed. Two short cans (such as soup cans) can be taped together to form a chimney.

If the candle does not produce sufficient smoke for observation, add a separate smoke source, such as a burning piece of paper, piece of rope, or incense. The candle should remain in the system to provide heat for the convective action. Be sure that all burning material is placed on the pan or other protective surface.

As students observe the upward movement of the warm air, evidenced by the smoke movement, then see it reverse directions after the positions of the ice and heat source are exchanged, they should begin forming the concept that warm air rises. Those who continue with the challenge to set up a similar system with water should be able to generalize and have an increased understanding of what convection currents are.

Skills: Observing, inferring, communicating, controlling variables

V. THE WATER CYCLE

ACTIVITY 21-4:
WHERE DOES THE WATER GO WHEN IT LEAVES THE CHALKBOARD?

Materials Needed:

Wet cloth or sponge

Chalkboard

Procedure:

1. Wipe the wet cloth across the chalkboard. Predict what will happen to the water. Wait a few minutes.
2. What did happen to the water? Were you right in your prediction?
3. Where do you think the water went? Share your ideas with your group.

For Problem Solvers:

Find a spray bottle and put some water in it. Go out to the sidewalk on a warm afternoon and write your initials on the sidewalk with water, using the spray bottle. Predict how long it will take for the water to evaporate, and write your prediction. Time it. How close were you? Adjust the bottle to a finer spray, then predict again and write your name on a new section of the sidewalk. Do it a third time if you have time. Are you doing better with your predictions? Compare your findings and observations with others who are doing the same activity.

Teacher Information:

Students are learning that water evaporates into the air. They should understand that the water is still water—it has gone into the air as water vapor, and we can't see it, but it's still there and it's still water.

What if water did not evaporate? Consider what changes that would create and how it would affect our lives. Discuss your ideas with your group.

Integrating: Social studies, math

Skills: Observing, inferring, using numbers, predicting, communicating, controlling variables, using space-time relationships

ACTIVITY 21-5:
DOES THE WATER REALLY GET OUT OF THE JAR?

Materials Needed:

Clear jar with lid

Ice

Water

Food coloring

White paper

Towel

Procedure:

1. Fill the jar about half full with ice, then fill it on up with water.
2. Put several drops of food coloring in the water and put the lid on the jar.
3. Place the jar on a flat surface on top of the white paper.
4. Dry the outside of the jar with the towel.
5. Check the jar every few minutes and see if it is still dry.
6. Explain your observations and share your ideas with your group. Is the jar leaking?

For Problem Solvers:

Chill a plate by putting it in the freezer. Ask an adult to help you put a pan of water on the stove and make it boil. After the water begins to boil, remove the plate from the refrigerator and hold it over the steam that is coming from the pan of water. Explain what happens and why you think it worked that way.

Teacher Information:

Having learned earlier that water evaporates into the air, students now learn one of the ways that water vapor can be brought back into liquid form. The cold jar cools the air around it, which has a similar effect to squeezing a wet sponge, and water comes out of the air and collects on the jar.

If the activity is done as written, it can help to allay some misconceptions. Note that the water in the jar is colored, the jar is sealed with a lid, and it is on white paper. Students who are inclined to think that the water that is on the outside of the jar somehow came out of the jar can see that this couldn't happen because the lid is on the jar. Those who think the water must have seeped through the walls of the jar can see that the water on the outside is clear, while the water inside the jar is colored. If enough water collects on the outside of the jar to run down onto the paper, it will be easy to see that the water on the paper is not colored water.

Those who do the extension for problem solvers should be closely supervised, as boiling water is involved and serious injury could result from carelessness. This activity shows evaporation and condensation occurring simultaneously.

Skills: Observing, inferring, communicating, using space-time relationships, formulating hypotheses

---

ACTIVITY 21-6:
HOW CAN YOU MAKE A CLOUD?
(Teacher-supervised activity)

Materials Needed:

2-liter plastic soda bottle (clear, not colored) with lid

Match

Water

Procedure:

1. Put a small amount of water in the bottom of the bottle.
2. Light the match, then blow it out and hold the end of the match in the opening of the bottle, allowing some smoke to go inside the bottle. It only needs a little bit of smoke.
3. Discard the match safely and put the lid on the bottle.
4. Squeeze the bottle tightly, then quickly release it.
5. What did you see inside the bottle?
6. Do it again and watch closely.
7. Share your observations and ideas with your group.

For Problem Solvers:

Study about clouds in your encyclopedia or other references that are available. Learn what the major cloud types are, and what the differences are between them. Find a way to make a model of the different cloud types, perhaps with cotton or other material. Observe the sky often and see if you can identify the cloud types that you see.

Teacher Information:

Close supervision is needed as students prepare the bottle for this activity, as it involves a match. You might even choose to prepare the bottle for the students, and avoid the risk of injury.

Formation of clouds is influenced by rapidly decreasing pressure. When the bottle is squeezed, then quickly released, a real cloud forms in the bottle. The smoke provides condensation nuclei, just as it does in the atmosphere, so the water vapor has something to collect on.

Integrating: Reading, art

Skills: Observing, inferring, communicating, researching

VI. ELEMENTS OF WEATHER

ACTIVITY 21-7: WHAT IS A TORNADO?

Materials Needed:

Two 2-liter soda bottles (clear), without lids

Strong tape

Procedure:

1. Fill one of the bottles about two-thirds full of water.
2. Stand the second bottle upside down on the first, so the openings are together, and wrap the bottle necks with tape. Be sure they are joined securely together (see Figure 21A-1).
3. Holding the taped joint with one hand and placing the other hand under the lower bottle for support, pick up the bottles.
4. Turn the system upside down, so the bottle with water is upside down over the other bottle.
5. As water begins to run into the lower bottle, move the top bottle around and around in a circular motion until the water swirls distinctly, then just hold the bottles steady and watch what happens.
6. Do it again and explain your observations. Share your ideas with your group.

Figure 21A-1

Two 2-liter bottles are joined with tape for use as a tornado model.

For Problem Solvers:

Go to your encyclopedias or other references that are available and learn about tornadoes. Find out what the word "vortex" means, and explain what a vortex has to do with a tornado. Do you recognize any problem with the 2-liter bottle model of a tornado? What have you learned about the action of a tornado? In what ways does the model show tornado action correctly, and in what ways does it not?

Teacher Information:

A whirlpool action is called a vortex, and it occurs when a fluid (such as water or air) moves rapidly through a small opening from a larger pool. Water draining from a bathtub or sink often swirls in a vortex action. In the atmosphere, a mass of low-pressure air sometimes gets trapped under a high-pressure area, then finds a weak spot and moves upward through the heavier air in a violent, swirling, vortex action. This vortex is called a tornado. The 2-liter bottle model shows the vortex action, but it is in a downward motion. Care should be taken to be sure students understand that the movement of air in a tornado is an upward movement.

Commercial plastic "Tornado Tubes" might be available from your science supply sources. The important thing is to get the two bottles firmly attached together, nose-to-nose, without leaks. The commercial device also further constricts the opening between the bottles, which enhances the vortex action and prolongs the flow time.

Integrating: Reading

Skills: Observing, inferring, communicating, researching

VII. FORECASTING THE WEATHER

ACTIVITY 21-8: HOW CAN WE MAKE A THERMOMETER THAT WORKS?

Materials Needed:

Small bottle (juice bottle, soda bottle, or the like)

One-hole rubber stopper to fit bottle (#6 1/2 fits many juice bottles)

Balloon stick (white)

Food coloring

Water

Sink or dishpan

Poster paper

Commercial thermometer

Procedure:

1. Insert the balloon stick through the stopper so that it extends slightly (about 1 centimeter) out the bottom of the stopper.
2. Do the following over a sink or dishpan:
   a. Fill the bottle to the brim with water.
   b. Add several drops of food coloring to the water.
   c. Push the stopper into the mouth of the bottle. Some water will spill, and that's okay. Twist slightly on the stopper as you push it into the bottle, forcing the liquid up the tube about 10 centimeters (4 inches) or so.
3. You now have a thermometer, but you must calibrate it before it is useful. Here's how to calibrate your thermometer, but wait until the colored water has been in the bottle at least two hours, so it has had plenty of time to adjust to room temperature.
   a. Place your thermometer on a table against a wall.
   b. Fasten the poster paper to the wall behind the thermometer tube.
   c. Make a mark on the paper at the water level. Read the temperature on the commercial thermometer and write that temperature beside the mark.

d. Later in the day, or when the temperature has gone up or down a bit, make a new mark at the water level and again record the temperature as indicated by the commercial thermometer.

e. Check your thermometer several times a day for several days. Whenever the water level in the tube rises or falls to a new position, mark the paper and record the temperature.

f. After you have several temperatures recorded, you can put the commercial thermometer away and use your homemade thermometer to read the current temperature.

4. Water will evaporate slowly from the opening in the tube. You will eventually need to add water, then re-calibrate your thermometer.

For Problem Solvers:

Do some research and learn all you can about thermometers. How and when was the thermometer invented, and who invented it? Why is the thermometer important to society? To measure temperature we need a device that is sensitive to temperature change, but is colored water the only material that is sensitive to change in temperature? What other materials and devices are used for measuring temperature? Can you design a different thermometer? Try it. As you use the one described above, notice any problems that it has and try to redesign it to correct the problems. Set up an experiment to test your new thermometer.

Teacher Information:

Of the many styles of homemade thermometers that have been tried, this is one that works. This thermometer works on the same principle as do commercial liquid thermometers. A soda straw can be used instead of the balloon stick, and modeling clay can be used to make a seal between the mouth of the bottle and the straw, but getting it to seal is often a problem. Balloon sticks are available from party supply outlets and they fit snugly into a one-hole stopper.

It is important that students calibrate their thermometer, and it is important that they allow plenty of time for the water to adjust to room temperature before they calibrate it. The commercial thermometer is needed only in calibrating the homemade thermometer, then the commercial thermometer can be put away.

With this activity students get a firsthand experience with the expansion and contraction of liquids, and with the useful application of that principle in measuring temperature. This experience should also help them to avoid the common misconception that water always expands as it gets colder. Water expands as it freezes, but at higher temperatures it expands as it gets warmer and contracts as it cools, like other materials do.

Those who accept the challenge for problem solvers will learn about the background of the thermometer. They will learn about the bi-metal material (two different metals laminated together) used in many thermometers. They will also stretch their inventiveness as they create a new design, hopefully a better one.

Integrating: Reading, social studies, math, art

Skills: Observing, inferring, using numbers, identifying and controlling variables, experimenting, researching

ACTIVITY 21-9: HOW CAN WE MAKE A BAROMETER?

Materials Needed:

Fruit jar (any wide-mouth jar)

Balloon (11 inches)

Heavy-duty rubber band

Soda straw

Glue

3 by 5 card

Scissors

Commercial barometer

Procedure:

1. Cut the neck off the balloon with the scissors and stretch the balloon over the mouth of the jar.
2. Secure the balloon with the rubber band to assure that the balloon won't slip. The balloon is now the diaphragm of the barometer.
3. Cut one end of the soda straw to a point and glue the other end to the center of the diaphragm. Mount the card on the wall or on a stand and place your barometer near it, so the pointer points to the card.
4. Mark the card at the position of the pointer, check the current atmospheric pressure on a commercial barometer, and record that number.
5. As the atmospheric pressure changes, the diaphragm will move up and down slightly, changing the position of the pointer.
6. Calibrate your barometer by marking several readings from the commercial barometer, as the pressure changes. Then you can put your commercial barometer away and use your home-made barometer to signal you of changes in barometric pressure.

Teacher Information:

This barometer is reliable as long as it is kept in constant temperature conditions. Any change in temperature will cause the air inside the jar to expand or contract, raising or lowering the diaphragm and causing it to give false barometric readings. If it is kept in constant temperature conditions, the only movement of the diaphragm will be from change in atmospheric pressure.

Integrating: Math

Skills: Observing, using numbers

ACTIVITY 21-10: HOW CAN WE MAKE A WIND VANE?

Materials Needed:

Pencil with eraser

Long straight pin

Soda straw

Construction paper

Procedure:

1. Push the pin through the straw and into the eraser of the pencil. The pencil is the handle of your wind vane.
2. Using the scissors, cut a vertical slot in each end of the straw.
3. Cut a pointer and a tail fin from construction paper. The tail fin must be larger than the pointer.
4. Slide the pointer into the vertical slot at one end of the straw and slide the tail fin

into the vertical slot at the other end of the straw (see Figure 21A-2).

5. Your wind vane should now be ready to use. If it isn't balanced, remove the pin from the straw and put it in again at a point that will make the arrow balance.
6. Test your wind vane by blowing on it or by putting it in front of a fan. If it doesn't turn freely, work the pin around in the straw to make the hole slightly larger.

Figure 21A-2

Your completed wind vane should look like this.

For Problem Solvers:

Wind vanes can be made in many different sizes and many different designs. As long as it is free to turn on its pivot, and as long as the flat surface on one end is larger than the flat surface on the other end, the small end should point into the wind. Make your own design for a wind vane. Find materials to make it and decorate it. You might even consider making one that can be permanently mounted in front of your home or in another good location.

Teacher Information:

With the tail fin larger than the pointer, the arrow will point into the wind. Since a wind is named for the direction from which it comes, the arrow points to the name of the wind. If the arrow points north, it is in a north wind, and so on.

Integrating: Art

Skills: Observing, controlling variables

VIII. SEASONS

ACTIVITY 21-11: WHAT CAUSES THE SEASONS?

Materials Needed:

Earth globe

Basketball (or other object to represent the sun)

Procedure:

1. Review what you learned from the activity dealing with direct light rays and slanted light rays at the beginning of this unit.
2. Place the basketball on a desk or table in the middle of the room.
3. Hold the Earth globe across the room from the basketball, with the earth's axis pointing north.
4. Find where you are on the earth and put a marker, such as a piece of tape, on that spot. Turn the globe slowly on its axis. From what you know about direct rays and slanted rays, does this position show your part of the earth getting the most heat that it can get from the sun?
5. Walk around the "sun" with the Earth globe, keeping the axis pointing toward the north. Find the place where you think your part of the earth is getting the most heat that it can get.
6. Standing in that position, turn the globe slowly on its axis and talk about what

you think the temperatures would be on different parts of the earth.

7. Walk slowly around the room with the globe, keeping the axis pointing toward the north. As you move around the sun, find the positions that you think would represent spring, summer, fall, and winter for the northern hemisphere and explain why. From each position, tell what season it would be in the southern hemisphere and explain why.
8. How would our lives be different if the earth's axis was perpendicular instead of tilted? Think about that question and discuss it with your group.

For Problem Solvers:

Select a time of day that you can check and record outdoor temperatures. It needs to be about the same time of day each day. Keep daily record of temperatures for a week, then compute average temperature for the week. Continue recording weekly averages throughout the year. Plot these on a graph. Share your results with the class, being sure to notice seasonal trends.

Teacher Information:

With some guidance in this activity, students should improve their understanding of the cause of the seasons. A common misconception is that the earth is closer to the sun in the summer than it is in the winter. That would not explain why one hemisphere has winter at the same time as the other hemisphere is having summer. Actually, when the northern hemisphere is having winter, the earth is slightly closer to the sun in its orbit than it is during the northern hemisphere's summer. The seasons are caused by the tilt of the earth's axis. Since the earth's axis is tilted toward the North Star, and remains fixed in that position, different portions of the earth receive direct rays from the sun at different times of the year. With more direct rays, the heat is more concentrated. The cycle of seasons is repeated as we progress around and around the sun.

Integrating: Social studies

Skills: Observing, inferring, communicating, using space-time relations

IX. CLIMATE

ACTIVITY 21-12: WHAT SEEMS TO AFFECT CLIMATE THE MOST?

Materials Needed:

Encyclopedias and other resources

Earth globe

Paper and pencil

Procedure:

1. Study about climates in the encyclopedia, or other sources you have available, and learn what you can about this topic.
2. Find a chart that shows average temperatures and average rainfall for many cities around the world.
3. Locate four or five major cities around the world that are at about the same latitude (distance from the equator). Write the names of these cities on your paper.
4. Write your best estimate of average temperature and average rainfall for each of these cities, then look at the chart to check the accuracy of your estimate.
5. Repeat steps 3 and 4, selecting cities at a different latitude than those of the first group.
6. Repeat the process one more time.
7. Do you see any trends that are consistent within each latitude? Did you find any surprises? Does latitude seem to have an

influence on climate? Do cities near the ocean have the same climate as inland cities that are at about the same latitude? How much do you think climate influences where people live? Does it have more or less of an influence than it had hundreds of years ago? Discuss your thoughts with your group.

8. Study this information and share with your group what you learn about factors that influences climate and how climate influences where and how people live.

Teacher Information:

As students do their research, they will find that latitude has a strong influence on climate, but that there are other factors that have an impact as well. These include elevation, ocean currents, wind patterns, mountain ranges, and proximity of the city to the ocean.

Integrating: Reading, social studies

Skills: Communicating, researching

CHAPTER

THE EARTH

CHAPTER OUTLINE:

- INTRODUCTION
- THE EARTH'S EARLY HISTORY
  - Precambrian Time
  - Paleozoic Era
  - Mesozoic Era
  - Cenozoic Era
- LAYERS OF THE EARTH
- ROCKS
  - Sedimentary Rock
  - Igneous Rock
    - Extrusive rock
    - Intrusive rock
  - Metamorphic Rock
- MINERALS
  - Types of Minerals
    - Silicate minerals
    - Nonmetallic minerals
    - Metallic minerals
    - Gem minerals
  - Identifying Minerals
    - Color test
    - Streak test
    - Hardness test
    - Other tests
- FORCES THAT CHANGE THE EARTH
  - Forces of Construction
    - Earthquakes
    - Volcanoes
    - Mountains formed by forces of construction
  - Forces of Destruction
    - Weathering
    - Erosion
    - Glaciers
- SOIL FORMATION
- IN CLOSING
- LIST OF RESOURCES
- ACTIVITIES

I WONDER . . .

When did it all begin?
How did it start?
Has the earth always been here? If not, where did it come from? If so, how long is "always"?
How can we illustrate geologic time?
What is the earth made of?
What are the major types of rocks and minerals?
What are some common and easy tests used for rock classification?
What are the major forces that change the earth's surface?
How is soil formed?

I. INTRODUCTION

Some of the "I Wonder" questions above have puzzled humankind since the beginning of time. Will they ever really be answered in a way that we can verify and agree on? Perhaps not, but thanks to the perpetual curiosity and persistent efforts of scientists cooperating around the world, much has been learned and much continues to be learned about this planet and its relationship to other elements of the universe.

Thanks to electronic means of research and data analysis, knowledge is expanding at an alarming rate, and among the exciting new information being acquired is data from space exploration. Along with earthbound research, this knowledge adds meaningfully to scientific insights into the mystery of the origin of this planet. Scientists do not claim infallible answers to the above questions, but their search for clues is untiring. New information raises new questions and further fuels the fires of scientific curiosity. This chapter describes some of the ideas put forth by scientists regarding the earth's early history, then proceeds to describe its makeup and the changes that continue to occur. Although the atmosphere is an important part of the earth, it is only briefly mentioned in this chapter. For information about Earth's atmosphere, see chapter 21.

II. THE EARTH'S EARLY HISTORY

Determining the origin of the cosmos and its parts is an enormous and elusive undertaking. Careful study by many great and curious minds has given rise to several theories. As each new hypothesis is studied and tested, new insights are acquired while the hypothesis either gains or loses support.

Scientists once believed the earth began as a huge, glowing ball of very hot, white gases. Theories have suggested that the planets of our solar system condensed from rings of matter that were thrown off by the sun due to its spin, or that the gravitational attraction of a more massive passing star extracted chunks of matter from the sun that subsequently combined to form the planets. Scientists today favor the idea that planets grow by gravitational accumulations of matter in space, in some cases from gaseous materials collecting together, and in other cases from aggregations of chunks of matter, some of which might have started from colliding dust particles (Cloud, 1988).

Over long periods of time changes occurred: continents were formed, mountains were raised and leveled, highs became lows, lowlands were lifted by mighty forces within the earth, seas were formed and drained off as land forms were altered, climatic changes occurred, and rivers carried vast amounts of material from highlands to lower elevations.

Geologists have discovered that throughout its history, Mother Earth has kept a journal—recorded in the rocks, which have trapped evidences of physical changes, climatic alterations, and life forms that have come and gone with changing conditions. Geologists have developed an insatiable fascination with reading and interpreting the story in the rocks, and ancient episodes slowly take form as geologic evidence continues to accumulate.

Scientists believe processes that are shaping the earth's surface today have been at work throughout its history. They explain clues in rocks based on current observations of those processes. They believe in the *principle of uniformitarianism,* which states that the natural laws of chemistry, physics, and biology operated historically the same as they do today. Stated another way, they believe the present is the best key to the past and to the future. One example of this principle is the process of ripples forming from wave action, as sand is moved along by water currents at the bottom of a stream or lake. If a slab of rock has ripple marks on it, that could be a clue that the rock was once sand that was moved along by waves, by a current of water, or by wind action.

Stories of life long ago are told in the form of fossils. A fossil is any evidence of prehistoric life found in the rocks, whether it might be the form of an animal's body, a tooth, or a piece of bone. Even the footprint of a dinosaur, the print of a leaf, or the trail of a worm found in rock are fossils because they are signs of prehistoric life.

Usually when fossils are discovered, they are found in sedimentary rocks, as the heat and pressure by which metamorphic rocks are formed generally destroy any fossilized remains of living things. When animals die, occasionally their bodies are covered by sediment, perhaps by sand in a desert wind, or at the bottom of a sea by mud and sand stirred up by water currents. The soft body parts typically decompose rather quickly, but sometimes the teeth and skeleton are preserved under the protection of a covering of sediment. Usually the skeleton eventually decomposes too, but it can happen so slowly that mineral-laden water infiltrates into the bones and replaces the bone material with minerals, leaving a perfect cast replica of the hard body parts such as teeth and bones. Some trees and other plants have left casts in the same way, as in the Petrified Forest of Arizona. Petrified wood is not wood at all, but a stone replica of the wood, consisting of minerals that have replaced the wood, molecule by molecule, and therefore shows the exact form of the wood, including the tree's growth rings. When the sediment deposits eventually turn to rock, the fossils in them are permanently preserved. Small plants and animals sometimes also get trapped in plant resin and become permanently preserved in fossilized resin, called amber.

Fossils help scientists determine the ages of rocks and the times at which various plants and animals lived. They can also infer environmental conditions of the times from such clues as plant and animal types found, and evidence of the presence of water. Fossils of the simplest forms of life are found in the oldest rocks. Rocks formed more recently contain fossils of plants and animals much like those living today.

Fossils also provide clues to structural changes that have taken place in the surface of the earth. Fossilized seashells are sometimes found high on a mountain top, far from any ocean. Scientists then know that these elevated rock layers were once a part of an ocean bottom, long before the material was raised to form a mountain.

In describing the earth's history, developmental periods are divided into time segments called *eras.* Eras are divided into *periods,* and the periods of the most recent era are further divided into *epochs.* Detailed descriptions of the eras, periods, and epochs of the earth's history are beyond the scope of this book. This section will say no more about epochs, and give only minimal attention to geologic periods. But it will provide a brief sketch of the eras that have been identified, in hopes of providing some insight to the sequence of events believed to have occurred, the vast amount of time involved, and the brevity of the segment of time we usually think of as history.

Before we begin discussing the geologic eras, let's devise a mental model of the estimated time of the earth's existence. Pretend that a complete history of the earth is written, with all of the events of each 100-year time segment written on one side of one sheet of paper. Each sheet of paper, then, represents 200 years. The history of 100,000 years is recorded on just 500 sheets of paper with the pages numbered front and back, the way pages of books are normally numbered. One ream of standard copy paper is about 5 centimeters (2 inches) thick and has 500 sheets. Ten reams, or a stack of paper 50 centimeters (20 inches) high, will be needed to record the events of 1 million years. The history of 1 billion years would require a book 500 meters (1,667 feet) thick. The estimated age of the earth is 4.5 billion years, so our book will be approximately 2.25 kilometers (1.4 miles) thick.

Precambrian Time

One thing scientists agree on is that the earth is very, very old, and that life as we know it has only existed during the relatively recent history of this planet. The first 4 billion years are considered together as *Precambrian time.* It is thought that during these years the earth's crust formed, the atmosphere developed, and oceans and continents were formed and reformed. Also, during this era, the first forms of life appeared.

It is thought that life began in the ocean, first as bacteria, perhaps as long as 3.5 billion years ago, and during the last half-billion years or so of Precambrian time, other sea life appeared, including jellyfish, worms, and many otherwise unknown types.

Paleozoic Era

The *Paleozoic era* began about 570 million years ago. It ended about 245 million years ago, so the record of this era begins about 285 meters (935 feet) from the end of the book that is 2.25 kilometers (1.4 miles) thick, and goes to about 123 meters (403 feet) from the end.

Fossils of Precambrian life forms are scarce, but fossils of sea life from the early part of the Paleozoic era are plentiful. During the first period of this era, called the Cambrian period, shelled animals such as mollusks and trilobites were common in the sea. Jawless fish also appeared during the Cambrian period. Throughout other periods of the Paleozoic era, many other life forms developed, including insects, amphibians, reptiles, and many kinds of fish. Plants of many types appeared during this time, including ferns and cone-bearing trees, which were the first seed plants. Thick beds of accumulated dead plants from this era later formed into coal deposits.

If we think these 162 meters (533 feet) of book pages would lack interest, that only reflects how little we know about the events of that time. Imagine the changes that must have occurred in the earth's surface during those 325 million years, the many life forms that came about, and the evolutionary processes that were at work in the various species of living organisms. Such a record would captivate readers for hours at a time. Much of the history has been eroded away or deeply buried.

Even so, many thousands of pages have been written about this segment of time.

Mesozoic Era

The *Mesozoic era* lasted about 179 million years, extending from about 245 million years ago to about 66 million years ago. In our historical record, the Mesazoic era begins 123 meters (403 feet) from the end and extends to about 33 meters (110 feet) from the end of the book.

Recorded on these pages is the account of many life forms, including the further development of cone-bearing trees and insects, both becoming plentiful during this time. Many fish of the Mesozoic era resembled those of today. The first turtles, crocodiles, mammals, birds, and flowering plants appeared. The Mesozoic era is known as the age of the reptiles, because they began during the first period (Triassic), flourished and reached their largest size during the second period (Jurassic), and completely died out during the third and final period (Cretaceous) of the Mesozoic era.

Why the dinosaur suddenly became extinct after ruling the land for such a long period of time is still a mystery, though scientists have theories about it. Land forms continued to change, and the continents we know today are believed to have formed during the Mesozoic era. If we could only make our book a reality, readers would be spellbound with this era of the earth's history!

Cenozoic Era

We live in the *Cenozoic era,* which extends from about 66 million years ago to the present time. Having begun when the Mesozoic era ended, the Cenozoic era is recorded in the last 33 meters (108 feet) of the book. That still represents a lot of reading, but considering that our book is over 2 kilometers (nearly 1 1/2 miles) thick, we're already approaching the end of it. Two periods, called the *Tertiary period* and the *Quaternary period,* are included in this era. The Quaternary period, the one in which we live, began only about 1.6 million years ago. All of this is recorded in the last 80 centimeters (32 inches) of our book. That leaves about 32 meters (105 feet) of the last 33 meters (108 feet) of the book to the Tertiary period.

Flowering plants became plentiful during the late Cretaceous and the first part of the Tertiary period. Invertebrates, fish, amphibians, reptiles, small mammals, and birds were common. The ancestors of many of today's animals appeared during this time, including cats, dogs, horses, monkeys, and whales. Primitive bears and raccoons appeared toward the middle of this period, and flowering plants resembled those of today. Before the end of the Tertiary period, birds and many mammals became like those of today and spread around the world. Early ancestors of humans are thought to have appeared toward the end of the Tertiary period.

The Quaternary period represents the most recent 1.6 million years, and is recorded in the last 80 centimeters (32 inches) of the book. On these pages we find record of the most recent ice age; some scientists believe it is still going on. This period can be thought of as the age of the humans, for it is only in the relatively recent history of the earth that human beings are thought to have existed on this planet—a brief moment among the billions of years during which the earth has developed. In fact, it was only during the past few thousand years that humans began developing a less primitive lifestyle, hunting and taming animals, developing agricultural skills, and learning to use the earth's natural resources, such as metal, coal, and oil.

Hang onto your seat, because now we're going to take another look at our history book and consider some of the events that have occurred during the period of time we usually think of as history. Remember, we began with a book that was more than 2 kilometers (nearly

1- 1/2 miles) thick to record the history of the earth, with each page containing the history of 100 years. The entire time of humans on the earth is represented by the last 32 inches or so. About forty-seven pages from the end, the Egyptians began building pyramids. The meridian of time is only twenty pages from the end of the book! Muhammed appears only six pages later, and the famed era of the Vikings began one page after that. Just five pages from the end, we find record of Columbus's discovery of America. The signing of the Declaration of Independence is recorded toward the bottom of the third page from the end. At the beginning of the next page we read about Robert Fulton and the first steam-powered ship. More than halfway down the second to last page, we find record of the Civil War. A few lines further down is the story of Thomas Edison in the process of inventing the electric light. In the last few lines of this page it tells about the automobile—so new and so strange that it was shown at circuses!

The print on the last page must be very small to record the story of the Wright Brothers' famous flight at Kitty Hawk, two world wars, and a myriad of other history-making events and inventions. Look carefully and you will find record of the first computer about halfway down the last page, followed by the invasion of the mighty micro-chip in everything from toys to telephones, and from automobiles to space ships. And don't forget to notice you and me, for our entire lives are represented by a portion of the last page. Very few of us, in fact, will live to see one full page written in this book.

III. LAYERS OF THE EARTH

The earth has three layers: the crust, the mantle, and the core. It can be compared to an apple, with the thin skin representing the crust and the apple core representing the core of the earth. In a way, this is a poor analogy, because the earth is not shaped like an apple and it doesn't have the consistency of an apple. However, like the apple, the thickest part of the earth lies between the crust and the core, so the meat of the apple represents the mantle. A boiled egg also makes an excellent model of Earth's layers (if you think of an egg that is shaped more like a golf ball than like a typical egg), with the shell as the crust and the yolk as the core. The earth's crust is very thin, but fortunately it provides effective insulation from the extremely hot temperatures just a few miles below. Geologists think the temperatures within the deepest parts of the crust may be as high as 870 degrees Celsius (1,600 degrees Fahrenheit)—hot enough to melt iron!

Let's set up another paper-stack model, this time to help us visualize a cross-section of the earth (this is written as a problem-solving activity at the end of this chapter). The diameter of the earth at the poles is 7,900 miles. Make a stack of sixteen reams of copy paper, then open the top package, remove 100 sheets of paper, and set them aside, as they won't be needed in this model. Each of the remaining 7,900 sheets of paper represents 1 mile of the earth's diameter. The deepest part of the ocean (the Marianas trench) is 11,033 meters (36,198 feet) below sea level, and the highest mountain (Mt. Everest) is 8,840 meters (29,002 feet) above sea level. The maximum irregularity at the surface of the earth, then, is 19,873 meters (65,200 feet, or 12.3 miles). Lift twelve sheets of paper and place a colored paper under them to show the deepest part of the ocean. Place a piece of blue paper under the first five sheets of paper to represent sea level. Now remember, the top of the stack is at the top of Mt. Everest and the lower divider is at the deepest part of the ocean. Most land elevations and ocean floor areas are much closer to sea level than are these points.

The earth is said to be somewhat egg-shaped—slightly squashed at the poles. But wait—just how squashed is it? Would it be noticeably irregular from outer space? The diameter of the earth at the poles is 7,900 miles.

At the equator, the diameter is 7,927 miles. The actual difference is 26.58 miles. That's about 0.3 percent of the earth's diameter, and is represented by twenty-seven sheets of paper, or about 0.1 inch in our model. To think of the earth as really being egg-shaped is a misconception.

The earth's crust varies from about 8 kilometers (5 miles) to 40 kilometers (25 miles) in thickness. At the thickest points, that's 25 sheets of paper in our model.

The mantle is about 2,900 kilometers (1,800 miles) thick. In our model, that's a little more than three and a half reams of paper. It's temperature near the crust is about 870 degrees Celsius (1,600 degrees Fahrenheit), increasing to about 2,200 degrees Celsius (4,000 degrees Fahrenheit) near the core. The outer core is about 2,250 kilometers (1,400 miles) thick (three reams of paper), made of melted iron and nickel, with temperatures ranging from about 2,200 degrees Celsius (4,000 degrees Fahrenheit) to 5,000 degrees Celsius (9,000 degrees Fahrenheit). The inner core has a radius of about 1,300 kilometers (800 miles), is made of solid iron and nickel, with temperatures as high as 5,000 degrees Celsius (9,000 degrees Fahrenheit)—about the same as the inner part of the outer core.

The crust of the earth consists basically of rock—mostly granite (about 90 percent) and basalt. Most of the crust is covered with water and soil, and within it are the coal, oil, gas, and minerals that are used by people for fuel and for other purposes. Tremendous forces inside the earth continue to put pressure on the crust, causing it to bend and crack, raising mountains and producing volcanoes and earthquakes.

Some 90 chemical elements exist in the crust, but five of them account for about 92 percent of the crust weight. The five dominant elements in or on the crust are: oxygen (about 47 percent, found mostly in air, water, and sand); silicon (28 percent, found mostly in sand, quartz, and clay); aluminum (8 percent—the earth's most abundant metal); iron (5 percent, usually found in combination with oxygen and sulfur); and calcium (4 percent, found with limestone and other materials).

The mantle consists of rock that is heavier than the rock in the earth's crust. Scientists believe the mantle is solid because of the great pressure exerted on it, and that when deep cracks develop and the pressure is somewhat reduced, the solid rock turns to liquid, called magma.

The core is believed to consist of iron (90 percent) and nickel (10 percent). The heavier matter settled to the center and the lighter matter floated toward the surface, as the earth formed and temperatures reached the melting point of these materials.

IV. ROCKS

Rocks of the earth's crust are commonly classified into three groups, according to their origin. *Igneous rock* forms from molten rock material, called *magma,* that is forced to the surface by tremendous pressures from within the earth. *Sedimentary rock* forms from layers of sediment that accumulate on the earth's surface and are cemented together by pressure and chemicals. As igneous and sedimentary rock are exposed to extreme temperatures and pressures, they undergo changes, perhaps physically and perhaps chemically. They are then known as *metamorphic rock,* a name that implies a change in form. Let's take a closer look at each of these separately.

Sedimentary Rock

As the name implies, *sedimentary rocks* are formed from sediments, such as materials in sand dunes and those that settle to the bottom of stream beds, lakes, oceans, and so on. These materials accumulate for thousands of years, and are cemented together by a combination of pressure and natural chemicals dissolved in the water. Sedimentary rocks are classified according to the type of material in them.

One type of sedimentary rock is formed from materials such as gravel, sand, clay, and silt, carried by rivers and streams to lakes and oceans, where they settle to the bottom and accumulate over long periods of time. As the sediments accumulate, layers are formed and the materials in the lower layers are pressed tightly together by great pressure from the layers above.

Chemicals dissolved in the water are deposited in the sediment and act as a cementing material, and the sediment eventually changes into solid rock. Examples of sedimentary rock formed in this way include conglomerate, sandstone, and shale. Conglomerate consists of coarse material such as pebbles and gravel. Sandstone is formed from sand that has been cemented together. Its hardness and color depend on the mineral fragments and the cementing chemicals that are in the sand. Shale is made of clay or mud that has formed into sedimentary rock. Shale usually splits easily into thin, flat pieces. Its color is usually gray or green, but other colors also occur.

Another type of sedimentary rock forms from the remains of plants and animals that live in the ocean. The shells and skeletons of billions of ocean animals and certain plants, such as coral, accumulate, harden, and form great beds of calcium carbonate, commonly called limestone. Soft coal is a sedimentary rock formed from the remains of plants in swampy areas. Accumulations of dead plants were covered by other sediments and formed layers that were changed, in time, by heat and pressure, into coal.

A third type of material that forms sedimentary rock includes chemicals, such as salt and calcium carbonate, that were at one time dissolved in sea water. Under certain conditions, these chemicals are deposited out of the water, accumulate on the ocean floor, and eventually harden into rock. Such rocks include rock salt and a fine form of limestone.

Igneous Rock

Igneous rock is formed from magma that comes from within the earth's surface. The word *igneous* means "formed from fire." When cracks form and conditions are right, pressures force this liquid rock upward. Sometimes it flows out onto the surface and sometimes the upper rock layers prevent it from reaching the surface.

Extrusive rock

Rock formed from *lava* (magma that reaches the surface) is called *extrusive rock.* This rock cools so quickly that large crystals do not have time to form, and extrusive rock is therefore usually glassy or made of very fine crystals. One common igneous extrusive rock, basalt, is dark in color and heavier than granite. Geologists believe that huge masses of basalt form the floors of the oceans.

Igneous extrusive rocks also form from lava that is thrown violently from volcanoes. These include pumice, a light-colored spongy rock that comes from lava that had many hot gases in it and cooled so quickly the gases did not have time to escape. Some pumice is so light it will actually float on water. A second example of igneous extrusive rock is obsidian, sometimes called *volcanic glass,* also from lava that cooled very quickly. Obsidian is black and glassy, with a chemical composition similar to that of commercial glass.

Intrusive rock

Rock formed from magma that cools and solidifies beneath the surface is called *intrusive rock.* Intrusive rocks have large, coarse crystals, due to the slow cooling of the magma. Sometimes the overlying material is eroded away, exposing the intrusive rock masses.

The most common igneous intrusive rock is granite, easily recognized by its speckled appearance, which is due to the presence of two minerals—quartz and feldspar. Quartz has glasslike crystals that are usually either milky or colorless. Feldspar is usually white or red, though it can be any of a variety of colors. Granite is a favorite material for construction of buildings and monuments.

Metamorphic Rock

The term *metamorphic* implies a change in form. Igneous and sedimentary rock are sometimes exposed to extreme heat and pressure and undergo physical changes, with a rearranging of the minerals, or chemical changes wherein new minerals are formed. Rocks that have undergone such changes are called *Metamorphic rocks*. A few common examples include *quartzite, marble, gneiss, slate, and anthracite* (hard coal).

Quartzite is formed from sandstone and it is very hard. Marble has large crystals and is formed from limestone. Gneiss can be formed from granite or from other forms of igneous or sedimentary rock and is characterized by parallel bands or streaks of mineral. Slate is formed from shale and maintains the characteristic of easily splitting into thin sheets. Hard coal is formed from soft coal and it contains much more carbon. Hard coal is sometimes further changed, by additional heat and pressure, into graphite, which is pure carbon and is used in making pencil leads and for lubricant and other purposes. (As you can see, pencil "lead" is not lead at all, but carbon.)

V. MINERALS

Minerals are chemical elements or compounds that are found in the earth's crust, and they have a definite crystal structure. They are the building blocks of rocks, with most rocks consisting of more than one mineral. More than 2,000 different minerals have been identified in the rocks of the earth's crust, yet a mere ten minerals make up about 90 percent of the rocks.

Types of Minerals

Minerals do not come from living things. Neither pearls nor coal are minerals, because pearls are produced by oysters and coal is formed from plant material. Geologists classify minerals into four major categories, depending on the chemicals in them and the structure of the crystals they form.

Silicate minerals

The first category, called the *silicate* minerals, are those that contain the chemical element silicon. Common examples of this group include quartz, feldspar, mica, garnet, hornblende, augite, and talc. About 40 percent of the commonly known minerals are of this group, including the minerals found in granite.

Nonmetallic minerals

The second category is called the *nonmetallic* minerals, although some of them contain metals, such as calcium or magnesium. This group includes such well-known minerals as sulfur, rock salt, gypsum, calcite, dolomite, fluorite, graphite, and apatite.

Metallic minerals

Third is the category of *metal ore* minerals. These include gold, silver, copper, iron, lead, zinc, aluminum, tin, mercury, uranium, and titanium.

Gem minerals

In the fourth category are the *gem* minerals, which are those that are made into precious and semiprecious stones. These include diamond, emerald, ruby, opal, topaz, jade, sapphire, and others.

Identifying Minerals

Each mineral has its own unique characteristics, and several tests can be used to distinguish one mineral from another. However, a particular mineral can resemble one or more others in some ways, and frequently even geologists must apply more than one test—even several—to be sure of accurate identification. The following are some tests that are commonly used.

Color test

For the *color test,* it is important to look at a fresh surface of the mineral, rather than a surface that is soiled or has been tarnished and dulled by time. A fresh surface shows the true color of the mineral. Even when acquainted with the common colors of a mineral, the untrained eye can be easily confused by impurities that change the true color.

Streak test

A second color test is the *streak test.* The mineral is used to scratch a piece of unglazed porcelain tile, called a *streak plate,* and the color of the streak produced is a clue to the mineral's identification.

Hardness test

One of the very common tests is the *hardness test.* Certain minerals are used as standards of hardness, and all other minerals are compared with these standards. A commonly used hardness scale is *Mohs' scale,* which includes a list of ten minerals arranged in order of their hardness, with the softest (talc) at the top of the list and the hardest (diamond) at the bottom. Mohs' scale includes the following minerals:

1. *Talc*
2. *Gypsum*
3. *Calcite*
4. *Fluorite*
5. *Apatite*
6. *Feldspar (orthoclase)*
7. *Quartz*
8. *Topaz*
9. *Corundum*
10. *Diamond*

The scratch test is a very simple process. A mineral will scratch those minerals that are softer, but not those that are harder, than it is. In using Mohs' scale, the mineral in question is used to scratch the minerals in the list. If a mineral will scratch gypsum, but will not scratch calcite, the mineral has a hardness of between two and three.

For convenience, a few common materials have been ranked with Mohs' scale as follows, and can be used to make preliminary judgments as to the hardness of a mineral.

- *Fingernail* *about 2.5*
- *Penny* *about 3*
- *Glass* *about 5.5*

- *Steel knife blade* *about 6*
- *Steel file* *about 7*

Other tests

Other tests used by geologists include: *luster* or shine of the mineral, which might be described as dull, silky, metallic, pearly, glassy, and so on; *crystal form,* as each mineral has distinct crystal forms, such as square, cubical, triangular, pyramid, and so on; by the way they split or break when struck; and by specific gravity, or heaviness.

Additional tests are used to identify certain groups of minerals. For example, some minerals (lodestone or magnetite) are attracted by a magnet, and some (sulfur) are electrically charged when rubbed. Other minerals glow in the presence of ultraviolet light. Limestone gives off bubbles of carbon dioxide gas when a drop of dilute hydrochloric acid is placed on it.

VI. FORCES THAT CHANGE THE EARTH

Perhaps a person living in the Great Plains and never venturing far from home could get the impression that the earth is flat and unchanging. One can scarcely drive through the Rocky Mountains or along the rim of the Grand Canyon, however, without being in awe at the mighty forces that have shaped the earth. And any awareness at all of the thousands of tons of material moved to the ocean daily by the Colorado River, the earthquake that rocked San Francisco, or the volcanic activity that forever altered the shape of Mt. St. Helens, can leave no question that the forces that have historically shaped the earth are very much at work today. With some forces lifting and other forces wearing away, the earth's surface is indeed in a state of constant transition. Considering the changes that we are aware of in a single lifetime, it's easy to understand that the surface of the earth is quite different from the way it was half a billion years ago, and that in another half billion years it will be different still.

Forces of Construction

The forces that lift up land masses to produce forms such as mountains are called *constructive forces.* Some of the constructive forces most responsible for changes in the earth's surface, and certainly the most violent and best known, are earthquakes and volcanoes. Scientists have discovered that the crust of the earth is only a thin skin that envelopes the globe, vulnerable to the motions of hot, semifluid material underneath. They have also learned that the *lithosphere,* which is the rigid upper 100 kilometers (66 miles) containing the crust and the uppermost part of the mantle, is broken into sections, called plates, and that those plates move—ever so slowly, but they move. As they do, some areas are lifted up, and fractures are sometimes formed in the earth's surface.

This shifting action of the plates is detected by sensing devices called *seismometers,* and the movements create shock waves called *earthquakes.* Rock layers crack, spread apart, or are weakened by this activity, allowing magma to come to the surface, sometimes discharged under great pressure in the form of volcanoes. Earthquakes and volcanoes are only partially predictable. From surface structure and seismic activity, scientists can usually determine the areas that are likely to experience such activity, but predicting just when Mother Nature will release that energy poses a great challenge.

Earthquakes

When the plates of the earth's crust shift, either toward each other (convergent movement), away from each other (divergent movement), or past each other (lateral or *transform* movement), vibrations are sent out in the form of shock waves that can shake the surface, sometimes slightly and sometimes severely. Even a slight movement in the earth's crust can destroy cities that rest on or near the area that shifts. These movements usually take place predictably along fractures that are weakened areas in the earth's crust. Such fractures in the earth are called *faults,* and movement along a fault is called *faulting.* The wave-like vibrations that are sent out from faulting, and sometimes from folding, as the surface yields to pressures and buckles, are called *earthquakes.*

Many earthquakes take place in remote areas, or they are weak and go quite unnoticed. Those that are strong and occur in populated areas often cause great damage to property, as well as injury and loss of lives. In 1976 alone, earthquakes claimed more than 23,000 lives in Guatemala and 750,000 lives in China, along with widespread destruction of property. The earthquake that hit the Mexico City area in 1985 killed about 9,000 people and left parts of the city in shambles.

The great majority of the earthquakes and volcanoes occur in two geographic belts. One belt rings both sides of the Pacific Ocean and includes the San Andreas Fault. Movements along this fault have rocked both Los Angeles and San Francisco in recent years. The other extends from the Mediterranean eastward across Asia Minor and the southern part of Asia. Certain other areas of the world are at high risk for earthquake activity, including the area of the Wasatch Fault, which runs along the base of the Wasatch Mountains in Utah. Overall, submarine earthquakes outnumber those on the surface of the earth.

Earthquakes are monitored and measured by *seismographs,* which are strategically placed in earthquake-prone regions of the world. The intensity of earthquakes is compared by using the *Richter scale,* which ranges from 1 to 10. An increase of one unit on the Richter scale represents a tenfold increase in the magnitude of the earthquake. A magnitude of 8 suggests an earthquake 10 times as powerful as one with a magnitude of 7, and 1000 times as powerful as an earthquake with a magnitude of 5.

Volcanoes

The material in the earth's mantle is very hot. It is solid because it is under great pressure, but when pressures are reduced, such as from a crack in the earth's crust, it becomes a liquid, called magma, and pressures can force it to the surface through cracks or weak spots in the earth's crust. Magma that has come to the surface is called *lava.* A *volcano* is a hill or a mountain formed by magma around a crack in the earth's crust. Sometimes the lava flows quietly from a volcano, such as those in the Hawaiian Islands and Iceland. With others, including those in the Mediterranean, the molten rock is released with such pressure that it is thrown many miles.

Volcanic action can occur on land or at sea. The Hawaiian Islands and the Aleutians are the eroded tops of volcanic mountains. Mt. St. Helens, in central Washington, is an example of an active inland volcano. The great majority of the volcanoes occur in the regions of the earthquake belts, mentioned above. Weak areas in the earth's crust are conducive to both the shifting of plates and the release of molten material from beneath the surface.

Mountains formed by forces of construction

Mountains are great masses of rock that have been raised up by forces inside the earth.

Fold Mountains.

Surface layers are sometimes subjected to such pressures that they are lifted up and form *fold mountains.* This action is responsible for many of the formations that make up the Rocky Mountain Range.

Block-Fault Mountains.

Sometimes the uplifting force will cause a break in the earth's crust, fracturing the rock layers and lifting the material on one side of the fracture higher than that on the other side, and *block-fault mountains* are formed. Such was the case in the forming of the Sierra Nevadas, with the elevated side facing east and forming the western border of the Great Basin.

Volcanic Mountains.

Volcanic mountains are formed as lava and other materials accumulate from volcanic eruptions. The Hawaiian Islands are the eroded tops of volcanic mountains.

The constructive forces of earthquakes and volcanoes are rarely seen, but when they occur, the results are easily noticed and sometimes the landscape is visibly altered in a very short time.

Forces of Destruction

The erosive action of running water and the scouring of the land by glaciers are among the *destructive forces,* meaning those that wear away the land areas.

Destructive forces can also quickly reshape the landscape. For example, a river overflowing its banks can leave a devastating layer of trees, mud, and other debris in its path. Some areas might be built up, as silt and other materials are deposited, while other areas are eroded away. These actions can bring widespread destruction to farmland and communities. The midwestern United States was victimized by such forces in the summer of 1993.

Usually, though, the destructive forces go about their work so quietly and slowly that they are mostly unnoticed. The Grand Canyon is being carved into the Colorado Plateau by the Colorado River, but to those who visit year after year it still looks the same as it did the first time they saw it. The "setting hen," the "mittens," and other monolithic attractions of Monument Valley (southern Utah) are being worn away constantly by the forces of wind, rain, and frost, but they appear unchanged to the human admirer of nature's artwork.

If we could turn back a few hundred pages in the history book described at the beginning of this chapter, comparisons with current formations would reveal visible differences, and in some places the changes would be dramatic. The same forces are still at work, with more material being washed out of the Grand Canyon every day, and scales of sandstone, loosened by the actions of moisture and frost, crumbling occasionally from the mittens of Monument Valley. Still, many of us are willing to assume that what we see has always been the way it appears now and that it will always be that way.

Weathering

The process of breaking down rocks is called *weathering,* and it is caused by water and atmosphere as they interact with the surface of the earth.

Mechanical Weathering.

Mechanical weathering occurs as water seeps into cracks and pores of rocks, and then freezes, acting as a wedge and breaking off pieces of rock, or even splitting huge boulders by the unyielding expansion of water in the process of freezing. Mechanical weathering is also caused by plants, as roots work into cracks and openings and apply pressure as they grow. This process is even aided by animals, which dig and expose new surfaces of rock and make passages that allow water to move easily into the soil.

Chemical Weathering.

Chemical weathering takes place as various materials combine chemically with minerals in rock, causing them to dissolve or soften and leaving them more vulnerable to other weathering forces and to erosion. For example, carbon dioxide in the air combines with water to form a weak acid called *carbonic acid,* which attacks certain rocks, such as limestone. This is how the Carlsbad Caverns, and many other huge caves were formed in limestone formations. Carbonic acid also reacts with feldspar, a mineral found in granite, causing it to decompose. Oxygen in the air reacts with iron that is present in many rocks, forming iron oxide, or rust, and having a decaying effect on the rock. Lichens that live on rocks produce acids that attack and dissolve the surface of the rock, making it possible for these plants to absorb needed minerals from the rock and deteriorating the rock surface. As plants and animals decay, acids are produced that attack rock material and cause it to soften and crumble.

Erosion

Erosion is a working partner to weathering, as it carries away the products of weathering through the forces of water, wind, and ice. A great deal of material is carried away as rainwater runs across fields and down hillsides. Streams carry small rocks, soil, and sand to the rivers, and rivers carry the material to the ocean. Rivers also constantly change the river channels, wearing away at their banks, eroding where the water moves swiftly and depositing materials wherever the water flows more slowly. Wind also carries sand and soil particles from one place to another, doing its part to change the landscape. As it picks up grains of sand and whirls them around rocks, it can aid the process of weathering by a sandblasting action. Sandstone is especially vulnerable to this process.

Glaciers

Another form of erosion, though less commonly recognized as such, is caused by *glaciers,* which begin as huge snow fields in areas that are so cold the snow stays year-round. More snow accumulates year after year, until the snow at the bottom melts from intense pressure, then refreezes, and fuses as one solid mass of ice. The weight can become so great that the glacier begins to move by the force of gravity. Those formed in mountain valleys slowly move down the canyon, carving the canyon into a U-shape, picking up soil, trees, and even huge boulders in its path. Debris picked up by the glacier is dropped at the point at which temperatures are warm enough to melt the ice. With climatic changes through the past few million years, glaciers have come and gone in different locations on the earth, resulting in deposits of glacial debris, called *moraines,* in many parts of the globe. Glaciers near the poles move outward toward the seacoast, break off in large pieces into the ocean and become icebergs. Glaciers in Glacier National Park and many other places in the western United States and other locations around the earth, provide plenty of opportunity for scientists to study current glacial action.

VII. SOIL FORMATION

The weathering processes discussed above eventually reduce rock material to particles so fine that it becomes soil. Scientists estimate that it may take up to 500 years, though, for one inch of topsoil to be produced by natural processes. Since our lives depend on food that is raised from the soil, this is an extremely precious resource and must be conserved, cared for, and used wisely.

Over the many millions of years that the forces of nature have been working on the rock layers at the earth's surface, enough rock has been turned to soil that most of the land area of the earth is covered by a layer of this life-giving material. To be effective for plant growth, soil must contain more than finely ground rock material; it must contain a good portion of *humus,* which is the decayed remains of dead plants and animals. Typically, the top several inches of soil is rich in humus; this layer is called *topsoil.* Earthworms help to build topsoil by stirring up and aerating the soil and by the organic castings they leave behind. The next layer is called *subsoil,* usually much thicker than the topsoil and containing a lot of rock and little or no humus. Beneath the subsoil can be found still coarser material, which is rock that is partially weathered. Next is solid bedrock.

The thickness and composition of each of these layers varies greatly from one area to another. Some soil contains more sand, some more humus, and some has more clay or pebbles. The materials in soil can easily be sorted for examination by placing a sample of soil in a jar of water, shaking it up, and allowing it to settle. The coarser rock material is heavier and will quickly sink to the bottom. The sand will settle next, then the silt. Most humus will float. Soil that is ideal for growing crops is called *loam,* and has proper amounts of gravel, sand, and clay, and abundant humus. Exact proportions for the "ideal" soil varies according to the type of plant to be raised in it; some plants need sandy soil and some do better in heavier clay soil. Acidic needs also vary from one plant to another. Strawberry plants, for instance, thrive in acidic soil, where many grasses would not do well.

VIII. IN CLOSING

With modern means of geologic dating and other studies and observations, some rock formations are calculated to be about 4.5 billion years old. The formation and changes of the structures of the earth have been going on for a long, long time, and these changes continue today.

Rocks provide many learning experiences for children, from beginning classification skills and other process skills, to a study of mineral types, to speculation of the origin of the rocks themselves.

LIST OF RESOURCES

Cloud, Preston, *Oasis in Space: Earth History from the Beginning* (New York: W. W. Norton & Co., 1988).

Earth Quakes (Washington, D.C.: National Science Teachers Association, 1988).

Hamblin, W. Kenneth, *Earth's Dynamic Systems, Sixth Edition* (New York: Macmillan Publishing Co., 1992).

Hardy, Garry R., and Marvin N. Tolman, "Cakequake! An Earth-Shaking Experience," *Science and Children* 29, no. 1 (September 1991): 18–21.

Tillery, Bill W., *Physical Science, Second Edition* (Dubuque, IA: Wm. C. Brown Publishers, 1993).

Tolman, Marvin N., and James O. Morton, *Earth Science Activities for Grades 2–8* (West Nyack, NY: Parker Publishing Co., 1986).

Victor, Edward, *Science for the Elementary School, Sixth Edition* (New York: Macmillan Publishing Co., 1989).

World Book Encyclopedia, 1989.

CHAPTER

THE EARTH

ACTIVITIES

II. THE EARTH'S EARLY HISTORY

ACTIVITY 22-1: HOW OLD IS THE EARTH?

Materials Needed:

10 meters of butcher paper

Markers (crayons)

Meter sticks

Procedure:

1. You are about to show the age of the earth on butcher paper.
2. Draw four lines the length of the paper, with each line being 10 meters long. Space them evenly down the paper.
3. Draw one more line at the bottom. This one is only 5 meters long.
4. Scientists think the earth is about 4.5 billion years old—that's 4,500 million. On these lines, each centimeter represents one million years.
5. Mark off each line in centimeters.
6. At the left end of the top line, make a mark and write, "The Earth Began About 4.5 Billion Years Ago. Each Centimeter Represents 1 Million Years."
7. At the right end of the bottom line, make a box 1 square centimeter. Color the box with yellow or some other light color. Above this box write, "The Last Million Years."
8. In the box, at the right end, make a narrow, red vertical line, just about the width of a pencil line.
9. Below the box write, "This Is How Long People Have Been on the Earth." Draw an arrow from these words to the narrow line.
10. Talk with your group about all of the things you know people have done. They have lived in caves, hunted with spears and bows, invented electricity, and so on. All of these things were done within the time shown by the narrow red line.

For Problem Solvers:

Add to the time line. With each centimeter representing 1 million years, it should be fairly easy to find specific time periods. For example, the first life began in the water just before the Cambrian period, which began about 570 million years ago. Dinosaurs lived during the Mesozoic era, which began about 245 million years ago and ended about 66 million years ago.

Find library books and reference books that will help you to identify major events throughout history and about when they happened. Add some of them to the time line. With major events from recent history you can just draw an arrow to the narrow line in the box.

Teacher Information:

Students will get a feel for what a very large time the earth has been here and what a very small part of that time people have been included on it. Students should recognize that information about conditions long ago is not complete, and that scientists continue to study and learn. They will change what they teach as they get new information.

Integrating: Reading, writing, math, art

Skills: Communicating, researching

ACTIVITY 22-2:
HOW CAN YOU MAKE A "FOSSIL"?

Materials Needed:

Seashell

Pie tin

Petroleum jelly

Plaster of Paris

Water

Paper towels

Newspapers

Procedure:

1. Coat the inside (both bottom and sides) of the pie tin with a thin layer of petroleum jelly so the plaster will release easily.
2. Coat your shell with a thin layer of petroleum jelly.
3. Lay your shell in the bottom of the pie tin. Place it with the rounded side up (see Figure 22A-1).

Figure 22A-1

Lay your shell in the pan with the rounded side up.

4. Mix plaster with water according to the instructions on the package. Prepare sufficient plaster to make a layer in the pan about 15 millimeters (at least $^{1}/_{2}$ inch) thick.
5. Pour the plaster carefully over the shell and let it harden (leave it at least one hour).
6. Turn the pie tin upside down on a table covered with newspaper and tap it lightly. The plaster cast with shell should fall out onto the table.
7. Remove the shell but handle the plaster cast very carefully. The plaster will be quite soft until it has had at least a day to cure (harden).
8. After at least one day of curing time, carefully wipe the excess petroleum jelly off the plaster cast with a paper towel. Then wash the rest off lightly with warm water.
9. You now have an imprint of the shell in plaster, much like those often found in limestone and other sedimentary rock. When found in rock, this imprint is called a fossil because it is evidence of an ancient animal (see Figure 22A-2).

For Problem Solvers:

Look for a chance to begin your own fossil collection. Meanwhile, learn what you can about fossils by visiting someone who has a collection and knows about them. Interview that person and write notes about what you

Figure 22A-2

Your shell imprint in plaster is much like a fossil.

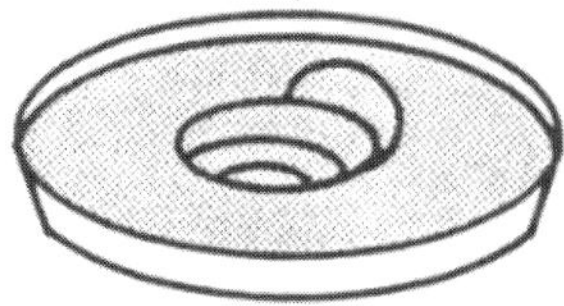

learned. Ask the person especially to tell about his or her favorite ones. Draw pictures of the fossils. Read about fossils in library books and encyclopedias. Try to find a field guide that will help you identify fossils you have or that you will have in the future.

From all of the fossils you learn about, pick out one favorite and do more research about that particular one. Where did it come from? What kind of animal or plant was it? How long ago did it live? What was the earth like at that time? Did this plant or animal live in water? Is the area where it was found covered with water now? What changes have occurred? How do scientists know whether the area was covered with water long ago or not? What clues do they look for?

Teacher Information:

You can obtain plaster of Paris at a local builder's supply store or craft shop. It is easy to work with, and if students follow the directions, the project should be successful. As the plaster cures, it will become quite warm, then will cool. It should be allowed to cool completely before being removed from the mold (pie tin).

If you have an area nearby where fossils can be found, that would be an excellent field trip. Otherwise, perhaps a few fossil samples could be borrowed from a friend or purchased from a science supply house. The experience of making a "fossil" will make a more lasting impression on the minds of students if they can see just how similar their "fossil" is to the real fossil formed by nature.

The imprint resulting from the above activity is a negative imprint. If a positive image is desired, spread a thin layer of petroleum jelly on the entire surface of the plaster cast, wrap and tie a piece of cardboard around it to provide sideboards to hold the plaster, and pour another layer of plaster on top of the first. After it has cured, remove the cardboard, separate the two pieces of plaster with a knife blade, and presto—you have both a positive and a negative of the shell. Clean up the petroleum jelly after the plaster has cured thoroughly, as indicated above.

You can make an imprint of a leaf following the same steps.

Integrating: Reading, writing, art

Skills: Observing, inferring, communicating, using space-time relationships, researching

(Except for addition of the sections "For Problem Solvers," "Integrating," and "Skills," this activity was reprinted from Activity 109, "How Can You Make a Permanent Shell Imprint?" in Tolman and Morton, 1986.)

III. LAYERS OF THE EARTH

ACTIVITY 22-3:

WHAT DOES A CROSS-SECTION OF THE EARTH LOOK LIKE?

Materials Needed:

Sixteen reams of paper

One sheet of blue paper

Two sheets of black paper (or other dark color)

One sheet of red paper

One sheet of orange paper

Ruler
Marker

Procedure:

1. Put all sixteen reams of paper in one stack.
2. Open the top package and leave the other fifteen reams wrapped and sealed.
3. The stack has a total of 8,000 sheets of paper. Each sheet represents 1 mile of the earth's diameter. Since the diameter of the earth at the poles is about 7,900 miles, remove 100 sheets of paper from the top of the stack.
4. Remove thirty-seven sheets of paper from the top and set them aside.
5. Place one black sheet of paper on the top of the stack.
6. Put twenty-five of the sheets you removed on top of the black paper.
7. Place another black sheet of paper on the top of the stack.
8. Put five of the remaining sheets you removed on top of the black paper.
9. Put the blue sheet on top of the stack and put the other 7 sheets you removed on top of the blue paper.
10. The blue paper represents sea level. Slide the top seven sheets to the side to show that some of the earth's surface is covered with ocean water.
11. The top of the stack now represents the top of Mt. Everest—the highest point on the earth's surface.
12. The first black paper represents the lowest point at the bottom of the sea. (The average depth of the sea is about 4 kilometers [2.5 miles]).
13. Notice that from the highest point on the earth to the bottom of the ocean is represented by only twelve sheets of paper. When you stand back and consider the size of the earth, you can see that the surface isn't really very distorted.
14. The bottom black paper represents the bottom of the earth's crust at the thickest places. The crust ranges from 5 miles thick to 25 miles thick.
15. Make a circle of orange paper 6 inches in diameter. Tape this circle right in the center of the stack of paper.
16. Make a circle of red paper 3 inches in diameter. Tape this circle in the center of the orange circle.
17. The red circle represents the inner core and the orange ring represents the outer core. From the orange ring to the bottom black paper is the mantle.
18. Talk about this with your group. Notice how thin the earth's crust really is. Under it is molten material. Why do we have earthquakes and volcanoes? Why does the earth's crust move sometimes?

For Problem Solvers:

Find out more about the earth and add to the paper model. People say the earth isn't really round, but slightly oblong. Find out the earth's diameter at the poles and the diameter at the equator and find a way to show on the model how much difference there really is. Find out what the temperatures of the mantle and the core are and include them on the model.

Some people say the land mass of the earth was together at one time. Do some research and find out about this. Make a puzzle showing how the continents really do seem to almost fit together. Considering how thin the earth's crust is, and considering what's under it, do you think it's possible that the surface has shifted that much?

Teacher Information:

In doing this activity, students should realize that even though some mountains are very high and the ocean is very deep, the total distortion of the earth's surface is very slight, when we consider the size of the earth. Also, recognizing how thin the earth's crust is and the vast amount of hot, molten material under it, one wonders why we don't have more volcanoes and earthquakes than we do. Students who continue with the extension for problem solvers can add much more information to the model, limited only by their interest and willingness to continue their research.

Integrating: Reading, writing, math, art

Skills: Measuring, communicating, researching

IV. ROCKS

ACTIVITY 22-4: WHAT CHARACTERISTICS DO ROCKS HAVE?

Materials Needed:

Collection of rocks

Procedure:

1. Look at the rocks and think about what is the same or different about them.
2. Put the rocks in two groups. Be sure that in each group there is something the same about all of the rocks in that group and that no rock in the other group has that particular characteristic.
3. Have someone else look at your groups of rocks and try to guess what criteria you used in grouping them.
4. Change roles and have your partner group the rocks. Then you try to decide what criteria was used.
5. Think of another way to sort the rocks into two groups and repeat the process.
6. Discuss what you did and what you were thinking. Talk about some other ways the rocks could be classified.

For Problem Solvers:

After you get the rocks sorted into two groups, think of a way to sort each group into two more groups. Can you do it again with each of the smaller groups? How far can you go with it and still find likenesses and differences?

Do some research on the ways that scientists classify rocks. In some ways, your ideas might be just as good as theirs, but try to find out how rocks are classified.

Try to get a little bit of vinegar and an eyedropper. Put just a drop or two of vinegar on each rock. Before putting the vinegar on a rock, scratch the rock with something—perhaps another rock. Put the vinegar on the fresh scratch. Record what happens. Is it the same for each rock?

Examine the rocks with a hand lens and see what colors and textures you can find in them. Does the rock seem to be made of just one material, or do you see evidence of more than one? If you have a piece of granite, check your books and find out what the speckles are and what the white part is.

Teacher Information:

Given an opportunity to study and compare rocks, and to classify them in their own ways time after time, students will use some of the same classification characteristics that geologists use. They will probably consider color and texture, for instance, and they might even discover that some rocks are harder than others.

Students should begin to recognize that rocks usually contain two or more minerals. When they really examine the rocks closely they will find, within some of them, differences in luster, color, and texture. This will become more apparent as students examine the rocks with a hand lens.

Integrating: Reading

Skills: Observing, inferring, classifying, communicating, researching

V. MINERALS

ACTIVITY 22-5:
HOW DO MINERALS COMPARE IN HARDNESS?

Materials Needed:

Collection of minerals

Procedure:

1. Select two minerals from your collection and try to scratch one of them with the other. The mineral that will scratch the other one is the harder of the two.
2. Keep the harder of the two minerals and select another mineral to test it with.
3. Again keep the harder one and continue until you have found the hardest mineral in the collection.
4. Set the hardest mineral aside. Then continue the process of comparing until you have found the next hardest. Put that one next to the hardest mineral.
5. Continue until you have all of the minerals in the collection lined up in order of hardness. If two minerals seem to be equal, place them side by side.
6. Now compare your fingernail. Where does your fingernail fit with the series of minerals?
7. Compare other materials you find, such as a piece of plastic, a penny, and other coins.

For Problem Solvers:

Do some research in your library books and find out what the Mohs' hardness scale is and how it is used to compare the hardness of minerals. Also learn about the streak test and try it with your mineral collection. What are other ways you might compare minerals?

Read about growing crystals. Try growing crystals of salt and alum. What else can you use to grow crystals? Compare your crystals with a hand lens or a low-power microscope. Can you see definite shapes in the crystals? Draw them. Compare the shapes of crystals that are grown from different substances. What if you mix substances? Do you think you can force the substances to form new shapes? Remember to write your hypothesis each time you begin testing something new—what effect do you think it will have? Then test your hypothesis by carrying out your experiment.

Teacher Information:

As they begin to think in terms of minerals, students will expand their recognition that minerals are contained within rocks. Tests of characteristics such as hardness and streak, for instance, are often meaningless for rocks, because the rocks contain more than one mineral and both the hardness and the streak might be different for each mineral. With these tests we usually think in terms of minerals, then, not in terms of rocks.

Students also might test various minerals for magnetic properties and for electrical conductivity. For testing electrical conductivity, students need a dry cell, a bulb (in bulb holder), and some insulated wire.

As your motivated students get into crystal growth, they will find a new form of art in nature. Encourage students to research, explore, and experiment.

Integrating: Reading, writing, math, art

Skills: Observing, inferring, classifying, communicating, formulating hypotheses, identifying and controlling variables, experimenting, researching

(Adapted from Activity 98, "How Do Rocks Compare in Hardness?" in Tolman and Morton, 1986.)

VI. FORCES THAT CHANGE THE EARTH

ACTIVITY 22-6:

WHERE DO MOUNTAINS COME FROM?

Materials Needed:

Several towels of different colors

Procedure:

1. Lay several towels of different colors out flat on a table, stacked one on top of the other.
2. The towels represent rock layers.
3. Place both hands on top of the stack, about 25 centimeters (10 inches) apart.
4. With both hands, press down and slide slowly toward the middle.
5. What happened? Compare this with what you think would happen if rock layers move together slowly. Discuss your ideas with your group.

For Problem Solvers:

Read from library books and learn about some other ways to show the movement of rock layers.

Make a model volcano and demonstrate it to the class. The volcano can be molded with plaster or papier-mâché on a wire frame. Nest a soup can in the top, then you can make your volcano erupt by using baking soda, vinegar, and red food coloring. You could also install a tube in the bottom of the can, extending out the bottom and out from under the volcano. Then put sand or puffed rice in the can and show an eruption by blowing on the tube.

Set up a way to demonstrate the effect of erosion. One way to do this is to put soil in the bottom of a tray, cover the soil with small rocks, leaves, and twigs, tilt the tray, and sprinkle water over the surface. Compare this surface with the same stream of water running over a grass-covered surface. Talk about differences.

Teacher Information:

With some help and encouragement in preparation, students can demonstrate lateral movement, convergent movement, and divergent movement of rock layer using layer cakes. Information for this activity can be found in the *Science and Children* magazine in an article referenced at the end of this chapter (Hardy and Tolman, 1991).

In their research, interested students will find a variety of ways to construct and use model volcanoes, in addition to those suggested in the extension for problem solvers. Some sources suggest using potassium permanganate. This material can be used in the models suggested above, and it produces a realistic reaction, but if it is used be sure it is done in a well-ventilated area, as the fumes are toxic.

Erosion is easily shown by most any water running over a soil surface. The effect of water running over a bare surface should be compared with the same stream running over a sod-covered surface, to show the soil-holding effect of plant growth.

Integrating: Reading, writing, math, art

Skills: Observing, inferring

VII. SOIL FORMATION

ACTIVITY 22-7:
HOW IS SOIL MADE?

Materials Needed:

Rocks
Sand
Magnifying glass
Leaves
Soil
Dishpan or bucket

Procedure:

1. Examine the rocks and sand with the magnifying glass.
2. How are the rocks and sand alike? How are they different?
3. Each grain of sand was once a part of a rock and was broken off by natural forces. As the sand is ground finer and finer and mixed with organic material, such as decaying plant material, soil is formed. This process takes a long time for nature to perform.
4. Put a thick layer of sand in the pan or bucket.
5. Break up some leaves, or other plant material, into tiny pieces. You could even grind this material up between two rocks.
6. Mix the fine plant material into the sand. Use about the same amount of this material as sand.
7. Compare your mixture with the soil. What likenesses do you observe? What differences?
8. If you can, set your mixture and soil aside for several weeks. Then compare them again.

Teacher Information:

Soil begins to form when rocks and similar materials on or near the earth's surface are broken down by environmental forces. The substance that results from this action is called *parent material.* Parent material is broken down into mineral particles through a process called *weathering.* There are two kinds of weathering: *physical disintegration* (caused by such forces as ice and rain) and *chemical decomposition* (such as when water dissolves certain minerals in a rock). Through the centuries, organic material mixes with the parent material and the resultant matter resembles the parent material less and less.

Various environmental factors affect soil formation, including climate, land surface features, plants and animals present, kinds of parent material, and time. The mineral content of parent material helps determine the kinds of plants that grow in the soil.

Just as soil is constantly being formed, it is also constantly being destroyed by erosive forces such as wind and water.

Although this activity will not produce real soil, it will result in a soil-like material and will provide a glimpse of nature's soil-making process. If circumstances will allow, let the mixture stand for a period of several weeks or months. Leaves break down quite rapidly and the substance will appear more like soil than when first mixed.

Consider having students crush their own rocks by using other rocks or hammers. If this is done, however, be sure adequate protection from flying chips is provided, especially for the eyes. Also be cautious of possible injury to fingers in the pounding process. Sand can similarly be ground into powder, resulting in a more soil-like mixture.

Other organic matter can be substituted for the leaves, or added to them.

Skills: Observing, Inferring

(This activity was reprinted from Activity 112, "How Is Soil Made?" in Tolman and Morton, 1986.)

CHAPTER

BEYOND THE EARTH

CHAPTER OUTLINE:

- INTRODUCTION
- THE MOON
  - Earth's Natural Satellite
  - Direction and Distance
  - Gravity Pulls Both Ways
  - Second Brightest Object
  - Lunar Month
  - We See Only One Side
  - Why It Rises and Sets
  - Looks as Big as the Sun
  - Changes Colors
  - Lunar Phases
    - The waxing moon
    - The waning moon
  - Nature of the Moon
  - Eclipses
    - Lunar eclipse
    - Solar eclipse
  - The Moon's Effect on the Tides
- EARTH AS A PLANET
  - Measurement of Time on Earth
    - Day and night
    - Year
    - Seasons
- THE SOLAR SYSTEM
  - Relative Positions of the Planets
  - Differences Between Stars and Planets
  - Motions of the Planets
  - Nature of the Planets Gravity and Planetary Orbits
  - Asteroids, Comets, and Meteors
    - Asteroids
    - Comet
    - Meteors
- ARTIFICIAL SATELLITES
- ROCKETS
- OUR SUN
  - Source of Energy
  - Sunspots
- THE UNIVERSE
  - Constellations
- IN CLOSING
- LIST OF RESOURCES
- ACTIVITIES

I WONDER . . .

What is a light-year?
How big is space?
Why doesn't the moon have an atmosphere?
Why does the moon appear to go through phases?
What causes eclipses?
What does the moon have to do with ocean tides?
What do the earth's movements have to do with seasons and measurement of time?
Do all planets move in the same direction?
What are the differences between asteroids, comets, and meteors?
What is an artificial satellite?
The Big Dipper resembles a dipper. Why doesn't the Great Bear resemble a bear?

I. INTRODUCTION

The immensity of space is far beyond human capacity to comprehend. Distances are measured in light-years, in some cases millions and even billions of them. The distance of a single light-year boggles the mind, as light travels at a speed of about 300,000 kilometers (186,000 miles) per second. That's equivalent to more than seven times around the earth in a single second! At that speed one light-year, or the distance light travels in a year, is approximately 9.6 trillion kilometers (6 trillion miles). The nearest star to our sun is more than 4 light-years away. And even that represents but a small step across our spiral-shaped Milky Way Galaxy, which is thought to be 100,000 light-years from side to side. The Andromeda galaxy, located in the constellation Andromeda, is one of the nearest and best-known galaxies; it's about 2.2 million light-years away! That's one of the *nearest* of the billions of galaxies known to exist in space. When you stop to think about it, we can only presume that the Andromeda galaxy is still there; the light from it that reaches our eyes today left the galaxy 2,200,000 years ago. That was long before the first humans roamed this planet. Perhaps that galaxy disintegrated long ago. Not likely, but if that happened, light from it could still be seen from the earth for more than 2 million years after the galaxy's demise. Let's leave such questions to the astronomers while we take a look at a little corner of space much closer to home.

People have probably been intrigued with the heavens since the beginning of human life, and have studied the movements of objects in the sky. Evidence of these curious investigations is included in the history of the Greeks, the Egyptians, and the early American Indians, as well as many other early civilizations. Over 400 years ago (a mere moment in astronomical time), Copernicus suggested that the earth revolves around the sun, and he published that idea in the mid-1500s. During the early 1600s, Galileo, an Italian scientist, taught the Copernican theory. In 1633 Galileo was punished and imprisoned for defying the commonly held "truth" that the earth is the center of the universe and that all celestial bodies revolve around it. Revolutionary ideas about the universe were not well received. Copernicus, Galileo, and other early scientists were heavily criticized, and they taught what they believed in the face of much opposition.

II. THE MOON

The moon seems to have mystified humans since they first looked skyward. What is that yellow disk in the sky, seemingly keeping watch as it appears to go around and around us daily? It mysteriously changes shape as the days go by—narrows to a sliver, disappears, then gradually grows to its full size again. It even changes color and brightness, from time to time, and it has been known to be apparently swallowed up, only to emerge again unharmed, just as mysteriously as it disappeared. When it is low on the horizon, the moon fools the unwary observer into thinking it is larger than when it is alone, high in the sky. Can you imagine the mystery of a lunar eclipse in those days?

As humankind learned more about the universe, and methods of gathering information improved, the moon became less of a mystery. More and more, it beckoned curious minds for further exploration. Even though today the distance between the earth and the moon has been conquered and Earthlings have explored part of its surface, still it begs for continued exploration and promises to add vital information to existing knowledge of the planet Earth.

Earth's Natural Satellite

Today we perceive the moon, not as a mysterious light in the sky, but as a natural satellite of the earth, placed in its position and set into motion long ago, by forces and events that are still the objects of many unanswered questions and a great deal of study. Some people prefer to think of the earth and moon as being more of a dual-planet system than a planet and its satellite, because most moons in the solar system are much smaller with respect to their mother planet. We will take the conventional position of the moon as a natural satellite of the earth.

Direction and Distance

The moon orbits the earth in a counterclockwise direction, in a somewhat elliptical path and at a speed of about 3,500 kilometers (2,200 miles) per hour. Its distance from the earth ranges from about 350,000 kilometers (220,000 miles) to 400,000 kilometers (250,000 miles), the average distance being about 384,000 kilometers (240,000 miles). About thirty Earth-sized planets could fit bumper-to-bumper between the earth and the moon.

Gravity Pulls Both Ways

The moon is held in its elliptical orbit by the gravitational attraction between the earth and the moon. Although the earth exerts a much greater gravitational force than does the moon, the attraction between these two bodies pulls on the earth with the same force that it pulls on the moon. For a comparison of this effect, think of a 300-pound person and a 50-pound person at opposite ends of a rope. If each person pulls on the rope with 50 pounds of force, the smaller person will be pulled toward the larger person while the larger person moves very little, even though the same amount of force is being applied to both. Similarly, the distortion of the earth's orbit due to the moon's gravitational pull is relatively slight.

Second Brightest Object

Because it is so close to the earth, the moon is the second brightest object in the sky. Yet the moon does not produce light; the light we see from it is sunlight that is reflected by the moon's surface. It outshines the stars only because it is so close and they are so far away.

Lunar Month

The time needed for the moon to travel once around the earth in its orbit is its period of revolution, which is called a *lunar month.* Actually it takes the moon about twenty-seven and one-third days to circle the earth once (relative to the stars), but because the earth is not standing still, but is revolving around the sun in the same direction (counterclockwise), the moon takes a little longer (twenty-nine and a half days) to get back to the same position relative to the earth and sun (see Figure 23-1).

Figure 23-1

Since the earth is moving in its orbit, the moon must travel more than 360 degrees around the earth to complete its cycle of phases.

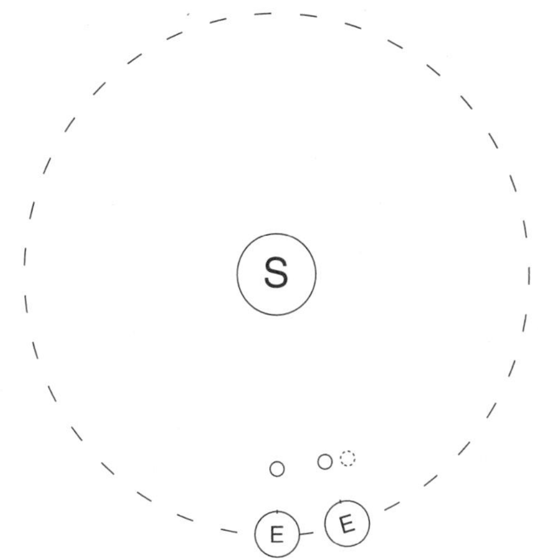

Calendars use twenty-nine and a half days as the time for one lunar month, because that is the period of time from one full moon to the next. Also, because the earth rotates in the same direction as the moon moves in its orbit (counterclockwise), the moon rises and sets about fifty minutes later each day.

We See Only One Side

The moon's period of rotation is equal to its period of revolution, so we see only one side of the moon. Explorations have shown that the other side of the moon looks much the same as the side that faces the earth. Since its period of rotation is approximately four weeks, any given point on the moon has about two weeks of daylight, followed by about two weeks of darkness.

Why It Rises and Sets

Because the earth makes one complete rotation each day in a counterclockwise direction, the moon appears to travel around the earth every day, rising in the east, moving across the sky, and setting in the west. Actually, if the earth suddenly stopped rotating, the moon would continue to rise and set, but it would happen on a four-week cycle instead of daily, and the moon would rise in the west and set in the east, due to its counterclockwise orbital movement.

Looks as Big as the Sun

The moon looks bigger when it is near the horizon, as it rises and sets, because it is seen against a background of buildings, trees, mountains, and other objects. Because it is relatively near, the moon appears to us to be as large as the sun and much larger than any other star. Our sun, which is a medium-sized star, is actually millions of times larger than the moon. Similarly, many stars are much larger than our sun; but because of their great distance, they appear to be only tiny points of light.

Changes Colors

The moon often appears yellow, or even orange, when it is near the horizon. This is because red light rays pass through the earth's atmosphere more easily than do blue light rays. Light rays reflected from the moon must travel through more atmosphere to reach our eyes when the moon is low on the horizon than when it is overhead. Blue light rays are scattered by the thicker atmosphere more than are light rays of other colors. Thus the light reaching our eyes has less blue in it, allowing yellow and orange to dominate.

Lunar Phases

The side of the moon that faces the sun is brightly lighted. The side away from the sun is in the darkness of the moon's own shadow (see Figure 23-2). As the moon travels around the earth, we see differing amounts of the moon's lighted surface. We do not see the moon's shadowed part except when it is slightly lit up by light reflected from the earth, called "earthlight." The varying portions of the moon's lighted surface that we can see are called the moon's phases (see Figure 23-3). During the twenty-nine-and-a-half day lunar month, the moon passes from full moon, through all of its phases, and back to full moon again.

When the moon is approximately between the earth and the sun, its shadowed side is turned toward the earth and we cannot see the moon at all. This is called the new moon. The new moon rises at sunrise and sets at sunset.

The waxing moon

A day or two later, as the moon continues in its orbit around the earth, a small amount of the lighted side of the moon becomes visible from Earth. The part of the moon that can then be seen is shaped like a thin crescent, and is called a crescent moon. The rest of the moon, which is in the moon's own shadow, can sometimes be seen faintly because of earthlight. The "horns" of the crescent point away from the sun. The waxing crescent moon is seen in the west shortly after sunset.

About a week after the new moon, one-half of the lighted side of the moon is visible from the earth. This is called the first quarter. The first quarter moon rises in the east at noon and sets in the west at midnight. A few days later, most of the moon's lighted side can be seen from the earth. This phase is called the *gibbous* moon. The full range between quarter and full is called gibbous.

Figure 23-2

Half of the moon is always lighted. The other half is in the moon's own shadow.

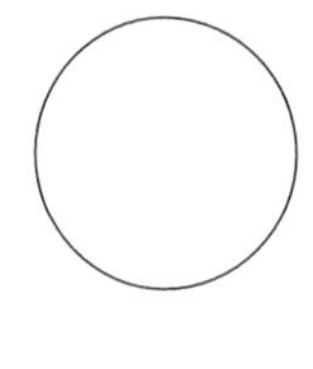

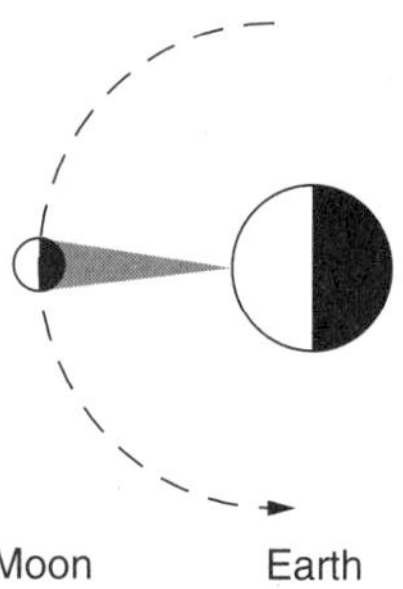

Figure 23-3 *Different portions of the moon's lighted surface are visible from Earth as the moon progresses around the earth, resulting in the moon's phases.*

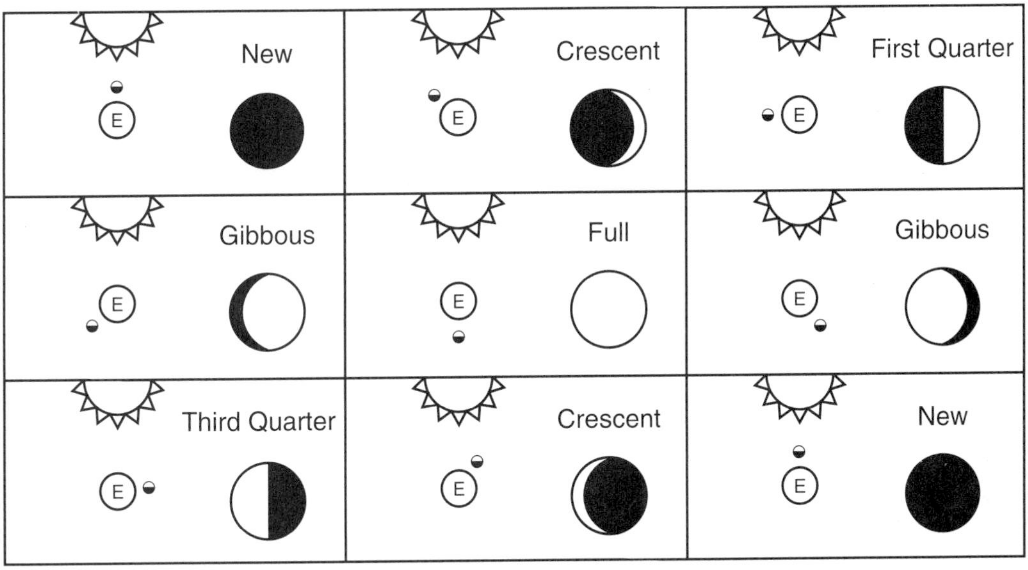

New (E)	Crescent (E)	First Quarter (E)
Gibbous (E)	Full (E)	Gibbous (E)
Third Quarter (E)	Crescent (E)	New (E)

Two weeks after the new moon, the entire lighted side of the moon is visible from the earth. This phase is called the full moon. At that time, the earth is approximately between the moon and the sun. The full moon rises at sunset and sets at sunrise. At this phase, a lunar eclipse is possible, but occurs only occasionally.

The waning moon

One or two days after the full moon, the amount of the lighted side we can see grows visibly smaller, and once again we see a gibbous moon. A week after the full moon, only one-half of the moon's lighted side is visible from the earth. This phase is called the third quarter, or last quarter. The moon in the last quarter rises at midnight and sets at noon.

After the last quarter the portion of the moon that we see grows smaller and is soon shaped like a crescent again. About one week after the last quarter, the moon has completed one revolution around the earth since the last new moon, and it is again in the new moon phase; it cannot be seen from the earth because the lighted half is turned away from the earth, and the cycle begins again. At the new moon phase a solar eclipse is possible, but rarely occurs.

The moon continues to repeat the cycle of phases, as it has for eons, making journey after journey around the earth, always keeping the same side toward its mother planet Earth, almost as though it dare not turn its back.

Nature of the Moon

The moon is a very large ball of rock, approximately 3,500 kilometers (2,150 miles) in diameter, or about one-fourth the diameter of the earth. It is about one-fiftieth the volume of the earth, and its mass is about one-eightieth of that of its mother planet. Gravity on the moon is about one-sixth that of the earth. A broad jumper who can jump 7 meters (23 feet) on the earth could jump 42 meters (138 feet) on the moon. A high jumper who can jump 2 meters

(6.5 feet) on the earth could jump 12 meters (39 feet) on the moon, and land with about the same impact.

The moon has no atmosphere (actually trace amounts of no significance) and no wind, no water, and no water vapor. There are no rivers, oceans, rain, snow, or clouds. Temperatures on the moon are much more extreme than are those on the earth, as high as 127 degrees Celsius (261 degrees Fahrenheit) during the day, and as low as -173 degrees Celsius (-279 degrees Fahrenheit) at night. Lunar landings are made at times and locations that avoid the most extreme temperatures. Notice the length of the shadows in the photograph (Figure 23-4), indicating that the sun is low in the sky. An additional benefit to this planning is that the shadows provide visual contrast. Without the shadows, surface features are difficult to distinguish. The timing of lunar observations from Earth is also important for the same reason; surface features are much more easily seen at the time of a quarter moon than at the time of a full moon, due to contrast provided by shadows of mountains, crater walls, and other irregular surface features.

The lunar surface has many smooth plains, jagged mountains, and craters. The plains appear dark from the earth because they reflect less light than do the mountains. Early astronomers thought the dark areas were seas and the light areas were continents, and thus they were identified by those early scientists, and the names are still used. Some of the mountains are more than 7,500 meters (25,000 feet) high—nearly as tall as Mt. Everest. They are very jagged because there is no wind or water to wear them down. Over 30,000 craters exist on the moon's surface, the largest being about 240 kilometers (150 miles) across. Most of these craters are thought to be the result of meteorites striking the moon's surface.

Eclipses

As the sun shines on the earth and the moon, long shadows are cast into space. Each shadow is cone-shaped and has two parts, like a cone within a larger cone. The inner cone-shaped shadow is completely dark and is called the umbra. The umbra's widest part is at the object that casts the shadow, and it tapers down to a point in space. The larger, semi-dark outer cone is called the penumbra. The object casting the shadow is at the point of the penumbral cone, and this cone becomes larger as it projects out

Figure 23-4

Neil Armstrong and Edwin Aldrin on the moon.

NASA photograph

through space. The sun's light is only partially blocked in the area of the penumbra (see Figure 23-5).

The moon's orbital plane around the earth is tilted about 5 degrees from the earth's plane of orbit around the sun. Therefore the moon and the earth are usually a little above or below each other's shadow as the moon circles the earth. At such times no eclipse occurs, as neither the moon nor the earth is within the shadow of the other.

Lunar eclipse

Earth's umbra is about 1,400,000 kilometers (866,000 miles) long, far beyond the distance to the moon. Occasionally, the earth passes directly between the sun and the moon, in such a way that the moon is within the earth's umbral shadow. This phenomenon is called an eclipse of the moon, or a lunar eclipse. If the moon passes directly through the earth's umbra, such that sunlight is completely blocked from the moon by the earth's dark shadow, a total lunar eclipse occurs (see Figure 23-6). This happens only rarely. More frequently, however, the moon passes partially through the earth's umbra, resulting in a partial lunar eclipse. A lunar eclipse can occur only at the full-moon phase, since that is the phase of the moon when the earth is between the sun and the moon.

Maps that illustrate lunar eclipses visible from North and South America from November 29, 1993 through December 21, 2010 are provided in Appendix M. Other lunar eclipses occur during these years, visible from various parts of the world. Information for these maps was taken from NASA Publication 1216 (see Espenak, 1989).

Figure 23-5 *In this diagram the sun and an unidentified sphere show the umbra and penumbra.*

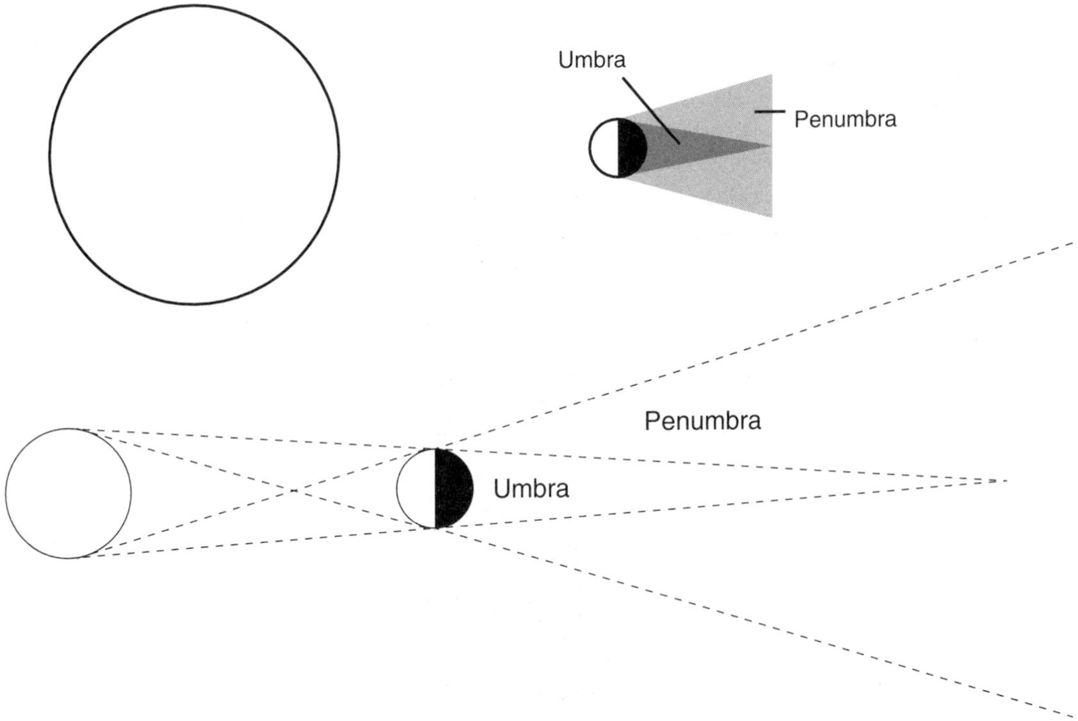

Umbra

Penumbra

Penumbra

Umbra

Figure 23-6

Occasionally, the moon passes within the earth's shadow, resulting in a lunar eclipse.

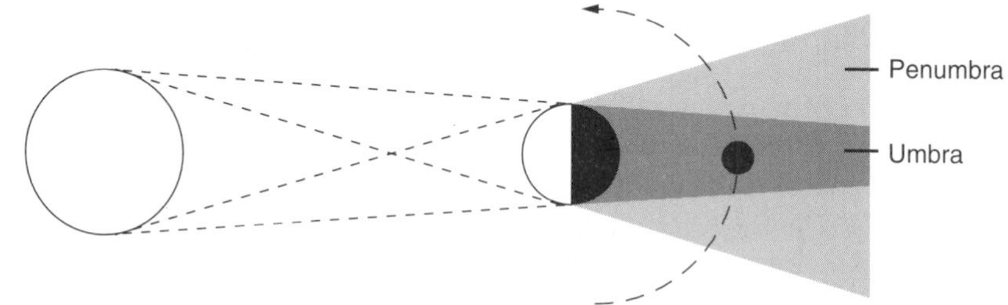

Solar eclipse

The moon's umbra is about 384,000 kilometers (240,000 miles) long, which is the approximate average distance between the earth and the moon. On rare occasions, the moon passes between the earth and the sun in such a way that the moon's umbral shadow reaches the earth. At the moon's perigee (the point in its orbit that is closest to the earth), the tip of the umbra covers a very small part of the earth's surface (usually in the range of a few hundred kilometers), darkening that part of the earth in a total solar eclipse, which lasts a maximum of about eight minutes at any given point on the earth. If the moon is near apogee (the point in its orbit that is farthest from the earth), the moon's umbra may not reach the earth's surface at all, even if the moon is directly between the earth and the sun. A solar eclipse can occur only at the new moon phase (see Figure 23-7).

The moon's penumbra covers a much larger part of the earth's surface. At locations on the earth that are inside the moon's penumbra, the sun is partially blocked by the moon. We call this a partial solar eclipse.

During a total solar eclipse, the sun's *corona* (outer atmosphere) can be seen outlining the moon. We should *never* look directly at the sun. Even during a total solar eclipse, the eyes can be seriously damaged. Methods of safely observing a solar eclipse are described in the activities at the end of this chapter. Sunglasses **do not** provide sufficient protection for observing the sun at any time, including during a solar eclipse.

At the time of a total solar eclipse, the moon's umbral shadow crosses the earth in a narrow path. Along this path, darkness is experienced briefly during daylight hours. Figure 23-8 shows the path of the total solar eclipse of July 11, 1991. The path of the total solar eclipse passed through part of the Hawaiian Islands, and Hawaii had great publicity as a viewing location for the eclipse because of its popularity as a tourist attraction. But, as you can see from the map, the path crossed the ocean, the tip of the Baja Peninsula, through much of

Figure 23-7

The moon rarely casts its shadow on the earth. When it does, the shaded part of the earth experiences a solar eclipse.

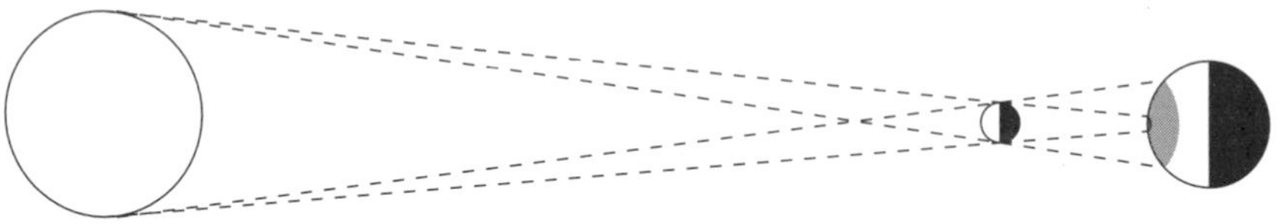

Figure 23-8

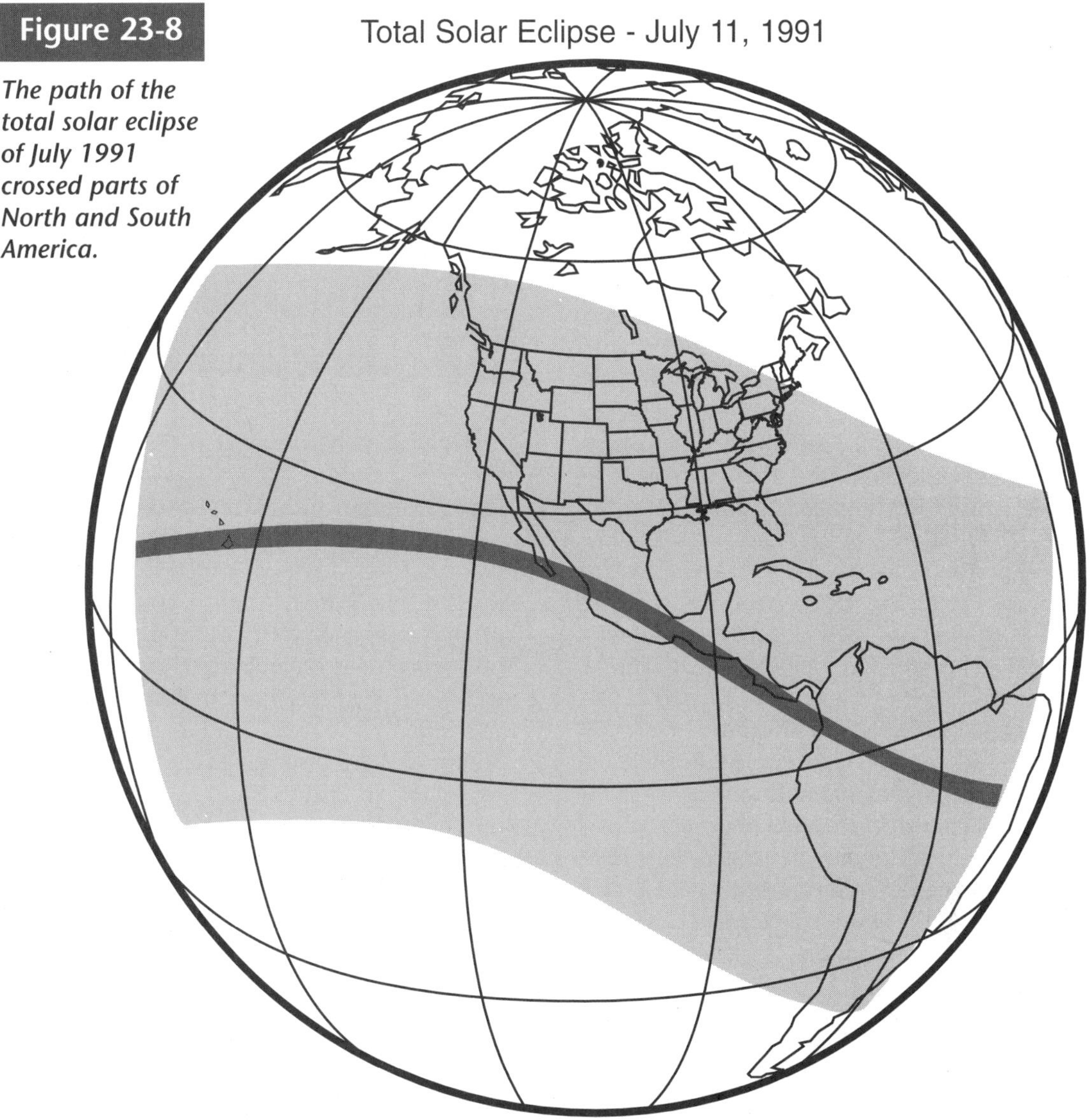

The path of the total solar eclipse of July 1991 crossed parts of North and South America.

Mexico, and across the northern part of South America. The total solar eclipse was experienced by anyone who was along that path at the time.

Maps that illustrate some of the more spectacular solar eclipses visible from North and South America from May 10, 1994, through April 8, 2024, are provided in Appendix M. Other solar eclipses occur during these years, visible from different parts of the world. Information for these maps was taken from NASA Publication 1278 (see Espenak, 1987).

The Moon's Effect on the Tides

The moon's gravitational pull on the earth is evidenced by the tides—the rise and fall of the oceans twice each day. The moon's strongest pull is at the near side of the earth, and its weakest attraction is at the far side of the earth. The earth's waters bulge slightly, producing a high tide at both of these points, as the earth turns on its axis. On the moon's side of the earth, the tide is called a *direct tide,* and at the opposite side of the earth it is called an *indirect tide.* At points on the earth halfway between the direct and indirect tides, the waters recede slightly, forming low tides. This effect results in two high tides and two low tides each day, at any given point on the earth. Since the moon is constantly moving in its orbit around the earth, in the same direction as the earth rotates on its axis (counterclockwise), the tides come and go about fifty minutes later each day.

The gravitational pull of the sun also produces tides on the earth. While these tides are less prominent than those produced by the moon's gravitation, their effect is still significant. When the sun and moon are at 90 degrees from each other, with respect to the earth, the sun has the effect of diminishing the tides caused by the moon. This occurs at the first and third quarter phases of the moon, and these less-prominent tides are called *neap tides.* When the earth, sun, and moon are in line with each other, however, as occurs at both new moon and full moon, the effect is accentuated and the tides are more prominent. These are called *spring tides.*

Tides are also affected by the moon's eliptical orbit. At the moon's perigee (closest to the earth), the tides are usually higher and lower than when the moon is at its apogee (farthest from the earth).

The amount of rise and fall of water level, as tides come and go, is also affected by the shoreline, ocean floor, and depth of the water. In the open sea, the tides typically rise only about one meter (3 feet). At the shorelines, water might rise from 3 meters (10 feet) to 15 meters (50 feet) at different points around the globe.

Both the atmosphere around the earth and the land-covered areas on the earth's surface respond to the gravitational pull of the sun and the moon, as well. Neither of these gets very much attention, however, because though detected by scientists, they are not noticed by the general public. Although the atmospheric tide is quite pronounced, there is no noticeable change in the atmosphere at the earth's surface. The land tide is so slight that it also goes unnoticed.

III. EARTH AS A PLANET

You say you don't travel very much? Well, my friend, fasten your seatbelt and hang on tight, because you are riding on a huge space ship, traveling at mind-boggling speeds. Did you know that you make a complete trip around the earth every day? Even if you do nothing but lie in bed and watch TV, you are traveling hundreds of miles each hour (about 1,000 miles per hour if you live near the equator) as the earth spins on its axis. And at the same time you are moving through space fast enough to travel clear around the sun every year of your life! That's more than half a billion miles in a single year—over 66,000 miles per hour—and all this time you thought you weren't really going anywhere. In addition to that, the sun and all the planets are moving within the Milky Way Galaxy, and the galaxy itself is hurling through space at phenomenal speeds. Wow—you can get dizzy just thinking about it! We don't notice these movements because motion is relative, and everything on the earth is moving with us—the buildings, the trees, the mountains, everything—so we don't realize we are moving at all.

Measurement of Time on Earth

Throughout history humans have devised measurements to aid communication. Just as distances and weights are measured, so is time. Otherwise we would have no use for calendars, clocks, or even sundials. Efforts to communicate about some past or upcoming event would be very frustrating without ways to measure time.

Day and night

Earth spins like a top, or rotates, counterclockwise (from west to east) around an imaginary line called an axis, which runs through the north and south poles of the earth. The time needed to make one complete rotation is called the earth's day, or period of rotation. Each day is divided into twenty-four equal segments, called hours, for our convenience in keeping track of time.

As the earth rotates from west to east, the sun appears to rise in the east, travel across the sky, and set in the west. At any given time, one side of the earth is in daylight, as it faces the sun, and the opposite side is in darkness, as it passes through its own shadow. Each part of the earth passes through one period of daylight and one period of darkness during any twenty-four-hour day; that is, of course, with the exception that at the poles constant daylight or constant darkness occur at certain times of the year.

Year

The earth travels around the sun, or revolves, in a counterclockwise direction. It takes the earth 365 1/4 days to make one complete revolution. This is called the earth's year, or period of revolution.

Seasons

The earth's axis is tilted 23.5 degrees, and always points toward a point near Polaris, or the North Star. Therefore, as the earth revolves around the sun, the northern hemisphere is sometimes tilted toward the sun, sometimes tilted away from the sun, and sometimes is neither tilted toward nor away from the sun. When the northern hemisphere is tilted toward the sun, it gets more direct rays from the sun and has more hours of daylight during each twenty-four-hour period. During this period the northern hemisphere is warmer, and we call it the summer season. When the northern hemisphere is tilted away from the sun, the rays from the sun are more slanted and that hemisphere has fewer hours of daylight (see Figure 23-9). The northern hemisphere is thus colder, and we call it the winter season. When the northern hemisphere has winter the southern hemisphere has summer, and when the

Figure 23-9 ***This diagram shows the sun centered with Earth in its June and December positions.***

Summer for
Northern Hemisphere

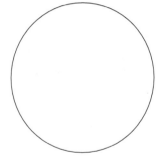

Winter for
Northern Hemisphere

northern hemisphere has summer the southern hemisphere has winter. In the spring and fall the northern hemisphere is neither tilted toward nor away from the sun, and temperatures are more mild than in either summer or winter (see Figure 23-10).

IV. THE SOLAR SYSTEM

The major members of the solar system are the sun and a group of nine planets that move around the sun. Moons of the planets are also part of the solar system, however, as are comets and asteroids. Any heavenly body that orbits another heavenly body is called a satellite. The principle satellites of the sun are the nine planets.

The word *planet* means "wanderer." The planets were given this name because to early astronomers they appeared to wander around the sky, instead of remaining in a fixed position as the stars appear to do.

Most of the planets have smaller satellites, called moons, that revolve around them. Earth has one moon. Some planets have several moons.

Relative Positions of the Planets

The names of the planets, in order of increasing distance from the sun, are Mercury, Venus, Earth, Mars, Jupiter, Saturn, Uranus, Neptune, and Pluto. Various mnemonics have been used to assist people in learning these names in order. One of them is *My Very Educated Mother Just Served Us Nine Pizzas.* Another is *Mary Valentine Eats Moldy Jello,* followed by the word *SUN* (to represent *S*aturn, *U*ranus, and *N*eptune) and remembering that Pluto is farthest away from the sun. Perhaps you can think of one you like better.

Although Pluto is the farthest planet from the sun most of the time, right now and for several years to come Neptune is farther away from the sun than is Pluto. This is because the orbits of Neptune and Pluto cross each other (see Figure 23-11). However, this condition only exists for a small portion of Pluto's orbital period, so Pluto is still considered to be the planet farthest from the sun.

Differences Between Stars and Planets

Stars shine because they produce light, while planets shine because they reflect sunlight. Planets are much smaller than the sun or other stars. Stars (other than our sun) are much farther away from the earth than are the planets.

Figure 23-10 *This diagram shows the Earth in its March and September positions.*

Figure 23-11 *A part of Pluto's orbit overlaps that of Neptune.*

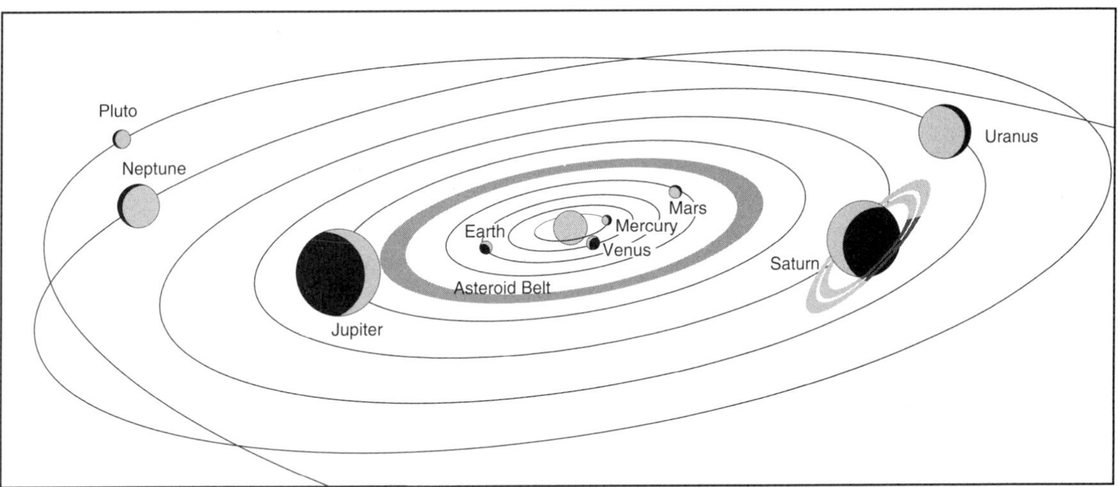

Motions of the Planets

All nine planets revolve around the sun in a counterclockwise (west to east) direction. The time needed for a planet to make one complete trip around the sun, or the period of revolution, is called the planet's year.

The planets rotate, or spin like a top, as they travel around the sun. They rotate around an imaginary line, called an axis, which runs through the north and south poles of the planet. The time needed for a planet to make one complete rotation on its axis, or period of rotation, is called the planet's day.

Nature of the Planets

The planets differ greatly in size, mass, distance from the sun, temperature, and other characteristics. See Figure 23-12 for characteristics of the members of the solar system.

Gravity and Planetary Orbits

Each planet is kept in orbit around the sun by a balance between inertia and the force of gravity. According to Newton's law of gravity, every body in the universe has a gravitational attraction for every other body. The heavier a body, the greater is its gravitational pull. The planets pull against the sun as the sun pulls against the planets. The sun is so much more massive than any of the planets, however, that the resultant movement of the sun is relatively slight.

The planets remain in orbit instead of being pulled into the sun because of inertia. Inertia is not a force; it is the tendency of a body in motion to continue moving in the same direction and at the same speed unless some force causes it to change direction or speed (Newton's first law of motion). The planets are moving at tremendous speed, with nothing to slow them down. Due to their forward motion and the gravitational attraction between them and the sun, the planets remain in orbit around the

Figure 23-12

This solar system fact sheet was produced by Hansen Planetarium, in Salt Lake City, Utah, with data provided by NASA/Ames and NASA/JPL.

The known satellites of the Solar System shown here next to their planets with their sizes (in kilometers.) The satellites are depicted in approximately relative sizes and are arranged in order by their distance from the planet with the closest at the top.

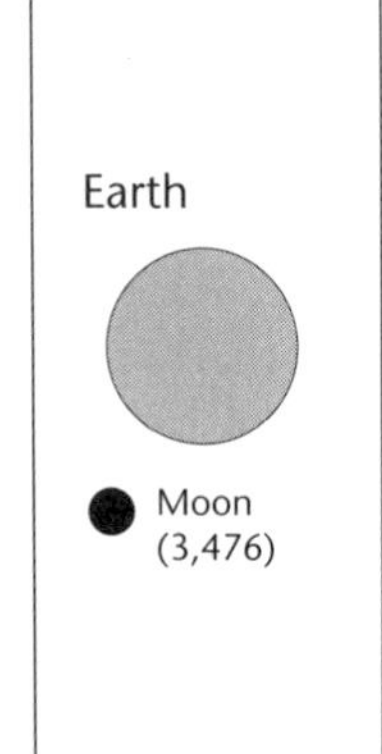

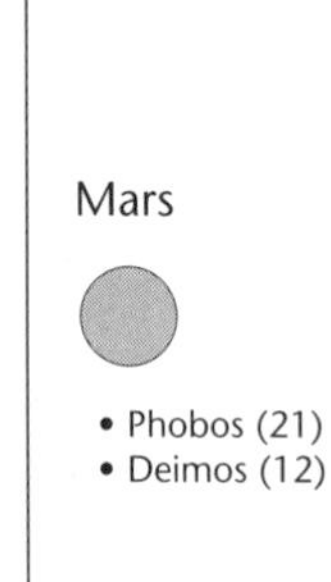

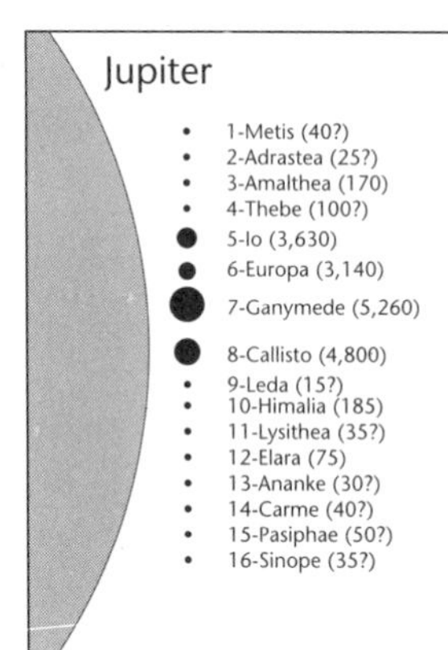

		Mercury	Venus	Earth	Moon	Mars
Average Distance from Sun	Kilometers (in millions)	57.9	108.2	149.6	0.3844 from Earth	227.9
	Light Travel Time	3^m13^s	6^m1^s	8^m19^s	1.3^s from Earth	12^m40^s
	Astronomical Units	0.387	0.723	1.0	0.0026 from Earth	1.523
Length of Year	(Period of Orbit)	87.97d	224.7d	365.26d	27.32d to orbit Earth	1.88y
Length of Day	(Period of Rotation)	$58^d15^h36^m$	$243^d0^h14^m$R	$23^h56^m04^s$	$27^d7^h43^m$	$24^h37^m48^s$
		y=years	d=days	m=minutes	s=seconds	
Average Orbital Velocity	Kilometers per second	47.89	35.03	29.79	1.023	24.13
	Kilometers per hour	172,404	126,108	107,244	3,683	86,868
Equatorial Diameter	Kilometers	4,878	12,102	12,756	3,476	6,786
	Sun=1	0.0035	0.0087	0.0092	0.0025	0.0049
	Earth=1	0.382	0.949	1.0	0.2725	0.532
Mass	Earth=1	0.055	0.815	1.0	0.012	0.107
Volume	Earth=1	0.056	0.857	1.0	0.02	0.15
Mean Density	Grams per cubic centimeter Water=1	5.43	5.25	5.52	3.34	3.95
Surface Gravity	Earth=1	0.38	0.91	1.0	0.17	0.38
Escape Velocity	Kilometers per second	4.3	10.4	11.2	2.38	5.0
	Kilometers per hour	15,480	37,440	40,320	8,568	18,000
Temperature Extremes	High °C	425	462	58	127	17
	High °K	698	735	331	400	290
	Low °C	-173	462	-88	-173	-143
	Low °K	100	735	185	100	130
	*Core	**At 1 atmosphere (altitude where barometric pressure equals Earth's barometric pressure at sea level—1.013				
Atmosphere	Principal Gases	Na	CO_2	N_2O_2	none	CO_2
# of Known Satellites		0	0	1	0	2
Eccentricity of Orbit	Circular Orbit=0	0.206	0.007	0.017	0.055	0.093
Inclination of Equator	To Planet's Orbital Plane	2.0°	177.3°	23.45°	6.68°	23.98°
Oblateness of Planet	Spherical Planet=0	0.	0.	0.003	0.002	0.006

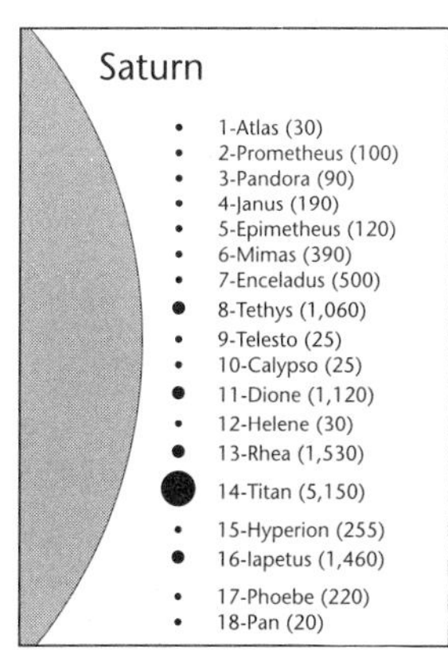

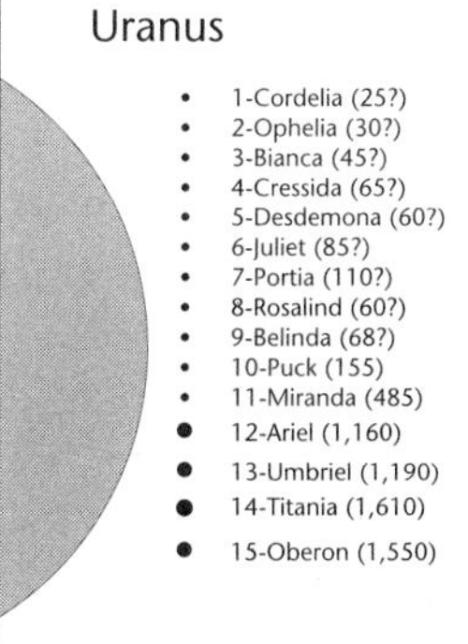

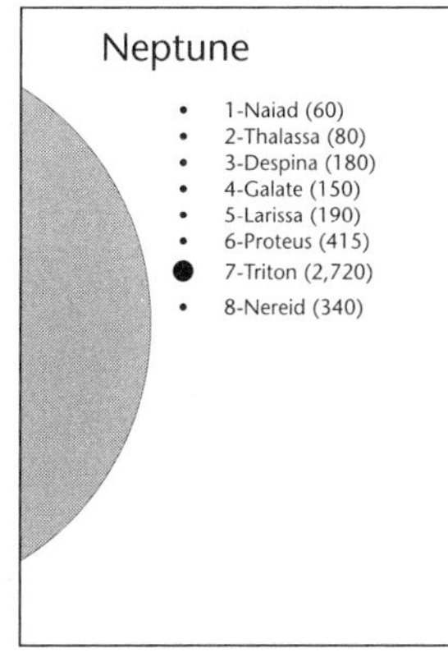

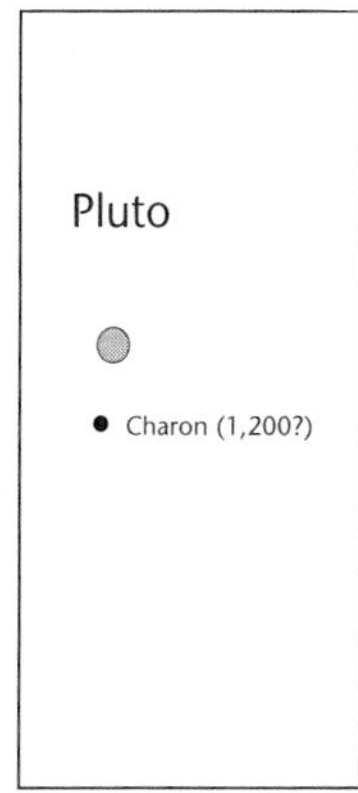

Jupiter	Saturn	Uranus	Neptune	Pluto	Sun
778.3	1,427	2,870	4,504	5,900	41 trillion to nearest star
43^m17^s	$1^h19^m21^s$	$2^h39^m35^s$	$4^h10^m24^s$	$5^h28^m4^s$	4.3y to nearest star
5.203	9.539	19.184	30.107	39.47	275,000 to nearest star
11.86y	29.45y	84.01y	164.79y	247.99y	220 million y to orbit galaxy
$9^h55^m30^s$	$10^h39^m22^s$	17^h14^mR	16^h7^m	$6^d9^h18^m$	25–35d+
R=Retrograde		+=Depending on latitude		?=Exact value not known	
13.06	9.64	6.81	5.43	4.7	250 around center of galaxy
47,016	34,704	24,516	19,548	16,920	900,000 around center of galaxy
142,984**	120,536**	51,118**	49,528**	2,300	1,392,000
0.1027**	0.0866**	0.0367**	0.0356**	0.0017	1.0
11.209**	9.449**	4.007**	3.883**	0.18	109
317.892	95.184	14.536	17.148	0.003	332,946
1,321.30	763.6	63.1	57.7	0.006	1,300,000
1.33	0.69	1.27	1.64	2.03	1.41
2.53	1.07	0.91	1.14	0.077	27.9
59.6	35.5	21.3	24.7	1.32	617.5
214,560	127,800	76,800	88,750	4,752	2,223,000
20,000*	12,000*	6,000*	6,000*	-218	15,000,000*
20,000*	12,000*	6,000*	6,000*	55	15,000,000*
438**	407**	346**	347**	-228	4,000**
711**	680**	619**	620**	45	4,000**
H_2He	H_2He	H_2He	H_2He	CH_4?	H_2He
16? plus rings	18? plus rings	15? plus rings	8? plus rings	1	9 planets
0.049	0.056	0.047	0.009	0.249	—
3.08°	26.73°	97.92°	28.8°	118.0°	7.25° Sun's equator to ecliptic
0.065	0.098	0.024	0.017	0?	0

sun. If the planets were not moving forward they would be pulled into the sun and would be consumed by it. Without gravity, on the other hand, the planets would move out into space away from the sun.

Asteroids, Comets, and Meteors

In addition to the sun and the planets, our solar system includes asteroids, comets, and meteors.

Asteroids

The asteroids are objects that revolve around the sun in a belt between the orbits of Mars and Jupiter. There are thousands of them; some are several hundred miles in diameter and are sometimes referred to as minor planets. They are smaller than any of the planets. Scientists think that craters on the moon and on Mars, and perhaps even some on the earth, are the result of collisions with asteroids.

Comets

Comets, made of ice and rock (sometimes referred to as "dirty snowballs"), are also a part of the solar system. They have long, oval-shaped orbits that bring them very close to the sun, then far out into the solar system. When a comet comes near the sun (perhaps within Jupiter's orbit) some of its ice is vaporized by solar energy, and gas and dust are ejected to form the tail of the comet. The tail points away from the sun whether the comet is approaching the sun or receding away from it. Some comets take many, many years to make a single trip around the sun. Halley's Comet is one of the best known comets. Named after a seventeenth-century astronomer, Edmond Halley, who accurately calculated its seventy-six year cycle and predicted its 1758 return, this comet last visited the solar system in 1986 (see Figure 23-13).

Meteors

In addition to the planets, asteroids, and comets, there are also billions of fast-moving objects

Figure 23-13

Th orbit of a comet within the solar system.

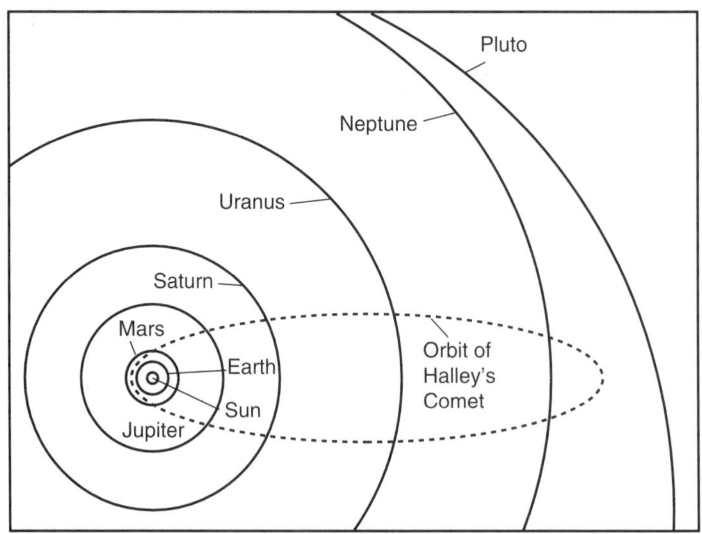

called meteors. Meteors consist of rock and/or iron and vary greatly in size, ranging in mass from less than a gram to many thousand kilograms. Of those that enter the earth's atmosphere, most are burned up by the friction of moving through the atmosphere; some are seen as "falling stars," most of which are about the size of a grain of sand. The few that reach the earth's surface are called meteorites. It is thought that Meteor Crater, near Flagstaff, Arizona, is a result of a collision with a meteorite.

V. ARTIFICIAL SATELLITES

Any heavenly body that revolves around a planet is called a satellite. The moon is a satellite of the earth. The first artificial satellite (made by humans) was *Sputnik I*, launched by the Soviet Union on October 4, 1957. About one month later, *Sputnik II* was launched with a canine passenger—the world's first astronaut! On January 31, 1958, the United States sent up its first satellite, called *Explorer I*. Since that time, many such satellites have been put into orbit around the earth. Some have been of short duration and have had people aboard. Some of those without human occupants are intended to remain in orbit for many years. These satellites serve various purposes; for example they assist in worldwide communications, provide weather information, and help nations to spy on each other.

VI. ROCKETS

Both jet engines and rocket engines burn fuels to produce hot, expanding gases to propel the engine forward, applying Newton's third law of motion—for every action there is an equal and opposite reaction. As the burning fuel is thrust out the back of the engine with great force, an equal force is applied on the engine itself in the opposite direction. As the engine moves forward, it takes with it the airplane or rocket that is attached to it.

The major difference between jet engines and rocket engines is in the source of oxygen. Fuel cannot burn without oxygen. The jet engine uses oxygen from the air, while the rocket engine carries its own supply of oxygen, either in the form of liquid oxygen that is mixed with the fuel as it burns, or as a solid fuel that includes a chemical that contains a ready supply of oxygen. The jet engine is therefore confined to the earth's atmosphere, while the rocket engine, with its own supply of oxygen, is able to operate outside the atmosphere. By attaining sufficient speed to escape the earth's gravitational pull (called *escape velocity*), a rocket can continue out into space. The engines can still be fired to provide the thrust necessary for controlling the rocket's speed and direction.

VII. OUR SUN

The sun looks bigger when it is just rising or setting, as it is seen among buildings, trees, or other objects on the horizon, than it does when it is by itself high in the sky. The sun also looks more orange or reddish when it is near the horizon. When the sun is low in the sky, the light rays must travel through more atmosphere. Red light rays penetrate the atmosphere more easily than do blue light rays. The blue light is scattered and a greater concentration of red light rays reaches our eyes, causing the beautiful orange and red displays we often see at sunrise or sunset. The more brilliant sunsets are also influenced by particulate matter in the atmosphere, such as dust and sand, thus sunsets in the desert areas of the southwestern United States are often spectacular.

The sun is one of billions of stars in the universe. It is a medium-size star, but it looks much larger to us than other stars because it is so much closer to the earth. The sun is about

150 million kilometers (93 million miles) from the earth.

The sun has a diameter of about 1,380,000 kilometers (860,000 miles), about 109 times the diameter of the earth. If the sun were a hollow ball, it would hold more than 1 million Earths.

Source of Energy

The sun is a huge ball of very hot gases. The outer layers of gases are referred to as the sun's atmosphere. These layers are called the chromosphere and the corona, with the corona being the outermost layer. The sun's surface, called the photosphere, is sometimes referred to as the innermost layer of the sun's atmosphere. Like all other stars, the sun gives off vast amounts of energy, including heat and light. The surface is about 6,000 degrees Celsius (10,800 degrees Fahrenheit). Scientists estimate that the center of the sun is about 15 million degrees Celsius (27 million degrees Fahrenheit).

The sun, which is the earth's energy source, has been producing energy for billions of years. It will continue to produce energy for many billions of years yet to come.

Sunspots

Dark spots appear on the surface of the sun, near the sun's equator. These spots look dark because they are somewhat cooler than the surrounding, glowing gases. Sunspots are associated with magnetic storms within the sun, which send out electrified particles. These particles strike the earth's ionosphere and sometimes interfere with radio, TV, and long-distance telephone communications on the earth. These particles also strike the lower atmosphere and produce a brilliant show of colored lights near the north and south poles. These colored lights are called the northern lights (aurora borealis) and the southern lights (aurora australis). Scientists have found that the northern and southern lights are much more active during periods of high solar activity.

VIII. THE UNIVERSE

The actual number of stars is not known, but about 3,000 can be seen from the earth with the naked eye. With the aid of telescopes, we see more and more stars. We now know there are billions of galaxies, each containing billions of stars. Our solar system is in the Milky Way galaxy.

Constellations

Ancient people divided stars into groups, called constellations (see Figure 23-14). Modern astronomers expanded on their work and mapped the entire sky. Each constellation has been given a name, such as Ursa Major (Great Bear), Ursa Minor (Little Bear), Pegasus, Orion, Taurus, and so on. The Big Dipper and the Little Dipper are not really constellations, but are part of Ursa Major and Ursa Minor.

Most constellations do not resemble their name. This is a frustration to many people, and they wonder why the constellation was given the name of something that it does not resemble. The constellations are labeled to make it easier to describe the location of the stars, just like places on the earth are named so people can communicate about them. Buffalo, New York, does not look like a buffalo, but giving the city a name simplifies communication in reference to that city, and knowing it is in the state of New York gives one an immediate approximation of its location on this planet.

Because the earth travels around the sun, different constellations are seen at different times of the year. Also, different constellations are seen from the northern hemisphere than are seen from the southern hemisphere.

Figure 23-14

This diagram shows Orion and other well-known constellations, as seen from the northern hemisphere in December.

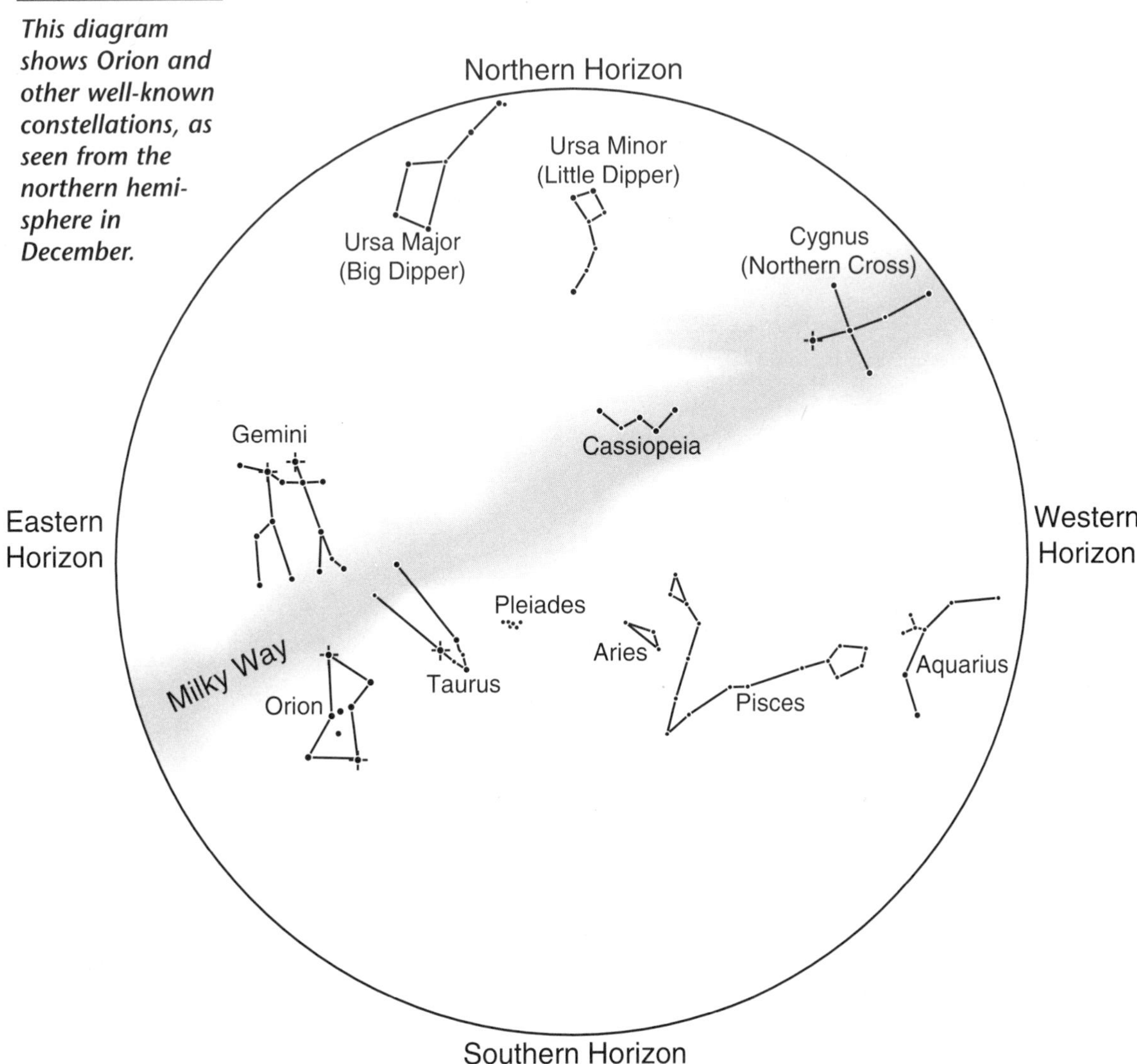

IX. IN CLOSING

Space exploration has beckoned humankind throughout history, and it will surely continue to capture the curiosities of most people and the energies of many. Even with all of our advances in space exploration, future generations will no doubt look back on our era as a time of scientific infants, plodding along with crude instruments and inefficient equipment. Progress comes slowly, and we must build our knowledge concept upon concept, with each new insight pointing the way to steps for acquiring the next.

LIST OF RESOURCES

Branley, Franklyn M., *Mysteries of the Planets* (New York: Lodestar Books, 1988).

Espenak, Fred, *Fifty Year Canon of Lunar Eclipses: 1986–2035* (Greenbelt, MD: NASA, Goddard Space Flight Center, 1989. NASA Reference Publication 1216 Revised March 1989. Contact NASA, Washington, D.C.).

Espenak, Fred, *Fifty Year Canon of Solar Eclipses: 1986–2035* (Greenbelt, MD: NASA, 1987. NASA Reference Publication 1178 Revised July 1987. Contact NASA, Washington, D.C.).

Gallant, Roy A., *National Geographic Picture Atlas of Our Universe* (Washington, D.C.: National Geographic Society, 1986).

Mayall, R. Newton, *et al.*, *The Sky Observer's Guide* (New York: Golden Press, 1985).

National Geographic (December 1969. Feature issue on the first lunar landing). (Washington, D.C.: National Geographic Society).

The Royal Astronomical Society of Canada, *Observer's Handbook, 1991* (Toronto, Ontario: University of Toronto Press, 1990).

Tolman, Marvin N., and James O. Morton, *Earth Science Activities for Grades 2–8* (West Nyack, NY: Parker Publishing Co., 1986).

CHAPTER

BEYOND THE EARTH

ACTIVITIES

II. THE MOON

ACTIVITY 23-1: DOES THE MOON COME UP EARLIER EACH DAY, OR LATER?

Materials Needed:

Paper and pencil

Procedure:

1. At the next full moon, write down the time when the moon first appears at the eastern horizon. Then write it down again the next day, and the next.
2. Does the moon come up earlier each day, or later? How much difference is there from day to day?
3. Using your moonrise times from three days in a row, predict the time the moon will rise on the fourth day. Check and see if you were right.
4. What do you think might cause these changes in the moonrise time? Discuss your ideas with your group.

For Problem Solvers:

Get an Earth globe and two balls—a large one to represent the sun and a small one to represent the moon. Using these, demonstrate what happens as the full moon comes up. Tape a piece of paper on the Earth globe to represent you on Earth. As you do this, use the information you collected for the above activity, and determine whether the moon revolves around the earth in a clockwise direction or in a counterclockwise direction.

Teacher Information:

In this activity, students will learn that the moon rises about fifty minutes later each day. The "problem solvers" should be able to determine that the moon revolves around the earth in a counterclockwise direction. This means that if you were above the north pole of the earth, looking down, the moon would appear to revolve counterclockwise.

Integrating: Math

Skills: Observing, inferring, using numbers, predicting, formulating hypotheses

ACTIVITY 23-2:
HOW CAN WE ROLE-PLAY THE MOVEMENTS OF THE EARTH AND MOON?

Materials Needed:

Three students

Procedure:

1. Three students should work together to role-play the movements of the earth and the moon as they together orbit the sun. One person is the earth, one is the moon, and the other is the sun.
2. The sun should stand in a stationary position. The earth should be several feet away from the sun.
3. The earth should walk around the sun in a big circle, showing that the earth revolves around the sun. The earth turns around (rotates) slowly as it revolves slowly around the sun.
4. Now put the moon in orbit around the earth. This person should face the earth constantly as he or she revolves around the earth.
5. Notice that the moon rotates on its axis exactly one time as it revolves once around the earth.
6. Notice also that all sides of the moon face the sun at some time as it moves around the earth.

For Problem Solvers:

This time your challenge as problem solvers is to clear up some misconceptions for other people. Select at least two people who were not involved in the above activity. These can be your friends from another class, members of your family, or anyone else. Do the above activity with them and help them to understand the movements of the earth and the moon. Be sure they understand that the moon always keeps its same side toward the earth and that the moon does not have a dark side.

Are you ready for another challenge? Repeat the above activity with the earth and moon rotating the right number of times as they orbit the sun together, and the earth progressing appropriately in its orbit around the sun.

Teacher Information:

The basic movements of the earth as it rotates on its axis and revolves around the sun seem simple enough to demonstrate and conceptualize, but it took thousands of years for humans to really understand that these movements were occurring as the sun appeared to pass around the earth day after day throughout the year.

This activity is best done in a gymnasium or on the playground, where plenty of space is available. As students role-play the movements of the earth and moon, the "moon" should constantly face the "earth," showing that the moon always has the same side toward the earth. Many people think that the moon does not rotate on its axis and that it has a dark side. These are two common misconceptions that should be more clear from this experience. The moon's period of rotation equals its period of revolution, thus it faces the earth with the same side all the time, but it does rotate on its axis. Students should also note that the "moon's" back and front have equal exposure to the sun, thus the moon does not have a dark side. The fact that the moon has its face, back, and both sides toward the sun at some time during each revolution verifies that the moon does rotate on its axis; while rotating it also revolves around the earth.

For the last problem-solving challenge, students should determine that the earth rotates on its axis twenty-eight times as the moon revolves once around the earth. During this same period of time the earth should progress slightly less than one-twelfth the distance of its orbit around the sun.

Integrating: Physical education

Skills: Observing, communicating, using space-time relationships

ACTIVITY 23-3:
HOW CAN WE WATCH THE MOON PASS THROUGH ITS PHASES?

Materials Needed:

Dim lamp (about 15-watt to 25-watt bulb)

Ball

Dark room

Procedure:

1. Place the lamp on a table or other support so that the bulb slightly higher than eye level for you.
2. Turn the lamp on and turn the room lights off.
3. Hold the ball at arm's length away from the lamp. You should be between the lamp and the ball. Hold the ball high enough that it is not in your shadow.
4. For the rest of this activity, pretend that the ball is the moon and you are the earth.
5. How much of the moon is lighted? How much of the lighted side do you see? Letting the ball represent the moon, you should now see a full moon.
6. Hold the ball at arm's length between you and the lamp.
7. Now how much of the moon is lighted? How much of the lighted side do you see? This is a new moon.
8. From the new moon position, move the "moon" slowly, counterclockwise, and you will see the moon pass through all of its phases. Try to identify the new moon, crescent, quarter, gibbous, full, gibbous, quarter, crescent, and new moon again.
9. Discuss with your group the real reason the moon passes through its phases.

For Problem Solvers:

Notice the next time a full moon comes up over the horizon. Will it be in the east or in the west? Will it happen in the evening, or morning, or what time of day? Think about how the sun, earth, and moon must line up in order for you to see a full moon. At what time of day, then, will the full moon appear on the horizon? Identify the rising and setting time for the new moon, the first quarter, the full moon, and the last quarter.

Use this activity with your family and friends, to help them understand the real reason the moon passes through its phases.

Teacher Information:

Some very common science misconceptions are associated with the phases of the moon. Many people think the moon goes through its phases because of the earth's shadow being cast on the moon. We see the moon in different phases because we see varying portions of the moon's lighted side, according to the relative positions of the earth, moon, and sun at any given time.

This activity provides an effective and inexpensive way to illustrate the cause of the lunar phases, as the moon progresses in its orbit around the earth. Students see the "moon" go through phases in a very real way, and for the same reason the moon really does go through its phases. It's very important that this activity be done in a dark room, in order to have a distinct shadow effect.

Sometimes with this activity, the shadow from the hand holding the ball gets in the way, making it difficult to see clearly the effect of the moon's own shadow. This problem can be avoided by using a Styrofoam ball, spearing the ball with a popsicle stick, and using the stick as a handle.

The problem solvers should determine that the new moon rises at sunrise and sets at sunset. However, we do not see the new moon because at that time the moon is approximately between us and the sun, and the entire shadowed side of the moon is toward the earth. The first quarter moon rises at noon and sets at midnight. The full moon rises at sunset and sets at sunrise. The third quarter rises at midnight and sets at noon. The moon between quarter and full is called *gibbous,* and between new moon and quarter it is called *crescent.*

This activity presents another great opportunity for learning by teaching, as the problem solvers accept the challenge to share their newly acquired insights with others.

Integrating: Social studies

Skills: Observing, inferring, predicting, communicating, using space-time relationships

ACTIVITY 23-4:
HOW CAN WE MAKE OUR OWN LUNAR PHASE CALENDAR?

Materials Needed:

White paper

Yellow construction paper

Pencil

Ruler

Scissors

Procedure:

1. Draw horizontal and vertical lines on the white paper to divide it into five rows and seven columns.
2. Make a calendar out of the paper by numbering the days of the next new month.
3. Next, cut the yellow paper into squares that are a bit smaller than the squares on the calendar.
4. On the first day of the new month, find the moon in the sky and draw its shape on a piece of scratch paper. Then cut one of the yellow squares in the shape of the moon.
5. Paste your moon on the first day of your calendar.
6. Repeat this each day of the month, making a moon for your calendar to match the real moon in the sky.
7. Repeat the entire calendar for a second month and compare the phases with the first month. During the second month, try to predict the phase of the moon one or more days in advance.

Teacher Information:

As students prepare their own lunar calendar, they will acquire insights as to the sequence of lunar phases. As they continue the calendar for a second month, they will recognize a repeating pattern. This will add meaning to their earlier experiences with the moon and its phases.

Integrating: Art

Skills: Observing, inferring, predicting, communicating, using space-time relationships

ACTIVITY 23-5:
WHAT IS AN ECLIPSE?

Materials Needed:

Flashlight or lamp

Ball, about 5 centimeters (2 inches) in diameter

Marble

Table

Procedure:

1. Place the ball on the table.
2. Turn the room lights off.
3. Hold the flashlight about 1 meter (1 yard) away from the ball. Adjust the position of the flashlight to show a clear cone-shaped shadow of the ball across the table top.
4. Place the marble on the table so that it rests just inside the tip of the cone-shaped shadow of the ball. The ball represents the earth and the marble represents the moon.
5. This arrangement illustrates a lunar eclipse; the moon is eclipsed, or blocked from view, by the shadow of the earth. Notice that the moon also has a cone-shaped shadow.
6. Now move the marble halfway around the ball so the cone-shaped shadow of the marble barely touches the ball.
7. This arrangement illustrates a solar eclipse; the sun is eclipsed, or blocked from view, by the moon. As the moon moves in its orbit, the shadow of the moon travels in a path across the earth. Notice that only the people on the earth who are along the path experience the solar eclipse.

For Problem Solvers:

Study from an encyclopedia or other available sources and learn all you can about eclipses, both lunar and solar. Find out how often each type occurs, and when the next will be. Communicate this information to others and help them to be prepared to share the experience with you.

Teacher Information:

In addition to the procedure described above, you might also point out that the cone-shaped shadows have a dark inner part, called the umbra, and a lighter outer part called the penumbra. People who are in the penumbral shadow of the moon during a solar eclipse can see a partial eclipse if they are equipped to view it. Caution students never to look at the sun without proper eye protection. Dark sunglasses *do not* provide adequate protection.

Integrating: Reading

Process Skills: Observing, communicating, researching

ACTIVITY 23-6:
WHAT IS A SAFE WAY TO VIEW A SOLAR ECLIPSE?

Materials:

Card

White paper

Straight pin

Aluminum foil

Tape

Scissors

Procedure:

1. Cut a hole in the card with the scissors.

2. Cut a piece of aluminum foil large enough to cover the hole, and tape the foil over the hole.
3. Make a hole in the foil with the pin.
4. During a solar eclipse, stand with your back to the sun and hold the card in one hand and the paper in the other. Position the card and paper so that sunlight passes through the pinhole in the foil and onto the paper below. The paper is your screen.
5. The spot of light you see on the paper is more than a spot of light—it is an image of the sun. As the moon moves across in front of the sun during a partial solar eclipse, the spot of light will appear to have a bite taken out of it, and the bite will move across the edge of the sun slowly enough to allow plenty of viewing time.

Teacher Information:

Caution students never to look at the sun without proper eye protection. Special glasses are sometimes available at the time of a solar eclipse, with which the eclipse can be safely viewed. If there is a planetarium nearby, ask them about the special glasses. Even if proper eyeware is available for viewing the eclipse, you will want to also give your students the experience described above. Actually, most any small hole that allows sunlight to pass through will show an eclipse on the surface it contacts, whether it shines on the white paper described above, the sidewalk, or whatever. If you ignore the aluminum foil and just make a pinhole in the card, the image will be a bit sharper if a thinner material is used. Have students try a variety of ways to make a small opening for sunlight to pass through during the eclipse, including the card with and without the foil, and a hole punched in a paper with a paper punch. Crossing the fingers of the two hands can produce an array of spots on the sidewalk, each of which will show the eclipse. These are not in sharp focus, but they are distinctly images of the eclipsing sun. Notice the light on the sidewalk where sunlight passes between the leaves of a tree—each spot of light will show the eclipse. Also use a small mirror to reflect sunlight on a wall. Be prepared with a variety of sizes of mirrors to experiment with—some should be as small as 1 centimeter (1/2 inch) in diameter. You can put tape on larger mirrors to provide the effect of small mirrors, rather than cutting the larger mirrors.

Process Skills: Observing, controlling variables, researching

III. EARTH AS A PLANET

ACTIVITY 23-7:

HOW DO THE MOTIONS OF THE EARTH CAUSE DAY AND NIGHT?

Materials Needed:

Earth globe

Dim lamp

Procedure:

1. Place the lamp in the center of the room. The lamp represents the sun for this activity.
2. Holding the Earth globe in your hand, stand three or four meters (yards) from the "sun."
3. Think of a position in space above the north pole, about where you think the North Star would be located. Point the axis of the globe in that direction.

4. As you slowly spin the globe, think of yourself as being on the globe, in your own state or country. Can you visualize yourself experiencing day and night each time the globe rotates once on its axis?
5. Discuss with your group what causes day and night. Take turns explaining it to each other.
6. Also discuss this question, "How would your life be different if the earth did not rotate on its axis?"

For Problem Solvers:

Continue with the activity, thinking of yourself as being at a location on the earth farther north or farther south from your home. How are the days and nights different at that location?

Next, think of yourself as being at the north pole. Continue to spin the globe slowly and consider what the days and nights are like. How are they different from the days and nights at your home? Now move yourself to the south pole and consider the question again.

Move the globe slowly halfway around the sun, keeping the axis pointed toward the north star. Discuss what the days and nights are like from your home, from the north pole, and from the south pole, with the globe in this position.

Teacher Information:

Students should be able to conceptualize that day and night are caused by the rotation of the earth on its axis. Help students to notice that nighttime occurs when we are in the earth's shadow.

If they can really think of themselves as being at the poles with this experience, students will begin to understand that from near the poles the sun never appears to rise high in the sky, and that directly at the poles the sun appears to go around and around just above the horizon or just below the horizon, depending on the time of year, making for very long days and very long nights.

Integrating: Social studies

Skills: Observing, inferring, communicating

IV. THE SOLAR SYSTEM

ACTIVITY 23-8:

HOW CAN WE MAKE A SCALE MODEL OF THE SOLAR SYSTEM?

Materials Needed:

Football field or large playground

At least ten students to work together

A large sign for each planet and one for the sun

Measuring tape

Procedure:

1. Go to a football field, or measure off 100 yards on the school playground.
2. Assign one person to represent each planet, and one person to represent the sun. Each person should take a sign to show what he or she represents.
3. Assign the person representing the sun to stand at one goal line and the person representing Pluto to stand at the 1-yard line on the other end of the field—99 yards from the sun.
4. Those representing the other planets are to stand the following distances from the sun:

Mercury	*1 yard*
Venus	*1.8 yards*
Earth	*2.5 yards*
Mars	*4 yards*
Jupiter	*13 yards*

Saturn *24 yards*
Uranus *48 yards*
Neptune *75 yards*

5. At these distances the sun will be slightly less than one inch in diameter. The diameter of the earth will be about equal to the thickness of two sheets of typing paper, and the diameter of Pluto will be about half the thickness of a sheet of typing paper!

Teacher Information:

Here we are using the football field to illustrate size and distance, in an effort to relate the activity to a familiar distance. Since the standard unit of measure for football fields is the yard, all measurements are given in yards. If using metric units, simply replace "yard" with "meter" in all cases, in which case a slightly longer space will be needed.

Students in the upper grades might enjoy computing their own models to represent the relative sizes and distances of the planets. Here's a convenient scale on which your students can base other models, whether the unit of measure to be used is centimeter, millimeter, inch, marble, BB, and so on. The relative diameters of the sun and the planets are shown below, with the diameter of the earth being one unit. Distances from the sun are shown in astronomical units (AU), which is the distance from the earth to the sun. If distance scale is to correspond to size scale, each AU will need to be about 11,734 diameter units.

	Diameter	*AU*
Sun	*109.0*	
Mercury	*0.38*	*0.39*
Venus	*0.95*	*0.72*
Earth	*1.0*	*1.0*
Moon	*0.27*	*0.0026 (from Earth)*
Mars	*0.53*	*1.52*
Jupiter	*11.27*	*5.20*
Saturn	*9.44*	*9.54*
Uranus	*4.10*	*19.18*
Neptune	*3.88*	*30.06*
Pluto	*0.24*	*39.44*

Using this scale, if you let Pluto be the size of a BB, the sun and the planets would have roughly the following diameters. Approximate distances from the sun at this scale are also given. Note that by reducing Pluto to the size of a BB, the sun is more than six feet in diameter and Pluto is a little more than five miles (91 football fields) from the sun! All distance measures in this example are given in football-field units in order to relate directly to the above activity.

	Diameter	*Distance from the sun*
Sun	*6.4 ft.*	
Mercury	*0.3 in.*	*90 yards*
Venus	*0.7 in.*	*1.7 football fields*
Earth	*0.7 in.*	*2.3 football fields*
Moon	*0.19 in.*	*1.8 feet*
Mars	*0.4 in.*	*3.5 football fields*
Jupiter	*7.9 in.*	*12 football fields*
Saturn	*6.6 in.*	*22 football fields*
Uranus	*2.9 in.*	*44 football fields*
Neptune	*2.7 in.*	*69 football fields*
Pluto	*.17 in. (1 BB)*	*91 football fields*

Integrating: Physical education

Skills: Observing, inferring, measuring, communicating

V. ARTIFICIAL SATELLITES

ACTIVITY 23-9: HOW DO ARTIFICIAL SATELLITES HELP US?

Materials Needed:

Globe of the earth

1-centimeter (1/4-inch) ball of aluminum foil

Bits of gummed paper

Pencil

Procedure:

1. Attach a small piece of gummed paper on the globe to mark the spot where you live and, with the point of your pencil, make a tiny dot on the paper. If your globe is an average size, 30 to 40 centimeters (12 to 16 inches), you, your school, and your community could fit within the tiny dot on the paper. In fact, the dot represents the greatest portion of the earth's surface that can be seen from any given location on the earth. Can you think of ways to help you see a greater distance?
2. Since television, radio, and other communication signals travel in a straight line, they can travel only short distances without being relayed (passed on) in some way. Hold the aluminum foil ball above the spot you marked on your globe. Have someone slowly turn the globe while you keep the foil ball directly above the mark. Notice that the foil ball is moving at a speed that matches the rotation of the earth. This is the way communication satellites work. If you were very small, standing at the marked point, would the foil ball appear to be moving? Why? Look at Figure 23A-1. With the ball acting as a reflector, television signals could be sent to you from a great distance away, in the same way that a mirror reflects light.
3. Look at Figure 23A-2. The orbit of this satellite is elliptical. At one point, the satellite comes very near the earth. This is called the *perigee.* The greatest distance a satellite moves away from a par-

Figure 23A-1 *This communication satellite, in orbit around the earth, enables television signals to be sent from great distances.*

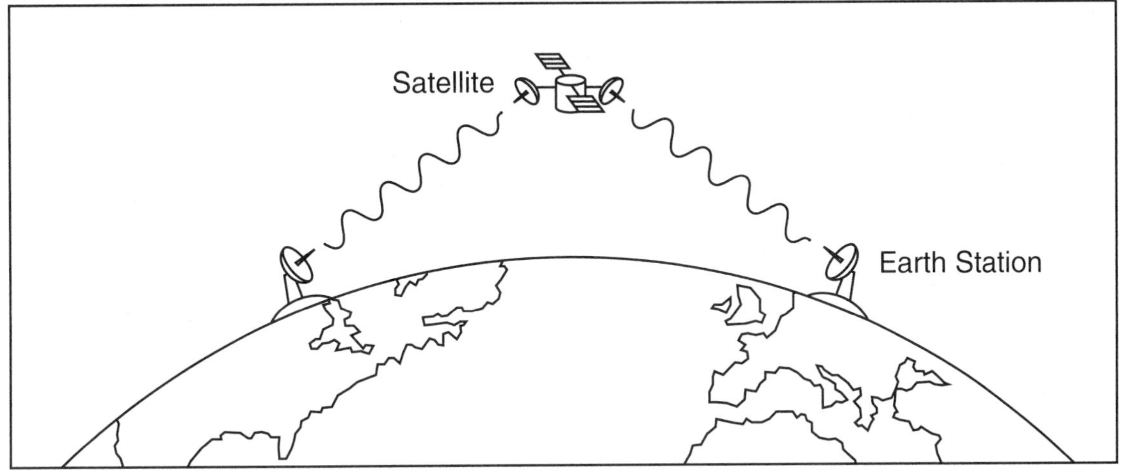

Figure 23A-2

This satellite is in an elliptical orbit around the earth.

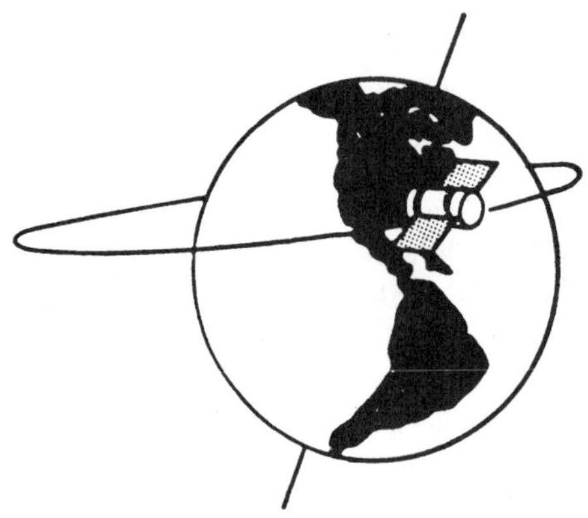

ent body is called the *apogee.* Scientists often put satellites in elliptical orbits to study a specific area of the earth or sky.

Teacher Information:

Although the foil ball is too large to be to scale, it would appear to be stationary. To be in scale it would need to be of microscopic size.

Orbits of satellites launched into space by NASA (National Aeronautics and Space Administration) vary according to the purpose of the satellite. Some are in "stationary" orbits that are almost round and almost exactly match the speed of the earth's rotation. These communication satellites appear to "hang" stationary in the sky and reflect and relay television signals around the earth. Telecommunications for the entire world depend on these satellites. Some satellites are put in greatly elongated orbits in order to come very near the earth at a specific point. Satellites are also used to relay weather information, specific geographic data (including geothermal and faulting), and for military purposes.

In an elliptical orbit, the point at which a satellite is closest to its parent body is called the *perigee.* The point furthest from the parent body is called the *apogee.* Thousands of man-made satellites have been launched in orbit around the earth since the 1950s. Many of them are no longer useful. See the encyclopedia and library books for further information.

Integrating: Reading, social studies

Skills: Communicating, researching

(Except for addition of the sections "For Problem Solvers," "Integrating," and "Skills," this activity was reprinted from Activity 159, "How Do Man-Made Satellites Help Us," in Tolman and Morton, 1986.)

VI. ROCKETS

ACTIVITY 23-10:
HOW CAN A BALLOON BECOME A ROCKET?

Materials Needed:

Long balloon

Fishing line (or light string or strong thread)

Soda straw

Tape

Procedure:

1. Thread the fishing line through the soda straw and attach it, tightly stretched, to opposite sides of the classroom.
2. Blow up the balloon and hold its mouth closed with your fingers.
3. Slide the soda straw to one end of the line.
4. Tape the soda straw to the balloon, with the mouth of the balloon pointed toward the near end of the line.
5. Release the balloon.

6. What happened? Why? Share your ideas with your group and try to explain what happened.

For Problem Solvers:

Try different sizes and shapes of balloons. Try paper straws and plastic straws. Experiment with different types of string and fishing line. Measure and compare the distances, record and chart your results, and find out which combinations tend to make the balloon go farther.

Use your encyclopedia and other available resources and learn all you can about Newton's law of action-reaction. Try to think of other ways to demonstrate this principle, in addition to the balloon rocket.

Teacher Information:

One of Newton's many contributions to the world of science was a better understanding of motion, including the notion that for every action there is an equal and opposite reaction. Rocket engines and jet engines are among the best-known applications of this principle. Students will learn first-hand about action-reaction, as they investigate with the balloon rocket and as they devise other ways to show action-reaction.

Integrating: Reading, math

Skills: Measuring, communicating, identifying and controlling variables, experimenting

(Adapted from Activity 150, "How Do Other Forces Affect Our Rocket's Performance," in Tolman and Morton, 1986.)

VII. OUR SUN

ACTIVITY 23-11:

HOW CAN WE MAKE A SHADOW CLOCK?

Materials Needed:

Pencil

Clay

Poster paper

Procedure:

1. Find an open area on the playground where you can place your poster paper in the sunlight at any time of the day.
2. Stand your pencil in a piece of clay at the center of your poster paper.
3. Find a way to remember the exact position of the poster paper on the playground, and the exact position of the pencil on the poster paper. This system will be your shadow clock, and it is very important that each time you use it, it is set up in exactly the same place.
4. At 9:00 A.M. make a mark on the paper at the tip of the pencil's shadow. Label the mark "9:00 A.M."
5. At 10:00 A.M. set up your shadow clock, making certain that it is in exactly the same position that it was in the first time. Make a mark at the tip of the pencil's shadow, and label the mark "10:00 A.M."
6. Repeat this process each hour throughout the day.
7. Predict where the shadow will be at 9:00 A.M. tomorrow. Check and see if your estimate was right.
8. Use your shadow clock to tell time for several days.
9. Discuss with your group why the shadow clock works day after day. When the shadow shifts a bit, which it will do after many days, try to find out why and explain.

For Problem Solvers:

Extend the above activity by making new marks on your shadow clock at the beginning of each month, using a different color marker each month. Notice the changes in the position of the shadow's tip hour by hour, from month to month.

Use your own shadow to make a human shadow clock. Get a piece of calculator paper (or other paper) that is at least as long as your 9:00 A.M. shadow. Stand in the sunlight at 9:00 A.M. and notice the direction of your shadow. Lay the strip of paper on the ground in the direction of your shadow, and stand with your toes touching the end of your paper and your shadow extending over the paper. Standing straight and tall, notice where the top of the shadow is on the paper. Mark that spot and write "9:00 A.M." Mark the paper again for each hour throughout the day. Use a different color marker for the afternoon hours.

See if your human shadow clock is accurate for a few days. Use it at least at the beginning of each month for two or three days. What changes do you notice? Explain why you think this happens. Get more information and find out if your explanation is accurate.

Teacher Information:

A paper plate can substitute for the poster paper in this activity, and a ruler or stick can substitute for the pencil. If a pencil is used, it must be one that is not used for writing, in order that it will not be shortened by sharpening. It is very important that the shadow clock be set up in exactly the same position each time it is used.

A tetherball pole or flagpole on the playground can be used for this activity if permanent or semipermanent marks can be made on the surrounding blacktop or other surface. This would not give a child his or her personal shadow clock, but it would permit the entire school to share in the experience.

If your area uses Daylight Savings Time during the summer months, it might be best to do this activity only during the months Standard Time is in effect, or only during the months Daylight Savings Time is in effect, to avoid confusion.

As the sun appears to move across the sky, it does so in a higher arch during the summer and in the winter it is lower in the sky. This will have an effect on the position of the tips of the shadow. Shadows are longer in the winter than they are in the summer. Another caution for students who make the human shadow clock has to do with the rapid growth of some students, which will obviously effect the length of their shadow.

Integrating: Reading, writing, math, social studies

Skills: Observing, inferring, measuring, predicting, communicating, using space-time relationships, using variables

VIII. THE UNIVERSE

ACTIVITY 23-12:
HOW CAN WE VIEW CONSTELLATIONS?

Materials Needed:

Map of the sky
Card stock
Pencil
Straight pin
Overhead projector

Procedure:

1. Select one constellation and locate it on your map of the sky.
2. Copying from the map, make dots on the card stock with the pencil, showing

the position of each of the stars of the constellation you chose.

3. Make a pinhole in the card stock at the position of each star.
4. On the card stock, draw lines to form the image that is often associated with that constellation.
5. Place the card stock on the overhead projector and project your constellation on the wall.
6. Repeat the procedure for other constellations of your choosing.

For Problem Solvers:

Cover the ends of cardboard tubes (toilet tissue tubes, paper towel tubes) with aluminum foil. Make pinholes in the foil to mark the positions of stars for one of the constellations. Hold the tube up to the light and look through the other end of the tube. You now have your own constellation viewer!

Do some research to learn all you can about constellations. How did they get their names? Why do we name clusters of stars in the first place? Why doesn't the Big Bear look like a bear?

Teacher Information:

Students enjoy studying about constellations, the stories behind them, and having ways to view them one by one and become acquainted with them. Groups of stars are named to make it easier to communicate about them, just as cities are named, and for the same reason people are named. Just as Bear Lake doesn't look like a bear, neither does the constellation Big Bear. By giving that cluster of stars a name, it can be used as a reference to help locate and communicate about celestial objects.

Integrating: Reading, social studies

Skills: Observing, researching

APPENDIXES

APPENDIX

LIST OF SUPPLIES AND EQUIPMENT COMMONLY USED IN ELEMENTARY SCIENCE ACTIVITIES

Aluminum foil
Aquarium
Baby food jars
Baking soda
Bags (paper, plastic)
Balances
Balloons
Balls
Barometer
Buttons
Cages
Candles
Clothespins
Coat hangers
Compasses
Construction paper
Copper wire
Cotton
Craft sticks
Dowels
Dry cells
Egg cartons
Extension cords
Flashlight
Flashlight bulbs
Food coloring
Funnels
Gallon cans
Glass jars
Glue
Hammer
Hotplate
Iron filings
Lenses
Magnets
Magnifiers
Matches
Measuring cups
Mechanical toys
Medicine droppers
Metersticks
Metric weights
Microscopes
Mirrors
Modeling clay
Paper cups
Paper towels
Pill bottles
Pipe cleaners
Plastic spoons
Plastic tubing
Plastic wrap
Pliers
Pulleys
Rock collections
Rope
Rubber bands
Rulers (metric)
Salt
Sand
Sandpaper
Saw
Screwdriver
Scissors
Seeds
Shoe boxes
Soda straws
Sponges
Steel wool
String
Styrofoam cups
Sugar
Tape (masking, cellophane)
Thermometers
(Celsius and Fahrenheit)
Tongs
Toothpicks
Tuning fork
Tweezers
Vinegar
Wax
Waxed paper
Wind vane

APPENDIX 

SELECTED SOURCES OF SUPPLIES AND EQUIPMENT

American Science & Surplus/Jerryco
601 Linden Place
Evanston, IL 60202

Arbor Scientific
P.O. Box 2750
Ann Arbor, MI 48106-2750

Astronomical Society of the Pacific
390 Ashton Ave.
San Francisco, CA 94112

Baxter Diagnostics, Inc.
Scientific Products Division
1430 Waukegan Rd.
McGaw Park, IL 60085-6787

Brock Optical
P.O. Box 940831
Maitland, FL 32794

Carolina Biological Supply Co.
2700 York Rd.
Burlington, NC 27215

Celestial Products, Inc.
P.O. Box 801
Middleburg, VA 22117

Central Scientific Co. (CENCO)
11222 Melrose Ave
Franklin Park, IL 60131

Chem Scientific, Inc.
67 Chapel St.
Newton, MA 02158

Chem Shop
1151 S. Redwood Rd.
Salt Lake City, UT 84104

Creative Teaching Associates
P.O. Box 7766
Fresno, CA 93747

Cuisenaire Co. of America, Inc.
P.O. Box 5026
White Plains, NY 10602-5026

Cynmar Scientific
131 N. Broad St.
P.O. Box 530
Carlinville, IL 62626

Dale Seymour Publications
P.O. Box 10888
Palo Alto, CA 94303-0879

Delta Education
P.O. Box 915
Hudson, NH 03051-0915

Denoyer-Geppert Science Co.
5225 Ravenswood Ave.
Chicago, IL 60640-2028

Didax Educational Resources
One Centennial Dr.
Peabody, MA 01960

Discovery Corner
Lawrence Hall of Science
University of California
Berkeley, CA 94720

Edmund Scientific
101 E. Gloucester Pike
Barrington, NJ 08007-1380

Educational Rocks & Minerals
P.O. Box 574
Florence, MA 01060

Energy Sciences
16728 Oakmont Ave.
Gaithersburg, MD 20877

Estes Industries
1295 H St.
Penrose, CO 81240

Fisher Scientific
4901 W. LeMoyne St.
Chicago, IL 60651

Flinn Scientific, Inc.
131 Flinn St.
P.O. Box 219
Batavia, IL 60510

Forestry Suppliers, Inc.
P.O. Box 8397
Jackson, MS 39284-8397

Frey Scientific
905 Hickory Lane
P.O. Box 8101
Mansfield, OH 44901-8101

General Supply Corp.
303 Commerce Park Dr.
P.O. Box 9347
Jackson, MS 39286-9347

Grau-Hall Scientific
6501 Elvas Ave.
Sacramento, CA 95819

Hach Co.
P.O. Box 389
Loveland, CO 80539

Hawks, Owls & Wildlife
R.D. 1, Box 293
Buskirk, NY 12028

Hubbard
P.O. Box 104
Northbrook, IL 60065

Hubbard Scientific
3101 Iris Ave., Suite 215
Boulder, CO 80301

Idea Factory, Inc.
10710 Dixon Dr.
Riverview, FL 33569

Ideal School Supply Co.
11000 S. Lavergne Ave.
Oak Lawn, IL 60453

Innovative Plastic Design
7045 S. State
Salt Lake City, UT 84047

Insights Visual Productions
P.O. Box 230644
Encinitas, CA 92023-0644

Learning Alternatives, Inc.
2305 Elm Rd., NE
Cortland, OH 44410

Learning Things, Inc.
68A Broadway
P.O. Box 436
Arlington, MA 02174

Let's Get Growing
1900-B Commercial Way
Santa Cruz, CA 95065

Nasco
901 Janesville Ave.
Fort Atkinson, WI 53538-0901

National Geographic Society
1145 17th St, NW
Washington, D.C. 20036

National Wildlife Federation
1400 Sixteenth St. NW
Washington, D.C. 20036-2266

Northwest Laboratories, Inc.
#20—255 Great Arrow Dr.
Buffalo, NY 14207

Northwest Scientific Supply Co., Inc.
4311 Anthony Ct., #700
P.O. Box 305
Rocklin, CA 95677

Nurnberg Scientific Co.
6310 SW Virginia Ave.
Portland, OR 97201

Ohaus Corp.
29 Hanover Rd.
Florham Park, NJ 07932

Pasco Scientific
10101 Foothills Blvd.
Roseville, CA 95678

Pitsco
P.O. Box 1188
Pittsburg, KS 66762

Quest Aerospace Education, Inc.
P.O. Box 42390
Phoenix, AZ 85080-2390

Radio Shack
Tandy Corp.
Fort Worth, TX 76102

Sargent-Welch Scientific Co.
911 Commerce Ct.
Buffalo Grove, IL 60089

Schoolmasters Science
745 State Circle
Box 1941
Ann Arbor, MI 48106

Science Kit
777 E. Park Dr.
Tonawanda, NY 14150

Science Man, The
P.O. Box 56036
Harwood Hts., IL 60656

Scott Resources
P.O. Box 2121F
Ft. Collins, CO 80522

Southwest Mineral Supply
P.O. Box 323
Santa Fe, NM 87504

Summit Learning
P.O. Box 493F
Ft. Collins, CO 80522

Tap Plastics
6475 Sierra Lane
Dublin, CA 94568

Teachers' Laboratory, Inc.
P.O. Box 6480
Brattleboro, VT 05302-6480

Tops Learning Systems
10970 S. Mulino Rd.
Canby, OR 97013

Uptown Sales, Inc.
33 N. Main St.
Chambersburg, PA 17201

Ward's National Science, Inc.
P.O. Box 92912
Rochester, NY 14692-9012

APPENDIX

SELECTED SOURCES OF FREE AND INEXPENSIVE SCIENCE MATERIALS

Requests for free materials should be made in writing and on school or district letterhead. Only one letter per class should be sent to a given organization. It is a courtesy, when requesting free materials, to provide postage and a return envelope. It is most important to send a thank-you letter when you have received free materials.

The following list includes only those organizations and agencies that specifically approved being included in the list.

American Gas Association
Education Programs
1515 Wilson Blvd.
Arlington, VA 22209

American Museum of Natural History
Education Dept.
Central Park W. at 79th St.
New York, NY 10024-5192

American Petroleum Institute
Public Relations Dept.
1220 L St. NW
Washington, D.C. 20005

American Water Works Association
Student Programs Manager
6666 W. Quincy Ave.
Denver, CO 80235

Animal Welfare Institute
P.O. Box 3650
Washington, D.C. 20007

Freebies: The Magazine with Something for Nothing
1145 Eugenia Place
Carpinteria, CA 93013

National Aeronautics & Space Administration
Education Services Branch FEE
Washington, D.C. 20546

National Cotton Council of America
Communications Services
P.O. Box 12285
Memphis, TN 38182-0285

National Geographic Society
1145 17th St, NW
Washington, D.C. 20036

National Institute of Dental Research
P.O. Box 547-93
Washington, D.C. 20032

Procter & Gamble
Educational Services
P.O. Box 599
Cincinnati, OH 45201-0599

For more comprehensive listings of sources of free and inexpensive materials, see the following sources. Annual editions are available for purchase from: Educators Progress Service, 214 Center St., Randolph, WI 53956.

- *Educators Guide to Free Audio and Visual Materials*
- *Educators Guide to Free Films*
- *Educators Guide to Free Filmstrips and Slides*
- *Educators Guide to Free Science Materials*

APPENDIX

SELECTED SUPPLIERS OF VIDEOTAPES, VIDEODISCS, AND CD-ROM FOR ELEMENTARY SCIENCE

Beacon Films
1560 Sherman Ave., Suite 100
Evanston, IL 60201

Carolina Biological Supply Co.
2700 York Road
Burlington, NC 27215

Churchill Media
12210 Nebraska Ave.
Los Angeles, CA 90025-3600

Elementary Specialties
917 Hickory Lane
Mansfield, OH 44901-8105

Emerging Technology Consultants, Inc.
P.O. Box 120444
St. Paul, MN 55112

Encyclopaedia Britannica Educational Corp.
310 S. Michigan Ave.
Chicago, IL 60604

Everyday Weather Project
State University of New York College at Brockport
Brockport, NY 14420

Frey Scientific
905 Hickory Ln.
Mansfield, OH 44905

GPN
P.O. Box 80669
Lincoln, NE 68501

Hubbard Scientific, Inc.
1120 Halbleib Rd.
P.O. Box 760
Chippewa Falls, WI 54729

Insights Visual Productions, Inc.
P.O. Box 230644
Encinitas, CA 92023

Instructional Video
P.O. Box 21
Maumee, OH 43537

Kons Scientific Co., Inc.
P.O. Box 3
Germantown, WI 53022-0003

MECC
6160 Summit Drive N.
Minneapolis, MN 55430-4003

Miramar Productions
200 Second Ave., W.
Seattle, WA 98119-4204

MMI Corp.
2950 Wyman Pkwy.
P.O. Box 19970
Baltimore, MD 21211

Modern Talking Picture Service, Inc.
5000 Park St. N.
St. Petersburg, FL 33709

Nasco
P.O. Box 901
Fort Atkinson, WI 53538-0901

National Geographic Society
Educational Services
1145 17th St, NW
Washington, D.C. 20036-4688

Optical Data Corporation
30 Technology Drive
Warren, NJ 07059

Phoenix/BFA Films and Video, Inc.
2349 Chaffee Dr.
St. Louis, MO 63146

The Planetary Society, Education Div.
65 N. Catalina
Pasadena, CA 91106

Sargent-Welch Scientific Co.
911 Commerce Ct.
Buffalo Grove, IL 60089

Scholastic Software
730 Broadway
New York, NY 10003

Science for Kids
9950 Concord Church Rd.
Lewisville, NC 27023

Scott Resources
P.O. Box 2121F
Ft. Collins, CO 80522

Society for Visual Education
1345 Diversey Parkway
Chicago, IL 60614-1299

Tom Snyder Productions
80 Coolidge Hill Rd.
Watertown, MA 02172

Videodiscovery, Inc.
1700 Westlake Ave. N.
Suite 600
Seattle, WA 98109-3012

APPENDIX

SELECTED SUPPLIERS OF COMPUTER SOFTWARE FOR ELEMENTARY SCIENCE

Apple Computer Co.
20525 Mariana Ave.
Cupertino, CA 95014

American Water Works Assoc.
6666 W. Quincy
Denver, CO 80235

Carolina Biological Supply Co.
2700 York Rd.
Burlington, NC 27215

Central Scientific Co. (CENCO)
11222 Melrose Ave.
Franklin Park, IL 60131

Churchill Media
12210 Nebraska Ave.
Los Angeles, CA 90025-3600

Curriculum Research & Development Group
University of Hawaii
1776 University Ave.
Honolulu, HI 96822

Denoyer-Geppert Science Co.
5225 Ravenswood Ave.
Chicago, IL 60640-2028

Educational Activities, Inc.
P.O. Box 392
Freeport, NY 11520

EME
P.O. Box 2805
Danbury, CT 06813

Emerging Technology Consultants, Inc.
P.O. Box 120444
St. Paul, MN 55112

Eureka!
Lawrence Hall of Science
University of California
Berkeley, CA 94720

MECC
6160 Summit Dr. North
Minneapolis, MN 55430-4003

Milliken Pub. Co.
P.O. Box 21579
St. Louis, MO 63132-0579

Nasco
P.O. Box 901
Fort Atkinson, WI 53538-0901

National Geographic Society
1145 17th St, NW
Washington, D.C. 20036

Opportunities for Learning, Inc.
20417 Nordhoff St.
Chatsworth, CA 91311

Optical Data Corp.
30 Technology Dr.
Warren, NJ 07059

Scholastic Software
730 Broadway
New York, NY 10003

Science for Kids
9950 Concord Church Rd.
Lewisville, NC 27023

Society for Visual Education
1345 Diversey Parkway
Chicago, IL 60614-1299

Special Times, Special Education Software
Cambridge Development Laboratory, Inc.
214 Third Ave.
Waltham, MA 02154

Wings for Learning/Sunburst
1600 Green Hills Rd.
P.O. Box 660002
Scotts Valley, CA 95067-9908

Videodiscovery, Inc.
1700 Westlake Ave. N., Suite 600
Seattle, WA 98109-3012

APPENDIX

SELECTED PUBLISHERS OF NONFICTION SCIENCE TRADE BOOKS

Charles Scribner's
866 Third Ave.
New York, NY 10022

Crowell Junior Books
Education Dept.
10 E. 53rd St.
New York, NY 10022

HarperCollins Publishers
10 E. 53rd St.
New York, NY 10022

Learning Spectrum
1390 Westridge
Portola Valley, CA 94025

National Geographic Society
1145 17th St, NW
Washington, D.C. 20036

Raintree Publishers, Inc.
310 W. Wisconsin Ave
Milwaukee, WI 53203

Troll Associates
100 Corporate Dr.
Mahwah, NJ 07430

APPENDIX

SELECTED PUBLISHERS OF ELEMENTARY SCIENCE TEXTBOOKS AND KITS

Addison-Wesley Publishing Co.
2725 Sand Hill Rd.
Menlo Park, CA 94025

Biological Sciences Curriculum Study (BSCS)
830 N. Tejon St., Suite 405
Colorado Springs, CO 80903-4720

Charles E. Merrill Books
1300 Alum Creek Dr.
Columbus, OH 43216

D. C. Heath and Co.
125 Spring St.
Lexington, MA 02173

Delta Education
P.O. Box 915
Hudson, NH 03051-0915

Harcourt Brace Jovanovich
School Dept.
Orlando, FL 32887

Holt, Rinehart and Winston
1120 South Capital of Texas Hwy.
Austin, TX 78746-6487

Kendall-Hunt Publishing Co.
4050 Westmark Dr.
P.O. Box 1840
Dubuque, IA 52004-1840

Macmillan/McGraw-Hill
4635 Hilton Corporate Dr.
Columbus, OH 43232-4163

Scholastic, Inc.
730 Broadway
New York, NY 10003

Scott, Foresman and Co.
1900 E. Lake Ave.
Glenview, IL 60025

Silver Burdett and Ginn
250 James St.
Morristown, NJ 07960-1918

The Wild Goose Co.
5181 S. 300 W.
Murray, UT 84107

APPENDIX

SAFETY TIPS FOR ELEMENTARY SCIENCE

1. Carefully label equipment and materials.
2. Train students in the use of any science-supplies or equipment before they are allowed to handle them. This is especially true of all sharp instruments, such as pins, knives, or scissors.
3. Instruct students to report to the teacher immediately any personal injury, damage to clothing, or equipment that appears unusual or functions abnormally.
4. Caution students never to touch, taste, or inhale unknown substances.
5. Minimize use of chemicals at the elementary level.
6. Store chemicals and dispose of chemical waste material in a manner prescribed by state, federal, and school district regulations.
7. Potentially harmful chemicals, hazardous equipment, or flame used at the elementary level should be handled only by the teacher.
8. Do not keep highly corrosive or volatile materials in the elementary school.
9. Take steps to assure that students with special needs or handicapping conditions have safe and easy access to science facilities to the extent that is advisable according to their circumstances. Any special needs that are anticipated for these students in emergency situations should be provided on standby.
10. Provide adequate lighting for science activities.
11. If any living organisms are to be handled or cared for by students, provide proper training for these students.
12. Electrical wiring, switches, outlets, plugs, and so on, should be kept in good repair.
13. Instruct students in the location and proper use of eye baths, fire extinguishers, and any other safety equipment that is available and that might be needed in the science area.
14. Provide eye protection devices and instruct students to use them during any activity that involves a potential risk to eye safety.
15. Store heavy objects on lower shelves.
16. Whenever possible, use plastic containers instead of glassware.
17. Avoid activities that put the safety of children at risk.
18. Teachers should be trained in basic first aid techniques.

For additional information on safety in the elementary science classroom, see *Safety in the Elementary Science Classroom,* a booklet available from NSTA, 1742 Connecticut Ave. NW, Washington, D.C. 20009.

APPENDIX

CARE AND TREATMENT OF ANIMALS IN THE CLASSROOM

Laws and policies pertaining to keeping animals in the classroom vary from district to district and from one state to another. It is the teacher's responsibility to become acquainted with such regulations before inviting these guests into the classroom.

Some children do not have pets at home, and their experience with animals is very limited. Especially for these children, having animals in the classroom can fill an emptiness of longing for such interaction. For all children, their active involvement in the proper care of animals can potentially enrich their lives as they learn about food and housing requirements of certain animals. Firsthand experiences enhance the meaningfulness of lessons about natural selection, adaptation, and changes that occur as young animals progress through their developmental stages of growth. Observing animal behaviors provides firsthand evidence of the unique and varied instincts of different species. Children can also learn about the realities of reproduction in a meaningful way as they see new life come about and experience nature's determination to perpetuate life. Over time, children will also learn about death as a natural part of life.

This section of the appendix provides brief suggestions regarding food and housing requirements for a few animals that are frequently found in elementary classrooms. It ends with guidelines and precautions from the National Science Teachers Association. These are provided in hopes of helping the elementary teacher to foresee and avoid potential problems, while increasing the likelihood of a successful experience in the effort to provide a new dimension in the lives of children.

Many different animals appropriate for the classroom can be obtained from pet stores. Pet stores are also a ready source for food, which can be a great advantage, especially for unusual items. It is very important to follow instructions provided with food, as overfeeding can be as harmful as underfeeding. If students bring animals from home it is probably best if the care and handling are done by the owner. With those brought in from the wild it must be recognized that there is increased risk of disease.

BASIC FOOD AND SHELTER REQUIREMENTS OF A FEW SPECIFIC ANIMALS

Ants

Food: Dead insects, food scraps, water.

Shelter: Glass jar filled with material from ant pile. Cover the jar with black paper except during observation.

Birds

Food: Birdseed, cereal, nuts.

Shelter: Commercial bird cage or equivalent, large enough for the bird to move about freely.

Butterflies

Food: Thick sugar-water.

Shelter: Insect cage. This may be a screen-covered frame or simply a glass jar with vent holes in the lid.

Caterpillars

Food: Leaves upon which the caterpillar was found.

Shelter: Glass jar with vent holes in lid.

Crayfish

Food: Meat, insects, water plants.

Shelter: Aquarium, large heavy-duty glass jar, bottom half of plastic jug, or child's wading pool, with washed sand in bottom. Provide rocks to hide under.

Frogs and Toads

Food: Live insects and worms (mealworms, caterpillars), raw chopped meat.

Shelter: Aquarium with top and with the floor covered with water. Provide rocks that are large enough for the animal to crawl out of the water.

Fruit Flies

Food: Fruit (over-ripe).

Shelter: Small plastic jars or tall baby food jars (*tiny* vent holes—perhaps cover with pantyhose fabric).

Goldfish or Guppies

Food: Dry commercial fish food.

Shelter: Aquarium, large heavy-duty glass jar, bottom half of plastic jug, or child's wading pool, with washed sand in bottom. Provide rocks to hide under.

Grasshoppers

Food: Leaves and grass.

Shelter: Insect cage. This may be a screen-covered frame or simply a glass jar with vent holes in the lid.

Guinea Pigs, Hamsters, Gerbils

Food: Corn, wheat, oats, dry cereal, green or leafy vegetables, carrots, corn, grass, hay, water.

Shelter: Large animal cage or commercial shelters. Exercise wheels should be provided for interest of the animal and of the observer.

Isopods and Crickets

Food: Crushed seeds, fruit.

Shelter: Terrarium or plastic sweater box (be sure to provide vents).

Lizards, Chameleons, and Salamanders

Food: Live insects and mealworms.

Shelter: Terrarium (aquarium) with vented lid. Cover the bottom with sand and coarse gravel. Add soil and plants.

Mealworms

Food: Apple slice.

Shelter: Plastic jar or bucket, with cheese-cloth cover and layer of bran flakes or rolled oats covering the bottom. Cover the container with cheese-cloth or towel.

Rabbits

Food: Rabbit pellets, grass, green or leafy vegetables, carrots, fresh corn, grains, hay, water, salt.

Shelter: Large animal cage.

Snakes

Food: Live insects, earthworms, live mice (consult a pet store for unique needs of your speific snake).

Shelter: Terrarium (aquarium) with vented lid. Cover the bottom with sand and coarse gravel. Add soil and plants.

Spiders

Food: Live insects.

Shelter: Glass jar with *tiny* vent holes in lid.

Tadpoles

Food: Cooked cereal, raw ground beef.

Shelter: Aquarium with top and with the floor covered with water. Provide rocks that are large enough for the adult to crawl out of the water.

Turtles

Food: Insects, worms, mealworms, night crawlers, fresh fruits and vegetables, commercial food.

Shelter: Aquarium or other large container, mostly water-covered but with some dry area.

GUIDELINES FOR RESPONSIBLE USE OF ANIMALS IN THE CLASSROOM (NSTA POSITION STATEMENT)

The following NSTA Position Statement is reprinted with permission from NSTA Publications, copyright 1992, from *NSTA Handbook 1991–92,* National Science Teachers Association, 1742 Connecticut Avenue, NW, Washington, D.C. 20009-1171.

These guidelines are recommended by the National Science Teachers Association for use by science educators and students. It applies, in particular, to the use of nonhuman animals in instructional activities planned or supervised by teachers who teach science at the precollege level.

Observation and experimentation with living organisms give students unique perspectives of life processes that are not provided by other modes of instruction. Studying animals in the classroom enables students to develop skills of observation and comparison, a sense of stewardship, and an appreciation for the unity, interrelationships, and complexity of life. This study, however, requires appropriate, humane care of the organism. Teachers are expected to be knowledgeable about the proper care of organisms under study and the safety of their students.

These are the guidelines recommended by NSTA concerning the responsible use of animals in a school classroom laboratory:

- *Acquisition and care of animals must be appropriate to the species.*
- *Student classwork and science projects involving animals must be under the supervision of a science teacher or other trained professional.*
- *Teachers sponsoring or supervising the use of animals in instructional activities, including acquisition, care, and disposition, will adhere to local, state, and national laws, policies, and regulations regarding species of organisms.*
- *Teachers must instruct students on safety precautions for handling live animals or animal specimens.*
- *Plans for the future care or disposition of animals at the conclusion of the study must be developed and implemented.*
- *Laboratory and dissection activities must be conducted with consideration and appreciation for the organism.*
- *Laboratory and dissection activities must be conducted in a clean and organized work space with care and laboratory precision.*
- *Laboratory and dissection activities must be based on carefully planned objectives.*
- *Laboratory and dissection objectives must be appropriate to the maturity level of the student.*
- *Student views or beliefs sensitive to dissection must be considered; the teacher will respond appropriately.*

Adopted by the NSTA Board of Directors in July, 1991.

APPENDIX

SELECTED PERIODICALS FOR ELEMENTARY TEACHERS AND STUDENTS

3-2-1 Contact, Children's Television Workshop, P.O. Box 2933, Boulder, CO 80322. Published monthly during the regular school year.

Cricket, Open Court Publishing Co., Box 100, LaSalle, IL 61301. Published monthly.

The Curious Naturalist, Massachusetts Audubon Society, South Lincoln, MA 01773. Nine issues per year.

Ladybug, Carus Publishing Co., 315 Fifth St., Peru, IL 61354. Published monthly.

Odyssey, AstroMedia, 625 E. St. Paul Ave. Milwaukee, WI 53202. Published monthly.

National Geographic School Bulletin, Washington, D.C., National Geographic Society. Published weekly during the regular school year.

National Geographic World, 17th and M St. NW, Washington, D.C. 20036.

Ranger Rick, 1412 16th St. NW, Washington, D.C. 20036. Eight issues per year.

School Science and Mathematics, Menasha, WI. Published monthly during the regular school year.

Science and Children, National Science Teachers Association, 1742 Connecticut Ave. NW, Washington, D.C. 20009. Published monthly during the regular school year.

Science Digest, Published monthly.

Science Scope, National Science Teachers Association. Published monthly during the regular school year.

Super Science, Scholastic, Inc., 730 Broadway, New York, NY 10003-9538.

APPENDIX

PROFESSIONAL ASSOCIATIONS FOR TEACHERS OF ELEMENTARY SCIENCE

American Association for the Advancement of Science (AAAS)
1515 Massachusetts Ave. NW
Washington, D.C. 20005

Association for Supervision and Curriculum Development (ASCD)
1201 16th St. NW
Washington, D.C. 20036

National Science Teachers Association (NSTA)
1742 Connecticut Ave. NW
Washington, D.C. 20036

NSTA affiliates (contact NSTA for information):
- Association for the Education of Teachers in Science (AETS)
- Council for Elementary Science International (CESI)
- National Association for Research in Science Teaching (NARST)

APPENDIX L

STANDARD MEASUREMENTS

Metric Prefixes

milli = *one thousandth*
centi = *one hundredth*
deci = *one tenth*
kilo = *one thousand*

Metric and English Units of Measure

METRIC UNITS		ENGLISH UNITS	
Weight			
mg	= *milligram*	*oz.*	= *ounce*
g	= *gram*	*lb.*	= *pound*
kg	= *kilogram*	*t.*	= *ton*
T	= *metric tonne*		
Length			
mm	= *millimeter*	*in.*	= *inch*
cm	= *centimeter*	*ft.*	= *foot*
m	= *meter*	*yd.*	= *yard*
km	= *kilometer*	*mi.*	= *mile*
Liquid Volume			
ml	= *milliliter*	*oz.*	= *ounce*
l	= *liter*	*pt.*	= *pint*
kl	= *kiloliter*	*qt.*	= *quart*
		gal.	= *gallon*

Commonly Used Equivalents within Systems

METRIC SYSTEM		ENGLISH SYSTEM	
Weight			
1 g	= *1000 mg*	*1 lb.*	= *16 oz.*
1 kg	= *1000 g*	*1 t.*	= *2000 lb.*
1 T	= *1000 kg*		

Length

1 cm	=	*10 mm*	*1 ft.*	=	*12 in.*
1 m	=	*100 cm; 1000 mm*	*1 yd.*	=	*3 ft.*
1 km	=	*1000 m*	*1 mi.*	=	*1,760 yd.; 5,280 ft.*

Liquid Volume

1 l	=	*1000 ml*	*1 pt.*	=	*16 oz.*
1 kl	=	*1000 l*	*1 qt.*	=	*2 pt.; 32 oz.*
			1 gal.	=	*4 qt.*

Commonly Used Metric and English Equivalents

METRIC		ENGLISH
Weight		
1 g	=	*0.035 oz.*
1 kg	=	*2.205 lb.*
1 T	=	*1.102 t.*
28.35 g	=	*1 oz.*
454 g	=	*1 lb.*
0.907 T	=	*1 t.*
Length		
1 mm	=	*0.0394 in.*
1 cm	=	*0.394 in.*
1 m	=	*39.37 in.; 1.094 yd.*
1 km	=	*0.621 mi.*
2.54 cm	=	*1 in.*
0.305 m	=	*1 ft.*
0.9144 m	=	*1 yd.*
1.609 km	=	*1 mi.*
Liquid Volume		
1 ml	=	*0.0338 oz.*
1 l	=	*1.06 qt.*
29.57 ml	=	*1 oz.*
0.473 l	=	*1 pt.*
0.946 l	=	*1 qt.*
3.785 l	=	*1 gal.*

APPENDIX M

ECLIPSE MAPS

Lunar Eclipses

The following maps illustrate lunar eclipses from November 29, 1993, through December 21, 2010. Other lunar eclipses occur during these years, visible from various parts of the world. Information for these maps was taken from NASA Publication 1216 (see Espenak, 1989). A total lunar eclipse is visible from the nonshaded region, and a partial eclipse is visible from the light-shaded region. The dark-shaded portion of each map is the area from which the lunar eclipse is *not* visible.

Total Lunar Eclipse — November 29, 1993

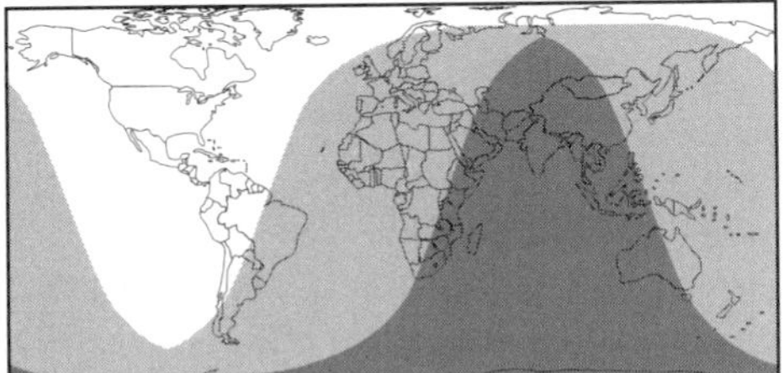

Moon enters Earth's umbral shadow 4:40.2 UT
Moon exits Earth's umbral shadow 8:12.0 UT

Total Lunar Eclipse — April 4, 1996

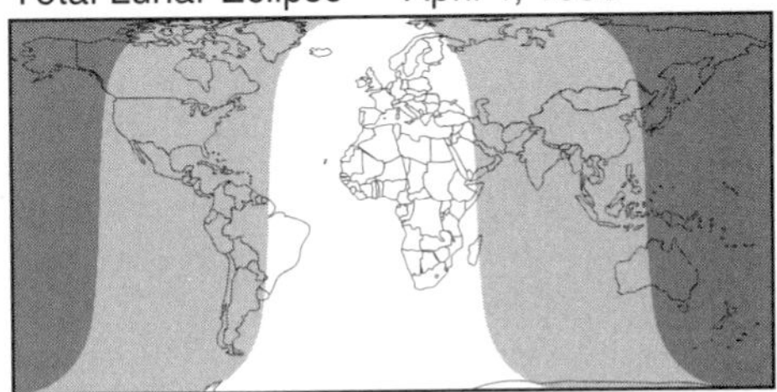

Moon enters Earth's umbral shadow 22:20.7 UT
Moon exits Earth's umbral shadow 1:58.8 UT

Total Lunar Eclipse — September 27, 1996

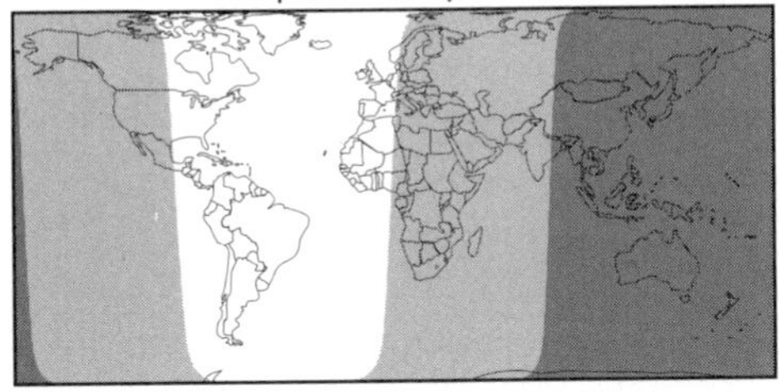

Moon enters Earth's umbral shadow 1:12.1 UT
Moon exits Earth's umbral shadow 4:36.4 UT

Partial Lunar Eclipse — March 24, 1997

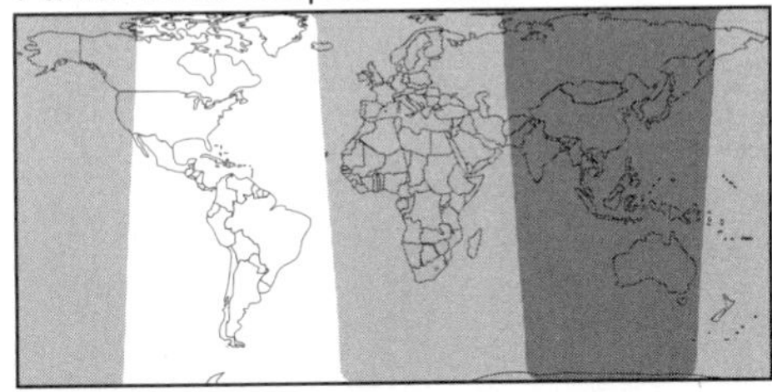

Moon enters Earth's umbral shadow 2:57.6 UT
Moon exits Earth's umbral shadow 6:21.5 UT

Partial Lunar Eclipse — January 21, 2000

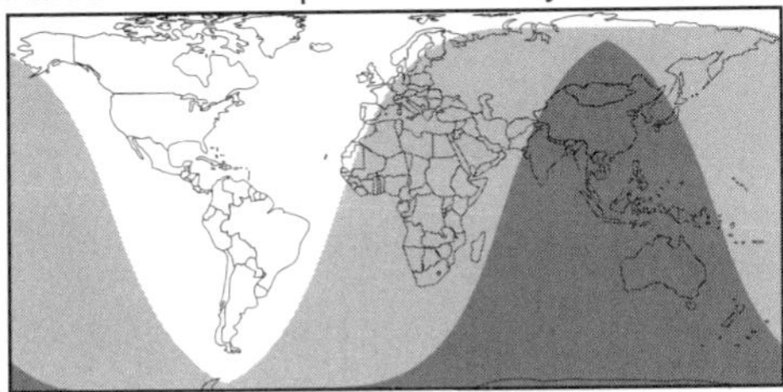

Moon enters Earth's umbral shadow 3:01.3 UT
Moon exits Earth's umbral shadow 6:25.6 UT

Total Lunar Eclipse — May 16, 2003

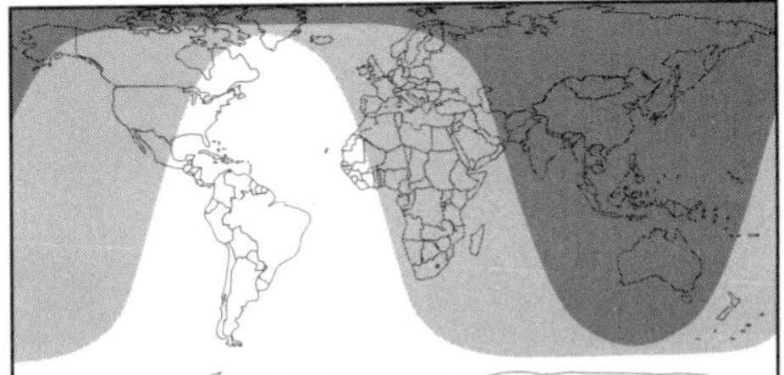

Moon enters Earth's umbral shadow 2:02.7 UT
Moon exits Earth's umbral shadow 5:17.6 UT

Total Lunar Eclipse — November 9, 2003

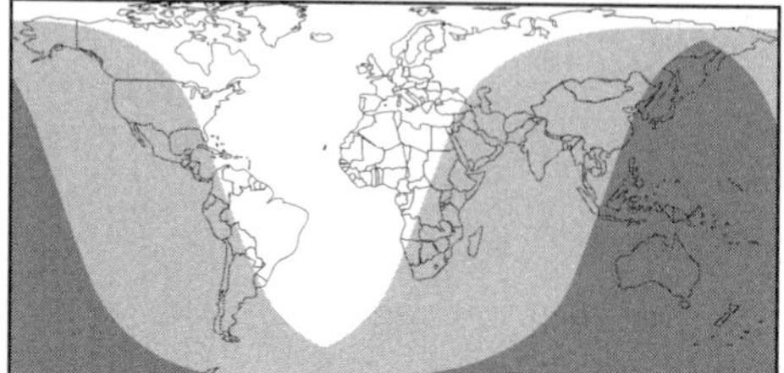

Moon enters Earth's umbral shadow 23:32.4 UT
Moon exits Earth's umbral shadow 3:04.7 UT

Total Lunar Eclipse — October 28, 2004

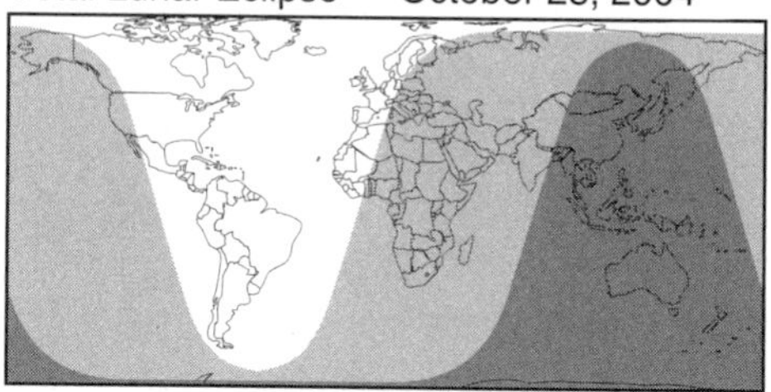

Moon enters Earth's umbral shadow 1:14.1 UT
Moon exits Earth's umbral shadow 4:53.7 UT

Total Lunar Eclipse — March 3, 2007

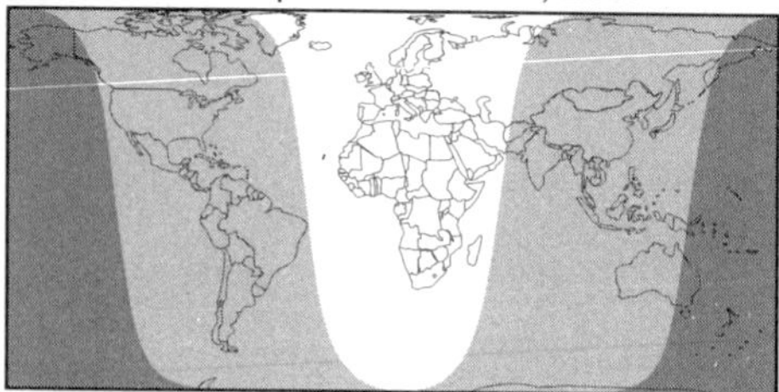

Moon enters Earth's umbral shadow 21:29.9 UT
Moon exits Earth's umbral shadow 1:11.8 UT

Total Lunar Eclipse — August 28, 2007

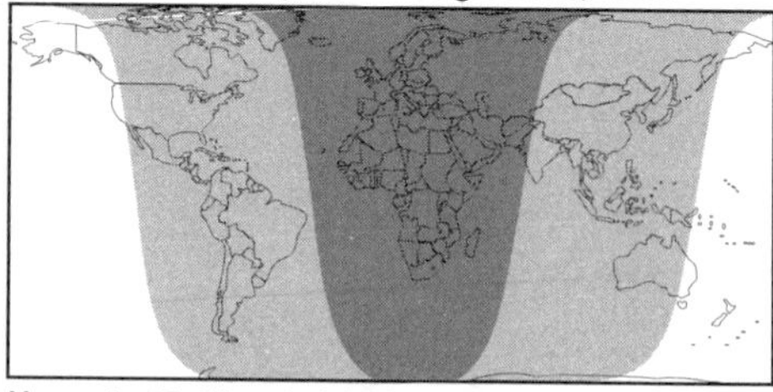

Moon enters Earth's umbral shadow 8:50.8 UT
Moon exits Earth's umbral shadow 12:23.9 UT

Total Lunar Eclipse — February 21, 2008

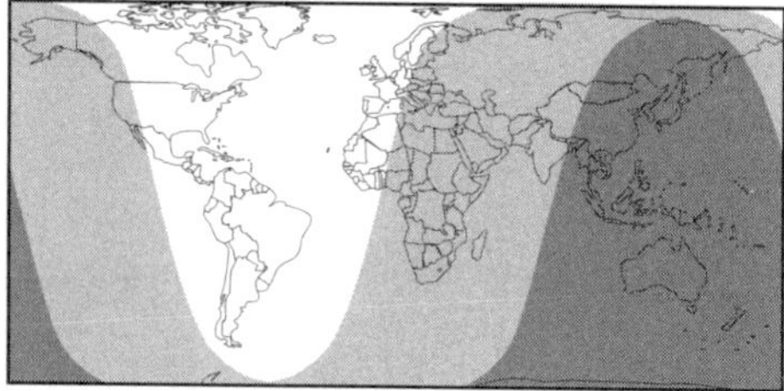

Moon enters Earth's umbral shadow 1:42.6 UT
Moon exits Earth's umbral shadow 5:08.9 UT

Total Lunar Eclipse — December 21, 2010

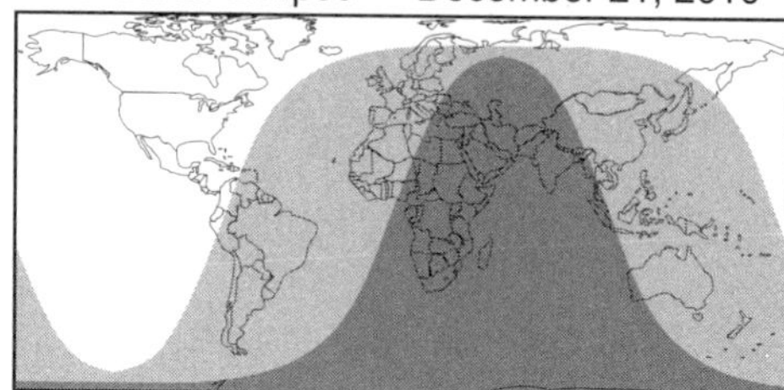

Moon enters Earth's umbral shadow 6:32.0 UT
Moon exits Earth's umbral shadow 10:01.7 UT

Solar Eclipses

The following maps illustrate some of the more spectacular solar eclipses visible from North and South America from May 10, 1994, through April 8, 2024. Other solar eclipses occur during these years, visible from various parts of the world. Information for these maps was taken from NASA Publication 1278 (see Espenak, 1987.)

Some solar eclipses are only partial, as shown for December 25, 2000, and for October 23, 2014. Where a total or an annular eclipse occurs, its path is shown on the map. During an annualar eclipse, a ring of the sun is visible around the moon. The final map compiles the paths of several total and annular eclipses.

Paths of Total and Annular Solar Eclipses

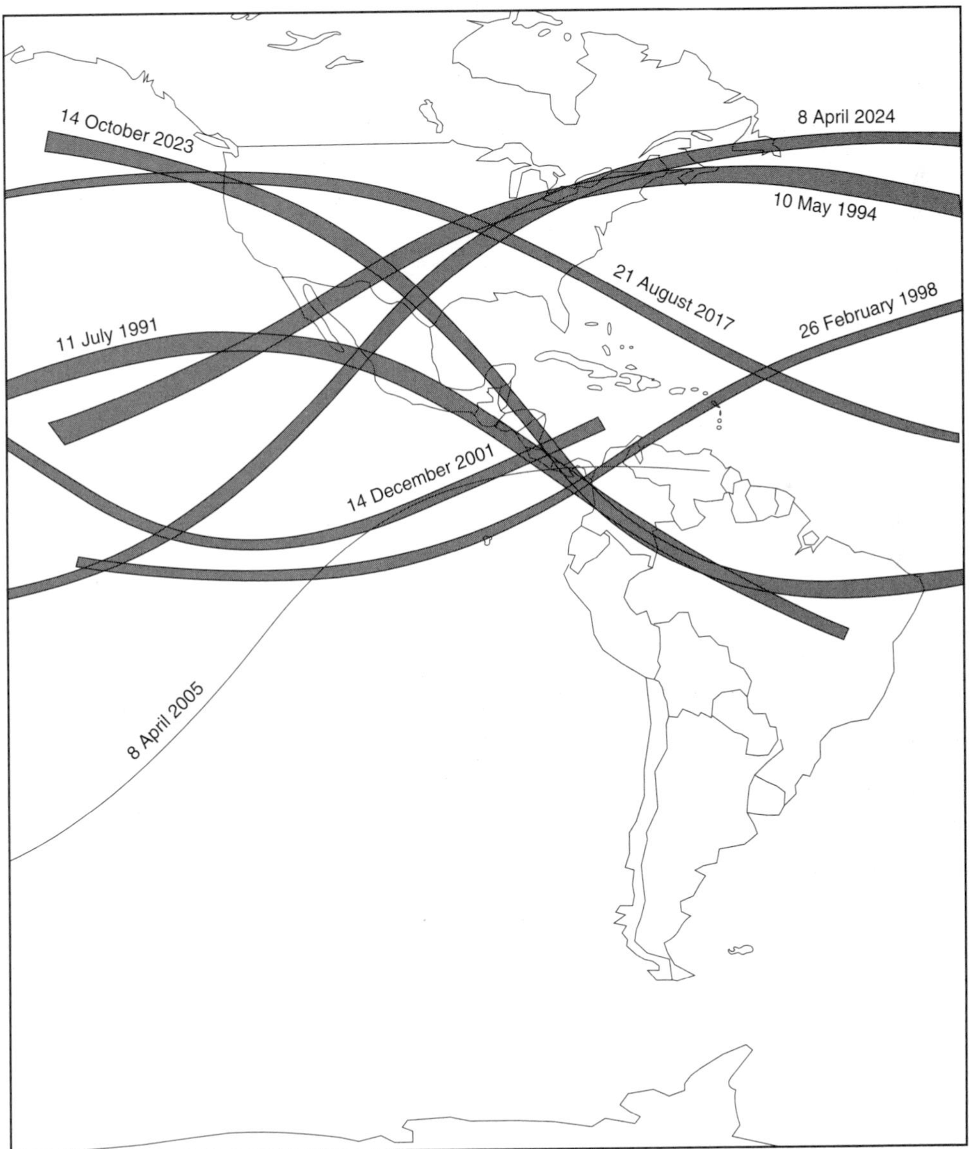

Annular Solar Eclipse
May 10, 1994

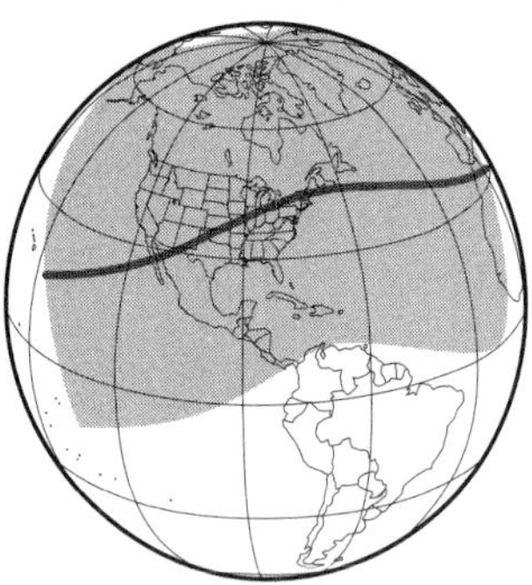

Total Solar Eclipse
February 26, 1998

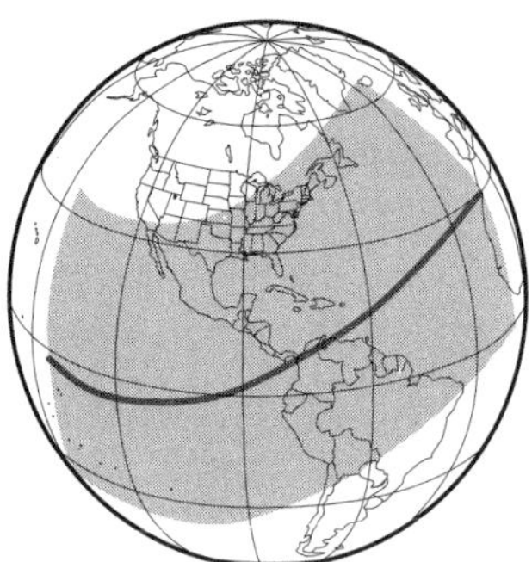

Partial Solar Eclipse
December 25, 2000

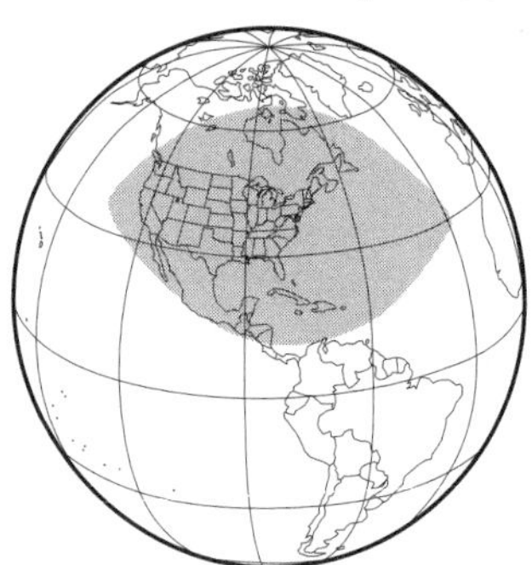

Annular Solar Eclipse
December 14, 2001

ANN/TOT Solar Eclipse
April 8, 2005

Partial Solar Eclipse
October 23, 2014

Total Solar Eclipse
August 21, 2017

Annular Solar Eclipse
October 14, 2023

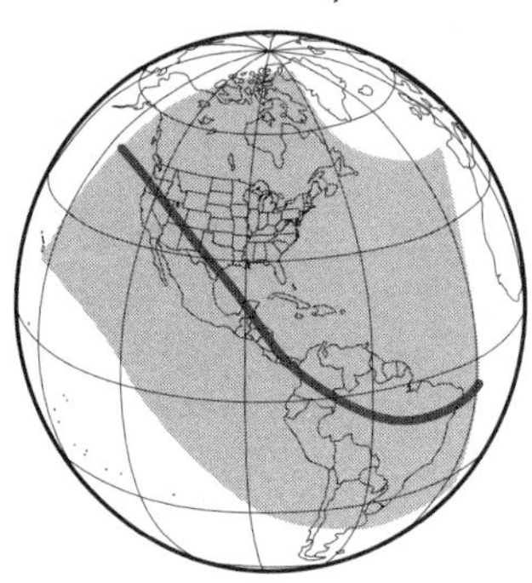

Total Solar Eclipse
April 8, 2024

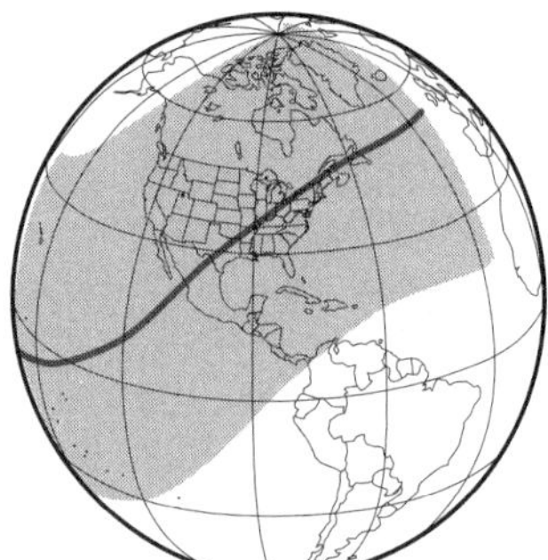

INDEX

A

B

C

D

E

N

O

P

T

U

V

W